DATA MINING AND PREDICTIVE ANALYTICS

WILEY SERIES ON METHODS AND APPLICATIONS IN DATA MINING

Series Editor: **Daniel T. Larose**

DATA MINING AND PREDICTIVE ANALYTICS

Second Edition

DANIEL T. LAROSE
CHANTAL D. LAROSE

For general information on our other products and services or for technical support, please contact our Customer Care Department within the United States at (800) 762-2974, outside the United States at (317) 572-3993 or fax (317) 572-4002.

Wiley also publishes its books in a variety of electronic formats. Some content that appears in print may not be available in electronic formats. For more information about Wiley products, visit our web site at www.wiley.com.

Library of Congress Cataloging-in-Publication Data:

Larose, Daniel T.
  Data mining and predictive analytics / Daniel T. Larose, Chantal D. Larose.
     pages cm. – (Wiley series on methods and applications in data mining)
  Includes bibliographical references and index.
  ISBN 978-1-118-11619-7 (cloth)
1. Data mining. 2. Prediction theory. I. Larose, Chantal D. II. Title.
  QA76.9.D343L3776 2015
  006.3′12–dc23

                              2014043340

Set in 10/12pt Times by Laserwords Private Limited, Chennai, India

Printed in the United States of America

10 9 8 7 6 5

To those who have gone before us,
And to those who come after us,
In the Family Tree of Life ...

CONTENTS

CHAPTER 15   *MODEL EVALUATION TECHNIQUES*   451

CHAPTER 16   *COST-BENEFIT ANALYSIS USING DATA-DRIVEN COSTS*   471

PREFACE

WHAT IS DATA MINING? WHAT IS PREDICTIVE ANALYTICS?

Data mining is the process of discovering useful patterns and trends in large data sets.

Predictive analytics is the process of extracting information from large data sets in order to make predictions and estimates about future outcomes.

Data Mining and Predictive Analytics, by Daniel Larose and Chantal Larose, will enable you to become an expert in these cutting-edge, profitable fields.

WHY IS THIS BOOK NEEDED?

According to the research firm MarketsandMarkets, the global big data market is expected to grow by 26% per year from 2013 to 2018, from $14.87 billion in 2013 to $46.34 billion in 2018.[1] Corporations and institutions worldwide are learning to apply data mining and predictive analytics, in order to increase profits. Companies that do not apply these methods will be left behind in the global competition of the twenty-first-century economy.

Humans are inundated with data in most fields. Unfortunately, most of this valuable data, which cost firms millions to collect and collate, are languishing in warehouses and repositories. *The problem is that there are not enough trained human analysts available who are skilled at translating all of this data into knowledge*, and thence up the taxonomy tree into wisdom. This is why this book is needed.

The McKinsey Global Institute reports[2]:

There will be a shortage of talent necessary for organizations to take advantage of big data. A significant constraint on realizing value from big data will be a shortage of talent, particularly of people with deep expertise in statistics and machine learning, and the

---

[1] *Big Data Market to Reach $46.34 Billion by 2018*, by Darryl K. Taft, *eWeek*, www.eweek.com/database/big-data-market-to-reach-46.34-billion-by-2018.html, posted September 1, 2013, last accessed March 23, 2014.

[2] *Big data: The next frontier for innovation, competition, and productivity*, by James Manyika *et al.*, Mckinsey Global Institute, www.mckinsey.com, May, 2011. Last accessed March 16, 2014.

managers and analysts who know how to operate companies by using insights from big data.... We project that demand for deep analytical positions in a big data world could exceed the supply being produced on current trends by 140,000 to 190,000 positions. ... In addition, we project a need for 1.5 million additional managers and analysts in the United States who can ask the right questions and consume the results of the analysis of big data effectively.

This book is an attempt to help alleviate this critical shortage of data analysts.

Data mining is becoming more widespread every day, because it empowers companies to uncover profitable patterns and trends from their existing databases. Companies and institutions have spent millions of dollars to collect gigabytes and terabytes of data, but are not taking advantage of the valuable and actionable information hidden deep within their data repositories. However, as the practice of data mining becomes more widespread, companies that do not apply these techniques are in danger of falling behind, and losing market share, because their competitors are applying data mining, and thereby gaining the competitive edge.

WHO WILL BENEFIT FROM THIS BOOK?

In *Data Mining and Predictive Analytics*, the step-by-step hands-on solutions of real-world business problems using widely available data mining techniques applied to real-world data sets will appeal to managers, CIOs, CEOs, CFOs, data analysts, database analysts, and others who need to keep abreast of the latest methods for enhancing return on investment.

Using *Data Mining and Predictive Analytics*, you will learn what types of analysis will uncover the most profitable nuggets of knowledge from the data, while avoiding the potential pitfalls that may cost your company millions of dollars. *You will* learn *data mining and predictive analytics* by doing *data mining and predictive analytics*.

DANGER! DATA MINING IS EASY TO DO BADLY

The growth of new off-the-shelf software platforms for performing data mining has kindled a new kind of danger. The ease with which these applications can manipulate data, combined with the power of the formidable data mining algorithms embedded in the black-box software, make their misuse proportionally more hazardous.

In short, *data mining is easy to do badly*. A little knowledge is especially dangerous when it comes to applying powerful models based on huge data sets. For example, analyses carried out on unpreprocessed data can lead to erroneous conclusions, or inappropriate analysis may be applied to data sets that call for a completely different approach, or models may be derived that are built on wholly unwarranted specious assumptions. If deployed, these errors in analysis can lead to very expensive failures. *Data Mining and Predictive Analytics* will help make you a savvy analyst, who will avoid these costly pitfalls.

"WHITE-BOX" APPROACH

Understanding the Underlying Algorithmic and Model Structures

The best way to avoid costly errors stemming from a blind black-box approach to data mining and predictive analytics is to instead apply a "white-box" methodology, which emphasizes an understanding of the algorithmic and statistical model structures underlying the software.

Data Mining and Predictive Analytics applies this white-box approach by

- clearly explaining *why* a particular method or algorithm is needed;
- getting the reader acquainted with *how* a method or algorithm works, using a toy example (tiny data set), so that the reader may follow the logic step by step, and thus gain a *white-box insight* into the inner workings of the method or algorithm;
- providing an application of the method to a large, real-world data set;
- using exercises to test the reader's level of understanding of the concepts and algorithms;
- providing an opportunity for the reader to experience doing some real data mining on large data sets.

ALGORITHM WALK-THROUGHS

Data Mining Methods and Models walks the reader through the operations and nuances of the various algorithms, using small data sets, so that the reader gets a true appreciation of what is really going on inside the algorithm. For example, in Chapter 21, we follow step by step as the balanced iterative reducing and clustering using hierarchies (BIRCH) algorithm works through a tiny data set, showing precisely how BIRCH chooses the optimal clustering solution for this data, from start to finish. As far as we know, such a demonstration is unique to this book for the BIRCH algorithm. Also, in Chapter 27, we proceed step by step to find the optimal solution using the selection, crossover, and mutation operators, using a tiny data set, so that the reader may better understand the underlying processes.

Applications of the Algorithms and Models to Large Data Sets

Data Mining and Predictive Analytics provides examples of the application of data analytic methods on actual large data sets. For example, in Chapter 9, we analytically unlock the relationship between nutrition rating and cereal content using a real-world data set. In Chapter 4, we apply principal components analysis to real-world census data about California. All data sets are available from the book series web site: www.dataminingconsultant.com.

Chapter Exercises: Checking to Make Sure You Understand It

Data Mining and Predictive Analytics includes over 750 chapter exercises, which allow readers to assess their depth of understanding of the material, as well as have a little fun playing with numbers and data. These include *Clarifying the Concept* exercises, which help to clarify some of the more challenging concepts in data mining, and *Working with the Data* exercises, which challenge the reader to apply the particular data mining algorithm to a small data set, and, step by step, to arrive at a computationally sound solution. For example, in Chapter 14, readers are asked to find the *maximum a posteriori* classification for the data set and network provided in the chapter.

Hands-On Analysis: Learn Data Mining by Doing Data Mining

Most chapters provide the reader with *Hands-On Analysis* problems, representing an opportunity for the reader to apply his or her newly acquired data mining expertise to solving real problems using large data sets. Many people learn by doing. *Data Mining and Predictive Analytics* provides a framework where the reader can learn data mining by doing data mining. For example, in Chapter 13, readers are challenged to approach a real-world credit approval classification data set, and construct their best possible logistic regression model, using the methods learned in this chapter as possible, providing strong interpretive support for the model, including explanations of derived variables and indicator variables.

EXCITING NEW TOPICS

Data Mining and Predictive Analytics contains many exciting new topics, including the following:

- Cost-benefit analysis using data-driven misclassification costs.
- Cost-benefit analysis for trinary and *k*-nary classification models.
- Graphical evaluation of classification models.
- BIRCH clustering.
- Segmentation models.
- Ensemble methods: Bagging and boosting.
- Model voting and propensity averaging.
- Imputation of missing data.

THE R ZONE

R is a powerful, open-source language for exploring and analyzing data sets (www.r-project.org). Analysts using *R* can take advantage of many freely available packages, routines, and graphical user interfaces to tackle most data analysis problems. In most chapters of this book, the reader will find *The R Zone*, which provides the actual *R* code needed to obtain the results shown in the chapter, along with screenshots of some of the output.

APPENDIX: DATA SUMMARIZATION AND VISUALIZATION

Some readers may be a bit rusty on some statistical and graphical concepts, usually encountered in an introductory statistics course. *Data Mining and Predictive Analytics* contains an appendix that provides a review of the most common concepts and terminology helpful for readers to hit the ground running in their understanding of the material in this book.

THE CASE STUDY: BRINGING IT ALL TOGETHER

Data Mining and Predictive Analytics culminates in a detailed Case Study. Here the reader has the opportunity to see how everything he or she has learned is brought all together to create actionable and profitable solutions. This detailed Case Study ranges over four chapters, and is as follows:

- Chapter 29: *Case Study, Part 1: Business Understanding, Data Preparation, and EDA*
- Chapter 30: *Case Study, Part 2: Clustering and Principal Components Analysis*
- Chapter 31: *Case Study, Part 3: Modeling and Evaluation for Performance and Interpretability*
- Chapter 32: *Case Study, Part 4: Modeling and Evaluation for High Performance Only*

The Case Study includes dozens of pages of graphical, exploratory data analysis (EDA), predictive modeling, customer profiling, and offers different solutions, depending on the requisites of the client. The models are evaluated using a custom-built data-driven cost-benefit table, reflecting the true costs of classification errors, rather than the usual methods such as overall error rate. Thus, the analyst can compare models using the estimated profit per customer contacted, and can predict how much money the models will earn, based on the number of customers contacted.

HOW THE BOOK IS STRUCTURED

Data Mining and Predictive Analytics is structured in a way that the reader will hopefully find logical and straightforward. There are 32 chapters, divided into eight major parts.

- Part 1, *Data Preparation*, consists of chapters on data preparation, EDA, and dimension reduction.

- Part 2, *Statistical Analysis*, provides classical statistical approaches to data analysis, including chapters on univariate and multivariate statistical analysis, simple and multiple linear regression, preparing to model the data, and model building.

- Part 3, *Classification*, contains nine chapters, making it the largest section of the book. Chapters include k-nearest neighbor, decision trees, neural networks, logistic regression, naïve Bayes, Bayesian networks, model evaluation techniques, cost-benefit analysis using data-driven misclassification costs, trinary and k-nary classification models, and graphical evaluation of classification models.

- Part 4, *Clustering*, contains chapters on hierarchical clustering, k-means clustering, Kohonen networks clustering, BIRCH clustering, and measuring cluster goodness.

- Part 5, *Association Rules*, consists of a single chapter covering a priori association rules and generalized rule induction.

- Part 6, *Enhancing Model Performance*, provides chapters on segmentation models, ensemble methods: bagging and boosting, model voting, and propensity averaging.

- Part 7, *Further Methods in Predictive Modeling*, contains a chapter on imputation of missing data, along with a chapter on genetic algorithms.

- Part 8, *Case Study: Predicting Response to Direct-Mail Marketing*, consists of four chapters presenting a start-to-finish detailed Case Study of how to generate the greatest profit from a direct-mail marketing campaign.

THE SOFTWARE

The software used in this book includes the following:

- *IBM SPSS Modeler* data mining software suite
- *R* open source statistical software
- *SAS Enterprise Miner*
- *SPSS* statistical software
- *Minitab* statistical software
- *WEKA* open source data mining software.

IBM SPSS Modeler (www-01.ibm.com/software/analytics/spss/products/modeler/) is one of the most widely used data mining software suites, and is distributed by *SPSS*, whose base software is also used in this book. *SAS Enterprise Miner* is probably more powerful than *Modeler*, but the learning curve is also steeper. *SPSS* is available for download on a trial basis as well (Google "spss" download). *Minitab* is an easy-to-use statistical software package that is available for download on a trial basis from their web site at www.minitab.com.

WEKA: THE OPEN-SOURCE ALTERNATIVE

The Weka (Waikato Environment for Knowledge Analysis) machine learning workbench is open-source software issued under the GNU General Public License, which includes a collection of tools for completing many data mining tasks. *Data Mining and Predictive Modeling* presents several hands-on, step-by-step tutorial examples using Weka 3.6, along with input files available from the book's companion web site www.dataminingconsultant.com. The reader is shown how to carry out the following types of analysis, using WEKA: Logistic Regression (Chapter 13), Naïve Bayes classification (Chapter 14), Bayesian Networks classification (Chapter 14), and Genetic Algorithms (Chapter 27). For more information regarding Weka, see www.cs.waikato.ac.nz/ml/weka/. The author is deeply grateful to James Steck for providing these WEKA examples and exercises. James Steck (james_steck@comcast.net) was one of the first students to complete the master of science in data mining from Central Connecticut State University in 2005 (GPA 4.0), and received the first data mining Graduate Academic Award. James lives with his wife and son in Issaquah, WA.

THE COMPANION WEB SITE: WWW.DATAMININGCONSULTANT.COM

The reader will find supporting materials, both for this book and for the other data mining books written by Daniel Larose and Chantal Larose for *Wiley InterScience*, at the companion web site, www.dataminingconsultant.com. There one may download the many data sets used in the book, so that the reader may develop a hands-on feel for the analytic methods and models encountered throughout the book. Errata are also available, as is a comprehensive set of data mining resources, including links to data sets, data mining groups, and research papers.

However, the real power of the companion web site is available to faculty adopters of the textbook, who will have access to the following resources:

- Solutions to all the exercises, including the hands-on analyses.
- PowerPoint® presentations of each chapter, ready for deployment in the classroom.
- Sample data mining course projects, written by the author for use in his own courses, and ready to be adapted for your course.
- Real-world data sets, to be used with the course projects.
- Multiple-choice chapter quizzes.
- Chapter-by-chapter web resources.

Adopters may e-mail Daniel Larose at larosed@ccsu.edu to request access information for the adopters' resources.

DATA MINING AND PREDICTIVE ANALYTICS AS A TEXTBOOK

Data Mining and Predictive Analytics naturally fits the role of textbook for a one-semester course or two-semester sequences of courses in introductory and intermediate data mining. Instructors may appreciate

- the presentation of data mining as a *process*;
- the "white-box" approach, emphasizing an understanding of the underlying algorithmic structures;
  - — Algorithm walk-throughs with toy data sets
  - — Application of the algorithms to large real-world data sets
  - — Over 300 figures and over 275 tables
  - — Over 750 chapter exercises and hands-on analysis
- the many exciting new topics, such as cost-benefit analysis using data-driven misclassification costs;
- the detailed *Case Study*, bringing together many of the lessons learned from the earlier 28 chapters;
- the Appendix: Data Summarization and Visualization, containing a review of statistical and graphical concepts readers may be a bit rusty on;
- the companion web site, providing the array of resources for adopters detailed above.

Data Mining and Predictive Analytics is appropriate for advanced undergraduate- or graduate-level courses. An introductory statistics course would be nice, but is not required. No computer programming or database expertise is required.

ACKNOWLEDGMENTS

DANIEL'S ACKNOWLEDGMENTS

I would first like to thank my mentor Dr. Dipak K. Dey, distinguished professor of statistics, and associate dean of the College of Liberal Arts and Sciences at the University of Connecticut, as well as Dr. John Judge, professor of statistics in the Department of Mathematics at Westfield State College. My debt to the two of you is boundless, and now extends beyond one lifetime. Also, I wish to thank my colleagues in the data mining programs at Central Connecticut State University, Dr. Chun Jin, Dr. Daniel S. Miller, Dr. Roger Bilisoly, Dr. Darius Dziuda, and Dr. Krishna Saha. Thanks to my daughter Chantal, and to my twin children, Tristan Spring and Ravel Renaissance, for providing perspective on what life is about.

DANIEL T. LAROSE, PhD

Professor of Statistics and Data Mining
Director, Data Mining @CCSU
www.math.ccsu.edu/larose

CHANTAL'S ACKNOWLEDGMENTS

I would first like to thank my PhD advisors, Dr. Dipak Dey, distinguished professor and associate dean, and Dr. Ofer Harel, associate professor, both of the Department of Statistics at the University of Connecticut. Their insight and understanding have framed and sculpted our exciting research program, including my PhD dissertation, "Model-Based Clustering of Incomplete Data." Thanks also to my father, Daniel, for kindling my enduring love of data analysis, and to my mother, Debra, for her care and patience through many statistics-filled conversations. Finally, thanks to my siblings, Ravel and Tristan, for perspective, music, and friendship.

CHANTAL D. LAROSE, MS

Department of Statistics
University of Connecticut

PART I

DATA PREPARATION

## CHAPTER 1

AN INTRODUCTION TO DATA MINING AND PREDICTIVE ANALYTICS

1.1 WHAT IS DATA MINING? WHAT IS PREDICTIVE ANALYTICS?

Recently, the computer manufacturer Dell was interested in improving the productivity of its sales workforce. It therefore turned to data mining and predictive analytics to analyze its database of potential customers, in order to identify the most likely respondents. Researching the social network activity of potential leads, using LinkedIn and other sites, provided a richer amount of information about the potential customers, thereby allowing Dell to develop more personalized sales pitches to their clients. This is an example of mining customer data to help identify the type of marketing approach for a particular customer, based on customer's individual profile. What is the bottom line? The number of prospects that needed to be contacted was cut by 50%, leaving only the most promising prospects, leading to a near doubling of the productivity and efficiency of the sales workforce, with a similar increase in revenue for Dell.[1]

The Commonwealth of Massachusetts is wielding predictive analytics as a tool to cut down on the number of cases of Medicaid fraud in the state. When a Medicaid claim is made, the state now immediately passes it in real time to a predictive analytics model, in order to detect any anomalies. During its first 6 months of operation, the new system has "been able to recover $2 million in improper payments, and has avoided paying hundreds of thousands of dollars in fraudulent claims," according to Joan Senatore, Director of the Massachusetts Medicaid Fraud Unit.[2]

---

[1] *How Dell Predicts Which Customers Are Most Likely to Buy*, by Rachael King, CIO Journal, Wall Street Journal, December 5, 2012.

[2] *How MassHealth cut Medicaid fraud with predictive analytics*, by Rutrell Yasin, GCN, February 24, 2014.

The McKinsey Global Institute (MGI) reports[3] that most American companies with more than 1000 employees had an average of at least 200 TB of stored data. MGI projects that the amount of data generated worldwide will increase by 40% annually, creating profitable opportunities for companies to leverage their data to reduce costs and increase their bottom line. For example, retailers harnessing this "big data" to best advantage could expect to realize an increase in their operating margin of more than 60%, according to the MGI report. And health-care providers and health maintenance organizations (HMOs) that properly leverage their data storehouses could achieve $300 in cost savings annually, through improved efficiency and quality.

Forbes magazine reports[4] that the use of data mining and predictive analytics has helped to identify patients who have been of the greatest risk of developing congestive heart failure. IBM collected 3 years of data pertaining to 350,000 patients, and including measurements on over 200 factors, including things such as blood pressure, weight, and drugs prescribed. Using predictive analytics, IBM was able to identify the 8500 patients most at risk of dying of congestive heart failure within 1 year.

The *MIT Technology Review* reports[5] that it was the Obama campaign's effective use of data mining that helped President Obama win the 2012 presidential election over Mitt Romney. They first identified likely Obama voters using a data mining model, and then made sure that these voters actually got to the polls. The campaign also used a separate data mining model to predict the polling outcomes county by county. In the important swing county of Hamilton County, Ohio, the model predicted that Obama would receive 56.4% of the vote; the Obama share of the actual vote was 56.6%, so that the prediction was off by only 0.02%. Such precise predictive power allowed the campaign staff to allocate scarce resources more efficiently.

Data mining is the process of discovering useful patterns and trends in large data sets.

Predictive analytics is the process of extracting information from large data sets in order to make predictions and estimates about future outcomes.

So, what is data mining? What is predictive analytics?

While waiting in line at a large supermarket, have you ever just closed your eyes and listened? You might hear the beep, beep, beep of the supermarket scanners, reading the bar codes on the grocery items, ringing up on the register, and storing the data on company servers. Each beep indicates a new row in the database, a new

---

[3] *Big data: The next frontier for innovation, competition, and productivity*, by James Manyika *et al.*, Mckinsey Global Institute, www.mckinsey.com, May, 2011. Last accessed March 16, 2014.

[4] *IBM and Epic Apply Predictive Analytics to Electronic Health Records*, by Zina Moukheiber, *Forbes* magazine, February 19, 2014.

[5] *How President Obama's campaign used big data to rally individual voters*, by Sasha Issenberg, *MIT Technology Review*, December 19, 2012.

"observation" in the information being collected about the shopping habits of your family, and the other families who are checking out.

Clearly, a lot of data is being collected. However, what is being learned from all this data? What knowledge are we gaining from all this information? Probably not as much as you might think, because there is a serious shortage of skilled data analysts.

1.2   WANTED: DATA MINERS

As early as 1984, in his book *Megatrends*,[6] John Naisbitt observed that "We are drowning in information but starved for knowledge." The problem today is not that there is not enough data and information streaming in. We are in fact inundated with data in most fields. Rather, the problem is that there are not enough trained *human* analysts available who are skilled at translating all of this data into knowledge, and thence up the taxonomy tree into wisdom.

The ongoing remarkable growth in the field of data mining and knowledge discovery has been fueled by a fortunate confluence of a variety of factors:

- The explosive growth in data collection, as exemplified by the supermarket scanners above.
- The storing of the data in data warehouses, so that the entire enterprise has access to a reliable, current database.
- The availability of increased access to data from web navigation and intranets.
- The competitive pressure to increase market share in a globalized economy.
- The development of "off-the-shelf" commercial data mining software suites.
- The tremendous growth in computing power and storage capacity.

Unfortunately, according to the McKinsey report,[7]

There will be a shortage of talent necessary for organizations to take advantage of big data. A significant constraint on realizing value from big data will be a shortage of talent, particularly of people with deep expertise in statistics and machine learning, and the managers and analysts who know how to operate companies by using insights from big data.... We project that demand for deep analytical positions in a big data world could exceed the supply being produced on current trends by 140,000 to 190,000 positions. ... In addition, we project a need for 1.5 million additional managers and analysts in the United States who can ask the right questions and consume the results of the analysis of big data effectively.

This book is an attempt to help alleviate this critical shortage of data analysts.

[6]*Megatrends*, John Naisbitt, Warner Books, 1984.

[7]*Big data: The next frontier for innovation, competition, and productivity*, by James Manyika *et al.*, Mckinsey Global Institute, www.mckinsey.com, May, 2011. Last accessed March 16, 2014.

1.3 THE NEED FOR HUMAN DIRECTION OF DATA MINING

Automation is no substitute for human oversight. Humans need to be actively involved at every phase of the data mining process. Rather than asking where humans fit into data mining, we should instead inquire about how we may design data mining into the very human process of problem solving.

Further, the very power of the formidable data mining algorithms embedded in the black box software currently available makes their misuse proportionally more dangerous. Just as with any new information technology, *data mining is easy to do badly*. Researchers may apply inappropriate analysis to data sets that call for a completely different approach, for example, or models may be derived that are built on wholly specious assumptions. Therefore, an understanding of the statistical and mathematical model structures underlying the software is required.

1.4 THE CROSS-INDUSTRY STANDARD PROCESS FOR DATA MINING: CRISP-DM

There is a temptation in some companies, due to departmental inertia and compartmentalization, to approach data mining haphazardly, to reinvent the wheel and duplicate effort. A cross-industry standard was clearly required, that is industry-neutral, tool-neutral, and application-neutral. The Cross-Industry Standard Process for Data Mining (CRISP-DM[8]) was developed by analysts representing Daimler-Chrysler, SPSS, and NCR. CRISP provides a nonproprietary and freely available standard process for fitting data mining into the general problem-solving strategy of a business or research unit.

According to CRISP-DM, a given data mining project has a life cycle consisting of six phases, as illustrated in Figure 1.1. Note that the phase-sequence is *adaptive*. That is, the next phase in the sequence often depends on the outcomes associated with the previous phase. The most significant dependencies between phases are indicated by the arrows. For example, suppose we are in the modeling phase. Depending on the behavior and characteristics of the model, we may have to return to the data preparation phase for further refinement before moving forward to the model evaluation phase.

The iterative nature of CRISP is symbolized by the outer circle in Figure 1.1. Often, the solution to a particular business or research problem leads to further questions of interest, which may then be attacked using the same general process as before. Lessons learned from past projects should always be brought to bear as input into new projects. Here is an outline of each phase. (Issues encountered during the evaluation phase can conceivably send the analyst back to any of the previous phases for amelioration.)

---

[8]Peter Chapman, Julian Clinton, Randy Kerber, Thomas Khabaza, Thomas Reinart, Colin Shearer, Rudiger Wirth, *CRISP-DM Step-by-Step Data Mining Guide*, 2000.

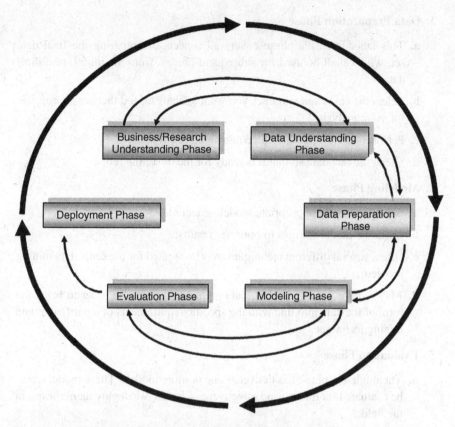

Figure 1.1   CRISP-DM is an iterative, adaptive process.

1.4.1   CRISP-DM: The Six Phases

1. Business/Research Understanding Phase

a. First, clearly enunciate the project objectives and requirements in terms of the business or research unit as a whole.

b. Then, translate these goals and restrictions into the formulation of a data mining problem definition.

c. Finally, prepare a preliminary strategy for achieving these objectives.

2. Data Understanding Phase

a. First, collect the data.

b. Then, use exploratory data analysis to familiarize yourself with the data, and discover initial insights.

c. Evaluate the quality of the data.

d. Finally, if desired, select interesting subsets that may contain actionable patterns.

3. Data Preparation Phase

a. This labor-intensive phase covers all aspects of preparing the final data set, which shall be used for subsequent phases, from the initial, raw, dirty data.

b. Select the cases and variables you want to analyze, and that are appropriate for your analysis.

c. Perform transformations on certain variables, if needed.

d. Clean the raw data so that it is ready for the modeling tools.

4. Modeling Phase

a. Select and apply appropriate modeling techniques.

b. Calibrate model settings to optimize results.

c. Often, several different techniques may be applied for the same data mining problem.

d. May require looping back to data preparation phase, in order to bring the form of the data into line with the specific requirements of a particular data mining technique.

5. Evaluation Phase

a. The modeling phase has delivered one or more models. These models must be evaluated for quality and effectiveness, before we deploy them for use in the field.

b. Also, determine whether the model in fact achieves the objectives set for it in phase 1.

c. Establish whether some important facet of the business or research problem has not been sufficiently accounted for.

d. Finally, come to a decision regarding the use of the data mining results.

6. Deployment Phase

a. Model creation does not signify the completion of the project. Need to make use of created models.

b. Example of a simple deployment: Generate a report.

c. Example of a more complex deployment: Implement a parallel data mining process in another department.

d. For businesses, the customer often carries out the deployment based on your model.

This book broadly follows CRISP-DM, with some modifications. For example, we prefer to clean the data (Chapter 2) before performing exploratory data analysis (Chapter 3).

1.5 FALLACIES OF DATA MINING

Speaking before the US House of Representatives Subcommittee on Technology, Information Policy, Intergovernmental Relations, and Census, Jen Que Louie, President of Nautilus Systems, Inc., described four fallacies of data mining.[9] Two of these fallacies parallel the warnings we have described above.

- **Fallacy 1.** There are data mining tools that we can turn loose on our data repositories, and find answers to our problems.
  - *Reality.* There are no automatic data mining tools, which will mechanically solve your problems "while you wait." Rather data mining is a process. CRISP-DM is one method for fitting the data mining process into the overall business or research plan of action.
- **Fallacy 2.** The data mining process is autonomous, requiring little or no human oversight.
  - *Reality.* Data mining is not magic. Without skilled human supervision, blind use of data mining software will only provide you with the wrong answer to the wrong question applied to the wrong type of data. Further, the wrong analysis is worse than no analysis, because it leads to policy recommendations that will probably turn out to be expensive failures. Even after the model is deployed, the introduction of new data often requires an updating of the model. Continuous quality monitoring and other evaluative measures must be assessed, by human analysts.
- **Fallacy 3.** Data mining pays for itself quite quickly.
  - *Reality.* The return rates vary, depending on the start-up costs, analysis personnel costs, data warehousing preparation costs, and so on.
- **Fallacy 4.** Data mining software packages are intuitive and easy to use.
  - *Reality.* Again, ease of use varies. However, regardless of what some software vendor advertisements may claim, you cannot just purchase some data mining software, install it, sit back, and watch it solve all your problems. For example, the algorithms require specific data formats, which may require substantial preprocessing. Data analysts must combine subject matter knowledge with an analytical mind, and a familiarity with the overall business or research model.

To the above list, we add three further common fallacies:

- **Fallacy 5.** Data mining will identify the causes of our business or research problems.
  - *Reality.* The knowledge discovery process will help you to uncover patterns of behavior. Again, it is up to the humans to identify the causes.

[9] Jen Que Louie, President of Nautilus Systems, Inc. (www.nautilus-systems.com), Testimony before the US House of Representatives Subcommittee on Technology, Information Policy, Intergovernmental Relations, and Census, Federal Document Clearing House, Congressional Testimony, March 25, 2003.

- **Fallacy 6.** Data mining will automatically clean up our messy database.
  - *Reality.* Well, not automatically. As a preliminary phase in the data mining process, data preparation often deals with data that has not been examined or used in years. Therefore, organizations beginning a new data mining operation will often be confronted with the problem of data that has been lying around for years, is stale, and needs considerable updating.
- **Fallacy 7.** Data mining always provides positive results.
  - *Reality.* There is no guarantee of positive results when mining data for actionable knowledge. Data mining is not a panacea for solving business problems. But, used properly, by people who understand the models involved, the data requirements, and the overall project objectives, data mining can indeed provide actionable and highly profitable results.

The above discussion may have been termed *what data mining cannot or should not do*. Next we turn to a discussion of what data mining can do.

1.6 WHAT TASKS CAN DATA MINING ACCOMPLISH

The following listing shows the most common data mining tasks.

Data Mining Tasks
> Description
> Estimation
> Prediction
> Classification
> Clustering
> Association.

1.6.1 Description

Sometimes researchers and analysts are simply trying to find ways to *describe* patterns and trends lying within the data. For example, a pollster may uncover evidence that those who have been laid off are less likely to support the present incumbent in the presidential election. Descriptions of patterns and trends often suggest possible explanations for such patterns and trends. For example, those who are laid off are now less well-off financially than before the incumbent was elected, and so would tend to prefer an alternative.

Data mining models should be as *transparent* as possible. That is, the results of the data mining model should describe clear patterns that are amenable to intuitive interpretation and explanation. Some data mining methods are more suited to transparent interpretation than others. For example, decision trees provide an intuitive and human-friendly explanation of their results. However, neural networks are comparatively opaque to nonspecialists, due to the nonlinearity and complexity of the model.

High-quality description can often be accomplished with *exploratory data analysis*, a graphical method of exploring the data in search of patterns and trends. We look at exploratory data analysis in Chapter 3.

1.6.2   Estimation

In estimation, we approximate the value of a numeric target variable using a set of numeric and/or categorical predictor variables. Models are built using "complete" records, which provide the value of the target variable, as well as the predictors. Then, for new observations, estimates of the value of the target variable are made, based on the values of the predictors.

For example, we might be interested in estimating the systolic blood pressure reading of a hospital patient, based on the patient's age, gender, body mass index, and blood sodium levels. The relationship between systolic blood pressure and the predictor variables in the training set would provide us with an estimation model. We can then apply that model to new cases.

Examples of estimation tasks in business and research include

- estimating the amount of money a randomly chosen family of four will spend for back-to-school shopping this fall;
- estimating the percentage decrease in rotary movement sustained by a National Football League (NFL) running back with a knee injury;
- estimating the number of points per game LeBron James will score when double-teamed in the play-offs;
- estimating the grade point average (GPA) of a graduate student, based on that student's undergraduate GPA.

Consider Figure 1.2, where we have a scatter plot of the graduate GPAs against the undergraduate GPAs for 1000 students. Simple linear regression allows us to find the line that best approximates the relationship between these two variables, according to the least-squares criterion. The regression line, indicated in blue in Figure 1.2, may then be used to estimate the graduate GPA of a student, given that student's undergraduate GPA.

Here, the equation of the regression line (as produced by the statistical package *Minitab*, which also produced the graph) is $\hat{y} = 1.24 + 0.67x$. This tells us that the estimated graduate GPA $\hat{y}$ equals 1.24 plus 0.67 times the student's undergrad GPA. For example, if your undergrad GPA is 3.0, then your estimated graduate GPA is $\hat{y} = 1.24 + 0.67(3) = 3.25$. Note that this point $(x = 3.0, \hat{y} = 3.25)$ lies precisely on the regression line, as do all of the linear regression predictions.

The field of statistical analysis supplies several venerable and widely used estimation methods. These include point estimation and confidence interval estimations, simple linear regression and correlation, and multiple regression. We examine these methods and more in Chapters 5, 6, 8, and 9. Chapter 12 may also be used for estimation.

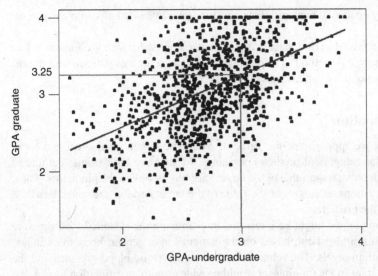

Figure 1.2   Regression estimates lie on the regression line.

1.6.3 Prediction

Prediction is similar to classification and estimation, except that for prediction, the results lie in the future. Examples of prediction tasks in business and research include

- predicting the price of a stock 3 months into the future;
- predicting the percentage increase in traffic deaths next year if the speed limit is increased;
- predicting the winner of this fall's World Series, based on a comparison of the team statistics;
- predicting whether a particular molecule in drug discovery will lead to a profitable new drug for a pharmaceutical company.

Any of the methods and techniques used for classification and estimation may also be used, under appropriate circumstances, for prediction. These include the traditional statistical methods of point estimation and confidence interval estimations, simple linear regression and correlation, and multiple regression, investigated in Chapters 5, 6, 8, and 9, as well as data mining and knowledge discovery methods such as k-nearest neighbor methods (Chapter 10), decision trees (Chapter 11), and neural networks (Chapter 12).

1.6.4 Classification

Classification is similar to estimation, except that the target variable is categorical rather than numeric. In classification, there is a target categorical variable, such as *income bracket*, which, for example, could be partitioned into three classes or categories: high income, middle income, and low income. The data mining model examines a large set of records, each record containing information on the target variable as well as a set of input or predictor variables. For example, consider the excerpt from a data set in Table 1.1.

TABLE 1.1   Excerpt from dataset for classifying income

Subject	Age	Gender	Occupation	Income Bracket
001	47	F	Software Engineer	High
002	28	M	Marketing Consultant	Middle
003	35	M	Unemployed	Low
...	...	...	...	...

Suppose the researcher would like to be able to *classify* the income bracket of new individuals, not currently in the above database, based on the other characteristics associated with that individual, such as age, gender, and occupation. This task is a classification task, very nicely suited to data mining methods and techniques.

The algorithm would proceed roughly as follows. First, examine the data set containing both the predictor variables and the (already classified) target variable, *income bracket*. In this way, the algorithm (software) "learns about" which combinations of variables are associated with which income brackets. For example, older females may be associated with the high-income bracket. This data set is called the *training set*.

Then the algorithm would look at new records, for which no information about income bracket is available. On the basis of the classifications in the training set, the algorithm would assign classifications to the new records. For example, a 63-year-old female professor might be classified in the high-income bracket.

Examples of classification tasks in business and research include

- determining whether a particular credit card transaction is fraudulent;
- placing a new student into a particular track with regard to special needs;
- assessing whether a mortgage application is a good or bad credit risk;
- diagnosing whether a particular disease is present;
- determining whether a will was written by the actual deceased, or fraudulently by someone else;
- identifying whether or not certain financial or personal behavior indicates a possible terrorist threat.

For example, in the medical field, suppose we are interested in classifying the type of drug a patient should be prescribed, based on certain patient characteristics, such as the age of the patient, and the patient's sodium/potassium ratio. For a sample of 200 patients, Figure 1.3 presents a scatter plot of the patients' sodium/potassium ratio against the patients' age. The particular drug prescribed is symbolized by the shade of the points. Light gray points indicate drug Y; medium gray points indicate drugs A or X; dark gray points indicate drugs B or C. In this scatter plot, Na/K

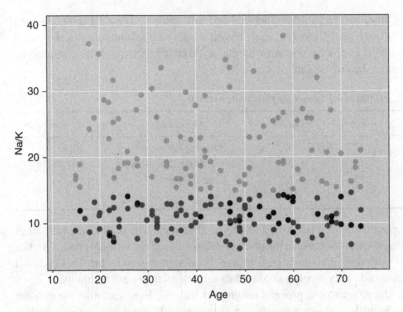

Figure 1.3　Which drug should be prescribed for which type of patient?

(sodium/potassium ratio) is plotted on the Y (vertical) axis and age is plotted on the X (horizontal) axis.

Suppose that we will base our prescription recommendation based on this data set.

1. Which drug should be prescribed for a young patient with high sodium/ potassium ratio?

   Young patients are on the left in the graph, and high sodium/potassium ratios are in the upper half, which indicates that previous young patients with high sodium/potassium ratios were prescribed drug Y (light gray points). The recommended prediction classification for such patients is drug Y.

2. Which drug should be prescribed for older patients with low sodium/potassium ratios?

   Patients in the lower right of the graph have been taking different prescriptions, indicated by either dark gray (drugs B or C) or medium gray (drugs A or X). Without more specific information, a definitive classification cannot be made here. For example, perhaps these drugs have varying interactions with beta-blockers, estrogens, or other medications, or are contraindicated for conditions such as asthma or heart disease.

Graphs and plots are helpful for understanding two- and three-dimensional relationships in data. But sometimes classifications need to be based on many different predictors, requiring a multidimensional plot. Therefore, we need to turn to more sophisticated models to perform our classification tasks. Common data mining methods used for classification are covered in Chapters 10–14.

1.6.5 Clustering

Clustering refers to the grouping of records, observations, or cases into classes of similar objects. A *cluster* is a collection of records that are similar to one another, and dissimilar to records in other clusters. Clustering differs from classification in that there is no target variable for clustering. The clustering task does not try to classify, estimate, or predict the value of a target variable. Instead, clustering algorithms seek to segment the whole data set into relatively homogeneous subgroups or clusters, where the similarity of the records within the cluster is maximized, and the similarity to records outside of this cluster is minimized.

Nielsen Claritas is in the clustering business. Among the services they provide is a demographic profile of each of the geographic areas in the country, as defined by zip code. One of the clustering mechanisms they use is the *PRIZM* segmentation system, which describes every American zip code area in terms of distinct lifestyle types. The 66 distinct clusters are shown in Table 1.2.

For illustration, the clusters for zip code 90210, Beverly Hills, California, are as follows:

- Cluster # 01: Upper Crust Estates
- Cluster # 03: Movers and Shakers

TABLE 1.2   The 66 clusters used by the *PRIZM* segmentation system

01 Upper Crust	02 Blue Blood Estates	03 Movers and Shakers
04 Young Digerati	05 Country Squires	06 Winner's Circle
07 Money and Brains	08 Executive Suites	09 Big Fish, Small Pond
10 Second City Elite	11 God's Country	12 Brite Lites, Little City
13 Upward Bound	14 New Empty Nests	15 Pools and Patios
16 Bohemian Mix	17 Beltway Boomers	18 Kids and Cul-de-sacs
19 Home Sweet Home	20 Fast-Track Families	21 Gray Power
22 Young Influentials	23 Greenbelt Sports	24 Up-and-Comers
25 Country Casuals	26 The Cosmopolitans	27 Middleburg Managers
28 Traditional Times	29 American Dreams	30 Suburban Sprawl
31 Urban Achievers	32 New Homesteaders	33 Big Sky Families
34 White Picket Fences	35 Boomtown Singles	36 Blue-Chip Blues
37 Mayberry-ville	38 Simple Pleasures	39 Domestic Duos
40 Close-in Couples	41 Sunset City Blues	42 Red, White and Blues
43 Heartlanders	44 New Beginnings	45 Blue Highways
46 Old Glories	47 City Startups	48 Young and Rustic
49 American Classics	50 Kid Country, USA	51 Shotguns and Pickups
52 Suburban Pioneers	53 Mobility Blues	54 Multi-Culti Mosaic
55 Golden Ponds	56 Crossroads Villagers	57 Old Milltowns
58 Back Country Folks	59 Urban Elders	60 Park Bench Seniors
61 City Roots	62 Hometown Retired	63 Family Thrifts
64 Bedrock America	65 Big City Blues	66 Low-Rise Living

- Cluster # 04: Young Digerati
- Cluster # 07: Money and Brains
- Cluster # 16: Bohemian Mix.

The description for Cluster # 01: Upper Crust is "The nation's most exclusive address, Upper Crust is the wealthiest lifestyle in America, a haven for empty-nesting couples between the ages of 45 and 64. No segment has a higher concentration of residents earning over $100,000 a year and possessing a postgraduate degree. And none has a more opulent standard of living."

Examples of clustering tasks in business and research include the following:

- Target marketing of a niche product for a small-cap business which does not have a large marketing budget.
- For accounting auditing purposes, to segmentize financial behavior into benign and suspicious categories.
- As a dimension-reduction tool when the data set has hundreds of attributes.
- For gene expression clustering, where very large quantities of genes may exhibit similar behavior.

Clustering is often performed as a preliminary step in a data mining process, with the resulting clusters being used as further inputs into a different technique downstream, such as neural networks. We discuss hierarchical and k-means clustering in Chapter 19, Kohonen networks in Chapter 20, and balanced iterative reducing and clustering using hierarchies (BIRCH) clustering in Chapter 21.

1.6.6 Association

The association task for data mining is the job of finding which attributes "go together." Most prevalent in the business world, where it is known as affinity analysis or market basket analysis, the task of association seeks to uncover rules for quantifying the relationship between two or more attributes. Association rules are of the form "If *antecedent* then *consequent*," together with a measure of the support and confidence associated with the rule. For example, a particular supermarket may find that, of the 1000 customers shopping on a Thursday night, 200 bought diapers, and of those 200 who bought diapers, 50 bought beer. Thus, the association rule would be "If buy diapers, then buy beer," with a support of $200/1000 = 20\%$ and a confidence of $50/200 = 25\%$.

Examples of association tasks in business and research include

- investigating the proportion of subscribers to your company's cell phone plan that respond positively to an offer of a service upgrade;
- examining the proportion of children whose parents read to them who are themselves good readers;
- predicting degradation in telecommunications networks;
- finding out which items in a supermarket are purchased together, and which items are never purchased together;

- determining the proportion of cases in which a new drug will exhibit dangerous side effects.

We discuss two algorithms for generating association rules, the a priori algorithm, and the generalized rule induction (GRI) algorithm, in Chapter 22.

THE R ZONE

Getting Started with R

Comments, indents, and semicolons

```
# Anything prefaced by a pound sign (#) is a comment.
# Comments are not executed by R. Instead, they explain what the code is doing.
# Indented code (that is not a comment) will run in R as if it was on one line
# Code separated by semicolons will run as if the code was on separate lines,
# with the semicolon marking the line break
```

Open a dataset and display the data

```
# Replace "C:/ … /" with the exact location of the file you want to open
cars <- read.csv(file = "C:/ … /cars.txt",
    stringsAsFactors = FALSE)
cars # To display the whole dataset, type the dataset name
head(cars) # Display the first few records of a dataset
names(cars) # Display variable names of a data frame, one kind of data in R
cars$weight # Look at only the weight variable within data frame cars
```

Matrices

```
# Create a matrix with three rows, two columns, and every value equal to 0.0
mat <- matrix(0.0, nrow = 3, ncol = 2); mat
colnames(mat) <- c("Var 1", "Var 2") # Give a matrix variable names
colnames(mat) # Display variable names of a matrix
```

Subset data and declare new variables

```
cars.rsub <- cars[1:50,] # Subset the data by rows
cars.csub <- cars[,1:3] # Subset by columns
cars.rcsub <- cars[c(1,3,5), c(2,4)] # Subset by specific rows and columns
cars.vsub <- cars[which(cars$mpg > 30),] # Subset by a logical condition
# To declare new variables, type the
  variable name, a left-arrow, then the value of the variable
firstletter <- "a"
weight <- cars$weight
```

Display more than one figure at a time

par(mfrow=c(1,1)) # plots one figure; the default setting
par(mfrow=c(2,3)) # plots six figures: three in the top row, three in the bottom row
Plots will fill the plot space row by row

Download and install an R Package

# Example: *ggplot2*, from Chapter 3.
install.packages("ggplot2")
# Pick any CRAN mirror, as shown
# Open the new package
library(ggplot2)

```
79: USA (CA 1)          80: USA (CA 2)
81: USA (IA)            82: USA (IN)
83: USA (KS)            84: USA (MD)
85: USA (MI)            86: USA (MO)
87: USA (OH)            88: USA (OR)
89: USA (PA 1)          90: USA (PA 2)
91: USA (TN)            92: USA (TX 1)
93: USA (WA 1)          94: USA (WA 2)
95: Venezuela           96: Vietnam
.
Selection: 79
```

R REFERENCES

Wickham H. *ggplot2: Elegant Graphics for Data Analysis*. New York: Springer; 2009.

R Core Team. *R: A Language and Environment for Statistical Computing*. Vienna, Austria: R Foundation for Statistical Computing; 2012. ISBN: 3-900051-07-0, http://www. R-project.org/.

EXERCISES

1. For each of the following, identify the relevant data mining task(s):
   a. The Boston Celtics would like to approximate how many points their next opponent will score against them.
   b. A military intelligence officer is interested in learning about the respective proportions of Sunnis and Shias in a particular strategic region.
   c. A NORAD defense computer must decide immediately whether a blip on the radar is a flock of geese or an incoming nuclear missile.
   d. A political strategist is seeking the best groups to canvass for donations in a particular county.
   e. A Homeland Security official would like to determine whether a certain sequence of financial and residence moves implies a tendency to terrorist acts.
   f. A Wall Street analyst has been asked to find out the expected change in stock price for a set of companies with similar price/earnings ratios.

2. For each of the following meetings, explain which phase in the CRISP-DM process is represented:
   a. Managers want to know by next week whether deployment will take place. Therefore, analysts meet to discuss how useful and accurate their model is.

b. The data mining project manager meets with the data warehousing manager to discuss how the data will be collected.

c. The data mining consultant meets with the vice president for marketing, who says that he would like to move forward with customer relationship management.

d. The data mining project manager meets with the production line supervisor, to discuss implementation of changes and improvements.

e. The analysts meet to discuss whether the neural network or decision tree models should be applied.

3. Discuss the need for human direction of data mining. Describe the possible consequences of relying on completely automatic data analysis tools.

4. CRISP-DM is not the only standard process for data mining. Research an alternative methodology (Hint: Sample, Explore, Modify, Model and Assess (SEMMA), from the SAS Institute). Discuss the similarities and differences with CRISP-DM.

## CHAPTER 2

DATA PREPROCESSING

Chapter 1 introduced us to data mining, and the cross-industry standard process for data mining (CRISP-DM) standard process for data mining model development. In phase 1 of the data mining process, *business understanding* or *research understanding,* businesses and researchers first enunciate project objectives, then translate these objectives into the formulation of a data mining problem definition, and finally prepare a preliminary strategy for achieving these objectives.

Here in this chapter, we examine the next two phases of the CRISP-DM standard process, *data understanding* and *data preparation.* We will show how to evaluate the quality of the data, clean the raw data, deal with missing data, and perform transformations on certain variables. All of Chapter 3 is devoted to this very important aspect of the *data understanding* phase. The heart of any data mining project is the *modeling* phase, which we begin examining in Chapter 7.

2.1   WHY DO WE NEED TO PREPROCESS THE DATA?

Much of the raw data contained in databases is unpreprocessed, incomplete, and noisy. For example, the databases may contain

- fields that are obsolete or redundant;
- missing values;
- outliers;
- data in a form not suitable for the data mining models;
- values not consistent with policy or common sense.

In order to be useful for data mining purposes, the databases need to undergo preprocessing, in the form of *data cleaning* and *data transformation.* Data mining often deals with data that has not been looked at for years, so that much of the data contains field values that have expired, are no longer relevant, or are simply missing. The overriding objective is to *minimize garbage in, garbage out (GIGO),* to minimize the Garbage that gets Into our model, so that we can minimize the amount of Garbage that our models give Out.

Depending on the data set, data preprocessing alone can account for 10–60% of all the time and effort for the entire data mining process. In this chapter, we shall examine several ways to preprocess the data for further analysis downstream.

2.2   DATA CLEANING

To illustrate the need for cleaning up the data, let us take a look at some of the kinds of errors that could creep into even a tiny data set, such as that in Table 2.1.

Let us discuss, attribute by attribute, some of the problems that have found their way into the data set in Table 2.1. The *customer ID* variable seems to be fine. What about *zip*?

Let us assume that we are expecting all of the customers in the database to have the usual five-numeral American zip code. Now, customer 1002 has this strange (to American eyes) zip code of *J2S7K7*. If we were not careful, we might be tempted to classify this unusual value as an error, and toss it out, until we stop to think that not all countries use the same zip code format. Actually, this is the zip code (*known as* postal code in Canada) of St. Hyancinthe, Quebec, Canada, and so probably represents real data from a real customer. What has evidently occurred is that a French-Canadian customer has made a purchase, and put their home zip code down in the required field. In the era of free trade, we must be ready to expect unusual values in fields such as zip codes that vary from country to country.

What about the zip code for customer 1004? We are unaware of any countries that have four-digit zip codes, such as the *6269* indicated here, so this must be an error, right? Probably not. Zip codes for the New England states begin with the numeral *0*. Unless the zip code field is defined to be *character* (text) and not *numeric*, the software will most likely chop off the leading zero, which is apparently what happened here. The zip code may well be *06269,* which refers to Storrs, Connecticut, home of the University of Connecticut.

The next field, *gender,* contains a missing value for customer 1003. We shall detail the methods for dealing with missing values later in this chapter.

The income field has three potentially anomalous values. First, customer 1003 is shown as having an income of $10,000,000 per year. While entirely possible, especially when considering the customer's zip code (*90210,* Beverly Hills), this value of income is nevertheless an *outlier,* an extreme data value. Certain statistical and data mining modeling techniques do not function smoothly in the presence of outliers; therefore, we shall examine the methods of handling outliers later in this chapter.

TABLE 2.1   Can you find any problems in this tiny data set?

Customer ID	Zip	Gender	Income	Age	Marital Status	Transaction Amount
1001	10048	M	75,000	C	M	5000
1002	J2S7K7	F	−40,000	40	W	4000
1003	90210		10,000,000	45	S	7000
1004	6269	M	50,000	0	S	1000
1005	55101	F	99,999	30	D	3000

Poverty is one thing, but it is rare to find an income that is negative, as our poor customer 1002 has. Unlike customer 1003's income, customer 1002's reported income of −$40,000 lies beyond the field bounds for income, and therefore must be an error. It is unclear how this error crept in, with perhaps the most likely explanation being that the negative sign is a stray data entry error. However, we cannot be sure, and hence should approach this value cautiously, and attempt to communicate with the database manager most familiar with the database history.

So what is wrong with customer 1005's income of $99,999? Perhaps nothing; it may in fact be valid. But, if all the other incomes are rounded to the nearest $5000, why the precision with customer 1005's income? Often, in legacy databases, certain specified values are meant to be codes for anomalous entries, such as missing values. Perhaps *99,999* was coded in an old database to mean *missing*. Again, we cannot be sure, and should again refer to the database administrator.

Finally, are we clear regarding, which unit of measure the income variable is measured in? Databases often get merged, sometimes without bothering to check whether such merges are entirely appropriate for all fields. For example, it is quite possible that customer 1002, with the Canadian zip code, has an income measured in Canadian dollars, not U.S. dollars.

The *age* field has a couple of problems. Although all the other customers have numeric values for *age,* customer 1001's "age" of *C* probably reflects an earlier categorization of this man's age into a bin labeled *C.* The data mining software will definitely not allow this categorical value in an otherwise numeric field, and we will have to resolve this problem somehow. How about customer 1004's age of *0*? Perhaps, there is a *newborn* male living in Storrs, Connecticut, who has made a transaction of $1000. More likely, the age of this person is probably missing, and was coded as *0* to indicate this or some other anomalous condition (e.g., refused to provide the age information).

Of course, keeping an *age* field in a database is a minefield in itself, as the passage of time will quickly make the field values obsolete and misleading. It is better to keep *date*-type fields (such as birthdate) in a database, as these are constant, and may be transformed into ages when needed.

The *marital status* field seems fine, right? Maybe not. The problem lies in the meaning behind these symbols. We all think we know what these symbols mean, but are sometimes surprised. For example, if you are in search of cold water in a restroom in Montreal, and turn on the faucet marked *C,* you may be in for a surprise, as the *C* stands for *chaude,* which is French for *hot.* There is also the problem of ambiguity. In Table 2.1, for example, does the *S* for customers 1003 and 1004 stand for *single* or *separated*?

The *transaction amount* field seems satisfactory, as long as we are confident that we know what unit of measure is being used, and that all records are transacted in this unit.

2.3 HANDLING MISSING DATA

Missing data is a problem that continues to plague data analysis methods. Even as our analysis methods gain sophistication, we nevertheless continue to encounter missing values in fields, especially in databases with a large number of fields. The absence of information is rarely beneficial. All things being equal, more information is almost always better. Therefore, we should think carefully about how we handle the thorny issue of missing data.

To help us tackle this problem, we will introduce ourselves to a new data set, the *cars* data set, originally compiled by Barry Becker and Ronny Kohavi of Silicon Graphics, and available for download at the book series web site www.dataminingconsultant.com. The data set consists of information about 261 automobiles manufactured in the 1970s and 1980s, including gas mileage, number of cylinders, cubic inches, horsepower, and so on.

Suppose, however, that some of the field values were missing for certain records. Figure 2.1 provides a peek at the first 10 records in the data set, with two of the field values missing.

	mpg	cubicinches	hp	brand
1	14.000	350	165	US
2	31.900		71	Europe
3	17.000	302	140	US
4	15.000	400	150	
5	37.700	89	62	Japan

Figure 2.1   Some of our field values are missing.

A common method of "handling" missing values is simply to omit the records or fields with missing values from the analysis. However, this may be dangerous, as the pattern of missing values may in fact be systematic, and simply deleting the records with missing values would lead to a biased subset of the data. Further, it seems like a waste to omit the information in all the other fields, just because one field value is missing. In fact, Schmueli, Patel, and Bruce[1] state that if only 5% of data values are missing from a data set of 30 variables, and the missing values are spread evenly throughout the data, almost 80% of the records would have at least one missing value. Therefore, data analysts have turned to methods that would replace the missing value with a value substituted according to various criteria.

Some common criteria for choosing replacement values for missing data are as follows:

1. Replace the missing value with some constant, specified by the analyst.
2. Replace the missing value with the field mean[2] (for numeric variables) or the mode (for categorical variables).
3. Replace the missing values with a value generated at random from the observed distribution of the variable.
4. Replace the missing values with *imputed* values based on the other character- istics of the record.

---

[1]Gallit Shmueli, Nitin Patel, and Peter Bruce, *Data Mining for Business Intelligence,* 2nd edition, John Wiley and Sons, 2010.

[2]See the Appendix for the definition of *mean* and *mode*.

Let us examine each of the first three methods, none of which is entirely satisfactory, as we shall see. Figure 2.2 shows the result of replacing the missing values with the constant 0 for the numerical variable *cubicinches* and the label *missing* for the categorical variable *brand*.

	mpg	cubicinches	hp	brand
1	14.000	350	165	US
2	31.900	0	71	Europe
3	17.000	302	140	US
4	15.000	400	150	Missing
5	37.700	89	62	Japan

Figure 2.2   Replacing missing field values with user-defined constants.

Figure 2.3 illustrates how the missing values may be replaced with the respective field means and modes.

	mpg	cubicinches	hp	brand
1	14.000	350	165	US
2	31.900	200.65	71	Europe
3	17.000	302	140	US
4	15.000	400	150	US
5	37.700	89	62	Japan

Figure 2.3   Replacing missing field values with means or modes.

The variable *brand* is categorical, with mode *US,* so the software replaces the missing *brand* value with *brand = US. Cubicinches,* however, is continuous (numeric), so that the software replaces the missing *cubicinches* values with *cubicinches = 200.65,* which is the mean of all 258 non-missing values of that variable.

Is it not nice to have the software take care of your missing data problems like this? In a way, certainly. However, do not lose sight of the fact that the software is creating information on the spot, actually fabricating data to fill in the holes in our data set. Choosing the field mean as a substitute for whatever value would have been there may sometimes work out well. However, the end-user needs to be informed that this process has taken place.

Further, the mean may not always be the best choice for what constitutes a "typical" value. For example, Larose[3] examines a data set where the mean is greater than the 81st percentile. Also, if many missing values are replaced with the mean, the resulting confidence levels for statistical inference will be overoptimistic, as measures

[3] *Discovering Statistics*, 2nd edition, by Daniel Larose, W.H. Freeman and Company, Publishers, 2013.

of spread will be artificially reduced. It must be stressed that replacing missing values is a gamble, and the benefits must be weighed against the possible invalidity of the results.

Finally, Figure 2.4 demonstrates how missing values can be replaced with values generated at random from the observed distribution of the variable.

	mpg	cubicinches	hp	brand
1	14.000	350	165	US
2	31.900	450	71	Europe
3	17.000	302	140	US
4	15.000	400	150	Japan
5	37.700	89	62	Japan

Figure 2.4   Replacing missing field values with random draws from the distribution of the variable.

One benefit of this method is that the measures of center and spread should remain closer to the original, when compared to the mean replacement method. However, there is no guarantee that the resulting records would make sense. For example, the random values drawn in Figure 2.4 has led to at least one car that does not in fact exist! There is no Japanese-made car in the database that has an engine size of 400 cubic inches.

We therefore need *data imputation methods* that take advantage of the knowledge that the car is Japanese when calculating its missing cubic inches. In data imputation, we ask "What would be the most likely value for this missing value, given all the other attributes for a particular record?" For instance, an American car with 300 cubic inches and 150 horsepower would probably be expected to have more cylinders than a Japanese car with 100 cubic inches and 90 horsepower. This is called *imputation of missing data*. Before we can profitably discuss data imputation, however, we need to learn the tools needed to do so, such as multiple regression or classification and regression trees. Therefore, to learn about the imputation of missing data, see Chapter 27.

2.4   IDENTIFYING MISCLASSIFICATIONS

Let us look at an example of checking the classification labels on the categorical variables, to make sure that they are all valid and consistent. Suppose that a frequency distribution of the variable *brand* was as shown in Table 2.2.

The frequency distribution shows five classes, USA, France, US, Europe, and Japan. However, two of the classes, USA and France, have a count of only one automobile each. What is clearly happening here is that two of the records have been inconsistently classified with respect to the origin of manufacture. To maintain consistency with the remainder of the data set, the record with origin *USA* should have been labeled *US,* and the record with origin *France* should have been labeled *Europe.*

TABLE 2.2 Notice anything strange about this frequency distribution?

Brand	Frequency
USA	1
France	1
US	156
Europe	46
Japan	51

2.5 GRAPHICAL METHODS FOR IDENTIFYING OUTLIERS

Outliers are extreme values that go against the trend of the remaining data. Identifying outliers is important because they may represent errors in data entry. Also, even if an outlier is a valid data point and not an error, certain statistical methods are sensitive to the presence of outliers, and may deliver unreliable results.

One graphical method for identifying outliers for numeric variables is to examine a *histogram*[4] of the variable. Figure 2.5 shows a histogram of the vehicle weights from the (slightly amended) *cars* data set. (Note: This slightly amended data set is available as *cars2* from the series web site.)

There appears to be one lonely vehicle in the extreme left tail of the distribution, with a vehicle weight in the hundreds of pounds rather than in the thousands. Further investigation (not shown) tells us that the minimum weight is 192.5 pounds, which is

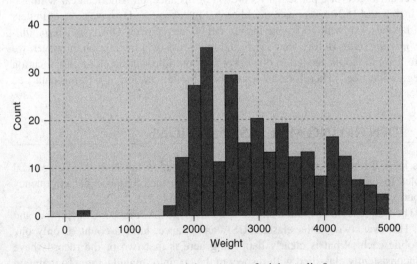

Figure 2.5 Histogram of vehicle weights: can you find the outlier?

[4]See the Appendix for more on histograms, including a caution on their interpretation.

undoubtedly our little outlier in the lower tail. As 192.5 pounds is rather light for an automobile, we would tend to doubt the validity of this information.

We can surmise that perhaps the weight was originally 1925 pounds, with the decimal inserted somewhere along the line. We cannot be certain, however, and further investigation into the data sources is called for.

Sometimes two-dimensional scatter plots[5] can help to reveal outliers in more than one variable. Figure 2.6, a scatter plot of *mpg* against *weightlbs,* seems to have netted two outliers.

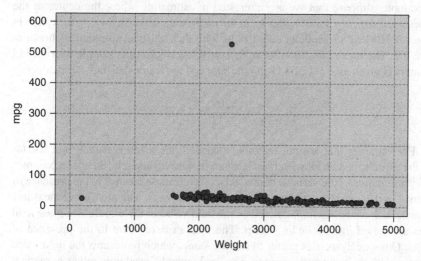

Figure 2.6   Scatter plot of *mpg* against *weightlbs* shows two outliers.

Most of the data points cluster together along the horizontal axis, except for two outliers. The one on the left is the same vehicle we identified in Figure 2.6, weighing only 192.5 pounds. The outlier near the top is something new: a car that gets over 500 miles per gallon! Clearly, unless this vehicle runs on dilithium crystals, we are looking at a data entry error.

Note that the 192.5-pound vehicle is an outlier with respect to weight but not with respect to mileage. Similarly, the 500-mpg car is an outlier with respect to mileage but not with respect to weight. Thus, a record may be an outlier in a particular dimension but not in another. We shall examine numeric methods for identifying outliers, but we need to pick up a few tools first.

2.6   MEASURES OF CENTER AND SPREAD

Suppose that we are interested in estimating where the center of a particular variable lies, as measured by one of the numerical *measures of center,* the most common of which are the mean, median, and mode. The measures of center are a special case of

---

[5] See the Appendix for more on scatter plots.

measures of location, numerical summaries that indicate *where* on a number line a certain characteristic of the variable lies. Examples of the measures of location are percentiles and quantiles.

The *mean* of a variable is simply the average of the valid values taken by the variable. To find the mean, simply add up all the field values and divide by the sample size. Here, we introduce a bit of notation. The sample mean is denoted as $\bar{x}$ ("*x-bar*") and is computed as $\bar{x} = \Sigma x/n$, where Σ (capital sigma, the Greek letter "S," for "summation") represents "sum all the values," and n represents the sample size. For example, suppose that we are interested in estimating where the center of the *customer service calls* variable lies from the *churn* data set, which we will explore in Chapter 3. IBM/SPSS Modeler supplies us with the statistical summaries shown in Figure 2.7. The mean number of customer service calls for this sample of $n = 3333$ customers is given as $\bar{x} = 1.563$ Using the *sum* and the *count* statistics, we can verify that

$$\bar{x} = \frac{\Sigma x}{n} = \frac{5209}{3333} = 1.563$$

For variables that are not extremely skewed, the mean is usually not too far from the variable center. However, for extremely skewed data sets, the mean becomes less representative of the variable center. Also, the mean is sensitive to the presence of outliers. For this reason, analysts sometimes prefer to work with alternative measures of center, such as the *median,* defined as the field value in the middle when the field values are sorted into ascending order. The median is resistant to the presence of outliers. Other analysts may prefer to use the *mode*, which represents the field value occurring with the greatest frequency. The mode may be used with either numerical or categorical data, but is not always associated with the variable center.

Note that the measures of center do not always concur as to where the center of the data set lies. In Figure 2.7, the median is 1, which means that half of the customers made at least one customer service call; the mode is also 1, which means that the most frequent number of customer service calls was 1. The median and mode agree. However, the mean is 1.563, which is 56.3% higher than the other measures. This is due to the mean's sensitivity to the right-skewness of the data.

Measures of location are not sufficient to summarize a variable effectively. In fact, two variables may have the very same values for the mean, median, and mode, and yet have different natures. For example, suppose that stock portfolio A and stock

⊟ Customer Service Calls
  ⊟ Statistics

Count	3333
Mean	1.563
Sum	5209.000
Median	1
Mode	1

Figure 2.7   Statistical summary of *customer service calls.*

TABLE 2.3   The two portfolios have the same mean, median, and mode, but are clearly different

Stock Portfolio A	Stock Portfolio B
1	7
11	8
11	11
11	11
16	13

portfolio B contained five stocks each, with the price/earnings (P/E) ratios as shown in Table 2.3. The portfolios are distinctly different in terms of P/E ratios. Portfolio A includes one stock that has a very small P/E ratio and another with a rather large P/E ratio. However, portfolio B's P/E ratios are more tightly clustered around the mean. However, despite these differences, the mean, median, and mode P/E ratios of the portfolios are precisely the same: The mean P/E ratio is 10, the median is 11, and the mode is 11 for each portfolio.

Clearly, these measures of center do not provide us with a complete picture. What are missing are the *measures of spread* or the *measures of variability,* which will describe how spread out the data values are. Portfolio A's P/E ratios are more spread out than those of portfolio B, so the measures of variability for portfolio A should be larger than those of B.

Typical measures of variability include the *range* (maximum − minimum), the standard deviation (SD), the mean absolute deviation, and the interquartile range (IQR). The sample *SD* is perhaps the most widespread measure of variability and is defined by

$$s = \sqrt{\frac{\Sigma(x - \bar{x})^2}{n - 1}}$$

Because of the squaring involved, the SD is sensitive to the presence of outliers, leading analysts to prefer other measures of spread, such as the *mean absolute deviation,* in situations involving extreme values.

The SD can be interpreted as the "typical" distance between a field value and the mean, and most field values lie within two SDs of the mean. From Figure 2.7 we can state that the number of customer service calls made by most customers lies within $2(1.315) = 2.63$ of the mean of 1.563 calls. In other words, most of the number of customer service calls lie within the interval $(-1.067, 4.193)$, that is, $(0, 4)$. (This can be verified by examining the histogram of customer service calls in Figure 3.12.)

More information about these statistics may be found in the Appendix. A more complete discussion of measures of location and variability can be found in any introductory statistics textbook, such as Larose.[6]

---

[6]*Discovering Statistics*, 2nd edition, by Daniel Larose, W.H. Freeman and Company, Publishers, 2013.

2.7   DATA TRANSFORMATION

Variables tend to have ranges that vary greatly from each other. For example, if we are interested in major league baseball, players' batting averages will range from zero to less than 0.400, while the number of home runs hit in a season will range from zero to around 70. For some data mining algorithms, such differences in the ranges will lead to a tendency for the variable with greater range to have undue influence on the results. That is, the greater variability in home runs will dominate the lesser variability in batting averages.

Therefore, data miners should *normalize* their numeric variables, in order to standardize the scale of effect each variable has on the results. Neural networks benefit from *normalization,* as do algorithms that make use of distance measures, such as the *k*-nearest neighbors algorithm. There are several techniques for normalization, and we shall examine two of the more prevalent methods. Let X refer to our original field value, and X^* refer to the normalized field value.

2.8   MIN–MAX NORMALIZATION

Min–max normalization works by seeing how much greater the field value is than the minimum value $min(X)$, and scaling this difference by the range. That is,

$$X^*_{mm} = \frac{X - \min(X)}{range(X)} = \frac{X - \min(X)}{\max(X) - \min(X)}$$

The summary statistics for *weight* are shown in Figure 2.8. The minimum weight is 1613 pounds, and the range $= \max(X) - \min(X) = 4997 - 1613 = 3384$ pounds.

Let us find the min–max normalization for three automobiles weighing 1613, 3384, and 4997 pounds, respectively.

- For an ultralight vehicle, weighing only 1613 pounds (the field minimum), the min–max normalization is

$$X^*_{mm} = \frac{X - \min(X)}{range(X)} = \frac{1613 - 1613}{3384} = 0$$

Thus, data values which represent the minimum for the variable will have a min–max normalization value of 0.

weightlbs	
Statistics	
Mean	3005.490
Min	1613
Max	4997
Range	3384
Standard Deviation	852.646

Figure 2.8   Summary statistics for *weight*.

- The *midrange* equals the average of the maximum and minimum values in a data set. That is,

$$\text{Midrange}(X) = \frac{\max(X) + \min(X)}{2} = \frac{4997 + 1613}{2} = 3305 \text{ pounds}$$

For a "midrange" vehicle (if any), which weighs exactly halfway between the minimum weight and the maximum weight, the min–max normalization is

$$X^*_{mm} = \frac{X - \min(X)}{\text{range}(X)} = \frac{3305 - 1613}{3384} = 0.5$$

So the midrange data value has a min–max normalization value of 0.5.

- The heaviest vehicle has a min–max normalization value of

$$X^*_{mm} = \frac{X - \min(X)}{\text{range}(X)} = \frac{4497 - 1613}{3384} = 1$$

That is, data values representing the field maximum will have a min–max normalization of 1. To summarize, min–max normalization values will range from 0 to 1.

2.9   Z-SCORE STANDARDIZATION

Z-score standardization, which is very widespread in the world of statistical analysis, works by taking the difference between the field value and the field mean value, and scaling this difference by the SD of the field values. That is

$$\text{Z-score} = \frac{X - \text{mean}(X)}{\text{SD}(X)}$$

Figure 2.8 tells us that mean(weight) = 3005.49 and SD(weight) = 852.49.

- For the vehicle weighing only 1613 pounds, the Z-score standardization is

$$\text{Z-score} = \frac{X - \text{mean}(X)}{\text{SD}(X)} = \frac{1613 - 3005.49}{852.49} \approx -1.63$$

Thus, data values that lie below the mean will have a negative Z-score standardization.

- For an "average" vehicle (if any), with a weight equal to mean(X) = 3005.49 pounds, the Z-score standardization is

$$\text{Z-score} = \frac{X - \text{mean}(X)}{\text{SD}(X)} = \frac{3005.49 - 3005.49}{852.49} = 0$$

That is, values falling exactly on the mean will have a Z-score standardization of zero.

- For the heaviest car, the Z-score standardization is

$$\text{Z-score} = \frac{X - \text{mean}(X)}{\text{SD}(X)} = \frac{4997 - 3005.49}{852.49} \approx 2.34$$

That is, data values that lie above the mean will have a positive Z-score standardization.[7]

2.10   DECIMAL SCALING

Decimal scaling ensures that every normalized value lies between −1 and 1.

$$X^*_{\text{decimal}} = \frac{X}{10^d}$$

where d represents the number of digits in the data value with the largest absolute value. For the weight data, the largest absolute value is $|4997| = 4997$, which has $d = 4$ digits. The decimal scaling for the minimum and maximum weight are

$$\text{Min} : X^*_{\text{decimal}} = \frac{1613}{10^4} = 0.1613 \quad \text{Max} : X^*_{\text{decimal}} = \frac{4997}{10^4} = 0.4997$$

2.11   TRANSFORMATIONS TO ACHIEVE NORMALITY

Some data mining algorithms and statistical methods require that the variables be *normally distributed*. The normal distribution is a continuous probability distribution commonly *known as* the bell curve, which is symmetric. It is centered at mean μ ("mew") and has its spread determined by SD σ (sigma). Figure 2.9 shows the normal distribution that has mean $\mu = 0$ and SD $\sigma = 1$, *known as* the *standard normal distribution Z*.

It is a common misconception that variables that have had the Z-score standardization applied to them follow the standard normal Z distribution. This is not correct! It is true that the Z-standardized data will have mean 0 and SD = 1

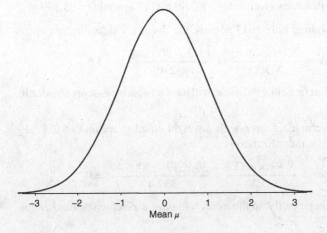

Figure 2.9   Standard normal Z distribution.

[7]Also, for a given Z-score, we may find its associated data value. See the Appendix.

but the distribution may still be skewed. Compare the histogram of the original *weight* data in Figure 2.10 with the Z-standardized data in Figure 2.11. Both histograms are right-skewed; in particular, Figure 2.10 is not symmetric, and so cannot be normally distributed.

We use the following statistic to measure the *skewness* of a distribution[8]:

$$\text{Skewness} = \frac{3(\text{mean} - \text{median})}{\text{standard deviation}}$$

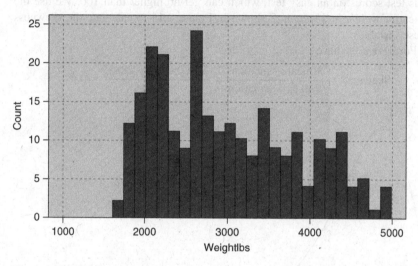

Figure 2.10   Original data.

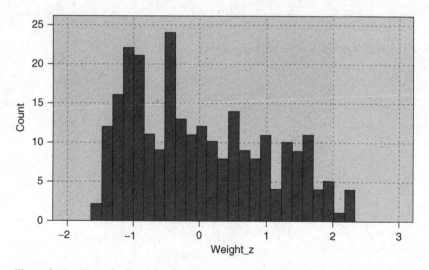

Figure 2.11   Z-standardized data is still right-skewed, not normally distributed.

[8]Find more about standard deviations in the Appendix.

For right-skewed data, the mean is greater than the median, and thus the skewness will be positive (Figure 2.12), while for left-skewed data, the mean is smaller than the median, generating negative values for skewness (Figure 2.13). For perfectly symmetric (and unimodal) data (Figure 2.9) of course, the mean, median, and mode are all equal, and so the skewness equals zero.

Much real-world data is right-skewed, including most financial data. Left-skewed data is not as common, but often occurs when the data is right-censored, such as test scores on an easy test, which can get no higher than 100. We use the statistics for *weight* and *weight_Z* shown in Figure 2.14 to calculate the skewness for these variables.

For *weight* we have

$$\text{Skewness} = \frac{3(\text{mean} - \text{median})}{\text{standard deviation}} = \frac{3(3005.490 - 2835)}{852.646} = 0.6$$

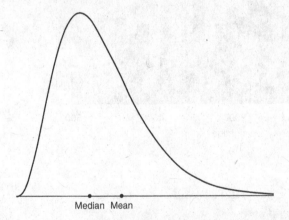

Median Mean

Figure 2.12   Right-skewed data has positive skewness.

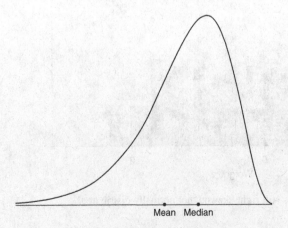

Mean Median

Figure 2.13   Left-skewed data has negative skewness.

⊟ weightlbs	
⊟ Statistics	
Mean	3005.490
Standard Deviation	852.646
Median	2835

⊟ weight_Z	
⊟ Statistics	
Mean	0.000
Standard Deviation	1.000
Median	-0.200

Figure 2.14   Statistics for calculating skewness.

For *weight_Z* we have

$$\text{Skewness} = \frac{3(\text{mean} - \text{median})}{\text{standard deviation}} = \frac{3(0 - (-0.2))}{1} = 0.6$$

Thus, Z-score standardization has *no effect* on skewness.

To make our data "more normally distributed," we must first make it symmetric, which means eliminating the skewness. To eliminate skewness, we apply a *transformation* to the data. Common transformations are the natural log transformation ln(weight), the square root transformation $\sqrt{\text{weight}}$, and the inverse square root transformation $1/\sqrt{\text{weight}}$. Application of the square root transformation (Figure 2.15) somewhat reduces the skewness, while applying the *ln* transformation (Figure 2.16) reduces skewness even further.

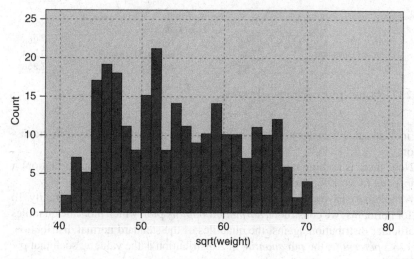

Figure 2.15   Square root transformation somewhat reduces skewness.

The statistics in Figure 2.17 are used to calculate the reduction in skewness:

$$\text{Skewness (sqrt(weight))} = \frac{3(54.280 - 53.245)}{7.709} \approx 0.40$$

$$\text{Skewness (ln(weight))} = \frac{3(7.968 - 7.950)}{0.284} \approx 0.19$$

Finally, we try the inverse square root transformation $1/\sqrt{\text{weight}}$, which gives us the distribution in Figure 2.18. The statistics in Figure 2.19 give us

$$\text{Skewness (inverse\_sqrt(weight))} = \frac{3(0.019 - 0.019)}{0.003} = 0$$

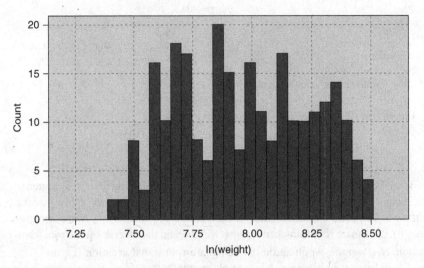

Figure 2.16   Natural log transformation reduces skewness even further.

⊟ sqrt(weight)	
⊟ Statistics	
Mean	54.280
Standard Deviation	7.709
Median	53.245

⊟ ln(weight)	
⊟ Statistics	
Mean	7.968
Standard Deviation	0.284
Median	7.950

Figure 2.17   Statistics for calculating skewness.

which indicates that we have eliminated the skewness and achieved a symmetric distribution.

Now, there is nothing magical about the inverse square root transformation; it just happened to work for this variable.

Although we have achieved symmetry, we still have not arrived at normality. To check for normality, we construct a *normal probability plot,* which plots the quantiles of a particular distribution against the quantiles of the standard normal distribution. Similar to a *percentile,* the *p*th *quantile* of a distribution is the value x_p such that $p\%$ of the distribution values are less than or equal to x_p.

In a normal probability plot, if the distribution is normal, the bulk of the points in the plot should fall on a straight line; systematic deviations from linearity in this plot indicate nonnormality. Note from Figure 2.18 that the distribution is not a good fit for the normal distribution curve shown. Thus, we would not expect our normal probability plot to exhibit normality. As expected, the normal probability plot of *inverse_sqrt(weight)* in Figure 2.20 shows systematic deviations from linearity, indicating nonnormality. For contrast, a normal probability plot of normally distributed data is shown in Figure 2.21; this graph shows no systematic deviations from linearity.

Experimentation with further transformations (not shown) did not yield acceptable normality for *inverse_sqrt(weight)*. Fortunately, algorithms requiring normality usually do fine when supplied with data that is symmetric and unimodal.

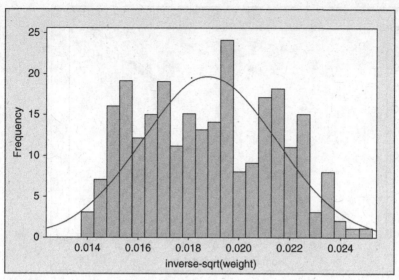

Figure 2.18   The transformation *inverse_sqrt*(*weight*) has eliminated the skewness, but is still not normal.

⊟ inverse_sqrt(weight)
   ⊟ Statistics

Mean	0.019
Standard Deviation	0.003
Median	0.019

Figure 2.19   Statistics for *inverse_sqrt*(*weight*).

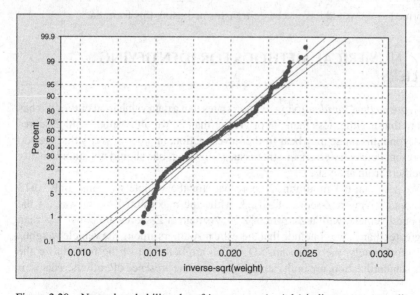

Figure 2.20   Normal probability plot of *inverse_sqrt*(*weight*) indicates nonnormality.

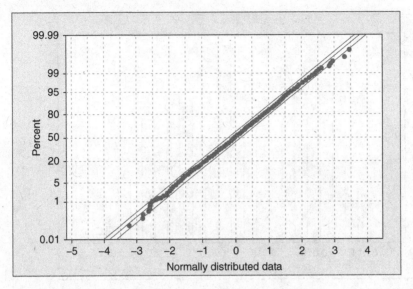

Figure 2.21 Normal probability plot of normally distributed data.

Finally, when the algorithm is done with its analysis, *don't forget to "de-transform" the data.* Let x represent the original variable, and y represent the transformed variable. Then, for the inverse square root transformation we have

$$y = \frac{1}{\sqrt{x}}$$

"de-transforming," we obtain: $x = \frac{1}{y^2}$. Results that your algorithm provided on the transformed scale would have to be de-transformed using this formula.[9]

2.12 NUMERICAL METHODS FOR IDENTIFYING OUTLIERS

The *Z-score method for identifying outliers* states that a data value is an outlier if it has a Z-score that is either less than -3 or greater than 3. Variable values with Z-scores much beyond this range may bear further investigation, in order to verify that they do not represent data entry errors or other issues. However, one should not automatically omit outliers from analysis.

We saw that the minimum Z-score was for the vehicle weighing only 1613 pounds, and having a Z-score of -1.63, while the maximum Z-score was for the 4997-pound vehicle, with a Z-score of 2.34. As neither Z-scores are either less than -3 or greater than 3, we conclude that there are no outliers among the vehicle weights.

Unfortunately, the mean and SD, which are both part of the formula for the Z-score standardization, are both rather *sensitive* to the presence of outliers. That is, if

[9]For more on data transformations, see Chapter 8.

an outlier is added to (or deleted from) a data set, then the values of mean and SD will both be unduly affected by the presence (or absence) of this new data value. Therefore, when choosing a method for evaluating outliers, it may not seem appropriate to use measures that are themselves sensitive to their presence.

Therefore, data analysts have developed more *robust* statistical methods for outlier detection, which are less sensitive to the presence of the outliers themselves. One elementary robust method is to use the IQR. The *quartiles* of a data set divide the data set into the following four parts, each containing 25% of the data:

- The *first quartile* (Q1) is the 25th percentile.
- The *second quartile* (Q2) is the 50th percentile, that is, the median.
- The *third quartile* (Q3) is the 75th percentile.

Then, the *IQR* is a measure of variability, much more robust than the SD. The *IQR* is calculated as *IQR = Q3 − Q1*, and may be interpreted to represent the spread of the middle 50% of the data.

A robust measure of outlier detection is therefore defined as follows. A data value is an outlier if

a. it is located 1.5(IQR) or more below Q1, or

b. it is located 1.5(IQR) or more above Q3.

For example, suppose for a set of test scores, the 25th percentile was *Q1 = 70* and the 75th percentile was *Q3 = 80,* so that half of all the test scores fell between 70 and 80. Then the *interquartile range,* or the difference between these quartiles was *IQR = 80 − 70 = 10.*

A test score would be robustly identified as an outlier if

a. it is lower than *Q1 − 1.5(IQR) = 70 − 1.5(10) = 55,* or

b. it is higher than *Q3 + 1.5(IQR) = 80 + 1.5(10) = 95.*

2.13   FLAG VARIABLES

Some analytical methods, such as regression, require predictors to be numeric. Thus, analysts wishing to use categorical predictors in regression need to recode the categorical variable into one or more *flag variables.* A *flag variable* (or *dummy variable,* or *indicator variable*) is a categorical variable taking only two values, 0 and 1. For example, the categorical predictor *sex,* taking values for *female* and *male,* could be recoded into the flag variable *sex_flag* as follows:

If *sex = female =* then *sex_flag = 0*; if *sex = male* then *sex_flag = 1.*

When a categorical predictor takes $k \geq 3$ possible values, then define $k − 1$ dummy variables, and use the unassigned category as the *reference category.* For example, if a categorical predictor *region* has $k = 4$ possible categories, {*north, east, south, west*}, then the analyst could define the following $k − 1 = 3$ flag variables.

north_flag: If *region* = *north* then *north_flag* = 1; otherwise *north_flag* = 0.

east_flag: If *region* = *east* then *east_flag* = 1; otherwise *east_flag* = 0.

south_flag: If *region* = *south* then *south_flag* = 1; otherwise *south_flag* = 0.

The flag variable for the west is not needed, as *region* = *west* is already uniquely identified by zero values for each of the three existing flag variables.[10] Instead, the unassigned category becomes the reference category, meaning that, the interpretation of the value of *north_flag* is *region* = *north* <u>compared to</u> *region* = *west*. For example, if we are running a regression analysis with income as the target variable, and the regression coefficient (see Chapter 8) for *north_flag* equals $1000, then the estimated income for *region* = *north* is $1000 greater than for *region* = *west*, when all other predictors are held constant.

2.14 TRANSFORMING CATEGORICAL VARIABLES INTO NUMERICAL VARIABLES

Would it not be easier to simply transform the categorical variable *region* into a single numerical variable rather than using several different flag variables? For example, suppose we defined the quantitative variable *region_num* as follows:

Region	Region_num
North	1
East	2
South	3
West	4

Unfortunately, this is a *common and hazardous error*. The algorithm now erroneously thinks the following:

- The four regions are ordered.
- West > South > East > North.
- West is three times closer to South compared to North, and so on.

So, in most instances, the data analyst should avoid transforming categorical variables to numerical variables. The exception is for categorical variables that are clearly ordered, such as the variable *survey_response*, taking values *always*, *usually*, *sometimes*, *never*. In this case, one could assign numerical values to the responses, although one may bicker with the actual values assigned, such as:

---

[10]Further, inclusion of the fourth flag variable will cause some algorithms to fail, because of the singularity of the $(X'X)^{-1}$ matrix in regression, for instance.

Survey response	Survey Response_num
Always	4
Usually	3
Sometimes	2
Never	1

Should *never* be "0" rather than "1"? Is *always* closer to *usually* than *usually* is to *sometimes*? Careful assignment of the numerical values is important.

2.15 BINNING NUMERICAL VARIABLES

Some algorithms prefer categorical rather than continuous predictors,[11] in which case we would need to partition any numerical predictors into *bins* or *bands*. For example, we may wish to partition the numerical predictor *house value* into *low, medium,* and *high*. There are the following four common methods for binning numerical predictors:

1. *Equal width binning* divides the numerical predictor into k categories of equal width, where k is chosen by the client or analyst.

2. *Equal frequency binning* divides the numerical predictor into k categories, each having k/n records, where n is the total number of records.

3. *Binning by clustering* uses a clustering algorithm, such as k-*means clustering* (Chapter 19) to automatically calculate the "optimal" partitioning.

4. *Binning based on predictive value.* Methods (1)–(3) ignore the target variable; binning based on predictive value partitions the numerical predictor based on the effect each partition has on the value of the target variable. Chapter 3 contains an example of this.

Equal width binning is not recommended for most data mining applications, as the width of the categories can be greatly affected by the presence of outliers. Equal frequency distribution assumes that each category is equally likely, an assumption which is usually not warranted. Therefore, methods (3) and (4) are preferred.

Suppose we have the following tiny data set, which we would like to discretize into $k = 3$ categories: $X = \{1, 1, 1, 1, 1, 1, 2, 2, 11, 11, 12, 12, 44\}$.

1. Using equal width binning, we partition X into the following categories of equal width, illustrated in Figure 2.22a:

   o *Low:* $0 \le X < 15$, which contains all the data values except one.

---

[11]For further information about discrete and continuous variables, as well as other ways of classifying variables, see the Appendix.

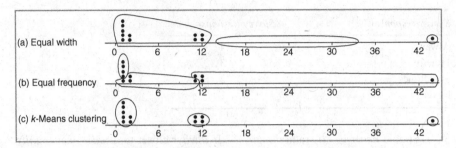

Figure 2.22 (a–c) Illustration of binning methods.

- o *Medium*: $15 \leq X < 30$, which contains no data values at all.
- o *High*: $30 \leq X < 45$, which contains a single outlier.

2. Using equal frequency binning, we have $n = 12$, $k = 3$, and $n/k = 4$. The partition is illustrated in Figure 2.22b.

- o *Low*: Contains the first four data values, all $X = 1$.
- o *Medium*: Contains the next four data values, $\{1, 2, 2, 11\}$.
- o *High*: Contains the last four data values, $\{11, 12, 12, 44\}$.

Note that one of the *medium* data values equals a data value in the *low* category, and another equals a data value in the *high* category. This violates what should be a self-evident heuristic: Equal data values should belong to the same category.

3. Finally, k-means clustering identifies what seems to be the intuitively correct partition, as shown in Figure 2.22c.

We provide two examples of binning based on predictive value in Chapter 3.

2.16 RECLASSIFYING CATEGORICAL VARIABLES

Reclassifying categorical variables is the categorical equivalent of binning numerical variables. Often, a categorical variable will contain too many easily analyzable field values. For example, the predictor *state* could contain 50 different field values. Data mining methods such as logistic regression and the C4.5 decision tree algorithm perform suboptimally when confronted with predictors containing too many field values. In such a case, the data analyst should reclassify the field values. For example, the 50 states could each be reclassified as the variable *region*, containing field values *Northeast, Southeast, North Central, Southwest,* and *West.* Thus, instead of 50 different field values, the analyst (and algorithm) is faced with only 5. Alternatively, the 50 states could be reclassified as the variable *economic_level*, with three field values containing the richer states, the midrange states, and the poorer states. The data analyst should choose a reclassification that supports the objectives of the business problem or research question.

2.17   ADDING AN INDEX FIELD

It is recommended that the data analyst create an index field, which tracks the sort order of the records in the database. Data mining data gets partitioned at least once (and sometimes several times). It is helpful to have an index field so that the original sort order may be recreated. For example, using IBM/SPSS Modeler, you can use the @*Index* function in the *Derive* node to create an index field.

2.18   REMOVING VARIABLES THAT ARE NOT USEFUL

The data analyst may wish to remove variables that will not help the analysis, regardless of the proposed data mining task or algorithm. Such variables include

- unary variables and
- variables that are very nearly unary.

Unary variables take on only a single value, so a unary variable is not so much a variable as a *constant*. For example, data collection on a sample of students at an all-girls private school would find that the *sex* variable would be unary, as every subject would be female. As *sex* is constant across all observations, it cannot have any effect on any data mining algorithm or statistical tool. The variable should be removed.

Sometimes a variable can be very nearly unary. For example, suppose that 99.95% of the players in a field hockey league are female, with the remaining 0.05% male. The variable *sex* is therefore very nearly, but not quite, unary. While it may be useful to investigate the male players, some algorithms will tend to treat the variable as essentially unary. For example, a classification algorithm can be better than 99.9% confident that a given player is female. So, the data analyst needs to weigh how close to unary a given variable is, and whether such a variable should be retained or removed.

2.19   VARIABLES THAT SHOULD PROBABLY NOT BE REMOVED

It is (unfortunately) a common – although questionable – practice to remove from analysis the following types of variables:

- Variables for which 90% or more of the values are missing.
- Variables that are strongly correlated.

Before you remove a variable because it has 90% or more missing values, consider that there may be a pattern in the missingness, and therefore useful information, that you may be jettisoning. Variables that contain 90% missing values present a challenge to any strategy for imputation of missing data (see Chapter 27). For example, are the remaining 10% of the cases truly representative of the missing data, or are the missing values occurring due to some systematic but unobserved phenomenon? For example, suppose we have a field called *donation_dollars* in a self-reported survey database. Conceivably, those who donate a lot would be inclined to report their donations, while those who do not donate much may be inclined to skip this survey question. Thus, the 10% who report are not representative of the whole. In this case, it may be preferable to construct a flag variable, *donation_flag*, as there is a pattern in the missingness which may turn out to have predictive power.

However, if the data analyst has reason to believe that the 10% are representative, then he or she may choose to proceed with the imputation of the missing 90%. It is strongly recommended that the imputation be based on the regression or decision tree methods shown in Chapter 27. Regardless of whether the 10% are representative of the whole or not, the data analyst may decide that it is wise to construct a flag variable for the non-missing values, as they may very well be useful for prediction or classification. Also, there is nothing special about the 90% figure; the data analyst may use any large proportion he or she considers warranted. Bottom line: One should avoid removing variables just because they have lots of missing values.

An example of correlated variables may be precipitation and attendance at a state beach. As precipitation increases, attendance at the beach tends to decrease, so that the variables are negatively correlated.[12] Inclusion of correlated variables may at best double-count a particular aspect of the analysis, and at worst lead to instability of the model results. When confronted with two strongly correlated variables, therefore, some data analysts may decide to simply remove one of the variables. We advise against doing so, as important information may thereby be discarded. Instead, it is suggested that principal components analysis be applied, where the common variability in correlated predictors may be translated into a set of uncorrelated principal components.[13]

2.20 REMOVAL OF DUPLICATE RECORDS

During a database's history, records may have been inadvertently copied, thus creating duplicate records. Duplicate records lead to an overweighting of the data values in those records, so, if the records are truly duplicate, only one set of them should be retained. For example, if the ID field is duplicated, then definitely remove the duplicate records. However, the data analyst should apply common sense. To take an extreme case, suppose a data set contains three nominal fields, and each field takes only three values. Then there are only $3 \times 3 \times 3 = 27$ possible different sets of observations. In other words, if there are more than 27 records, at least one of them has

---

[12]For more on correlation, see the Appendix.

[13]For more on principal components analysis, see Chapter 4.

to be a duplicate. So, the data analyst should weigh the likelihood that the duplicates represent truly different records against the likelihood that the duplicates are indeed just duplicated records.

2.21   A WORD ABOUT ID FIELDS

Because ID fields have a different value for each record, they will not be helpful for your downstream data mining algorithms. They may even be hurtful, with the algorithm finding some spurious relationship between ID field and your target. Thus, it is recommended that ID fields should be filtered out from the data mining algorithms, but should not be removed from the data, so that the data analyst can differentiate between similar records.

In Chapter 3, we apply some basic graphical and statistical tools to help us begin to uncover simple patterns and trends in the data structure.

THE R ZONE

Read in the Cars and Cars2 datasets

```
cars <- read.csv("C:/ … /cars.txt",
  stringsAsFactors = FALSE)
cars2 <- read.csv("C:/ … /cars2.txt",
  stringsAsFactors = FALSE)
```

Missing data

Look at four variables from *cars*
```
cars.4var <- cars[, c(1, 3, 4, 8)]
head(cars.4var)
```

```
> head(cars.4var)
   mpg cubicinches  hp   brand
1 14.0         350 165      US
2 31.9          89  71  Europe
3 17.0         302 140      US
4 15.0         400 150      US
5 30.5          98  63      US
6 23.0         350 125      US
```

Make certain entries missing
```
cars.4var[2,2] <- cars.4var[4,4] <- NA
head(cars.4var)
```

```
> head(cars.4var)
   mpg cubicinches  hp   brand
1 14.0         350 165      US
2 31.9          NA  71  Europe
3 17.0         302 140      US
4 15.0         400 150    <NA>
5 30.5          98  63      US
6 23.0         350 125      US
```

```
# Replace missing values with constants
cars.4var[2,2] <- 0
cars.4var[4,4] <- "Missing"
head(cars.4var)
```

```
> head(cars.4var)
   mpg cubicinches  hp    brand
1 14.0        350  165       US
2 31.9          0   71   Europe
3 17.0        302  140       US
4 15.0        400  150  Missing
5 30.5         98   63       US
6 23.0        350  125       US
```

```
# Replace values with mean and mode
cars.4var[2,2] <-
  mean(na.omit(cars.4var$cubicinches))
our_table <- table(cars.4var$brand)
our_mode <- names(our_table)
  [our_table ==
    max(our_table)]
cars.4var[4,4] <- our_mode
head(cars.4var)
```

```
> head(cars.4var)
   mpg cubicinches    hp   brand
1 14.0    350.0000   165      US
2 31.9    201.5346    71  Europe
3 17.0    302.0000   140      US
4 15.0    400.0000   150      US
5 30.5     98.0000    63      US
6 23.0    350.0000   125      US
```

```
# Generate random observations
obs_brand <-
  sample(na.omit(cars.4var$brand), 1)
obs_cubicinches <-
  sample(na.omit(cars.4var$cubicinches), 1)
cars.4var[2,2] <- obs_cubicinches
cars.4var[4,4] <- obs_brand
head(cars.4var)
```

```
> head(cars.4var)
   mpg cubicinches  hp    brand
1 14.0        350  165       US
2 31.9         86   71   Europe
3 17.0        302  140       US
4 15.0        400  150   Europe
5 30.5         98   63       US
6 23.0        350  125       US
```

Create a Histogram

```
# Set up the plot area
par(mfrow = c(1,1))
# Create the
  histogram bars
hist(cars2$weight,
  breaks = 30,
  xlim = c(0, 5000),
  col = "blue",
  border = "black",
  ylim = c(0, 40),
  xlab = "Weight",
  ylab = "Counts",
  main = "Histogram
    of Car Weights")
# Make a box around
# the plot
box(which = "plot",
  lty = "solid",
  col = "black")
```

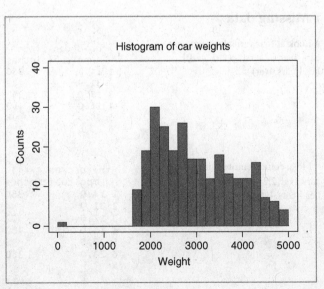

Create a Scatterplot

```
plot(cars2$weight,
   cars2$mpg,
   xlim = c(0, 5000),
   ylim = c(0, 600),
   xlab = "Weight",
   ylab = "MPG",
   main = "Scatterplot
     of MPG by
     Weight",
   type = "p",
   pch = 16,
   col = "blue")
#Add open black
# circles
points(cars2$weight,
   cars2$mpg,
   type = "p",
   col = "black")
```

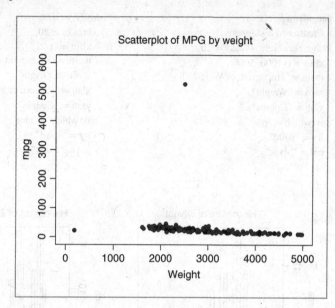

Descriptive Statistics

```
mean(cars$weight) # Mean
median(cars$weight) # Median
length(cars$weight) # Number of observations
sd(cars$weight) # Standard deviation
summary(cars$weight) # Min, Q1, Median, Mean, Q3, Max
```

Transformations

```
# Min-max normalization
summary(cars$weight)
mi <- min(cars$weight)
ma <- max(cars$weight)
minmax.weight <- (cars$weight - mi)/(ma - mi)
minmax.weight
```

```
# Z-score standarization
m <- mean(cars$weight); s <- sd(cars$weight)
z.weight <- (cars$weight - m)/s
z.weight
length(cars$weight)
```

```
# Decimal scaling
max(abs(cars$weight)) # 4 digits
d.weight <- cars$weight/(10^4); d.weight
```

Side-by-Side Histograms

```
par(mfrow = c(1,2))                    hist(z.weight,
# Create two histograms                  breaks = 20,
hist(cars$weight, breaks = 20,           xlim = c(-2, 3),
  xlim = c(1000, 5000),                  main = "Histogram of Z-
  main = "Histogram of Weight",          score of Weight",
  xlab = "Weight",                       xlab = "Z-score of Weight",
  ylab = "Counts")                       ylab = "Counts")
box(which = "plot",                    box(which = "plot",
  lty = "solid",                         lty = "solid",
  col = "black")                         col = "black")
```

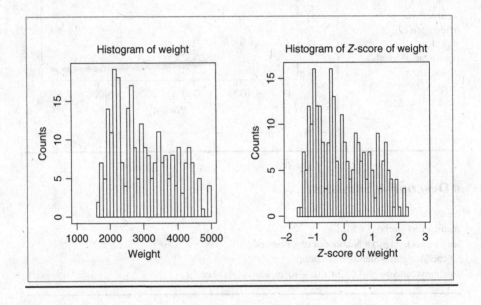

Skewness

```
(3*(mean(cars$weight) - median(cars$weight)))/sd(cars$weight)
(3*(mean(z.weight) - median(z.weight)))/sd(z.weight)
```

Transformations for Normality

```
sqrt.weight <- sqrt(cars$weight) # Square root
sqrt.weight_skew <- (3*(mean(sqrt.weight) - median(sqrt.weight))) / sd(sqrt.weight)
ln.weight <- log(cars$weight) # Natural log
ln.weight_skew <- (3*(mean(ln.weight) - median(ln.weight))) / sd(ln.weight)
invsqrt.weight <- 1 / sqrt(cars$weight) # Inverse square root
invsqrt.weight_skew <- (3*(mean(invsqrt.weight) - median(invsqrt.weight))) /sd(invsqrt.weight)
```

Histogram with Normal Distribution Overlay

```
par(mfrow=c(1,1))
x <- rnorm(1000000,
   mean = mean
   (invsqrt.weight),
sd = sd(invsqrt.weight))
hist(invsqrt.weight,
   breaks = 30,
   xlim = c(0.0125, 0.0275),
   col = "lightblue",
   prob = TRUE,
   border = "black",
   xlab = "Inverse Square
      Root of Weight",
   ylab = "Counts",
   main = "Histogram of
      Inverse Square Root
      of Weight")
box(which = "plot",
   lty = "solid",
   col="black")
# Overlay with
   Normal density
lines(density(x), col = "red")
```

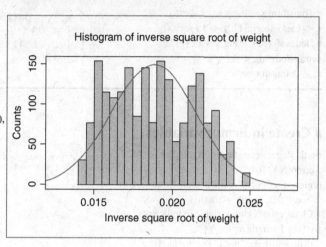

Normal Q-Q Plot

```
qqnorm(invsqrt.weight,
   datax = TRUE,
   col = "red",
   ylim = c(0.01, 0.03),
   main = "Normal
   Q-Q Plot of Inverse
   Square Root of Weight")
qqline(invsqrt.weight,
   col = "blue",
   datax = TRUE)
```

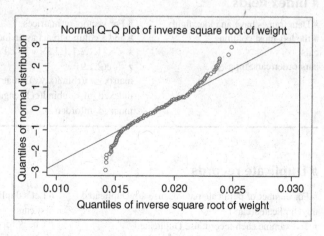

De-transform data

```
# Transform x using y = 1 / sqrt(x)
x <- cars$weight[1]; y <- 1 / sqrt(x)
# Detransform x using x = 1 / (y)^2
detransformedx <- 1 / y^2
x; y; detransformedx
```

```
> x; y; detransformedx
[1] 4209
[1] 0.01541383
[1] 4209
```

Create indicator variables

```
north_flag <- east_flag <- south_flag <-
  c(rep(NA, 10))
region <- c(rep(c("north", "south", "east",
  "west"),2), "north", "south")
# Change the region variable to indicators
for (i in 1:length(region)) {
  if(region[i] == "north") north_flag[i] = 1
  else north_flag[i] = 0
  if(region[i] == "east") east_flag[i] = 1
  else east_flag[i] = 0
  if(region[i] == "south") south_flag[i] = 1
  else south_flag[i] = 0
}
  north_flag; east_flag; south_flag
```

```
> north_flag; east_flag; south_flag
[1] 1 0 0 0 1 0 0 0 1 0
[1] 0 0 1 0 0 0 1 0 0 0
[1] 0 1 0 0 0 1 0 0 0 1
```

Index fields

```
# Data frames have an index field;
# the left-most column
cars
cars[order(cars$mpg),]
```

```
# For vectors or matrices,
# add a column to act as an index field
x <- c(1,1,3:1,1:4,3); y <- c(9,9:1)
z <- c(2,1:9)
matrix <- t(rbind(x,y,z)); matrix
indexed_m <- cbind(c(1:length(x)), matrix); indexed_m
indexed_m[order(z),]
```

Duplicate records

```
# For number of duplicate records, use anyDuplicated
anyDuplicated(cars)
# To examine each record, use Duplicated
duplicated(cars)
# 'True': record is a duplicate,
# 'False': record is not a duplicate
```

```
# Let's duplicate the first record
new.cars <- rbind(cars, cars[1,])
# Check for duplicates
anyDuplicated(new.cars)
# The 262nd record is a duplicate
duplicated(new.cars)
```

R REFERENCE

R Core Team. *R: A Language and Environment for Statistical Computing*. Vienna, Austria: R Foundation for Statistical Computing; 2012. ISBN: 3-900051-07-0, http://www.R-project.org/.

EXERCISES

CLARIFYING THE CONCEPTS

1. Describe the possible negative effects of proceeding directly to mine data that has not been preprocessed.

2. Refer to the income attribute of the five customers in Table 2.1, before preprocessing.
   a. Find the mean income before preprocessing.
   b. What does this number actually mean?
   c. Now, calculate the mean income for the three values left after preprocessing. Does this value have a meaning?

3. Explain why zip codes should be considered text variables rather than numeric.

4. What is an outlier? Why do we need to treat outliers carefully?

5. Explain why a birthdate variable would be preferred to an age variable in a database.

6. True or false: All things being equal, more information is almost always better.

7. Explain why it is not recommended, as a strategy for dealing with missing data, to simply omit the records or fields with missing values from the analysis.

8. Which of the four methods for handling missing data would tend to lead to an underestimate of the spread (e.g., SD) of the variable? What are some benefits to this method?

9. What are some of the benefits and drawbacks for the method for handling missing data that chooses values at random from the variable distribution?

10. Of the four methods for handling missing data, which method is preferred?

11. Make up a classification scheme that is inherently flawed, and would lead to misclassification, as we find in Table 2.2. For example, classes of items bought in a grocery store.

12. Make up a data set, consisting of the heights and weights of six children, in which one of the children is an outlier with respect to one of the variables, but not the other. Then alter this data set so that the child is an outlier with respect to both variables.

WORKING WITH THE DATA

Use the following stock price data (in dollars) for Exercises 13–18.

10	7	20	12	75	15	9	18	4	12	8	14

13. Calculate the mean, median, and mode stock price.

14. Compute the SD of the stock price. Interpret what this number means.

15. Find the min–max normalized stock price for the stock price $20.

16. Calculate the midrange stock price.

17. Compute the Z-score standardized stock price for the stock price $20.

18. Find the decimal scaling stock price for the stock price $20.

19. Calculate the skewness of the stock price data.

20. Explain why data analysts need to normalize their numeric variables.

21. Describe three characteristics of the standard normal distribution.

22. If a distribution is symmetric, does it follow that it is normal? Give a counterexample.

23. What do we look for in a normal probability plot to indicate nonnormality?
    Use the stock price data for Exercises 24–26.

24. Do the following.
    a. Identify the outlier.
    b. Verify that this value is an outlier, using the Z-score method.
    c. Verify that this value is an outlier, using the IQR method.

25. Identify all possible stock prices that would be outliers, using:
    a. The Z-score method.
    b. The IQR method.

26. Investigate how the outlier affects the mean and median by doing the following:
    a. Find the mean score and the median score, with and without the outlier.
    b. State which measure, the mean or the median, the presence of the outlier affects more, and why.

27. What are the four common methods for binning numerical predictors? Which of these are preferred?
    Use the following data set for Exercises 28–30:

1	1	1	3	3	7

28. Bin the data into three bins of equal width (width = 3).

29. Bin the data into three bins of two records each.

30. Clarify why each of the binning solutions above are not optimal.

31. Explain why we might not want to remove a variable that had 90% or more missing values.

32. Explain why we might not want to remove a variable just because it is highly correlated with another variable.

HANDS-ON ANALYSIS

Use the *churn* data set[14] on the book series web site for the following exercises:

33. Explore whether there are missing values for any of the variables.

34. Compare the area code and state fields. Discuss any apparent abnormalities.

35. Use a graph to visually determine whether there are any outliers among the number of calls to customer service.

36. Identify the range of customer service calls that should be considered outliers, using:
    a. the Z-score method;
    b. the IQR method.

37. Transform the *day minutes* attribute using Z-score standardization.

38. Work with skewness as follows:
    a. Calculate the skewness of *day* minutes.
    b. Then calculate the skewness of the Z-score standardized *day minutes*. Comment.
    c. Based on the skewness value, would you consider *day minutes* to be skewed or nearly perfectly symmetric?

39. Construct a normal probability plot of *day minutes*. Comment on the normality of the data.

40. Work with *international minutes* as follows:
    a. Construct a normal probability plot of *international minutes*.
    b. What is preventing this variable from being normally distributed.
    c. Construct a flag variable to deal with the situation in (b).
    d. Construct a normal probability plot of the derived variable *nonzero international minutes*. Comment on the normality of the derived variable.

41. Transform the *night minutes* attribute using Z-score standardization. Using a graph, describe the range of the standardized values.

[14]Churn data set. Blake, C.L. & Merz, C.J. UCI Repository of machine learning databases [kdd.ics.uci.edu/]. Irvine, CA: University of California, Department of Information and Computer Science, 1998.

CHAPTER 3

EXPLORATORY DATA ANALYSIS

3.1 HYPOTHESIS TESTING VERSUS EXPLORATORY DATA ANALYSIS

When approaching a data mining problem, a data mining analyst may already have some a priori hypotheses that he or she would like to test regarding the relationships between the variables. For example, suppose that cell-phone executives are interested in whether a recent increase in the fee structure has led to a decrease in market share. In this case, the analyst would *test* the *hypothesis* that market share has decreased, and would therefore use *hypothesis testing* procedures.

A myriad of statistical hypothesis testing procedures are available through the traditional statistical analysis literature. We cover many of these in Chapters 5 and 6. However, analysts do not always have *a priori* notions of the expected relationships among the variables. Especially when confronted with unknown, large databases, analysts often prefer to use *exploratory data analysis* (EDA), or *graphical data analysis*. EDA allows the analyst to

- delve into the data set;
- examine the interrelationships among the attributes;
- identify interesting subsets of the observations;
- develop an initial idea of possible associations amongst the predictors, as well as between the predictors and the target variable.

3.2 GETTING TO KNOW THE DATA SET

Graphs, plots, and tables often uncover important relationships that could indicate important areas for further investigation. In Chapter 3, we use exploratory methods to delve into the *churn* data set[1] from the UCI Repository of Machine Learning

---

[1] Churn data set. Blake, C.L. & Merz, C.J. UCI Repository of machine learning databases [kdd.ics.uci.edu/]. Irvine, CA: University of California, Department of Information and Computer Science, 1998.

Data Mining and Predictive Analytics, First Edition. Daniel T. Larose and Chantal D. Larose.
© 2015 John Wiley & Sons, Inc. Published 2015 by John Wiley & Sons, Inc.

Databases at the University of California, Irvine. The data set is also available on the book series web site, www.dataminingconsultant.com. *Churn,* also called attrition, is a term used to indicate a customer leaving the service of one company in favor of another company. The data set contains 20 predictors worth of information about 3333 customers, along with the target variable, *churn,* an indication of whether that customer churned (left the company) or not.

The variables are as follows:

- *State*: Categorical, for the 50 states and the District of Columbia.
- *Account length*: Integer-valued, how long account has been active.
- *Area code*: Categorical
- *Phone number*: Essentially a surrogate for customer ID.
- *International plan*: Dichotomous categorical, yes or no.
- *Voice mail plan*: Dichotomous categorical, yes or no.
- *Number of voice mail messages*: Integer-valued.
- *Total day minutes*: Continuous, minutes customer used service during the day.
- *Total day calls*: Integer-valued.
- *Total day charge*: Continuous, perhaps based on above two variables.
- *Total eve minutes*: Continuous, minutes customer used service during the evening.
- *Total eve calls*: Integer-valued.
- *Total eve charge*: Continuous, perhaps based on above two variables.
- *Total night minutes*: Continuous, minutes customer used service during the night.
- *Total night calls*: Integer-valued.
- *Total night charge*: Continuous, perhaps based on above two variables.
- *Total international minutes*: Continuous, minutes customer used service to make international calls.
- *Total international calls*: Integer-valued.
- *Total international charge*: Continuous, perhaps based on above two variables.
- *Number of calls to customer service*: Integer-valued.
- *Churn*: Target. Indicator of whether the customer has left the company (true or false).

To begin, it is often best to simply take a look at the field values for some of the records. Figure 3.1 shows the variable values for the first 10 records of the *churn* data set.

We can begin to get a feel for the data by looking at Figure 3.1. We note, for example:

- The variable *Phone* uses only seven digits.
- There are two flag variables.

	State	Account Length	Area Code	Phone	Intl Plan	VMail Plan	VMail Message	Day Mins	Day Calls	Day Charge	Eve Mins
1	KS	128	415	382-4657	no	yes	25	265.100	110	45.070	197.400
2	OH	107	415	371-7191	no	yes	26	161.600	123	27.470	195.500
3	NJ	137	415	358-1921	no	no	0	243.400	114	41.380	121.200
4	OH	84	408	375-9999	yes	no	0	299.400	71	50.900	61.900
5	OK	75	415	330-6626	yes	no	0	166.700	113	28.340	148.300
6	AL	118	510	391-8027	yes	no	0	223.400	98	37.980	220.600
7	MA	121	510	355-9993	no	yes	24	218.200	88	37.090	348.500
8	MO	147	415	329-9001	yes	no	0	157.000	79	26.690	103.100
9	LA	117	408	335-4719	no	no	0	184.500	97	31.370	351.600
(a) 10	WV	141	415	330-8173	yes	yes	37	258.600	84	43.960	222.000

	Eve Calls	Eve Charge	Night Mins	Night Calls	Night Charge	Intl Mins	Intl Calls	Intl Charge	CustServ Calls	Churn
1	99	16.780	244.700	91	11.010	10.000	3	2.700	1	False
2	103	16.620	254.400	103	11.450	13.700	3	3.700	1	False
3	110	10.300	162.600	104	7.320	12.200	5	3.290	0	False
4	88	5.260	196.900	89	8.860	6.600	7	1.780	2	False
5	122	12.610	186.900	121	8.410	10.100	3	2.730	3	False
6	101	18.750	203.900	118	9.180	6.300	6	1.700	0	False
7	108	29.620	212.600	118	9.570	7.500	7	2.030	3	False
8	94	8.760	211.800	96	9.530	7.100	6	1.920	0	False
9	80	29.890	215.900	90	9.710	8.700	4	2.350	1	False
(b) 10	111	18.870	326.400	97	14.690	11.200	5	3.020	0	False

Figure 3.1   (a,b) Field values of the first 10 records in the *churn* data set.

- Most of our variables are continuous.
- The response variable *Churn* is a flag variable having two values, *True* and *False*.

Next, we turn to summarization and visualization (see Appendix). Figure 3.2 shows graphs (either histograms or bar charts) and summary statistics for each variable in the data set, except *Phone*, which is an identification field. The variable types for this software (Modeler, by IBM/SPSS) are shown (*set* for categorical, *flag* for flag, and *range* for continuous). We may note that *vmail messages* have a spike on the length, and that most quantitative variables seem to be normally distributed, except for *Intl Calls* and *CustServ Calls*, which are right-skewed (note that the skewness statistic is larger for these variables).*Unique* represents the number of distinct field values. We wonder how it can be that there are 51 distinct values for *State*, but only three distinct values for *Area Code*. Also, the mode of *State* being West Virginia may have us scratching our heads a bit. More on this will be discussed later. We are still just getting to know the data set.

3.3   EXPLORING CATEGORICAL VARIABLES

The bar graph in Figure 3.3 shows the counts and percentages of customers who churned (true) and who did not churn (false). Fortunately, only a minority (14.49%) of our customers have left our service. *Our task is to identify patterns in the data that will help to reduce the proportion of churners.*

One of the primary reasons for performing EDA is to investigate the variables, examine the distributions of the categorical variables, look at the histograms of the numeric variables, and explore the relationships among sets of variables. However, our overall objective for the data mining project as a whole (not just the EDA phase) is to develop a model of the type of customer likely to churn (jump from your company's

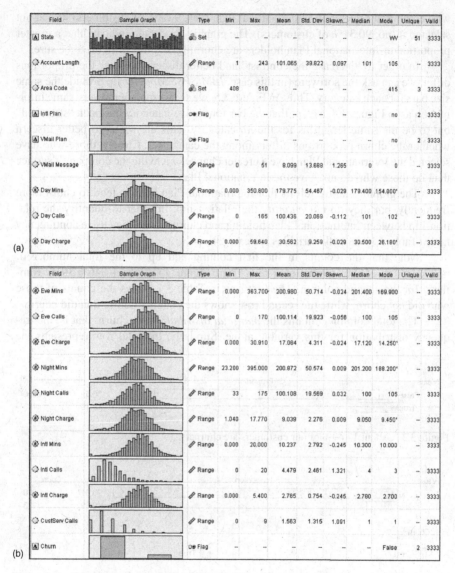

Figure 3.2 Summarization and visualization of the *churn* data set.

service to another company's service). Today's software packages allow us to become familiar with the variables, while at the same time allowing us to begin to see which variables are associated with churn. In this way, we can explore the data while keeping an eye on our overall goal. We begin by considering the categorical variables, and their relationship to *churn*.

The first categorical variable we investigate is *International Plan*. Figure 3.4 shows a bar chart of the International Plan, with an *overlay* of churn, and represents a comparison of the proportion of churners and non-churners, among customers who either had selected the International Plan (yes, 9.69% of customers) or had not selected it (no, 90.31% of customers). The graphic appears to indicate that a greater proportion of International Plan holders are churning, but it is difficult to be sure.

In order to "increase the contrast" and better discern whether the proportions differ, we can ask the software (in this case, *IBM/SPSS Modeler*) to provide the same size bars for each category. Thus, in Figure 3.5, we see a graph of the very same information as in Figure 3.4, except that the bar for the *yes* category has been "stretched" out to be the same length as for the *no* category. This allows us to better discern whether the churn proportions differ among the categories. Clearly, those who have selected the International Plan have a greater chance of leaving the company's service than do those who do not have the International Plan.

The graphics above tell us that International Plan holders tend to churn more frequently, but they do not *quantify* the relationship. In order to quantify the relationship between International Plan holding and churning, we may use a contingency table (Table 3.1), as both variables are categorical.

Note that the counts in the first column add up to the total number of non-selectors of the international plan from Figure 3.4: 2664 + 346 = 3010. Similarly for the second column. The first row in Table 3.1 shows the counts of those who did not churn, while the second row shows the counts of those that did churn.

The total column contains the *marginal distribution* for churn, that is, the frequency distribution for this variable alone. Similarly, the total row represents the

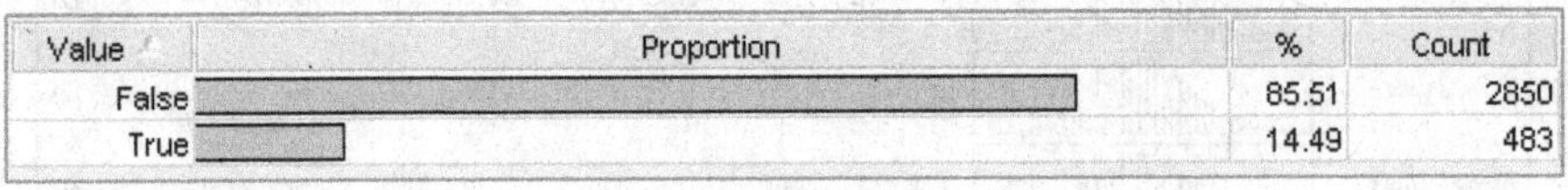

Value	Proportion	%	Count
False		85.51	2850
True		14.49	483

Figure 3.3   About 14.49% of our customers are churners.

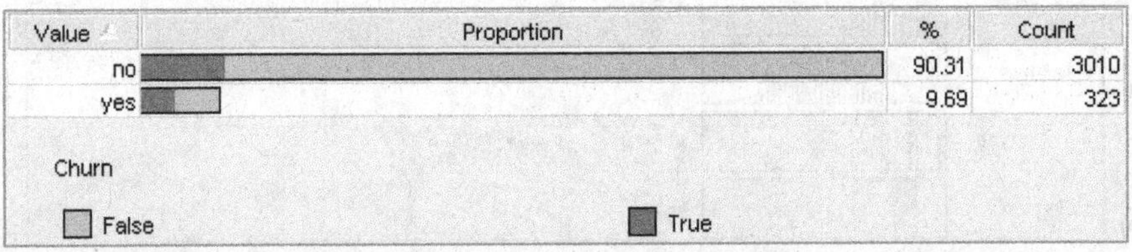

Value	Proportion	%	Count
no		90.31	3010
yes		9.69	323

Churn

☐ False   ■ True

Figure 3.4   Comparison bar chart of churn proportions, by international plan participation.

Value	Proportion	%	Count
no		90.31	3010
yes		9.69	323

Churn

☐ False   ■ True

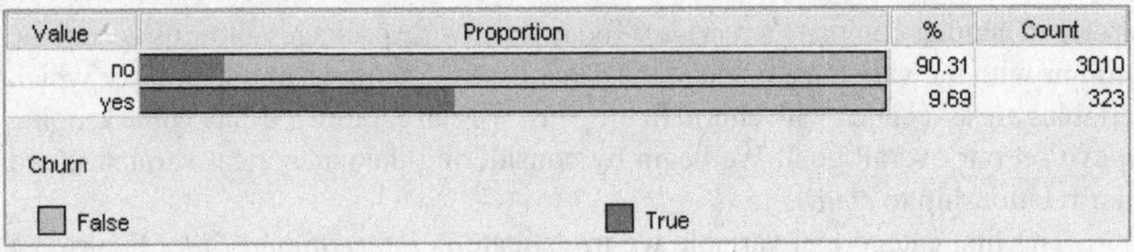

Figure 3.5   Comparison bar chart of churn proportions, by international plan participation, with equal bar length.

marginal distribution for International Plan. Note that the marginal distribution for International Plan concurs with the counts in Figure 3.5.

We may enhance Table 3.1 with percentages, depending on our question of interest. For example, Table 3.2 adds *column percentages*, which indicate, for each cell, the percentage of the column total.

We calculate the column percentages whenever we are interested in comparing the percentages of the row variable for each value of the column variable. For example, here we are interested in comparing the proportions of churners (row variable) for those who belong or do not belong to the International Plan (column variable). Note that 137/(137 + 186) = 42.4% of the International Plan holders churned, as compared to only 346/(346 + 2664) = 11.5% of those without the International Plan. Customers selecting the International Plan are more than three times as likely to leave the company's service and those without the plan. Thus, we have now quantified the relationship that we uncovered graphically earlier.

The graphical counterpart of the contingency table is the *clustered bar chart*. Figure 3.6 shows a Minitab bar chart of churn, *clustered by* International Plan. The first set of two bars represents those who do not belong to the plan, and is associated with the "No" column in Table 3.2. The second set of two bars represents those who do belong to the International Plan, and is associated with the "Yes" column in Table 3.2. Clearly, the proportion of churners is greater among those belonging to the plan.

Another useful graphic for comparing two categorical variables is the *comparative pie chart*. Figure 3.7 shows a comparative pie chart of churn, for those who do not ("no") and those who do ("yes") belong to the International Plan. The clustered bar chart is usually preferred, because it conveys counts as well as proportions, while the comparative pie chart conveys only proportions.

TABLE 3.1   Contingency table of International Plan with churn

		International Plan		
		No	Yes	Total
Churn	False	2664	186	2850
	True	346	137	483
	Total	3010	323	3333

TABLE 3.2   Contingency table with column percentages

		International Plan		
		No	Yes	Total
Churn	False	Count 2664	Count 186	Count 2850
		Col% 88.5%	Col% 57.6%	Col% 85.5%
	True	Count 346	Count 137	Count 483
		Col% 11.5%	Col% 42.4%	Col% 14.5%
	Total	3010	323	3333

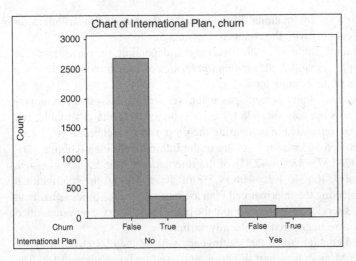

Figure 3.6   The clustered bar chart is the graphical counterpart of the contingency table.

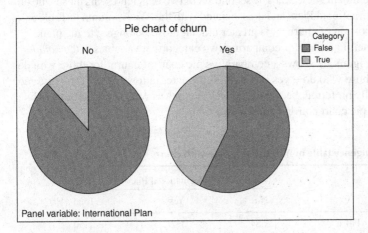

Figure 3.7   Comparative pie chart associated with Table 3.2.

Contrast Table 3.2 with Table 3.3, the contingency table with *row percentages*, which indicate, for each cell, the percentage of the row total. We calculate the row percentages whenever we are interested in comparing the percentages of the column variable for each value of the row variable. Table 3.3 indicates, for example, that 28.4% of churners belong to the International Plan, compared to 6.5% of non-churners.

Figure 3.8 contains the bar chart of International Plan, clustered by Churn, and represents the graphical counterpart of the contingency table with row percentages in Table 3.3. The first set of bars represents non-churners, and is associated with the "False" row in Table 3.3. The second set of bars represents churners, and is associated with the "True" row in Table 3.3. Clearly, the proportion of International Plan holders is greater among the churners. Similarly for Figure 3.9, which shows the comparative

TABLE 3.3   Contingency table with row percentages

		International Plan		
		No	Yes	Total
Churn	False	Count 2664 Row% 93.5%	Count 186 Row% 6.5%	2850
	True	Count 346 Row% 71.6%	Count 137 Row% 28.4%	483
	Total	Count 3010 Row% 90.3%	Count 323 Row% 9.7%	3333

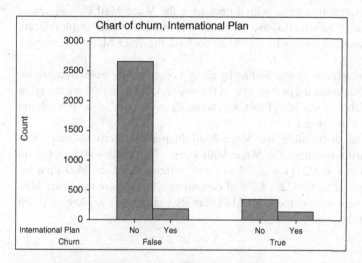

Figure 3.8   Clustered bar chart associated with Table 3.3.

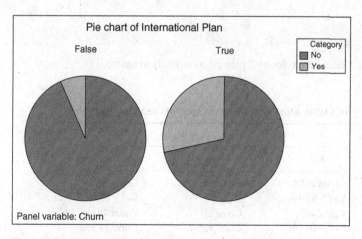

Figure 3.9   Comparative pie chart associated with Table 3.3.

bar chart of International Plan holders, by whether or not they have churned ("True" or "False").

To summarize, this EDA on the International Plan has indicated that

1. perhaps we should investigate what is it about our international plan that is inducing our customers to leave;

2. we should expect that, whatever data mining algorithms we use to predict churn, the model will probably include whether or not the customer selected the International Plan.

Let us now turn to the Voice Mail Plan. Figure 3.10 shows, using a bar graph with equalized lengths, that those who do not have the Voice Mail Plan are more likely to churn than those who do have the plan. (The numbers in the graph indicate proportions and counts of those who do and do not have the Voice Mail Plan, without reference to churning.)

Again, we may quantify this finding by using a contingency table. Because we are interested in comparing the percentages of the row variable (Churn) for each value of the column variable (Voice Mail Plan), we choose a contingency table with column percentages, shown in Table 3.4.

The marginal distribution for Voice Mail Plan (row total) indicates that $842 + 80 = 922$ customers have the Voice Mail Plan, while $2008 + 403 = 2411$ do not. We then find that $403/2411 = 16.7\%$ of those without the Voice Mail Plan are churners, as compared to $80/922 = 8.7\%$ of customers who do have the Voice Mail Plan. Thus, customers without the Voice Mail Plan are nearly twice as likely to churn as customers with the plan.

Value	Proportion	%	Count
no		72.34	2411
yes		27.66	922

Churn

☐ False   ■ True

Figure 3.10   Those without the voice mail plan are more likely to churn.

TABLE 3.4   **Contingency table with column percentages for the Voice Mail Plan**

		Voice Mail Plan		
		No	Yes	Total
Churn	False	Count 2008 Col% 83.3%	Count 842 Col% 91.3%	Count 2850 Col% 85.5%
	True	Count 403 Col% 16.7%	Count 80 Col% 8.7%	Count 483 Col% 14.5%
	Total	2411	922	3333

To summarize, this EDA on the Voice Mail Plan has indicated that

1. perhaps we should enhance our Voice Mail Plan still further, or make it easier for customers to join it, as an instrument for increasing customer loyalty;

2. we should expect that, whatever data mining algorithms we use to predict churn, the model will probably include whether or not the customer selected the Voice Mail Plan. Our confidence in this expectation is perhaps not quite as high as for the International Plan.

We may also explore the *two-way interactions* among categorical variables with respect to churn. For example, Figure 3.11 shows a multilayer clustered bar chart of churn, clustered by *both* International Plan and Voice Mail Plan.

The statistics associated with Figure 3.11 are shown in Table 3.5. Note that there are many more customers who have neither plan $(1878 + 302 = 2180)$ than have the international plan only $(130 + 101 = 231)$. More importantly, among customers with no voice mail plan, the proportion of churners is greater for those who do have an international plan $(101/231 = 44\%)$ than for those who do not $(302/2180 = 14\%)$. There are many more customers who have the voice mail plan only $(786 + 44 = 830)$ than have both plans $(56 + 36 = 92)$. Again, however, among customers with the voice mail plan, the proportion of churners is much greater for those who also select the international plan $(36/92 = 39\%)$ than for those who do not $(44/830 = 5\%)$. Note also that there is no interaction among the categorical variables. That is, international plan holders have greater churn regardless of whether they are Voice Mail plan adopters or not.

Finally, Figure 3.12 shows a *directed web graph* of the relationships between International Plan holders, Voice Mail Plan holders, and churners. Web graphs are graphical representations of the relationships between categorical variables. Note that three lines lead to the Churn = False node, which is good. However, note that one faint line leads to the Churn = True node, that of the International Plan holders, indicating

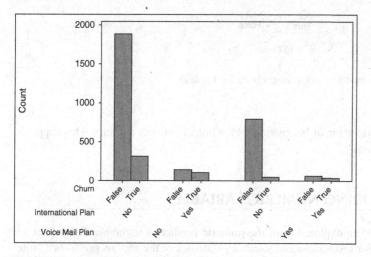

Figure 3.11   Multilayer clustered bar chart.

TABLE 3.5   Statistics for multilayer clustered bar chart

Results for Voice Mail Plan = no

```
Rows: Churn    Columns: International Plan

            no   yes   All

False     1878   130  2008
True       302   101   403
All       2180   231  2411
```

Results for Voice Mail Plan = yes

```
Rows: Churn    Columns: International Plan

            no   yes   All

False      786    56   842
True        44    36    80
All        830    92   922
```

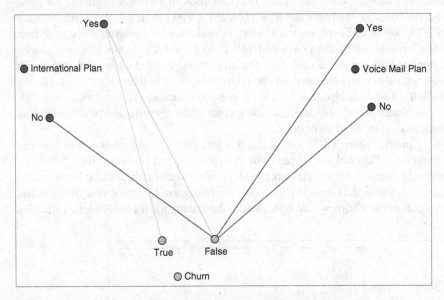

Figure 3.12   Directed web graph supports earlier findings.

that a greater proportion of International Plan holders choose to churn. This supports our earlier findings.

3.4   EXPLORING NUMERIC VARIABLES

Next, we turn to an exploration of the numeric predictive variables. Refer back to Figure 3.2 and for histograms and summary statistics of the various predictors. Note that many fields show evidence of symmetry, such as *account length* and all of the *minutes, charge,* and *call* fields. Fields not showing evidence of symmetry include *voice mail messages* and *customer service calls.* The median for *voice mail messages* is zero, indicating that at least half of all customers had no voice mail messages. This results of course from fewer than half of the customers selecting the Voice Mail Plan, as we saw above. The mean of *customer service calls* (1.563) is greater than the median (1.0), indicating some right-skewness, as also indicated by the maximum number of customer service calls being nine.

Unfortunately, the usual type of histogram (such as those in Figure 3.2) does not help us determine whether the predictor variables are associated with the target variable. To explore whether a predictor is useful for predicting the target variable, we should use an *overlay histogram,* which is a histogram where the rectangles are colored according to the values of the target variable. For example, Figure 3.13 shows a histogram of the predictor variable *customer service calls,* with no overlay. We can see that the distribution is right skewed with a mode of one call, but we have no information on whether this variable is useful for predicting churn. Next, Figure 3.14 shows a histogram of customer service calls, with an overlay of the target variable *churn.*

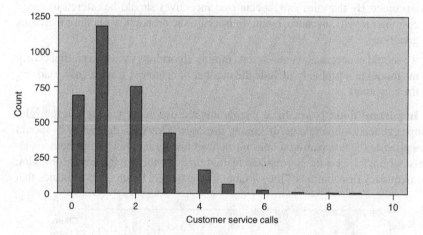

Figure 3.13   Histogram of customer service calls with no overlay.

Figure 3.14 hints that the churn proportion may be greater for higher numbers of customer service calls, but it is difficult to discern this result unequivocally. We therefore turn to the "normalized" histogram, where every rectangle has the same height and width, as shown in Figure 3.15. Note that the *proportions* of churners versus non-churners in Figure 3.15 is exactly the same as in Figure 3.14; it is just that "stretching out" the rectangles that have low counts enables better definition and contrast.

The pattern now becomes crystal clear. Customers who have called customer service three times or less have a markedly lower churn rate (red part of the rectangle) than customers who have called customer service four or more times.

This EDA on the customer service calls has indicated that

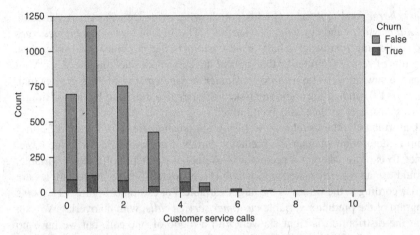

Figure 3.14   Histogram of customer service calls with churn overlay.

1. we should carefully track the number of customer service calls made by each customer. By the third call, specialized incentives should be offered to retain customer loyalty, because, by the fourth call, the probability of churn increases greatly;

2. we should expect that, whatever data mining algorithms we use to predict churn, the model will probably include the number of customer service calls made by the customer.

Important note: Normalized histograms are useful for teasing out the relationship between a numerical predictor and the target. However, data analysts should always provide the companion a non-normalized histogram along with the normalized histogram, because the normalized histogram does not provide any information on the frequency distribution of the variable. For example, Figure 3.15 indicates that

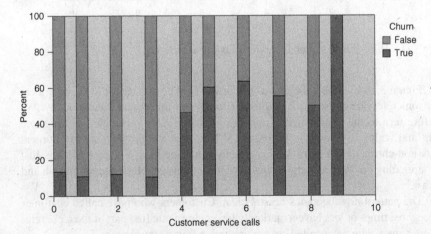

Figure 3.15   "Normalized" histogram of customer service calls with churn overlay.

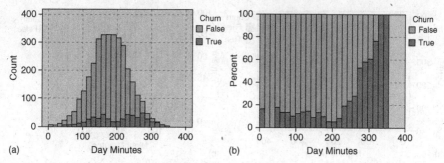

Figure 3.16   (a) Non-normalized histogram of day minutes. (b) Normalized histogram of day minutes.

the churn rate for customers logging nine service calls is 100%; but Figure 3.14 shows that there are only two customers with this number of calls.

Let us now turn to the remaining numerical predictors. The normalized histogram of *Day Minutes* in Figure 3.16b shows that high day-users tend to churn at a higher rate. Therefore,

1. we should carefully track the number of day minutes used by each customer. As the number of day minutes passes 200, we should consider special incentives;

2. we should investigate why heavy day-users are tempted to leave;

3. we should expect that our eventual data mining model will include *day minutes* as a predictor of churn.

Figure 3.17b shows a slight tendency for customers with higher *evening minutes* to churn. Based solely on the graphical evidence, however, we cannot conclude beyond a reasonable doubt that such an effect exists. Therefore, we shall hold off on formulating policy recommendations on evening cell-phone use until our data mining models offer firmer evidence that the putative effect is in fact present.

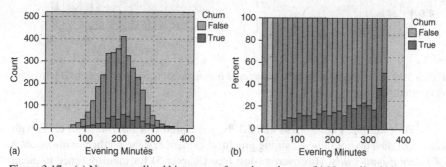

Figure 3.17   (a) Non-normalized histogram of evening minutes. (b) Normalized histogram of evening minutes.

Figures 3.18b indicates that there is no obvious association between churn and *night minutes*, as the pattern is relatively flat. In fact, EDA would indicate no obvious

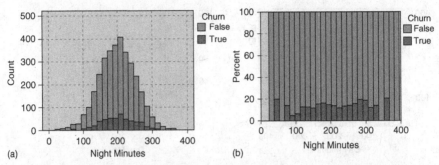

Figure 3.18   (a) Non-normalized histogram of night minutes. (b) Normalized histogram of night minutes.

association with the target for any of the remaining numeric variables in the data set (except one), although showing this is left as an exercise.

   Note: *The lack of obvious association at the EDA stage between a predictor and a target variable is not sufficient reason to omit that predictor from the model.* For example, based on the lack of evident association between *churn* and *night minutes*, we will not necessarily expect the data mining models to uncover valuable predictive information using this predictor. However, we should nevertheless retain the predictor as an input variable for the data mining models, because actionable associations may still exist for identifiable subsets of the records, and they may be involved in higher-dimension associations and interactions. In any case, unless there is a good reason for eliminating the variable before modeling, then we should probably allow the modeling process to identify which variables are predictive and which are not.

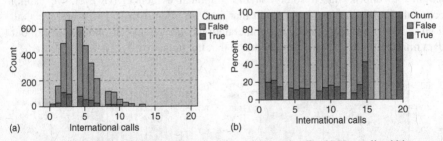

Figure 3.19   (a) Non-normalized histogram of *international calls*. (b) Normalized histogram of *international calls*.

   For example, Figure 3.19a and 3.19b, of the predictor *International Calls* with *churn* overlay, do not indicate strong graphical evidence of the predictive importance of *International Calls*. However, a *t*-test (see Chapter 5) for the difference in mean number of international calls for churners and non-churners is statistically significant (Table 3.6, p-value $= 0.003$; p-values larger than, say, 0.10 are not considered significant; see Chapter 5), meaning that this variable is indeed useful for predicting churn: Churners tend to place a lower mean number of international calls. Thus, had we omitted *International Calls* from the analysis based on the seeming lack of graphical

TABLE 3.6   *t*-test is significant for difference in mean international calls for churners and non-churners

```
Two-Sample T-Test and CI: Intl Calls, Churn

Two-sample T for Intl Calls

Churn     N   Mean  StDev  SE Mean
False  2850   4.53   2.44    0.046
True    483   4.16   2.55    0.12


Difference = mu (False) - mu (True)
Estimate for difference:  0.369
95% CI for difference:   (0.124, 0.614)
T-Test of difference = 0 (vs not =): T-Value = 2.96  P-Value = 0.003  DF = 640
```

evidence, we would have committed a mistake, and our predictive model would not perform as well.

A hypothesis test, such as this *t*-test, represents statistical inference and model building, and as such lies beyond the scope of EDA. We mention it here merely to underscore the importance of not omitting predictors, merely because their relationship with the target is nonobvious using EDA.

3.5   EXPLORING MULTIVARIATE RELATIONSHIPS

We next turn to an examination of the possible multivariate associations of numeric variables with churn, using scatter plots. Multivariate graphics can uncover new interaction effects which our univariate exploration missed.

Figure 3.20 shows a scatter plot of *day minutes* versus *evenings minutes*, with churners indicated by the darker circles. Note the straight line partitioning off the upper right section of the graph. Records above this diagonal line, representing customers with both high day minutes and high evening minutes, appear to have a higher proportion of churners than records below the line. The univariate evidence for a high churn rate for high evening minutes was not conclusive (Figure 3.17b), so it is nice to have a multivariate graph that supports the association, at least for customers with high day minutes.

Figure 3.21 shows a scatter plot of *customer service calls* versus *day minutes*. Churners and non-churners are indicated with large and small circles, respectively. Consider the records inside the rectangle partition shown in the scatter plot, which indicates a high-churn area in the upper left section of the graph. These records represent customers who have a combination of a high number of customer service calls and a low number of day minutes used. Note that this group of customers could not have been identified had we restricted ourselves to univariate exploration (exploring variable by single variable). This is because of the *interaction* between the variables.

In general, customers with higher numbers of customer service calls tend to churn at a higher rate, as we learned earlier in the univariate analysis. However,

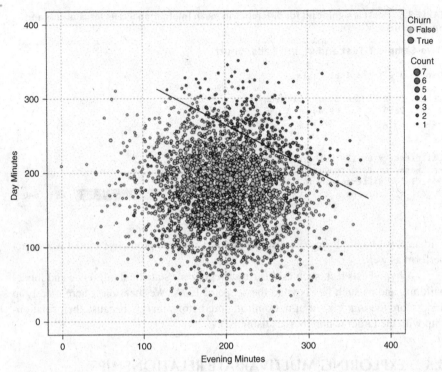

Figure 3.20 Customers with both high day minutes and high evening minutes are at greater risk of churning.

Figure 3.21 shows that, of these customers with high numbers of customer service calls, those who also have high day minutes are somewhat "protected" from this high churn rate. The customers in the upper right of the scatter plot exhibit a lower churn rate than those in the upper left. But how do we quantify these graphical findings?

3.6 SELECTING INTERESTING SUBSETS OF THE DATA FOR FURTHER INVESTIGATION

Graphical EDA can uncover subsets of records that call for further investigation, as the rectangle in Figure 3.21 illustrates. Let us examine the records in the rectangle more closely. *IBM/SPSS Modeler* allows the user to click and drag a box around data points of interest, and select them for further investigation. Here, we select the records within the rectangular box in the upper left. Figure 3.22 shows that about 65% (115 of 177) of the selected records are churners. That is, those with high customer service calls and low day minutes have a 65% probability of churning. Compare this to the records with high customer service calls and high day minutes (essentially the data points to the right of the rectangle). Figure 3.23 shows that only about 26% of customers with high customer service calls and high day minutes are churners. Thus, it is recommended that we red-flag customers with low day minutes who have a high number of customer service calls, as they are at much higher risk of leaving

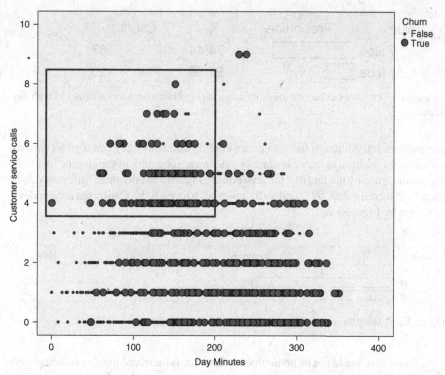

Figure 3.21   There is an interaction effect between *customer service calls* and *day minutes* with respect to churn.

Value	Proportion	%	Count
False		35.03	62
True		64.97	115

Figure 3.22   Very high proportion of churners for high customer service calls and low day minutes.

the company's service than the customers with the same number of customer service calls, but higher day minutes.

To summarize, the strategy we implemented here is as follows:

1. Generate multivariate graphical EDA, such as scatter plots with a flag overlay.
2. Use these plots to uncover subsets of interesting records.
3. Quantify the differences by analyzing the subsets of records.

3.7   USING EDA TO UNCOVER ANOMALOUS FIELDS

EDA will sometimes uncover strange or anomalous records or fields that the earlier data cleaning phase may have missed. Consider, for example, the *area code* field in the

Value	Proportion	%	Count
False		74.44	67
True		25.56	23

Figure 3.23   Much lower proportion of churners for high customer service calls and high day minutes.

present data set. Although the area codes contain numerals, they can also be used as categorical variables, as they can classify customers according to geographic location. We are intrigued by the fact that the area code field contains only three different values for all the records, *408, 415*, and *510* (which all happen to be California area codes), as shown by Figure 3.24.

Value	Proportion	%	Count
408		25.14	838
415		49.65	1655
510		25.2	840

Figure 3.24   Only three area codes for all records.

Now, this would not be anomalous if the records indicated that the customers all lived in California. However, as shown in the contingency table in Figure 3.25 (shown only up to Georgia, to save space), the three area codes seem to be distributed more or less evenly across all the states and the District of Columbia. Also, the chi-square test (see Chapter 6) has a *p*-value of 0.608, supporting the suspicion that the area codes are distributed randomly across all the states. Now, it is possible that domain experts might be able to explain this type of behavior, but it is also possible that the field just contains bad data.

We should therefore be wary of this *area code* field, and should not include it as input to the data mining models in the next phase. Further, the *state* field may be in error as well. Either way, further communication with someone familiar with the data history, or a domain expert, is called for before inclusion of these variables in the data mining models.

3.8   BINNING BASED ON PREDICTIVE VALUE

Chapter 2 discussed four methods for binning numerical variables. Here we provide two examples of the fourth method: Binning based on predictive value. Recall Figure 3.15, where we saw that customers with less than four calls to customer service had a lower churn rate than customers who had four or more calls to customer service. We may therefore decide to bin the *customer service calls* variable into two classes, *low* (fewer than four) and *high* (four or more). Table 3.7 shows that the churn rate for customers with a low number of calls to customer service is 11.3%, while the

		Area Code	
State	408	415	510
AK	14	24	14
AL	25	40	15
AR	13	27	15
AZ	15	36	13
CA	7	17	10
CO	25	29	12
CT	22	39	13
DC	14	27	13
DE	13	31	17
FL	12	31	20
GA	15	21	18
...	..	--	-

Cells contain: cross-tabulation of fields

Chi-square = 95.518, df = 100, probability = 0.608

Figure 3.25   Anomaly: three area codes distributed randomly across all 50 states.

TABLE 3.7   Binning customer service calls shows difference in churn rates

		CustServPlan_Bin	
		Low	High
Churn	False	Count 2721 Col% 88.7%	Count 129 Col% 48.3%
	True	Count 345 Col% 11.3%	Count 138 Col% 51.7%

churn rate for customers with a high number of calls to customer service is 51.7%, more than four times higher.

This binning of customer service calls created a flag variable with two values, high and low. Our next example of binning creates an ordinal categorical variable with three values, low, medium, and high. Recall that we are trying to determine whether there is a relationship between *evening minutes* and *churn*. Figure 3.17b hinted at a relationship, but inconclusively. Can we use binning to help tease out a signal from this noise? We reproduce Figure 3.17b here as Figure 3.26, somewhat enlarged, and with the boundaries between the bins indicated.

Binning is an art, requiring judgment. *Where can I insert boundaries between the bins that will maximize the difference in churn proportions?* The first boundary is inserted at *evening minutes* = 160, as the group of rectangles to the right of this boundary seem to have a higher proportion of churners than the group of rectangles to the left. And the second boundary is inserted at *evening minutes* = 240 for the same reason. (Analysts may fine tune these boundaries for maximum contrast, but for now these boundary values will do just fine; remember that we need to explain

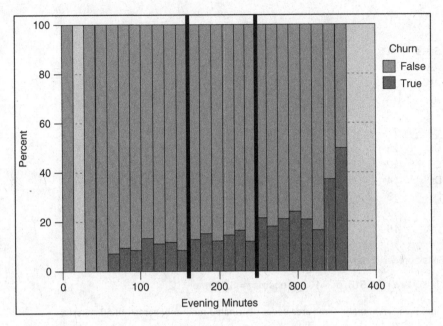

Figure 3.26 Binning *evening minutes* helps to tease out a signal from the noise.

TABLE 3.8 Bin values for *Evening Minutes*

Bin for Categorical Variable *Evening Minutes_Bin*	Values of Numerical Variable *Evening Minutes*
Low	*Evening minutes* ≤ 160
Medium	160 < *Evening minutes* ≤ 240
High	*Evening minutes* > 240

our results to the client, and that nice round numbers are more easily explained.) These boundaries thus define three bins, or categories, shown in Table 3.8.

Did the binning manage to tease out a signal? We can answer this by constructing a contingency table of *EveningMinutes_Bin* with *Churn*, shown in Table 3.9.

About half of the customers have medium amounts of evening minutes (1626/3333 = 48.8%), with about one-quarter each having low and high evening minutes. Recall that the *baseline churn rate* for all customers is 14.49% (Figure 3.3). The *medium* group comes in very close to this baseline rate, 14.1%. However, the *high* evening minutes group has nearly double the churn proportion compared to the *low* evening minutes group, 19.5–10%. The chi-square test (Chapter 6) is significant, meaning that these results are most likely real and not due to chance alone. In other words, we have succeeded in teasing out a signal from the *evening minutes* versus *churn* relationship.

TABLE 3.9 We have uncovered significant differences in churn rates among the three categories

		EveningMinutes_Bin		
		Low	Medium	High
Churn	False	Count 618	Count 1626	Count 606
		Col% 90.0%	Col% 85.9%	Col% 80.5%
	True	Count 69	Count 138	Count 138
		Col% 10.0%	Col% 14.1%	Col% 19.5%

3.9 DERIVING NEW VARIABLES: FLAG VARIABLES

Strictly speaking, deriving new variables is a data preparation activity. However, we cover it here in the EDA chapter to illustrate how the usefulness of the new derived variables in predicting the target variable may be assessed. We begin with an example of a derived variable which is not particularly useful. Figure 3.2 shows a spike in the distribution of the variable *Voice Mail Messages*, which makes its analysis problematic. We therefore derive a flag variable (see Chapter 2), *VoiceMailMessages_Flag*, to address this problem, as follows:

```
If Voice Mail Messages> 0 then
VoiceMailMessages_Flag=1;
otherwiseVoiceMailMessages_Flag = 0.
```

The resulting contingency table is shown in Table 3.10. Compare the results with those from Table 3.4, the contingency table for the Voice Mail Plan. The results are exactly the same, which is not surprising, as those without the plan can have no voice mail messages. Thus, as *VoiceMailMessages_Flag* has identical values as the flag variable *Voice Mail Plan*, it is not deemed to be a useful derived variable.

TABLE 3.10 Contingency table for *VoiceMailMessages_Flag*

		VoiceMailMessages_Flag	
		0	1
Churn	False	Count 2008 Col% 83.3%	Count 842 Col% 91.3%
	True	Count 403 Col% 16.7%	Count 80 Col% 8.7%

Recall Figure 3.20 (reproduced here as Figure 3.27), showing a scatter plot of *day minutes* versus *evening minutes*, with a straight line separating a group in the upper right(with both high day minutes and high evening minutes) that apparently churns at a greater rate. It would be nice to quantify this claim. We do so by selecting the records in the upper right, and compare their churn rate to that of the other records. One way to do this in IBM/SPSS Modeler is to draw an oval around the desired records, which the software then selects (not shown). However, this method is *ad hoc*, and not portable to a different data set (say the validation set). A better idea is to

1. estimate the equation of the straight line;
2. use the equation to separate the records, via a flag variable.

This method is portable to a validation set or other related data set.
We estimate the equation of the line in Figure 3.27 to be:

$$\hat{y} = 400 - 0.6x$$

That is, for each customer, the estimated day minutes equals 400 min minus 0.6 times the evening minutes. We may then create a flag variable *HighDayEveMins_Flag* as follows:

```
If Day Minutes > 400-0.6 Evening Minutes then
HighDayEveMins_Flag = 1;
otherwiseHighDayEveMins_Flag = 0.
```

Then each data point above the line will have *HighDayEveMins_Flag* = 1, while the data points below the line will have *HighDayEveMins_Flag* = 0. The resulting contingency table (Table 3.11) shows the highest churn proportion of any

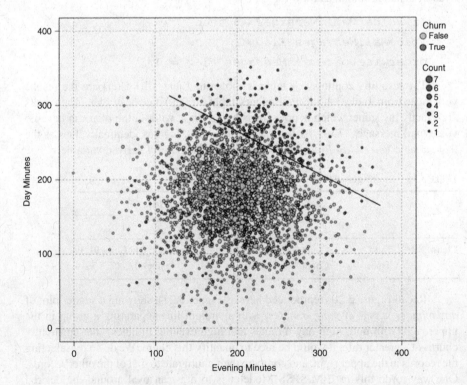

Figure 3.27   Use the equation of the line to separate the records via a flag variable.

TABLE 3.11   Contingency table for *HighDayEveMins_Flag*

		HighDayEveMins_Flag	
		0	1
Churn	False	Count 2792 Col% 89.0%	Count 58 Col% 29.6%
	True	Count 345 Col% 11.0%	Count 138 Col% 70.4%

variable we have studied thus far, 70.4 versus 11%, a more than sixfold difference. However, this 70.4% churn rate is restricted to a subset of fewer than 200 records, fortunately for the company.

A NOTE ABOUT CRISP-DM FOR DATA MINERS: BE STRUCTURED BUT FLEXIBLE

For *EveningMinutes_Bin* we referred to the chi-square significance test (Chapter 6), which really belongs to the modeling phase of data analysis. Also, our derived variable really belongs to the data preparation phase. These examples illustrate the flexibility of the cross-industry standard process for data mining (CRISP-DM) standard practice (or indeed any well-structured standard practice) of data mining. The assorted phases are interdependent, and should not be viewed as isolated from each other. For example, deriving variables is a data preparation activity, but derived variables need to be explored using EDA and (sometimes) significance tests. The data miner needs to be as flexible as CRISP-DM.

However, some data analysts fall victim to the opposite problem, interminably iterating back and forth between data preparation and EDA, getting lost in the details, and never advancing toward the research objectives. When this happens, CRISP-DM can serve as a useful road map, a structure to keep the data miner organized and moving toward the fulfillment of the research goals.

3.10 DERIVING NEW VARIABLES: NUMERICAL VARIABLES

Suppose we would like to derive a new numerical variable which combines *Customer Service Calls* and *International Calls*, and whose values will be the mean of the two fields. Now, as *International Calls* have a larger mean and standard deviation than *Customer Service Calls*, it would be unwise to take the mean of the raw field values, as *International Calls* would thereby be more heavily weighted. Instead, when combining numerical variables, we first need to standardize. The new derived variable therefore takes the form:

$$CSCInternational\_Z = \frac{(CSC\_Z + International\_Z)}{2}$$

where *CSC_Z* represents the z-score standardization of *Customer Service Calls* and *International_Z* represents the z-score standardization of *International Calls*. The

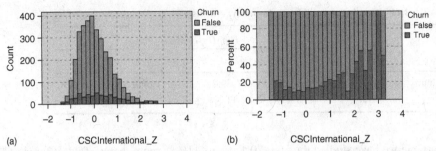

(a) CSCInternational_Z (b) CSCInternational_Z

Figure 3.28 (a) Non-normalized histogram of *CSCInternational_Z*. (b) Normalized histogram of *CSCInternational_Z*.

resulting normalized histogram of *CSCInternational_Z* indicates that it will be useful for predicting churn, as shown in Figure 3.28b.

3.11 USING EDA TO INVESTIGATE CORRELATED PREDICTOR VARIABLES

Two variables x and y are linearly correlated if an increase in x is associated with either an increase in y or a decrease in y. The *correlation coefficient r* quantifies the strength and direction of the linear relationship between x and y. The threshold for significance of the correlation coefficient r depends not only on the sample size but also on data mining, where there are a large number of records (over 1000), even small values of r, such as $-0.1 \le r \le 0.1$ may be statistically significant.

One should take care to avoid feeding correlated variables to one's data mining and statistical models. At best, using correlated variables will overemphasize one data component; at worst, using correlated variables will cause the model to become unstable and deliver unreliable results. However, *just because two variables are correlated does not mean that we should omit one of them*. Instead, while in the EDA stage, we should apply the following strategy.

STRATEGY FOR HANDLING CORRELATED PREDICTOR VARIABLES AT THE EDA STAGE

1. Identify any variables that are *perfectly* correlated (i.e., $r = 1.0$ or $r = -1.0$). Do not retain both variables in the model, but rather omit one.

2. Identify groups of variables that are correlated with each other. Then, later, during the modeling phase, apply *dimension-reduction methods*, such as *principal components analysis*,[2] to these variables.

[2]For more on dimension reductions and principal components analysis, see Chapter 4.

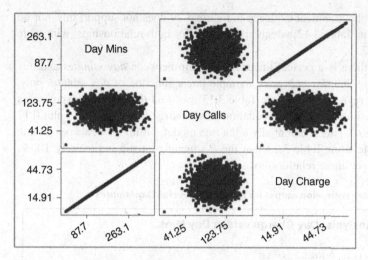

Figure 3.29   Matrix plot of *day minutes*, *day calls*, and *day charge*.

Note that this strategy applies to uncovering correlation among the predictors alone, not between a given predictor and the target variable.

Turning to our data set, for each of *day*, *evening*, *night*, and *international*, the data set contains three variables, *minutes*, *calls*, and *charge*. The data description indicates that the *charge* variable may be a function of *minutes* and *calls*, with the result that the variables would be correlated. We investigate using a *matrix plot* (Figure 3.29), which is a matrix of scatter plots for a set of numeric variables, in this case for *day minutes*, *day calls*, and *day charge*. Table 3.12 contains the correlation coefficient values and the *p*-values for each pairwise set of variables.

There does not seem to be any relationship between *day minutes* and *day calls*, nor between *day calls* and *day charge*. This we find to be rather odd, as one may have expected that, as the number of calls increased, the number of minutes would tend to increase (and similarly for charge), resulting in a positive correlation between these

TABLE 3.12   **Correlations and *p*-values**

```
Correlations: Day Mins, Day Calls, Day Charge

                Day Mins    Day Calls
Day Calls        0.007
                 0.697

Day Charge       1.000       0.007
                 0.000       0.697



Cell Contents:  Pearson correlation
                P-Value
```

fields. However, the graphical evidence in Figure 3.29 does not support this, nor do the correlations in Table 3.12, which are $r = 0.07$ for both relationships, with large p-values of 0.697.

However, there is a perfect linear relationship between *day minutes* and *day charge*, indicating that *day charge* is a simple linear function of *day minutes* only. Using Minitab's regression tool (see Table 3.13), we find that we may express this function as the estimated regression equation: "*Day charge* equals 0.000613 plus 0.17 times *day minutes*." This is essentially a flat rate model, billing 17 cents per minute for day use. Note from Table 3.13 that the R-squared statistic is precisely 100%, indicating a perfect linear relationship.

TABLE 3.13 *Minitab regression output for Day Charge versus Day Minutes*

```
Regression Analysis: Day Charge versus Day Mins

The regression equation is
Day Charge =0.000613 + 0.170 Day Mins

Predictor          Coef      SE Coef          T         P
Constant       0.0006134    0.0001711       3.59     0.000
Day Mins       0.170000     0.000001   186644.31     0.000

S = 0.002864    R-Sq = 100.0%    R-Sq(adj) = 100.0%
```

As *day charge* is perfectly correlated with *day minutes*, we should eliminate one of the two variables. We do so, arbitrarily choosing to eliminate *day charge* and retain *day minutes*. Investigation of the *evening*, *night*, and *international* components reflected similar findings, and we thus also eliminate *evening charge*, *night charge*, and *international charge*. Note that, had we proceeded to the modeling phase without first uncovering these correlations, our data mining and statistical models may have returned incoherent results, due, for example, to multicollinearity in multiple regression. We have therefore reduced the number of predictors from 20 to 16 by eliminating one of each pair of perfectly correlated predictors. A further benefit of doing so is that the dimensionality of the solution space is reduced so that certain data mining algorithms may more efficiently find the globally optimal solution.

After dealing with the perfectly correlated predictors, the data analyst should turn to step 2 of the strategy, and *identify any other correlated predictors*, for later handling with principal components analysis. The correlation of each numerical predictor with every other numerical predictor should be checked, if feasible. Correlations with small p-values should be identified. A subset of this procedure is shown here in Table 3.14. Note that the correlation coefficient 0.038 between *account length* and *day calls* has a small p-value of 0.026, telling us that account length and day calls are positively correlated. The data analyst should note this, and prepare to apply the principal components analysis during the modeling phase.

TABLE 3.14   *Account length* is positively correlated with *day calls*

```
Correlations: Account Leng, VMail Messag, Day Mins, Day Calls, CustServ Cal

                Account Length   VMail Message      Day Mins      Day Calls
VMail Message          -0.005
                        0.789

Day Mins                0.006           0.001
                        0.720           0.964

Day Calls               0.038          -0.010         0.007
                        0.026           0.582         0.697

CustServ Calls         -0.004          -0.013        -0.013         -0.019
                        0.827           0.444         0.439          0.274


Cell Contents: Pearson correlation
               P-Value
```

3.12   SUMMARY OF OUR EDA

Let us consider some of the insights we have gained into the *churn* data set through the use of EDA. We have examined each of the variables (here and in the exercises), and have taken a preliminary look at their relationship with *churn*.

- The four *charge* fields are linear functions of the *minute* fields, and should be omitted.
- The *area code* field and/or the *state* field are anomalous, and should be omitted until further clarification is obtained.

  Insights with respect to *churn* are as follows:

- Customers with the *International Plan* tend to churn more frequently.
- Customers with the *Voice Mail Plan* tend to churn less frequently.
- Customers with four or more *Customer Service Calls* churn more than four times as often as the other customers.
- Customers with both high *Day Minutes* and high *Evening Minutes* tend to churn at a higher rate than the other customers.
- Customers with both high *Day Minutes* and high *Evening Minutes* churn at a rate about six times greater than the other customers.
- Customers with low *Day Minutes* and high *Customer Service Calls* churn at a higher rate than the other customers.
- Customers with lower numbers of *International Calls* churn at a higher rate than do customers with more international calls.
- For the remaining predictors, EDA uncovers no obvious association of *churn*. However, these variables are still retained for input to downstream data mining models and techniques.

Note the power of EDA. We have not applied any high-powered data mining algorithms yet on this data set, such as decision trees or neural network algorithms. Yet, we have still gained considerable insight into the attributes that are associated with the customers leaving the company, simply by careful application of EDA. These insights can be easily formulated into actionable recommendations so that the company can take action to lower the churn rate among its customer base.

THE R ZONE

Read in the Churn data set

```
churn <- read.csv(file =
       "C:/ . . . /churn.txt",
    stringsAsFactors=TRUE)
# Show the first ten records
churn[1:10,]
```

```
> churn[1:10,]
   State Account.Length Area.Code    Phone Int.1.Plan
1     KS            128      415 382-4657         no
2     OH            107      415 371-7191         no
3     NJ            137      415 358-1921         no
4     OH             84      408 375-9999        yes
5     OK             75      415 330-6626        yes
6     AL            118      510 391-8027        yes
7     MA            121      510 355-9993         no
8     MO            147      415 329-9001        yes
9     LA            117      408 335-4719         no
10    WV            141      415 330-8173        yes
```

```
# Summarize the Churn variable

sum.churn <- summary(churn$Churn)
sum.churn
```

```
# Calculate proportion of churners

prop.churn <- sum(churn$Churn ==
       "True") / length(churn$Churn)
prop.churn
```

Bar chart of variable Churn

```
barplot(sum.churn,
     ylim = c(0, 3000),
     main = "Bar Graph of Churners and
     Non-Churners",
     col = "lightblue")
box(which = "plot",
     lty = "solid",
     col="black")
```

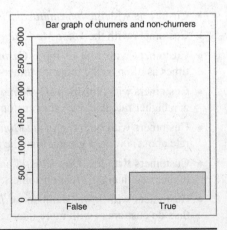

Make a table for counts of Churn and International Plan

```
counts <- table(churn$Churn,
    churn$Int.l.Plan,
        dnn=c("Churn", "International Plan"))
counts
```

```
> counts
            International Plan
churn     no   yes
    False 2664  186
    True   346  137
```

#Overlayed bar chart

```
barplot(counts,
    legend = rownames(counts),
    col = c("blue", "red"),
    ylim = c(0, 3300),
    ylab = "Count",
    xlab = "International Plan",
    main = "Comparison Bar Chart:
        Churn Proportions by
        International Plan")
box(which = "plot",
    lty = "solid",
    col="black")
```

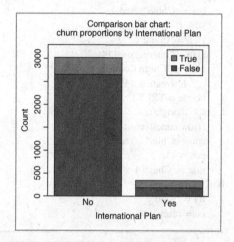

Create a table with sums for both variables

```
sumtable <- addmargins(counts,
    FUN = sum)
sumtable
```

```
> sumtable
            International Plan
churn     no   yes  sum
    False 2664  186 2850
    True   346  137  483
    sum   3010  323 3333
```

Create a table of proportions over rows

```
row.margin <- round(prop.table(counts,
        margin = 1),
    4)*100
row.margin
```

```
> row.margin
            International Plan
churn     no    yes
    False 93.47  6.53
    True  71.64 28.36
```

Create a table of proportions over columns

```
col.margin <- round(prop.table(counts,
        margin = 2),
    4)*100
col.margin
```

```
> col.margin
              International Plan
Churn       no     yes
  False 88.50  57.59
  True  11.50  42.41
```

Clustered Bar Chart, with legend

```
barplot(counts,
    col = c("blue", "red"),
    ylim = c(0, 3300),
    ylab = "Count",
    xlab = "International Plan",
    main = "Churn Count by
        International Plan",
    beside = TRUE)
legend("topright",
    c(rownames(counts)),
    col = c("blue", "red"),
    pch = 15,
    title = "Churn")
box(which = "plot",
    lty = "solid",
    col="black")
```

Clustered Bar Chart of Churn and International Plan with legend

```
barplot(t(counts),
    col = c("blue", "green"),
    ylim = c(0, 3300),
    ylab = "Counts",
    xlab = "Churn",
    main = "International Plan Count by
        Churn",
    beside = TRUE)
legend("topright",
    c(rownames(counts)),
    col = c("blue", "green"),
    pch = 15,
    title = "Int'l Plan")
box(which = "plot",
    lty = "solid",
    col="black")
```

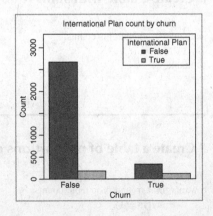

Histogram of non-overlayed Customer Service Calls

```
hist(churn$CustServ.Calls,
      xlim = c(0,10),
      col = "lightblue",
      ylab = "Count",
      xlab = "Customer Service Calls",
      main = "Histogram of Customer Service
            Calls")
```

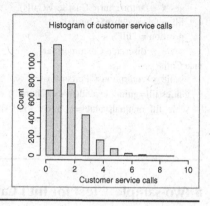

Download and install the R Package *ggplot2*

```
install.packages("ggplot2")
# Pick any CRAN mirror
# (see example image)
# Open the new package
library(ggplot2)
```

```
79: USA (CA 1)        80: USA (CA 2)
81: USA (IA)          82: USA (IN)
83: USA (KS)          84: USA (MD)
85: USA (MI)          86: USA (MO)
87: USA (OH)          88: USA (OR)
89: USA (PA 1)        90: USA (PA 2)
91: USA (TN)          92: USA (TX 1)
93: USA (WA 1)        94: USA (WA 2)
95: Venezuela         96: Vietnam

Selection: 79
```

Overlayed bar charts

```
ggplot() +
      geom_bar(data = churn,
      aes(x = factor(churn$CustServ.Calls),
      fill = factor(churn$Churn)),
      position = "stack") +
      scale_x_discrete("Customer Service Calls") +
      scale_y_continuous("Percent") +
      guides(fill=guide_legend(title="Churn")) +
      scale_fill_manual(values=c("blue", "red"))
```

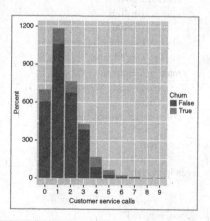

```
ggplot() +
    geom_bar(data=churn,
    aes(x = factor(churn$CustServ.Calls),
    fill = factor(churn$Churn)),
    position = "fill") +
    scale_x_discrete("Customer Ser-
vice Calls") +
    scale_y_continuous("Percent") +
    guides(fill=guide_legend(title="Churn")) +
    scale_fill_manual(values=c("blue", "red"))
```

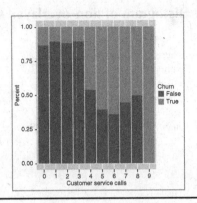

Two-sample T-Test for Int'l Calls

```
# Partition data
churn.false <- subset(churn,
    churn$Churn ==
        "False")
churn.true <- subset(churn,
    churn$Churn ==
        "True")
# Run the test
t.test(churn.false$Intl.Calls,
    churn.true$Intl.Calls)
```

```
> t.test(churn.false$Intl.Calls,
+          churn.true$Intl.Calls)

    welch Two Sample t-test

data:  churn.false$Intl.Calls and churn.true$Intl.Calls
t = 2.9604, df = 640.643, p-value = 0.003186
alternative hypothesis: true difference in means is not
equal to 0
95 percent confidence interval:
 0.1243807 0.6144620
sample estimates:
mean of x mean of y
 4.532982  4.163561
```

Scatterplot of Evening Minutes and Day Minutes, colored by Churn

```
plot(churn$Eve.Mins,
    churn$Day.Mins,
    xlim = c(0, 400),
    ylim = c(0, 400),
    xlab = "Evening Minutes",
    ylab = "Day Minutes",
    main = "Scatterplot of Day
        and Evening Minutes by
        Churn",
    col = ifelse(churn$Churn==
        "True",
        "red",
        "blue"))
legend("topright",
        c("True",
        "False"),
    col = c("red",
        "blue"),
    pch = 1,
    title = "Churn")
```

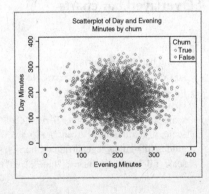

Scatterplot of Day Minutes and Customer Service Calls, colored by Churn

```
plot(churn$Day.Mins,
    churn$CustServ.Calls,
    xlim = c(0, 400),
    xlab = "Day Minutes",
    ylab = "Customer Service Calls",
    main = "Scatterplot of Day Minutes and
        Customer Service Calls by Churn",
    col = ifelse(churn$Churn=="True",
        "red",
        "blue"),
    pch = ifelse(churn$Churn=="True",
        16, 20))
legend("topright",
    c("True",
        "False"),
    col = c("red",
        "blue"),
    pch = c(16, 20),
    title = "Churn")
```

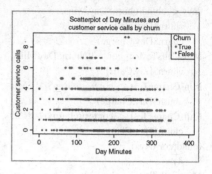

Scatterplot matrix

```
pairs(~churn$Day.Mins+
    churn$Day.Calls+
    churn$Day.Charge)
```

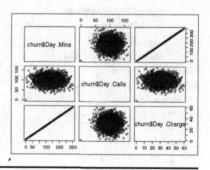

Regression of Day Charge vs Day Minutes

```
fit <- lm(churn$Day.Charge ~
        churn$Day.Mins)
summary(fit)
```

```
> summary(fit)

Call:
lm(formula = churn$Day.charge ~ churn$Day.Mins)

Residuals:
      Min         1Q     Median         3Q        Max
-0.0045935 -0.0025391  0.0004326  0.0024587  0.0045224

Coefficients:
                 Estimate Std. Error   t value Pr(>|t|)
(Intercept)     6.134e-04  1.711e-04 3.585e+00 0.000341 ***
churn$Day.Mins 1.700e-01  9.108e-07 1.866e+05  < 2e-16 ***
---
Signif. codes:  0 '***' 0.001 '**' 0.01 '*' 0.05 '.' 0.1 ' ' 1

Residual standard error: 0.002864 on 3331 degrees of freedom
Multiple R-squared:     1,  Adjusted R-squared:     1
F-statistic: 3.484e+10 on 1 and 3331 DF,  p-value: < 2.2e-16
```

Correlation values, with p-values

```
days <- cbind(churn$Day.Mins,
       churn$Day.Calls,
       churn$Day.Charge)
MinsCallsTest <- cor.test(churn$Day.Mins,
       churn$Day.Calls)
MinsChargeTest <- cor.test(churn$Day.Mins,
       churn$Day.Charge)
CallsChargeTest <- cor.test(churn$Day.Calls,
       churn$Day.Charge)
round(cor(days),
       4)
MinsCallsTest$p.value
MinsChargeTest$p.value
CallsChargeTest$p.value
```

```
> round(cor(days), 4)
        [,1]   [,2]   [,3]
[1,] 1.0000 0.0068 1.0000
[2,] 0.0068 1.0000 0.0068
[3,] 1.0000 0.0068 1.0000
> MinsCallsTest$p.value
[1] 0.6968515
> MinsChargeTest$p.value
[1] 0
> CallsChargeTest$p.value
[1] 0.6967428
```

Correlation values and p-values in matrix form

```
# Collect variables of interest
corrdata <-
       cbind(churn$Account.Length,
          churn$VMail.Message,
          churn$Day.Mins,
          churn$Day.Calls,
          churn$CustServ.Calls)
# Declare the matrix
corrpvalues <- matrix(rep(0, 25),
       ncol = 5)
# Fill the matrix with correlations
for (i in 1:4) {
    for (j in (i+1):5) {
        corrpvalues[i,j] <-
        corrpvalues[j,i] <-
            round(cor.test(corrdata[,i],
                corrdata[,j])$p.value,
                4)
    }
}
round(cor(corrdata), 4)
corrpvalues
```

```
> round(cor(corrdata), 4)
        [,1]    [,2]    [,3]    [,4]    [,5]
[1,]  1.0000 -0.0046  0.0062  0.0385 -0.0038
[2,] -0.0046  1.0000  0.0008 -0.0095 -0.0133
[3,]  0.0062  0.0008  1.0000  0.0068 -0.0134
[4,]  0.0385 -0.0095  0.0068  1.0000 -0.0189
[5,] -0.0038 -0.0133 -0.0134 -0.0189  1.0000
> corrpvalues
        [,1]   [,2]   [,3]   [,4]   [,5]
[1,] 0.0000 0.7894 0.7198 0.0264 0.8266
[2,] 0.7894 0.0000 0.9642 0.5816 0.4440
[3,] 0.7198 0.9642 0.0000 0.6969 0.4385
[4,] 0.0264 0.5816 0.6969 0.0000 0.2743
[5,] 0.8266 0.4440 0.4385 0.2743 0.0000
```

R REFERENCES

Wickham H. *ggplot2: Elegant Graphics for Data Analysis*. New York: Springer; 2009.

R Core Team. *R: A Language and Environment for Statistical Computing*. Vienna, Austria: R Foundation for Statistical Computing; 2012. ISBN: 3-900051-07-0, http://www.R-project.org/.

EXERCISES

1. Explain the difference between EDA and hypothesis testing, and why analysts may prefer EDA when doing data mining.

2. Why do we need to perform EDA? Why should not we simply proceed directly to the modeling phase and start applying our high-powered data mining software?

3. Why do we use contingency tables, instead of just presenting the graphical results?

4. How can we find the marginal distribution of each variable in a contingency table?

5. What is the difference between taking row percentages and taking column percentages in a contingency table?

6. What is the graphical counterpart of a contingency table?

7. Describe what it would mean for interaction to take place between two categorical variables, using an example.

8. What type of histogram is useful for examining the relationship between a numerical predictor and the target?

9. Explain one benefit and one drawback of using a normalized histogram. Should we ever present a normalized histogram without showing its non-normalized counterpart?

10. Explain whether we should omit a predictor from the modeling stage if it does not show any relationship with the target variable in the EDA stage, and why.

11. Describe how scatter plots can uncover patterns in two-dimensions that would be invisible from one-dimensional EDA.

12. Make up a fictional data set (attributes with no records is fine) with a pair of anomalous attributes. Describe how EDA would help to uncover the anomaly.

13. Explain the objective and the method of binning based on predictive value.

14. Why is binning based on predictive value considered to be somewhat of an art?

15. What step should precede the deriving of a new numerical variable representing the mean of two other numerical variables?

16. What does it mean to say that two variables are correlated?

17. Describe the possible consequences of allowing correlated variables to remain in the model.

18. A common practice among some analysts when they encounter two correlated predictors is to omit one of them from the analysis. Is this practice recommended?

19. Describe the strategy for handing correlated predictor variables at the EDA stage.

20. For each of the following descriptive methods, state whether it may be applied to categorical data, continuous numerical data, or both.

    a. Bar charts
    b. Histograms
    c. Summary statistics
    d. Cross tabulations
    e. Correlation analysis
    f. Scatter plots
    g. Web graphs
    h. Binning.

HANDS-ON ANALYSIS

21. Using the *churn* data set, develop EDA which shows that the remaining numeric variables in the data set (apart from those covered in the text above) indicate no obvious association with the target variable.
    Use the *adult* data set from the book series web site for the following exercises. The target variable is *income*, and the goal is to classify income based on the other variables.

22. Which variables are categorical and which are continuous?

23. Using software, construct a table of the first 10 records of the data set, in order to get a feel for the data.

24. Investigate whether we have any correlated variables.

25. For each of the categorical variables, construct a bar chart of the variable, with an overlay of the target variable. Normalize if necessary.

    a. Discuss the relationship, if any, each of these variables has with the target variables.

    b. Which variables would you expect to make a significant appearance in any data mining classification model we work with?

26. For each pair of categorical variables, construct a cross tabulation. Discuss your salient results.

27. (If your software supports this.) Construct a web graph of the categorical variables. Fine tune the graph so that interesting results emerge. Discuss your findings.

28. Report on whether anomalous fields exist in this data set, based on your EDA, which fields these are, and what we should do about it.

29. Report the mean, median, minimum, maximum, and standard deviation for each of the numerical variables.

30. Construct a histogram of each numerical variables, with an overlay of the target variable *income*. Normalize if necessary.

    a. Discuss the relationship, if any, each of these variables has with the target variables.

    b. Which variables would you expect to make a significant appearance in any data mining classification model we work with?

31. For each pair of numerical variables, construct a scatter plot of the variables. Discuss your salient results.

32. Based on your EDA so far, identify interesting sub-groups of records within the data set that would be worth further investigation.

33. Apply binning to one of the numerical variables. Do it in such a way as to maximize the effect of the classes thus created (following the suggestions in the text). Now do it in such a way as to minimize the effect of the classes so that the difference between the classes is diminished. Comment.

34. Refer to the previous exercise. Apply the other two binning methods (equal width, and equal number of records) to this same variable. Compare the results and discuss the differences. Which method do you prefer?

35. Summarize your salient EDA findings from the above exercises, just as if you were writing a report.

## CHAPTER 4

DIMENSION-REDUCTION METHODS

4.1 NEED FOR DIMENSION-REDUCTION IN DATA MINING

The databases typically used in data mining may have millions of records and thousands of variables. It is unlikely that all of the variables are independent, with no correlation structure among them. Data analysts need to guard against *multicollinearity*, a condition where some of the predictor variables are strongly correlated with each other. Multicollinearity leads to instability in the solution space, leading to possible incoherent results, such as in multiple regression, where a multicollinear set of predictors can result in a regression which is significant overall, even when none of the individual variables is significant. Even if such instability is avoided, inclusion of variables which are highly correlated tends to overemphasize a particular component of the model, as the component is essentially being double counted.

Bellman[1] noted that the sample size needed to fit a multivariate function grows exponentially with the number of variables. In other words, higher-dimension spaces are inherently sparse. For example, the empirical rule tells us that, in one-dimension, about 68% of normally distributed variates lie between one and negative one standard deviation from the mean; while, for a 10-dimension multivariate normal distribution, only 2% of the data lies within the analogous hypersphere.[2]

The use of too many predictor variables to model a relationship with a response variable can unnecessarily complicate the interpretation of the analysis, and violates the principle of parsimony, that one should consider keeping the number of predictors to such a size that would be easily interpreted. Also, retaining too many variables may lead to overfitting, in which the generality of the findings is hindered because new data do not behave the same as the training data for all the variables.

---

[1] Bellman, R., *Adaptive Control Processes: A Guided Tour*, Princeton University Press, 1961.

[2] Pace, R. Kelley and Ronald Berry, 1997. Sparse Spatial Autoregressions, *Statistics and Probability Letters*, Vol 33, Number 3, May 5, 1997, pp. 291–297.

Data Mining and Predictive Analytics, First Edition. Daniel T. Larose and Chantal D. Larose.
© 2015 John Wiley & Sons, Inc. Published 2015 by John Wiley & Sons, Inc.

Further, analysis solely at the variable-level might miss the fundamental under-lying relationships among the predictors. For example, several predictors might fall naturally into a single group, (a *factor* or a *component*), which addresses a single aspect of the data. For example, the variables savings account balance, checking account balance, home equity, stock portfolio value, and 401k balance might all fall together under the single component, *assets*.

In some applications, such as image analysis, retaining full dimensionality would make most problems intractable. For example, a face classification system based on 256×256 pixel images could potentially require vectors of dimension 65,536.

Humans are innately endowed with visual pattern recognition abilities, which enable us in an intuitive manner to discern patterns in graphic images at a glance: the patterns that might elude us if presented algebraically or textually. However, even the most advanced data visualization techniques do not go much beyond five dimensions. How, then, can we hope to visualize the relationship among the hundreds of variables in our massive data sets?

Dimension-reduction methods have the goal of using the correlation structure among the predictor variables to accomplish the following:

- To reduce the number of predictor items.
- To help ensure that these predictor items are independent.
- To provide a framework for interpretability of the results.

In this chapter, we examine the following dimension-reduction methods:

- Principal components analysis (PCA)
- Factor analysis
- User-defined composites

This next section calls upon knowledge of matrix algebra. For those of you whose matrix algebra may be rusty, concentrate on the meaning of Results 1–3 (see below).[3] Immediately after, we shall apply all of the following terminologies and notations in terms of a concrete example, using the real-world data.

4.2   PRINCIPAL COMPONENTS ANALYSIS

PCA seeks to explain the correlation structure of a set of predictor variables, using a smaller set of linear combinations of these variables. These linear combinations are called *components*. The total variability of a data set produced by the complete set of m variables can often be mostly accounted for by a smaller set of k linear combinations of these variables, which would mean that there is almost as much information in the k components as there is in the original m variables. If desired, the analyst can then replace the original m variables with the $k < m$ components, so that the working data

---

[3] Johnson and Wichern, *Applied Multivariate Statistical Analysis*, 6th edition, Prentice Hall, Upper Saddle River, New Jersey, 2007.

set now consists of n records on k components, rather than n records on m variables. The analyst should note that PCA acts solely on the predictor variables, and ignores the target variable.

Suppose that the original variables $X_1, X_2, \ldots, X_m$ form a coordinate system in m-dimensional space. The principal components represent a new coordinate system, found by rotating the original system along the directions of maximum variability.

When preparing to perform data reduction, the analyst should first standardize the data, so that the mean for each variable is zero, and the standard deviation is one. Let each variable X_i represent an $n \times 1$ vector, where n is the number of records. Then, represent the standardized variable as the $n \times 1$ vector Z_i, where $Z_i = \frac{(X_i - \mu_i)}{\sigma_{ii}}$, μ_i is the mean of X_i, and σ_{ii} is the standard deviation of X_i. In matrix notation, this standardization is expressed as $\mathbf{Z} = (\mathbf{V}^{1/2})^{-1}(\mathbf{X} - \boldsymbol{\mu})$, where the "$-1$" exponent refers to the matrix inverse, and $\mathbf{V}^{1/2}$ is a diagonal matrix (nonzero entries only on the diagonal); the $m \times m$ *standard deviation matrix* is:

$$\mathbf{V}^{1/2} = \begin{bmatrix} \sigma_{11} & 0 & \cdots & 0 \\ 0 & \sigma_{22} & \cdots & 0 \\ \vdots & \vdots & \ddots & \vdots \\ 0 & 0 & \cdots & \sigma_{mm} \end{bmatrix}$$

Let Σ refer to the symmetric *covariance matrix*:

$$\Sigma = \begin{bmatrix} \sigma_{11}^2 & \sigma_{12}^2 & \cdots & \sigma_{1m}^2 \\ \sigma_{12}^2 & \sigma_{22}^2 & \cdots & \sigma_{2m}^2 \\ \vdots & \vdots & \ddots & \vdots \\ \sigma_{1m}^2 & \sigma_{2m}^2 & \cdots & \sigma_{mm}^2 \end{bmatrix},$$

where σ_{ij}^2, $i \neq j$ refers to the *covariance* between X_i and X_j.

$$\sigma_{ij}^2 = \frac{\sum_{k=1}^n (x_{ki} - \mu_i)(x_{kj} - \mu_j)}{n}$$

The covariance is a measure of the degree to which two variables vary together. A positive covariance indicates that, when one variable increases, the other tends to increase, while a negative covariance indicates that, when one variable increases, the other tends to decrease. The notation σ_{ii}^2 is used to denote the variance of X_i. If X_i and X_j are independent, then $\sigma_{ij}^2 = 0$; but $\sigma_{ij}^2 = 0$ does not imply that X_i and X_j are independent. Note that the covariance measure is not scaled, so that changing the units of measure would change the value of the covariance.

The *correlation coefficient* r_{ij} avoids this difficulty by scaling the covariance by each of the standard deviations:

$$r_{ij} = \frac{\sigma_{ij}^2}{\sigma_{ii}\sigma_{jj}}$$

Then, the *correlation matrix* is denoted as ρ (*rho*, the Greek letter for *r*):

$$\rho = \begin{bmatrix} \dfrac{\sigma_{11}^2}{\sigma_{11}\sigma_{11}} & \dfrac{\sigma_{12}^2}{\sigma_{11}\sigma_{22}} & \cdots & \dfrac{\sigma_{1m}^2}{\sigma_{11}\sigma_{mm}} \\[2mm] \dfrac{\sigma_{12}^2}{\sigma_{11}\sigma_{22}} & \dfrac{\sigma_{22}^2}{\sigma_{22}\sigma_{22}} & \cdots & \dfrac{\sigma_{2m}^2}{\sigma_{22}\sigma_{mm}} \\[2mm] \vdots & \vdots & \ddots & \vdots \\[2mm] \dfrac{\sigma_{1m}^2}{\sigma_{11}\sigma_{mm}} & \dfrac{\sigma_{2m}^2}{\sigma_{22}\sigma_{mm}} & \cdots & \dfrac{\sigma_{mm}^2}{\sigma_{mm}\sigma_{mm}} \end{bmatrix}.$$

Consider again the standardized data matrix $\mathbf{Z} = (\mathbf{V}^{1/2})^{-1}(\mathbf{X} - \boldsymbol{\mu})$. Then, as each variable has been standardized we have $E(\mathbf{Z}) = \mathbf{0}$, where $\mathbf{0}$ denotes an $n \times m$ matrix of zeroes, and $\mathbf{Z}$ has covariance matrix $\text{Cov}(\mathbf{Z}) = (\mathbf{V}^{1/2})^{-1}\Sigma(\mathbf{V}^{1/2})^{-1} = \rho$. Thus, for the standardized data set, the covariance matrix and the correlation matrix are the same.

The *i*th *principal component* of the standardized data matrix $\mathbf{Z} = [Z_1, Z_2, \ldots, Z_m]$ is given by: $Y_i = \mathbf{e}_i'\mathbf{Z}$, where $\mathbf{e}_i$ refers to the *i*th *eigenvector* (discussed below), and $\mathbf{e}_i'$ refers to the transpose of $\mathbf{e}_i$. The principal components $Y_1, Y_2, \ldots, Y_k$ are linear combinations of the standardized variables in $\mathbf{Z}$, such that (a) the variances of the Y_i are as large as possible, and (b) the Y_i's are uncorrelated.

The first principal component is the linear combination $Y_1 = \mathbf{e}_1'\mathbf{Z} = e_{11}Z_1 + e_{21}Z_2 + \cdots + e_{m1}Z_m$ that has greater variability than any other possible linear combination of the Z variables. Thus,

- the first principal component is the linear combination $Y_1 = \mathbf{e}_1'\mathbf{Z}$ that maximizes $\text{Var}(Y_1) = \mathbf{e}_1'\rho\mathbf{e}_1$;
- the second principal component is the linear combination $Y_2 = \mathbf{e}_2'\mathbf{Z}$ that *is independent of* Y_1, and maximizes $\text{Var}(Y_2) = \mathbf{e}_2'\rho\mathbf{e}_2$;
- in general, the *i*th principal component is the linear combination $Y_i = \mathbf{e}_i'\mathbf{Z}$ that *is independent of all the other principal components* Y_j, $j < i$, and maximizes $\text{Var}(Y_i) = \mathbf{e}_i'\rho\mathbf{e}_i$.

Eigenvalues. Let $\mathbf{B}$ be an $m \times m$ matrix, and let $\mathbf{I}$ be the $m \times m$ identity matrix (diagonal matrix with 1's on the diagonal). Then the scalars (numbers of dimension 1×1) $\lambda_1, \lambda_2, \ldots, \lambda_m$ are said to be the *eigenvalues* of $\mathbf{B}$ if they satisfy $|\mathbf{B} - \lambda\mathbf{I}| = 0$, where $|\mathbf{Q}|$ denotes the determinant of $\mathbf{Q}$.

Eigenvectors. Let $\mathbf{B}$ be an $m \times m$ matrix, and let λ be an eigenvalue of $\mathbf{B}$. Then nonzero $m \times 1$ vector $\mathbf{e}$ is said to be an *eigenvector* of $\mathbf{B}$, if $\mathbf{Be} = \lambda\mathbf{e}$.

The following results are very important for our PCA analysis.

Result 1

The total variability in the standardized set of predictors equals the sum of the variances of the Z-vectors, which equals the sum of the variances of the components, which equals the sum of the eigenvalues, which equals the number of predictors. That is,

$$\sum_{i=1}^{m} \text{Var}(Y_i) = \sum_{i=1}^{m} \text{Var}(Z_i) = \sum_{i=1}^{m} \lambda_i = m.$$

Result 2

The partial correlation between a given component and a given predictor variable is a function of an eigenvector and an eigenvalue. Specifically, $\text{Corr}(Y_i, Z_j) = e_{ij}\sqrt{\lambda_i}; \quad i, j = 1, 2, \ldots, m,$ where $(\lambda_1, \mathbf{e}_1), (\lambda_2, \mathbf{e}_2), \ldots, (\lambda_m, \mathbf{e}_m)$ are the eigenvalue–eigenvector pairs for the correlation matrix ρ, and we note that $\lambda_1 \geq \lambda_2 \geq \ldots \geq \lambda_m$. In other words, the eigenvalues are ordered by size. (A *partial correlation coefficient* is a correlation coefficient that takes into account the effect of all the other variables.)

Result 3

The proportion of the total variability in $\mathbf{Z}$ that is explained by the ith principal component is the ratio of the ith eigenvalue to the number of variables, that is, the ratio $\frac{\lambda_i}{m}$.

Next, to illustrate how to apply PCA on real data, we turn to an example.

4.3 APPLYING PCA TO THE *HOUSES* DATA SET

We turn to the *Houses* data set,[4] which provides census information from all the block groups from the 1990 California census. For this data set, a block group has an average of 1425.5 people living in an area that is geographically compact. Block groups were excluded that contained zero entries for any of the variables. Median house value is the response variable; the predictor variables are the following:

Median income	Population
Housing median age	Households
Total rooms	Latitude
Total bedrooms	Longitude

The original data set had 20,640 records, of which 18,540 were randomly selected for a training data set, and 2100 held out for a test data set. A quick look at the variables is provided in Figure 4.1. ("Range" indicates *IBM Modeler's* type label for continuous variables.)

Median house value appears to be in dollars, but *median income* has been scaled to a 0–15 continuous scale. Note that *longitude* is expressed in negative terms, meaning west of Greenwich. Larger absolute values for longitude indicate geographic locations further west.

---

[4]Data set available from StatLib: http://lib.stat.cmu.edu/datasets/houses.zip. Also available at textbook website: www.DataMiningConsultant.com.

Field	Sample Graph	Type	Min	Max	Mean	Std. Dev
median_house_value		Range	14999	500001	206918.067	115485.040
median_income		Range	0.500	15.000	3.873	1.906
housing_median_age		Range	1	52	28.656	12.582
total_rooms		Range	2	37937	2621.653	2131.644
total_bedrooms		Range	1	6445	535.096	413.541
population		Range	3	35682	1418.971	1122.534
households		Range	1	6082	497.332	377.378
latitude		Range	32.540	41.950	35.630	2.137
longitude		Range	-124.350	-114.310	-119.567	2.003

Figure 4.1   A quick look at the houses data set.

Relating this data set to our earlier notation, we have $X_1 = $ *median income*, $X_2 = $ *housing median age*, $\ldots$, $X_8 = $ *longitude*, so that $m = 8$, and $n = 18{,}540$. A glimpse of the first 20 records in the training data set looks like Figure 4.2. So, for example, for the first block group, the *median house value* is \$425,600, the *median income* is 8.3252 (on the census scale), the *housing median age* is 41, the *total rooms* is 880, the *total bedrooms* is 129, the *population* is 322, the *number of households*

	median_house_value	median_income	housing_median_age	total_rooms	total_bedrooms	population	households	latitude	longitude
1	452600	8.325	41	880	129	322	126	37.880	-122.230
2	358500	8.301	21	7099	1106	2401	1138	37.860	-122.220
3	352100	7.257	52	1467	190	496	177	37.850	-122.240
4	342200	3.846	52	1627	280	565	259	37.850	-122.250
5	299200	3.659	52	2535	489	1094	514	37.840	-122.250
6	241400	3.120	52	3104	687	1157	647	37.840	-122.250
7	226700	2.080	42	2555	665	1206	595	37.840	-122.250
8	261100	3.691	52	3549	707	1551	714	37.840	-122.250
9	241800	3.270	52	3503	752	1504	734	37.850	-122.260
10	191300	2.674	52	696	191	345	174	37.840	-122.260
11	159200	1.917	52	2643	626	1212	620	37.850	-122.260
12	140000	2.125	50	1120	283	697	264	37.850	-122.260
13	152500	2.775	52	1966	347	793	331	37.850	-122.270
14	155500	2.120	52	1228	293	648	303	37.850	-122.270
15	158700	1.991	50	2239	455	990	419	37.840	-122.260
16	147500	1.358	40	751	184	409	166	37.850	-122.270
17	159800	1.714	42	1639	367	929	366	37.850	-122.270
18	99700	2.181	52	1688	337	853	325	37.840	-122.270
19	132600	2.600	52	2224	437	1006	422	37.840	-122.270
20	107500	2.404	41	535	123	317	119	37.850	-122.280

Figure 4.2   A glimpse of the first twenty records in the houses data set.

is 126, the *latitude* is 37.88 north, and the *longitude* is 122.23 west. Clearly, this is a smallish block group with high median house value. A map search reveals that this block group is centered between the University of California at Berkeley and Tilden Regional Park.

Note from Figure 4.1 the great disparity in variability among the predictors. The *median income* has a standard deviation less than 2, while the *total rooms* has a standard deviation over 2100. If we proceeded to apply PCA without first standardizing the variables, *total rooms* would dominate *median income*'s influence, and similarly across the spectrum of variabilities. Therefore, standardization is called for. The variables were standardized, and the Z-vectors found, $Z_i = \frac{(X_i - \mu_i)}{\sigma_{ii}}$, using the means and standard deviations from Figure 4.1.

Note that normality of the data is not strictly required to perform non-inferential PCA (Johnson and Wichern, 2006),[5] but that strong departures from normality may diminish the observed correlations (Hair *et al.*, 2006).[6] As data mining applications usually do not involve inference, we will not worry about normality.

Next, we examine the matrix plot of the predictors in Figure 4.3 to explore whether correlations exist. Diagonally from left to right, we have the standardized variables *minc_z* (median income), *hage_z* (housing median age), *rooms_z* (total rooms), *bedrms_z* (total bedrooms), *popn_z* (population), *hhlds_z* (number of households), *lat_z* (latitude), and *long_z* (longitude). What does the matrix plot tell us about the correlation among the variables? Rooms, bedrooms, population, and households all appear to be positively correlated. Latitude and longitude appear to be negatively correlated. (What does the plot of latitude vs longitude look like? Did you say the State of California?) Which variable appears to be correlated the least with the other predictors? Probably *housing median age*. Table 4.1 shows the correlation matrix æ for the predictors. Note that the matrix is symmetrical, and that the diagonal elements all equal one. A matrix plot and the correlation matrix are two ways of looking at the same thing: the correlation structure among the predictor variables. Note that the cells for the correlation matrix ρ line up one-to-one with the graphs in the matrix plot.

What would happen if we performed, say, a multiple regression analysis of *median housing value* on the predictors, despite the strong evidence for multicollinearity in the data set? The regression results would become quite unstable, with (among other things) tiny shifts in the predictors leading to large changes in the regression coefficients. In short, we could not use the regression results for profiling.

This is where PCA comes in. PCA can sift through the correlation structure, and identify the components underlying the correlated variables. Then, the principal components can be used for further analysis downstream, such as in regression analysis, classification, and so on.

PCA was carried out on the eight predictors in the *house* data set. The *component matrix* is shown in Table 4.2. Each of the columns in Table 4.2 represents one of

---

[5] Johnson and Wichern, *Applied Multivariate Statistical Analysis*, 6th edition. Prentice Hall, Upper Saddle River, New Jersey, 2007.

[6] Hair, Black, Babin, Anderson, and Tatham, *Multivariate Data Analysis*, 6th edition, Prentice Hall, Upper Saddle River, New Jersey, 2006.

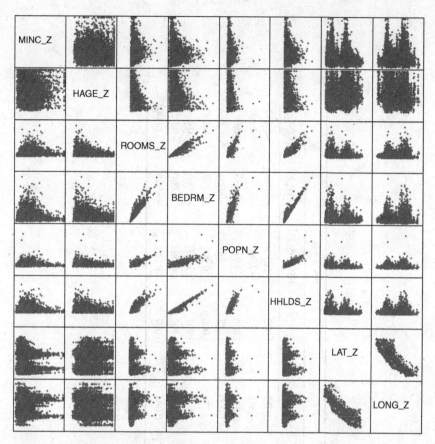

Figure 4.3   Matrix plot of the predictor variables.

the components $Y_i = \mathbf{e}_i'\mathbf{Z}$. The cell entries are called the *component weights*, and represent the partial correlation between the variable and the component. *Result 2* tells us that these component weights therefore equal $\mathrm{Corr}(Y_i, Z_j) = e_{ij}\sqrt{\lambda_i}$, a product involving the ith eigenvector and eigenvalue. As the component weights are correlations, they range between one and negative one.

In general, the first principal component may be viewed as the single best summary of the correlations among the predictors. Specifically, this particular linear combination of the variables accounts for more variability than any other linear combination. It has maximized the variance $\mathrm{Var}(Y_1) = \mathbf{e}_1'\rho\mathbf{e}_1$. As we suspected from the matrix plot and the correlation matrix, there is evidence that *total rooms*, *total bedrooms*, *population*, and *households* vary together. Here, they all have very high (and very similar) component weights, indicating that all four variables are highly correlated with the first principal component.

Let us examine Table 4.3, which shows the eigenvalues for each component, along with the percentage of the total variance explained by that component. Recall that *Result 3* showed us that the proportion of the total variability in $\mathbf{Z}$ that is explained

TABLE 4.1 The correlation matrix ρ

					Correlations			
	MINC_Z	HAGE_Z	ROOMS_Z	BEDRMS_Z	POPN_Z	HHLDS_Z	LAT_Z	LONG_Z
MINC_Z	1.000	-0.117	0.199	-0.012	0.002	0.010	-0.083	-0.012
HAGE_Z	-0.117	1.000	-0.360	-0.318	-0.292	-0.300	0.011	-0.107
ROOMS_Z	0.199	-0.360	1.000	0.928	0.856	0.919	-0.035	0.041
BEDRMS_Z	-0.012	-0.318	0.928	1.000	0.878	0.981	-0.064	0.064
POPN_Z	0.002	-0.292	0.856	0.878	1.000	0.907	-0.107	0.097
HHLDS_Z	0.010	-0.300	0.919	0.981	0.907	1.000	-0.069	0.051
LAT_Z	-0.083	0.011	-0.035	-0.064	-0.107	-0.069	1.000	-0.925
LONG_Z	-0.012	-0.107	0.041	0.064	0.097	0.051	-0.925	1.000

TABLE 4.2   The component matrix

Component Matrix[a]

	Component							
	1	2	3	4	5	6	7	8
MINC_Z	0.086	−0.058	0.922	0.370	−0.02	−0.018	0.037	−0.004
HAGE_Z	−0.429	0.025	−0.407	0.806	0.014	0.026	0.009	−0.001
ROOMS_Z	0.956	0.100	0.102	0.104	0.120	0.162	−0.119	0.015
BEDRMS_Z	0.970	0.083	−0.121	0.056	0.144	−0.068	0.051	−0.083
POPN_Z	0.933	0.034	−0.121	0.076	−0.327	0.034	0.006	−0.015
HHLDS_Z	0.972	0.086	−0.113	0.087	0.058	−0.112	0.061	0.083
LAT_Z	−0.140	0.970	0.017	−0.088	0.017	0.132	0.113	0.005
LONG_Z	0.144	−0.969	−0.062	−0.063	0.037	0.136	0.109	0.007

Extraction method: Principal component analysis.

[a]Eight components extracted.

TABLE 4.3   Eigenvalues and proportion of variance explained by each component

	Initial Eigenvalues		
Component	Total	% of Variance	Cumulative%
1	3.901	48.767	48.767
2	1.910	23.881	72.648
3	1.073	13.409	86.057
4	0.825	10.311	96.368
5	0.148	1.847	98.215
6	0.082	1.020	99.235
7	0.047	0.586	99.821
8	0.014	0.179	100.000

by the ith principal component is $\frac{\lambda_i}{m}$, the ratio of the ith eigenvalue to the number of variables. Here, we see that the first eigenvalue is 3.901, and as there are eight predictor variables, this first component explains $3.901/8 = 48.767\%$ of the variance, as shown in Table 4.3 (allowing for rounding). So, a single component accounts for nearly half of the variability in the set of eight predictor variables, meaning that *this single component by itself carries about half of the information in all eight predictors.* Notice also that the eigenvalues decrease in magnitude, $\lambda_1 \geq \lambda_2 \geq \ldots \geq \lambda_m$, $\lambda_1 \geq \lambda_2 \geq \ldots \geq \lambda_8$, as we noted in *Result 2*.

The second principal component Y_2 is the second-best linear combination of the variables, on the condition that it is *orthogonal* to the first principal component. Two vectors are *orthogonal* if they are mathematically independent, have no correlation, and are at right angles to each other. The second component is derived from the variability that is left over, once the first component has been accounted for. The third component is the third-best linear combination of the variables, on the condition that it is orthogonal to the first two components. The third component is derived from the variance remaining after the first two components have been extracted. The remaining components are defined similarly.

4.4 HOW MANY COMPONENTS SHOULD WE EXTRACT?

Next, recall that one of the motivations for PCA was to reduce the number of distinct explanatory elements. The question arises, "How do we determine how many components to extract?" For example, should we retain only the first principal component, as it explains nearly half the variability? Or, should we retain all eight components, as they explain 100% of the variability? Well, clearly, retaining all eight components does not help us to reduce the number of distinct explanatory elements. As usual, the answer lies somewhere between these two extremes. Note from Table 4.3 that the eigenvalues for several of the components are rather low, explaining less than 2% of the variability in the Z-variables. Perhaps these would be the components we should consider not retaining in our analysis?

The criteria used for deciding how many components to extract are the following:

- The Eigenvalue Criterion
- The Proportion of Variance Explained Criterion
- The Minimum Communality Criterion
- The Scree Plot Criterion.

4.4.1 The Eigenvalue Criterion

Recall from *Result 1* that the sum of the eigenvalues represents the number of variables entered into the PCA. An eigenvalue of *1* would then mean that the component would explain about "one variable's worth" of the variability. The rationale for using the eigenvalue criterion is that each component should explain at least one variable's worth of the variability, and therefore, the eigenvalue criterion states that only components with eigenvalues greater than 1 should be retained. Note that, if there are fewer than 20 variables, the eigenvalue criterion tends to recommend extracting too few components, while, if there are more than 50 variables, this criterion may recommend extracting too many. From Table 4.3, we see that three components have eigenvalues greater than 1, and are therefore retained. Component 4 has an eigenvalue of 0.825, which is not too far from one, so that we may decide to consider retaining this component as well, if other criteria support such a decision, especially in view of the tendency of this criterion to recommend extracting too few components.

4.4.2 The Proportion of Variance Explained Criterion

First, the analyst specifies how much of the total variability that he or she would like the principal components to account for. Then, the analyst simply selects the components one by one until the desired proportion of variability explained is attained. For example, suppose we would like our components to explain 85% of the variability in the variables. Then, from Table 4.3, we would choose components 1–3, which together explain 86.057% of the variability. However, if we wanted our components to explain 90% or 95% of the variability, then we would need to include component 4 along with components 1–3, which together would explain 96.368% of the variability. Again, as with the eigenvalue criterion, how large a proportion is enough?

This question is akin to asking how large a value of r^2 (coefficient of determination) is enough in the realm of linear regression. The answer depends in part on the field of study. Social scientists may be content for their components to explain only 60% or so of the variability, as human response factors are so unpredictable, while natural scientists might expect their components to explain 90–95% of the variability, as their measurements are often less variable. Other factors also affect how large a proportion is needed. For example, if the principal components are being used for descriptive purposes only, such as customer profiling, then the proportion of variability explained may be a shade lower than otherwise. However, if the principal components are to be used as replacements for the original (standardized) data set, and used for further inference in models downstream, then the proportion of variability explained should be as much as can conveniently be achieved, given the constraints of the other criteria.

4.4.3 The Minimum Communality Criterion

For now, we postpone discussion of this criterion until we introduce the concept of *communality* below.

4.4.4 The Scree Plot Criterion

A scree plot is a graphical plot of the eigenvalues against the component number. Scree plots are useful for finding an upper bound (maximum) for the number of components that should be retained. See Figure 4.4 for the scree plot for this example. Most scree plots look broadly similar in shape, starting high on the left, falling rather quickly, and then flattening out at some point. This is because the first component usually explains much of the variability, the next few components explain a moderate amount, and the latter components only explain a small amount of the variability. The scree plot criterion is this: The maximum number of components that should be extracted is *just before* where the plot first begins to straighten out into a horizontal line. (Sometimes, the curve in a scree plot is so gradual that no such elbow point is evident; in that case, turn to the other criteria.) For example, in Figure 4.4, the plot straightens out horizontally starting at component 5. The line is nearly horizontal because the components all explain approximately the same amount of variance,

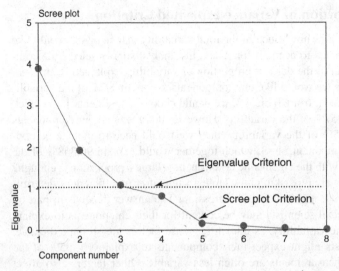

Figure 4.4   Scree plot. Stop extracting components before the line flattens out.

which is not much. Therefore, the scree plot criterion would indicate that the maximum number of components we should extract is four, as the fourth component occurs just before where the line first begins to straighten out.

To summarize, the recommendations of our criteria are as follows:

- The Eigenvalue Criterion:
  - Retain components 1–3, but do not throw away component 4 yet.
- The Proportion of Variance Explained Criterion
  - Components 1–3 account for a solid 86% of the variability, and tacking on component 4 gives us a superb 96% of the variability.
- The Scree Plot Criterion
  - Do not extract more than four components.

So, we will extract at least three but no more than four components. Which is it to be, three or four? As in much of data analysis, there is no absolute answer in this case to the question of how many components to extract. This is what makes data mining an art as well as a science, and this is another reason why data mining requires human direction. The data miner or data analyst must weigh all the factors involved in a decision, and apply his or her judgment, tempered by experience.

In a case like this, where there is no clear-cut best solution, why not try it both ways and see what happens? Consider Tables 4.4a and 4.4b, which compares the component matrices when three and four components are extracted, respectively. The component weights smaller than 0.15 are suppressed to ease the component interpretation. Note that the first three components are each exactly the same in both cases, and each is the same as when we extracted all eight components, as shown in Table 4.2 above (after suppressing the small weights). This is because each component extracts its portion of the variability sequentially, so that later component extractions do not affect the earlier ones.

TABLE 4.4a   Component matrix for extracting three components

	Component Matrix[a]		
	Component		
	1	2	3
MINC_Z			0.922
HAGE_Z	−0.429		−0.407
ROOMS_Z	0.956		
BEDRMS_Z	0.970		
POPN_Z	0.933		
HHLDS_Z	0.972		
LAT_Z		0.970	
LONG_Z		−0.969	

Extraction method: PCA.
[a]Three components extracted.

TABLE 4.4b   Component matrix for extracting four components

	Component Matrix[a]			
	Component			
	1	2	3	4
MINC_Z			0.922	0.370
HAGE_Z	−0.429		−0.407	0.806
ROOMS_Z	0.956			
BEDRMS_Z	0.970			
POPN_Z	0.933			
HHLDS_Z	0.972			
LAT_Z		0.970		
LONG_Z		−0.969		

Extraction method: PCA.
[a]Four components extracted.

4.5   PROFILING THE PRINCIPAL COMPONENTS

The client may be interested in detailed profiles of the principal components the analyst has uncovered. Let us now examine the salient characteristics of each principal component, giving each component a title for ease of interpretation.

- *The Size Component.* Principal component 1, as we saw earlier, is largely composed of the "block-group-size"-type variables, *total rooms*, *total bedrooms*, *population*, and *households*, which are all either large or small together. That is, large block groups have a strong tendency to have large values for all four variables, while small block groups tend to have small values for all four variables. *Median housing age* is a smaller, lonely counterweight to these four variables, tending to be low (recently built housing) for large block groups, and high (older, established housing) for smaller block groups.

- *The Geographical Component.* Principal component 2 is a "geographical" component, composed solely of the *latitude* and *longitude* variables, which are strongly negatively correlated, as we can tell by the opposite signs of their component weights. This supports our earlier exploratory data analysis (EDA) regarding these two variables in Figure 4.3 and Table 4.1. The negative correlation is because of the way latitude and longitude are signed by definition, and because California is broadly situated from northwest to southeast. If California was situated from northeast to southwest, then latitude and longitude would be positively correlated.

- *Income and Age 1.* Principal component 3 refers chiefly to the *median income* of the block group, with a smaller effect due to the *housing median age* of the block group. That is, in the data set, high median income is associated with more recently built housing, while lower median income is associated with older housing.

- *Income and Age 2.* Principal component 4 is of interest, because it is the one that we have not decided whether or not to retain. Again, it focuses on the combination of *housing median age* and *median income*. Here, we see that, *once the negative correlation between these two variables has been accounted for*, there is left over a positive relationship between these variables. That is, once the association between, for example, high incomes and recent housing has been extracted, there is left over some further association between higher incomes and older housing.

To further investigate the relationship between *principal components 3* and *4*, and their constituent variables, we next consider factor scores. *Factor scores* are estimated values of the factors for each observation, and are based on *factor analysis*, discussed in the next section. For the derivation of factor scores, see Johnson and Wichern.[7]

Consider Figure 4.5, which provides two matrix plots. The matrix plot on the left displays the relationships among *median income*, *housing median age*, and the factor scores for *component 3*, while the matrix plot on the right displays the relationships among *median income*, *housing median age*, and the factor scores for *component 4*. Tables 4.4a and 4.4b showed that *components 3* and *4* both included each of these variables as constituents. However, there seemed to be a large difference in

---

[7]Johnson and Wichern, *Applied Multivariate Statistical Analysis*, 6th edition, Prentice Hall, Upper Saddle River, New Jersey, 2007.

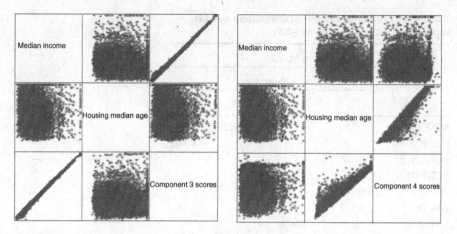

Figure 4.5   Correlations between *components 3* and *4*, and their variables.

the absolute component weights, as for example, 0.922 having a greater amplitude than −0.407 for the *component 3* component weights. Is this difference in magnitude reflected in the matrix plots?

Consider the left side of Figure 4.5. The strong positive correlation between *component 3* and *median income* is strikingly evident, reflecting the 0.922 positive correlation. But the relationship between *component 3* and *housing median age* is rather amorphous. It would be difficult to estimate the correlation between *component 3* and *housing median age* as being −0.407, with only the scatter plot to guide us. Similarly for the right side of Figure 4.5, the relationship between *component 4* and *housing median age* is crystal clear, reflecting the 0.806 positive correlation, while the relationship between *component 3* and *median income* is not entirely clear, reflecting its lower positive correlation of 0.370. We conclude, therefore, that the component weight of −0.407 for *housing median age* in *component 3* is not of practical significance, and similarly for the component weight for *median income* in *component 4*.

This discussion leads us to the following criterion for assessing the component weights. For a component weight to be considered of practical significance, it should exceed ±0.50 in magnitude. Note that the component weight represents the correlation between the component and the variable; thus, the squared component weight represents the amount of the variable's total variability that is explained by the component. Thus, this threshold value of ±0.50 requires that at least 25% of the variable's variance be explained by a particular component.

Table 4.5 therefore presents the component matrix from Tables 4.4a and 4.4b, this time suppressing the component weights below ±0.50 in magnitude. The component profiles should now be clear, and uncluttered:

- *The Size Component*. Principal component 1 represents the "block group size" component, consisting of four variables: *total rooms*, *total bedrooms*, *population*, and *households*.
- *The Geographical Component*. Principal component 2 represents the "geographical" component, consisting of two variables: *latitude* and *longitude*.

TABLE 4.5   Component matrix of component weights, suppressing magnitudes below ±0.50

	Component Matrix[a]			
	Component			
	1	2	3	4
MINC_Z			0.922	
HAGE_Z				0.806
ROOMS_Z	0.956			
BEDRMS_Z	0.970			
POPN_Z	0.933			
HHLDS_Z	0.972			
LAT_Z		0.970		
LONG_Z		−0.969		

Extraction method: Principal component analysis.

[a]Four components extracted.

- *Median Income.* Principal component 3 represents the "income" component, and consists of only one variable: *median income.*
- *Housing Median Age.* Principal component 4 represents the "housing age" component, and consists of only one variable: *housing median age.*

Note that the partition of the variables among the four components is *mutually exclusive,* meaning that no variable is shared (after suppression) by any two components, and *exhaustive,* meaning that all eight variables are contained in the four components. Further, support for this $4 - 2 - 1 - 1$ partition of the variables among the first four components is found in the similar relationship identified among the first four eigenvalues: $3.901 - 1.910 - 1.073 - 0.825$ (see Table 4.3).

4.6   COMMUNALITIES

We are moving toward a decision regarding how many components to retain. One more piece of the puzzle needs to be set in place: *Communality.* Now, PCA does not extract all the variance from the variables, but only that proportion of the variance that is shared by several variables. *Communality* represents the proportion of variance of a particular variable that is shared with other variables.

The communalities represent the overall importance of each of the variables in the PCA as a whole. For example, a variable with a communality much smaller than the other variables indicates that this variable shares much less of the common variability among the variables, and contributes less to the PCA solution. Communalities that are very low for a particular variable should be an indication to the analyst that the particular variable might not participate in the PCA solution (i.e., might not be a member of any of the principal components). Overall, large communality values indicate that the principal components have successfully extracted a large proportion of the variability in the original variables, while small communality values show that there is still much variation in the data set that has not been accounted for by the principal components.

Communality values are calculated as the sum of squared component weights, for a given variable. We are trying to determine whether to retain *component 4*, the "housing age" component. Thus, we calculate the commonality value for the variable *housing median age*, using the component weights for this variable ($hage\_z$) from Table 4.2. Two communality values for *housing median age* are calculated, one for retaining three components, and the other for retaining four components.

- Communality (*housing median age*, three components) $= (-0.429)^2 + (0.025)^2 + (-0.407)^2 = 0.350315$.
- Communality (*housing median age*, four components) $= (-0.429)^2 + (0.025)^2 + (-0.407)^2 + (0.806)^2 = 0.999951$.

Communalities less than 0.5 can be considered to be too low, as this would mean that the variable shares less than half of its variability in common with the other variables. Now, suppose that for some reason we wanted or needed to keep the variable *housing median age* as an active part of the analysis. Then, extracting only three components would not be adequate, as *housing median age* shares only 35% of its variance with the other variables. If we wanted to keep this variable in the analysis, we would need to extract the fourth component, which lifts the communality for *housing median age* over the 50% threshold. This leads us to the statement of the *minimum communality criterion* for component selection, which we alluded to earlier.

4.6.1 Minimum Communality Criterion

Suppose that it is required to keep a certain set of variables in the analysis. Then, enough components should be extracted so that the communalities for each of these variables exceed a certain threshold (e.g., 50%).

Hence, we are finally ready to decide how many components to retain. We have decided to retain four components, for the following reasons:

- The Eigenvalue Criterion recommended three components, but did not absolutely reject the fourth component. Also, for small numbers of variables, this criterion can underestimate the best number of components to extract.
- The Proportion of Variance Explained Criterion stated that we needed to use four components if we wanted to account for that superb 96% of the variability. *As our ultimate goal is to substitute these components for the original data and use them in further modeling downstream*, being able to explain so much of the variability in the original data is very attractive.
- The Scree Plot Criterion said not to exceed four components. We have not.
- The Minimum Communality Criterion stated that, if we wanted to keep *housing median age* in the analysis, we had to extract the fourth component. As we intend to substitute the components for the original data, then we need to keep this variable, and therefore we need to extract the fourth component.

4.7 VALIDATION OF THE PRINCIPAL COMPONENTS

Recall that the original data set was divided into a training data set and a test data set. All of the above analysis has been carried out on the training data set. In order to validate the principal components uncovered here, we now perform PCA on the standardized variables for the test data set. The resulting component matrix is shown in Table 4.6, with component weights smaller than ± 0.50 suppressed.

TABLE 4.6 Validating the PCA: component matrix of component weights for test set

	Component Matrix[a]			
	Component			
	1	2	3	4
MINC_Z			0.920	
HAGE_Z				0.785
ROOMS_Z	0.957			
BEDRMS_Z	0.967			
POPN_Z	0.935			
HHLDS_Z	0.968			
LAT_Z		0.962		
LONG_Z		−0.961		

Extraction method: PCA.
[a]Four components extracted.

Although the component weights do not exactly equal those of the training set, nevertheless the same four components were extracted, with a one-to-one correspondence in terms of which variables are associated with which component. This may be considered validation of the PCA performed. Therefore, we shall substitute these principal components for the standardized variables in the further analysis we undertake on this data set later on. Specifically, we shall investigate whether the components are useful for estimating *median house value*.

If the split sample method described here does not successfully provide validation, then the analyst should take this as an indication that the results (for the data set as a whole) are not generalizable, and the results should not be reported as valid. If the lack of validation stems from a subset of the variables, then the analyst may consider omitting these variables, and performing the PCA again.

An example of the use of PCA in multiple regression is provided in Chapter 9.

4.8 FACTOR ANALYSIS

Factor analysis is related to principal components, but the two methods have different goals. Principal components seek to identify orthogonal linear combinations of the variables, to be used either for descriptive purposes or to substitute a smaller number of uncorrelated components for the original variables. In contrast, factor analysis represents a *model* for the data, and as such is more elaborate. Keep in mind that the primary reason we as data miners are learning about factor analysis is so that we may apply *factor rotation* (see below).

The *factor analysis model* hypothesizes that the response vector $X_1, X_2, \ldots, X_m$ can be modeled as linear combinations of a smaller set of k unobserved, "latent" random variables $F_1, F_2, \ldots, F_k$, called *common factors*, along with an error term $\varepsilon = \varepsilon_1, \varepsilon_2, \ldots, \varepsilon_m$. Specifically, the factor analysis model is

$$\underset{m \times 1}{X} - \mu = \underset{m \times k}{L} \underset{k \times 1}{F} + \underset{m \times 1}{\varepsilon}$$

where $\underset{m \times 1}{X} - \mu$ is the response vector, centered by the mean vector, $\underset{m \times k}{L}$ is the matrix of *factor loadings*, with l_{ij} representing the factor loading of the ith variable on the jth factor, $\underset{k \times 1}{F}$ represents the vector of unobservable common factors, and $\underset{m \times 1}{\varepsilon}$ represents the error vector. The factor analysis model differs from other models, such as the linear regression model, in that the *predictor variables $F_1, F_2, \ldots, F_k$ are unobservable*.

Because so many terms are unobserved, further assumptions must be made before we may uncover the factors from the observed responses alone. These assumptions are that $E(F) = 0$, $Cov(F) = I$, $E(\varepsilon) = 0$, and $Cov(\varepsilon)$ is a diagonal matrix. See Johnson and Wichern[2] for further elucidation of the factor analysis model.

Unfortunately, the factor solutions provided by factor analysis are invariant to transformations. Two models, $X - \mu = LF + \varepsilon$ and $X - \mu = (LT)(TF) + \varepsilon$, where T represents an orthogonal transformations matrix, both will provide the same results. Hence, the factors uncovered by the model are in essence nonunique, without further constraints. This indistinctness provides the motivation for factor rotation, which we will examine shortly.

4.9 APPLYING FACTOR ANALYSIS TO THE *ADULT* DATA SET

The *Adult* data set[8] was extracted from data provided by the U.S. Census Bureau. The intended task is to find the set of demographic characteristics that can best predict whether or not the individual has an income of over \$50,000 per year. For this example, we shall use only the following variables for the purpose of our factor analysis: *age*, *demogweight* (a measure of the socioeconomic status of the individual's district), *education_num*, *hours-per-week*, and *capnet* ($=$ *capital gain* $-$ *capital loss*). The training data set contains 25,000 records, and the test data set contains 7561 records.

The variables were standardized, and the Z-vectors found, $Z_i = \frac{(X_i - \mu_i)}{\sigma_{ii}}$. The correlation matrix is shown in Table 4.7.

[8]Blake and Merz, 1998. UCI Repository of machine learning databases [http://www.ics.uci.edu/'mlearn/MLRepository.html]. Irvine, CA: University of California, Department of Information and Computer Science. *Adult* data set donated by Ron Kohavi. Also available at textbook website: www.DataMiningConsultant.com.

TABLE 4.7   Correlation matrix for factor analysis example

		Correlations			
	AGE_Z	DEM_Z	EDUC_Z	CAPNET_Z	HOURS_Z
AGE_Z	1.000	-0.076^b	0.033^b	0.070^b	0.069^b
DEM_Z	-0.076^b	1.000	-0.044^b	0.005	-0.015^a
EDUC_Z	0.033^b	-0.044^b	1.000	0.116^b	0.146^b
CAPNET_Z	0.070^b	0.005	0.116^b	1.000	0.077^b
HOURS_Z	0.069^b	-0.015^a	0.146^b	0.077^b	1.000

[a]Correlation is significant at the 0.05 level (2-tailed).
[b]Correlation is significant at the 0.01 level (2-tailed).

Note that the correlations, although statistically significant in several cases, are overall much weaker than the correlations from the *houses* data set. A weaker correlation structure should pose more of a challenge for the dimension-reduction method.

Factor analysis requires a certain level of correlation in order to function appropriately. The following tests have been developed to ascertain whether there exists sufficiently high correlation to perform factor analysis.[9]

- The proportion of variability within the standardized predictor variables which is shared in common, and therefore might be caused by underlying factors, is measured by the Kaiser–Meyer–Olkin (KMO) Measure of Sampling Adequacy. Values of the *KMO* statistic less than 0.50 indicate that factor analysis may not be appropriate.

- Bartlett's Test of Sphericity tests the null hypothesis that the correlation matrix is an identity matrix, that is, that the variables are really uncorrelated. The statistic reported is the *p*-value, so that very small values would indicate evidence against the null hypothesis, that is, the variables really are correlated. For *p*-values much larger than 0.10, there is insufficient evidence that the variables are correlated, and so factor analysis may not be suitable.

Table 4.8 provides the results of these statistical tests. The *KMO* statistic has a value of 0.549, which is not less than 0.5, meaning that this test does not find the level of correlation to be too low for factor analysis. The *p*-value for Bartlett's Test of Sphericity rounds to zero, so that the null hypothesis that no correlation exists among the variables is rejected. We therefore proceed with the factor analysis.

To allow us to view the results using a scatter plot, we decide a priori to extract only two factors. The following factor analysis is performed using the *principal axis factoring* option. In principal axis factoring, an iterative procedure is used to estimate the communalities and the factor solution. This particular analysis required 152 such iterations before reaching convergence. The eigenvalues and the proportions of the variance explained by each factor are shown in Table 4.9.

---

[9]Note, however, that statistical tests in the context of huge data sets can be misleading. With huge sample sizes, even the smallest effect sizes become statistically significant. This is why data mining methods rely on cross-validation methodologies, not statistical inference.

TABLE 4.8   Is there sufficiently high correlation to run factor analysis?

KMO and Bartlett's Test

Kaiser–Meyer–Olkin measure of sampling adequacy		0.549
Bartlett's test of sphericity	Approx. Chi-square	1397.824
	df	10
	p-Value	0.000

TABLE 4.9   Eigenvalues and proportions of variance explained, factor analysis

	Total Variance Explained		
	Initial Eigenvalues		
Factor	Total	% of Variance	Cumulative%
1	1.277	25.533	25.533
2	1.036	20.715	46.248
3	0.951	19.028	65.276
4	0.912	18.241	83.517
5	0.824	16.483	100.000

Extraction method: Principal axis factoring.

Note that the first two factors extract less than half of the total variability in the variables, as contrasted with the *houses* data set, where the first two components extracted over 72% of the variability. This is due to the weaker correlation structure inherent in the original data.

The *factor loadings* $\mathbf{L}_{m \times k}$ are shown in Table 4.10. Factor loadings are analogous to the component weights in PCA, and represent the correlation between the *i*th

TABLE 4.10   Factor loadings are much weaker than previous example

	Factor Matrix[a]	
	Factor	
	1	2
AGE_Z	0.590	−0.329
EDUC_Z	0.295	0.424
CAPNET_Z	0.193	0.142
HOURS_Z	0.224	0.193
DEM_Z	−0.115	0.013

Extraction method: Principal axis factoring.

[a]Two factors extracted. 152 iterations required.

variable and the jth factor. Notice that the factor loadings are much weaker than the previous *houses* example, again due to the weaker correlations among the standardized variables.

The communalities are also much weaker than the *houses* example, as shown in Table 4.11. The low communality values reflect the fact that there is not much shared correlation among the variables. Note that the factor extraction increases the shared correlation.

TABLE 4.11 Communalities are low, reflecting not much shared correlation

	Communalities	
	Initial	Extraction
AGE_Z	0.015	0.457
EDUC_Z	0.034	0.267
CAPNET_Z	0.021	0.058
HOURS_Z	0.029	0.087
DEM_Z	0.008	0.013

Extraction method: Principal axis factoring.

4.10 FACTOR ROTATION

To assist in the interpretation of the factors, *factor rotation* may be performed. Factor rotation corresponds to a transformation (usually orthogonal) of the coordinate axes, leading to a different set of factor loadings. We may look upon factor rotation as analogous to a scientist attempting to elicit greater contrast and detail by adjusting the focus of the microscope.

The sharpest focus occurs when each variable has high factor loadings on a single factor, with low-to-moderate loadings on the other factors. For the *houses* example, this sharp focus occurred already on the unrotated factor loadings (e.g., Table 4.5), so rotation was not necessary. However, Table 4.10 shows that we should perhaps try factor rotation for the *adult* data set, in order to help improve our interpretation of the two factors.

Figure 4.6 shows the graphical view of the vectors of factors of loadings for each variable from Table 4.10. Note that most vectors do not closely follow the coordinate axes, which means that there is poor "contrast" among the variables for each factor, thereby reducing interpretability.

Next, a *varimax* rotation (discussed shortly) was applied to the matrix of factor loadings, resulting in the new set of factor loadings found in Table 4.12. Note that the contrast has been increased for most variables, which is perhaps made clearer by Figure 4.7, the graphical view of the rotated vectors of factor loadings.

Figure 4.7 shows that the factor loadings have been rotated along the axes of maximum variability, represented by *Factor 1* and *Factor 2*. Often, the first factor extracted represents a "general factor," and accounts for much of the total variability.

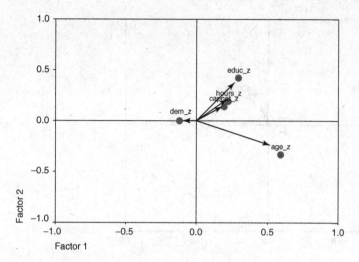

Figure 4.6   Unrotated vectors of factor loadings do not follow coordinate axes.

TABLE 4.12   The factor loadings after varimax rotation

	Rotated Factor Matrix[a]	
	Factor	
	1	2
AGE_Z	0.675	0.041
EDUC_Z	0.020	0.516
CAPNET_Z	0.086	0.224
HOURS_Z	0.084	0.283
DEM_Z	−0.104	−0.051

Extraction method: Principal axis factoring.

Rotation method: Varimax with Kaiser normalization.

[a]Rotation converged in three iterations.

The effect of factor rotation is to redistribute this first factor's variability explained among the second, third, and subsequent factors. For example, consider Table 4.13, which shows the percent of variance explained by *Factors 1* and *2*, for the initial unrotated extraction (left side) and the rotated version (right side).

The sums of squared loadings for *Factor 1* for the unrotated case is (using Table 4.10 and allowing for rounding, as always) $0.590^2 + 0.295^2 + 0.193^2 + 0.224^2 + -0.115^2 = 0.536$.

This represents 10.7% of the total variability, and about 61% of the variance explained by the first two factors. For the rotated case, *Factor 1*'s influence has been partially redistributed to *Factor 2* in this simplified example, now accounting for

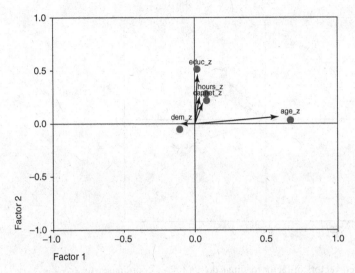

Figure 4.7 Rotated vectors of factor loadings more closely follow coordinate axes.

TABLE 4.13 **Factor rotation redistributes the percentage of variance explained**

			Total Variance Explained			
	Extraction Sums of Squared Loadings			Rotation Sums of Squared Loadings		
Factor	Total	% of Variance	Cumulative%	Total	% of Variance	Cumulative%
1	0.536	10.722	10.722	0.481	9.616	9.616
2	0.346	6.912	17.635	0.401	8.019	17.635

Extraction method: Principal axis factoring.

9.6% of the total variability and about 55% of the variance explained by the first two factors.

We now describe three methods for *orthogonal rotation*, in which the axes are rigidly maintained at 90°. The goal when rotating the matrix of factor loadings is to ease interpretability by simplifying the rows and columns of the column matrix. In the following discussion, we assume that the columns in a matrix of factor loadings represent the factors, and that the rows represent the variables, just as in Table 4.10, for example. Simplifying the rows of this matrix would entail maximizing the loading of a particular variable on one particular factor, and keeping the loadings for this variable on the other factors as low as possible (ideal: row of zeroes and ones). Similarly, simplifying the columns of this matrix would entail maximizing the loading of a particular factor on one particular variable, and keeping the loadings for this factor on the other variables as low as possible (ideal: column of zeroes and ones).

- *Quartimax Rotation* seeks to simplify the rows of a matrix of factor loadings. Quartimax rotation tends to rotate the axes so that the variables have high loadings for the first factor, and low loadings thereafter. The difficulty is that it can generate a strong "general" first factor, in which many variables have high loadings.

- *Varimax Rotation* prefers to simplify the column of the factor loading matrix. Varimax rotation maximizes the variability in the loadings for the factors, with a goal of working toward the ideal column of zeroes and ones for each variable. The rationale for varimax rotation is that we can best interpret the factors when they are strongly associated with some variable and strongly not associated with other variables. Kaiser[10] showed that the varimax rotation is more invariant than the quartimax rotation.

- *Equimax Rotation* seeks to compromise between simplifying the columns and the rows.

The researcher may prefer to avoid the requirement that the rotated factors remain orthogonal (independent). In this case, *oblique rotation* methods are available, in which the factors may be correlated with each other. This rotation method is called oblique because the axes are no longer required to be at 90°, but may form an oblique angle. For more on oblique rotation methods, see Harmon.[11]

4.11 USER-DEFINED COMPOSITES

Factor analysis continues to be controversial, in part due to the lack of invariance under transformation, and the consequent nonuniqueness of the factor solutions. Analysts may prefer a much more straightforward alternative: *User-Defined Composites*. A user-defined composite is simply a linear combination of the variables, which combines several variables together into a single composite measure. In the behavior science literature, user-defined composites are known as *summated scales* (e.g., Robinson *et al.*, 1991).[12]

User-defined composites take the form $W = \mathbf{a}'Z = a_1Z_1 + a_2Z_2 + \cdots + a_kZ_k$, where $\sum_{i=1}^{k} a_i = 1, k \leq m$, and the Z_i are the standardized variables. Whichever form the linear combination takes, however, the variables should be standardized first, so that one variable with high dispersion does not overwhelm the others.

The simplest user-defined composite is simply the mean of the variables. In this case, $a_i = 1/k, \quad i = 1, 2, \ldots, k$. However, if the analyst has prior information or expert knowledge available to indicate that the variables should not be all equally weighted, then each coefficient a_i can be chosen to reflect the relative weight of that variable, with more important variables receiving higher weights.

---

[10]Kaiser, H.F., A Second-Generation Little Jiffy, in *Psychometrika*, 35, 401–415, 1970. Also Kaiser, H.F., Little Jiffy, Mark IV, in *Educational and Psychology Measurement*, 34, 111–117.

[11]Harman, H.H., *Modern Factor Analysis*, 3rd edition, University of Chicago Press, Chicago, 1976.

[12]Robinson, Shaver, and Wrigtsman, Criteria for Scale Selection and Evaluation, in *Measures of Personality and Social Psychological Attitudes*, Academy Press, San Diego, 1991.

What are the benefits of utilizing user-defined composites? When compared to the use of individual variables, user-defined composites provide a way to diminish the effect of measurement error. *Measurement error* refers to the disparity between the observed variable values, and the "true" variable value. Such disparity can be due to a variety of reasons, including mistranscription and instrument failure. Measurement error contributes to the background error noise, interfering with the ability of models to accurately process the signal provided by the data, with the result that truly significant relationships may be missed. User-defined composites reduce measurement error by combining multiple variables into a single measure.

Appropriately constructed user-defined composites allow the analyst to represent the manifold aspects of a particular concept using a single measure. Thus, user-defined composites enable the analyst to embrace the range of model characteristics, while retaining the benefits of a parsimonious model.

Analysts should ensure that the conceptual definition for their user-defined composites lies grounded in prior research or established practice. The conceptual definition of a composite refers to the theoretical foundations for the composite. For example, have other researchers used the same composite, or does this composite follow from best practices in one's field of business? If the analyst is aware of no such precedent for his or her user-defined composite, then a solid rationale should be provided to support the conceptual definition of the composite.

The variables comprising the user-defined composite should be highly correlated with each other and uncorrelated with other variables used in the analysis. This unidimensionality should be confirmed empirically, perhaps through the use of PCA, with the variables having high loadings on a single component and low-to-moderate loadings on the other components.

4.12 AN EXAMPLE OF A USER-DEFINED COMPOSITE

Consider again the *houses* data set. Suppose that the analyst had reason to believe that the four variables, *total rooms*, *total bedrooms*, *population*, and *households*, were highly correlated with each other and not with other variables. The analyst could then construct the following user-defined composite:

$$W = \mathbf{a'}Z = a_1(totalrooms) + a_2(totalbedrooms) + a_3(population) + a_2(households)$$

with $a_i = 1/4$, $i = 1, \ldots, 4$, so that *Composite W* represented the mean of the four (standardized) variables.

The conceptual definition of *Composite W* is "block group size," a natural and straightforward concept. It is unlikely that all block groups have exactly the same size, and that therefore, differences in block group size may account for part of the variability in the other variables. We might expect large block groups tending to have large values for all four variables, and small block groups tending to have small values for all four variables.

The analyst should seek out support in the research or business literature for the conceptual definition of the composite. The evidence for the existence and relevance of the user-defined composite should be clear and convincing. For example, for *Composite W*, the analyst may cite the study from the *National Academy of Sciences* by Hope *et al.* (2003),[13] which states that block groups in urban areas average 5.3 km^2 in size while block groups outside urban areas averaged 168 km^2 in size. As we may not presume that block groups inside and outside urban areas have exactly similar characteristics, this may mean that block group size could conceivably be associated with differences in block group characteristics, including *median housing value*, the response variable. Further, the analyst could cite the *U.S. Census Bureau*'s notice in the *Federal Register* (2002)[14] that population density was much lower for block groups whose size was greater than 2 square miles. Hence, block group size may be considered a "real" and relevant concept to be used in further analysis downstream.

THE R ZONE

Read in the Houses dataset and prepare the data

```
houses <- read.csv(file="C:/ … /houses.csv",
   stringsAsFactors = FALSE, header = FALSE)
names(houses) <- c("MVAL", "MINC", "HAGE", "ROOMS", "BEDRMS", "POPN" ,
   "HHLDS", "LAT", "LONG")
# Standardize the variables
houses$MINC_Z <- (houses$MINC - mean(houses$MINC))/(sd(houses$MINC))
houses$HAGE_Z <- (houses$HAGE - mean(houses$HAGE))/(sd(houses$HAGE))
# Do the same for the remaining variables
# Randomly select 90% for the Training dataset
choose <- runif(dim(houses)[1],0, 1)
test.house <- houses[which(choose < .1),]
train.house <- houses[which(choose <= .1),]
```

Principal Component Analysis

```
# Requires library "psych"
library(psych)
pca1 <- principal(train.house[,c(10:17)],
   nfactors=8,
   rotate="none",
   scores=TRUE)
```

---

[13] Hope, Gries, Zhu, Fagan, Redman, Grimm, Nelson, Martin, and Kinzig, Socioeconomics Drive Urban Plant Diversity, in *Proceedings of the National Academy of Sciences*, Volume **100**, Number 15, pages 8788–8792, July 22, 2003.

[14] Bureau of the Census, Urban Area Criteria for Census 2000, *Federal Register*, Volume **67**, Number 51, March 15, 2002.

PCA results

```
# Eigenvalues:
pca1$values
# Loadings matrix,
# variance explained,
pca1$loadings
```

```
> pca1$values
[1] 3.91572423 1.90929235 1.07366473 0.81878484 0.13983203
[6] 0.08106670 0.04667528 0.01499984
> pca1$loadings

Loadings:
         PC1    PC2    PC3    PC4    PC5    PC6    PC7    PC8
MINC_Z                 0.922  0.370
HAGE_Z  -0.434        -0.410  0.801
ROOMS_Z  0.956  0.102         0.106  0.129  0.155 -0.119
BEDRMS_Z 0.970        -0.122         0.139
POPN_Z   0.937        -0.118        -0.314
HHLDS_Z  0.972        -0.113               -0.116
LAT_Z   -0.140  0.970                       0.131  0.113
LONG_Z   0.147 -0.969                       0.135  0.109

                PC1    PC2    PC3    PC4    PC5    PC6    PC7    PC8
SS loadings    3.916  1.909  1.074  0.819  0.140  0.081  0.047  0.015
Proportion Var 0.489  0.239  0.134  0.102  0.017  0.010  0.006  0.002
Cumulative Var 0.489  0.728  0.862  0.965  0.982  0.992  0.998  1.000
```

Scree plot

```
plot(pca1$values,
    type = "b",
    main = "Scree Plot for Houses
        Data")
```

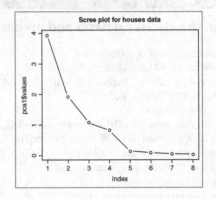

Plot factor scores

```
pairs(~train.house$MINC+
train.house$HAGE+pca1$scores[,3],
    labels = c("Median Income",
        "Housing Median Age",
        "Component 3 Scores"))
```

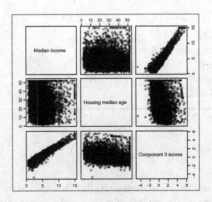

```
pairs(~train.house$MINC+
    train.house$HAGE+pca1$scores[,4],
    labels = c("Median Income",
     "Housing Median Age",
     "Component 4 Scores"))
```

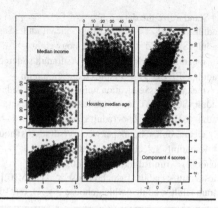

Calculate communalities

```
comm3 <- loadings(pca1)[2,1]^2+
    loadings(pca1)[2,2]^2 + loadings(pca1)[2,3]^2
comm4 <- loadings(pca1)[2,1]^2+
    loadings(pca1)[2,2]^2+ loadings(pca1)[2,3]^2+
    loadings(pca1)[2,4]^2
comm3; comm4
```

```
> comm3; comm4
[1] 0.3571416
[1] 0.9990797
```

Validation of the Principal Components

```
pca2 <-
    principal(test.house[,c(10:17)],
    nfactors=4,
    rotate="none",
    scores=TRUE)
pca2$loadings
```

```
> pca2$loadings
Loadings:
         PC1    PC2    PC3    PC4
MINC_Z   0.117         0.923  0.361
HAGE_Z  -0.412        -0.387  0.824
ROOMS_Z  0.958  0.110
BEDRMS_Z 0.967               -0.111
POPN_Z   0.906               -0.140
HHLDS_Z  0.968         0.104 -0.112
LAT_Z   -0.177  0.964
LONG_Z   0.167 -0.965

               PC1   PC2   PC3   PC4
SS loadings    3.853 1.897 1.058 0.847
Proportion Var 0.482 0.237 0.132 0.106
Cumulative Var 0.482 0.719 0.851 0.957
```

Read in and prepare data for factor analysis

```
adult <- read.csv(file="C:/ ... /adult.txt",
    stringsAsFactors = FALSE)
adult$"capnet"<- adult$capital.gain-adult$capital.loss
adult.s <- adult[,c(1,3,5,13,16)]
```

```
# Standardize the data:
adult.s$AGE_Z <- (adult.s$age - mean(adult.s$age))/(sd(adult.s$age))
adult.s$DEM_Z <- (adult.s$demogweight –
   mean(adult.s$demogweight))/(sd(adult.s$demogweight))
adult.s$EDUC_Z <- (adult.s$education.num –
   mean(adult.s$education.num))/(sd(adult.s$education.num))
adult.s$CAPNET_Z <- (adult.s$capnet - mean(adult.s$capnet))/(sd(adult.s$capnet))
adult.s$HOURS_Z <- (adult.s$hours.per.week –
   mean(adult.s$hours.per.week))/(sd(adult.s$hours.per.week))
# Randomly select a Training dataset
choose <- runif(dim(adult.s)[1],0, 1)
test.adult <- adult.s[which(choose < .1), c(6:10)]
train.adult < adult.s[which(choose >= .1), c(6:10)]
```

Bartlett's test for Sphericity

```
# Requires package psych
library(psych)
corrmat1 <- cor(train.adult,
   method = "pearson")
cortest.bartlett(corrmat1,
   n = dim(train.adult)[1])
```

```
> cortest.bartlett(corrmat1,
+            n = dim(train.adult)[1])
$chisq
[1] 1227.187

$p.value
[1] 1.967231e-257

$df
[1] 10
```

Factor analysis with five components

```
# Requires psych, GPArotation
library(GPArotation)
fa1 <- fa(train.adult, nfactors=5,
   fm = "pa", rotate="none")
fa1$values # Eigenvalues
fa1$loadings # Loadings,
# proportion of variance,
# and cumulative variance
```

```
> fa1$values
[1] 1.2714050 1.0330490 0.9575673 0.9156883
[5] 0.8222904
> fa1$loadings

Loadings:
           PA1     PA2     PA3     PA4     PA5
AGE_Z     0.426  -0.530   0.547   0.370   0.319
DEM_Z    -0.256   0.760   0.423   0.333   0.258
EDUC_Z    0.626   0.257  -0.385  -0.214   0.589
CAPNET_Z  0.531   0.244   0.512  -0.532  -0.337
HOURS_Z   0.591   0.220  -0.263   0.582  -0.440

                 PA1    PA2    PA3    PA4
SS loadings     1.271  1.033  0.958  0.916
Proportion Var  0.254  0.207  0.192  0.183
Cumulative Var  0.254  0.461  0.652  0.836
                 PA5
SS loadings     0.822
Proportion Var  0.164
Cumulative Var  1.000
```

Factor analysis with two components

```
fa2 <- fa(train.adult, nfactors=2,
    fm = "pa", max.iter = 200,
    rotate="none")
fa2$values # Eigenvalues
fa2$loadings # Loadings
fa2$communality # Communality
```

```
> fa2$values
[1]  0.525535230  0.355071207  0.032759632
[4] -0.005213205 -0.028543798
> fa2$loadings

Loadings:
        PA1    PA2
AGE_Z    0.554 -0.364
DEM_Z   -0.119
EDUC_Z   0.336  0.428
CAPNET_Z 0.200  0.112
HOURS_Z  0.227  0.162

                 PA1   PA2
SS loadings     0.526 0.355
Proportion Var  0.105 0.071
Cumulative Var  0.105 0.176
> fa2$communality
      AGE_Z      DEM_Z      EDUC_Z     CAPNET_Z
 0.43915473 0.01429767 0.29655977  0.05273470
     HOURS_Z
  0.07785957
```

Varimax rotation

```
fa2v <- fa(train.adult,
    nfactors = 2,
    fm = "pa", max.iter = 200,
    rotate="varimax")
fa2v$loadings
fa2v$communality
```

```
> fa2v$loadings

Loadings:
        PA1    PA2
AGE_Z    0.662
DEM_Z   -0.104
EDUC_Z          0.544
CAPNET_Z        0.210
HOURS_Z         0.266

                 PA1   PA2
SS loadings     0.465 0.416
Proportion Var  0.093 0.083
Cumulative Var  0.093 0.176
```

User-defined composites

```
small.houses <- houses[,c(4:7)]
a <- c(1/4, 1/4, 1/4, 1/4)
W <- t(a)*small.houses
```

R REFERENCES

Bernaards CA, Jennrich RI. 2005. Gradient projection algorithms and software for arbitrary rotation criteria in factor analysis, *Educational and Psychological Measurement*: 65, 676-696. http://www.stat.ucla.edu/research/gpa.

R Core Team. *R: A Language and Environment for Statistical Computing*. Vienna, Austria: R Foundation for Statistical Computing; 2012. ISBN: 3-900051-07-0http://www.R-project .org/.

Revelle W. 2013. *psych: Procedures for Personality and Psychological Research*, Northwestern University, Evanston, Illinois, USA, http://CRAN.R-project.org/package=psychVersion =1.4.2.

EXERCISES

CLARIFYING THE CONCEPTS

1. Determine whether the following statements are true or false. If false, explain why the statement is false, and how one could alter the statement to make it true.

   a. Positive correlation indicates that, as one variable increases, the other variable increases as well.

   b. Changing the scale of measurement for the covariance matrix, for example, from meters to kilometers, will change the value of the covariance.

   c. The total variability in the data set equals the number of records.

   d. The value of the ith principal component equals the ith eigenvalue divided by the number of variables.

   e. The second principal component represents any linear combination of the variables that accounts for the most variability in the data, once the first principal component has been extracted.

   f. For a component weight to be considered of practical significance, it should exceed ± 0.50 in magnitude.

   g. The principal components are always mutually exclusive and exhaustive of the variables.

   h. When validating the principal components, we would expect the component weights from the training and test data sets to have the same signs.

   i. For factor analysis to function properly, the predictor variables should not be highly correlated.

2. For what type of data are the covariance and correlation matrices identical? In this case, what is Σ?

3. What is special about the first principal component, in terms of variability?

4. Describe the four criteria for choosing how many components to extract. Explain the rationale for each.

5. Explain the concept of communality, so that someone new to the field could understand it.

6. Explain the difference between PCA and factor analysis. What is a drawback of factor analysis?

7. Describe two tests for determining whether there exists sufficient correlation within a data set for factor analysis to proceed. Which results from these tests would allow us to proceed?

8. Explain why we perform factor rotation. Describe three different methods for factor rotation.

9. What is a user-define composite, and what is the benefit of using it in place of individual variables?

WORKING WITH THE DATA

The following computer output explores the application of PCA to the Churn data set.[15]

10. Based on the following information, does there exists an adequate amount of correlation among the predictors to pursue PCA? Explain how you know this, and how we may be getting mixed signals.

KMO and Bartlett's Test

Kaiser–Meyer–Olkin measure of sampling adequacy		0.512
Bartlett's test of sphericity	Approx. Chi–square	34.908
	df	55
	Sig.	0.984

11. Suppose that we go ahead and perform the PCA, in this case using seven components. Considering the following information, which variable or variables might we be well advised to omit from the PCA, and why? If we really need all these variables in the analysis, then what should we do?

Communalities

	Initial	Extraction
ZACCTLEN	1.000	0.606
ZVMAILME	1.000	0.836
ZDAYCALL	1.000	0.528
ZDAYCHAR	1.000	0.954
ZEVECALL	1.000	0.704
ZEVECHAR	1.000	0.621
ZNITECAL	1.000	0.543
ZNITECHA	1.000	0.637
ZINTCALL	1.000	0.439
ZINTCHAR	1.000	0.588
ZCSC	1.000	0.710

Extraction method: Principal component analysis.

[15]Blake and Merz, 1998. UCI Repository of machine learning databases [http://www.ics.uci.edu/'mlearn/MLRepository.html]. Irvine, CA: University of California, Department of Information and Computer Science. Also available at textbook website: www.DataMiningConsultant.com.

12. Based on the following information, how many components should be extracted, using (a) the eigenvalue criterion and (b) the proportion of variance explained criterion?

	Initial Eigenvalues		
Component	Total	% of Variance	Cumulative %
1	1.088	9.890	9.890
2	1.056	9.596	19.486
3	1.040	9.454	28.939
4	1.023	9.296	38.236
5	1.000	9.094	47.329
6	0.989	8.987	56.317
7	0.972	8.834	65.151
8	0.969	8.811	73.961
9	0.963	8.754	82.715
10	0.962	8.747	91.462
11	0.939	8.538	100.000

13. Based on the following scree plot, how many components should be extracted using the scree plot criterion? Now, based on the three criteria, work toward a decision on the number of components to extract.

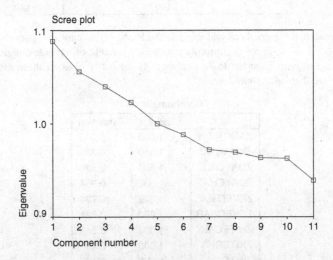

14. Based on the following rotated component matrix:

   a. Provide a quick profile of the first four components.

   b. If we extracted an eighth component, describe how the first component would change.

   c. What is your considered opinion on the usefulness of applying PCA on this data set?

HANDS-ON ANALYSIS

For Exercises 15–20, work with the *baseball* data set, available from the textbook web site, www.DataMiningConsultant.com.

15. First, filter out all batters with fewer than 100 at bats. Next, standardize all the numerical variables using z-scores.

16. Now, suppose we are interested in estimating the number of home runs, based on the other numerical variables in the data set. So all the other numeric variables will be our predictors. Investigate whether sufficient variability exists among the predictors to perform PCA.

17. How many components should be extracted according to
    a. The Eigenvalue Criterion?
    b. The Proportion of Variance Explained Criterion?
    c. The Scree Plot Criterion?
    d. The Communality Criterion?

18. Based on the information from the previous exercise, make a decision about how many components you shall extract.

19. Apply PCA using varimax rotation, with your chosen number of components. Write up a short profile of the first few components extracted.

20. Construct a useful user-defined composite using the predictors. Describe situations where the composite would be more appropriate or useful than the principal components, and vice versa.

Use the *wine_quality_training* data set, available at the textbook web site, for the remaining exercises. The data consist of chemical data about some wines from Portugal. The target variable is *quality*. Remember to omit the target variable from the dimension-reduction analysis. Unless otherwise indicated, use only the white wines for the analysis.

21. Standardize the predictors.

22. Construct a matrix plot of the predictors. Provide a table showing the correlation coefficients of each predictor with each other predictor. Color code your table so that the reader can easily see at a glance which are the strongest correlations. What you are doing here is doing EDA for the principal components later on. Using the matrix plot and the table of coefficients, discuss which sets of predictors seem to "vary together."

23. Suppose we eventually would like to perform linear regression analysis of *quality* versus these predictors. Clearly explain why we should beware of using a set of predictors that are highly correlated.

24. Run a multiple regression of the predictors on *quality*. Get the variance inflation factor (VIF) measures of the predictors. Explain what these mean in the context of this problem. Explain whether they support or undermine the need for PCA in this problem.

25. Clearly explain how PCA can solve the problem of collinear predictors.

26. Determine the optimal number of components to extract, using
    a. The Eigenvalue Criterion;
    b. The Proportion of Variance Explained Criterion;
    c. The Minimum Communality Criterion;

    d. The Scree Plot Criterion;

    e. Try to arrive at a consensus among the four criteria as to the optimal number of components to extract.

27. Proceed to apply PCA to the predictors, using varimax rotation. In the output, suppress factor loadings less than $|0.5|$.

    a. Provide both the unrotated and the rotated component matrices.

    b. Use the results in (a) to demonstrate how varimax rotation eases interpretability of the components.

    c. Report detailed profiles of the components, including a descriptive title. It is important that you be able to explain to your client with crystal clarity what your results mean. It may be worth your while to do some research on wine.

28. Compare your principal components in one-to-one manner with your EDA earlier. Discuss.

29. Run a multiple regression of the principal components predictors on *quality*.

    a. Get the VIF measures of the components. Comment.

    b. Compare the regression standard error for the two regression models. Comment.

    c. Compare the R^2 for the two regression models. Comment.

30. Provide a table showing the correlation coefficients of each principal component with each other principal component. Comment.

31. Discuss the question of whether we should add principal components to increase the predictive power of the regression model and/or reduce the standard error. Arm yourself for this discussion by incrementing your optimal number of components by 1, running the PCA, performing the regression with the additional component, and then comparing your standard error and R^2 to the earlier model.

32. Repeat Exercises 21–31 using the red wines only. Compare your principal component profiles and the performance of your regression models.

PART II

STATISTICAL ANALYSIS

## CHAPTER 5

UNIVARIATE STATISTICAL ANALYSIS

5.1 DATA MINING TASKS IN DISCOVERING KNOWLEDGE IN DATA

In Chapter 1, we were introduced to the six data mining tasks, which are as follows:

- Description
- Estimation
- Prediction
- Classification
- Clustering
- Association.

In the description task, analysts try to find ways to describe patterns and trends lying within the data. Descriptions of patterns and trends often suggest possible explanations for such patterns and trends, as well as possible recommendations for policy changes. This description task can be accomplished capably with exploratory data analysis (EDA), as we saw in Chapter 3. The description task may also be performed using descriptive statistics, such as the sample proportion or the regression equation, which we learn about in Chapter 8. Of course, the data mining methods are not restricted to one task only, which results in a fair amount of overlap among data mining methods and tasks. For example, decision trees may be used for classification, estimation, or prediction.

5.2 STATISTICAL APPROACHES TO ESTIMATION AND PREDICTION

If estimation and prediction are considered to be data mining tasks, statistical analysts have been performing data mining for over a century. In this chapter and Chapter 6,

---

we examine some of the more widespread and traditional methods of estimation and prediction, drawn from the world of statistical analysis. Here, in this chapter, we examine univariate methods, statistical estimation, and prediction methods that analyze one variable at a time. These methods include point estimation and confidence interval estimation for population means and proportions. We discuss ways of reducing the margin of error of a confidence interval estimate. Then we turn to hypothesis testing, examining hypothesis tests for population means and proportions. Then, in Chapter 6, we consider multivariate methods for statistical estimation and prediction.

5.3 STATISTICAL INFERENCE

Consider our roles as data miners. We have been presented with a data set with which we are presumably unfamiliar. We have completed the data understanding and data preparation phases and have gathered some descriptive information using EDA. Next, we would like to perform univariate estimation and prediction. A widespread tool for performing estimation and prediction is *statistical inference*.

Statistical inference consists of methods for estimating and testing hypotheses about population characteristics based on the information contained in the sample. A *population* is the collection of *all* elements (persons, items, or data) of interest in a particular study.

For example, presumably, the cell phone company does not want to restrict its actionable results to the sample of 3333 customers from which it gathered the data. Rather, it would prefer to deploy its churn model to *all* of its present and future cell phone customers, which would therefore represent the population. A *parameter* is a characteristic of a population, such as the mean number of customer service calls of all cell phone customers.

A *sample* is simply a subset of the population, preferably a representative subset. If the sample is not representative of the population, that is, if the sample characteristics deviate systematically from the population characteristics, *statistical inference should not be applied*. A *statistic* is a characteristic of a sample, such as the mean number of customer service calls of the 3333 customers in the sample (1.563).

Note that the values of population parameters are *unknown* for most interesting problems. Specifically, the value of the population mean is usually unknown. For example, we do not know the true mean number of customer service calls to be made by all of the company's cell phone customers. To represent their unknown nature, population parameters are often denoted with Greek letters. For example, the population mean is symbolized using the Greek lowercase letter μ (pronounced "mew"), which is the Greek letter for "m" ("mean").

The value of the population mean number of customer service calls μ is unknown for a variety of reasons, including the fact that the data may not yet have been collected or warehoused. Instead, data analysts would use *estimation*. For example, they would estimate the unknown value of the population mean μ by obtaining a sample and computing the sample mean $\bar{x}$, which would be used to estimate μ. Thus, we would estimate the mean number of customer service calls for all customers to be 1.563, because this is the value of our observed sample mean.

An important *caveat* is that estimation is valid only as long as the sample is truly representative of the population. For example, suppose for a moment that the *churn* data set represents a sample of 3333 disgruntled customers. Then this sample would not be representative (one hopes!) of the population of all the company's customers, and none of the EDA that we performed in Chapter 3 would be actionable with respect to the population of all customers.

Analysts may also be interested in proportions, such as the proportion of customers who churn. The sample proportion p is the statistic used to measure the unknown value of the population proportion π. For example, in Chapter 3, we found that the proportion of churners in the data set was $p = 0.145$, which could be used to estimate the true proportion of churners for the population of all customers, keeping in mind the caveats above.

Point estimation refers to the use of a single known value of a statistic to estimate the associated population parameter. The observed value of the statistic is called the *point estimate*. We may summarize estimation of the population mean, standard deviation, and proportion using Table 5.1.

TABLE 5.1   Use observed sample statistics to estimate unknown population parameters

	Sample Statistic	... Estimates	Population Parameter
Mean	$\bar{x}$	$\rightarrow$	μ
Standard deviation	s	$\rightarrow$	σ
Proportion	p	$\rightarrow$	π

Estimation need not be restricted to the parameters in Table 5.1. Any statistic observed from sample data may be used to estimate the analogous parameter in the population. For example, we may use the sample maximum to estimate the population maximum, or we could use the sample 27th percentile to estimate the population 27th percentile. *Any* sample characteristic is a statistic, which, under the appropriate circumstances, can be used to estimate its respective parameter.

More specifically, for example, we could use the sample churn proportion of customers who did select the VoiceMail Plan, but did not select the International Plan, and who made three customer service calls to estimate the population churn proportion of all such customers. Or, we could use the sample 99th percentile of day minutes used for customers without the VoiceMail Plan to estimate the population 99th percentile of day minutes used for all customers without the VoiceMail Plan.

5.4   HOW CONFIDENT ARE WE IN OUR ESTIMATES?

Let us face it: Anyone can make estimates. Crystal ball gazers will be happy (for a price) to provide you with an estimate of the parameter in which you are interested. The question is: *How confident can we be in the accuracy of the estimate?*

Do you think that the population mean number of customer service calls made by all of the company's customers is exactly the same as the sample mean $\bar{x} = 1.563$? Probably not. In general, because the sample is a subset of the population, inevitably the population contains more information than the sample about any given characteristic. Hence, unfortunately, our point estimates will nearly always "miss" the target parameter by a certain amount, and thus be in error by this amount, which is probably, although not necessarily, small.

This distance between the observed value of the point estimate and the unknown value of its target parameter is called *sampling error*, defined as |statistic − parameter|. For example, the sampling error for the mean is $|\bar{x} - \mu|$, the distance (always positive) between the observed sample mean and the unknown population mean. As the true values of the parameter are usually unknown, the value of the sampling error is usually unknown in real-world problems. In fact, for continuous variables, the probability that the observed value of a point estimate exactly equals its target parameter is precisely zero. This is because probability represents area above an interval for continuous variables, and there is no area above a point.

Point estimates have no measure of confidence in their accuracy; there is no probability statement associated with the estimate. All we know is that the estimate is probably close to the value of the target parameter (small sampling error) but that possibly may be far away (large sampling error). In fact, point estimation has been likened to a dart thrower, throwing darts with infinitesimally small tips (the point estimates) toward a vanishingly small bull's-eye (the target parameter). Worse, the bull's-eye is hidden, and the thrower will never know for sure how close the darts are coming to the target.

The dart thrower could perhaps be forgiven for tossing a beer mug in frustration rather than a dart. But wait! As the beer mug has width, there does indeed exist a positive probability that some portion of the mug has hit the hidden bull's-eye. We still do not know for sure, but we can have a certain degree of confidence that the target has been hit. Very roughly, the beer mug represents our next estimation method, *confidence intervals*.

5.5 CONFIDENCE INTERVAL ESTIMATION OF THE MEAN

A *confidence interval estimate* of a population parameter consists of an interval of numbers produced by a point estimate, together with an associated *confidence level* specifying the probability that the interval contains the parameter. Most confidence intervals take the general form

$$\text{point estimate} \pm \text{margin of error}$$

where the margin of error is a measure of the precision of the interval estimate. Smaller margins of error indicate greater precision. For example, the *t-interval* for the population mean is given by

$$\bar{x} \pm t_{\alpha/2}\left(\frac{s}{\sqrt{n}}\right)$$

where the sample mean $\bar{x}$ is the point estimate and the quantity $t_{\alpha/2}(s/\sqrt{n})$ represents the margin of error. The t-interval for the mean may be used when either the population is normal or the sample size is large.

Under what conditions will this confidence interval provide precise estimation? That is, when will the margin of error $t_{\alpha/2}(s/\sqrt{n})$ be small? The quantity $s/\sqrt{n}$ represents the standard error of the sample mean (the standard deviation of the sampling distribution of $\bar{x}$) and is small whenever the sample size is large or the sample variability is small. The multiplier $t_{\alpha/2}$ is associated with the sample size and the confidence level (usually 90–99%) specified by the analyst, and is smaller for lower confidence levels. As we cannot influence the sample variability directly, and we hesitate to lower our confidence level, we must turn to increasing the sample size should we seek to provide more precise confidence interval estimation.

Usually, finding a large sample size is not a problem for many data mining scenarios. For example, using the statistics in Figure 5.1, we can find the 95% t-interval for the mean number of customer service calls for all customers as follows:

$$\bar{x} \pm t_{\alpha/2}(s/\sqrt{n})$$

$$1.563 \pm 1.96(1.315/\sqrt{3333})$$

$$1.563 \pm 0.045$$

$$(1.518, 1.608)$$

We are 95% confident that the population mean number of customer service calls for all customers falls between 1.518 and 1.608 calls. Here, the margin of error is 0.045 customer service calls.

However, data miners are often called on to perform *subgroup analyses* (see also Chapter 24, *Segmentation Models*.); that is, to estimate the behavior of specific subsets of customers instead of the entire customer base, as in the example above. For example, suppose that we are interested in estimating the mean number of customer service calls for customers who have both the International Plan and the VoiceMail Plan and who have more than 220 day minutes. This reduces the sample size to 28 (Figure 5.2), which, however, is still large enough to construct the confidence interval.

There are only 28 customers in the sample who have both plans and who logged more than 220 minutes of day use. The point estimate for the population mean number of customer service calls for all such customers is the sample mean 1.607. We may

⊟ Customer Service Calls
   ⊟ Statistics

Count	3333
Mean	1.563
Sum	5209.000
Median	1
Mode	1

Figure 5.1   Summary statistics of customer service calls.

⊟ Customer Service Calls
  ⊟ Statistics

Count	28
Mean	1.607
Standard Deviation	1.892

Figure 5.2   Summary statistics of customer service calls for those with both the International Plan and VoiceMail Plan and with more than 200 day minutes.

find the 95% t-confidence interval estimate as follows:

$$\bar{x} \pm t_{\alpha/2}(s/\sqrt{n})$$

$$1.607 \pm 2.052(1.892/\sqrt{28})$$

$$1.607 \pm 0.734$$

$$(0.873, 2.341)$$

We are 95% confident that the population mean number of customer service calls for all customers who have both plans and who have more than 220 minutes of day use falls between 0.873 and 2.341 calls. Here, 0.873 is called the *lower bound* and 2.341 is called the *upper bound* of the confidence interval. The margin of error for this specific subset of customers is 0.734, which indicates that our estimate of the mean number of customer service calls for this subset of customers is much less precise than for the customer base as a whole.

Confidence interval estimation can be applied to any desired target parameter. The most widespread interval estimates are for the population mean and the population proportion.

5.6   HOW TO REDUCE THE MARGIN OF ERROR

The margin of error E for a 95% confidence interval for the population mean μ is $E = t_{\alpha/2}(s/\sqrt{n})$ and may be interpreted as follows:
We can estimate μ to within E units with 95% confidence.

For example, the margin of error above the number of customer service calls for all customers equals 0.045 service calls, which may be interpreted as, "We can estimate the mean number of customer service calls for all customers to within 0.045 calls with 95% confidence."

Now, the smaller the margin of error, the more precise our estimation is. So the question arises, *how can we reduce our margin of error*? Now the margin of error E contains three quantities, which are as follows:

- $t_{\alpha/2}$, which depends on the confidence level and the sample size.
- the sample standard deviation s, which is a characteristic of the data, and may not be changed.

- n, the sample size.

Thus, we may decrease our margin of error in two ways, which are as follows:

- By decreasing the confidence level, which reduces the value of $t_{\alpha/2}$, and therefore reduces E. *Not recommended.*
- By increasing the sample size. *Recommended.* Increasing the sample size is the only way to decrease the margin of error while maintaining a constant level of confidence.

For example, had we procured a new sample of 5000 customers, with the same standard deviation $s = 1.315$, then the margin of error for a 95% confidence interval would be

$$E = t_{\alpha/2}(s/\sqrt{n}) = 1.96(1.315/\sqrt{5000}) = 0.036.$$

Owing to the $\sqrt{n}$ in the formula for E, an increase of a in the sample size leads to a reduction in margin of error of $\sqrt{a}$.

5.7   CONFIDENCE INTERVAL ESTIMATION OF THE PROPORTION

Figure 3.3 showed that 483 of 3333 customers had churned, so that an estimate of the *population proportion* π of all of the company's customers who churn is

$$p = \frac{\text{number who churn}}{\text{sample size}} = \frac{x}{n} = \frac{483}{3333} = 0.1449$$

Unfortunately, with respect to the population of our entire customer base, we have no measure of our confidence in the accuracy of this estimate. In fact, it is nearly impossible that this value exactly equals π. Thus, we would prefer a *confidence interval for the population proportion* π, given as follows:

$$p \pm Z_{\alpha/2}\sqrt{\frac{p \cdot (1-p)}{n}}$$

where the sample proportion p is the point estimate of π and the quantity $Z_{\alpha/2}\sqrt{\frac{p\cdot(1-p)}{n}}$ represents the margin of error. The quantity $Z_{\alpha/2}$ depends on the confidence level: for 90% confidence, $Z_{\alpha/2} = 1.645$; for 95% confidence, $Z_{\alpha/2} = 1.96$; and for 99% confidence, $Z_{\alpha/2} = 2.576$. This Z-interval for π may be used whenever both $np \geq 5$ and $n(1-p) \geq 5$.

For example, a 95% confidence interval for the proportion π of churners among the entire population of the company's customers is given by

$$p \pm Z_{\alpha/2}\sqrt{\frac{p \cdot (1-p)}{n}} = 0.1149 \pm 1.96\sqrt{\frac{(0.1449)(0.8551)}{3333}}$$

$$= 0.1149 \pm 0.012$$

$$= (0.1329,\ 0.1569)$$

We are 95% confident that this interval captures the population proportion π. Note that the confidence interval for π takes the form

$$p \pm E = 0.1149 \pm 0.012$$

where the margin of error E for a 95% confidence interval for the population mean π is $E = Z_{\alpha/2}\sqrt{\frac{p \cdot (1-p)}{n}}$. The margin of error may be interpreted as follows:

We can estimate π to within E with 95% confidence.

In this case, we can estimate the population proportion of churners to with 0.012 (or 1.2%) with 95% confidence. For a given confidence level, the margin of error can be reduced only by taking a larger sample size.

5.8 HYPOTHESIS TESTING FOR THE MEAN

Hypothesis testing is a procedure where claims about the value of a population parameter (such as μ or π) may be considered using the evidence from the sample. Two competing statements, or *hypotheses*, are crafted about the parameter value, which are as follows:

- The *null hypothesis* H_0 is the status quo hypothesis, representing what has been assumed about the value of the parameter.
- The *alternative hypothesis* or *research hypothesis* H_a represents an alternative claim about the value of the parameter.

The two possible conclusions are (i) reject H_0 and (b) do not reject H_0. A criminal trial is a form of a hypothesis test, with the following hypotheses:

$$H_0 : \text{Defendant is innocent} \quad H_a : \text{Defendant is guilty}$$

Table 5.2 illustrates the four possible outcomes of the criminal trial with respect to the jury's decision, and what is true in reality.

- *Type I error*: Reject H_0 when H_0 is true. The jury convicts an innocent person.
- *Type II error*: Do not reject H_0 when H_0 is false. The jury acquits a guilty person.

TABLE 5.2   Four possible outcomes of the criminal trial hypothesis test

		Reality	
		H_0 true: Defendant did not commit crime	H_0 false: Defendant did commit crime
Jury's Decision	Reject H_0: Find defendant guilty	Type I error	Correct decision
	Do not reject H_0: Find defendant not guilty	Correct decision	Type II error

- Correct decisions:
  - Reject H_0 when H_0 is false. The jury convicts a guilty person.
  - Do not reject H_0 when H_0 is true. The jury acquits an innocent person.

The probability of a Type I error is denoted α, while the probability of a Type II error is denoted β. For a constant sample size, a decrease in α is associated with an increase in β, and vice versa. In statistical analysis, α is usually fixed at some small value, such as 0.05, and called the *level of significance*.

A common treatment of hypothesis testing for the mean is to restrict the hypotheses to the following three forms.

- Left-tailed test. $H_0 : \mu \geq \mu_0$ versus $H_a : \mu < \mu_0$
- Right-tailed test. $H_0 : \mu \leq \mu_0$ versus $H_a : \mu > \mu_0$
- Two-tailed test. $H_0 : \mu = \mu_0$ versus $H_a : \mu \neq \mu_0$

where μ_0 represents a hypothesized value of μ.

When the sample size is large or the population is normally distributed, the test statistic

$$t_{\text{data}} = \frac{\bar{x} - \mu_0}{s/\sqrt{n}}$$

follows a t distribution, with $n - 1$ degrees of freedom. The value of t_{data} is interpreted as the number of standard errors above or below the hypothesized mean μ, that the sample mean $\bar{x}$ resides, where the standard error equals $s/\sqrt{n}$. (Roughly, the *standard error* represents a measure of spread of the distribution of a statistic.) When the value of t_{data} is extreme, this indicates a conflict between the null hypothesis (with the hypothesized value μ_0) and the observed data. As the data represent empirical evidence whereas the null hypothesis represents merely a claim, such conflicts are resolved in favor of the data, so that, when t_{data} is extreme, the null hypothesis H_0 is rejected. How extreme is extreme? This is measured using the *p-value*.

The *p-value* is the probability of observing a sample statistic (such as $\bar{x}$ or t_{data}) at least as extreme as the statistic actually observed, if we assume that the null hypothesis is true. As the p-value ("probability value") represents a probability, its value must always fall between 0 and 1. Table 5.3 indicates how to calculate the p-value for each form of the hypothesis test.

TABLE 5.3   How to calculate *p*-value

Form of Hypothesis Test	*p*-Value
Left-tailed test. $H_0 : \mu \geq \mu_0$ versus $H_a : \mu < \mu_0$	$P(t < t_{\text{data}})$
Right-tailed test. $H_0 : \mu \leq \mu_0$ versus $H_a : \mu > \mu_0$	$P(t > t_{\text{data}})$
Two-tailed test. $H_0 : \mu = \mu_0$ versus $H_a : \mu \neq \mu_0$	If $t_{\text{data}} < 0$, then *p*-value $= 2 \cdot P(t < t_{\text{data}})$. If $t_{\text{data}} > 0$, then *p*-value $= 2 \cdot P(t > t_{\text{data}})$.

The names of the forms of the hypothesis test indicate in which tail or tails of the t distribution the p-value will be found.

A small p-value will indicate conflict between the data and the null hypothesis. Thus, we will reject H_0 if the p-value is small. How small is small? As researchers set the level of significance α at some small value (such as 0.05), we consider the p-value to be small if it is less than α. This leads us to the rejection rule:

$$\text{Reject } H_0 \text{ if the } p\text{-value is} < \alpha.$$

For example, recall our subgroup of customers who have both the International Plan and the Voice Mail Plan and who have more than 220 day minutes. Suppose we would like to test whether the mean number of customer service calls of all such customers differs from 2.4, and we set the level of significance α to be 0.05. We would have a two-tailed hypothesis test:

$$H_0 : \mu = 2.4 \text{ versus } H_a : \mu \neq 2.4$$

The null hypothesis will be rejected if the p-value is less than 0.05. Here we have $\mu_0 = 2.4$, and earlier, we saw that $\bar{x} = 1.607$, $s = 1.892$, and $n = 28$. Thus,

$$t_{\text{data}} = \frac{\bar{x} - \mu_0}{s/\sqrt{n}} = \frac{1.607 - 2.4}{1.892/\sqrt{28}} = -2.2178$$

As $t_{\text{data}} < 0$, we have

$$p\text{-value} = 2 \cdot P(t < t_{\text{data}}) = 2 \cdot P(t < -2.2178) = 2 \cdot 0.01758 = 0.035$$

As the p-value of 0.035 is less than the level of significance $\alpha = 0.05$, we reject H_0. The interpretation of this conclusion is that there is evidence at level of significance $\alpha = 0.05$ that the population mean number of customer service calls of all such customers differs from 2.4. Had we not rejected H_0, we could simply insert the word "insufficient" before "evidence" in the previous sentence.

5.9 ASSESSING THE STRENGTH OF EVIDENCE AGAINST THE NULL HYPOTHESIS

However, there is nothing written in stone saying that the level of significance α must be 0.05. What if we had chosen $\alpha = 0.01$ in this example? Then the p-value 0.035 would not have been less than $\alpha = 0.01$, and we would not have rejected H_0. Note that *the hypotheses have not changed and the data have not changed, but the conclusion has been reversed simply by changing the value of* α.

Further, consider that hypothesis testing restricts us to a simple "yes-or-no" decision: to either reject H_0 or not reject H_0. But this dichotomous conclusion provides no indication of the strength of evidence against the null hypothesis residing in the data. For example, for level of significance $\alpha = 0.05$, one set of data may return a p-value of 0.06 while another set of data provides a p-value of 0.96. Both p-values lead to the same conclusion – do not reject H_0. However, the first data set came close to rejecting H_0, and shows a fair amount of evidence against the null hypothesis, while the second data set shows no evidence at all against the null hypothesis. A simple "yes-or-no" decision misses the distinction between these two scenarios. The p-value provides extra information that a dichotomous conclusion does not take advantage of.

Some data analysts do not think in terms of whether or not to reject the null hypothesis so much as to *assess the strength of evidence against the null hypothesis.* Table 5.4 provides a thumbnail interpretation of the strength of evidence against H_0 for various p-values. For certain data domains, such as physics and chemistry, the interpretations may differ.

Thus, for the hypothesis test $H_0 : \mu = 2.4$ versus $H_a : \mu \neq 2.4$, where the p-value equals 0.035, we would not provide a conclusion as to whether or not to reject H_0. Instead, we would simply state that there is *solid evidence against the null hypothesis.*

TABLE 5.4   Strength of evidence against H_0 for various p-values

p-Value	Strength of Evidence Against H_0
p-value ≤ 0.001	Extremely strong evidence
$0.001 < p$-value ≤ 0.01	Very strong evidence
$0.01 < p$-value ≤ 0.05	Solid evidence
$0.05 < p$-value ≤ 0.10	Mild evidence
$0.10 < p$-value ≤ 0.15	Slight evidence
$0.15 < p$-value	No evidence

5.10   USING CONFIDENCE INTERVALS TO PERFORM HYPOTHESIS TESTS

Did you know that one confidence interval is worth 1000 hypothesis tests? Because the t confidence interval and the t hypothesis test are both based on the same distribution with the same assumptions, we may state the following:

A $100(1 - \alpha)\%$ confidence interval for μ is equivalent to a two-tailed hypothesis test for μ, with level of significance α.

Table 5.5 shows the equivalent confidence levels and levels of significance.

TABLE 5.5   Confidence levels and levels of significance for equivalent confidence intervals and hypothesis tests

Confidence Level $100(1 - \alpha)\%$	Level of Significance α
90%	0.10
95%	0.05
99%	0.01

The equivalency is stated as follows (see Figure 5.3):

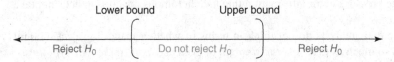

Figure 5.3 Reject values of μ_0 that would fall outside the equivalent confidence interval.

- If a certain hypothesized value for μ_0 falls *outside* the confidence interval with confidence level $100(1 - \alpha)\%$, then the two-tailed hypothesis test with level of significance α will reject H_0 for that value of μ_0.
- If the hypothesized value for μ_0 falls *inside* the confidence interval with confidence level $100(1 - \alpha)\%$, then the two-tailed hypothesis test with level of significance α will not reject H_0 for that value of μ_0.

For example, recall that our 95% confidence interval for the population mean number of customer service calls for all customers who have the International Plan and the Voice Mail plan and who have more than 220 minutes of day use is

$$(\text{lower bound, upper bound}) = (0.875, 2.339)$$

We may use this confidence interval to test any number of possible values of μ_0, as long as the test is two-tailed with level of significance $\alpha = 0.05$. For example, use level of significance $\alpha = 0.05$ to test whether the mean number of customer service calls for such customers differs from the following values:

a. 0.5

b. 1.0

c. 2.4

The solution is as follows. We have the following hypothesis tests:

a. $H_0: \mu = 0.5$ versus $H_a: \mu \neq 0.5$
b. $H_0: \mu = 1.0$ versus $H_a: \mu \neq 1.0$
c. $H_0: \mu = 2.4$ versus $H_a: \mu \neq 2.4$

We construct the 95% confidence interval, and place the hypothesized values of μ_0 on the number line, as shown in Figure 5.4.

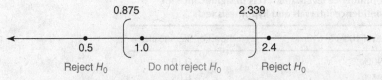

Figure 5.4 Placing the hypothesized values of μ_0 on the number line in relation to the confidence interval informs us immediately of the conclusion.

Their placement in relation to the confidence interval allows us to immediately state the conclusion of the two-tailed hypothesis test with level of significance $\alpha = 0.05$, as shown in Table 5.6.

TABLE 5.6 Conclusions for three hypothesis tests using the confidence interval

μ_0	Hypotheses with $\alpha = 0.05$	Position in Relation to 95% Confidence Interval	Conclusion
0.5	$H_0:\mu = 0.5$ vs $H_a:\mu \neq 0.5$	Outside	Reject H_0
1.0	$H_0:\mu = 1.0$ vs $H_a:\mu \neq 1.0$	Inside	Do not reject H_0
2.4	$H_0:\mu = 2.4$ vs $H_a:\mu \neq 2.4$	Outside	Reject H_0

5.11 HYPOTHESIS TESTING FOR THE PROPORTION

Hypothesis tests may also be performed about the population proportion π. The test statistic is

$$Z_{\text{data}} = \frac{p - \pi_0}{\sqrt{(\pi_0(1 - \pi_0)/n)}}$$

where π_0 is the hypothesized value of π, and p is the sample proportion

$$p = \frac{\text{number of successes}}{n}$$

The hypotheses and p-values are shown in Table 5.7.

For example, recall that 483 of 3333 customers in our sample had churned, so that an estimate of the population proportion π of all of the company's customers who churn is

$$p = \frac{\text{number who churn}}{\text{sample size}} = \frac{x}{n} = \frac{483}{3333} = 0.1449$$

Suppose we would like to test using level of significance $\alpha = 0.10$ whether π differs from 0.15. The hypotheses are

$$H_0:\pi = 0.15 \text{ versus } H_a:\pi \neq 0.15$$

TABLE 5.7 Hypotheses and p-values for hypothesis tests about π

Hypotheses with $\alpha = 0.05$	p-Value
Left-tailed test. $H_0:\pi \geq \pi_0$ versus $H_a:\pi < \pi_0$	$P(Z < Z_{\text{data}})$
Right-tailed test. $H_0:\pi \leq \pi_0$ versus $H_a:\pi > \pi_0$	$P(Z > Z_{\text{data}})$
Two-tailed test. $H_0:\pi = \pi_0$ versus $H_a:\pi \neq \pi_0$	If $Z_{\text{data}} < 0$, then p-value $= 2 \cdot P(Z < Z_{\text{data}})$. If $Z_{\text{data}} > 0$, then p-value $= 2 \cdot P(Z > Z_{\text{data}})$.

The test statistic is

$$Z_{\text{data}} = \frac{p - \pi_0}{\sqrt{(\pi_0(1 - \pi_0)/n)}} = \frac{0.1449 - 0.15}{\sqrt{(0.15(0.85)/3333)}} = -0.8246$$

As $Z_{\text{data}} < 0$ the p-value $= 2 \cdot P(Z < Z_{\text{data}}) = 2 \cdot P(Z < -0.8246) = 2 \cdot 0.2048 = 0.4096$.

As the p-value is not less than $\alpha = 0.10$, we would not reject H_0. There is insufficient evidence that the proportion of all our customers who churn differs from 15%. Further, assessing the strength of evidence against the null hypothesis using Table 5.5 would lead us to state that there is no evidence against H_0. Also, given a confidence interval, we may perform two-tailed hypothesis tests for π, just as we did for μ.

REFERENCE

Much more information regarding the topics covered in this chapter may be found in any introductory statistics textbook, such as *Discovering Statistics*, 2nd edition, by Daniel T. Larose, W. H. Freeman, New York, 2013.

THE R ZONE

Input the Churn dataset

```
churn <- read.csv(file = "C:/ ... /churn.txt",
    stringsAsFactors=TRUE)
```

Analyze a subgroup of data

```
subchurn <- subset(churn,
    churn$Int.l.Plan == "yes" &
    churn$VMail.Plan == "yes" &
    churn$Day.Mins>220)
summary(subchurn$CustServ.Calls)
length(subchurn$CustServ.Calls)
```

```
> summary(subchurn$CustServ.Calls)
   Min. 1st Qu.  Median    Mean 3rd Qu.    Max.
  0.000   0.750   1.000   1.607   2.000   9.000
> length(subchurn$CustServ.Calls)
[1] 28
```

One Sample T-test and Confidence Interval for Mean

```
mean.test <- t.test(x= subchurn$CustServ.Calls,
    mu=2.4, conf.level= 0.95)
mean.test$statistic
mean.test$p.value
mean.test$conf.int
```

```
> mean.test$statistic
       t
-2.217128
> mean.test$p.value
[1] 0.03522289
> mean.test$conf.int
[1] 0.8733969 2.3408888
attr(,"conf.level")
[1] 0.95
```

One sample Proportion Test and Confidence Interval

```
num.churn <- sum(churn$Churn == "True") # Churners
sample.size <- dim(churn)[1] # Sample size
p <- num.churn/sample.size # Point estimate
Z_data <- (p - 0.15) / sqrt((0.15*(1-0.15))/sample.size)
error <- qnorm(0.975, mean = 0, sd = 1)*
    sqrt((p*(1-p))/sample.size)
lower.bound <- p – error; upper.bound <- p + error
p.value <- 2*pnorm(Z_data, mean = 0, sd = 1)
Z_data; p.value # Test statistic, p-value
lower.bound; upper.bound # Confidence interval
```

```
> z_data; p.value
[1] -0.8222369
[1] 0.4109421
> lower.bound; upper.bound
[1] 0.1329639
[1] 0.1568651
```

R REFERENCE

R Core Team. *R: A Language and Environment for Statistical Computing.* Vienna, Austria: R Foundation for Statistical Computing; 2012. ISBN: 3-900051-07-0, http://www.R-project.org/.

EXERCISES

CLARIFYING THE CONCEPTS

1. Explain what is meant by statistical inference. Give an example of statistical inference from everyday life, say, a political poll.

2. What is the difference between a population and a sample?

3. Describe the difference between a parameter and a statistic.

4. When should statistical inference not be applied?

5. What is the difference between point estimation and confidence interval estimation?

6. Discuss the relationship between the width of a confidence interval and the confidence level associated with it.

7. Discuss the relationship between the sample size and the width of a confidence interval. Which is better, a wide interval or a tight interval? Why?

8. Explain what we mean by sampling error.

9. What is the meaning of the term *margin of error*?

10. What are the two ways to reduce margin of error, and what is the recommended way?

11. A political poll has a margin of error of 3%. How do we interpret this number?

12. What is hypothesis testing?

13. Describe the two ways a correct conclusion can be made, and the two ways an incorrect conclusion can be made.

14. Explain clearly why a small p-value leads to rejection of the null hypothesis.

15. Explain why it may not always be desirable to draw a black-and-white, up-or-down conclusion in a hypothesis test. What can we do instead?

16. How can we use a confidence interval to conduct hypothesis tests?

WORKING WITH THE DATA

17. The duration customer service calls to an insurance company is normally distributed, with mean 20 minutes, and standard deviation 5 minutes. For the following sample sizes, construct a 95% confidence interval for the population mean duration of customer service calls.
    a. $n = 25$
    b. $n = 100$
    c. $n = 400$.

18. For each of the confidence intervals in the previous exercise, calculate and interpret the margin of error.

19. Refer to the previous exercise. Describe the relationship between margin of error and sample size.

20. Of 1000 customers who received promotional materials for a marketing campaign, 100 responded to the promotion. For the following confidence levels, construct a confidence interval for the population proportion who would respond to the promotion.
    a. 90%
    b. 95%
    c. 99%.

21. For each of the confidence intervals in the previous exercise, calculate and interpret the margin of error.

22. Refer to the previous exercise. Describe the relationship between margin of error and confidence level.

23. A sample of 100 donors to a charity has a mean donation amount of $55 with a sample standard deviation of $25. Test using $\alpha = 0.05$ whether the population mean donation amount exceeds $50.

    a. Provide the hypotheses. State the meaning of μ.

    b. What is the rejection rule?

    c. What is the meaning of the test statistic t_{data}?

    d. Is the value of the test statistic t_{data} extreme? How can we tell?

    e. What is the meaning of the p-value in this example?

    f. What is our conclusion?

    g. Interpret our conclusion so that a nonspecialist could understand it.

24. Refer to the hypothesis test in the previous exercise. Suppose we now set $\alpha = 0.01$.

    a. What would our conclusion now be? Interpret this conclusion.

    b. Note that the conclusion has been reversed simply because we have changed the value of α. But have the data changed? No, simply our level of what we consider to be significance. Instead, go ahead and assess the strength of evidence against the null hypothesis.

25. Refer to the first confidence interval you calculated for the population mean duration of customer service calls. Use this confidence interval to test whether this population mean differs from the following values, using level of significance $\alpha = 0.05$.

    a. 15 minutes

    b. 20 minutes

    c. 25 minutes.

26. In a sample of 100 customers, 240 churned when the company raised rates. Test whether the population proportion of churners is less than 25%, using level of significance $\alpha = 0.01$.

CHAPTER **6**

MULTIVARIATE STATISTICS

So far we have discussed inference methods for one variable at a time. Data analysts are also interested in multivariate inferential methods, where the relationships between two variables, or between one target variable and a set of predictor variables, are analyzed.

We begin with bivariate analysis, where we have two independent samples and wish to test for significant differences in the means or proportions of the two samples. When would data miners be interested in using bivariate analysis? In Chapter 6, we illustrate how the data is partitioned into a training data set and a test data set for cross-validation purposes. Data miners can use the hypothesis tests shown here to determine whether significant differences exist between the means of various variables in the training and test data sets. If such differences exist, then the cross-validation is invalid, because the training data set is nonrepresentative of the test data set.

- For a continuous variable, use the *two-sample t-test for the difference in means*.
- For a flag variable, use the *two-sample Z-test for the difference in proportions*.
- For a multinomial variable, use the *test for the homogeneity of proportions*.

Of course, there are presumably many variables in each of the training set and test set. However, spot-checking of a few randomly chosen variables is usually sufficient.

6.1 TWO-SAMPLE T-TEST FOR DIFFERENCE IN MEANS

To test for the difference in population means, we use the following test statistic:

$$t_{\text{data}} = \frac{\bar{x}_1 - \bar{x}_2}{\sqrt{(s_1^2/n_1) + (s_2^2/n_2)}}$$

which follows an approximate t distribution with degrees of freedom the smaller of $n_1 - 1$ and $n_2 - 1$, whenever either both populations are normally distributed or both samples are large.

Data Mining and Predictive Analytics, First Edition. Daniel T. Larose and Chantal D. Larose.
© 2015 John Wiley & Sons, Inc. Published 2015 by John Wiley & Sons, Inc.

For example, we partitioned the churn data set into a training set of 2529 records and a test set of 804 records (the reader's partition will differ). We would like to assess the validity of the partition by testing whether the population mean number of customer service calls differs between the two data sets. The summary statistics are given in Table 6.1.

TABLE 6.1   Summary statistics for customer service calls, training data set, and test data set

Data Set	Sample Mean	Sample Standard Deviation	Sample Size
Training set	$\bar{x}_1 = 1.5714$	$s_1 = 1.3126$	$n_1 = 2529$
Test set	$\bar{x}_2 = 1.5361$	$s_2 = 1.3251$	$n_2 = 804$

Now, the sample means do not look very different, but we would like to have the results of the hypothesis test just to make sure. The hypotheses are

$$H_0 : \mu_1 = \mu_2 \text{ versus } H_a : \mu_1 \neq \mu_2$$

The test statistic is

$$t_{\text{data}} = \frac{\bar{x}_1 - \bar{x}_2}{\sqrt{(s_1^2/n_1) + (s_2^2/n_2)}} = \frac{1.5714 - 1.5361}{\sqrt{(1.3126^2/2529) + (1.3251^2/804)}} = 0.6595$$

The two-tailed p-value for $t_{\text{data}} = 0.6594$ is

$$p - \text{value} = 2 \cdot P(t > 0.6595) = 0.5098$$

Since the p-value is large, there is no evidence that the mean number of customer service calls differs between the training data set and the test data set. For this variable at least, the partition seems valid.

6.2   TWO-SAMPLE Z-TEST FOR DIFFERENCE IN PROPORTIONS

Of course not all variables are numeric, like customer service calls. What if we have a 0/1 flag variable – such as membership in the Voice Mail Plan – and wish to test whether the proportions of records with value 1 differ between the training data set and test data set? We could turn to the two-sample Z-test for the difference in proportions. The test statistic is

$$Z_{\text{data}} = \frac{p_1 - p_2}{\sqrt{p_{\text{pooled}} \cdot (1 - p_{\text{pooled}})((1/n_1) + (1/n_2))}}$$

where $p_{\text{pooled}} = \frac{x_1 + x_2}{n_1 + n_2}$, and x_i and p_i represents the number of and proportion of records with value 1 for sample i, respectively.

For example, our partition resulted in $x_1 = 707$ of $n_1 = 2529$ customers in the training set belonging to the Voice Mail Plan, while $x_2 = 215$ of $n_2 = 804$ customers in the test set belonging, so that $p_1 = \frac{x_1}{n_1} = \frac{707}{2529} = 0.2796$, $p_2 = \frac{x_2}{n_2} = \frac{215}{804} = 0.2674$, and $p_{pooled} = \frac{x_1+x_2}{n_1+n_2} = \frac{707+215}{2529+804} = 0.2766$.

The hypotheses are

$$H_0 : \pi_1 = \pi_2 \quad \text{versus} \quad H_a : \pi_1 \neq \pi_2$$

The test statistic is

$$Z_{data} = \frac{p_1 - p_2}{\sqrt{p_{pooled} \cdot (1 - p_{pooled})((1/n_1) + (1/n_2))}}$$

$$= \frac{0.2796 - 0.2674}{\sqrt{0.2766 \cdot (0.7234)((1/2529) + (1/804))}} = 0.6736$$

The p-value is

$$p - \text{value} = 2 \cdot P(Z > 0.6736) = 0.5006$$

Thus, there is no evidence that the proportion of Voice Mail Plan members differs between the training and test data sets. For this variable, the partition is valid.

6.3   TEST FOR THE HOMOGENEITY OF PROPORTIONS

Multinomial data is an extension of binomial data to $k > 2$ categories. For example, suppose a multinomial variable *marital status* takes the values *married*, *single*, and *other*. Suppose we have a training set of 1000 people and a test set of 250 people, with the frequencies shown in Table 6.2.

To determine whether significant differences exist between the multinomial proportions of the two data sets, we could turn to the test for the homogeneity of proportions.[1] The hypotheses are

$$H_0 : p_{married,training} = p_{married,test},$$

$$p_{single,training} = p_{single,test},$$

$$p_{other,training} = p_{other,test}$$

H_a : At least one of the claims in H_0 is wrong.

TABLE 6.2   Observed frequencies

Data Set	Married	Single	Other	Total
Training set	410	340	250	1000
Test set	95	85	70	250
Total	505	425	320	**1250**

---

[1] Thanks to Dr. Daniel S. Miller for helpful discussions on this topic.

To determine whether these *observed frequencies* represent proportions that are significantly different for the training and test data sets, we compare these observed frequencies with the *expected frequencies* that we would expect if H_0 were true. For example, to find the expected frequency for the number of married people in the training set, we (i) find the overall proportion of married people in both the training and test sets, $\frac{505}{1250}$, and (ii) we multiply this overall proportion by the number of people in the training set, 1000, giving us the expected proportion of married people in the training set to be

$$\text{Expected frequency}_{\text{married,training}} = \frac{(1000)(505)}{1250} = 404$$

We use the overall proportion in (i) because H_0 states that the training and test proportions are equal. Generalizing, for each cell in the table, the expected frequencies are calculated as follows:

$$\text{Expected frequency} = \frac{(\text{row total})(\text{column total})}{\text{grand total}}$$

Applying this formula to each cell in the table gives us the table of expected frequencies in Table 6.3.

The observed frequencies (O) and the expected frequencies (E) are compared using a test statistic from the χ^2 (chi-square) distribution:

$$\chi^2_{\text{data}} = \sum \frac{(O - E)^2}{E}$$

Large differences between the observed and expected frequencies, and thus a large value for χ^2_{data}, will lead to a small p-value, and a rejection of the null hypothesis. Table 6.4 illustrates how the test statistic is calculated.

The p-value is the area to the right of χ^2_{data} under the χ^2 curve with degrees of freedom equal to (number of rows $- 1$) (number of columns $- 1$) $= (1)(2) = 2$:

$$p\text{-value} = P(\chi^2 > \chi^2_{\text{data}}) = P(\chi^2 > 1.15) = 0.5627$$

Because this p-value is large, there is no evidence that the observed frequencies represent proportions that are significantly different for the training and test data sets. In other words, for this variable, the partition is valid.

This concludes our coverage of the tests to apply when checking the validity of a partition.

TABLE 6.3   Expected frequencies

Data Set	Married	Single	Other	Total
Training set	404	340	256	1000
Test set	101	85	64	250
Total	505	425	320	**1250**

TABLE 6.4   Calculating the test statistic χ^2_{data}

Cell	Observed Frequency	Expected Frequency	$\dfrac{(\text{Obs} - \text{Exp})^2}{\text{Exp}}$
Married, training	410	404	$\dfrac{(410 - 404)^2}{404} = 0.09$
Married, test	95	101	$\dfrac{(95 - 101)^2}{101} = 0.36$
Single, training	340	340	$\dfrac{(340 - 340)^2}{340} = 0$
Single, test	85	85	$\dfrac{(85 - 85)^2}{85} = 0$
Other, training	250	256	$\dfrac{(250 - 256)^2}{256} = 0.14$
Other, test	70	64	$\dfrac{(70 - 64)^2}{64} = 0.56$
			Sum $= \chi^2_{data} = 1.15$

6.4   CHI-SQUARE TEST FOR GOODNESS OF FIT OF MULTINOMIAL DATA

Next, suppose a multinomial variable *marital status* takes the values *married*, *single*, and *other*, and suppose that we know that 40% of the individuals in the *population* are married, 35% are single, and 25% report another marital status. We are taking a sample and would like to determine whether the sample is representative of the population. We could turn to the χ^2 (chi-square) goodness of fit test.

The hypotheses for this χ^2 goodness of fit test would be as follows:

$$H_0 : p_{married} = 0.40, \quad p_{single} = 0.35, \quad p_{married} = 0.25$$

$$H_a : \text{At least one of the proportions in } H_0 \text{ is wrong.}$$

Our sample of size $n = 100$, yields the following *observed frequencies* (represented by the letter "O"):

$$O_{married} = 36, \quad O_{single} = 35, \quad O_{other} = 29$$

To determine whether these counts represent proportions that are significantly different from those expressed in H_0, we compare these observed frequencies with the *expected frequencies* that we would expect if H_0 were true. If H_0 were true, then we would expect 40% of our sample of 100 individuals to be married, that is, the expected frequency for *married* is

$$E_{married} = n \cdot p_{married} = 100 \cdot 0.40 = 40$$

Similarly,

$$E_{single} = n \cdot p_{single} = 100 \cdot 0.35 = 35$$

$$E_{other} = n \cdot p_{other} = 100 \cdot 0.25 = 25$$

These frequencies are compared using the test statistic:

$$\chi^2_{data} = \sum \frac{(O-E)^2}{E}$$

Again, large differences between the observed and expected frequencies, and thus a large value for χ^2_{data}, will lead to a small p-value, and a rejection of the null hypothesis. Table 6.5 illustrates how the test statistic is calculated.

The p-value is the area to the right of χ^2_{data} under the χ^2 curve with $k-1$ degrees of freedom, where k is the number of categories (here $k = 3$):

$$p - \text{value} = P(\chi^2 > \chi^2_{data}) = P(\chi^2 > 1.04) = 0.5945$$

Thus, there is no evidence that the observed frequencies represent proportions that differ significantly from those in the null hypothesis. In other words, our sample is representative of the population.

TABLE 6.5 Calculating the test statistic χ^2_{data}

Marital Status	Observed Frequency	Expected Frequency	$\frac{(\text{Obs} - \text{Exp})^2}{\text{Exp}}$
Married	36	40	$\frac{(36-40)^2}{40} = 0.4$
Single	35	35	$\frac{(35-35)^2}{35} = 0$
Other	29	25	$\frac{(29-25)^2}{25} = 0.64$
			$\text{Sum} = \chi^2_{data} = 1.04$

6.5 ANALYSIS OF VARIANCE

In an extension of the situation for the two-sample t-test, suppose that we have a three-fold partition of the data set, and wish to test whether the mean value of a continuous variable is the same across all three subsets. We could turn to one-way analysis of variance (ANOVA). To understand how ANOVA works, consider the following small example. We have samples from Groups A, B, and C, of four observations each, for the continuous variable *age*, shown in Table 6.6.

TABLE 6.6 Sample ages for Groups A, B, and C

Group A	Group B	Group C
30	25	25
40	30	30
50	50	40
60	55	45

The hypotheses are

$$H_0 : \mu_A = \mu_B = \mu_C$$

H_a : Not all the population means are equal.

The sample mean ages are $\overline{x}_A = 45$, $\overline{x}_B = 40$, and $\overline{x}_C = 35$. A comparison dot plot of the data (Figure 6.1) shows that there is a considerable amount of overlap among the three data sets. So, despite the difference in sample means, the dotplot offers little or no evidence to reject the null hypothesis that the population means are all equal.

Next, consider the following samples from Groups D, E, and F, for the continuous variable *age*, shown in Table 6.7.

Once again, the sample mean ages are $\overline{x}_D = 45$, $\overline{x}_E = 40$, and $\overline{x}_F = 35$. A comparison dot plot of this data (Figure 6.2) illustrates that there is very little overlap among the three data sets. Thus, Figure 6.2 offers good evidence to reject the null hypothesis that the population means are all equal.

To recapitulate, Figure 6.1 shows no evidence of difference in group means, while Figure 6.2 shows good evidence of differences in group means, *even though*

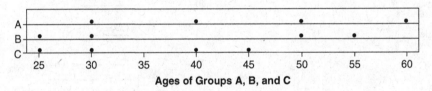

Figure 6.1 Dotplot of Groups A, B, and C shows considerable overlap.

TABLE 6.7 Sample ages for Groups D, E, and F

Group D	Group E	Group F
43	37	34
45	40	35
45	40	35
47	43	36

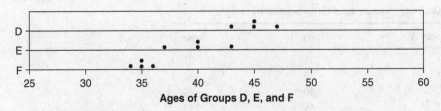

Figure 6.2 Dotplot of Groups D, E, and F shows little overlap.

the respective sample means are the same in both cases. The distinction stems from the overlap among the groups, which itself is a result of the *spread* within each group. Note that the spread is large for each group in Figure 6.1, and small for each group in Figure 6.2. When the spread within each sample is large (Figure 6.1), the difference in sample means seems small. When the spread within each sample is small (Figure 6.2), the difference in sample means seems large.

ANOVA works by performing the following comparison. Compare

1. the *between-sample variability*, that is, the variability in the sample means, such as $\bar{x}_A = 45$, $\bar{x}_B = 40$, and $\bar{x}_C = 35$, with

2. the *within-sample variability*, that is, the variability within each sample, measured, for example, by the sample standard deviations.

When (1) is much larger than (2), this represents evidence that the population means are not equal. Thus, the analysis depends on measuring variability, hence the term *analysis of variance.*

Let $\bar{\bar{x}}$ represent the overall sample mean, that is, the mean of all observations from all groups. We measure the between-sample variability by finding the variance of the k sample means, weighted by sample size, and expressed as the *mean square treatment* (MSTR):

$$\text{MSTR} = \frac{\sum n_i(\bar{x}_i - \bar{\bar{x}})^2}{k - 1}$$

We measure the within-sample variability by finding the weighted mean of the sample variances, expressed as the *mean square error* (MSE):

$$\text{MSTE} = \frac{\sum (n_i - 1)s_i^2}{n_t - k}$$

We compare these two quantities by taking their ratio:

$$F_{\text{data}} = \frac{\text{MSTR}}{\text{MSE}}$$

which follows an F distribution, with degrees of freedom $df_1 = k - 1$ and $df_2 = n_t - k$. The numerator of MSTR is the *sum of squares treatment*, SSTR, and the numerator of MSE is the *sum of squares error*, SSE. The total sum of squares (SST) is the sum of SSTR and SSE. A convenient way to display the above quantities is in the ANOVA table, shown in Table 6.8.

TABLE 6.8   ANOVA table

Source of Variation	Sum of Squares	Degrees of Freedom	Mean Square	F
Treatment	SSTR	$df_1 = k - 1$	$\text{MSTR} = \dfrac{\text{SSTR}}{df_1}$	$F_{\text{data}} = \dfrac{\text{MSTR}}{\text{MSE}}$
Error	SSE	$df_2 = n_t - k$	$\text{MSE} = \dfrac{\text{SSE}}{df_2}$	
Total	SST			

The test statistic F_{data} will be large when the between-sample variability is much greater than the within-sample variability, which is indicative of a situation calling for rejection of the null hypothesis. The p-value is $P(F > F_{data})$; reject the null hypothesis when the p-value is small, which happens when F_{data} is large.

For example, let us verify our claim that Figure 6.1 showed little or no evidence that the population means were not equal. Table 6.9 shows the Minitab ANOVA results.

TABLE 6.9   ANOVA results for $H_0 : \mu_A = \mu_B = \mu_C$

```
Source  DF    SS   MS     F      P
Factor   2   200  100   0.64  0.548
Error    9  1400  156
Total   11  1600
```

The p-value of 0.548 indicates that there is no evidence against the null hypothesis that all population means are equal. This bears out our earlier claim. Next let us verify our claim that Figure 6.2 showed evidence that the population means were not equal. Table 6.10 shows the Minitab ANOVA results.

TABLE 6.10   ANOVA results for $H_0 : \mu_D = \mu_E = \mu_F$

```
Source  DF      SS      MS      F      P
Factor   2  200.00  100.00  32.14  0.000
Error    9   28.00    3.11
Total   11  228.00
```

The p-value of approximately zero indicates that there is strong evidence that not all the population mean ages are equal, thus supporting our earlier claim. For more on ANOVA, see Larose (2013).[2]

Regression analysis represents another multivariate technique, comparing a single predictor with the target in the case of *Simple Linear Regression*, and comparing a set of predictors with the target in the case of *Multiple Regression*. We cover these topics in their own chapters, Chapters 8 and 9, respectively.

REFERENCE

Much more information regarding the topics covered in this chapter may be found in any introductory statistics textbook, such as *Discovering Statistics*, second edition, by Daniel T. Larose, W. H. Freeman, New York, 2013.

---

[2]Daniel Larose, *Discovering Statistics*, Second Edition, W.H. Freeman and Company, Publishers, New York, 2013.

THE R ZONE

Two-Sample *T*-Test for difference in means

```
# Input the summary statistics from Table 5.1
xbar1 <- 1.5714
xbar2 <- 1.5361
s1 <- 1.3126; s2 <- 1.3251
n1 <- 2529; n2 <- 804
dfs <- min(n1-1, n2-1)
tdata <- (xbar1 - xbar2) / sqrt((s1^2/n1)+(s2^2/n2))
pvalue <- 2*pt(tdata, df = dfs, lower.tail=FALSE)
tdata; pvalue # Test statistic and p-value
```

```
> tdata; pvalue
[1] 0.6594724
[1] 0.5097815
```

Two-Sample *Z* Test for Difference in Proportions

```
# Input the summary statistics
# Some of these will override the values
# from the previous example
x1 <- 707
x2 <- 215
n1 <- 2529
n2 <- 804
p1 <- x1 / n1
p2 <- x2 / n2
ppooled <- (x1+x2) / (n1+n2)
zdata <- (p1-p2) / sqrt(ppooled*(1-ppooled)
   *((1/n1)+(1/n2)))
pvalue <- 2*pnorm(abs(zdata), lower.tail = FALSE)
zdata; pvalue  # Test statistic and p-value
```

```
> zdata; pvalue
[1] 0.6705405
[1] 0.5025133
```

Chi Square Test for Homogeneity of Proportions

```
# Recreate Table 5.2
table5.2 <- as.table(rbind(c(410, 340, 250),
    c(95, 85, 70)))
dimnames(table5.2) <- list(Data.Set =
    c("Training Set", "Test Set"),
    Status = c("Married", "Single", "Other"))
Xsq_data <- chisq.test(table5.2)
Xsq_data$statistic # Test statistic
Xsq_data$p.value # p-value
Xsq_data$expected # Expected counts
```

```
> Xsq_data$statistic
X-squared
 1.14867
> Xsq_data$p.value
[1] 0.5630793
> Xsq_data$expected
                Status
Data.Set      Married Single Other
  Training Set    404    340   256
  Test Set        101     85    64
```

Chi-Square Goodness of Fit of Multinomial Data

# Population proportions
p_status <- c(0.40, 0.35, 0.25)
# Observed frequencies
o_status <- c(36, 35, 29)
chisq.test(o_status, p = p_status)

```
> chisq.test(o_status, p = p_status)

    Chi-squared test for given probabilities

data:  o_status
X-squared = 1.04, df = 2, p-value = 0.5945
```

ANOVA

a <- c(30, 40, 50, 60); b <- c(25, 30, 50, 55)
c <- c(25, 30, 40, 45)
ab <- append(a,b); datavalues <- append(ab, c)
datalabels <- factor(c(rep("a", length(a)),
    rep("b", length(b)), rep("c", length(c))))
anova.results <- aov(datavalues ~ datalabels)
summary(anova.results)

```
> summary(anova.results)
            Df Sum Sq Mean Sq F value Pr(>F)
datalabels   2    200   100.0   0.643  0.548
Residuals    9   1400   155.6
```

R REFERENCE

R Core Team. *R: A Language and Environment for Statistical Computing.* Vienna, Austria: R Foundation for Statistical Computing; 2012. ISBN: 3-900051-07-0, http://www. R-project.org/.

EXERCISES

1. In Chapter 7, we will learn to split the data set into a training data set and a test data set. To test whether there exist unwanted differences between the training and test set, which hypothesis test do we perform, for the following types of variables:

   a. Flag variable

   b. Multinomial variable

   c. Continuous variable

   Table 6.11 contains information on the mean duration of customer service calls between a training and a test data set. Test whether the partition is valid for this variable, using $\alpha = 0.10$.

2. Our partition shows that 800 of the 2000 customers in our test set own a tablet, while 230 of the 600 customers in our training set own a tablet. Test whether the partition is valid for this variable, using $\alpha = 0.10$.

   Table 6.12 contains the counts for the marital status variable for the training and test set data. Test whether the partition is valid for this variable, using $\alpha = 0.10$.

TABLE 6.11   Summary statistics for duration of customer service calls

Data Set	Sample Mean	Sample Standard Deviation	Sample Size
Training set	$\bar{x}_1 = 20.5$	$s_1 = 5.2$	$n_1 = 2000$
Test set	$\bar{x}_2 = 20.4$	$s_2 = 4.9$	$n_2 = 600$

TABLE 6.12   Observed frequencies for marital status

Data Set	Married	Single	Other	Total
Training set	800	750	450	2000
Test set	240	250	110	600
Total	1040	1000	560	**2600**

3. The multinomial variable *payment preference* takes the values *credit card*, *debit card*, and *check*. Now, suppose we know that 50% of the customers in our population prefer to pay by credit card, 20% prefer debit card, and 30% prefer to pay by check. We have taken a sample from our population, and would like to determine whether it is representative of the population. The sample of size 200 shows 125 customers preferring to pay by credit card, 25 by debit card, and 50 by check. Test whether the sample is representative of the population, using $\alpha = 0.05$.

4. Suppose we wish to test for difference in population means among three groups.
   a. Explain why it is not sufficient to simply look at the differences among the sample means, without taking into account the variability within each group.
   b. Describe what we mean by between-sample variability and within-sample variability.
   c. Which statistics measure the concepts in (b).
   d. Explain how ANOVA would work in this situation.

Table 6.13 contains the amount spent (in dollars) in a random sample of purchases where the payment was made by credit card, debit card, and check, respectively. Test whether the population mean amount spent differs among the three groups, using $\alpha = 0.05$. Refer to the previous exercise. Now test whether the population mean amount spent differs among the three groups, using $\alpha = 0.01$. Describe any conflict between your two conclusions. Suggest at least two courses of action to ameliorate the situation.

TABLE 6.13   Purchase amounts for three payment methods

Credit Card	Debit Card	Check
100	80	50
110	120	70
90	90	80
100	110	80

## CHAPTER 7

PREPARING TO MODEL THE DATA

7.1 SUPERVISED VERSUS UNSUPERVISED METHODS

Data mining methods may be categorized as either supervised or unsupervised. In *unsupervised methods*, no target variable is identified as such. Instead, the data mining algorithm searches for patterns and structures among all the variables. The most common unsupervised data mining method is clustering, our topic for Chapters 19–22. For example, political consultants may analyze congressional districts using clustering methods, to uncover the locations of voter clusters that may be responsive to a particular candidate's message. In this case, all appropriate variables (e.g., income, race, gender) would be input to the clustering algorithm, with no target variable specified, in order to develop accurate voter profiles for fund-raising and advertising purposes.

Another data mining method, which may be supervised or unsupervised, is association rule mining. In market basket analysis, for example, one may simply be interested in "which items are purchased together," in which case no target variable would be identified. The problem here, of course, is that there are so many items for sale, that searching for all possible associations may present a daunting task, due to the resulting combinatorial explosion. Nevertheless, certain algorithms, such as the a priori algorithm, attack this problem cleverly, as we shall see when we cover association rule mining in Chapter 23.

Most data mining methods are *supervised methods*, however, meaning that (i) there is a particular prespecified target variable, and (ii) the algorithm is given many examples where the value of the target variable is provided, so that the algorithm may learn which values of the target variable are associated with which values of the predictor variables. For example, the regression methods of Chapters 8 and 9 are supervised methods, as the observed values of the response variable y are provided to the least-squares algorithm, which seeks to minimize the squared distance between these y values and the y values predicted given the x-vector. All of the classification methods we examine in Chapters 10–18 are supervised methods, including decision trees, neural networks, and k-nearest neighbors.

Data Mining and Predictive Analytics, First Edition. Daniel T. Larose and Chantal D. Larose.
© 2015 John Wiley & Sons, Inc. Published 2015 by John Wiley & Sons, Inc.

Note: The terms *supervised* and *unsupervised* are widespread in the literature, and hence used here. However, we do not mean to imply that unsupervised methods require no human involvement. To the contrary, effective cluster analysis and association rule mining both require substantial human judgment and skill.

7.2   STATISTICAL METHODOLOGY AND DATA MINING METHODOLOGY

In Chapters 5 and 6, we were introduced to a wealth of statistical methods for performing inference, that is, for estimating or testing the unknown parameters of a population of interest. Statistical methodology and data mining methodology differ in the following two ways:

1. Applying statistical inference using the huge sample sizes encountered in data mining tends to result in statistical significance, even when the results are not of practical significance.

2. In statistical methodology, the data analyst has an a priori hypothesis in mind. Data mining procedures usually do not have an a priori hypothesis, instead freely trolling through the data for actionable results.

7.3   CROSS-VALIDATION

Unless properly conducted, data mining can become data dredging, whereby the analyst "uncovers" phantom spurious results, due to random variation rather than real effects. It is therefore crucial that data miners avoid data dredging. This is accomplished through *cross-validation*.

Cross-validation is a technique for insuring that the results uncovered in an analysis are generalizable to an independent, unseen, data set. In data mining, the most common methods are *twofold cross-validation* and *k-fold cross-validation*. In twofold cross-validation, the data are partitioned, using random assignment, into a *training data set* and a *test data set*. The test data set should then have the target variable omitted. Thus, the only systematic difference between the training data set and the test data set is that the training data includes the target variable and the test data does not. For example, if we are interested in classifying *income bracket*, based on *age, gender*, and *occupation*, our classification algorithm would need a large pool of records, containing complete (as complete as possible) information about every field, including the target field, *income bracket*. In other words, the records in the *training set* need to be *preclassified*. A provisional data mining model is then constructed using the training samples provided in the training data set.

However, the training set is necessarily incomplete; that is, it does not include the "new" or future data that the data modelers are really interested in classifying. Therefore, the algorithm needs to guard against "memorizing" the training set and blindly applying all patterns found in the training set to the future data. For example, it may happen that all customers named "David" in a training set may be in the high-income bracket. We would presumably not want our final model, to be applied to the new data, to include the pattern "If the customer's first name is David, the customer has a high income." Such a pattern is a spurious artifact of the training set and needs to be verified before deployment.

Therefore, the next step in supervised data mining methodology is to examine how the provisional data mining model performs on a *test set* of data. In the test set, a holdout data set, the values of the target variable are hidden temporarily from the provisional model, which then performs classification according to the patterns and structures it learned from the training set. The efficacy of the classifications is then evaluated by comparing them against the true values of the target variable. The provisional data mining model is then adjusted to minimize the error rate on the test set.

Estimates of model performance for future, unseen data can then be computed by observing various evaluative measures applied to the test data set. Such model evaluation techniques are covered in Chapters 15–18. The bottom line is that cross-validation guards against spurious results, as it is highly unlikely that the same random variation would be found to be significant in both the training set and the test set. For example, a spurious signal with 0.05 probability of being observed, if in fact no real signal existed, would have only $0.05^2 = 0.0025$ probability of being observed in both the training and test sets, because these data sets are independent. In other words, the data analyst could report an average 400 results before one would expect a spurious result to be reported.

But the data analyst must insure that the training and test data sets are indeed independent, by *validating the partition*. We validate the partition into training and test data sets by performing graphical and statistical comparisons between the two sets. For example, we may find that, even though the assignment of records was made randomly, a significantly higher proportion of positive values of an important flag variable were assigned to the training set, compared to the test set. This would bias our results, and hurt our prediction or classification accuracy on the test data set. It is especially important that the characteristics of the target variable be as similar as possible between the training and test data sets. Table 7.1 shows the suggested hypothesis test for validating the target variable, based on the type of target variable.

In *k*-fold cross validation, the original data is partitioned into *k* independent and similar subsets. The model is then built using the data from $k - 1$ subsets, using the *k*th subset as the test set. This is done iteratively until we have *k* different models. The results from the *k* models are then combined using averaging or voting. A popular choice for *k* is 10. A benefit of using *k*-fold cross-validation is that each record appears in the test set exactly once; a drawback is that the requisite validation task is made more difficult.

TABLE 7.1 Suggested hypothesis tests for validating different types of target variables

Type of Target Variable	Test from Chapter 5
Continuous	Two-sample *t*-test for difference in means
Flag	Two-sample *Z* test for difference in proportions
Multinomial	Test for homogeneity of proportions

To summarize, most supervised data mining methods apply the following methodology for building and evaluating a model:

METHODOLOGY FOR BUILDING AND EVALUATING A DATA MODEL

1. *Partition* the available data into a *training set* and a *test set*. Validate the partition.
2. Build a data mining model using the training set data.
3. Evaluate the data mining model using the test set data.

7.4 OVERFITTING

Usually, the accuracy of the provisional model is not as high on the test set as it is on the training set, often because the provisional model is *overfitting* on the training set. Overfitting results when the provisional model tries to account for every possible trend or structure in the training set, even idiosyncratic ones such as the "David" example above. There is an eternal tension in model building between model complexity (resulting in high accuracy on the training set) and generalizability to the test and validation sets. Increasing the complexity of the model in order to increase the accuracy on the training set eventually and inevitably leads to a degradation in the generalizability of the provisional model to the test set, as shown in Figure 7.1.

Figure 7.1 shows that as the provisional model begins to grow in complexity from the null model (with little or no complexity), the error rates on both the training

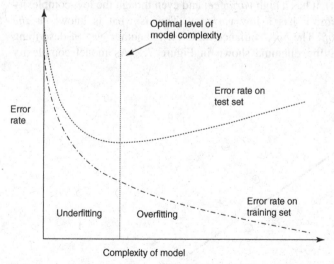

Figure 7.1 The optimal level of model complexity is at the minimum error rate on the test set.

set and the test set fall. As the model complexity increases, the error rate on the training set continues to fall in a monotone manner. However, as the model complexity increases, the test set error rate soon begins to flatten out and increase because the provisional model has memorized the training set rather than leaving room for generalizing to unseen data. The point where the minimal error rate on the test set is encountered is the optimal level of model complexity, as indicated in Figure 7.1. Complexity greater than this is considered to be overfitting; complexity less than this is considered to be underfitting.

7.5 BIAS–VARIANCE TRADE-OFF

Suppose that we have the scatter plot in Figure 7.2 and are interested in constructing the optimal curve (or straight line) that will separate the dark gray points from the light gray points. The straight line has the benefit of low complexity but suffers from some classification errors (points ending up on the wrong side of the line).

In Figure 7.3, we have reduced the classification error to zero but at the cost of a much more complex separation function (the curvy line). One might be tempted to adopt the greater complexity in order to reduce the error rate. However, one should be careful not to depend on the idiosyncrasies of the training set. For example, suppose that we now add more data points to the scatter plot, giving us the graph in Figure 7.4.

Note that the low-complexity separator (the straight line) need not change very much to accommodate the new data points. This means that this low-complexity separator has *low variance*. However, the high-complexity separator, the curvy line, must alter considerably if it is to maintain its pristine error rate. This high degree of change indicates that the high-complexity separator has a *high variance*.

Even though the high-complexity model has a low *bias* (in terms of the error rate on the training set), it has a high *variance*; and even though the low-complexity model has a high *bias*, it has a low *variance*. This is what is known as *the bias–variance trade-off*. The bias–variance trade-off is another way of describing the overfitting/underfitting dilemma shown in Figure 7.1. As model complexity

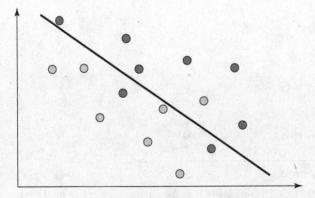

Figure 7.2 Low-complexity separator with high error rate.

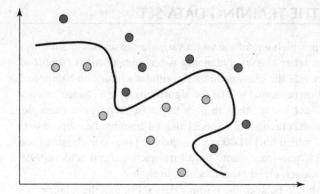

Figure 7.3   High-complexity separator with low error rate.

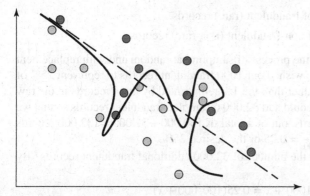

Figure 7.4   With more data: low-complexity separator need not change much; high-complexity separator needs much revision.

increases, the bias on the training set decreases but the variance increases. The goal is to construct a model in which neither the bias nor the variance is too high, but usually, minimizing one tends to increase the other.

For example, a common method of evaluating how accurate model estimation is proceeding for a continuous target variable is to use the *mean-squared error* (MSE). Between two competing models, one may select the better model as that model with the lower MSE. Why is MSE such a good evaluative measure? Because it combines both bias and variance. The MSE is a function of the estimation error (sum of squared errors, SSE) and the model complexity (e.g., degrees of freedom). It can be shown (e.g., Hand, Mannila, and Smyth.[1]) that the MSE can be partitioned using the following equation, which clearly indicates the complementary relationship between bias and variance:

$$MSE = variance + bias^2$$

[1]David Hand, Heikki Mannila, and Padhraic Smyth, *Principles of Data Mining*, MIT Press, Cambridge, MA, 2001.

7.6   BALANCING THE TRAINING DATA SET

For classification models, in which one of the target variable classes has much lower relative frequency than the other classes, balancing is recommended. A benefit of balancing the data is to provide the classification algorithms with a rich balance of records for each classification outcome, so that the algorithms have a chance to learn about all types of records, not just those with high target frequency. For example, suppose we are running a fraud classification model and our training data set consists of 100,000 transactions, of which only 1000 are fraudulent. Then, our classification model could simply predict "non-fraudulent" for all transactions, and achieve 99% classification accuracy. However, clearly this model is useless.

Instead, the analyst should balance the training data set so that the relative frequency of fraudulent transactions is increased. There are two ways to accomplish this, which are as follows:

1. Resample a number of fraudulent (rare) records.
2. Set aside a number of non-fraudulent (non-rare) records.

Resampling refers to the process of sampling at random and with replacement from a data set. Suppose we wished our 1000 fraudulent records to represent 25% of the balanced training set, rather than the 1% represented by these records in the raw training data set. Then, we could add 32,000 resampled fraudulent records so that we had 33,000 fraudulent records, out of a total of $100,000 + 32,000 = 132,000$ records in all. This represents $\frac{33,000}{132,000} = 0.25$ or the desired 25%.

How did we arrive at the number of 32,000 additional fraudulent records? By using the equation

$$1000 + x = 0.25(100,000 + x)$$

and solving for x, the required number of additional records to resample. In general, this equation is

$$\text{Rare} + x = p(\text{records} + x)$$

and solving for x gives us:

$$x = \frac{p(\text{records}) - \text{rare}}{1 - p}$$

where x is the required number of resampled records, p represents the desired proportion of rare values in the balanced data set, *records* represents the number of records in the unbalanced data set, and *rare* represents the current number of rare target values.

Some data miners have a philosophical aversion to resampling records to achieve balance, as they feel this amounts to fabricating data. In this case, a sufficient number of non-fraudulent transactions would instead be set aside, thereby increasing the proportion of fraudulent transactions. To achieve a 25% balance proportion, we would retain only 3000 non-fraudulent records. We would then need to discard from the analysis 96,000 of the 99,000 non-fraudulent records, using random selection. It would not be surprising if our data mining models would suffer as a result of starving them of data in this way. Instead, the data analyst would probably be well-advised either to decrease the desired balance proportion to something like 10% or to use resampling.

When choosing a desired balancing proportion, recall the rationale for doing so: in order to allow the model a sufficiently rich variety of records to learn how to classify the rarer value of the target variable across a range of situations. The balancing proportion can be relatively low (e.g., 10%) if the analyst is confident that the rare target value is exposed to a sufficiently rich variety of records. The balancing proportion should be higher (e.g., 25%) if the analyst is not so confident of this.

The test data set should never be balanced. The test data set represents new data that the models have not seen yet. Certainly, the real world will not balance tomorrow's data for the convenience of our classification models; therefore, the test data set itself should not be balanced. Note that all model evaluation will take place using the test data set, so that the evaluative measures will all be applied to unbalanced (real-world-like) data.

Because some predictor variables have higher correlation with the target variable than do other predictor variables, the character of the balanced data will change. For example, suppose we are working with the *Churn* data set, and suppose that churners have higher levels of *day minutes* than non-churners. Then, when we balance the data set, the overall mean of *day minutes* will increase, as we have eliminated so many non-churner records. *Such changes cannot be avoided when balancing data sets.* Thus, direct overall comparisons between the original and balanced data sets are futile, as changes in character are inevitable. However, apart from these unavoidable changes, and although the random sampling tends to protect against systematic deviations, data analysts should provide evidence that their balanced data sets do not otherwise differ systematically from the original data set. This can be accomplished by examining the graphics and summary statistics from the original and balanced data set, *partitioned on the categories of the target variable.* If desired, hypothesis tests such as those in Chapter 6 may be applied. If deviations are uncovered, the balancing should be reapplied. Cross-validation measures can be applied if the analyst is concerned about these deviations. Multiple randomly selected balanced data sets can be formed, and the results averaged, for example.

7.7   ESTABLISHING BASELINE PERFORMANCE

In *Star Trek IV: The Voyage Home*, Captain Kirk travels back in time to the 20th century, finds himself in need of cash, and pawns his eyeglasses. The buyer offers him $100, to which Captain Kirk responds, "Is that a lot?" Unfortunately, the Captain had no frame of reference to compare the $100 to, and so was unable to determine whether the $100 was a satisfactory offer or not. As data analysts we should do our best to avoid putting our clients into Captain Kirk's situation, by reporting results with no comparison to a baseline. Without comparison to a baseline, a client cannot determine whether our results are any good.

For example, suppose we naively report that "only" 28.4% of customers adopting our International Plan (see Table 3.3) will churn. That does not sound too bad, until we recall that, among all of our customers, the overall churn rate is only 14.49%

(Figure 3.3). This overall churn rate may be considered our *baseline*, against which any further results can be calibrated. Thus, belonging to the International Plan actually nearly doubles the churn rate, which is clearly not good.

The type of baseline one should use depends on the way the results are reported. For the churn example, we are interested in decreasing the overall churn rate, which is expressed as a percentage. So, our objective would be to report a decrease in the overall churn rate. Note the difference between an absolute difference in the churn rate versus a relative difference in the churn rate. Suppose our data mining model resulted in a predicted churn rate of 9.99%. This represents only a $14.49 - 9.99\% = 4.5\%$ absolute decrease in the churn rate, but a $4.5\%/14.49\% = 31\%$ relative decrease in the churn rate. The analyst should make it clear for the client which comparison method is being used.

Suppose our task is estimation, and we are using a regression model. Then, our baseline model may take the form of a "$\bar{y}$ model," that is, a model that simply finds the mean of the response variable, and predicts that value for every record. Clearly this is quite naïve, so any data mining model worth its salt should not have a problem beating this $\bar{y}$ model. By the same token, if your data mining model cannot outperform the $\bar{y}$ model, then something is clearly wrong. (We measure the goodness of a regression model using the standard error of the estimate s along with r^2.)

A more challenging yardstick against which to calibrate your model is to use existing research or results already existing in the field. For example, suppose the algorithm your analytics company currently uses succeeds in identifying 90% of all fraudulent online transactions. Then, your company will probably expect your new data mining model to outperform this 90% baseline.

THE R ZONE

Read in the data, partition Training and Testing data

```
adult <- read.csv(file = "C:/ .../adult.txt",
    stringsAsFactors=TRUE)
choose <- runif(length(adult$income),
    min = 0,
    max = 1)
training <- adult[choose <= 0.75,]
testing <- adult[choose > 0.75,]
adult[1:5, c(1,2,3)]
training[1:5, c(1,2,3)]
testing[1:5, c(1,2,3)]
```

```
> adult[1:5, c(1,2,3)]
  age       workclass demogweight
1  39       State-gov       77516
2  50 Self-emp-not-inc       83311
3  38         Private      215646
4  53         Private      234721
5  28         Private      338409
> training[1:5, c(1,2,3)]
  age       workclass demogweight
2  50 Self-emp-not-inc       83311
3  38         Private      215646
4  53         Private      234721
5  28         Private      338409
6  37         Private      284582
> testing[1:5, c(1,2,3)]
   age workclass demogweight
1   39 State-gov       77516
9   31   Private       45781
10  42   Private      159449
12  30 State-gov      141297
14  32   Private      205019
```

Remove the target variable, Income, from the testing data

names(testing)
# Target variable is in Column 15
testing <- testing[,-15]
names(testing)
# Target variable is no longer in
# the testing data

```
> names(testing)
 [1] "age"            "workclass"       "demogweight"
 [4] "education"      "education.num"   "marital.status"
 [7] "occupation"     "relationship"    "race"
[10] "sex"            "capital.gain"    "capital.loss"
[13] "hours.per.week" "native.country"  "income"
[16] "part"
> testing <- testing[,-15]
> names(testing)
 [1] "age"            "workclass"       "demogweight"
 [4] "education"      "education.num"   "marital.status"
 [7] "occupation"     "relationship"    "race"
[10] "sex"            "capital.gain"    "capital.loss"
[13] "hours.per.week" "native.country"  "part"
```

Remove the partitioning variable, Part, from both data sets

# Part is now the 15th variable
testing <- testing[,-15]
names(testing)
names(training)
# Part is the 16th variable
# in the training data set
training <- training[,-16]
names(training)

```
> names(testing)
 [1] "age"            "workclass"       "demogweight"
 [4] "education"      "education.num"   "marital.status"
 [7] "occupation"     "relationship"    "race"
[10] "sex"            "capital.gain"    "capital.loss"
[13] "hours.per.week" "native.country"
> names(training)
 [1] "age"            "workclass"       "demogweight"
 [4] "education"      "education.num"   "marital.status"
 [7] "occupation"     "relationship"    "race"
[10] "sex"            "capital.gain"    "capital.loss"
[13] "hours.per.week" "native.country"  "income"
[16] "part"
> training <- training[,-16]
> names(training)
 [1] "age"            "workclass"       "demogweight"
 [4] "education"      "education.num"   "marital.status"
 [7] "occupation"     "relationship"    "race"
[10] "sex"            "capital.gain"    "capital.loss"
[13] "hours.per.week" "native.country"  "income"
```

R REFERENCE

R Core Team. *R: A Language and Environment for Statistical Computing*. Vienna, Austria: R Foundation for Statistical Computing; 2012. ISBN: 3-900051-07-0, http://www. R-project.org/. Accessed 2014 Sep 30.

EXERCISES

1. Explain the difference between supervised and unsupervised methods. Which data mining tasks are associated with unsupervised methods? Supervised? Both?

2. Describe the differences between the training set, test set, and validation set.

3. Should we strive for the highest possible accuracy with the training set? Why or why not? How about the validation set?

4. How is the bias–variance trade-off related to the issue of overfitting and underfitting? Is high bias associated with overfitting and underfitting, and why? High variance?

5. Explain why we sometimes need to balance the data.

6. Suppose we are running a fraud classification model, with a training set of 10,000 records of which only 400 are fraudulent. How many fraudulent records need to be resampled if we would like the proportion of fraudulent records in the balanced data set to be 20%?

7. When should the test data set be balanced?

8. Explain why we should always report a baseline performance, rather than merely citing the uncalibrated results from our model.

9. Explain the distinction between reporting an absolute difference versus a relative difference.

10. If we are using a regression model, what form may our baseline model take?

## CHAPTER 8

SIMPLE LINEAR REGRESSION

Regression modeling represents a powerful and elegant method for estimating the value of a continuous target variable. In this chapter, we introduce regression modeling through simple linear regression, where a straight line is used to approximate the relationship between a single continuous predictor variable and a single continuous response variable. Later, in Chapter 9, we turn to multiple regression, where several predictor variables are used to estimate a single response.

8.1   AN EXAMPLE OF SIMPLE LINEAR REGRESSION

To develop the simple linear regression model, consider the *Cereals* data set,[1] an excerpt of which is presented in Table 8.1. The *Cereals* data set contains nutritional information for 77 breakfast cereals, and includes the following variables:

- Cereal name
- Cereal manufacturer
- Type (hot or cold)
- Calories per serving
- Grams of protein
- Grams of fat
- Milligrams of sodium
- Grams of fiber
- Grams of carbohydrates
- Grams of sugar
- Milligrams of potassium
- Percentage of recommended daily allowance of vitamins (0%, 25%, or 100%)

---

[1] Cereals data set, in Data and Story Library, http://lib.stat.cmu.edu/DASL. Also available at book web site www.DataMiningConsultant.com.

Data Mining and Predictive Analytics, First Edition. Daniel T. Larose and Chantal D. Larose.
© 2015 John Wiley & Sons, Inc. Published 2015 by John Wiley & Sons, Inc.

TABLE 8.1 Excerpt from *Cereals* data set: eight fields, first 16 cereals

Cereal Name	Manufacture	Sugars	Calories	Protein	Fat	Sodium	Rating
100% Bran	N	6	70	4	1	130	68.4030
100% Natural Bran	Q	8	120	3	5	15	33.9837
All-Bran	K	5	70	4	1	260	59.4255
All-Bran Extra Fiber	K	0	50	4	0	140	93.7049
Almond Delight	R	8	110	2	2	200	34.3848
Apple Cinnamon Cheerios	G	10	110	2	2	180	29.5095
Apple Jacks	K	14	110	2	0	125	33.1741
⋮	⋮	⋮	⋮	⋮	⋮	⋮	⋮

- Weight of one serving
- Number of cups per serving
- Shelf location (1 = bottom, 2 = middle, 3 = top)
- Nutritional rating, as calculated by Consumer Reports.

We are interested in estimating the nutritional *rating* of a cereal, given its *sugar* content. However, before we begin, it is important to note that this data set contains some missing data. The following four field values are missing:

- Potassium content of Almond Delight
- Potassium content of Cream of Wheat
- Carbohydrates and *sugars* content of Quaker Oatmeal.

We shall therefore not be able to use the sugar content of Quaker Oatmeal to help estimate nutrition rating using sugar content, and only 76 cereals are available for this purpose. Figure 8.1 presents a scatter plot of the nutritional rating versus the sugar content for the 76 cereals, along with the least-squares regression line.

The regression line is written in the form: $\hat{y} = b_0 + b_1 x$, called the *regression equation*, where:

- $\hat{y}$ is the estimated value of the response variable;
- b_0 is the *y-intercept* of the regression line;
- b_1 is the *slope* of the regression line;
- b_0 and b_1, together, are called the *regression coefficients*.

The regression equation for the relationship between sugars (x) and nutritional rating (y) for this sample of cereals is $\hat{y} = 59.853 - 2.4614x$. Below we demonstrate how this equation is calculated. This estimated regression equation can be interpreted as "the estimated cereal rating equals 59.953 minus 2.4614 times the sugar content in grams." The regression line and the regression equation are used as a *linear approximation* of the relationship between the x (predictor) and y (response) variables, that is, between sugar content and nutritional rating. We can then use the regression equation to make estimates or predictions.

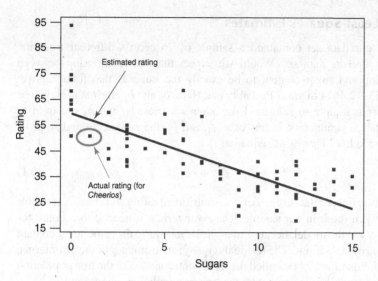

Figure 8.1   Scatter plot of nutritional rating versus sugar content for 77 cereals.

For example, suppose that we are interested in estimating the nutritional rating for a new cereal (not in the original data) that contains $x = 1$ gram of sugar. Using the regression equation, we find the estimated nutritional rating for a cereal with 1 gram of sugar to be $\widehat{y} = 59.853 - 2.4614(1) = 57.3916$. Note that this estimated value for the nutritional rating lies directly on the regression line, at the location $(x = 1, \widehat{y} = 57.3916)$, as shown in Figure 8.1. In fact, for any given value of x (sugar content), the estimated value for y (nutritional rating) lies precisely on the regression line.

Now, there is one cereal in our data set that does have a sugar content of 1 gram, Cheerios. Its nutrition rating, however, is 50.765, not 57.3916 as we estimated above for the new cereal with 1 gram of sugar. Cheerios' point in the scatter plot is located at $(x = 1, y = 50.765)$, within the oval in Figure 8.1. Now, the upper arrow in Figure 8.1 is pointing to a location on the regression line directly above the Cheerios point. This is where the regression equation predicted the nutrition rating to be for a cereal with a sugar content of 1 gram. The prediction was too high by $57.3916 - 50.765 = 6.6266$ rating points, which represents the vertical distance from the Cheerios data point to the regression line. This vertical distance of 6.6266 rating points, in general $(y - \widehat{y})$, is known variously as the *prediction error*, *estimation error*, or *residual*.

We of course seek to minimize the overall size of our prediction errors. *Least squares* regression works by choosing the unique regression line that minimizes the sum of squared residuals over all the data points. There are alternative methods of choosing the line that best approximates the linear relationship between the variables, such as median regression, although least squares remains the most common method. Note that we say we are performing a "regression of *rating* on *sugars*," where the y variable precedes the x variable in the statement.

8.1.1 The Least-Squares Estimates

Now, suppose our data set contained a sample of 76 cereals different from the sample in our *Cereals* data set. Would we expect that the relationship between nutritional rating and sugar content to be exactly the same as that found above: Rating $= 59.853 - 2.4614$ Sugars? Probably not. Here, b_0 and b_1 are *statistics*, whose values differ from sample to sample. Like other statistics, b_0 and b_1 are used to estimate population parameters, in this case, β_0 and β_1, the y-intercept and slope of the true regression line. That is, the equation

$$y = \beta_0 + \beta_1 x + \varepsilon \tag{8.1}$$

represents the true linear relationship between nutritional rating and sugar content for *all* cereals, not just those in our sample. The *error term* ε is needed to account for the indeterminacy in the model, because two cereals may have the same sugar content but different nutritional ratings. The residuals $(y_i - \hat{y})$ are estimates of the error terms, $\varepsilon_i, i = 1, \dots, n$. Equation (8.1) is called the regression equation or the true population regression equation; it is associated with the true or population regression line.

Earlier, we found the estimated regression equation for estimating the nutritional rating from sugar content to be $\hat{y} = 59.853 - 2.4614$(sugars). Where did these values for b_0 and b_1 come from? Let us now derive the formulas for estimating the y-intercept and slope of the estimated regression line, given the data.[2]

Suppose we have n observations from the model in equation (8.1); that is, we have

$$y_i = \beta_0 + \beta_1 x_i + \varepsilon_i, \quad i = 1, \dots, n$$

The least-squares line is that line that minimizes the population sum of squared errors, $\text{SSE}_p = \sum_{i=1}^{n} \varepsilon_i^2$. First, we re-express the population SSEs as

$$\text{SSE}_p = \sum_{i=1}^{n} \varepsilon_i^2 = \sum_{i=1}^{n} (y_i - \beta_0 - \beta_1 x_i)^2 \tag{8.2}$$

Then, recalling our differential calculus, we may find the values of β_0 and β_1 that minimize $\sum_{i=1}^{n} \varepsilon_i^2$ by differentiating equation (8.2) with respect to β_0 and β_1, and setting the results equal to zero. The partial derivatives of equation (8.2) with respect to β_0 and β_1 are, respectively:

$$\frac{\partial \text{SSE}_p}{\partial \beta_0} = -2 \sum_{i=1}^{n} (y_i - \beta_0 - \beta_1 x_i)$$

$$\frac{\partial \text{SSE}_p}{\partial \beta_1} = -2 \sum_{i=1}^{n} x_i (y_i - \beta_0 - \beta_1 x_i) \tag{8.3}$$

---

[2]These derivations assume calculus, but those whose calculus is rusty may skip ahead a couple of pages with little loss in understanding.

We are interested in the values for the estimates b_0 and b_1, so setting the equations in (8.3) equal to zero, we have

$$\sum_{i=1}^{n}(y_i - b_0 - b_1 x_i) = 0$$

$$\sum_{i=1}^{n} x_i(y_i - b_0 - b_1 x_i) = 0$$

Distributing the summation gives us

$$\sum_{i=1}^{n} y_i - nb_0 - b_1 \sum_{i=1}^{n} x_i = 0$$

$$\sum_{i=1}^{n} x_i y_i - b_0 \sum_{i=1}^{n} x_i - b_1 \sum_{i=1}^{n} x_i^2 = 0$$

which is re-expressed as

$$b_0 n + b_1 \sum_{i=1}^{n} x_i = \sum_{i=1}^{n} y_i$$

$$b_0 \sum_{i=1}^{n} x_i + b_1 \sum_{i=1}^{n} x_i^2 = \sum_{i=1}^{n} x_i y_i$$

(8.4)

Solving equation (8.4) for b_1 and b_0, we have

$$b_1 = \frac{\sum x_i y_i - \left[\left(\sum x_i\right)\left(\sum y_i\right)\right]/n}{\sum x_i^2 - \left(\sum x_i\right)^2/n}$$

(8.5)

$$b_0 = \bar{y} - b_1 \bar{x}$$

(8.6)

where n is the total number of observations, $\bar{x}$ is the mean value for the predictor variable and $\bar{y}$ is the mean value for the response variable, and the summations are $i = 1$ to n. The equations in (8.5) and (8.6) are therefore the least squares estimates for β_0 and β_1, the values that minimize the SSEs.

We now illustrate how we may find the values $b_0 = 59.853$ and $b_1 = -2.4614$, using equations (8.5), (8.6), and the summary statistics from Table 8.2, which shows the values for $x_i, y_i, x_i y_i$, and x_i^2, for the *Cereals* in the data set (note that only 16 of the 77 cereals are shown). It turns out that, for this data set, $\sum x_i = 534$, $\sum y_i = 3234.4309$, $\sum x_i y_i = 19,186.7401$, and $\sum x_i^2 = 5190$.

Plugging into formulas (8.5) and (8.6), we find:

$$b_1 = \frac{\sum x_i y_i - \left[\left(\sum x_i\right)\left(\sum y_i\right)\right]/n}{\sum x_i^2 - \left(\sum x_i\right)^2/n}$$

TABLE 8.2   Summary statistics for finding b_0 and b_1

Cereal Name	X = Sugars	Y = Rating	$X*Y$	X^2
100% Bran	6	68.4030	410.418	36
100% Natural Bran	8	33.9837	271.870	64
All-Bran	5	59.4255	297.128	25
All-Bran Extra Fiber	0	93.7049	0.000	0
Almond Delight	8	34.3848	275.078	64
Apple Cinnamon Cheerios	10	29.5095	295.095	100
Apple Jacks	14	33.1741	464.437	196
Basic 4	8	37.0386	296.309	64
Bran Chex	6	49.1203	294.722	36
Bran Flakes	5	53.3138	266.569	25
Cap'n Crunch	12	18.0429	216.515	144
Cheerios	1	50.7650	50.765	1
Cinnamon Toast Crunch	9	19.8236	178.412	81
Clusters	7	40.4002	282.801	49
Cocoa Puffs	13	22.7364	295.573	169
⋮	⋮	⋮		
Wheaties Honey Gold	8	36.1876	289.501	64

$$\sum x_i = 534 \qquad \sum y_i = 3234.4309$$
$$\bar{x} = 534/76 \qquad \bar{y} = 3234.4309/76 \qquad \sum x_i y_i \qquad \sum x_i^2 = 5190$$
$$= 7.0263 \qquad = 42.5583 \qquad = 19,186.7401$$

$$= \frac{19,186.7401 - (534)(3234.4309)/76}{5190 - (534)^2/76} = \frac{-3539.3928}{1437.9474}$$

$$= -2.4614 \tag{8.7}$$

and

$$b_0 = \bar{y} - b_1\bar{x} = 42.5583 + 2.4614(7.0263) = 59.853 \tag{8.8}$$

These values for the slope and y-intercept provide us with the estimated regression line indicated in Figure 8.1.

The y-intercept b_0 is the location on the y-axis where the regression line intercepts the y-axis; that is, the estimated value for the response variable when the predictor variable equals zero. The interpretation of the value of the y-intercept b_0 is as the estimated value of y, given $x = 0$. For example, for the *Cereals* data set, the y-intercept $b_0 = 59.853$ represents the estimated nutritional rating for cereals with zero sugar content. Now, in many regression situations, a value of zero for the predictor variable would not make sense. For example, suppose we were trying to predict elementary school students' weight (y) based on the students' height (x). The meaning of *height* = 0 is unclear, so that the denotative meaning of the y-intercept would not make interpretive sense in this case. However, for our data set, a value of zero for the sugar content does make sense, as several cereals contain 0 grams of sugar.

The slope of the regression line indicates the estimated change in y per unit increase in x. We interpret $b_1 = -2.4614$ to mean the following: "For each increase of 1 gram in sugar content, the estimated nutritional rating *decreases* by 2.4614 rating points." For example, Cereal A with five more grams of sugar than Cereal B would have an estimated nutritional rating $5(2.4614) = 12.307$ ratings points lower than Cereal B.

8.2   DANGERS OF EXTRAPOLATION

Suppose that a new cereal (say, the Chocolate Frosted Sugar Bombs loved by Calvin, the comic strip character written by Bill Watterson) arrives on the market with a very high sugar content of 30 grams per serving. Let us use our estimated regression equation to estimate the nutritional rating for Chocolate Frosted Sugar Bombs:

$$\hat{y} = 59.853 - 2.4614(\text{sugars}) = 59.4 - 2.4614(30) = -13.989.$$

In other words, Calvin's cereal has so much sugar that its nutritional rating is actually a negative number, unlike any of the other cereals in the data set (minimum $= 18$) and analogous to a student receiving a negative grade on an exam. What is going on here? The negative estimated nutritional rating for Chocolate Frosted Sugar Bombs is an example of the dangers of *extrapolation*.

Analysts should confine the estimates and predictions made using the regression equation to values of the predictor variable contained within the range of the values of x in the data set. For example, in the *Cereals* data set, the lowest sugar content is 0 grams and the highest is 15 grams, so that predictions of nutritional rating for any value of x (sugar content) between 0 and 15 grams would be appropriate. However, *extrapolation*, making predictions for x-values lying outside this range, can be dangerous, because we do not know the nature of the relationship between the response and predictor variables outside this range.

Extrapolation should be avoided if possible. If predictions outside the given range of x must be performed, the end-user of the prediction needs to be informed that no x-data is available to support such a prediction. The danger lies in the possibility that the relationship between x and y, which may be linear within the range of x in the data set, may no longer be linear outside these bounds.

Consider Figure 8.2. Suppose that our data set consisted only of the data points in black but that the true relationship between x and y consisted of both the black (observed) and the gray (unobserved) points. Then, a regression line based solely on the available (black dot) data would look approximately similar to the regression line indicated. Suppose that we were interested in predicting the value of y for an x-value located at the triangle. The prediction based on the available data would then be represented by the dot on the regression line indicated by the upper arrow. Clearly, this prediction has failed spectacularly, as shown by the vertical line indicating the huge prediction error. Of course, as the analyst would be completely unaware of the hidden data, he or she would hence be oblivious to the massive scope of the error

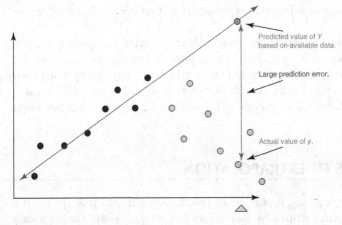

Figure 8.2 Dangers of extrapolation.

in prediction. Policy recommendations based on such erroneous predictions could certainly have costly results.

EXTRAPOLATION

- *Extrapolation* refers to estimates and predictions of the target variable made using the regression equation with values of the predictor variable outside of the range of the values of x in the data set.
- The analyst does not know the shape of the relationship between x and y in areas beyond the range of x. It may no longer be linear.
- Extrapolation should be avoided. If unable to avoid extrapolation, inform the end-user of the analysis that no x-data is available to support such a prediction.

8.3 HOW USEFUL IS THE REGRESSION? THE COEFFICIENT OF DETERMINATION, r^2

Of course, a least-squares regression line could be found to approximate the relationship between any two continuous variables, regardless of the quality of the relationship between them, but this does not guarantee that the regression will therefore be useful. The question therefore arises as to how we may determine whether a particular estimated regression equation is useful for making predictions.

We shall work toward developing a statistic, r^2, for measuring the goodness of fit of the regression. That is, r^2, known as the *coefficient of determination*, measures how well the linear approximation produced by the least-squares regression line actually fits the observed data.

Recall that $\hat{y}$ represents the estimated value of the response variable, and that $(y - \hat{y})$ represents the *prediction error* or *residual*. Consider the data set in Table 8.3, which shows the distance in kilometers traveled by a sample of 10 orienteering competitors, along with the elapsed time in hours. For example, the first competitor traveled 10 kilometers in 2 hours. On the basis of these 10 competitors, the estimated regression takes the form $\hat{y} = 6 + 2x$, so that the estimated distance traveled equals 6 kilometers plus twice the number of hours. You should verify that you can calculate this estimated regression equation, either using software, or using the equations in (8.7) and (8.8).

This estimated regression equation can be used to make predictions about the distance traveled for a given number of hours. These estimated values of y are given in the Predicted Score column in Table 8.3. The prediction error and squared prediction error may then be calculated. The sum of the squared prediction errors, or the sum of squares error, SSE $= \sum(y - \hat{y})^2$, represents an overall measure of the error in prediction resulting from the use of the estimated regression equation. Here we have SSE = 12. Is this value large? We are unable to state whether this value, SSE = 12, is large, because at this point we have no other measure to compare it to.

TABLE 8.3   Calculation of the SSE for the orienteering example

Subject	X = Time	Y = Distance	Predicted Score $\hat{y} = 6 + 2x$	Error in Prediction $(y - \hat{y})$	(Error in Prediction)^2 $(y - \hat{y})^2$
1	2	10	10	0	0
2	2	11	10	1	1
3	3	12	12	0	0
4	4	13	14	−1	1
5	4	14	14	0	0
6	5	15	16	−1	1
7	6	20	18	2	4
8	7	18	20	−2	4
9	8	22	22	0	0
10	9	25	24	1	1
					SSE $= \sum(y - \hat{y})^2 = 12$

Now, imagine for a moment that we were interested in estimating the distance traveled *without knowledge of the number of hours*. That is, suppose that we did not have access to the x-variable information for use in estimating the y-variable. Clearly, our estimates of the distance traveled would be degraded, on the whole, because less information usually results in less accurate estimates.

Because we lack access to the predictor information, our best estimate for y is simply $\bar{y}$, the sample mean of the number of hours traveled. We would be forced to use $\bar{y} = 16$ to estimate the number of kilometers traveled for every competitor, regardless of the number of hours that person had traveled.

Consider Figure 8.3. The estimates for distance traveled when ignoring the time information is shown by the horizontal line $\bar{y} = 16$ Disregarding the time information

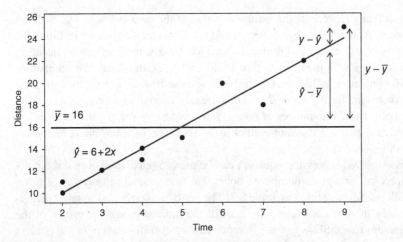

Figure 8.3 Overall, the regression line has smaller prediction error than the sample mean.

entails predicting $\bar{y} = 16$ kilometers for the distance traveled, for orienteering competitors who have been hiking only 2 or 3 hours, as well as for those who have been out all day (8 or 9 hours). This is clearly not optimal.

The data points in Figure 8.3 seem to "cluster" tighter around the estimated regression line than around the line $\bar{y} = 16$, which suggests that, overall, the prediction errors are smaller when we use the x-information than otherwise. For example, consider competitor #10, who hiked $y = 25$ kilometers in $x = 9$ hours. If we ignore the x-information, then the estimation error would be $(y - \bar{y}) = 25 - 16 = 9$ kilometers. This prediction error is indicated as the vertical line between the data point for this competitor and the horizontal line; that is, the vertical distance between the observed y and the predicted $\bar{y} = 16$.

Suppose that we proceeded to find $(y - \bar{y})$ for every record in the data set, and then found the sum of squares of these measures, just as we did for $(y - \hat{y})$ when we calculated the SSE. This would lead us to SST, the *sum of squares total*:

$$\text{SST} = \sum_{i=1}^{n} (y - \bar{y})^2$$

SST, also known as the *total sum of squares*, is a measure of the total variability in the values of the response variable alone, without reference to the predictor. Note that SST is a function of the *sample variance* of y, where the variance is the square of the standard deviation of y:

$$\text{SST} = \sum_{i=1}^{n} (y - \bar{y})^2 = (n - 1)s_y^2 = (n - 1)(s_y)^2$$

Thus, all three of these measures—SST, variance, and standard deviation—are univariate measures of the variability in y alone (although of course we could find the variance and standard deviation of the predictor as well).

Would we expect SST to be larger or smaller than SSE? Using the calculations shown in Table 8.4, we have SST $= 228$, which is much larger than SSE $= 12$. We now have something to compare SSE against. As SSE is so much smaller than SST, this indicates that using the predictor information in the regression results in much tighter estimates overall than ignoring the predictor information. These sums of squares measure errors in prediction, so that smaller is better. In other words, using the regression improves our estimates of the distance traveled.

TABLE 8.4 Finding SST for the orienteering example

Student	$X=$ Time	$Y=$ Distance	$\bar{y}$	$(y - \bar{y})$	$(y - \bar{y})^2$
1	2	10	16	−6	36
2	2	11	16	−5	25
3	3	12	16	−4	16
4	4	13	16	−3	9
5	4	14	16	−2	4
6	5	15	16	−1	1
7	6	20	16	4	16
8	7	18	16	2	4
9	8	22	16	6	36
10	9	25	16	9	81
				SST $= \sum (y - \bar{y})^2 = 228$	

Next, what we would like is a measure of how much the estimated regression equation improves the estimates. Once again examine Figure 8.3. For hiker #10, the estimation error when using the regression is $(y - \hat{y}) = 25 - 24 = 1$, while the estimation error when ignoring the time information is $(y - \bar{y}) = 25 - 16 = 9$. Therefore, the amount of *improvement* (reduction in estimation error) is $(\hat{y} - \bar{y}) = 24 - 16 = 8$.

Once again, we may proceed to construct a sum of squares statistic based on $(\hat{y} - \bar{y})$. Such a statistic is known as *SSR*, the *sum of squares regression*, a measure of the overall improvement in prediction accuracy when using the regression as opposed to ignoring the predictor information.

$$SSR = \sum_{i=1}^{n} (\hat{y} - \bar{y})^2$$

Observe from Figure 8.2 that the vertical distance $(y - \bar{y})$ may be partitioned into two "pieces," $(\hat{y} - \bar{y})$ and $(y - \hat{y})$. This follows from the following identity:

$$(y - \bar{y}) = (\hat{y} - \bar{y}) + (y - \hat{y}) \tag{8.9}$$

Now, suppose we square each side, and take the summation. We then obtain[3]:

$$\sum (y_i - \bar{y})^2 = \sum (\hat{y}_i - \bar{y})^2 + \sum (y_i - \hat{y}_i)^2 \tag{8.10}$$

---

[3] The cross-product term $2 \cdot \sum (\hat{y}_i - \bar{y})(y_i - \hat{y}_i)$ cancels out. For details, see Draper and Smith, *Applied Regression Analysis*, 3rd edition, Wiley Publishers, Hoboken, New Jersey, 1998.

We recognize from equation (8.8) the three sums of squares we have been developing, and can therefore express the relationship among them as follows:

$$SST = SSR + SSE \qquad (8.11)$$

We have seen that SST measures the total variability in the response variable. We may then think of SSR as the amount of variability in the response variable that is "explained" by the regression. In other words, SSR measures that portion of the variability in the response variable that is accounted for by the linear relationship between the response and the predictor.

However, as not all the data points lie precisely on the regression line, this means that there remains some variability in the y-variable that is not accounted for by the regression. SSE can be thought of as measuring all the variability in y from all sources, including random error, after the linear relationship between x and y has been accounted for by the regression.

Earlier, we found SST = 228 and SSE = 12. Then, using equation (8.11), we can find SSR to be SSR = SST − SSE = 228 − 12 = 216. Of course, these sums of squares must always be nonnegative. We are now ready to introduce the *coefficient of determination*, r^2, which measures the goodness of fit of the regression as an approximation of the linear relationship between the predictor and response variables.

$$r^2 = \frac{SSR}{SST}$$

As r^2 takes the form of a ratio of SSR to SST, we may interpret r^2 to represent the proportion of the variability in the y-variable that is explained by the regression; that is, by the linear relationship between the predictor and response variables.

What is the maximum value that r^2 can take? The maximum value for r^2 would occur when the regression is a perfect fit to the data set, which takes place when each of the data points lies precisely on the estimated regression line. In this optimal situation, there would be no estimation errors from using the regression, meaning that each of the residuals would equal zero, which in turn would mean that SSE would equal zero. From equation (8.11), we have that SST = SSR + SSE. If SSE = 0, then SST = SSR, so that r^2 would equal SSR/SST = 1. Thus, the maximum value for r^2 is 1, which occurs when the regression is a perfect fit.

What is the minimum value that r^2 can take? Suppose that the regression showed no improvement at all, that is, suppose that the regression explained none of the variability in y. This would result in SSR equaling zero, and consequently, r^2 would equal zero as well. Thus, r^2 is bounded between 0 and 1, inclusive.

How are we to interpret the value that r^2 takes? Essentially, the higher the value of r^2, the better the fit of the regression to the data set. Values of r^2 near one denote an extremely good fit of the regression to the data, while values near zero denote an extremely poor fit. In the physical sciences, one encounters relationships that elicit very high values of r^2, while in the social sciences, one may need to be content with lower values of r^2, because of person-to-person variability. As usual, the analyst's judgment should be tempered with the domain expert's experience.

8.4   STANDARD ERROR OF THE ESTIMATE, s

We have seen how the r^2 statistic measures the goodness of fit of the regression to the data set. Next, the s statistic, known as the *standard error of the estimate*, is a measure of the accuracy of the estimates produced by the regression. Clearly, s is one of the most important statistics to consider when performing a regression analysis. To find the value of s, we first find the *mean square error* (MSE):

$$MSE = \frac{SSE}{(n - m - 1)}$$

where m indicates the number of predictor variables, which is 1 for the simple linear regression case, and greater than 1 for the multiple regression case (Chapter 9). Like SSE, MSE represents a measure of the variability in the response variable left unexplained by the regression.

Then, *the standard error of the estimate* is given by

$$s = \sqrt{MSE} = \sqrt{\frac{SSE}{(n - m - 1)}}$$

The value of s provides an estimate of the size of the "typical" residual, much as the value of the standard deviation in univariate analysis provides an estimate of the size of the typical deviation. In other words, s is a measure of the typical error in estimation, the typical difference between the predicted response value and the actual response value. In this way, the standard error of the estimate s represents the precision of the predictions generated by the estimated regression equation. Smaller values of s are better, and s has the benefit of being expressed in the units of the response variable y.

For the orienteering example, we have

$$s = \sqrt{MSE} = \sqrt{\frac{12}{(10 - 1 - 1)}} = 1.2$$

Thus, the typical estimation error when using the regression model to predict distance is 1.2 kilometers. That is, if we are told how long a hiker has been traveling, then our estimate of the distance covered will typically differ from the actual distance by about 1.2 kilometers. Note from Table 8.3 that all of the residuals lie between 0 and 2 in absolute value, so that 1.2 may be considered a reasonable estimate of the typical residual. (Other measures, such as the mean absolute deviation of the residuals, may also be considered, but are not widely reported in commercial software packages.)

We may compare $s = 1.2$ kilometers against the typical estimation error obtained from ignoring the predictor data, obtained from the standard deviation of the response,

$$\sigma_y = \sqrt{\frac{\sum_{i=1}^{n}(y - \bar{y})^2}{n - 1}} = 5.0$$

The typical prediction error when ignoring the time data is 5 kilometers. Using the regression has reduced the typical prediction error from 5 to 1.2 kilometers.

In the absence of software, one may use the following computational formulas for calculating the values of SST and SSR. The formula for SSR is exactly the same as for the slope b_1, except that the numerator is squared.

$$SST = \sum y^2 - \frac{\left(\sum y\right)^2}{n}$$

$$SSR = \frac{\left[\sum xy - \left(\sum x\right)\left(\sum y\right)/n\right]^2}{\sum x^2 - \left(\sum x\right)^2/n}$$

Let us use these formulas for finding the values of SST and SSR for the orienteering example. You should verify that we have $\sum x = 50$, $\sum y = 160$, $\sum xy = 908$, $\sum x^2 = 304$, and $\sum y^2 = 2788$.

Then, $SST = \sum y^2 - \left(\sum y\right)^2/n = 2788 - (160)^2/10 = 2478 - 2560 = 228$.

And, $SSR = \dfrac{\left[\sum xy - \left(\sum x\right)\left(\sum y\right)/n\right]^2}{\sum x^2 - \left(\sum x\right)^2/n} = \dfrac{[908 - (50)(160)/10]^2}{304 - (50)^2/10} = \dfrac{108^2}{54} = 216$.

Of course, these are the same values found earlier using the more onerous tabular method. Finally, we calculate the value of the coefficient of determination r^2 to be

$$r^2 = \frac{SSR}{SST} = \frac{216}{228} = 0.9474$$

In other words, the linear relationship between time and distance accounts for 94.74% of the variability in the distances traveled. The regression model fits the data very nicely.

8.5   CORRELATION COEFFICIENT r

A common measure used to quantify the linear relationship between two quantitative variables is the *correlation coefficient*. The correlation coefficient r (also known as the *Pearson product moment correlation coefficient*) is an indication of the strength of the linear relationship between two quantitative variables, and is defined as follows:

$$r = \frac{\sum (x - \bar{x})(y - \bar{y})}{(n-1)s_x s_y}$$

where s_x and s_y represent the sample standard deviations of the x and y data values, respectively.

INTERPRETING CORRELATIONS

- When x and y are *positively correlated*, as the value of x increases, the value of y tends to increase as well.
- When x and y are *negatively correlated*, as the value of x increases, the value of y tends to decrease.
- When x and y are *uncorrelated*, as the value of x increases, the value of y tends to remain unaffected.

The correlation coefficient r always takes on values between 1 and -1, inclusive. Values of r close to 1 indicate that x and y are *positively correlated*, while values of r close to -1 indicate that x and y are *negatively correlated*. However, because of the large sample sizes associated with data mining, even values of r relatively small in absolute value may be considered statistically significant. For example, for a relatively modest-sized data set of about 1000 records, a correlation coefficient of $r = 0.07$ would be considered statistically significant. Later in this chapter, we learn how to construct a confidence interval for determining the statistical significance of the correlation coefficient r.

The definition formula for the correlation coefficient above may be tedious, because the numerator would require the calculation of the deviations for both the x-data and the y-data. We therefore have recourse, in the absence of software, to the following computational formula for r:

$$r = \frac{\sum xy - \left(\sum x\right)\left(\sum y\right)/n}{\sqrt{\sum x^2 - \left(\sum x\right)^2/n}\sqrt{\sum y^2 - \left(\sum y\right)^2/n}}$$

For the orienteering example, we have

$$r = \frac{\sum xy - \left(\sum x\right)\left(\sum y\right)/n}{\sqrt{\sum x^2 - \left(\sum x\right)^2/n}\sqrt{\sum y^2 - \left(\sum y\right)^2/n}}$$

$$= \frac{908 - (50)(160)/10}{\sqrt{304 - (50)^2/10}\sqrt{2788 - (160)^2/10}}$$

$$= \frac{108}{\sqrt{54}\sqrt{228}} = 0.9733$$

We would say that the time spent traveling and the distance traveled are strongly positively correlated. As the time spent hiking increases, the distance traveled tends to increase.

However, it is more convenient to express the correlation coefficient r as $r = \pm\sqrt{r^2}$. When the slope b_1 of the estimated regression line is positive, then the correlation coefficient is also positive, $r = \sqrt{r^2}$; when the slope is negative, then the correlation coefficient is also negative, $r = -\sqrt{r^2}$ In the orienteering example, we have $b_1 = 2$. This is positive, which means that the correlation coefficient will also be positive, $r = \sqrt{r^2} = \sqrt{0.9474} = 0.9733$.

It should be stressed here that the correlation coefficient r measures only the *linear* correlation between x and y. The predictor and target may be related in a curvilinear manner, for example, and r may not uncover the relationship.

8.6 ANOVA TABLE FOR SIMPLE LINEAR REGRESSION

Regression statistics may be succinctly presented in an analysis of variance (ANOVA) table, the general form of which is shown here in Table 8.5. Here, m represents the number of predictor variables, so that, for simple linear regression, $m = 1$.

TABLE 8.5 The ANOVA table for simple linear regression

Source of Variation	Sum of Squares	Degrees of Freedom	Mean Square	F
Regression	SSR	m	$MSR = \dfrac{SSR}{m}$	$F = \dfrac{MSR}{MSE}$
Error (or residual)	SSE	$n - m - 1$	$MSE = \dfrac{SSE}{n - m - 1}$	
Total	SST = SSR + SSE	$n - 1$		

The ANOVA table conveniently displays the relationships among several statistics, showing, for example, that the sums of squares add up to SST. The *mean squares* are presented as the ratios of the items to their left, and, for inference, the test statistic F is represented as the ratio of the mean squares. Tables 8.6 and 8.7 show the Minitab regression results, including the ANOVA tables, for the orienteering example and the cereal example, respectively.

8.7 OUTLIERS, HIGH LEVERAGE POINTS, AND INFLUENTIAL OBSERVATIONS

Next, we discuss the role of three types of observations that may or may not exert undue influence on the regression results. These are as follows:

- Outliers
- High leverage points
- Influential observations.

An *outlier* is an observation that has a very large standardized residual in absolute value. Consider the scatter plot of nutritional rating against sugars in Figure 8.4.

TABLE 8.6   Results for regression of *distance* versus *time* for the orienteering example

```
The regression equation is
Distance = 6.00 + 2.00 Time


Predictor     Coef    SE Coef      T        P
Constant    6.0000     0.9189    6.53    0.000
Time        2.0000     0.1667   12.00    0.000



S = 1.22474    R-Sq = 94.7%    R-Sq(adj) = 94.1%


Analysis of Variance

Source           DF       SS       MS        F       P
Regression        1   216.00   216.00   144.00   0.000
Residual Error    8    12.00     1.50
Total             9   228.00
```

TABLE 8.7   Results for regression of *nutritional rating* versus *sugar content*

```
The regression equation is
Rating = 59.9 - 2.46 Sugars


Predictor     Coef    SE Coef      T        P
Constant    59.853      1.998    29.96   0.000
Sugars     -2.4614      0.2417  -10.18   0.000


S = 9.16616    R-Sq = 58.4%    R-Sq(adj) = 57.8%


Analysis of Variance

Source           DF       SS       MS        F       P
Regression        1    8711.9   8711.9   103.69   0.000
Residual Error   74    6217.4     84.0
Total            75   14929.3



Unusual Observations

Obs   Sugars   Rating     Fit   SE Fit   Residual   St Resid
  1      6.0    68.40   45.08     1.08      23.32      2.56R
  4      0.0    93.70   59.85     2.00      33.85      3.78R

R denotes an observation with a large standardized residual.
```

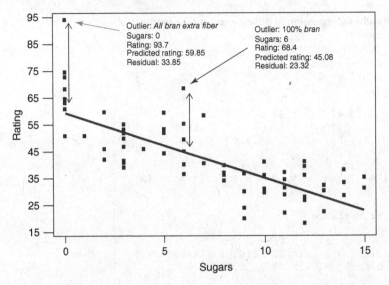

Figure 8.4 Identifying the outliers in regression of *nutritional rating* versus *sugars*.

The two observations with the largest absolute residuals are identified as *All Bran Extra Fiber* and *100% Bran*. Note that the vertical distance away from the regression line (indicated by the vertical arrows) is greater for these two observations than for any other cereals, indicating the largest residuals.

For example, the nutritional rating for *All Bran Extra Fiber* (93.7) is much higher than predicted (59.85), based on its sugar content alone (0 grams). Similarly, the nutritional rating for *100% Bran* (68.4) is much higher than would have been estimated (45.08) based on its sugar content alone (6 grams).

Residuals may have different variances, so that it is preferable to use the standardized residuals in order to identify outliers. Standardized residuals are residuals divided by their standard error, so that they are all on the same scale. Let $s_{i,\text{resid}}$ denote the standard error of the ith residual. Then

$$s_{i,\text{resid}} = s\sqrt{1 - h_i}$$

where h_i refers to the *leverage* of the ith observation (see below).

And the standardized residual equals:

$$\text{residual}_{i,\text{standardized}} = \frac{y_i - \widehat{y}_i}{s_{i,\text{resid}}}$$

A rough rule of thumb is to flag observations whose standardized residuals exceed 2 in absolute value as being outliers. For example, note from Table 8.7 that *Minitab* identifies observations 1 and 4 as outliers based on their large standardized residuals; these are *All Bran Extra Fiber* and *100% Bran*.

In general, if the residual is *positive*, we may say that the observed y-value is *higher* than the regression estimated, given the x-value. If the residual is *negative*, we may say that the observed y-value is *lower* than the regression estimated, given the x-value. For example, for *All Bran Extra Fiber* (which has a positive residual), we would say that the observed nutritional rating is higher than the regression estimated, given its sugars value. (This may presumably be because of all that extra fiber.)

A *high leverage point* is an observation that is extreme in the predictor space. In other words, a high leverage point takes on extreme values for the x-variable(s), without reference to the y-variable. That is, leverage takes into account only the x-variables, and ignores the y-variable. The term *leverage* is derived from the physics concept of the lever, which Archimedes asserted could move the Earth itself if only it were long enough.

The leverage h_i for the ith observation may be denoted as follows:

$$h_i = \frac{1}{n} + \frac{(x_i - \bar{x})^2}{\sum (x_i - \bar{x})^2}$$

For a given data set, the quantities $1/n$ and $\sum (x_i - \bar{x})^2$ may be considered to be constants, so that the leverage for the ith observation depends solely on $(x_i - \bar{x})^2$, the squared distance between the value of the predictor and the mean value of the predictor. The farther the observation differs from the mean of the observations, in the x-space, the greater the leverage. The lower bound on leverage values is $1/n$, and the upper bound is 1.0. An observation with leverage greater than about $2(m + 1)/n$ or $3(m + 1)/n$ may be considered to have high leverage (where m indicates the number of predictors).

For example, in the orienteering example, suppose that there was a new observation, a real hard-core orienteering competitor, who hiked for 16 hours and traveled 39 kilometers. Figure 8.5 shows the scatter plot, updated with this 11th hiker.

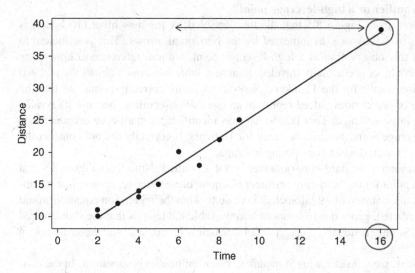

Figure 8.5   Scatter plot of distance versus time, with new competitor who hiked for 16 hours.

The Hard-Core Orienteer hiked 39 kilometers in 16 hours. Does he represent an outlier or a high-leverage point?

Note from Figure 8.5 that the time traveled by the new hiker (16 hours) is extreme in the x-space, as indicated by the horizontal arrows. This is sufficient to identify this observation as a high leverage point, without reference to how many kilometers he or she actually traveled. Examine Table 8.8, which shows the updated regression results for the 11 hikers. Note that *Minitab* correctly points out that the extreme orienteer does indeed represent an unusual observation, because its x-value gives it large leverage. That is, Minitab has identified the hard-core orienteer as a high leverage point, because he hiked for 16 hours. It correctly did not consider the distance (y-value) when considering leverage.

However, the hard-core orienteer is not an outlier. Note from Figure 8.5 that the data point for the hard-core orienteer lies quite close to the regression line, meaning that his distance of 39 kilometers is close to what the regression equation would have predicted, given the 16 hours of hiking. Table 8.8 tells us that the standardized residual is only $residual_{i,\text{standardized}} = 0.47$, which is less than 2, and therefore not an outlier.

Next, we consider what it means to be an influential observation. In the context of history, what does it mean to be an influential person? A person is influential if

TABLE 8.8   Updated regression results, including the hard-core hiker

```
The regression equation is
Distance = 5.73 + 2.06 Time


Predictor      Coef    SE Coef      T       P
Constant     5.7251    0.6513    8.79   0.000
Time        2.06098   0.09128   22.58   0.000


S = 1.16901    R-Sq = 98.3%    R-Sq(adj) = 98.1%


Analysis of Variance

Source          DF        SS       MS        F       P
Regression       1    696.61   696.61   509.74   0.000
Residual Error   9     12.30     1.37
Total           10    708.91


Unusual Observations

Obs   Time  Distance      Fit   SE Fit   Residual   St Resid
 11   16.0    39.000   38.701    0.979      0.299       0.47 X

X denotes an observation whose X value gives it large leverage.


Predicted Values for New Observations

New Obs     Fit   SE Fit        95% CI               95% PI
      1  18.091    0.352   (17.294, 18.888)   (15.329, 20.853)
```

their presence or absence significantly changes the history of the world. In the context of Bedford Falls (from the Christmas movie *It's a Wonderful Life*), George Bailey (played by James Stewart) discovers that he really was influential when an angel shows him how different (and poorer) the world would have been had he never been born. Similarly, in regression, an observation is *influential* if the regression parameters alter significantly based on the presence or absence of the observation in the data set.

An outlier may or may not be influential. Similarly, a high leverage point may or may not be influential. Usually, influential observations combine both the characteristics of large residual and high leverage. It is possible for an observation to be not-quite flagged as an outlier, and not-quite flagged as a high leverage point, but still be influential through the combination of the two characteristics.

First let us consider an example of an observation that is an outlier but is not influential. Suppose that we replace our 11th observation (no more hard-core guy) with someone who hiked 20 kilometers in 5 hours. Examine Table 8.9, which presents the regression results for these 11 hikers. Note from Table 8.9 that the new observation

TABLE 8.9 Regression results including person who hiked 20 kilometers in 5 hours

```
The regression equation is
Distance = 6.36 + 2.00 Time


Predictor      Coef  SE Coef      T      P
Constant      6.364    1.278   4.98  0.001
Time         2.0000   0.2337   8.56  0.000


S = 1.71741    R-Sq = 89.1%   R-Sq(adj) = 87.8%


Analysis of Variance

Source          DF       SS       MS      F      P
Regression       1   216.00   216.00  73.23  0.000
Residual Error   9    26.55     2.95
Total           10   242.55


Unusual Observations

Obs  Time  Distance     Fit  SE Fit  Residual  St Resid
 11  5.00    20.000  16.364   0.518     3.636     2.22R

R denotes an observation with a large standardized residual.
```

is flagged as an outlier (unusual observation with large standardized residual). This is because the distance traveled (20 kilometers) is higher than the regression predicted (16.364 kilometers), given the time (5 hours).

Now, would we consider this observation to be influential? Overall, probably not. Compare Table 8.9 (the regression output for the new hiker with 5 hours/20 kilometers) and Table 8.6 (the regression output for the original data set) to assess the effect the presence of this new observation has on the regression coefficients. The y-intercept changes from $b_0 = 6.00$ to $b_0 = 6.36$, but the slope does not change at all, remaining at $b_1 = 2.00$, regardless of the presence of the new hiker.

Figure 8.6 shows the relatively mild effect this outlier has on the estimated regression line, shifting it vertically a small amount, without affecting the slope at all. Although it is an outlier, this observation is not influential because it has very low leverage, being situated exactly on the mean of the x-values, so that it has the minimum possible leverage for a data set of size $n = 11$.

We can calculate the leverage for this observation ($x = 5$, $y = 20$) as follows. As $\bar{x} = 5$, we have

$$\sum (x_i - \bar{x})^2 = (2-5)^2 + (2-5)^2 + (3-5)^2 + \cdots + (9-5)^2 + (5-5)^2 = 54.$$

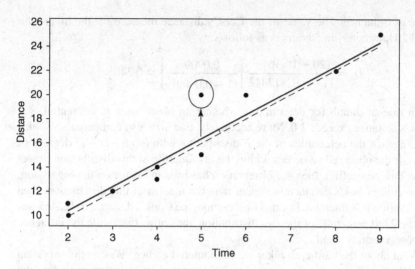

Figure 8.6   The mild outlier shifts the regression line only slightly.

Then the leverage for the new observation is

$$h_{(5,20)} = \frac{1}{11} + \frac{(5-5)^2}{54} = 0.0909.$$

Now that we have the leverage for this observation, we may also find the standardized residual, as follows. First, we have the standard error of the residual:

$$s_{(5,20),\text{resid}} = 1.71741\sqrt{1 - 0.0909} = 1.6375$$

So that the standardized residual equals:

$$\text{residual}_{(5,20),\text{standardized}} = \frac{y_i - \hat{y}_i}{s_{(5,20),\text{resid}}} = \frac{20 - 16.364}{1.6375} = 2.22,$$

as shown in Table 8.9. Note that the value of the standardized residual, 2.22, is only slightly larger than 2.0, so by our rule of thumb this observation may considered only a mild outlier.

   Cook's distance is the most common measure of the influence of an observation. It works by taking into account both the size of the residual and the amount of leverage for that observation. Cook's distance takes the following form, for the ith observation:

$$D_i = \frac{(y_i - \hat{y}_i)^2}{(m+1)s^2}\left[\frac{h_i}{(1-h_i)^2}\right]$$

where $(y_i - \hat{y}_i)$ represents the ith residual, s represents the standard error of the estimate, h_i represents the leverage of the ith observation, and m represents the number of predictors.

   The left-hand ratio in the formula for Cook's distance contains an element representing the residual, while the right-hand ratio contains functions of the leverage. Thus Cook's distance combines the two concepts of outlier and leverage into a single measure of influence. The value of the Cook's distance measure for the hiker who traveled 20 kilometers in 5 hours is as follows:

$$D_i = \frac{(20 - 16.364)^2}{(1 + 1)1.71741^2} \left[\frac{0.0909}{(1 - 0.0909)^2} \right] = 0.2465$$

A rough rule of thumb for determining whether an observation is influential is if its Cook's distance exceeds 1.0. More accurately, one may also compare the Cook's distance against the percentiles of the F-distribution with $(m, n - m - 1)$ degrees of freedom. If the observed value lies within the first quartile of this distribution (lower than the 25th percentile), then the observation has little influence on the regression; however, if the Cook's distance is greater than the median of this distribution, then the observation is influential. For this observation, the Cook's distance of 0.2465 lies within the 22nd percentile of the $F_{2,9}$ distribution, indicating that while the influence of the observation is small.

What about the hard-core hiker we encountered earlier? Was that observation influential? Recall that this hiker traveled 39 kilometers in 16 hours, providing the 11th observation in the results reported in Table 8.8. First, let us find the leverage.

We have $n = 11$ and $m = 1$, so that observations having $h_i > \frac{2(m+1)}{n} = 0.36$ or $h_i > \frac{3(m+1)}{n} = 0.55$ may be considered to have high leverage. This observation has $h_i = 0.7007$, which indicates that this durable hiker does indeed have high leverage, as mentioned earlier with reference to Figure 8.5. Figure 8.5 seems to indicate that this hiker ($x = 16$, $y = 39$) is not however an outlier, because the observation lies near the regression line. The standardized residual supports this, having a value of 0.46801. The reader will be asked to verify these values for leverage and standardized residual in the exercises. Finally, the Cook's distance for this observation is 0.2564, which is about the same as our previous example, indicating that the observation is not influential. Figure 8.7 shows the slight change in the regression with (solid line) and without (dotted line) this observation.

So we have seen that an observation that is an outlier with low influence, or an observation that is a high leverage point with a small residual may not be particularly influential. We next illustrate how a data point that has a moderately high residual and moderately high leverage may indeed be influential. Suppose that our 11th hiker had instead hiked for 10 hours, and traveled 23 kilometers. The regression analysis for these 11 hikers is then given in Table 8.10.

Note that *Minitab* does not identify the new observation as either an outlier or a high leverage point. This is because, as the reader is asked to verify in the exercises, the leverage of this new hiker is $h_i = 0.36019$, and the standardized residual equals -1.70831.

However, despite lacking either a particularly large leverage or large residual, this observation is nevertheless influential, as measured by its Cook's distance of $D_i = 0.821457$, which is in line with the 62nd percentile of the $F_{1,10}$ distribution.

The influence of this observation stems from the combination of its moderately large residual with its moderately large leverage. Figure 8.8 shows the influence this single hiker has on the regression line, pulling down on the right side to decrease the slope (from 2.00 to 1.82), and thereby increase the y-intercept (from 6.00 to 6.70).

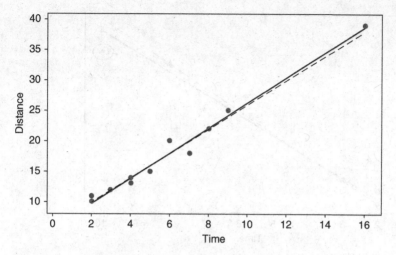

Figure 8.7   Slight change in regression line when hard-core hiker added.

TABLE 8.10   **Regression results for new observation with *time* = 10, *distance* = 23**

```
The regression equation is
Distance = 6.70 + 1.82 Time


Predictor     Coef    SE Coef       T      P
Constant     6.6967    0.9718    6.89   0.000
Time         1.8223    0.1604   11.36   0.000


S = 1.40469    R-Sq = 93.5%    R-Sq(adj) = 92.8%


Analysis of Variance

Source          DF      SS       MS       F      P
Regression       1   254.79   254.79   129.13  0.000
Residual Error   9    17.76     1.97
Total           10   272.55
```

8.8   POPULATION REGRESSION EQUATION

Least squares regression is a powerful and elegant methodology. However, if the assumptions of the regression model are not validated, then the resulting inference and model building are undermined. Deploying a model whose results are based on unverified assumptions may lead to expensive failures later on. The simple linear

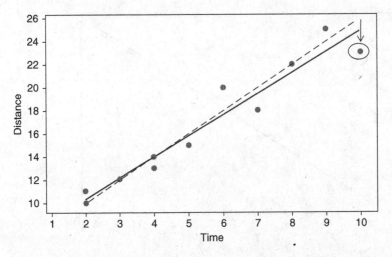

Figure 8.8 Moderate residual plus moderate leverage = influential observation.

regression model is given as follows. We have a set of n bivariate observations, with response value y_i related to predictor value x_i through the following linear relationship.

THE POPULATION REGRESSION EQUATION

$$y = \beta_0 + \beta_1 x + \varepsilon$$

where

- β_0 and β_1 represent the model parameters, for the y-intercept and slope respectively. These are constants, whose true value remains unknown, and which are estimated from the data using the least squares estimates.

- ε represents the error term. As most predictor–response relationships are not deterministic, a certain amount of error will be introduced by any linear approximation of the actual relationship. Therefore, an error term, modeled by a random variable, is needed.

THE ASSUMPTIONS ABOUT THE ERROR TERM

- **Zero-Mean Assumption.** The error term ε is a random variable, with mean or expected value equal to zero. In other words, $E(\varepsilon) = 0$.

- **Constant Variance Assumption.** The variance of ε, denoted by σ^2, is constant, regardless of the value of x.

- **Independence Assumption.** The values of ε are independent.

- **Normality Assumption.** The error term ε is a normally distributed random variable.

In other words, the values of the error term ε_i are independent normal random variables, with mean 0 and variance σ^2.

On the basis of these four assumptions, we can derive four implications for the behavior of the response variable, y, as follows.

IMPLICATIONS OF THE ASSUMPTIONS FOR THE BEHAVIOR OF THE RESPONSE VARIABLE y

---

1. On the basis of the Zero-Mean Assumption, we have

$$E(y) = E(\beta_0 + \beta_1 x + \varepsilon) = E(\beta_0) + E(\beta_1 x) + E(\varepsilon) = \beta_0 + \beta_1 x$$

That is, for each value of x, the mean of the y's lies on the regression line.

2. On the basis of the Constant Variance Assumption, we have the variance of y, Var(y), given as Var(y) = Var($\beta_0 + \beta_1 x + \varepsilon$) = Var($\varepsilon$) = σ^2. That is, regardless of which value taken by the predictor x, the variance of the y's is always constant.

3. On the basis of the Independence Assumption, it follows that, for any particular value of x, the values of y are independent as well.

4. Based on the normality assumption, it follows that y is also a normally distributed random variable.

In other words, the values of the response variable y_i are independent normal random variables, with mean $\beta_0 + \beta_1 x$ and variance σ^2.

Figure 8.9 illustrates graphically the normality of the y_i, with mean $\beta_0 + \beta_1 x$ and constant variance σ^2. Suppose we have a data set which includes predictor values at

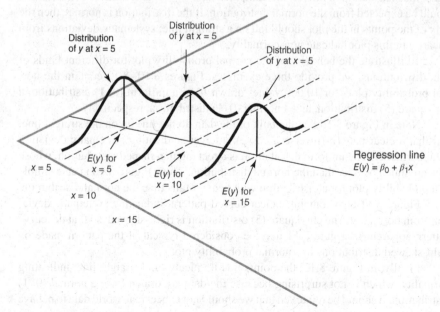

Figure 8.9   For each value of x, the y_i are normally distributed, with mean on the true regression line, and constant variance.

$x = 5, 10$, and 15, among other values. Then, at each of these values of x, the regression assumptions assert that observed values of y are samples from a normally distributed population with a mean on the regression line ($E(y) = \beta_0 + \beta_1 x$), and constant standard deviation σ^2. Note from Figure 8.9 that each of the normal curves has precisely the same shape, which indicates that the variance is constant for each value of x.

If one is interested in using regression analysis in a strictly descriptive manner, with no inference and no model building, then one need not worry quite so much about assumption validation. This is because the assumptions are about the error term. If the error term is not involved, then the assumptions are not needed. However, if one wishes to do inference or model building, then the assumptions must be verified.

8.9   VERIFYING THE REGRESSION ASSUMPTIONS

So, how does one go about verifying the regression assumptions? The two main graphical methods used to verify regression assumptions are as follows:

a. A normal probability plot of the residuals.

b. A plot of the standardized residuals against the fitted (predicted) values.

A *normal probability plot* is a quantile–quantile plot of the quantiles of a particular distribution against the quantiles of the standard normal distribution, for the purposes of determining whether the specified distribution deviates from normality. (Similar to a percentile, a *quantile* of a distribution is a value x_p such that $p\%$ of the distribution values are less than or equal to x_p.) In a normality plot, the observed values of the distribution of interest are compared against the same number of values that would be expected from the normal distribution. If the distribution is normal, then the bulk of the points in the plot should fall on a straight line; systematic deviations from linearity in this plot indicate non-normality.

To illustrate the behavior of the normal probability plot for different kinds of data distributions, we provide three examples. Figures 8.10–8.12 contain the normal probability plots for 10,000 values drawn from a uniform (0, 1) distribution, a chi-square (5) distribution, and a normal (0, 1) distribution, respectively.

Note in Figure 8.10 that the bulk of the data do not line up on the straight line, and that a clear pattern (reverse S curve) emerges, indicating systematic deviation from normality. The uniform distribution is a rectangular-shaped distribution, whose tails are much heavier than the normal distribution. Thus, Figure 8.10 is an example of a probability plot for a distribution with heavier tails than the normal distribution.

Figure 8.11 also contains a clear curved pattern, indicating systematic deviation from normality. The chi-square (5) distribution is right-skewed, so that the curve pattern apparent in Figure 8.11 may be considered typical of the pattern made by right-skewed distributions in a normal probability plot.

Finally, in Figure 8.12, the points line up nicely on a straight line, indicating normality, which is not surprising because the data are drawn from a normal (0, 1) distribution. It should be remarked that we should not expect real-world data to behave

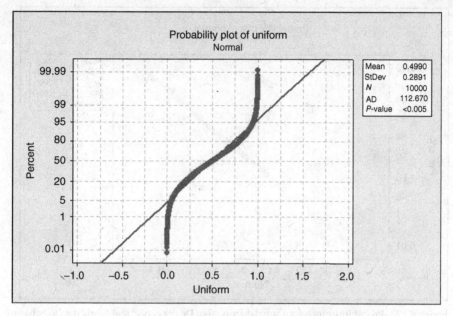

Figure 8.10   Normal probability plot for a uniform distribution: heavy tails.

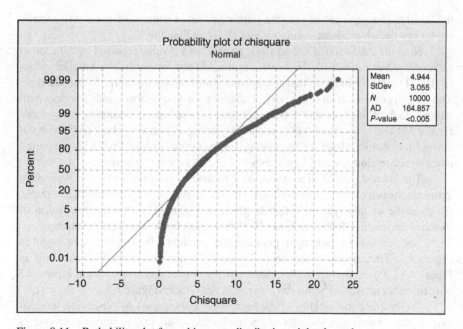

Figure 8.11   Probability plot for a chi-square distribution: right-skewed.

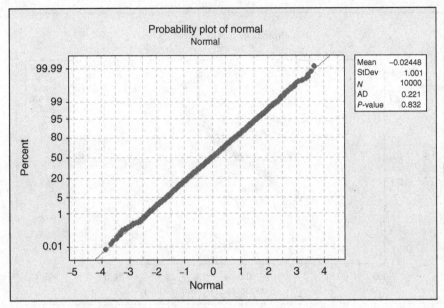

Figure 8.12 Probability plot for a normal distribution: Do not expect real-world data to behave this nicely.

this nicely. The presence of sampling error and other sources of noise will usually render our decisions about normality less clear-cut than this.

Note the Anderson–Darling (*AD*) statistic and *p*-value reported by *Minitab* in each of Figures 8.10–8.12. This refers to the AD test for normality. Smaller values of the AD statistic indicate that the normal distribution is a better fit for the data. The null hypothesis is that the normal distribution fits, so that small *p*-values will indicate lack of fit. Note that for the uniform and chi-square examples, the *p*-value for the AD test is less than 0.005, indicating strong evidence for lack of fit with the normal distribution. However, the *p*-value for the normal example is 0.832, indicating no evidence against the null hypothesis that the distribution is normal.

The second graphical method used to assess the validity of the regression assumptions is a plot of the standardized residuals against the fits (predicted values). An example of this type of graph is given in Figure 8.13, for the regression of *distance* versus *time* for the original 10 observations in the orienteering example.

Note the close relationship between this graph and the original scatter plot in Figure 8.3. The regression line from Figure 8.3 is now the horizontal zero line in Figure 8.13. Points that were either above/below/on the regression line in Figure 8.3 now lie either above/below/on the horizontal zero line in Figure 8.13.

We evaluate the validity of the regression assumptions by observing whether certain patterns exist in the plot of the residuals versus fits, in which case one of the assumptions has been violated, or whether no such discernible patterns exists, in which case the assumptions remain intact. The 10 data points in Figure 8.13 are really too few to try to determine whether any patterns exist. In data mining applications, of

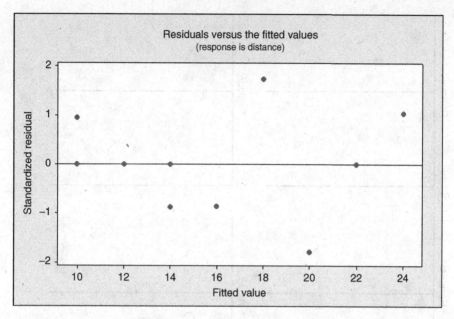

Figure 8.13   Plot of standardized residuals versus predicted values for orienteering example.

course, paucity of data is rarely the issue. Let us see what types of patterns we should watch out for. Figure 8.14 shows four pattern "archetypes" that may be observed in residual-fit plots. Plot (a) shows a "healthy" plot, where no noticeable patterns are observed, and the points display an essentially rectangular shape from left to right. Plot (b) exhibits curvature, which violates the independence assumption. Plot (c) displays a "funnel" pattern, which violates the constant variance assumption. Finally, plot (d) exhibits a pattern that increases from left to right, which violates the zero-mean assumption.

Why does plot (b) violate the independence assumption? Because the errors are assumed to be independent, the residuals (which estimate the errors) should exhibit independent behavior as well. However, if the residuals form a curved pattern, then, for a given residual, we may predict where its neighbors to the left and right will fall, within a certain margin of error. If the residuals were truly independent, then such a prediction would not be possible.

Why does plot (c) violate the constant variance assumption? Note from plot (a) that the variability in the residuals, as shown by the vertical distance, is fairly constant, regardless of the value of x. However, in plot (c), the variability of the residuals is smaller for smaller values of x, and larger for larger values of x. Therefore, the variability is non-constant, which violates the constant variance assumption.

Why does plot (d) violate the zero-mean assumption? The zero-mean assumption states that the mean of the error term is zero, regardless of the value of x. However, plot (d) shows that, for small values of x, the mean of the residuals is less than 0, while, for large values of x, the mean of the residuals is greater than 0. This is a violation of the zero-mean assumption, as well as a violation of the independence assumption.

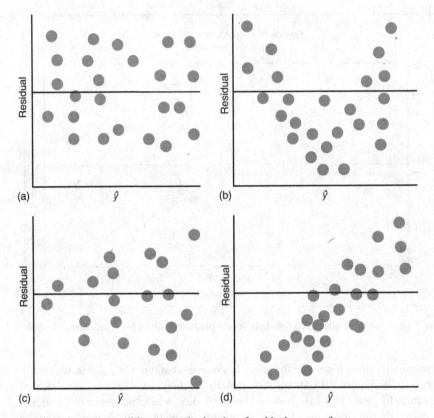

Figure 8.14 Four possible patterns in the plot of residuals versus fits.

When examining plots for patterns, beware of the "Rorschach effect" of seeing patterns in randomness. The null hypothesis when examining these plots is that the assumptions are intact; only systematic and clearly identifiable patterns in the residuals plots offer evidence to the contrary.

Apart from these graphical methods, there are also several diagnostic hypothesis tests that may be carried out to assess the validity of the regression assumptions. As mentioned above, the AD test may be used to indicate fit of the residuals to a normal distribution. For assessing whether the constant variance assumption has been violated, either Bartlett's test or Levene's test may be used. For determining whether the independence assumption has been violated, either the Durban–Watson test or the runs test may be applied. Information about all of these diagnostic tests may be found in Draper and Smith (1998).[4]

Note that these assumptions represent the structure needed to perform inference in regression. Descriptive methods in regression, such as point estimates, and simple reporting of such statistics, as the slope, correlation, standard error of the

---

[4]Draper and Smith, *Applied Regression Analysis*, 3rd edition, Wiley Publishers, Hoboken, New Jersey, 1998.

estimate, and r^2, may still be undertaken even if these assumptions are not met, if the results are cross-validated. What is not allowed by violated assumptions is statistical inference. But we as data miners and big data scientists understand that inference is not our primary *modus operandi*. Rather, data mining seeks confirmation through cross-validation of the results across data partitions. For example, if we are examining the relationship between *outdoor event ticket sales* and *rainfall amounts*, and if the training data set and test data set both report correlation coefficients of about -0.7, and there is graphical evidence to back this up, then we may feel confident in reporting to our client *in a descriptive manner* that the variables are negatively correlated, even if both variables are not normally distributed (which is the assumption for the correlation test). We just cannot say that the correlation coefficient has a statistically significant negative value, because the phrase "statistically significant" belongs to the realm of inference. So, for data miners, the keys are to (i) cross-validate the results across partitions, and (ii) restrict the interpretation of the results to descriptive language, and avoid inferential terminology.

8.10   INFERENCE IN REGRESSION

Inference in regression offers a systematic framework for assessing the significance of linear association between two variables. Of course, analysts need to keep in mind the usual caveats regarding the use of inference in general for big data problems. For very large sample sizes, even tiny effect sizes may be found to be statistically significant, even when their practical significance may not be clear.

We shall examine five inferential methods in this chapter, which are as follows:

1. The *t-test* for the relationship between the response variable and the predictor variable.
2. The correlation coefficient test.
3. The confidence interval for the slope, β_1.
4. The confidence interval for the mean of the response variable, given a particular value of the predictor.
5. The prediction interval for a random value of the response variable, given a particular value of the predictor.

In Chapter 9, we also investigate the *F-test* for the significance of the regression as a whole. However, for simple linear regression, the *t-test* and the *F-test* are equivalent.

How do we go about performing inference in regression? Take a moment to consider the form of the true (population) regression equation.

$$y = \beta_0 + \beta_1 x + \varepsilon$$

This equation asserts that there is a linear relationship between y on the one hand, and some function of x on the other. Now, β_1 is a model parameter, so that it is a constant whose value is unknown. Is there some value that β_1 could take such that, if β_1 took that value, there would no longer exist a linear relationship between x and y?

Consider what would happen if β_1 was zero. Then the true regression equation would be as follows:

$$y = \beta_0 + (0)x + \varepsilon$$

In other words, when $\beta_1 = 0$, the true regression equation becomes:

$$y = \beta_0 + \varepsilon$$

That is, a linear relationship between x and y no longer exists. However, if β_1 takes on any conceivable value other than zero, then a linear relationship of some kind exists between the response and the predictor. Much of our regression inference in this chapter is based on this key idea, that the linear relationship between x and y depends on the value of β_1.

8.11   *t*-TEST FOR THE RELATIONSHIP BETWEEN x AND y

Much of the inference we perform in this section refers to the regression of *rating* on *sugars*. The assumption is that the residuals (or standardized residuals) from the regression are approximately normally distributed. Figure 8.15 shows that this assumption is validated. There are some strays at either end, but the bulk of the data lie within the confidence bounds.

The least squares estimate of the slope, b_1, is a statistic, because its value varies from sample to sample. Like all statistics, it has a sampling distribution with

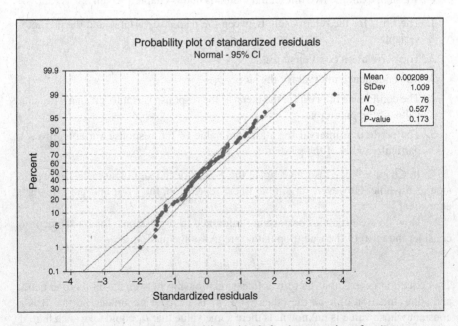

Figure 8.15   Normal probability plot of the residuals for the regression of *rating* on *sugars*.

a particular mean and standard error. The sampling distribution of b_1 has as its mean the (unknown) value of the true slope β_1, and has as its standard error, the following:

$$\sigma_{b_1} = \frac{\sigma}{\sqrt{\sum x^2 - \left(\sum x\right)^2 / n}}$$

Just as one-sample inference about the mean μ is based on the sampling distribution of $\bar{x}$, so regression inference about the slope β_1 is based on this sampling distribution of b_1. The point estimate of σ_{b_1} is s_{b_1}, given by

$$s_{b_1} = \frac{s}{\sqrt{\sum x^2 - \left(\sum x\right)^2 / n}}$$

where s is the standard error of the estimate, reported in the regression results. The s_{b_1} statistic is to be interpreted as a measure of the variability of the slope. Large values of s_{b_1} indicate that the estimate of the slope b_1 is unstable, while small values of s_{b_1} indicate that the estimate of the slope b_1 is precise. The *t*-test is based on the distribution of $t = \frac{(b_1 - \beta_1)}{s_{b_1}}$, which follows a *t*-distribution with $n - 2$ degrees of freedom. When the null hypothesis is true, the test statistic $t = \frac{b_1}{s_{b_1}}$ follows a *t*-distribution with $n - 2$ degrees of freedom. The *t*-test requires that the residuals be normally distributed.

To illustrate, we shall carry out the *t*-test using the results from Table 8.7, the regression of nutritional rating on sugar content. For convenience, Table 8.7 is reproduced here as Table 8.11. Consider the row in Table 8.11, labeled "Sugars."

- Under "Coef" is found the value of b_1, −2.4614.
- Under "SE Coef" is found the value of s_{b_1}, the standard error of the slope. Here, $s_{b_1} = 0.2417$.
- Under "T" is found the value of the *t-statistic*; that is, the test statistic for the *t-test*, $t = \frac{b_1}{s_{b_1}} = \frac{-2.4614}{0.2417} = -10.18$.
- Under "P" is found the *p*-value of the *t-statistic*. As this is a two-tailed test, this *p*-value takes the following form: *p*-value $= P(|t| > |t_{obs}|)$, where t_{obs} represent the observed value of the *t-statistic* from the regression results. Here, *p*-value $= P(|t| > |t_{obs}|) = P(|t| > |-10.18|) \approx 0.000$, although, of course, no continuous *p*-value ever precisely equals zero.

The hypotheses for this hypothesis test are as follows. The null hypothesis asserts that no linear relationship exists between the variables, while the alternative hypothesis states that such a relationship does indeed exist.

H_0: $\beta_1 = 0$ (There is no linear relationship between sugar content and nutritional rating.)

H_a: $\beta_1 \neq 0$ (Yes, there is a linear relationship between sugar content and nutritional rating.)

We shall carry out the hypothesis test using the *p*-value method, where the null hypothesis is rejected when the *p*-value of the test statistic is small. What determines

TABLE 8.11   Results for regression of *nutritional rating* versus *sugar content*

```
The regression equation is
Rating = 59.9 - 2.46 Sugars


Predictor      Coef   SE Coef        T       P
Constant     59.853     1.998    29.96   0.000
Sugars      -2.4614     0.2417  -10.18   0.000


S = 9.16616   R-Sq = 58.4%   R-Sq(adj) = 57.8%


Analysis of Variance

Source            DF       SS       MS        F       P
Regression         1   8711.9   8711.9   103.69   0.000
Residual Error    74   6217.4     84.0
Total             75  14929.3


Unusual Observations

Obs  Sugars  Rating     Fit  SE Fit  Residual  St Resid
  1     6.0   68.40   45.08    1.08     23.32      2.56R
  4     0.0   93.70   59.85    2.00     33.85      3.78R

R denotes an observation with a large standardized residual.
```

how small is small depends on the field of study, the analyst, and domain experts, although many analysts routinely use 0.05 as a threshold. Here, we have p-value $\approx$ 0.00, which is surely smaller than any reasonable threshold of significance. We therefore reject the null hypothesis, and conclude that a linear relationship exists between sugar content and nutritional rating.

8.12   CONFIDENCE INTERVAL FOR THE SLOPE OF THE REGRESSION LINE

Researohers may consider that hypothesis tests are too black-and-white in their conclusions, and prefer to estimate the slope of the regression line β_1, using a confidence interval. The interval used is a *t-interval*, and is based on the above sampling distribution for b_1. The form of the confidence interval is as follows.[5]

---

[5]The notation $100(1 - \alpha)\%$ notation may be confusing. But suppose we let $\alpha = 0.05$, then the confidence level will be $100(1 - \alpha)\% = 100(1 - 0.05)\% = 95\%$.

THE $100(1 - \alpha)\%$ CONFIDENCE INTERVAL FOR THE TRUE SLOPE β_1 OF THE REGRESSION LINE

We can be $100(1 - \alpha)\%$ confident that the true slope β_1 of the regression line lies between:

$$b_1 \pm (t_{\alpha/2,n-2})(s_{b_1})$$

where $t_{\alpha/2,n-2}$ is based on $n - 2$ degrees of freedom.

For example, let us construct a 95% confidence interval for the true slope of the regression line, β_1. We have the point estimate given as $b_1 = -2.4614$. The *t-critical* value for 95% confidence and $n - 2 = 75$ degrees of freedom is $t_{75,95\%} = 2.0$. From Figure 8.16, we have $s_{b_1} = 0.2417$. Thus, our confidence interval is as follows:

$$b_1 - (t_{n-2})(s_{b_1}) = -2.4614-(2.0)(0.2417) = -2.9448, \text{ and}$$

$$b_1 + (t_{n-2})(s_{b_1}) = -2.4614 + (2.0)(0.2417) = -1.9780.$$

We are 95% confident that the true slope of the regression line lies between -2.9448 and -1.9780. That is, for every additional gram of sugar, the nutritional rating will decrease by between 1.9780 and 2.9448 points. As the point $\beta_1 = 0$ is not contained within this interval, we can be sure of the significance of the relationship between the variables, with 95% confidence.

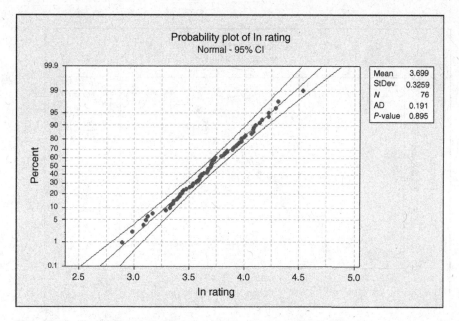

Figure 8.16   Probability plot of *ln rating* shows approximate normality.

8.13 CONFIDENCE INTERVAL FOR THE CORRELATION COEFFICIENT ρ

Let ρ ("rho") represent the population correlation coefficient between the x and y variables for the entire population. Then the confidence interval for ρ is as follows.

THE 100(1 − α)% CONFIDENCE INTERVAL FOR THE POPULATION CORRELATION COEFFICIENT ρ

We can be 100(1 − α)% confident that the population correlation coefficient ρ lies between:

$$r \pm t_{\alpha/2,\,n-2} \cdot \sqrt{\frac{1 - r^2}{n - 2}}$$

where $t_{\alpha/2,n-2}$ is based on $n - 2$ degrees of freedom.

This confidence interval requires that both the x and y variables be normally distributed. Now, *rating* is not normally distributed, but the transformed variable *ln rating* is normally distributed, as shown in Figure 8.16. However, neither *sugars* nor any transformation of *sugars* (see the *ladder of re-expressions* later in this chapter) is normally distributed. *Carbohydrates*, however, shows normality that is just barely acceptable, with an AD p-value of 0.081, as shown in Figure 8.17. Thus, the assumptions are met for calculating the confidence interval for the population correlation coefficient between *ln rating* and *carbohydrates*, but not between *ln rating*

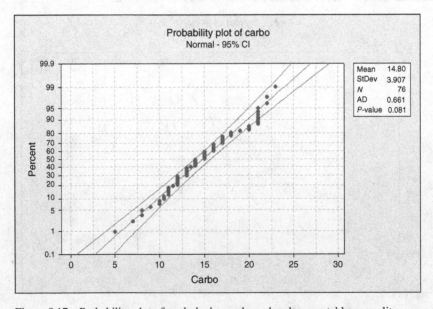

Figure 8.17 Probability plot of *carbohydrates* shows barely acceptable normality.

and *sugars*. Thus, let us proceed to construct a 95% confidence interval for ρ, the population correlation coefficient between *ln rating* and *carbohydrates*.

From Table 8.12, the regression output for the regression of *ln rating* on *carbohydrates*, we have $r^2 = 2.5\% = 0.025$, and the slope b_1 is positive, so that the sample correlation coefficient is $r = +\sqrt{r^2} = +\sqrt{0.025} = 0.1581$. The sample size is $n = 76$, so that $n - 2 = 74$. Finally, $t_{\alpha/2, n-2} = t_{0.025, 74}$ refers to the t-critical value with area 0.025 in the tail of the curve with 74 degrees of freedom. This value equals $1.99.$[6] Thus, our 95% confidence interval for ρ is given by

$$r \pm t_{\alpha/2, n-2} \cdot \sqrt{\frac{1 - r^2}{n - 2}}$$

$$= 0.1581 \pm 1.99 \cdot \sqrt{\frac{1 - 0.025}{74}}$$

$$= (-0.0703, \ 0.3865)$$

[6]Use software such as Excel or Minitab to obtain this value, if desired.

TABLE 8.12 Regression of *ln rating* on carbohydrates

```
The regression equation is
ln rating = 3.50 + 0.0131 Carbo


Predictor      Coef    SE Coef      T      P
Constant     3.5043     0.1465  23.91  0.000
Carbo      0.013137   0.009576   1.37  0.174


S = 0.324030   R-Sq = 2.5%   R-Sq(adj) = 1.2%


Analysis of Variance

Source           DF      SS      MS      F      P
Regression        1  0.1976  0.1976   1.88  0.174
Residual Error   74  7.7697  0.1050
Total            75  7.9673


Unusual Observations

Obs  Carbo  ln rating     Fit  SE Fit  Residual  St Resid
  1    5.0     4.2254  3.5699  0.1010    0.6555     2.13RX
  4    8.0     4.5402  3.6094  0.0750    0.9308     2.95R
 11   12.0     2.8927  3.6619  0.0458   -0.7692    -2.40R
 13   13.0     2.9869  3.6750  0.0410   -0.6882    -2.14R

R denotes an observation with a large standardized residual.
X denotes an observation whose X value gives it large leverage.
```

We are 95% confident that the population correlation coefficient lies between -0.0703 and 0.3865. As zero is included in this interval, then we conclude that *ln rating* and *carbohydrates* are not linearly correlated. We generalize this interpretation method as follows.

USING A CONFIDENCE INTERVAL TO ASSESS CORRELATION

- If both endpoints of the confidence interval are positive, then we conclude with confidence level $100(1 - \alpha)\%$ that x and y are positively correlated.
- If both endpoints of the confidence interval are negative, then we conclude with confidence level $100(1 - \alpha)\%$ that x and y are negatively correlated.
- If one endpoint is negative and one endpoint is positive, then we conclude with confidence level $100(1 - \alpha)\%$ that x and y are not linearly correlated.

8.14 CONFIDENCE INTERVAL FOR THE MEAN VALUE OF y GIVEN x

Point estimates for values of the response variable for a given value of the predictor value may be obtained by an application of the estimated regression equation $\widehat{y} = b_0 + b_1 x$. Unfortunately, these kinds of point estimates do not provide a probability statement regarding their accuracy. The analyst is therefore advised to provide for the end-user two types of intervals, which are as follows:

- A confidence interval for the mean value of y given x.
- A prediction interval for the value of a randomly chosen y, given x.

    Both of these intervals require that the residuals be normally distributed.

THE CONFIDENCE INTERVAL FOR THE MEAN VALUE OF y *FOR A GIVEN VALUE OF x*

$$\widehat{y}_p \pm t_{n-2}(s)\sqrt{\frac{1}{n} + \frac{(x_p - \overline{x})^2}{\sum (x_i - \overline{x})^2}}$$

where

x_p is the particular value of x for which the prediction is being made,

$\widehat{y}_p$ is the point estimate of y for a particular value of x,

t_{n-2} is a multiplier associated with the sample size and confidence level, and s is the standard error of the estimate.

Before we look at an example of this type of confidence interval, we are first introduced to a new type of interval, the prediction interval.

8.15   PREDICTION INTERVAL FOR A RANDOMLY CHOSEN VALUE OF *y* GIVEN *x*

Baseball buffs, which is easier to predict: the mean batting average for an entire team, or the batting average of a randomly chosen player? Perhaps, you may have noticed while perusing the weekly batting average statistics that the team batting averages (which each represent the mean batting average of all the players on a particular team) are more tightly bunched together than are the batting averages of the individual players themselves. This would indicate that an estimate of the team batting average would be more precise than an estimate of a randomly chosen baseball player, given the same confidence level. Thus, in general, it is easier to predict the mean value of a variable than to predict a randomly chosen value of that variable.

For another example of this phenomenon, consider exam scores. We would not think it unusual for a randomly chosen student's grade to exceed 98, but it would be quite remarkable for the class mean to exceed 98. Recall from elementary statistics that the variability associated with the mean of a variable is smaller than the variability associated with an individual observation of that variable. For example, the standard deviation of the univariate random variable x is σ, whereas the standard deviation of the sampling distribution of the sample mean $\bar{x}$ is $\sigma/\sqrt{n}$. Hence, predicting the class average on an exam is an easier task than predicting the grade of a randomly selected student.

In many situations, analysts are more interested in predicting an individual value, rather than the mean of all the values, given x. For example, an analyst may be more interested in predicting the credit score for a particular credit applicant, rather than predicting the mean credit score of all similar applicants. Or, a geneticist may be interested in the expression of a particular gene, rather than the mean expression of all similar genes.

Prediction intervals are used to estimate the value of a randomly chosen value of y, given x. Clearly, this is a more difficult task than estimating the mean, resulting in intervals of greater width (lower precision) than confidence intervals for the mean with the same confidence level.

THE PREDICTION INTERVAL FOR A RANDOMLY CHOSEN VALUE OF
y FOR A GIVEN VALUE OF x

$$\hat{y}_p \pm t_{n-2}(s)\sqrt{1 + \frac{1}{n} + \frac{(x_p - \bar{x})^2}{\sum (x_i - \bar{x})^2}}$$

Note that this formula is precisely the same as the formula for the confidence interval for the mean value of y, given x, except for the presence of the "1+" inside the square root. This reflects the greater variability associated with estimating a single value of y rather than the mean; it also ensures that the prediction interval is always wider than the analogous confidence interval.

Recall the orienteering example, where the time and distance traveled was observed for 10 hikers. Suppose we are interested in estimating the distance traveled for a hiker traveling for $y_p = 5$, $x = 5$ hours. The point estimate is easily obtained using the estimated regression equation, from Table 8.6: $\hat{y} = 6 + 2(x) = 6 + 2(5) = 16$. That is, the estimated distance traveled for a hiker walking for 5 hours is 16 kilometers. Note from Figure 8.3 that this prediction ($x = 5, y = 16$) falls directly on the regression line, as do all such predictions.

However, we must ask the question: How sure are we about the accuracy of our point estimate? That is, are we certain that this hiker will walk precisely 16 kilometers, and not 15.9 or 16.1 kilometers? As usual with point estimates, there is no measure of confidence associated with it, which limits the appicability and usefulness of the point estimate.

We would therefore like to construct a confidence interval. Recall that the regression model assumes that, at each of the x-values, the observed values of y are samples from a normally distributed population with a mean on the regression line ($E(y) = \beta_0 + \beta_1 x$), and constant variance σ^2, as illustrated in Figure 8.9. The point estimate represents the mean of this population, as estimated by the data.

Now, in this case, of course, we have only observed a single observation with the value $x = 5$ hours. Nevertheless, the regression model assumes the existence of an entire normally distributed population of possible hikers with this value for *time*. Of all possible hikers in this distribution, 95% will travel within a certain bounded distance (the margin of error) from the point estimate of 16 kilometers. We may therefore obtain a 95% confidence interval (or whatever confidence level is desired) for the mean distance traveled by all possible hikers who walked for 5 hours. We use the formula provided above, as follows:

$$\hat{y}_p \pm t_{n-2}(s)\sqrt{\frac{1}{n} + \frac{(x_p - \bar{x})^2}{\sum (x_i - \bar{x})^2}}$$

where

- $\hat{y}_p = 16$, the point estimate,
- $t_{n-2,\alpha} = t_{=8,95\%} = 2.306$,
- $s = 1.22474$, from Table 8.6,
- $n = 10$,
- $x_p = 5$, and
- $\bar{x} = 5$.

We have $\sum (x_i - \bar{x})^2 = (2 - 5)^2 + (2 - 5)^2 + (3 - 5)^2 + \cdots + (9 - 5)^2 = 54$, and we therefore calculate the 95% confidence interval as follows:

$$\hat{y}_p \pm t_{n-2}(s)\sqrt{\frac{1}{n} + \frac{(x_p - \bar{x})^2}{\sum (x_i - \bar{x})^2}}$$

$$= 16 \pm (2.306)(1.22474)\sqrt{\frac{1}{10} + \frac{(5 - 5)^2}{54}}$$

$$= 16 \pm 0.893$$
$$= (15.107, 16.893)$$

We are 95% confident that the mean distance traveled by all possible 5-hour hikers lies between 15.107 and 16.893 kilometers.

However, are we sure that this mean of all possible 5-hour hikers is the quantity that we really want to estimate? Wouldn't it be more useful to estimate the distance traveled by a particular randomly selected hiker? Many analysts would agree, and would therefore prefer a prediction interval for a single hiker rather than the above confidence interval for the mean of the hikers.

The calculation of the prediction interval is quite similar to the confidence interval above, but the interpretation is quite different. We have

$$\hat{y}_p \pm t_{n-2}(s) \sqrt{1 + \frac{1}{n} + \frac{(x_p - \bar{x})^2}{\sum (x_i - \bar{x})^2}}$$

$$= 16 \pm (2.306)(1.22474) \sqrt{1 + \frac{1}{10} + \frac{(5-5)^2}{54}}$$

$$= 16 \pm 2.962$$

$$= (13.038, 18.962)$$

In other words, we are 95% confident that the distance traveled by a randomly chosen hiker who had walked for 5 hours lies between 13.038 and 18.962 kilometers. Note that, as mentioned earlier, the prediction interval is wider than the confidence interval, because estimating a single response is more difficult than estimating the mean response. However, also note that the interpretation of the prediction interval is probably more useful for the data miner.

We verify our calculations by providing in Table 8.13 the *Minitab* results for the regression of distance on time, with the confidence interval and prediction interval indicated at the bottom ("Predicted Values for New Observations"). The *Fit* of 16 is the point estimate, the standard error of the fit equals $(s)\sqrt{\frac{1}{n} + \frac{(x_p - \bar{x})^2}{\sum (x_i - \bar{x})^2}}$, the 95% CI indicates the confidence interval for the mean distance of all 5-hour hikers, and the 95% PI indicates the prediction interval for the distance traveled by a randomly chosen 5-hour hiker.

8.16 TRANSFORMATIONS TO ACHIEVE LINEARITY

If the normal probability plot shows no systematic deviations from linearity, and the residuals-fits plot shows no discernible patterns, then we may conclude that there is no graphical evidence for the violation of the regression assumptions, and we may then proceed with the regression analysis. However, *what do we do if these graphs*

TABLE 8.13 **Regression of distance on time, with confidence interval and prediction interval shown at the bottom**

```
The regression equation is
Distance = 6.00 + 2.00 Time


Predictor     Coef   SE Coef      T      P
Constant    6.0000    0.9189   6.53  0.000
Time        2.0000    0.1667  12.00  0.000


S = 1.22474    R-Sq = 94.7%    R-Sq(adj) = 94.1%


Analysis of Variance

Source           DF       SS       MS       F      P
Regression        1   216.00   216.00  144.00  0.000
Residual Error    8    12.00     1.50
Total             9   228.00


Predicted Values for New Observations

New Obs     Fit  SE Fit       95% CI              95% PI
      1  16.000   0.387  (15.107, 16.893)  (13.038, 18.962)
```

indicate violations of the assumptions? For example, suppose our normal probability plot of the residuals looked something such as plot (c) in Figure 8.14, indicating non-constant variance? Then we may apply a transformation to the response variable *y*, such as the *ln* (natural log, log to the base *e*) transformation. We illustrate with an example drawn from the world of board games.

Have you ever played the game of Scrabble®? Scrabble is a game in which the players randomly select letters from a pool of letter tiles, and build crosswords. Each letter tile has a certain number of points associated with it. For instance, the letter "E" is worth 1 point, while the letter "Q" is worth 10 points. The point value of a letter tile is roughly related to its letter frequency, the number of times the letter appears in the pool.

Table 8.14 contains the frequency and point value of each letter in the game. Suppose we were interested in approximating the relationship between frequency and point value, using linear regression. As always when performing simple linear regression, the first thing an analyst should do is to construct a scatter plot of the response versus the predictor, in order to see if the relationship between the two variables is indeed linear. Figure 8.18 presents a scatter plot of the point value versus the frequency. Note that each dot may represent more than one letter.

TABLE 8.14   **Frequency in Scrabble®, and Scrabble® point value of the letters in the alphabet**

Letter	Frequency in Scrabble®	Point Value in Scrabble®
A	9	1
B	2	3
C	2	3
D	4	2
E	12	1
F	2	4
G	3	2
H	2	4
I	9	1
J	1	8
K	1	5
L	4	1
M	2	3
N	6	1
O	8	1
P	2	3
Q	1	10
R	6	1
S	4	1
T	6	1
U	4	1
V	2	4
W	2	4
X	1	8
Y	2	4
Z	1	10

Perusal of the scatter plot indicates clearly that there is a relationship between point value and letter frequency. However, the relationship is not linear, but rather *curvilinear*, in this case quadratic. It would not be appropriate to model the relationship between point value and letter frequency using a linear approximation such as simple linear regression. Such a model would lead to erroneous estimates and incorrect inference. Instead, the analyst may apply a transformation to achieve linearity in the relationship.

Frederick, Mosteller, and Tukey, in their book *Data Analysis and Regression*[4], suggest "the bulging rule" for finding transformations to achieve linearity. To understand the bulging rule for quadratic curves, consider Figure 8.19 (after Mosteller and Tukey[4]).

Compare the curve seen in our scatter plot, Figure 8.18, to the curves shown in Figure 8.19. It is most similar to the curve in the lower left quadrant, the one labeled

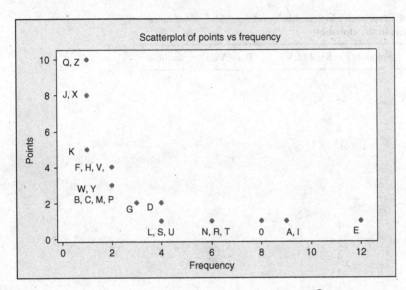

Figure 8.18   Scatter plot of *points* versus *frequency* in Scrabble®: nonlinear!

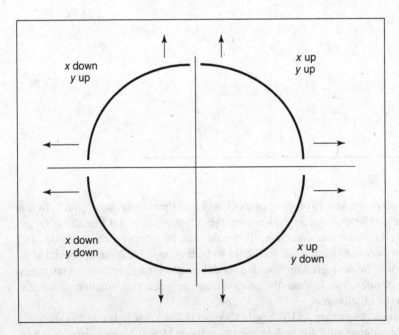

Figure 8.19   The bulging rule: a heuristic for variable transformation to achieve linearity.

"x down, y down." Mosteller and Tukey[7] propose a "ladder of re-expressions," which are essentially a set of power transformations, with one exception, $\ln(t)$.

LADDER OF RE-EXPRESSIONS (MOSTELLER AND TUKEY)

The ladder of re-expressions consists of the following ordered set of transformations for any continuous variable t.

$$t^{-3} \quad t^{-2} \quad t^{-1} \quad t^{-1/2} \quad \ln(t) \quad \sqrt{t} \quad t^1 \quad t^2 \quad t^3$$

For our curve, the heuristic from the bulging rule is "x down, y down." This means that we should transform the variable x, by going down one or more spots from x's present position on the ladder. Similarly, the same transformation is made for y. The present position for all untransformed variables is t^1. Thus, the bulging rule suggests that we apply either the square root transformation or the natural log transformation to both letter tile frequency and point value, in order to achieve a linear relationship between the two variables.

Thus, we apply the square root transformation to both *frequency* and *points*, and consider the scatter plot of *sqrt points* versus *sqrt frequency*, given in Figure 8.20. Unfortunately, the graph indicates that the relationship between sqrt points and sqrt frequency is still not linear, so that it would still be inappropriate to apply linear regression. Evidently, the square root transformation was too mild to effect linearity in this case.

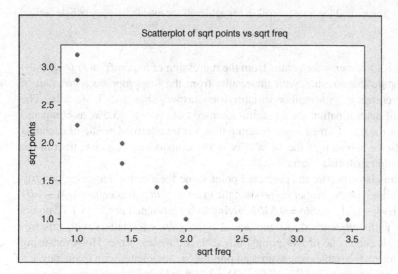

Figure 8.20   After applying square root transformation, still not linear.

---

[7]Mosteller and Tukey, *Data Analysis and Regression*, Addison-Wesley, Reading, MA, 1977.

We therefore move one more notch down the ladder of re-expressions, and apply the natural log transformation to each of frequency and point value, generating the transformed variables ln points and ln frequency. The scatter plot of *ln points* versus *ln frequency* is shown in Figure 8.21. This scatter plot exhibits acceptable linearity, although, as with any real-world scatter plot, the linearity is imperfect. We may therefore proceed with the regression analysis for *ln points* and *ln frequency*.

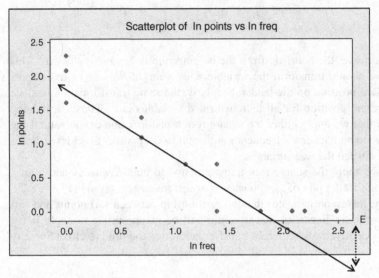

Figure 8.21   The natural log transformation has achieved acceptable linearity (single outlier, *E*, indicated).

Table 8.15 presents the results from the regression of *ln points* on *ln frequency*. Let us compare these results with the results from the inappropriate regression of points on frequency, with neither variable transformed, shown in Table 8.16. The coefficient of determination for the untransformed case is only 45.5%, as compared to 87.6% for the transformed case, meaning that, the transformed predictor accounts for nearly twice as much of the variability in the transformed response than in the case for the untransformed variables.

We can also compare the predicted point value for a given frequency, say frequency = 4 tiles. For the proper regression, the estimated *ln points* equals $1.94 - 1.01$ *(ln freq)* $= 1.94 - 1.01 (1.386) = 0.5401$, giving us an estimated $e^{0.5401} = 1.72$ points for a letter with frequency 4. As the actual point values for letters with this frequency are all either one or two points, this estimate makes sense. However, using the untransformed variables, the estimated point value for a letter with frequency 4 is $5.73 - 0.633$ (frequency) $= 5.73 - 0.633 (4) = 3.198$, which is much larger than any of the actual point values for letter with frequency 4. This exemplifies the danger of applying predictions from inappropriate models.

TABLE 8.15   Regression of *ln points* on *ln frequency*

```
The regression equation is
ln points = 1.94 - 1.01 ln freq


Predictor       Coef   SE Coef       T      P
Constant     1.94031   0.09916   19.57  0.000
ln freq     -1.00537   0.07710  -13.04  0.000


S = 0.293745   R-Sq = 87.6%   R-Sq(adj) = 87.1%


Analysis of Variance

Source          DF      SS      MS       F      P
Regression       1  14.671  14.671  170.03  0.000
Residual Error  24   2.071   0.086
Total           25  16.742


Unusual Observations

Obs  ln freq  ln points      Fit  SE Fit  Residual  St Resid
  5     2.48     0.0000  -0.5579  0.1250    0.5579      2.10R

R denotes an observation with a large standardized residual.
```

TABLE 8.16   Inappropriate regression of *points* on *frequency*

```
The regression equation is
Points = 5.73 - 0.633 Frequency


Predictor      Coef   SE Coef      T      P
Constant     5.7322    0.6743   8.50  0.000
Frequency   -0.6330    0.1413  -4.48  0.000


S = 2.10827   R-Sq = 45.5%   R-Sq(adj) = 43.3%


Analysis of Variance

Source          DF       SS      MS       F      P
Regression       1   89.209  89.209  20.07  0.000
Residual Error  24  106.676   4.445
Total           25  195.885
```

In Figure 8.21 and Table 8.15, there is a single outlier, the letter "E." As the standardized residual is positive, this indicates that the point value for E is higher than expected, given its frequency, which is the highest in the bunch, 12. The residual of 0.5579 is indicated by the dashed vertical line in Figure 8.21. The letter "E" is also the only "influential" observation, with a Cook's distance of 0.5081 (not shown), which just exceeds the 50th percentile of the $F_{1, 25}$ distribution.

8.17 BOX–COX TRANSFORMATIONS

Generalizing from the idea of a ladder of transformations, to admit powers of any continuous value, we may apply a Box–Cox transformation.[8] A Box–Cox transformation is of the form:

$$W = \begin{cases} \left(y^\lambda - 1\right)/\lambda, & \text{for } \lambda \neq 0, \\ \ln y, & \text{for } \lambda = 0 \end{cases}$$

For example, we could have $\lambda = 0.75$, giving us the following transformation, $W = (y^{0.75} - 1)/0.75$. Draper and Smith[9] provide a method of using maximum likelihood to choose the optimal value of λ. This method involves first choosing a set of candidate values for λ, and finding SSE for regressions performed using each value of λ. Then, plotting SSE_λ versus λ, find the lowest point of a curve through the points in the plot. This represents the maximum-likelihood estimate of λ.

THE R ZONE

Read in and prepare Cereals data

```
cereal <- read.csv(file = "C:/ .../cereals.txt",
    stringsAsFactors=TRUE, header=TRUE, sep="\t")
# Save Rating and Sugar as new variables
sugars <- cereal$Sugars; rating <- cereal$Rating
which(is.na(sugars)) # Record 58 is missing
sugars <- na.omit(sugars) # Delete missing value
rating <- rating[-58] # Delete Record 58 from Rating to match
```

[8] Box and Cox, An Analysis of Transformations, *Journal of the Royal Statistical Society, Series B*, Volume **26**, pages 2211—243, 1964. (This formula above is valid only for $y > 0$.)

[9] Draper and Smith, *Applied Regression Analysis*, 3rd edition, Wiley Publishers, Hoboken, New Jersey, 1998.

Run regression analysis

```
lm1<-
     lm(rating~sugars)
# Display summaries
summary(lm1)
anova(lm1)
```

```
> summary(lm1)

call:
lm(formula = rating ~ sugars)

Residuals:
    Min     1Q  Median     3Q     Max
-17.877  -5.612  -1.285   4.689  33.852

Coefficients:
            Estimate Std. Error t value Pr(>|t|)
(Intercept)  59.8530     1.9975   29.96  < 2e-16 ***
sugars       -2.4614     0.2417  -10.18 1.01e-15 ***
---
Signif. codes:  0 '***' 0.001 '**' 0.01 '*' 0.05 '.' 0.1 ' ' 1

Residual standard error: 9.166 on 74 degrees of freedom
Multiple R-squared: 0.5835,  Adjusted R-squared: 0.5779
F-statistic: 103.7 on 1 and 74 DF,  p-value: 1.006e-15

> anova(lm1)
Analysis of Variance Table

Response: rating
          Df Sum Sq Mean Sq F value    Pr(>F)
sugars     1 8711.9  8711.9  103.69 1.006e-15 ***
Residuals 74 6217.4    84.0
---
Signif. codes:  0 '***' 0.001 '**' 0.01 '*' 0.05 '.' 0.1 ' ' 1
```

Plot data with regression line

```
plot(sugars, rating,
     main = "Cereal Rating by Sugar Content",
     xlab = "Sugar Content", ylab = "Rating",
     pch = 16, col = "blue")
abline(lm1, col = "red")
```

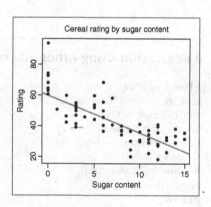

Residuals, r^2, standardized residuals, leverage

```
lm1$residuals # All residuals
lm1$residuals[12] # Residual of Cheerios, Record 12
a1 <- anova(lm1)
# Calculate r^2
r2.1 <- a1$"Sum Sq"[1] / (a1$"Sum Sq"[1] +
     a1$"Sum Sq"[2])
std.res1 <- rstandard(lm1) # Standardized residuals
lev <- hatvalues(lm1) # Leverage
```

```
> lm1$residuals[12]
       12
-6.626598
> r2.1
[1] 0.5835462
```

Orienteering example

```
# Input the data
x <- c(2, ...,9)
y <- c(10, ..., 25)
o.data <- data.frame(cbind(
    "Time" = x,
    "Distance" = y))
lm2 <- lm(Distance ~
    Time, data = o.data)
a2 <- anova(lm2)
# Directly calculate r^2
r2.2 <- a2$"Sum Sq"[1] /
    (a2$"Sum Sq"[1] +
    a2$"Sum Sq"[2])
# MSE
mse <- a2$"Mean Sq"[2]
s <- sqrt(mse) # s
# Std dev of Y
sd(o.data$Distance)
r <- sign(lm2$coefficients[2])* sqrt(r2.2) # r
```

```
> summary(lm2)

Call:
lm(formula = Distance ~ Time, data = o.data)

Residuals:
  Min    1Q Median    3Q   Max
-2.00 -0.75   0.00  0.75  2.00

Coefficients:
            Estimate Std. Error t value Pr(>|t|)
(Intercept)   6.0000     0.9189   6.529 0.000182 ***
Time          2.0000     0.1667  12.000 2.14e-06 ***
---
Signif. codes:  0 '***' 0.001 '**' 0.01 '*' 0.05 '.'
0.1 ' ' 1

Residual standard error: 1.225 on 8 degrees of freedom
Multiple R-squared: 0.9474,  Adjusted R-squared: 0.9408
F-statistic:  144 on 1 and 8 DF,  p-value: 2.144e-06

> a2
Analysis of Variance Table

Response: Distance
          Df Sum Sq Mean Sq F value   Pr(>F)
Time       1    216   216.0     144 2.144e-06 ***
Residuals  8     12     1.5
---
Signif. codes:  0 '***' 0.001 '**' 0.01 '*' 0.05 '.'
0.1 ' ' 1
> sd(o.data$Distance)
[1] 5.033223
> r2.2
[1] 0.9473684
> mse
[1] 1.5
> s
[1] 1.224745
> r
     Time
0.9733285
```

Regression using other hikers

```
# Hard-core hiker
hardcore <- cbind("Time" = 16,
    "Distance" = 39)
o.data <- rbind(o.data, hardcore)
lm3 <- lm(Distance ~ Time,
    data = o.data)
summary(lm3); anova(lm3)
hatvalues(lm3)
# Leverage
rstandard(lm3)
# Standardized residual
cooks.distance(lm3)
# Cook's Distance
# 5-hour, 20-km hiker
o.data[11,] <- cbind("Time" = 5, "Distance" = 20)
lm4 <- lm(Distance ~ Time, data = o.data)
summary(lm4); anova(lm4); rstandard(lm4) ;
hatvalues(lm4) ; cooks.distance(lm4)
# 10-hour, 23-km hiker
o.data[11,] <- cbind("Time" = 10, "Distance" = 23)
lm5 <- lm(Distance ~ Time, data = o.data)
summary(lm5); anova(lm5); hatvalues(lm5);
rstandard(lm5); cooks.distance(lm5)
```

```
> summary(lm3)

Call:
lm(formula = Distance ~ Time, data = o.data)

Residuals:
    Min     1Q Median    3Q    Max
-2.1786 -0.4286 0.1421 0.3044 1.8931

Coefficients:
            Estimate Std. Error t value Pr(>|t|)
(Intercept)  5.67666    0.57317   9.904 1.74e-06
Time         2.07171    0.06951  29.806 4.23e-11

> anova(lm3)
Analysis of Variance Table

Response: Distance
          Df  Sum Sq Mean Sq F value    Pr(>F)
Time       1 1097.31 1097.31  888.37 4.225e-11
Residuals 10   12.35    1.24

> hatvalues(lm3)
         1          2          3          4
0.17470665 0.17470665 0.14080834 0.11473272
         5          6          7          8
0.11473272 0.09647979 0.08604954 0.08344198
         9         10         11         12
0.08865711 0.10169492 0.41199478 0.41199478
> rstandard(lm3)
          1          2          3           4
0.17820117 1.16863808 0.10504338 -0.92138866
          5          6          7           8
0.03491053 -0.97991227 1.78172600 -2.04753860
          9         10         11          12
-0.23593694 0.64361631 0.20652794 0.20652794
> cooks.distance(lm3)
           1            2            3
3.361183e-03 1.445543e-01 9.041609e-04
           4            5            6
5.501342e-02 7.897612e-05 5.126759e-02
           7            8            9
1.494437e-01 1.908354e-01 2.707657e-03
          10           11           12
2.344766e-02 1.494301e-02 1.494301e-02
```

Verify the assumptions

```
par(mfrow=c(2,2)); plot(lm2)
# Normal probability plot: top-right
# Residuals vs Fitted: top-left
# Square root of absolute value
# of standardized residuals:
# bottom-left
# Reset the plot space
par(mfrow=c(1,1))
```

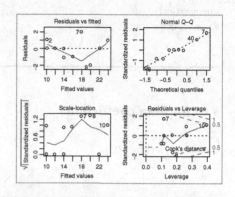

Plot Standardized residuals by fitted values

```
plot(lm2$fitted.values, rstandard(lm2),
    pch = 16, col = "red",
    main = "Standardized
        Residuals by Fitted Values",
    ylab  = "Standardized Residuals",
    xlab = "Fitted Values")
abline(0,0)
```

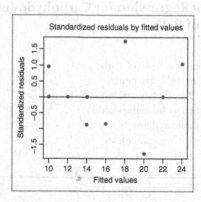

Check residuals are Normally distributed

```
# Normal Q-Q Plot
qqnorm(lm1$residuals, datax = TRUE)
qqline(lm1$residuals, datax = TRUE)
# Anderson-Darling test
# Requires "nortest" package
library("nortest")
ad.test(lm1$residuals)
```

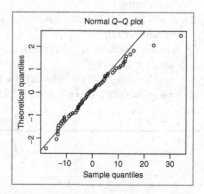

t-test

summary(lm1)
# t-test is in the 'sugars' row

```
Coefficients:
            Estimate Std. Error t value Pr(>|t|)
(Intercept) 59.8530    1.9975    29.96  < 2e-16
sugars      -2.4614    0.2417   -10.18 1.01e-15
```

CI for Beta coefficients

confint(lm1, level = 0.95)

```
> confint(lm1, level = 0.95)
                 2.5 %    97.5 %
(Intercept) 55.872858 63.833176
sugars      -2.943061 -1.979779
```

Regression for Carbohydrates and Natural Log of Rating

carbs <- cereal$"Carbo"[−58]
lrating <- log(rating)
ad.test(lrating); ad.test(carbs)
lm6 <- lm(lrating~carbs)
summary(lm6)
a6 <- anova(lm6); a6

```
Coefficients:
            Estimate Std. Error t value Pr(>|t|)
(Intercept) 3.504260   0.146539  23.913   <2e-16
carbs       0.013137   0.009576   1.372    0.174

Analysis of Variance Table

Response: lrating
          Df Sum Sq Mean Sq F value Pr(>F)
carbs      1 0.1976 0.19761  1.8821 0.1742
Residuals 74 7.7697 0.10500
```

CI for r

alpha <- 0.05
n <- length(lrating)
r2.6 <- a6$"Sum Sq"[1] / (a6$"Sum Sq"[1] +
    a6$"Sum Sq"[2])
r <- sign(lm6$coefficients[2])*sqrt(r2.6)
sr <- sqrt((1-r^2)/(n-2))
lb <- r - qt(p=alpha/2, df = n-2, lower.tail = FALSE)*sr
ub <- r + qt(p=alpha/2, df = n-2, lower.tail = FALSE)*sr
lb;ub

```
> lb;ub
      carbs
-0.07124931
      carbs
 0.3862266
```

Confidence and Prediction Intervals

```
newdata <- data.frame(cbind(Distance = 5, Time = 5))
conf.int <- predict(lm2, newdata,
    interval = "confidence")
pred.int <- predict(lm2, newdata,
    interval = "prediction")
conf.int; pred.int
```

```
> conf.int
    fit      lwr      upr
1   16 15.10689 16.89311
> pred.int
    fit      lwr      upr
1   16 13.03788 18.96212
```

Assess Normality in Scrabble example

```
# Scrabble data
s.freq <- c(9, … 1); s.point <- c(1, … 10)
scrabble <- data.frame("Frequency" = s.freq,
    "Points" = s.point)
plot(scrabble,
    main = "Scrabble Points vs Frequency",
    xlab = "Frequency", ylab = "Points",
    col = "red", pch = 16,
    xlim = c(0, 13), ylim = c(0,10))
sq.scrabble <- sqrt(scrabble)
plot(sq.scrabble,
    main = "Square Root of Scrabble Points
    vs Frequency",
    xlab = "Sqrt Frequency", ylab = "Sqrt
    Points", col = "red", pch = 16)
ln.scrabble <- log(scrabble)
plot(ln.scrabble, main = "Natural Log of
        Scrabble Points vs Frequency",
    xlab = "Ln Frequency", ylab = "Ln
    Points", col = "red", pch = 16)
```

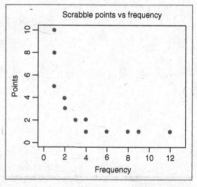

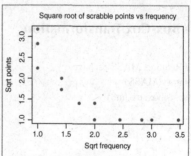

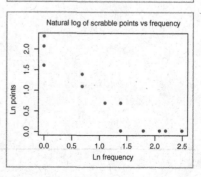

Run regression on Scrabble data, transformed and untransformed

```
lm7 <- lm(Points ~
    Frequency,
    data = ln.scrabble)
summary(lm7)
anova(lm7)
rstandard(lm7)
lm8 <- lm(Points ~
    Frequency,
    data = scrabble)
summary(lm8)
anova(lm8)
```

```
> summary(lm7)

Call:
lm(formula = Points ~ Frequency, data = ln.scrabble)

Residuals:
    Min      1Q  Median      3Q     Max
-0.5466 -0.1448  0.1391  0.1457  0.5579

Coefficients:
            Estimate Std. Error t value Pr(>|t|)
(Intercept)  1.94031    0.09916   19.57 2.94e-16 ***
Frequency   -1.00537    0.07710  -13.04 2.20e-12 ***

> anova(lm7)
Analysis of Variance Table

Response: Points
          Df  Sum Sq Mean Sq F value    Pr(>F)
Frequency  1 14.6711 14.6711  170.03 2.197e-12 ***
Residuals 24  2.0709  0.0863

> summary(lm8)

Call:
lm(formula = Points ~ Frequency, data = scrabble)

Residuals:
    Min      1Q  Median      3Q     Max
-2.2001 -1.4661 -0.4661  0.8068  4.9008

Coefficients:
            Estimate Std. Error t value Pr(>|t|)
(Intercept)  5.7322     0.6743    8.502 1.06e-08 ***
Frequency   -0.6330     0.1413   -4.480 0.000156 ***

> anova(lm8)
Analysis of Variance Table

Response: Points
          Df  Sum Sq Mean Sq F value    Pr(>F)
Frequency  1  89.209  89.209   20.07 0.0001558 ***
Residuals 24 106.676   4.445
```

Box-Cox Transformation

```
# Requires MASS package
library(MASS)
bc <- boxcox(lm8)
```

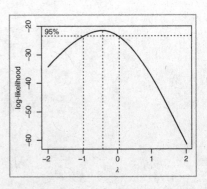

R REFERENCES

Juergen Gross and bug fixes by Uwe Ligges. 2012. nortest: Tests for normality. R package version 1.0-2. http://CRAN.R-project.org/package=nortest.

R Core Team. *R: A Language and Environment for Statistical Computing*. Vienna, Austria: R Foundation for Statistical Computing; 2012. ISBN: 3-900051-07-0, http://www .R-project.org/.

Venables WN, Ripley BD. *Modern Applied Statistics with S*. Fourth ed. New York: Springer; 2002. ISBN: 0-387-95457-0.

EXERCISES

CLARIFYING THE CONCEPTS

1. Indicate whether the following statements are true or false. If false, alter the statement to make it true.
   a. The least-squares line is that line that minimizes the sum of the residuals.
   b. If all the residuals equal zero, then SST = SSR.
   c. If the value of the correlation coefficient is negative, this indicates that the variables are negatively correlated.
   d. The value of the correlation coefficient can be calculated, given the value of r^2 alone.
   e. Outliers are influential observations.
   f. If the residual for an outlier is positive, we may say that the observed y-value is higher than the regression estimated, given the x-value.
   g. An observation may be influential even though it is neither an outlier nor a high leverage point.
   h. The best way of determining whether an observation is influential is to see whether its Cook's distance exceeds 1.0.
   i. If one is interested in using regression analysis in a strictly descriptive manner, with no inference and no model building, then one need not worry quite so much about assumption validation.
   j. In a normality plot, if the distribution is normal, then the bulk of the points should fall on a straight line.
   k. The chi-square distribution is left-skewed.
   l. Small p-values for the Anderson–Darling test statistic indicate that the data are right-skewed.
   m. A funnel pattern in the plot of residuals versus fits indicates a violation of the independence assumption.

2. Describe the difference between the estimated regression line and the true regression line.

3. Calculate the estimated regression equation for the orienteering example, using the data in Table 8.3. Use either the formulas or software of your choice.

4. Where would a data point be situated that has the smallest possible leverage?

5. Calculate the values for leverage, standardized residual, and Cook's distance for the hard-core hiker example in the text.

6. Calculate the values for leverage, standardized residual, and Cook's distance for the 11th hiker who had hiked for 10 hours and traveled 23 kilometers. Show that, while it is neither an outlier nor of high leverage, it is nevertheless influential.

7. Match each of the following regression terms with its definition.

Regression Term	Definition
a. Influential observation	Measures the typical difference between the predicted response value and the actual response value.
b. SSE	Represents the total variability in the values of the response variable alone, without reference to the predictor.
c. r^2	An observation that has a very large standardized residual in absolute value.
d. Residual	Measures the strength of the linear relationship between two quantitative variables, with values ranging from -1 to 1.
e. s	An observation that significantly alters the regression parameters based on its presence or absence in the data set.
f. High leverage point	Measures the level of influence of an observation, by taking into account both the size of the residual and the amount of leverage for that observation.
g. r	Represents an overall measure of the error in prediction resulting from the use of the estimated regression equation.
h. SST	An observation that is extreme in the predictor space, without reference to the response variable.
i. Outlier	Measures the overall improvement in prediction accuracy when using the regression as opposed to ignoring the predictor information.
j. SSR	The vertical distance between the predicted response and the actual response.
k. Cook's distance	The proportion of the variability in the response that is explained by the linear relationship between the predictor and response variables.

8. Explain in your own words the implications of the regression assumptions for the behavior of the response variable y.

9. Explain what statistics from Table 8.11 indicate to us that there may indeed be a linear relationship between x and y in this example, even though the value for r^2 is less than 1%.

10. Which values of the slope parameter indicate that no linear relationship exist between the predictor and response variables? Explain how this works.

11. Explain what information is conveyed by the value of the standard error of the slope estimate.

12. Describe the criterion for rejecting the null hypothesis when using the p-value method for hypothesis testing. Who chooses the value of the level of significance, α? Make up a situation (one p-value and two different values of α) where the very same data could lead to two different conclusions of the hypothesis test. Comment.

13. (a) Explain why an analyst may prefer a confidence interval to a hypothesis test. (b) Describe how a confidence interval may be used to assess significance.

14. Explain the difference between a confidence interval and a prediction interval. Which interval is always wider? Why? Which interval is probably, depending on the situation, more useful to the data miner? Why?

15. Clearly explain the correspondence between an original scatter plot of the data and a plot of the residuals versus fitted values.

16. What recourse do we have if the residual analysis indicates that the regression assumptions have been violated? Describe three different rules, heuristics, or family of functions that will help us.

17. A colleague would like to use linear regression to predict whether or not customers will make a purchase, based on some predictor variable. What would you explain to your colleague?

WORKING WITH THE DATA

For Exercises 18–23, refer to the scatterplot of attendance at football games versus winning percentage of the home team in Figure 8.22.

18. Describe any correlation between the variables. Interpret this correlation.

19. Estimate as best you can the values of the regression coefficients b_0 and b_1.

20. Will the p-value for the hypothesis test for the existence of a linear relationship between the variables be small or large? Explain.

21. Will the confidence interval for the slope parameter include zero or not? Explain.

22. Will the value of s be closer to 10, 100, 1000, or 10,000? Why?

23. Is there an observation that may look as though it is an outlier? Explain.

For Exercises 24 and 25, use the scatter plot in Figure 8.23 to answer the questions.

24. Is it appropriate to perform linear regression? Why or why not?

25. What type of transformation or transformations is called for? Use the bulging rule.

For Exercises 26–30, use the output from the regression of *z mail messages* on *z day calls* (from the *Churn* data set) in Table 8.17 to answer the questions.

26. Is there evidence of a linear relationship between *z vmail messages* (z-scores of the number of voice mail messages) and *z day calls* (z-scores of the number of day calls made)? Explain.

27. Use the data in the ANOVA table to find or calculate the following quantities:

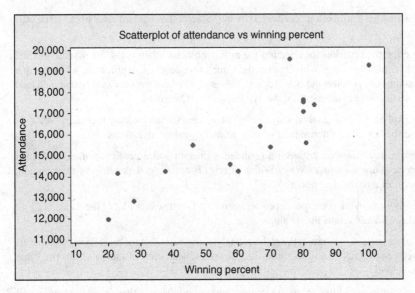

Figure 8.22   Scatter plot of attendance versus winning percentage.

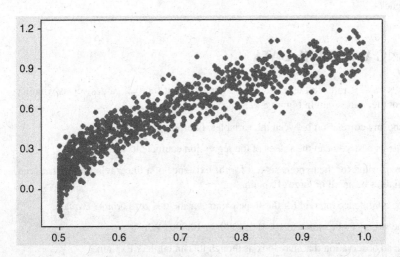

Figure 8.23   Scatter plot.

   a. SSE, SSR, and SST.

   b. Coefficient of determination, using the quantities in (a). Compare with the number reported by Minitab.

   c. Correlation coefficient r.

   d. Use SSE and the residual error degrees of freedom to calculate s, the standard error of the estimate. Interpret this value.

28. Assuming normality, construct and interpret a 95% confidence interval for the population correlation coefficient.

TABLE 8.17 Regression of *z vmail messages* on *z day calls*

```
The regression equation is
zvmail messages = 0.0000 - 0.0095 z day calls


Predictor          Coef   SECoef      T      P
Constant        0.00000  0.01732   0.00  1.000
z day calls    -0.00955  0.01733  -0.55  0.582


S = 1.00010   R-Sq = 0.0%   R-Sq(adj) = 0.0%


Analysis of Variance

Source          DF        SS      MS      F      P
Regression       1     0.304   0.304   0.30  0.582
Residual Error 3331  3331.693   1.000
Total          3332  3331.997
```

TABLE 8.18 Regression of an unspecified *y* on an unspecified *x*

```
The regression equation is
Y = 0.783 + 0.0559 X


Predictor       Coef  SE Coef       T      P
Constant     0.78262  0.03791   20.64  0.000
Y            0.05594  0.03056    1.83  0.067


S = 0.983986   R-Sq = 0.3%   R-Sq(adj) = 0.2%
```

29. Discuss the usefulness of the regression of *z mail messages* on *z day calls*.

30. As it has been standardized, the response *z vmail messages* has a standard deviation of 1.0. What would be the typical error in predicting *z vmail messages* if we simply used the sample mean response and no information about day calls? Now, from the printout, what is the typical error in predicting *z vmail messages*, given *z day calls*? Comment.

For Exercises 31–38, use the output from the regression of an unspecified *y* on an unspecified *x* in Table 8.18 to answer the questions.

31. Carefully state the regression equation, using words and numbers.

32. Interpret the value of the *y*-intercept b_0.

33. Interpret the value of the slope b_1.

34. Interpret the value of the standard error of the estimate, *s*.

35. Suppose we let $\alpha = 0.10$. Perform the hypothesis test to determine if a linear relationship exists between x and y. Assume the assumptions are met.

36. Calculate the correlation coefficient r.

37. Assume normality. Construct a 90% confidence interval for the population correlation coefficient. Interpret the result.

38. Compare your results for the hypothesis test and the confidence interval. Comment.

HANDS-ON ANALYSIS

Open the *Baseball* data set, a collection of batting statistics for 331 baseball players who played in the American League in 2002, available on the book website, www.DataMiningConsultant.com. Suppose we are interested in whether there is a relationship between batting average and the number of home runs a player hits. Some fans might argue, for example, that those who hit lots of home runs also tend to make a lot of strike outs, so that their batting average is lower. Let us check it out, using a regression of the number of home runs against the player's batting average (hits divided by at bats). Because baseball batting averages tend to be highly variable for low numbers of at bats, we restrict our data set to those players who had at least 100 at bats for the 2002 season. This leaves us with 209 players. Use this data set for Exercises 39–61.

39. Construct a scatter plot of *home runs* versus *batting average*.

40. Informally, is there evidence of a relationship between the variables?

41. What would you say about the variability of the number of home runs, for those with higher batting averages?

42. Refer to the previous exercise. Which regression assumption might this presage difficulty for?

43. Perform a regression of *home runs* on *batting average*. Obtain a normal probability plot of the standardized residuals from this regression. Does the normal probability plot indicate acceptable normality, or is there skewness? If skewed, what type of skewness?

44. Construct a plot of the residuals versus the fitted values (fitted values refers to the y's). What pattern do you see? What does this indicate regarding the regression assumptions?

45. Take the natural log of *home runs*, and perform a regression of *ln home runs* on *batting average*. Obtain a normal probability plot of the standardized residuals from this regression. Does the normal probability plot indicate acceptable normality?

46. Construct a plot of the residuals versus the fitted values. Do you see strong evidence that the constant variance assumption has been violated? (Remember to avoid the Rorschach effect.) Therefore conclude that the assumptions are validated.

47. Write the population regression equation for our model. Interpret the meaning of β_0 and β_1.

48. State the regression equation (from the regression results) in words and numbers.

49. Interpret the value of the y-intercept b_0.

50. Interpret the value of the slope b_1.

51. Estimate the number of *home runs* (not *ln home runs*) for a player with a *batting average* of 0.300.

52. What is the size of the typical error in predicting the number of *home runs*, based on the player's *batting average*?

53. What percentage of the variability in the *ln home runs* does *batting average* account for?

54. Perform the hypothesis test for determining whether a linear relationship exists between the variables.

55. Construct and interpret a 95% confidence interval for the unknown true slope of the regression line.

56. Calculate the correlation coefficient. Construct a 95% confidence interval for the population correlation coefficient. Interpret the result.

57. Construct and interpret a 95% confidence interval for the mean number of home runs for all players who had a batting average of 0.300.

58. Construct and interpret a 95% prediction interval for a randomly chosen player with a 0.300 batting average. Is this prediction interval useful?

59. List the outliers. What do all these outliers have in common? For Orlando Palmeiro, explain why he is an outlier.

60. List the high leverage points. Why is Greg Vaughn a high leverage point? Why is Bernie Williams a high leverage point?

61. List the influential observations, according to Cook's distance and the F criterion.

Next, subset the *Baseball* data set so that we are working with batters who have at least 100 at bats. Use this data set for Exercises 62–71.

62. We are interested in investigating whether there is a linear relationship between the number of times a player has been caught stealing and the number of stolen bases the player has. Construct a scatter plot, with "caught" as the response. Is there evidence of a linear relationship?

63. On the basis of the scatter plot, is a transformation to linearity called for? Why or why not?

64. Perform the regression of the number of times a player has been caught stealing versus the number of stolen bases the player has.

65. Find and interpret the statistic that tells you how well the data fit the model.

66. What is the typical error in predicting the number of times a player is caught stealing, given his number of stolen bases?

67. Interpret the *y*-intercept. Does this make any sense? Why or why not?

68. Inferentially, is there a significant relationship between the two variables? What tells you this?

69. Calculate and interpret the correlation coefficient.

70. Clearly interpret the meaning of the slope coefficient.

71. Suppose someone said that knowing the number of stolen bases a player has explains most of the variability in the number of times the player gets caught stealing. What would you say?

For Exercises 72–85, use the *Cereals* data set.

72. We are interested in predicting nutrition rating based on sodium content. Construct the appropriate scatter plot. Note that there is an outlier. Identify this outlier. Explain why this cereal is an outlier.

73. Perform the appropriate regression.

74. Omit the outlier. Perform the same regression. Compare the values of the slope and y-intercept for the two regressions.

75. Using the scatter plot, explain why the y-intercept changed more than the slope when the outlier was omitted.

76. Obtain the Cook's distance value for the outlier. Is it influential?

77. Put the outlier back in the data set for the rest of the analysis. On the basis of the scatter plot, is there evidence of a linear relationship between the variables? Discuss. Characterize their relationship, if any.

78. Construct the graphics for evaluating the regression assumptions. Are they validated?

79. What is the typical error in predicting rating based on sodium content?

80. Interpret the y-intercept. Does this make any sense? Why or why not?

81. Inferentially, is there a significant relationship between the two variables? What tells you this?

82. Calculate and interpret the correlation coefficient.

83. Clearly interpret the meaning of the slope coefficient.

84. Construct and interpret a 95% confidence interval for the true nutrition rating for all cereals with a sodium content of 100.

85. Construct and interpret a 95% confidence interval for the nutrition rating for a randomly chosen cereal with sodium content of 100.

Open the *California* data set (Source: US Census Bureau, www.census.gov, and available on the book website, www.DataMiningConsultant.com), which consists of some census information for 858 towns and cities in California. This example will give us a chance to investigate handling outliers and high leverage points as well as transformations of both the predictor and the response. We are interested in approximating the relationship, if any, between the percentage of townspeople who are senior citizens and the total population of the town. That is, do the towns with higher proportions of senior citizens (over 64 years of age) tend to be larger towns or smaller towns? Use the *California* data set for Exercises 86–92.

86. Construct a scatter plot of *percentage over 64* versus *popn*. Is this graph very helpful in describing the relationship between the variables?

87. Identify the four cities that appear larger than the bulk of the data in the scatter plot.

88. Apply the *ln* transformation to the predictor, giving us the transformed predictor variable *ln popn*. Note that the application of this transformation is due solely to the skewness inherent in the variable itself (shown by the scatter plot), and is not the result of any

regression diagnostics. Perform the regression of *percentage over 64* on *ln popn*, and obtain the regression diagnostics.

89. Describe the pattern in the normal probability plot of the residuals. What does this mean?

90. Describe the pattern in the plot of the residuals versus the fitted values. What does this mean? Are the assumptions validated?

91. Perform the regression of *ln pct* (*ln* of *percentage over 64*) on *ln popn*, and obtain the regression diagnostics. Explain how taking the *ln* of *percentage over 64* has tamed the residuals versus fitted values plot.

92. Identify the set of outliers in the lower right of the residuals versus fitted values plot. Have we uncovered a natural grouping? Explain how this group would end up in this place in the graph.

## CHAPTER 9

MULTIPLE REGRESSION AND MODEL BUILDING

9.1 AN EXAMPLE OF MULTIPLE REGRESSION

Chapter 8 examined regression modeling for the simple linear regression case of a single predictor and a single response. Clearly, however, data miners and predictive analysts are usually interested in the relationship between the target variable and a set of (two or more) predictor variables. Most data mining applications enjoy a wealth of data, with some data sets including hundreds or thousands of variables, many of which may have a linear relationship with the target (response) variable. *Multiple regression modeling* provides an elegant method of describing such relationships. Compared to simple linear regression, multiple regression models provide improved precision for estimation and prediction, analogous to the improved precision of regression estimates over univariate estimates. A *multiple regression model* uses a linear surface, such as a plane or hyperplane, to approximate the relationship between a continuous response (target) variable, and a set of predictor variables. While the predictor variables are typically continuous, categorical predictor variables may be included as well, through the use of indicator (dummy) variables.

In simple linear regression, we used a straight line (of dimension 1) to approximate the relationship between the response and one predictor. Now, suppose we would like to approximate the relationship between a response and two continuous predictors. In this case, we would need a plane to approximate such a relationship, because a plane is linear in two dimensions.

For example, returning to the *cereals* data set, suppose we are interested in trying to estimate the value of the target variable, *nutritional rating*, but this time using two variables, *sugars* and *fiber*, rather than sugars alone as in Chapter 8.[1] The three-dimensional scatter plot of the data is shown in Figure 9.1. High fiber levels seem to be associated with high nutritional rating, while high sugar levels seem to be associated with low nutritional rating.

---

[1] *Quaker Oats*, whose *sugars* value is missing, is not included in this analysis.

Data Mining and Predictive Analytics, First Edition. Daniel T. Larose and Chantal D. Larose.
© 2015 John Wiley & Sons, Inc. Published 2015 by John Wiley & Sons, Inc.

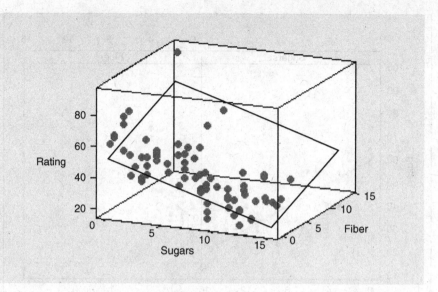

Figure 9.1 A plane approximates the linear relationship between one response and two continuous predictors.

These relationships are approximated by the plane that is shown in Figure 9.1, in a manner analogous to the straight-line approximation for simple linear regression. The plane tilts downward to the right (for high sugar levels) and toward the front (for low fiber levels).

We may also examine the relationship between *rating* and its predictors, *sugars*, and *fiber*, one at a time, as shown in Figure 9.2. This more clearly illustrates the negative relationship between *rating* and *sugars* and the positive relationship between *rating* and *fiber*. The multiple regression should reflect these relationships.

Let us examine the results (Table 9.1) of a multiple regression of nutritional *rating* on both predictor variables. The regression equation for multiple regression with two predictor variables takes the form:

$$\hat{y} = b_0 + b_1 x_1 + b_2 x_2$$

For a multiple regression with m variables, the regression equation takes the form:

$$\hat{y} = b_0 + b_1 x_1 + b_2 x_2 + \cdots + b_m x_m$$

From Table 9.1, we have

- x_1 = sugars,
- x_2 = fiber,
- $b_0 = 52.174$,
- $b_1 = -2.2436$,
- $b_2 = 2.8665$.

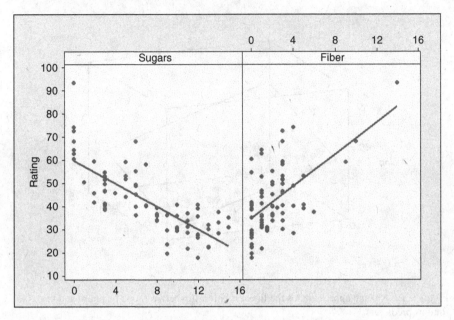

Figure 9.2 Individual variable scatter plots of *rating* versus *sugars* and *fiber*.

Thus, the regression equation for this example is

$$\hat{y} = 52.174 - 2.2436(\text{sugars}) + 2.8665(\text{fiber})$$

That is, the estimated nutritional rating equals 52.174 minus 2.2436 times the grams of sugar plus 2.8665 times the grams of fiber. Note that the coefficient for sugars is negative, indicating a negative relationship between sugars and rating, while the coefficient for fiber is positive, indicating a positive relationship. These results concur with the characteristics of the graphs in Figures 9.1 and 9.2. The straight lines shown in Figure 9.2 represent the value of the slope coefficients for each variable, -2.2436 for sugars and 2.8665 for fiber.

The interpretations of the slope coefficients b_1 and b_2 are slightly different than for the simple linear regression case. For example, to interpret $b_1 = -2.2436$, we say that "the estimated decrease in nutritional rating for a unit increase in sugar content is 2.2436 points, *when fiber content is held constant.*" Similarly, we interpret $b_2 = 2.8665$ as follows: "the estimated increase in nutritional rating for a unit increase in fiber content is 2.8408 points, *when sugar content is held constant.*" In general, for a multiple regression with m predictor variables, we would interpret coefficient b_i as follows: "the estimated change in the response variable for a unit increase in variable x_i is b_i, when all other predictor variables are held constant."

Recall that errors in prediction are measured by the *residual*, $y - \hat{y}$. In simple linear regression, this residual represented the vertical distance between the actual data point and the regression line. In multiple regression, the residual is represented by the vertical distance between the data point and the regression plane or hyperplane.

TABLE 9.1   Results from regression of nutritional *rating* on *sugars* and *fiber*

```
The regression equation is
Rating = 52.2 - 2.24 Sugars + 2.87 Fiber


Predictor      Coef  SE Coef       T       P
Constant     52.174    1.556   33.54   0.000
Sugars      -2.2436   0.1632  -13.75   0.000
Fiber        2.8665   0.2979    9.62   0.000


S = 6.12733   R-Sq = 81.6%   R-Sq(adj) = 81.1%


Analysis of Variance

Source            DF       SS      MS       F       P
Regression         2  12188.6  6094.3  162.32   0.000
Residual Error    73   2740.7    37.5
Total             75  14929.3


Source  DF  Seq SS
Sugars   1  8711.9
Fiber    1  3476.6


Predicted Values for New Observations

New Obs     Fit  SE Fit         95% CI              95% PI
      1  55.289   1.117  (53.062, 57.516)  (42.876, 67.702)


Values of Predictors for New Observations

New Obs  Sugars  Fiber
      1    5.00   5.00
```

For example, *Spoon Size Shredded Wheat* has $x_1 = 0$ grams of sugar, $x_2 = 3$ grams of fiber, and a nutritional rating of 72.8018. The estimated regression equation would predict, however, that the nutritional rating for this cereal would be

$$\hat{y} = 52.174 - 2.2436 \,(0) + 2.8665 \,(3) = 60.7735$$

Therefore, we have a residual for Spoon Size Shredded Wheat of $y - \hat{y} =$ 72.8018−60.7735 = 12.0283, illustrated in Figure 9.3. As the residual is positive, the data value lies above the regression plane.

Each observation has its own residual, which, taken together, leads to the calculation of the sum of squares error (SSE) as an overall measure of the estimation errors. Just as for the simple linear regression case, we may again calculate the three sums of squares, as follows:

- SSE $= \sum (y - \hat{y})^2$

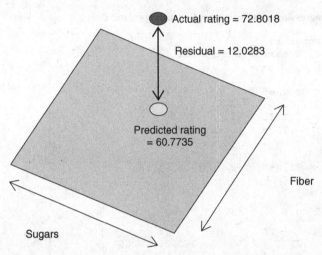

Figure 9.3 Estimation error is the vertical distance between the actual data point and the regression plane or hyperplane.

- $\text{SSR} = \sum (\hat{y} - \bar{y})^2$
- $\text{SST} = \sum (y - \bar{y})^2$

We may again present the regression statistics succinctly in a convenient analysis of variance (ANOVA) table, shown here in Table 9.2, where m represents the number of predictor variables. Finally, for multiple regression, we have the so-called multiple coefficient of determination,[2] which is simply

$$R^2 = \frac{\text{SSR}}{\text{SST}}$$

For multiple regression, R^2 is interpreted as the proportion of the variability in the target variable that is accounted for by its linear relationship with the set of predictor variables.

TABLE 9.2 The ANOVA table for multiple regression

Source of Variation	Sum of Squares	Degrees of Freedom	Mean Square	F
Regression	SSR	m	$\text{MSR} = \dfrac{\text{SSR}}{m}$	$F = \dfrac{\text{MSR}}{\text{MSE}}$
Error (or residual)	SSE	$n - m - 1$	$\text{MSE} = \dfrac{\text{SSE}}{n - m - 1}$	
Total	$\text{SST} = \text{SSR} + \text{SSE}$	$n - 1$		

[2]By convention, R^2 for multiple regression is indicated using a capital R.

From Table 9.1, we can see that the value of R^2 is 81.6%, which means that 81.6% of the variability in nutritional rating is accounted for by the linear relationship (the plane) between rating and the *set of predictors*, sugar content and fiber content. Now, would we expect R^2 to be greater than the value for the coefficient of determination we got from the simple linear regression of nutritional rating on sugars alone? The answer is yes. Whenever a new predictor variable is added to the model, the value of R^2 always goes up. If the new variable is useful, the value of R^2 will increase significantly; if the new variable is not useful, the value of R^2 may barely increase at all.

Table 8.7, here reproduced as Table 9.3, provides us with the coefficient of determination for the simple linear regression case, $r^2 = 58.4\%$. Thus, by adding the new predictor, fiber content, to the model, we can account for an additional $81.6 - 58.4\% = 23.2\%$ of the variability in the nutritional rating. This seems like a significant increase, but we shall defer this determination until later.

The typical error in estimation is provided by the standard error of the estimate, s. The value of s here is about 6.13 rating points. Therefore, our estimation of the nutritional rating of the cereals, based on sugar and fiber content, is typically in error by about 6.13 points. Now, would we expect this error to be greater or less than the value for s obtained by the simple linear regression of nutritional rating on sugars alone? In general, the answer depends on the usefulness of the new predictor. If the new variable is useful, then s will decrease, but if the new variable is not useful for

TABLE 9.3   Results for regression of *nutritional rating* versus *sugar content* alone

```
The regression equation is
Rating = 59.9 - 2.46 Sugars


Predictor     Coef    SE Coef      T       P
Constant    59.853     1.998    29.96   0.000
Sugars      -2.4614    0.2417  -10.18   0.000


S = 9.16616    R-Sq = 58.4%    R-Sq(adj) = 57.8%


Analysis of Variance

Source            DF       SS       MS       F        P
Regression         1    8711.9   8711.9   103.69   0.000
Residual Error    74    6217.4     84.0
Total             75   14929.3


Unusual Observations

Obs  Sugars  Rating    Fit   SE Fit  Residual  St Resid
  1     6.0   68.40   45.08   1.08     23.32      2.56R
  4     0.0   93.70   59.85   2.00     33.85      3.78R

R denotes an observation with a large standardized residual.
```

predicting the target variable, then s may in fact increase. This type of behavior makes s, the standard error of the estimate, a more attractive indicator than R^2 of whether a new variable should be added to the model, because R^2 always increases when a new variable is added, regardless of its usefulness.

Table 9.3 shows that the value for s from the regression of rating on sugars alone was about 9.17. Thus, the addition of fiber content as a predictor decreased the typical error in estimating nutritional content from 9.17 points to 6.13 points, a decrease of 3.04 points. Thus, adding a second predictor to our regression analysis decreased the prediction error (or, equivalently, increased the precision) by about three points.

Next, before we turn to inference in multiple regression, we first examine the details of the population multiple regression equation.

9.2 THE POPULATION MULTIPLE REGRESSION EQUATION

We have seen that, for simple linear regression, the regression model takes the form:

$$y = \beta_0 + \beta_1 x + \varepsilon, \tag{9.1}$$

with β_0 and β_1 as the unknown values of the true regression coefficients, and ε the error term, with its associated assumption discussed in Chapter 8. The multiple regression model is a straightforward extension of the simple linear regression model in equation (9.1), as follows.

THE POPULATION MULTIPLE REGRESSION EQUATION

$$y = \beta_0 + \beta_1 x_1 + \beta_2 x_2 + \cdots + \beta_m x_m + \varepsilon$$

where $\beta_0, \beta_1, \ldots, \beta_m$ represent the model parameters. These are constants, whose true value remains unknown, and which are estimated from the data using the least-squares estimates. ε represents the error term.

The Assumptions About The Error Term

1. **Zero-Mean Assumption.** The error term ε is a random variable, with mean or expected value equal to zero. In other words, $E(\varepsilon) = 0$.

2. **Constant Variance Assumption.** The variance of ε, denoted by σ^2, is constant, regardless of the value of $x_1, x_2, \ldots, x_m$.

3. **Independence Assumption.** The values of ε are independent.

4. **Normality Assumption.** The error term ε is a normally distributed random variable.

In other words, the values of the error term ε_i are independent normal random variables, with mean 0 and variance σ^2.

Just as we did for the simple linear regression case, we can derive four implications for the behavior of the response variable, y, as follows.

IMPLICATIONS OF THE ASSUMPTIONS FOR THE BEHAVIOR OF THE RESPONSE VARIABLE y

1. On the basis of Zero-Mean Assumption, we have:

$$
\begin{aligned}
E(y) &= E(\beta_0 + \beta_1 x_1 + \beta_2 x_2 + \cdots + \beta_m x_m + \varepsilon) \\
&= E(\beta_0) + E(\beta_1 x_1) + \cdots + E(\beta_m x_m) + E(\varepsilon) \\
&= \beta_0 + \beta_1 x_1 + \beta_2 x_2 + \cdots + \beta_m x_m
\end{aligned}
$$

   That is, for each set of values for $x_1, x_2, \ldots, x_m$, the mean of the y's lies on the regression line.

2. On the basis of Constant Variance Assumption, we have the variance of y, $\mathrm{Var}(y)$, given as $\mathrm{Var}(y) = \mathrm{Var}(\beta_0 + \beta_1 x_1 + \beta_2 x_2 + \cdots + \beta_m x_m + \varepsilon) = \mathrm{Var}(\varepsilon) = \sigma^2$.

   That is, regardless of which values are taken by the predictors $x_1, x_2, \ldots, x_m$, the variance of the y's is always constant.

3. On the basis of Independence Assumption, it follows that, for any particular set of values for $x_1, x_2, \ldots, x_m$, the values of y are independent as well.

4. On the basis of normality assumption, it follows that y is also a normally distributed random variable.

   In other words, the values of the response variable y_i are independent normal random variables, with mean $\beta_0 + \beta_1 x_1 + \beta_2 x_2 + \cdots + \beta_m x_m$ and variance σ^2.

9.3 INFERENCE IN MULTIPLE REGRESSION

We shall examine five inferential methods in this chapter, which are as follows:

1. The *t-test* for the relationship between the response variable y and a particular predictor variable x_i, in the presence of the other predictor variables, $x_{(i)}$, where $x_{(i)} = x_1, x_2, \ldots, x_{i-1}, x_{i+1}, \ldots, x_m$ denotes the set of all predictors, not including x_i.

2. The *F-test* for the significance of the regression as a whole.

3. The confidence interval, β_i, for the slope of the ith predictor variable.

4. The confidence interval for the mean of the response variable y, given a set of particular values for the predictor variables $x_1, x_2, \ldots, x_m$.

5. The prediction interval for a random value of the response variable y, given a set of particular values for the predictor variables $x_1, x_2, \ldots, x_m$.

9.3.1 The *t*-Test for the Relationship Between y and x_i

The hypotheses for this test are given by

$$
\begin{aligned}
H_0&: \beta_i = 0 \\
H_a&: \beta_i \neq 0
\end{aligned}
$$

The models implied by these hypotheses are given by

$$\text{Under } H_0: \beta_0 + \beta_1 x_1 + \cdots + 0 + \cdots + \beta_m x_m + \varepsilon$$
$$\text{Under } H_a: \beta_0 + \beta_1 x_1 + \cdots + \beta_i x_i + \cdots + \beta_m x_m + \varepsilon$$

Note that the only difference between the two models is the presence or absence of the ith term. All other terms are the same in both models. Therefore, interpretations of the results for this t-test must include some reference to the other predictor variables being held constant.

Under the null hypothesis, the test statistic $t = \frac{b_i}{s_{b_i}}$ follows a t distribution with $n - m - 1$ degrees of freedom, where s_{b_i} refers to the standard error of the slope for the ith predictor variable. We proceed to perform the t-test for each of the predictor variables in turn, using the results displayed in Table 9.1.

9.3.2 *t*-Test for Relationship Between Nutritional *Rating* and *Sugars*

- H_0: $\beta_1 = 0$ Model: $y = \beta_0 + \beta_2(\text{fiber}) + \varepsilon$
- H_a: $\beta_1 \neq 0$ Model: $y = \beta_0 + \beta_1(\text{sugars}) + \beta_2(\text{fiber}) + \varepsilon$
- In Table 9.1, under "Coef" in the "Sugars" row is found the value, $b_1 = -2.2436$.
- Under "SE Coef" in the "Sugars" row is found the value of the standard error of the slope for sugar content, $s_{b_1} = 0.1632$.
- Under "T" is found the value of the t-statistic; that is, the test statistic for the t-test, $t = \frac{b_1}{s_{b_1}} = \frac{-2.2436}{0.1632} = -13.75$.
- Under "P" is found the p-value of the t-statistic. As this is a two-tailed test, this p-value takes the following form: p-value $= P(|t| > |t_{\text{obs}}|)$, where t_{obs} represents the observed value of the t-statistic from the regression results. Here, p-value $= P(|t| > |t_{\text{obs}}|) = P(|t| > |-13.75|) \approx 0.000$, although, of course, no continuous p-value ever precisely equals zero.

The p-value method is used, whereby the null hypothesis is rejected when the p-value of the test statistic is small. Here, we have p-value $\cong 0$, which is smaller than any reasonable threshold of significance. Our conclusion is therefore to reject the null hypothesis. The interpretation of this conclusion is that there is evidence for a linear relationship between nutritional rating and sugar content, *in the presence of fiber content.*

9.3.3 *t*-Test for Relationship Between Nutritional *Rating* and *Fiber* Content

- H_0: $\beta_2 = 0$ Model: $y = \beta_0 + \beta_1(\text{sugars}) + \varepsilon$
- H_a: $\beta_2 \neq 0$ Model: $y = \beta_0 + \beta_1(\text{sugars}) + \beta_2(\text{fiber}) + \varepsilon$

- In Table 9.1, under "Coef" in the "Fibers" row is found the value, $b_2 = -2.8665$.
- Under "SE Coef" in the "Fiber" row is found the value of the standard error of the slope for fiber, $s_{b_1} = 0.2979$.
- Under "T" is found the test statistic for the *t-test*, $t = \dfrac{b_2}{s_{b_2}} = \dfrac{2.8665}{0.2979} = 9.62$.
- Under "P" is found the *p*-value of the *t*-statistic. Again, *p*-value ≈ 0.000.

Thus, our conclusion is again to reject the null hypothesis. We interpret this to mean that there is evidence for a linear relationship between nutritional rating and fiber content, in the presence of sugar content.

9.3.4   The *F*-Test for the Significance of the Overall Regression Model

Next, we introduce the *F-test* for the significance of the overall regression model. Figure 9.4 illustrates the difference between the *t-test* and the *F-test*. One may apply a separate *t-test* for each predictor x_1, x_2, or x_3, examining whether a linear relationship exists between the target variable y and that particular predictor. However, the *F-test* considers the linear relationship between the target variable y and the *set of predictors* (e.g., $\{x_1, x_2, x_3\}$), taken as a whole.

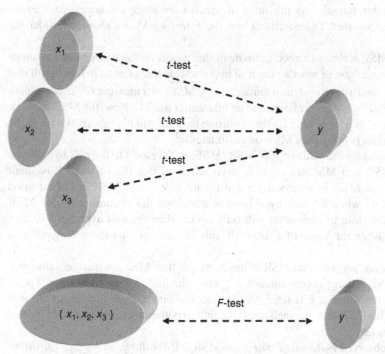

Figure 9.4   The *F*-test considers the relationship between the target and the set of predictors, taken as a whole.

The hypotheses for the *F-test* are given by

$$H_0: \beta_1 = \beta_2 = \ldots = \beta_m = 0$$

$$H_a: \text{At least one of the } \beta_i \text{ does not equal } 0$$

The null hypothesis asserts that there is no linear relationship between the target variable y, and the set of predictors, $x_1, x_2, \ldots, x_m$. Thus, the null hypothesis states that the coefficient β_i for each predictor x_i exactly equals zero, leaving the null model to be

$$\text{Model under } H_0: y = \beta_0 + \varepsilon$$

The alternative hypothesis does not assert that all the regression coefficients differ from zero. For the alternative hypothesis to be true, it is sufficient for a single, unspecified, regression coefficient to differ from zero. Hence, the alternative hypothesis for the *F-test* does not specify a particular model, because it would be true if any, some, or all of the coefficients differed from zero.

As shown in Table 9.2, the F-statistic consists of a ratio of two means squares, the mean square regression (MSR) and the mean square error (MSE). A *mean square* represents a sum of squares divided by the degrees of freedom associated with that sum of squares statistic. As the sums of squares are always nonnegative, then so are the mean squares. To understand how the *F-test* works, we should consider the following.

The MSE is always a good estimate of the overall variance (see model assumption 2) σ^2, regardless of whether the null hypothesis is true or not. (In fact, recall that we use the standard error of the estimate, $s = \sqrt{MSE}$, as a measure of the usefulness of the regression, without reference to an inferential model.) Now, the MSR is also a good estimate of σ^2, but only on the condition that the null hypothesis is true. If the null hypothesis is false, then MSR overestimates σ^2.

So, consider the value of $F = MSR/MSE$, with respect to the null hypothesis. Suppose MSR and MSE are close to each other, so that the value of F is small (near 1.0). As MSE is always a good estimate of σ^2, and MSR is only a good estimate of σ^2 when the null hypothesis is true, then the circumstance that MSR and MSE are close to each other will only occur when the null hypothesis is true. Therefore, when the value of F is small, this is evidence that the null hypothesis is true.

However, suppose that MSR is much greater than MSE, so that the value of F is large. MSR is large (overestimates σ^2) when the null hypothesis is false. Therefore, when the value of F is large, this is evidence that the null hypothesis is false. Therefore, for the F-test, we shall reject the null hypothesis when the value of the test statistic F is large.

The observed F-statistic $F = F_{obs} = MSR/MSE$ follows an $F_{m,n-m-1}$ distribution. As all F values are nonnegative, the *F-test* is a right-tailed test. Thus, we will reject the null hypothesis when the p-value is small, where the p-value is the area in the tail to the right of the observed F statistic. That is, p-value $= P(F_{m,n-m-1} > F_{obs})$, and we reject the null hypothesis when $P(F_{m,n-m-1} > F_{obs})$ is small.

9.3.5 *F*-Test for Relationship Between Nutritional Rating and {Sugar and Fiber}, Taken Together

- H_0: $\beta_1 = \beta_2 = 0$ Model : $y = \beta_0 + \varepsilon$.
- H_a: At least one of β_1 and β_2 does not equal 0
- The model implied by H_a is not specified, and may be any one of the following:
    - $y = \beta_0 + \beta_1(\text{sugars}) + \varepsilon$
    - $y = \beta_0 + \beta_2(\text{fiber}) + \varepsilon$
    - $y = \beta_0 + \beta_1(\text{sugars}) + \beta_2(\text{fiber}) + \varepsilon$.
- In Table 9.1, under "MS" in the "Regression" row of the "Analysis of Variance" table, is found the value of MSR, 6094.3.
- Under "MS" in the "Residual Error" row of the "Analysis of Variance" table is found the value of MSE, 37.5.
- Under "*F*" in the "Regression" row of the "Analysis of Variance" table is found the value of the test statistic $F = \dfrac{\text{MSR}}{\text{MSE}} = \dfrac{6094.3}{37.5} = 162.32$.
- The degrees of freedom for the F-statistic are given in the column marked "DF," so that we have $m = 2$, and $n - m - 1 = 73$.
- Under "*P*" in the "Regression" row of the "Analysis of Variance" table is found the p-value of the F-statistic. Here, the p-value is $P(F_{m,n-m-1} > F_{obs}) = P(F_{2,75} > 162.32) \approx 0.000$, although again no continuous p-value ever precisely equals zero.

This p-value of approximately zero is less than any reasonable threshold of significance. Our conclusion is therefore to reject the null hypothesis. The interpretation of this conclusion is the following. There is evidence for a linear relationship between nutritional rating on the one hand, and the set of predictors, sugar content and fiber content, on the other. More succinctly, we may simply say that the overall regression model is significant.

9.3.6 The Confidence Interval for a Particular Coefficient, β_i

Just as for simple linear regression, we may construct a $100(1 - \alpha)\%$ confidence interval for a particular coefficient, β_i, as follows. We can be $100(1 - \alpha)\%$ confident that the true value of a particular coefficient β_i lies within the following interval:

$$b_i \pm (t_{n-m-1})(s_{b_i})$$

where t_{n-m-1} is based on $n - m - 1$ degrees of freedom, and s_{b_i} represents the standard error of the ith coefficient estimate.

For example, let us construct a 95% confidence interval for the true value of the coefficient β_1 for x_1, sugar content. From Table 9.1, the point estimate is given as

$b_1 = -2.2436$. The t-critical value for 95% confidence and $n - m - 1 = 73$ degrees of freedom is $t_{n-m-1} = 1.99$. The standard error of the coefficient estimate is $s_{b_1} = 0.1632$. Thus, our confidence interval is as follows:

$$b_1 \pm t_{n-m-1}(s_{b_1})$$
$$= -2.2436 \pm 1.99(0.1632)$$
$$= (-2.57, -1.92)$$

We are 95% confident that the value for the coefficient β_1 lies between -2.57 and -1.92. In other words, for every additional gram of sugar, the nutritional rating will decrease by between 1.92 and 2.57 points, *when fiber content is held constant*. For example, suppose a nutrition researcher claimed that nutritional rating would fall two points for every additional gram of sugar, when fiber is held constant. As -2.0 lies within the 95% confidence interval, then we would not reject this hypothesis, with 95% confidence.

9.3.7 The Confidence Interval for the Mean Value of *y*, Given $x_1, x_2, \ldots, x_m$

We may find confidence intervals for the mean value of the target variable y, given a particular set of values for the predictors $x_1, x_2, \ldots, x_m$. The formula is a multivariate extension of the analogous formula from Chapter 8, requires matrix multiplication, and may be found in Draper and Smith.[3] For example, the bottom of Table 9.1 ("Values of Predictors for New Observations") shows that we are interested in finding the confidence interval for the mean of the distribution of all nutritional ratings, when the cereal contains 5.00 grams of sugar and 5.00 grams of fiber.

The resulting 95% confidence interval is given, under "Predicted Values for New Observations," as "95% CI" = (53.062, 57.516). That is, we can be 95% confident that the mean nutritional rating of all cereals with 5.00 grams of sugar and 5.00 grams of fiber lies between 55.062 points and 57.516 points.

9.3.8 The Prediction Interval for a Randomly Chosen Value of *y*, Given $x_1, x_2, \ldots, x_m$

Similarly, we may find a prediction interval for a randomly selected value of the target variable, given a particular set of values for the predictors $x_1, x_2, \ldots, x_m$. We refer to Table 9.1 for our example of interest: 5.00 grams of sugar and 5.00 grams of fiber. Under "95% PI," we find the prediction interval to be (42.876, 67.702). In other words, we can be 95% confident that the nutritional rating for a randomly chosen cereal with 5.00 grams of sugar and 5.00 grams of fiber lies between 42.876 points and 67.702 points. Again, note that the prediction interval is wider than the confidence interval, as expected.

---

[3]Draper and Smith, *Applied Regression Analysis*, John Wiley and Sons, New York, 1998.

9.4   REGRESSION WITH CATEGORICAL PREDICTORS, USING INDICATOR VARIABLES

Thus far, our predictors have all been continuous. However, categorical predictor variables may also be used as inputs to regression models, through the use of indicator variables (dummy variables). For example, in the *cereals* data set, consider the variable *shelf*, which indicates which supermarket shelf the particular cereal was located on. Of the 76 cereals, 19 were located on shelf 1, 21 were located on shelf 2, and 36 were located on shelf 3.

A dot plot of the nutritional rating for the cereals on each shelf is provided in Figure 9.5, with the shelf means indicated by the triangles. Now, if we were to use only the categorical variables (such as shelf and manufacturer) as predictors, then we could perform *ANOVA*.[4] However, we are interested in using the categorical variable *shelf* along with continuous variables such as sugar content and fiber content. Therefore, we shall use multiple regression analysis with indicator variables.

On the basis of comparison dot plot in Figure 9.5, does there seem to be evidence that shelf location affects nutritional rating? It would seem that shelf 2 cereals, with their average nutritional rating of 34.97, seem to lag somewhat behind the cereals on shelf 1 and shelf 3, with their respective average nutritional ratings of 45.90 and 45.22. However, it is not clear whether this difference is significant. Further, this dot plot does not take into account the other variables, such as sugar content and fiber

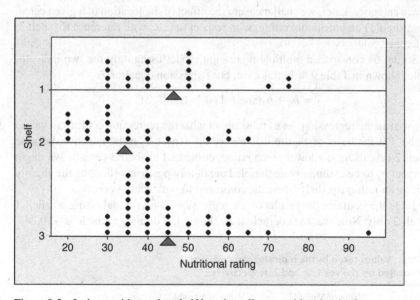

Figure 9.5   Is there evidence that shelf location affects nutritional rating?

[4]See Chapter 5, or Larose, *Discovering Statistics*, Second Edition, W.H. Freeman and Company, Publishers, New York, 2013.

content; it is unclear how any "shelf effect" would manifest itself, in the presence of these other variables.

For use in regression, a categorical variable with k categories must be transformed into a set of $k-1$ indicator variables. An *indicator variable*, also known as a *flag variable*, or a *dummy variable*, is a binary 0/1 variable, which takes the value 1 if the observation belongs to the given category, and takes the value 0 otherwise.

For the present example, we define the following indicator variables:

$$\text{Shelf } 1 = \begin{cases} 1 & \text{if cereal located on shelf 1} \\ 0 & \text{otherwise} \end{cases}$$

$$\text{Shelf } 2 = \begin{cases} 1 & \text{if cereal located on shelf 2} \\ 0 & \text{otherwise} \end{cases}$$

Table 9.4 indicates the values taken by these indicator variables, for cereals located on shelves 1, 2, and 3, respectively. Note that it is not necessary to define a third indicator variable "shelf 3," because cereals located on shelf 3 will have zero values for each of the shelf 1 and shelf 2 indicator variables, and this is sufficient to distinguish them. In fact, one should not define this third dummy variable because the resulting covariate matrix will be singular, and the regression will not work. The category that is not assigned an indicator variable is denoted the *reference category*. Here, shelf 3 is the reference category. Later, we shall measure the effect of the location of a given cereal (e.g., on shelf 1) on nutritional rating, with respect to (i.e., with reference to) shelf 3, the reference category.

So, let us construct a multiple regression model using only the two indicator variables shown in Table 9.4. In this case, our regression equation is

$$\hat{y} = b_0 + b_3(\text{shelf } 1) + b_4(\text{shelf } 2)$$

Before we run the regression, let us think about what the regression coefficient values might be. On the basis of Figure 9.5, we would expect b_4 to be negative, because the shelf 2 cereals have a lower mean rating, compared to shelf 3 cereals. We might also expect b_3 to be essentially negligible but slightly positive, reflecting the slightly greater mean rating for shelf 1 cereals, compared to with shelf 3 cereals.

Table 9.5 contains the results of the regression of nutritional rating on shelf 1 and shelf 2 only. Note that the coefficient for the shelf 2 dummy variable is -10.247,

TABLE 9.4 Values taken by the indicator variables, for cereals located on shelves 1, 2, and 3, respectively

Cereal Location	Value of Variable *Shelf 1*	Value of Variable *Shelf 2*
Shelf 1	1	0
Shelf 2	0	1
Shelf 3	0	0

TABLE 9.5   Results of regression of nutritional rating on shelf location only

```
The regression equation is
Rating = 45.2 + 0.68 Shelf 1 - 10.2 Shelf 2


Predictor      Coef   SE Coef        T       P
Constant     45.220     2.246    20.14   0.000
Shelf 1       0.679     3.821     0.18   0.859
Shelf 2     -10.247     3.700    -2.77   0.007


S = 13.4744    R-Sq = 11.2%    R-Sq(adj) = 8.8%


Analysis of Variance

Source          DF        SS      MS      F       P
Regression       2    1675.4   837.7   4.61   0.013
Residual Error  73   13253.9   181.6
Total           75   14929.3
```

which is equal (after rounding) to the difference in the mean nutritional ratings between cereals on shelves 2 and 3: $34.97 - 45.22$. Similarly, the coefficient for the shelf 1 dummy variable is 0.679, which equals (after rounding) the difference in the mean ratings between cereals on shelves 1 and 3: $45.90 - 45.22$. These values fulfill our expectations, based on Figure 9.5.

Next, let us proceed to perform multiple regression, for the linear relationship between nutritional rating and sugar content, fiber content, and shelf location, using the two dummy variables from Table 9.4. The regression equation is given as

$$\hat{y} = b_0 + b_1(\text{sugars}) + b_2(\text{fiber}) + b_3(\text{shelf } 1) + b_4(\text{shelf } 2)$$

For cereals located on shelf 1, regression equation looks like the following:

$$\hat{y} = b_0 + b_1(\text{sugars}) + b_2(\text{fiber}) + b_3(1) + b_4(0)$$
$$= (b_0 + b_3) + b_1(\text{sugars}) + b_2(\text{fiber})$$

For cereals located on shelf 2, the regression equation is

$$\hat{y} = b_0 + b_1(\text{sugars}) + b_2(\text{fiber}) + b_3(0) + b_4(1)$$
$$= (b_0 + b_4) + b_1(\text{sugars}) + b_2(\text{fiber})$$

Finally, for cereals located on shelf 3, the regression equation is as follows:

$$\hat{y} = b_0 + b_1(\text{sugars}) + b_2(\text{fiber}) + b_3(0) + b_4(0)$$
$$= b_0 + b_1(\text{sugars}) + b_2(\text{fiber})$$

Note the relationship of the model equations to each other. The three models represent parallel planes, as illustrated in Figure 9.6. (Note that the planes do not, of course, directly represent the shelves themselves, but the fit of the regression model to the

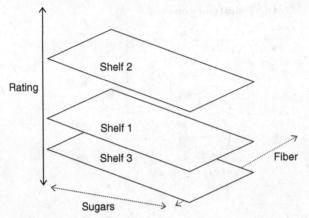

Figure 9.6 The use of indicator variables in multiple regression leads to a set of parallel planes (or hyperplanes).

nutritional rating, for the cereals on the various shelves.) The results for the regression of nutritional rating on sugar content, fiber content, and shelf location are provided in Table 9.6. The general form of the regression equation looks like:

$$\hat{y} = 50.525 - 2.3183(\text{sugars}) + 3.1314(\text{fiber}) + 2.101(\text{shelf } 1) + 3.915(\text{shelf } 2)$$

Thus, the regression equation for cereals located on the various shelves is given as the following:

$$\text{Shelf } 1 : \hat{y} = 50.525 - 2.3183(\text{sugars}) + 3.1314(\text{fiber}) + 2.101(1)$$
$$= 52.626 - 2.3183(\text{sugars}) + 3.1314(\text{fiber})$$

$$\text{Shelf } 2 : \hat{y} = 50.525 - 2.3183(\text{sugars}) + 3.1314(\text{fiber}) + 3.915(1)$$
$$= 54.44 - 2.3183(\text{sugars}) + 3.1314(\text{fiber})$$

$$\text{Shelf } 3 : \hat{y} = 50.525 - 2.3183(\text{sugars}) + 3.1314(\text{fiber})$$

Note that these estimated regression equations are exactly the same, except for the y-intercept. This means that cereals on each shelf are modeled as following the exact same slope in the sugars dimension (-2.3183) and the exact same slope in the fiber dimension (3.1314), which gives us the three parallel planes shown in Figure 9.6. The only difference lies in the value of the y-intercept for the cereals on the three shelves.

The reference category in this case is shelf 3. What is the vertical distance between the shelf 3 plane and, for example, the shelf 1 plane? Note from the derivations above that the estimated regression equation for the cereals on shelf 1 is given as

$$\hat{y} = (b_0 + b_3) + b_1(\text{sugars}) + b_2(\text{fiber})$$

TABLE 9.6   Results for the regression of nutritional rating on sugar content, fiber content, and shelf location

```
The regression equation is
Rating = 50.5 - 2.32 Sugars + 3.13 Fiber + 2.10 Shelf 1 + 3.92 Shelf 2


Predictor       Coef   SE Coef       T       P
Constant      50.525     1.851   27.29   0.000
Sugars       -2.3183     0.1729  -13.41   0.000
Fiber         3.1314     0.3186    9.83   0.000
Shelf 1       2.101      1.795     1.17   0.246
Shelf 2       3.915      1.865     2.10   0.039


S = 6.02092    R-Sq = 82.8%    R-Sq(adj) = 81.8%


Analysis of Variance

Source             DF        SS      MS       F       P
Regression          4   12355.4  3088.9   85.21   0.000
Residual Error     71    2573.9    36.3
Total              75   14929.3


Source     DF   Seq SS
Sugars      1   8711.9
Fiber       1   3476.6
Shelf 1     1      7.0
Shelf 2     1    159.9
```

so that the y-intercept is $b_0 + b_3$. We also have the estimated regression equation for the cereals on shelf 3 to be

$$\hat{y} = b_0 + b_1(\text{sugars}) + b_2(\text{fiber})$$

Thus, the difference between the y-intercepts is $(b_0 + b_3) - b_0 = b_3$. We can verify this by noting that $(b_0 + b_3) - b_0 = 52.626 - 50.525 = 2.101$, which is the value of b_3 reported in Table 9.6. The vertical distance between the planes representing shelves 1 and 3 is everywhere 2.101 rating points, as shown in Figure 9.7.

Of particular importance is the interpretation of this value for b_3. Now, the y-intercept represents the estimated nutritional rating when both sugars and fiber equal zero. However, as the planes are parallel, the difference in the y-intercepts among the shelves remains constant throughout the range of sugar and fiber values. Thus, the vertical distance between the parallel planes, as measured by the coefficient for the indicator variable, represents the estimated effect of the particular indicator variable on the target variable, with respect to the reference category.

In this example, $b_3 = 2.101$ represents the estimated difference in nutritional rating for cereals located on shelf 1, compared to the cereals on shelf 3. As b_3 is positive, this indicates that the estimated nutritional rating for shelf 1 cereals is higher. We thus interpret b_3 as follows: The estimated increase in nutritional rating for cereals located on shelf 1, as compared to cereals located on shelf 3, is $b_3 = 2.101$ points, when sugars and fiber content are held constant. It is similar for the cereals on shelf 2.

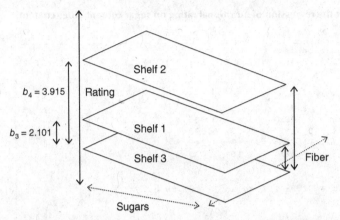

Figure 9.7 The indicator variables coefficients estimate the difference in the response value, compared to the reference category.

We have the estimated regression equation for these cereals as:

$$\hat{y} = (b_0 + b_4) + b_1(\text{sugars}) + b_2(\text{fiber})$$

so that the difference between the y-intercepts for the planes representing shelves 2 and 3 is $(b_0 + b_4) - b_0 = b_4$. We thus have $(b_0 + b_4) - b_0 = 54.44 - 50.525 = 3.915$, which is the value for b_4 reported in Table 9.6. That is, the vertical distance between the planes representing shelves 2 and 3 is everywhere 3.915 rating points, as shown in Figure 9.7. Therefore, the estimated increase in nutritional rating for cereals located on shelf 2, as compared to cereals located on shelf 3, is $b_4 = 3.915$ points, when sugars and fiber content are held constant.

We may then infer the estimated difference in nutritional rating between shelves 2 and 1. This is given as $(b_0 + b_4) - (b_0 + b_3) = b_4 - b_3 = 3.915 - 2.101 = 1.814$ points. The estimated increase in nutritional rating for cereals located on shelf 2, as compared to cereals located on shelf 1, is 1.814 points, when sugars and fiber content are held constant.

Now, recall Figure 9.5, where we encountered evidence that shelf 2 cereals had the lowest nutritional rating, with an average of about 35, compared to average ratings of 46 and 45 for the cereals on the other shelves. How can this knowledge be reconciled with the dummy variable results, which seem to show the highest rating for shelf 2?

The answer is that our indicator variable results are accounting for the presence of the other variables, sugar content and fiber content. It is true that the cereals on shelf 2 have the lowest nutritional rating; however, as shown in Table 9.7, these cereals also have the highest sugar content (average 9.62 grams, compared to 5.11 and 6.53 grams for shelves 1 and 3) and the lowest fiber content (average 0.91 grams, compared to 1.63 and 3.14 grams for shelves 1 and 3). Because of the negative correlation between sugar and rating, and the positive correlation between fiber and rating, the shelf 2 cereals already have a relatively low estimated nutritional rating based on these two predictors alone.

TABLE 9.7   Using sugars and fiber only, the regression model underestimates the nutritional rating of shelf 2 cereals

Shelf	Mean Sugars	Mean Fiber	Mean Rating	Mean Estimated Rating[a]	Mean Error
1	5.11	1.63	45.90	45.40	−0.50
2	9.62	0.91	34.97	33.19	−1.78
3	6.53	3.14	45.22	46.53	+1.31

[a]Rating estimated using sugars and fiber only, and not shelf location.[5]

Table 9.7 shows the mean fitted values (estimated ratings) for the cereals on the various shelves, when sugar and fiber content are included in the model, but shelf location is not included as a predictor. Note that, on average, the nutritional rating of the shelf 2 cereals is underestimated by 1.78 points. However, the nutritional rating of the shelf 3 cereals is overestimated by 1.31 points. Therefore, when shelf location is introduced into the model, these over-/underestimates can be compensated for. Note from Table 9.7 that the *relative* estimation error difference between shelves 2 and 3 is $1.31 + 1.78 = 3.09$. Thus, we would expect that if shelf location were going to compensate for the underestimate of shelf 2 cereals relative to shelf 3 cereals, it would add a factor in the neighborhood of 3.09 ratings points. Recall from Figure 9.6 that $b_4 = 3.915$, which is in the ballpark of 3.09. Also, note that the relative estimation error difference between shelves 1 and 3 is $1.31 + 0.50 = 1.81$. We would expect that the shelf indicator variable compensating for this estimation error would be not far from 1.81, and, indeed, we have the relevant coefficient as $b_3 = 2.101$.

This example illustrates the flavor of working with multiple regression, in that the relationship of the *set* of predictors with the target variable is not necessarily dictated by the individual bivariate relationships the target variable has with each of the predictors. For example, Figure 9.5 would have led us to believe that shelf 2 cereals would have had an indicator variable adjusting the estimated nutritional rating downward. But the actual multiple regression model, which included sugars, fiber, and shelf location, had an indicator variable adjusting the estimated nutritional rating upward, because of the effects of the other predictors.

Consider again Table 9.6. Note that the p-values for the sugars coefficient and the fiber coefficient are both quite small (near zero), so that we may include both of these predictors in the model. However, the p-value for the shelf 1 coefficient is somewhat large (0.246), indicating that the relationship between this variable is not statistically significant. In other words, in the presence of sugars and fiber content, the difference in nutritional rating between shelf 1 cereals and shelf 3 cereals is not significant. We may therefore consider eliminating the shelf 1 indicator variable from the model. Suppose we go ahead and eliminate the shelf 1 indicator variable from the model, because of its large p-value, but retain the shelf 2 indicator variable. The results from the regression of nutritional rating on sugar content, fiber content, and shelf 2 (compared to shelf 3) location are given in Table 9.8.

---

[5]To do this, store the predicted rating values from the regression of *rating* on *sugars* and *fiber*, and then find the mean predicted rating value, by shelf location.

TABLE 9.8 Results from regression of nutritional rating on sugars, fiber, and the shelf 2 indicator variable

```
The regression equation is
Rating = 51.7 + 3.03 Fiber - 2.35 Sugars + 3.12 Shelf 2


Predictor      Coef    SE Coef       T      P
Constant     51.709      1.554   33.27  0.000
Fiber        3.0283      0.3070    9.86  0.000
Sugars      -2.3496      0.1713  -13.72  0.000
Shelf 2       3.125       1.742    1.79  0.077



S = 6.03639    R-Sq = 82.4%    R-Sq(adj) = 81.7%


Analysis of Variance

Source            DF        SS       MS       F      P
Regression         3   12305.8   4101.9  112.57  0.000
Residual Error    72    2623.5     36.4
Total             75   14929.3
```

Note from Table 9.8 that the p-value for the shelf 2 dummy variable has increased from 0.039 to 0.077, indicating that it may no longer belong in the model. The effect of adding or removing predictors on the other predictors is not always predictable. This is why variable selection procedures exist to perform this task methodically, such as *stepwise regression*. We cover these methods later in this chapter.

9.5 ADJUSTING R^2: PENALIZING MODELS FOR INCLUDING PREDICTORS THAT ARE NOT USEFUL

Recall that adding a variable to the model will increase the value of the coefficient of determination R^2, regardless of the usefulness of the variable. This is not a particularly attractive feature of this measure, because it may lead us to prefer models with marginally larger values for R^2, simply because they have more variables, and not because the extra variables are useful. Therefore, in the interests of parsimony, we should find some way to penalize the R^2 measure for models that include predictors that are not useful. Fortunately, such a penalized form for R^2 does exist, and is known as the *adjusted R^2*. The formula for adjusted R^2 is as follows:

$$R^2_{adj} = 1 - (1 - R^2)\frac{n-1}{n-m-1}$$

If R^2_{adj} is much less than R^2, then this is an indication that at least one variable in the model may be extraneous, and the analyst should consider omitting that variable from the model.

As an example of calculating R^2_{adj}, consider Figure 9.10, where we have

- $R^2 = 0.828$
- $R^2_{adj} = 0.818$
- $n = 76$
- $m = 4$

Then, $R^2_{adj} = 1 - (1 - R^2)\frac{n-1}{n-m-1} = 1 - (1 - 0.828)\frac{75}{71} = 0.818$.

Let us now compare Tables 9.6 and 9.8, where the regression model was run with and without the shelf 1 indicator variable, respectively. The shelf 1 indicator variable was found to be not useful for estimating nutritional rating. How did this affect R^2 and R^2_{adj}?

- With shelf 1: Penalty $= R^2 - R^2_{adj} = 0.828 - 0.818 = 0.010$
- Without shelf 1: Penalty $= R^2 - R^2_{adj} = 0.824 - 0.817 = 0.007$

So, the regression model, not including shelf 1, suffers a smaller penalty than does the model that includes it, which would make sense if shelf 1 is not a helpful predictor. However, in this instance, the penalty is not very large in either case. Just remember: When one is building models in multiple regression, one should use R^2_{adj} and s, rather than the raw R^2.

9.6   SEQUENTIAL SUMS OF SQUARES

Some analysts use the information provided in the sequential sums of squares, provided by many software packages, to help them get a better idea of which variables to include in the model. The sequential sums of squares represent a partitioning of SSR, the regression sum of squares. Recall that SSR represents the proportion of the variability in the target variable that is explained by the linear relationship of the target variable with the set of predictor variables. The *sequential sums of squares* partition the SSR into the unique portions of the SSR that are explained by the particular predictors, given any earlier predictors. Thus, the values of the sequential sums of squares depend on the *order* that the variables are entered into the model. For example, the sequential sums of squares for the model:

$$y = \beta_0 + \beta_1(\text{sugars}) + \beta_2(\text{fiber}) + \beta_3(\text{Shelf 1}) + \beta_4(\text{Shelf 2}) + \varepsilon$$

are found in Table 9.6, and repeated here in Table 9.9. The sequential sum of squares shown for *sugars* is 8711.9, and represents the variability in *nutritional rating* that is explained by the linear relationship between *rating* and *sugar* content. In other words, this first sequential sum of squares is exactly the value for SSR from the simple linear regression of nutritional rating on *sugar* content.[6]

$$y = \beta_0 + \beta_1(\text{sugars}) + \beta_2(\text{fiber}) + \beta_3(\text{Shelf 1}) + \beta_4(\text{Shelf 2}) + \varepsilon$$

[6]Confirm this by comparing against Table 8.7.

TABLE 9.9 The sequential sums of squares for the model:
$y = \beta_0 + \beta_1(\text{sugars}) + \beta_2(\text{fiber}) + \beta_3(\text{Shelf 1}) + \beta_4(\text{Shelf 2}) + \varepsilon$

```
Source    DF   Seq SS
Sugars     1   8711.9
Fiber      1   3476.6
Shelf 1    1      7.0
Shelf 2    1    159.9
```

The second sequential sum of squares, for fiber content, equals 3476.6. This represents the amount of unique additional variability in nutritional *rating* that is explained by the linear relationship of *rating* with *fiber* content, given that the variability explained by *sugars* has already been extracted. The third sequential sum of squares, for shelf 1, is 7.0. This represents the amount of unique additional variability in nutritional rating that is accounted for by location on shelf 1 (compared to the reference class shelf 3), given that the variability accounted for by *sugars* and *fiber* has already been separated out. This tiny value for the sequential sum of squares for shelf 1 indicates that the variable is probably not useful for estimating nutritional *rating*. Finally, the sequential sum of squares for shelf 2 is a moderate 159.9.

Now, suppose we changed the ordering of the variables into the regression model. This would change the values of the sequential sums of squares. For example, suppose we perform an analysis based on the following model:

$$y = \beta_0 + \beta_1(\text{shelf 1}) + \beta_2(\text{shelf 2}) + \beta_3(\text{sugars}) + \beta_4(\text{fiber}) + \varepsilon$$

The results for this regression are provided in Table 9.10. Note that all the results in Table 9.10 are exactly the same as in Table 9.6 (apart from ordering), except the values of the sequential sums of squares. This time, the indicator variables are able to "claim" their unique portions of the variability before the other variables are entered, thus giving them larger values for their sequential sums of squares. See Neter, Wasserman, and Kutner[7] for more information on applying sequential sums of squares for variable selection. We use the sequential sums of squares, in the context of a partial *F-test*, to perform variable selection later on in this chapter.

9.7 MULTICOLLINEARITY

Suppose that we are now interested in adding the predictor *potassium* to the model, so that our new regression equation looks like:

$$\hat{y} = b_0 + b_1(\text{sugars}) + b_2(\text{fiber}) + b_3(\text{shelf 1}) + b_4(\text{potassium})$$

Now, data miners need to guard against *multicollinearity*, a condition where some of the predictor variables are correlated with each other. Multicollinearity leads to

[7]Neter, Wasserman, and Kutner, *Applied Linear Statistical Models*, 4th edition, McGraw-Hill/Irwin, 1996.

TABLE 9.10 Changing the ordering of the variables into the model changes nothing except the sequential sums of squares

```
The regression equation is
Rating = 50.5 + 2.10 Shelf 1 + 3.92 Shelf 2 - 2.32 Sugars + 3.13 Fiber


Predictor       Coef  SE Coef       T      P
Constant      50.525    1.851   27.29  0.000
Shelf 1        2.101    1.795    1.17  0.246
Shelf 2        3.915    1.865    2.10  0.039
Sugars       -2.3183   0.1729  -13.41  0.000
Fiber         3.1314   0.3186    9.83  0.000


S = 6.02092   R-Sq = 82.8%   R-Sq(adj) = 81.8%


Analysis of Variance

Source           DF       SS      MS      F      P
Regression        4  12355.4  3088.9  85.21  0.000
Residual Error   71   2573.9    36.3
Total            75  14929.3


Source   DF  Seq SS
Shelf 1   1   282.7
Shelf 2   1  1392.7
Sugars    1  7179.0
Fiber     1  3501.0
```

instability in the solution space, leading to possible incoherent results. For example, in a data set with severe multicollinearity, it is possible for the *F-test* for the overall regression to be significant, while none of the *t-tests* for the individual predictors are significant.

Consider Figures 9.8 and 9.9. Figure 9.8 illustrates a situation where the predictors x_1 and x_2 are not correlated with each other; that is, they are orthogonal, or independent. In such a case, the predictors form a solid basis, on which the response surface y may rest sturdily, thereby providing stable coefficient estimates b_1 and b_2, each with small variability s_{b_1} and s_{b_2}. However, Figure 9.9 illustrates a multicollinear situation where the predictors x_1 and x_2 are correlated with each other, so that as one of them increases, so does the other. In this case, the predictors no longer form a solid basis, on which the response surface may firmly rest. Instead, when the predictors are correlated, the response surface is unstable, providing highly variable coefficient estimates b_1 and b_2, because of the inflated values for s_{b_1} and s_{b_2}.

The high variability associated with the estimates means that *different samples may produce coefficient estimates with widely different values*. For example, one sample may produce a positive coefficient estimate for x_1, while a second sample may produce a negative coefficient estimate. This situation is unacceptable when the analytic task calls for an explanation of the relationship between the response and the predictors, individually. Even if such instability is avoided, inclusion of variables that

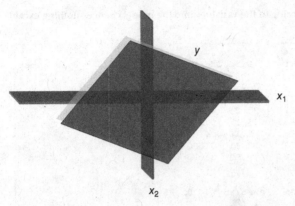

Figure 9.8 When the predictors x_1 and x_2 are uncorrelated, the response surface y rests on a solid basis, providing stable coefficient estimates.

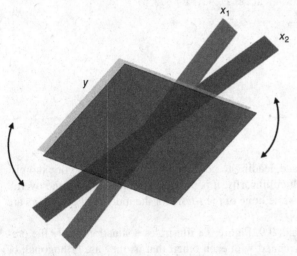

Figure 9.9 Multicollinearity: When the predictors are correlated, the response surface is unstable, resulting in dubious and highly variable coefficient estimates.

are highly correlated tends to overemphasize a particular component of the model, because the component is essentially being double counted.

To avoid multicollinearity, the analyst should investigate the correlation structure among the predictor variables (ignoring for the moment the target variable). Table 9.11[8] provides the correlation coefficients among the predictors for our present model. For example, the correlation coefficient between sugars and fiber is −0.139,

---

[8] *Shelf 2* is an indicator variable. No correlation inference should be carried out for indicator variables, as the normality assumption would be violated. However, using the correlation coefficient as a descriptive statistic for indicator variables is acceptable as an exploratory tool.

TABLE 9.11   Correlation coefficients among the predictors: We have a problem

	Sugars	Fiber	Shelf 2
Fiber	−0.139		
Shelf 2	0.368	−0.322	
Potass	0.001	0.912	−0.326

while the correlation coefficient between sugars and potassium is 0.001. Unfortunately, there is one pair of variables that are strongly correlated: fiber and potassium, with $r = 0.912$. Another method of assessing whether the predictors are correlated is to construct a matrix plot of the predictors, such as Figure 9.10. The matrix plot supports the finding that fiber and potassium are positively correlated.

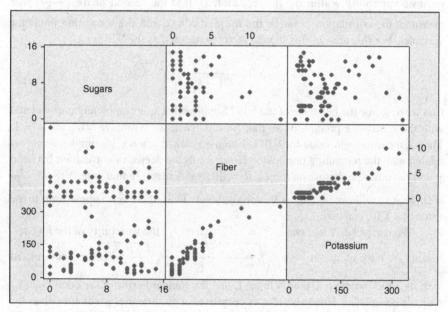

Figure 9.10   Matrix plot of the predictor variables shows correlation between fiber and potassium.

However, suppose we did not check for the presence of correlation among our predictors, and went ahead and performed the regression anyway. Is there some way that the regression results can warn us of the presence of multicollinearity? The answer is yes: We may ask for the *variance inflation factors* (VIFs) to be reported.

What do we mean by VIFs? First, recall that s_{b_i} represents the variability associated with the coefficient b_i for the ith predictor variable x_i. We may express s_{b_i} as a product of s, the standard error of the estimate, and c_i, which is a constant whose value depends on the observed predictor values. That is, $s_{b_i} = s \cdot c_i$. Now, s is fairly robust with respect to the inclusion of correlated variables in the model, so, in the presence of correlated predictors, we would look to c_i to help explain large changes in s_{b_i}.

We may express c_i as the following:

$$c_i = \sqrt{\frac{1}{(n-1)s_i^2} \cdot \frac{1}{1-R_i^2}}$$

where s_i^2 represents the sample variance of the observed values of ith predictor, x_i, and R_i^2 represents the R^2 value obtained by regressing x_i on the other predictor variables. Note that R_i^2 will be large when x_i is highly correlated with the other predictors.

Note that, of the two terms in c_i, the first factor $\left(\frac{1}{(n-1)s_i^2}\right)$ measures only the intrinsic variability within the ith predictor, x_i. It is the second factor $\left(\frac{1}{1-R_i^2}\right)$ that measures the correlation between the ith predictor x_i and the remaining predictor variables. For this reason, this second factor is denoted as the VIF for x_i:

$$VIF_i = \frac{1}{1-R_i^2}$$

Can we describe the behavior of the VIF? Suppose that x_i is completely uncorrelated with the remaining predictors, so that $R_i^2 = 0$. Then we will have $VIF_i = \frac{1}{1-0} = 1$. That is, the minimum value for VIF is 1, and is reached when x_i is completely uncorrelated with the remaining predictors. However, as the degree of correlation between x_i and the other predictors increases, R_i^2 will also increase. In that case, $VIF_i = \frac{1}{1-R_i^2}$ will increase without bound, as R_i^2 approaches 1. Thus, there is no upper limit to the value that VIF_i can take.

What effect do these changes in VIF_i have on s_{b_i}, the variability of the ith coefficient? We have $s_{b_i} = s \cdot c_i = s \cdot \sqrt{\frac{1}{(n-1)s_i^2} \cdot \frac{1}{1-R_i^2}} = s \cdot \sqrt{\frac{VIF_i}{(n-1)s_i^2}}$. If x_i is uncorrelated with the other predictors, then $VIF_i = 1$, and the standard error of the coefficient s_{b_i} will not be inflated. However, if x_i is correlated with the other predictors, then the large VIF_i will produce an inflation of the standard error of the coefficient s_{b_i}. As you know, inflating the variance estimates will result in a degradation in the precision of the estimation. A rough rule of thumb for interpreting the value of the VIF is to consider $VIF_i \geq 5$ to be an indicator of moderate multicollinearity, and to consider $VIF_i \geq 10$ to be an indicator of severe multicollinearity. A $VIF_i = 5$ corresponds to $R_i^2 = 0.80$, while $VIF_i = 10$ corresponds to $R_i^2 = 0.90$.

Getting back to our example, suppose we went ahead with the regression of nutritional rating on sugars, fiber, the shelf 2 indicator, and the new variable potassium, which is correlated with fiber. The results, including the observed VIFs, are shown in Table 9.12. The estimated regression equation for this model is

$$\hat{y} = 52.525 - 2.1476(\text{sugars}) + 4.2515(\text{fiber}) + 1.663(\text{shelf 2})$$
$$- 0.04656(\text{potassium})$$

TABLE 9.12   Regression results, with variance inflation factors indicating a multicollinearity problem[a]

```
The regression equation is
Rating = 52.5 - 2.15 Sugars + 4.25 Fiber + 1.66 Shelf 2 - 0.0466 Potass


74 cases used, 2 cases contain missing values


Predictor       Coef  SE Coef        T      P    VIF
Constant      52.525    1.698    30.94  0.000
Sugars       -2.1476   0.1937   -11.09  0.000  1.461
Fiber         4.2515   0.7602     5.59  0.000  6.952
Shelf 2        1.663    1.860     0.89  0.374  1.417
Potass      -0.04656  0.02637    -1.77  0.082  7.157


S = 5.96956   R-Sq = 82.9%   R-Sq(adj) = 81.9%


Analysis of Variance

Source          DF       SS       MS      F      P
Regression       4  11918.1   2979.5  83.61  0.000
Residual Error  69   2458.9     35.6
Total           73  14377.0
```

[a]Note that only 74 cases were used, because the *potassium* content of Almond Delight and Cream of Wheat are missing, along with the *sugar* content of Quaker Oats.

The p-value for potassium is not very small (0.082), so at first glance, the variable may or may not be included in the model. Also, the p-value for the shelf 2 indicator variable (0.374) has increased to such an extent that we should perhaps not include it in the model. However, we should probably not put too much credence into any of these results, because the observed VIFs seem to indicate the presence of a multicollinearity problem. We need to resolve the evident multicollinearity *before* moving forward with this model.

The VIF for fiber is 6.952 and the VIF for potassium is 7.157, with both values indicating moderate-to-strong multicollinearity. At least the problem is localized with these two variables only, as the other VIFs are reported at acceptably low values.

How shall we deal with this problem? Some texts suggest choosing one of the variables and eliminating it from the model. However, this should be viewed only as a last resort, because the omitted variable may have something to teach us. As we saw in Chapter 4, principal components can be a powerful method for using the correlation structure in a large group of predictors to produce a smaller set of independent components. Principal components analysis is a definite option here. Another option might be to construct a user-defined composite, as discussed in Chapter 4. Here, our user-defined composite will be as simple as possible, the mean of $fiber_z$ and $potassium_z$, where the z-subscript notation indicates that the variables have been standardized. Thus, our composite W is defined as $W = (fiber_z + potassium_z)/2$. Note that we need to standardize the variables involved in the composite, to avoid the possibility that the greater variability of one of the variables will overwhelm that of the other variable. For example, the standard deviation of fiber among all cereals is 2.38 grams, while the standard deviation of potassium is 71.29 milligrams. (The grams/milligrams scale difference is not at issue here. What is relevant is the difference in variability, even on their respective scales.) Figure 9.11 illustrates the difference in variability.[9]

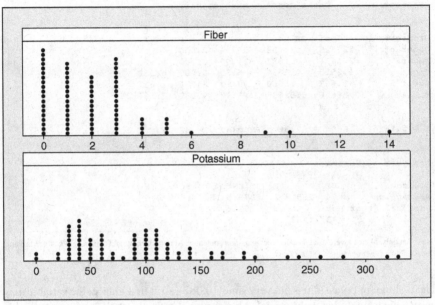

Figure 9.11 Fiber and potassium have different variabilities, thus requiring standardization before construction of user-defined composite.

We therefore proceed to perform the regression of nutritional rating on the following variables:

- Sugars$_z$
- Shelf 2
- $W = (\text{fiber}_z + \text{potassium}_z)/2$.

The results are provided in Table 9.13.

Note first that the multicollinearity problem seems to have been resolved, with the VIF values all near 1. Note also, however, that the regression results are rather disappointing, with the values of R^2, R^2_{adj}, and s all underperforming the model results found in Table 9.8, from the model, $y = \beta_0 + \beta_1(\text{sugars}) + \beta_2(\text{fiber}) + \beta_4(\text{shelf 2}) + \varepsilon$, which did not even include the potassium variable.

What is going on here? The problem stems from the fact that the fiber variable is a very good predictor of nutritional rating, especially when coupled with sugar

---

[9]Note that standardization by itself will not solve the multicollinearity issue. In fact, VIF values will not change at all if the predictors are standardized.

TABLE 9.13   Results from regression of rating on sugars, shelf 2, and the fiber/potassium composite

```
The regression equation is
Rating = 41.7 - 10.7 Sugarsz + 3.00 Shelf 2 + 7.07 W


74 cases used, 2 cases contain missing values


Predictor        Coef    SE Coef        T       P      VIF
Constant      41.7149     0.9242    45.14   0.000
Sugarsz      -10.6865     0.8443   -12.66   0.000    1.221
Shelf 2        3.000      1.987      1.51   0.136    1.365
W              7.0717     0.8226     8.60   0.000    1.130


S = 6.49820   R-Sq = 79.4%    R-Sq(adj) = 78.6%


Analysis of Variance

Source           DF       SS       MS       F       P
Regression        3   11421.1   3807.0   90.16   0.000
Residual Error   70    2955.9     42.2
Total            73   14377.0
```

content, as we shall see later on when we perform best subsets regression. Therefore, using the fiber variable to form a composite with a variable that has weaker correlation with rating dilutes the strength of fiber's strong association with rating, and so degrades the efficacy of the model.

Thus, reluctantly, we put aside this model $(y = \beta_0 + \beta_1(\text{sugars}_z) + \beta_4(\text{shelf } 2) + \beta_5(W) + \varepsilon)$. One possible alternative is to change the weights in the composite, to increase the weight of fiber with respect to potassium. For example, we could use $W_2 = (0.9 \times \text{fiber}_z + 0.1 \times \text{potassium}_z)$. However, the model performance would still be slightly below that of using fiber alone. Instead, the analyst may be better advised to pursue principal components.

Now, depending on the task confronting the analyst, multicollinearity may not in fact present a fatal defect. Weiss[10] notes that multicollinearity "does not adversely affect the ability of the sample regression equation to predict the response variable." He adds that multicollinearity does not significantly affect point estimates of the target variable, confidence intervals for the mean response value, or prediction intervals for a randomly selected response value. However, the data miner must therefore strictly limit the use of a multicollinear model to estimation and prediction of the target variable. Interpretation of the model would not be appropriate, because the individual coefficients may not make sense, in the presence of multicollinearity.

[10]Weiss, *Introductory Statistics*, 9th edition, Pearson, 2010.

9.8 VARIABLE SELECTION METHODS

To assist the data analyst in determining which variables should be included in a multiple regression model, several different *variable selection methods* have been developed, including

- forward selection;
- backward elimination;
- stepwise selection;
- best subsets.

These variable selection methods are essentially algorithms to help construct the model with the optimal set of predictors.

9.8.1 The Partial *F*-Test

In order to discuss variable selection methods, we first need to learn about the *partial F-test*. Suppose that we already have p variables in the model, $x_1, x_2, \ldots, x_p$, and we are interested in whether one extra variable x^* should be included in the model or not. Recall earlier where we discussed the sequential sums of squares. Here, we would calculate the extra (sequential) sum of squares from adding x^* to the model, given that $x_1, x_2, \ldots, x_p$ are already in the model. Denote this quantity by $SS_{Extra} = SS(x^* | x_1, x_2, \ldots, x_p)$. Now, this extra sum of squares is computed by finding the regression sum of squares for the full model (including $x_1, x_2, \ldots, x_p$ and x^*), denoted $SS_{Full} = SS(x_1, x_2, \ldots, x_p, x^*)$, and subtracting the regression sum of squares from the reduced model (including only $x_1, x_2, \ldots, x_p$), denoted $SS_{Reduced} = SS(x_1, x_2, \ldots, x_p)$. In other words:

$$SS_{Extra} = SS_{Full} - SS_{Reduced}$$

that is,

$$SS(x^* | x_1, x_2, \ldots, x_p) = SS(x_1, x_2, \ldots, x_p, x^*) - SS(x_1, x_2, \ldots, x_p)$$

The null hypothesis for the partial *F-test* is as follows:

H$_0$: No, the SS_{Extra} associated with x^* does not contribute significantly to the regression sum of squares for a model already containing $x_1, x_2, \ldots, x_p$. Therefore, do not include x^* in the model.

The alternative hypothesis is:

H$_a$: Yes, the SS_{Extra} associated with x^* does contribute significantly to the regression sum of squares for a model already containing $x_1, x_2, \ldots, x_p$. Therefore, do include x^* in the model.

The test statistic for the partial *F-test* is the following:

$$F(x^* | x_1, x_2, \ldots, x_p) = \frac{SS_{Extra}}{MSE_{Full}}$$

where MSE_{Full} denotes the mean square error term from the full model, including $x_1, x_2, \ldots, x_p$ and x^*. This is known as the partial F-statistic for x^*. When the null hypothesis is true, this test statistic follows an $F_{1;n-p-2}$ distribution. We would therefore reject the null hypothesis when $F(x^* | x_1, x_2, \ldots, x_p)$ is large, or when its associated p-value is small.

An alternative to the partial F-test is the t-test. Now, an F-test with 1 and $n - p - 2$ degrees of freedom is equivalent to a t-test with $n - p - 2$ degrees of freedom. This is due to the distributional relationship that $F_{1,n-p-2} = (t_{n-p-2})^2$. Thus, either the F-test or the t-test may be performed. Similarly to our treatment of the t-test earlier in the chapter, the hypotheses are given by

$$H_0: \beta^* = 0$$
$$H_a: \beta^* \neq 0$$

The associated models are

$$\text{Under } H_0: y = \beta_0 + \beta_1 x_1 + \cdots + \beta_p x_p + \varepsilon$$
$$\text{Under } H_a: y = \beta_0 + \beta_1 x_1 + \cdots + \beta_p x_p + \beta^* x^* + \varepsilon$$

Under the null hypothesis, the test statistic $t = \dfrac{b^*}{s_{b^*}}$ follows a t distribution with $n - p - 2$ degrees of freedom. Reject the null hypothesis when the two-tailed p-value, $P(|t| > |t_{obs}|)$, is small.

Finally, we need to discuss the difference between sequential sums of squares, and partial sums of squares. The sequential sums of squares are as described earlier in the chapter. As each variable is entered into the model, the sequential sum of squares represents the additional unique variability in the response explained by that variable, after the variability accounted for by variables entered earlier in the model has been extracted. That is, the *ordering* of the entry of the variables into the model is germane to the sequential sums of squares.

However, ordering is not relevant to the partial sums of squares. For a particular variable, the partial sum of squares represents the additional unique variability in the response explained by that variable, after the variability accounted for by all the other variables in the model has been extracted. Table 9.14 shows the difference between sequential and partial sums of squares, for a model with four predictors, x_1, x_2, x_3, x_4.

TABLE 9.14   The difference between sequential SS and partial SS

Variable	Sequential SS	Partial SS
x_1	$SS(x_1)$	$SS(x_1 | x_2, x_3, x_4)$
x_2	$SS(x_2 | x_1)$	$SS(x_2 | x_1, x_3, x_4)$
x_3	$SS(x_3 | x_1, x_2)$	$SS(x_3 | x_1, x_2, x_4)$
x_4	$SS(x_4 | x_1, x_2, x_3)$	$SS(x_4 | x_1, x_2, x_3)$

9.8.2 The Forward Selection Procedure

The forward selection procedure starts with no variables in the model.

- Step 1. For the first variable to enter the model, select the predictor most highly correlated with the target. (Without loss of generality, denote this variable x_1.) If the resulting model is not significant, then stop and report that no variables are important predictors; otherwise, proceed to step 2. Note that the analyst may choose the level of α; lower values make it more difficult to enter the model. A common choice is $\alpha = 0.05$, but this is not set in stone.

- Step 2. For each remaining variable, compute the sequential F-statistic for that variable, given the variables already in the model. For example, in this first pass through the algorithm, these sequential F-statistics would be $F(x_2|x_1)$, $F(x_3|x_1)$, and $F(x_4|x_1)$. On the second pass through the algorithm, these might be $F(x_3|x_1,x_2)$ and $F(x_4|x_1,x_2)$. Select the variable with the largest sequential F-statistic.

- Step 3. For the variable selected in step 2, test for the significance of the sequential F-statistic. If the resulting model is not significant, then stop, and report the current model without adding the variable from step 2. Otherwise, add the variable from step 2 into the model and return to step 2.

9.8.3 The Backward Elimination Procedure

The backward elimination procedure begins with all the variables, or all of a user-specified set of variables, in the model.

- Step 1. Perform the regression on the full model; that is, using all available variables. For example, perhaps the full model has four variables, x_1, x_2, x_3, x_4.

- Step 2. For each variable in the current model, compute the partial F-statistic. In the first pass through the algorithm, these would be $F(x_1|x_2,x_3,x_4)$, $F(x_2|x_1,x_3,x_4)$, $F(x_3|x_1,x_2,x_4)$, and $F(x_4|x_1,x_2,x_3)$. Select the variable with the smallest partial F-statistic. Denote this value F_{min}.

- Step 3. Test for the significance of F_{min}. If F_{min} is not significant, then remove the variable associated with F_{min} from the model, and return to step 2. If F_{min} is significant, then stop the algorithm and report the current model. If this is the first pass through the algorithm, then the current model is the full model. If this is not the first pass, then the current model has been reduced by one or more variables from the full model. Note that the analyst may choose the level of α needed to remove variables. Lower values make it more difficult to keep variables in the model.

9.8.4 The Stepwise Procedure

The stepwise procedure represents a modification of the forward selection procedure. A variable that has been entered into the model early in the forward selection process may turn out to be nonsignificant, once other variables have been entered into the model. The stepwise procedure checks on this possibility, by performing at each step a partial *F-test*, using the partial sum of squares, for each variable currently in the model. If there is a variable in the model that is no longer significant, then the variable with the smallest partial *F*-statistic is removed from the model. The procedure terminates when no further variables can be entered or removed. The analyst may choose both the level of α required to enter the model, and the level of α' needed to remove variables, with α' chosen to be somewhat large than α.

9.8.5 The Best Subsets Procedure

For data sets where the number of predictors is not too large, the best subsets procedure represents an attractive variable selection method. However, if there are more than 30 or so predictors, then the best subsets method encounters a combinatorial explosion, and becomes intractably slow.

The best subsets procedure works as follows:

- Step 1. The analyst specifies how many (k) models of each size he or she would like reported, as well as the maximum number of predictors (p) the analyst wants in the model.

- Step 2. All models of one predictor are built. Their R^2, R^2_{adj}, Mallows' C_p (see below), and s values are calculated. The best k models are reported, based on these measures.

- Step 3. Then all models of two predictors are built. Their R^2, R^2_{adj}, Mallows' C_p, and s values are calculated, and the best k models are reported.

- The procedure continues in this way until the maximum number of predictors (p) is reached. The analyst then has a listing of the best models of each size, 1, 2, ..., p, to assist in the selection of the best overall model.

9.8.6 The All-Possible-Subsets Procedure

The four methods of model selection we have discussed are essentially optimization algorithms over a large sample space. Because of that, there is no guarantee that the globally optimal model will be found; that is, there is no guarantee that these variable selection algorithms will uncover the model with the lowest s, the highest R^2_{adj}, and so on (Draper and Smith[11]; Kleinbaum, Kupper, Nizam, and Muller[12]). The only way to ensure that the absolute best model has been found is simply to perform all the possible regressions. Unfortunately, in data mining applications, there are usually so many candidate predictor variables available that this method is simply not practicable. Not counting the null model $y = \beta_0 + \varepsilon$, there are $2^p - 1$ possible models to be built, using p predictors.

[11]Draper and Smith, *Applied Regression Analysis*, 3rd edition, Wiley Publishers, Hoboken, New Jersey, 1998.

[12]Kleinbaum, Kupper, Nizam, and Muller, *Applied Regression Analysis and Multivariable Methods*, 4th edition, Cengage Learning, 2007.

For small numbers of predictors, it is not a problem to construct all possible regressions. For example, for $p = 5$ predictors, there are $2^5 - 1 = 31$ possible models. However, as the number of predictors starts to grow, the search space grows exponentially. For instance, for $p = 10$ predictors, there are $2^{10} - 1 = 1023$ possible models, while for $p = 20$ predictors, there are $2^{20} - 1 = 1,048,575$ possible models. Thus, for most data mining applications, in which there may be hundreds of predictors, the all-possible-regressions procedure is not applicable. Therefore, the data miner may be inclined to turn to one of the four variable selection procedures discussed above. Even though there is no guarantee that the globally best model is found, these methods usually provide a useful set of models, which can provide positive results. The analyst can then adopt these models as starting points, and apply tweaks and modifications to coax the best available performance out of them.

9.9 GAS MILEAGE DATA SET

At this point, it may be helpful to turn to a new data set to illustrate the nuts and bolts of variable selection methods. We shall use the *Gas Mileage* data set,[13] where the target variable *MPG* (miles per gallon) is estimated using four predictors: *cab space*, *horsepower*, *top speed*, and *weight*. Let us explore this data set a bit. Figure 9.12 shows scatter plots of the target *MPG* with each of the predictors. The relationship between *MPG* and *horsepower* does not appear to be linear. Using the bulging rule

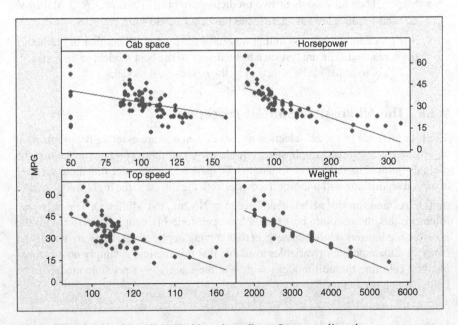

Figure 9.12   Scatter plots of MPG with each predictor. Some non-linearity.

[13]From the DASL web site (Data and Story Library), http://lib.stat.cmu.edu/DASL/.

from Chapter 8, we therefore take the *ln* of each variable. The resulting scatter plots, shown in Figure 9.13, show improved linearity. We therefore proceed to perform linear regression of *ln MPG* on *cab space, ln HP, top speed, and weight.*

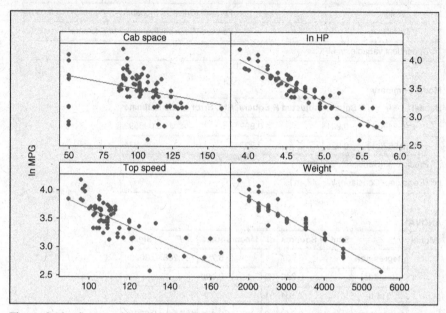

Figure 9.13   Scatter plots of *ln* MPG with each predictor (including *ln* HP). Improved linearity.

9.10   AN APPLICATION OF VARIABLE SELECTION METHODS

We would like the most parsimonious model that does not leave out any significant predictors. We shall apply the variable selection methods described above. We select the following commonly used thresholds of significance for variables entering and leaving the model: $\alpha = 0.05$ and $\alpha' = 0.10$.

9.10.1   Forward Selection Procedure Applied to the *Gas Mileage* Data Set

Table 9.15 shows the results for the forward selection method. We begin with no variables in the model. Then the variable most strongly correlated with *ln MPG* is selected, and, if significant, entered into the model. This variable is *weight*, which has the highest correlation with *ln MPG*, among the predictors. This is shown in the upper left of Table 9.15, showing *weight* as the first variable entered.

Then the sequential *F-tests* are performed, such as $F(\ln HP|weight)$, $F(cab\ space|weight)$, and so on. It turns out that the highest sequential *F*-statistic is

TABLE 9.15   Forward selection results

Variables Entered/Removed[a]

Model	Variables Entered	Variables Removed	Method
1	Weight	.	Forward (Criterion: Probability-of-F-to-enter <= 0.050).
2	ln HP	.	Forward (Criterion: Probability-of-F-to-enter <= 0.050).

[a] Dependent variable: ln MPG.

Model Summary

Model	R	R Square	Adjusted R Square	Std. Error of the Estimate
1	0.949(a)	0.901	0.899	0.096592
2	0.962(b)	0.925	0.923	0.084374

[a] Predictors: (Constant), Weight.

[b] Predictors: (Constant), Weight, ln HP.

ANOVA[a]

Model		Sum of Squares	df	Mean Square	F	Sig.
1	Regression	6.757	1	6.757	724.268	0.000(b)
	Residual	0.746	80	0.009		
	Total	7.504	81			
2	Regression	6.942	2	3.471	487.540	0.000(c)
	Residual	0.562	79	0.007		
	Total	7.504	81			

[a] Dependent Variable: ln MPG.

[b] Predictors: (Constant), Weight.

[c] Predictors: (Constant), Weight, ln HP.

given by the significance test of $F(\ln HP|weight)$, so that the variable $\ln HP$ becomes the second variable entered into the model, as shown in Table 9.15. Once again, the sequential *F-tests* are performed, but no further significant variables were found. Thus, the forward selection method prefers the following model:

$$\hat{y} = b_0 + b_1 \text{weight} + b_2 \ln HP$$

Table 9.15 contains the ANOVA tables for the two models selected by the forward selection procedure. We may use these ANOVA results to calculate the sequential *F*-statistics. Model 1 represents the model with *weight* as the only predictor. Model 2 represents the model with both *weight* and *ln HP* entered as predictors.

As $\text{SS}_{\text{Extra}} = \text{SS}_{\text{Full}} - \text{SS}_{\text{Reduced}}$, we have

$$\text{SS}_{\ln HP|\text{weight}} = \text{SS}_{\text{weight},\ln HP} - \text{SS}_{\text{weight}}$$

From Table 9.15, we have

- $SS_{sugars,fiber} = 6.942$, and
- $SS_{sugars} = 6.757$, giving us:
- $SS_{fiber|sugars} = SS_{sugars,fiber} - SS_{sugars} = 6.942 - 6.757 = 0.185$

The test statistic for the partial (or, in this case, sequential) *F-test* is the following:

$$F(\ln HP | weight) = \frac{SS_{\ln HP|weight}}{MSE_{weight,\ln HP}}$$

From Table 9.15, we have

- $MSE_{weight,\ln HP} = 0.007$, giving us:
- $F(\ln HP | weight) = \frac{SS_{\ln HP|weight}}{MSE_{weight,\ln HP}} = \frac{0.185}{0.007} = 26.4$

With a sample size of 82, and $p = 2$ parameters in the model, this test statistic follows an $F_{1,n-p-2} = F_{1,79}$ distribution. The *p*-value for this test statistic is approximately zero, thereby rejecting the null hypothesis that fiber should not be included after sugars.

9.10.2   Backward Elimination Procedure Applied to the *Gas Mileage* Data Set

In the backward elimination procedure, we begin with all of the variables in the model. The partial *F*-statistic is then calculated for each variable in the model (e.g., F(cab space|weight, ln HP, top speed). The variable with the smallest partial *F*-statistic, F_{min}, is examined, which in this case is *cab space*. If F_{min} is not significant, which is the case here, then the variable is dropped from the model. *Cab space* is the first variable to be removed, as is shown in Table 9.16. On the next pass, the variable with the smallest partial *F*-statistic is *top speed*, which again is not significant. Thus, *top speed* becomes the second variable omitted from the model. No other variables are removed from the model, so that the backward elimination method prefers the same model as the forward selection method.

9.10.3   The Stepwise Selection Procedure Applied to the *Gas Mileage* Data Set

The stepwise selection procedure is a modification of the forward selection procedure, where the algorithm checks at each step whether all variables currently in the model are still significant. In this example, each variable that had been entered remained significant when the other variables were also entered. Thus, for this example, the results were the same as for the forward selection procedure, with the same model summaries as shown in Table 9.15.

TABLE 9.16   Backward elimination results

Variables Entered/Removed[a]

Model	Variables Entered	Variables Removed	Method
1	ln HP, Cab Space, Weight, Top Speed(b)	.	Enter
2		Cab space	Backward (criterion: Probability of F-to-remove >= 0.100).
3		Top speed	Backward (criterion: Probability of F-to-remove >= 0.100).

[a] Dependent variable: ln MPG.

[b] All requested variables entered.

Model Summary

Model	R	R Square	Adjusted R Square	Std. Error of the Estimate
1	0.963(a)	0.927	0.924	0.084165
2	0.963(b)	0.927	0.924	0.083654
3	0.962(c)	0.925	0.923	0.084374

[a] Predictors: (Constant), ln HP, Cab Space, Weight, Top Speed.

[b] Predictors: (Constant), ln HP, Weight, Top Speed.

[c] Predictors: (Constant), ln HP, Weight.

ANOVA[a]

Model		Sum of Squares	df	Mean Square	F	Sig.
1	Regression	6.958	4	1.740	245.580	0.000(b)
	Residual	0.545	77	0.007		
	Total	7.504	81			
2	Regression	6.958	3	2.319	331.433	0.000(c)
	Residual	0.546	78	0.007		
	Total	7.504	81			
3	Regression	6.942	2	3.471	487.540	0.000(d)
	Residual	0.562	79	0.007		
	Total	7.504	81			

[a] Dependent variable: ln MPG.

[b] Predictors: (Constant), ln HP, Cab Space, Weight, Top Speed.

[c] Predictors: (Constant), ln HP, Weight, Top Speed.

[d] Predictors: (Constant), ln HP, Weight.

9.10.4   Best Subsets Procedure Applied to the *Gas Mileage* Data Set

Table 9.17 provides the results from *Minitab*'s application of the best subsets procedure on the *gas mileage* data set. The predictor variable names are given on the upper right, formatted vertically. Each horizontal line in the table represents a separate model, with the "X"s shown under the predictors included in a particular model. The best subsets procedure reports the two best models with $p = 1$ predictor, the two best models with $p = 2$ models, and so on. Thus, the first model has only *weight*; the second model has only *ln HP*; the third model has *ln HP* and *weight*; the fourth model has *top speed and weight*; and so on.

TABLE 9.17   Best subsets results for *Gas Mileage* data set ("best" model highlighed)

Vars	R-Sq	R-Sq(adj)	Mallows Cp	S	Cab space	lnHP	Speed	Top Weight
1	90.1	89.9	27.4	0.096592				X
1	83.7	83.5	95.1	0.12379	X			
2	92.5	92.3	3.4	0.084374	X			X
2	91.8	91.6	11.0	0.088310		X	X	
3	**92.7**	**92.4**	**3.1**	**0.083654**	**X**	**X**	**X**	
3	92.6	92.3	4.8	0.084576	X	X		X
4	92.7	92.4	5.0	0.084165	X	X	X	X

Four model selection criteria are reported for each model: R^2, R^2_{adj}, Mallows' C_p, and s.

9.10.5 Mallows' C_p Statistic

We now discuss the C_p statistic, developed by C. L. Mallows[14]. Mallows' C_p statistic takes the form:

$$C_p = \frac{\text{SSE}_p}{\text{MSE}_{\text{full}}} - [n - 2(p + 1)]$$

where p represents the number of predictors in the current (working) model, SSE_p represents the error sum of squares of the model with p predictors, and MSE_{full} represents the MSE of the full model; that is, the model with all predictors entered.

For a model that fits well, it can be shown[15] that $E(C_p) = p + 1$. Thus, we would expect the value of C_p for a well-fitting model to take a value not far from $p + 1$. However, models that show a considerable lack of fit will take values of C_p above (and sometimes far above) $p + 1$. The full model, with all variables entered, always has $C_p = p + 1$, but is often not the best model.

It is useful to plot the value of Mallows' C_p against the number of predictors, p. Figure 9.14 shows such a plot for the *gas mileage* data set regression. (To increase granularity, the model with $C_p = 95.1$ is omitted.) One heuristic for choosing the best model is to select the model where the value of C_p first approaches or crosses the line $C_p = p + 1$, as p increases.

[14]Mallows, Some comments on C_p, *Technometrics*, Volume 15, pages 661–675, 1973.

[15]Draper and Smith, *Applied Regression Analysis*, 3rd edition, Wiley Publishers, Hoboken, New Jersey, 1998.

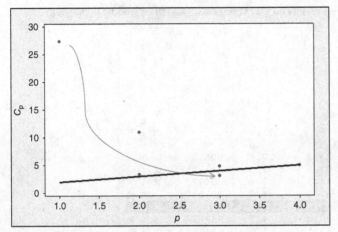

Figure 9.14   A plot of Mallows' C_p against the number of predictors, p, can help select the best model.

Consider Figure 9.14. However, the general trend for the values of C_p is to fall as p increases, as can be seen from Figure 9.17. As we reach $p = 2$, we have $C_p = 3.4$, which is approaching the line $C_p = p + 1$. This represents the model chosen by the other three variable selection methods.

Finally, when we reach $p = 3$, we have, for one of the models, $C_p = 3.1$, which is below the line $C_p = p + 1$. Therefore, the Mallows' C_p heuristic would be to select this model as the working model. This model contains *ln HP*, *top speed*, and *weight* as predictors.

Thus, we have two candidate working models:

$$\text{Model A: } \hat{y} = b_0 + b_1 \text{ weight} + b_2 \ln \text{HP}$$

$$\text{Model B: } \hat{y} = b_0 + b_1 \text{weight} + b_2 \ln \text{HP} + b_3 \text{ top speed}$$

Model A is supported by forward selection, backward elimination, and stepwise, and was nearly favored by best subsets. Model B is preferred by best subsets, but barely. Let us mention that one need not report only one model as a final model. Two or three models may be carried forward, and input sought from managers about which model may be most ameliorative of the business or research problem. However, it is often convenient to have one "working model" selected, because of the complexity of model building in the multivariate environment. However, recall the principal of *parsimony*, which states *All things being equal, choose the simpler model*. Because of parsimony, and because Model A did so well with most of the variable selection methods, it is recommended that we consider Model A to be our working model. The regression results for Model A are shown in Table 9.18.

Checking for the regression assumptions, each of the graphs in Figure 9.15 shows an outlier, the Subaru Loyale, which got lower gas mileage than expected, given its predictor values. Table 9.19 shows the regression results when this outlier is

TABLE 9.18   Regression results for model chosen by variable selection criteria

```
The regression equation is
ln MPG = 5.39 - 0.249 ln HP - 0.000242 Weight


Predictor           Coef     SE Coef        T       P    VIF
Constant          5.3858      0.1641    32.81   0.000
ln HP            -0.24895     0.04897    -5.08   0.000  4.728
Weight        -0.00024173  0.00002504    -9.65   0.000  4.728


S = 0.0843736   R-Sq = 92.5%   R-Sq(adj) = 92.3%


Analysis of Variance

Source           DF      SS      MS        F       P
Regression        2  6.9415  3.4708   487.54   0.000
Residual Error   79  0.5624  0.0071
Total            81  7.5039
```

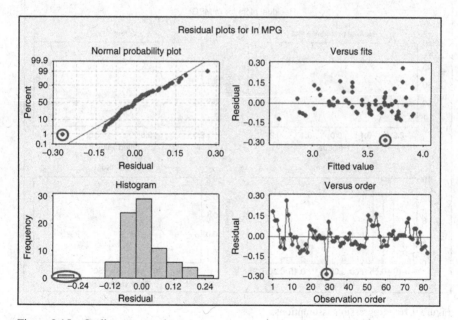

Figure 9.15   Outlier uncovered.

omitted. The precision of the regression is improved; for example, the standard error of the estimate, s, has decreased by 6.6%.

Figure 9.16 shows the plots for validation of the regression assumptions. With some slight right-skewness in the residuals, and some curvature in the residuals versus fitted values, these are not as tight as we might wish; in the exercises, we will

TABLE 9.19 Regression results improved a bit with outlier removed

```
The regression equation is
ln MPG = 5.37 - 0.240 ln HP - 0.000249 Weight


Predictor           Coef     SE Coef        T      P     VIF
Constant          5.3684      0.1533    35.01  0.000
ln HP            -0.23963     0.04579    -5.23  0.000   4.734
Weight        -0.00024908  0.00002347  -10.61  0.000   4.734


S = 0.0787767   R-Sq = 93.5%   R-Sq(adj) = 93.4%


Analysis of Variance

Source         DF       SS       MS       F      P
Regression      2   7.0114   3.5057  564.91  0.000
Residual Error 78   0.4841   0.0062
Total          80   7.4955
```

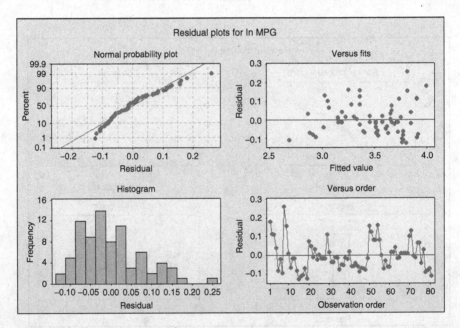

Figure 9.16 Regression assumptions.

try to deal with these issues. However, we are on the whole satisfied that our regression model provides a decent summary of the linear relationship between *ln* MPG and the predictors. Nevertheless, there still remains the problem of moderate multicollinearity, as shown by the VIF values close to 5 for the predictors. Thus, we now turn to a method made to deal with multicollinearity: principal components analysis.

9.11 USING THE PRINCIPAL COMPONENTS AS PREDICTORS IN MULTIPLE REGRESSION

Principal components[16] may be used as predictors in a multiple regression model. Each record has a component value for each principal component, as shown in the rightmost four columns in Table 9.20. These component values may be used as predictors in a regression model, or, indeed, any analytical model.

First, the predictors from the original data set are all standardized, using z-scores. Then principal components analysis is performed on the standardized predictors, with varimax rotation. The variance-explained results are shown in Table 9.21. The varimax-rotated solution has nearly attained 100% of variance explained by three components. We therefore extract three components, to be used as predictors for our regression model.[17]

Table 9.22 shows the unrotated and rotated component weights, with weights less than 0.5 hidden, for clarity. Brief component profiles for the rotated solution are as follows:

- *Component 1*: **Muscle.** This component combines *top speed* and *horsepower*.

- *Component 2*: **Roominess.** The only variable is *cab space*.

- *Component 3*: **Weight.** The only variable is *weight*.

Regression of *ln* MPG on the three principal components is performed, with the results shown in Table 9.23 and the residual plots shown in Figure 9.17. Note that the multicollinearity problem has been solved, because the VIF statistics all equal a perfect 1.0. However, the normal probability plot of the residuals shows concave curvature, indicating right-skewness. We therefore apply the following Box–Cox transformation to *MPG*, to reduce the skewness:

$$MPG_{BC\ 0.75} = \frac{(MPG^{0.75} - 1)}{0.75}$$

The residual plots for the resulting regression of $MPG_{BC\ 0.75}$ on the principal components are shown in Figure 9.18. The skewness has mostly been dealt with. These plots are not perfect. Specifically, there appears to be a systematic difference for the set of vehicles near the end of the data set in observation order. A glance at the data set indicates these are luxury cars, such as a Rolls–Royce and a Jaguar, which may follow a somewhat different gas mileage model. Overall, we find the plots indicate broad validation of the regression assumptions. Remember, in the world of dirty data, perfect validation of the assumptions may be elusive.

---

[16]Principal components analysis was covered in Chapter 5.

[17]In the exercises, we confirm that the four criteria for selecting the number of components can live with extracting three components, although an argument can be made for extracting two instead.

TABLE 9.20 Each record has component weight values for each component

Make/Model	MPG	ln HP	ln MPG	Cab Space_z	Horsepower_z	Top Speed_z	Weight_z	PrinComp1	PrinComp2	PrinComp3	PrinComp4
GM/GeoMetroXF1	65.400	3.892	4.181	−0.442	−1.199	−1.169	−1.648	−0.770	−0.246	−1.454	2.449
GM/GeoMetro	56.000	4.007	4.025	−0.307	−1.093	−1.098	−1.341	−0.805	−0.167	−1.081	1.896
GM/GeoMetroLSI	55.900	4.007	4.024	−0.307	−1.093	−1.098	−1.341	−0.805	−0.167	−1.081	1.896
SuzukiSwift	49.000	4.248	3.892	−0.307	−0.829	−0.528	−1.341	−0.173	−0.081	−1.518	0.115
DaihatsuCharade	46.500	3.970	3.839	−0.307	−1.128	−1.169	−1.341	−0.885	−0.177	−1.026	2.094
GM/GeoSprintTurbo	46.200	4.248	3.833	−0.442	−0.829	−0.528	−1.341	−0.199	−0.229	−1.450	0.079
GM/GeoSprint	45.400	4.007	3.816	−0.307	−1.093	−1.098	−1.341	−0.805	−0.167	−1.081	1.896
HondaCivicCRXHF	59.200	4.127	4.081	−2.202	−0.970	−1.027	−1.034	−1.229	−2.307	0.302	1.012
HondaCivicCRXHF	53.300	4.127	3.976	−2.202	−0.970	−1.027	−1.034	−1.229	−2.307	0.302	1.012
DaihatsuCharade	43.400	4.382	3.770	−0.217	−0.653	−0.386	−1.034	−0.118	−0.039	−1.189	−0.246
SubaruJusty	41.100	4.290	3.716	−0.442	−0.776	−0.671	−1.034	−0.473	−0.328	−0.860	0.686
HondaCivicCRX	40.900	4.522	3.711	−2.202	−0.442	0.042	−1.034	−0.027	−2.145	−0.528	−1.953

TABLE 9.21 Percentage of variance explained for the rotated solution for three components is nearly 100%

Total Variance Explained

Component	Initial Eigenvalues			Extraction Sums of Squared Loadings			Rotation Sums of Squared Loadings		
	Total	% of Variance	Cumulative %	Total	% of Variance	Cumulative %	Total	% of Variance	Cumulative %
1	2.689	67.236	67.236	2.689	67.236	67.236	2.002	50.054	50.054
2	1.100	27.511	94.747	1.100	27.511	94.747	1.057	26.436	76.490
3	0.205	5.137	99.884	0.205	5.137	99.884	0.935	23.386	99.876
4	0.005	0.116	100.000	0.005	0.116	100.000	0.005	0.124	100.000

Extraction method: Principal component analysis.

TABLE 9.22 Component weights, for the unrotated and rotated solutions

Component Matrix[a]

	Component			
	1	2	3	4
Horsepower_z	0.984			
Top Speed_z	0.921			
Weight_z	0.906			
Cab Space_z		0.958		

Extraction method: Principal component analysis.

[a] Four components extracted.

Rotated Component Matrix[a]

	Component			
	1	2	3	4
Top Speed_z	0.969			
Horsepower_z	0.892			
Cab Space_z		0.988		
Weight_z	0.517		0.809	

Extraction method: Principal component analysis. Rotation method: Varimax with Kaiser normalization.

[a] Rotation converged in five iterations.

TABLE 9.23 Regression using principal components solves the multicollinearity problem

```
The regression equation is
ln MPG = 3.48 - 0.184 PrinComp1 - 0.0751 PrinComp2 - 0.213 PrinComp3


Predictor       Coef     SE Coef        T       P     VIF
Constant     3.47571     0.00982   354.12   0.000
PrinComp1   -0.183916    0.009875   -18.62   0.000   1.000
PrinComp2   -0.075066    0.009875    -7.60   0.000   1.000
PrinComp3   -0.213480    0.009875   -21.62   0.000   1.000


S = 0.0888786   R-Sq = 91.8%   R-Sq(adj) = 91.5%


Analysis of Variance

Source           DF       SS       MS       F       P
Regression        3   6.8877   2.2959   290.64   0.000
Residual Error   78   0.6162   0.0079
Total            81   7.5039
```

The regression results for regression of $MPG_{BC\ 0.75}$ on the principal components are shown in Table 9.24. Note the following:

- Multicollinearity remains vanquished, with all VIF = 1.0.
- $R^2 = 92.1\%$, not quite as good as the 93.5% for the model not accounting for multicollinearity.
- Note the group of last four unusual observations, all high leverage points, consists of a Mercedes, a Jaguar, a BMW, and a Rolls–Royce. The Rolls–Royce is the most extreme outlier.

In the exercises, we invite the analyst to further improve this model, either by tweaking the Box–Cox transformation, or through an indicator variable for the luxury cars, or some other means.

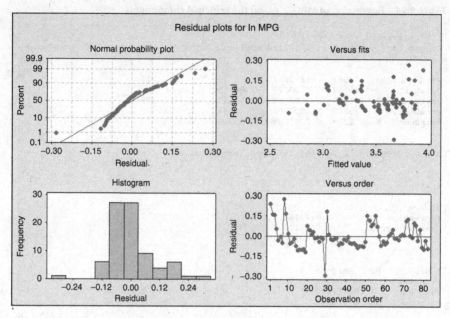

Figure 9.17   Normal probability plot shows skewness.

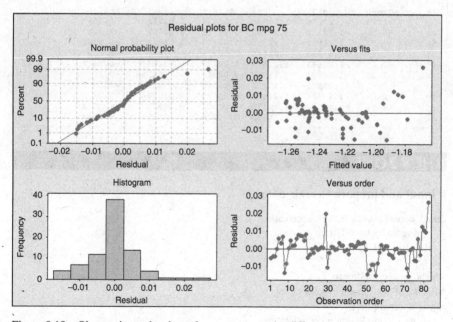

Figure 9.18   Observation order shows luxury cars may be different.

TABLE 9.24 Regression of MPG$_{BC\,0.75}$ on the principal components

```
The regression equation is
BC mpg 75 = - 1.23 + 0.0151 PrinComp1 + 0.00498 PrinComp2 + 0.0171 PrinComp3


Predictor          Coef     SE Coef         T      P     VIF
Constant       -1.23233     0.00077  -1596.15  0.000
PrinComp1      0.0151380   0.0007768     19.49  0.000   1.000
PrinComp2      0.0049782   0.0007768      6.41  0.000   1.000
PrinComp3      0.0171224   0.0007768     22.04  0.000   1.000


S = 0.00699137   R-Sq = 92.1%   R-Sq(adj) = 91.8%


Analysis of Variance

Source            DF        SS        MS       F      P
Regression         3  0.044316  0.014772  302.22  0.000
Residual Error    78  0.003813  0.000049
Total             81  0.048129


Source      DF    Seq SS
PrinComp1    1  0.018562
PrinComp2    1  0.002007
PrinComp3    1  0.023747


Unusual Observations

Obs  PrinComp1  BC mpg 75       Fit   SE Fit  Residual  St Resid
  8      -1.23   -1.27086  -1.25724  0.00218  -0.01362     -2.05R
 29      -0.01   -1.22800  -1.24803  0.00112   0.02003      2.90R
 51      -0.50   -1.23801  -1.22378  0.00114  -0.01423     -2.06R
 55       1.68   -1.23035  -1.21544  0.00174  -0.01490     -2.20R
 67      -0.05   -1.20881  -1.20665  0.00279  -0.00216     -0.34 X
 72       3.35   -1.20801  -1.19278  0.00319  -0.01523     -2.45RX
 78       3.69   -1.18139  -1.17819  0.00346  -0.00320     -0.53 X
 80       2.04   -1.17408  -1.18496  0.00289   0.01088      1.71 X
 81       3.56   -1.17193  -1.18170  0.00302   0.00977      1.55 X
 82       0.53   -1.14080  -1.16733  0.00276   0.02653      4.13RX
```

THE R ZONE

Input and prepare Cereals data

```
cereal <- read.csv(file = "C:/ ... /cereals.txt",
    stringsAsFactors=TRUE,
    header=TRUE,
    sep="\t")
which(is.na(cereal$Sugars))
# Record 58 has missing Sugars value
cereal <- cereal[-58,]
dat <- data.frame(Rating = cereal$Rating,
    Sugars = cereal$Sugars,
    Fiber = cereal$Fiber)
```

Three-Variable Scatterplot

```
library(scatterplot3d)
# Color by Rating
rg <- colorRampPalette(c("red",
    "green"))(76)
sp <- scatterplot3d(z=sort(cereal$Rating),
    y=cereal$Sugars,
    x=cereal$Fiber,
    color=rg,
    pch = 16,
    xlab = "Fiber",
    ylab = "Sugars",
    zlab = "Rating",
    main = "3D Scatterplot")
```

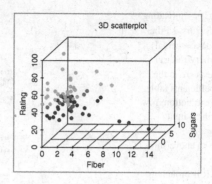

Individual Variable Scatter Plots of Rating vs. Sugars and Fiber

```
par(mfrow=c(1,2),
    mar = c(4.5,4,3,3),
    oma = c(0,1,0,0))
lm91 <- lm(Rating ~
    Sugars,
    data = cereal)
lm92 <- lm(Rating ~
    Fiber,
    data = cereal)
plot(Rating ~ Sugars,
    data = cereal,
    pch = 16,
    col = "red",
    ylab = "Rating")
abline(lm91, col = "blue")
plot(Rating ~ Fiber, data = cereal, pch = 16, col = "red")
abline(lm92, col = "blue")
# Reset plot area
par(mfrow=c(1,1))
```

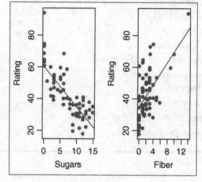

Multiple regression: <Insert carriage return.> # Output, *t*-Tests, F-Tests

```
mreg1 <- lm(Rating ~
    Sugars + Fiber,
    data = cereal)
summary(mreg1)
# t-tests are in the
# Coefficients table
# F-test: bottom row
# of the output

ma1 <- anova(mreg1)
ma1
# SSR is broken up
# between predictors
```

```
Call:
lm(formula = Rating ~ Sugars + Fiber, data = cereal)

Residuals:
    Min      1Q  Median      3Q     Max
-12.159  -4.415  -1.151   2.584  16.732

Coefficients:
            Estimate Std. Error t value Pr(>|t|)
(Intercept)  52.1742     1.5556  33.541  < 2e-16 ***
Sugars       -2.2436     0.1632 -13.750  < 2e-16 ***
Fiber         2.8665     0.2979   9.623 1.28e-14 ***
---
Signif. codes:  0 '***' 0.001 '**' 0.01 '*' 0.05 '.' 0.1 ' ' 1

Residual standard error: 6.127 on 73 degrees of freedom
Multiple R-squared: 0.8164,  Adjusted R-squared: 0.8114
F-statistic: 162.3 on 2 and 73 DF,  p-value: < 2.2e-16

Analysis of Variance Table

Response: Rating
          Df Sum Sq Mean Sq F value    Pr(>F)
Sugars     1 8711.9  8711.9 232.045 < 2.2e-16 ***
Fiber      1 3476.6  3476.6  92.601 1.276e-14 ***
Residuals 73 2740.7    37.5
---
Signif. codes:  0 '***' 0.001 '**' 0.01 '*' 0.05 '.' 0.1 ' ' 1
```

Confidence Intervals

```
# CI for Beta coefficients
confint(mreg1, level =0.95)
# Confidence Interval
predict(mreg1, newdata =
    data.frame(Sugars = 5, Fiber = 5),
    interval = c("confidence"))
# Prediction Interval
predict(mreg1, newdata =
    data.frame(Sugars = 5, Fiber = 5),
    interval = c("prediction"))
```

```
                 2.5 %    97.5 %
(Intercept) 49.074025 55.274460
Sugars      -2.568736 -1.918369
Fiber        2.272853  3.460221

       fit      lwr      upr
1 55.28916 53.06209 57.51623

       fit      lwr      upr
1 55.28916 42.876 67.70233
```

Dotplot of Rating by Shelf

```
# Create indicator variables
cereal$shelf1 <- ifelse(cereal$Shelf==1,
    1, 0)
cereal$shelf2 <- ifelse(cereal$Shelf==2,
    1, 0)
stripchart(Rating~Shelf,
    data = cereal,
    method = "stack",
    pch = 1,
    col=c("green", "blue", "red"),
main = "Rating by Shelf",
    offset=0.5,
    ylab = "Shelf")
```

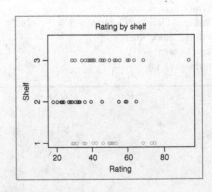

Regression including Shelf effect

```
# All shelves
mreg2 <- lm(Rating ~
    shelf1 + shelf2,
    data = cereal)
summary(mreg2)
anova(mreg2)
# One shelf
mreg3 <- lm(Rating ~
    Sugars + Fiber +
    shelf1 + shelf2,
    data = cereal)
summary(mreg3)
```

```
Call:
lm(formula = Rating ~ shelf1 + shelf2, data = cereal)

Residuals:
    Min     1Q  Median     3Q    Max
-17.157  -8.822  -4.254   5.984  48.485

Coefficients:
            Estimate Std. Error t value Pr(>|t|)
(Intercept)  45.2200     2.2457  20.136  < 2e-16 ***
shelf1        0.6789     3.8209   0.178  0.85946
shelf2      -10.2472     3.6999  -2.770  0.00711 **
---
Signif. codes:  0 '***' 0.001 '**' 0.01 '*' 0.05 '.' 0.1 ' ' 1

Residual standard error: 13.47 on 73 degrees of freedom
Multiple R-squared: 0.1122,  Adjusted R-squared: 0.0879
F-statistic: 4.614 on 2 and 73 DF,  p-value: 0.01297
Analysis of Variance Table

Response: Rating
          Df  Sum Sq Mean Sq F value   Pr(>F)
shelf1     1   282.7  282.72  1.5572 0.216067
shelf2     1  1392.7 1392.70  7.6708 0.007112 **
Residuals 73 13253.9  181.56
---
Signif. codes:  0 '***' 0.001 '**' 0.01 '*' 0.05 '.' 0.1 ' ' 1

Call:
lm(formula = Rating ~ Sugars + Fiber + shelf1 + shelf2, data = cereal)

Residuals:
    Min     1Q  Median     3Q    Max
-13.7512  -4.3085  -0.6918  2.9774 17.4020

Coefficients:
            Estimate Std. Error t value Pr(>|t|)
(Intercept)  50.5245     1.8512  27.293  < 2e-16 ***
Sugars       -2.3183     0.1729 -13.409  < 2e-16 ***
Fiber         3.1314     0.3186   9.827 7.08e-15 ***
shelf1        2.1011     1.7948   1.171  0.2457
shelf2        3.9154     1.8646   2.100  0.0393 *
---
Signif. codes:  0 '***' 0.001 '**' 0.01 '*' 0.05 '.' 0.1 ' ' 1

Residual standard error: 6.021 on 71 degrees of freedom
Multiple R-squared: 0.8276,  Adjusted R-squared: 0.8179
F-statistic: 85.21 on 4 and 71 DF,  p-value: < 2.2e-16
```

3D scatterplot with groups

```
sp <- scatterplot3d(z=
    sort(cereal$Rating),
    y=cereal$Sugars, x=cereal$Fiber,
    color=cereal$Shelf, pch = 16,
    xlab = "Fiber", ylab = "Sugars",
    zlab = "Rating",
    main = "3D Scatterplot")
```

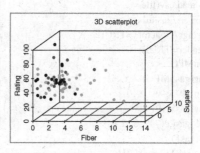

Sequential SS

```
mreg4.1 <- lm(Rating ~
    Sugars + Fiber + shelf2,
    data = cereal)
anova(mreg4.1)
mreg4.2 <- lm(Rating ~
    shelf1 + shelf2 +
    Sugars + Fiber,
    data = cereal)
anova(mreg4.2)
```

```
> anova(mreg4.1)
Analysis of Variance Table

Response: Rating
          Df Sum Sq Mean Sq F value   Pr(>F)
Sugars     1 8711.9  8711.9 239.0896 < 2.2e-16 ***
Fiber      1 3476.6  3476.6  95.4126 7.891e-15 ***
shelf2     1  117.2   117.2   3.2162  0.07711 .
Residuals 72 2623.5    36.4

> anova(mreg4.2)
Analysis of Variance Table

Response: Rating
          Df Sum Sq Mean Sq F value   Pr(>F)
shelf1     1  282.7   282.7   7.7989  0.006713 **
shelf2     1 1392.7  1392.7  38.4178 3.340e-08 ***
Sugars     1 7179.0  7179.0 198.0328 < 2.2e-16 ***
Fiber      1 3501.0  3501.0  96.5764 7.084e-15 ***
Residuals 71 2573.9    36.3
```

Multicollinearity

```
datam <- matrix(c(cereal$Fiber,
    cereal$Sugars,
    cereal$shelf2),
    ncol = 3)
colnames(datam)<- c("Fiber",
    "Sugars", "Shelf2")
cor(datam)
pairs(~Sugars+Fiber+Potass,
    data = cereal)
# VIFs
mreg5 <- lm(Rating ~ Sugars +
    Fiber + shelf2 + Potass,
    data = cereal)
library(car)
vif(mreg5)
```

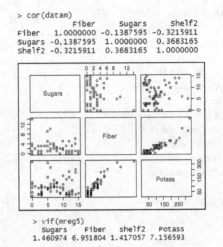

```
> cor(datam)
            Fiber      Sugars     Shelf2
Fiber   1.0000000 -0.1387595 -0.3215911
Sugars -0.1387595  1.0000000  0.3683165
Shelf2 -0.3215911  0.3683165  1.0000000
```

```
> vif(mreg5)
   Sugars     Fiber    shelf2    Potass
 1.460974  6.951804  1.417057  7.156593
```

Gas mileage data example

```
# Read in Gas data
gas <- read.csv(file =
    "C:/ ... /gasmilage.csv",
    stringsAsFactors=TRUE,
    header=TRUE)
gas$"lnMPG" <-
    log(gas$MPG)
gas$"lnHP" <-
    log(gas$HP)
gas1 <- gas[,c(7, 2, 8, 5, 6)]
names(gas1)
pairs(gas1[,1]~gas1[,2]+
    gas1[,3]+gas1[,4]+gas1[,5],
    labels = names(gas1),
    cex.labels = 1)
```

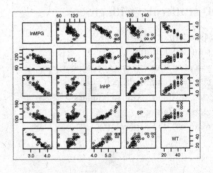

Model Selection: Forward

```
library(MASS)
# Declare empty model
mreg7.empty <- lm(lnMPG ~
    1, data = gas1)
stepF1 <- add1(mreg7.empty,
    scope = gas1[,-1],
    test = "F", trace = TRUE)
mreg7.empty2 <-
    lm(lnMPG ~ WT,
    data = gas1)
stepF2 <-
    add1(mreg7.empty2,
    scope = gas1[,-1],
    test = "F", trace = TRUE)
mreg7.empty3 <-
    lm(lnMPG ~ WT+lnHP,
    data = gas1)
stepF3<-
    add1(mreg7.empty3,
    scope = gas1[,-1],
    test = "F", trace = TRUE)
```

```
> stepF1
Single term additions

Model:
lnMPG ~ 1
       Df Sum of Sq     RSS     AIC F value      Pr(>F)
<none>              7.5039 -194.09
lnHP    1   6.2780 1.2259 -340.65 409.682 < 2.2e-16 ***
SP      1   4.1170 3.3869 -257.32  97.245 1.802e-15 ***
WT      1   6.7575 0.7464 -381.33 724.268 < 2.2e-16 ***

> stepF2
Single term additions

Model:
lnMPG ~ WT
       Df Sum of Sq     RSS     AIC F value      Pr(>F)
<none>              0.74641 -381.33
lnHP    1   0.18402 0.56239 -402.55 25.849 2.425e-06 ***
SP      1   0.13032 0.61609 -395.07 16.710 0.0001039 ***

> stepF3
Single term additions

Model:
lnMPG ~ WT + lnHP
       Df Sum of Sq     RSS     AIC F value Pr(>F)
<none>              0.56239 -402.55
SP      1   0.016553 0.54584 -403.00  2.3653 0.1281
```

Model Selection: Backward

```
# Declare full model
mreg7.full <- lm(lnMPG ~ .,
    data = gas1)
stepB1 <- drop1(mreg7.full,
    scope = gas1[,-1],
    test = "F",
    trace = TRUE)
mreg7.full2 <- lm(lnMPG ~
    lnHP+WT,
    data = gas1)
stepB2 <- drop1(mreg7.full2,
    scope = gas1[,-c(1,4)],
    test = "F",
    trace = TRUE)
```

```
> stepB1
Single term deletions

Model:
lnMPG ~ VOL + lnHP + SP + WT
       Df Sum of Sq     RSS     AIC F value     Pr(>F)
<none>              0.54544 -401.06
lnHP    1  0.063853 0.60930 -393.98  9.0141  0.003611 **
SP      1  0.012503 0.55795 -401.20  1.7651  0.187916
WT      1  0.170533 0.71598 -380.75 24.0741 5.058e-06 ***

> stepB2
Single term deletions

Model:
lnMPG ~ lnHP + WT
       Df Sum of Sq     RSS     AIC F value     Pr(>F)
<none>              0.56239 -402.55
lnHP    1   0.18401 0.74641 -381.33 25.849 2.425e-06 ***
WT      1   0.66353 1.22592 -340.65 93.207 5.163e-15 ***
```

Model Selection: Stepwise

```
library(rms)
mreg8 <- ols(lnMPG ~
    VOL+lnHP+SP+WT,
    data = gas1)
stepS <- fastbw(mreg8,
    rule="p")
# Your model is
# lnHP + WT
```

```
> stepS
 Deleted Chi-Sq d.f. P      Residual d.f. P      AIC   R2
 VOL     0.06   1    0.8130 0.06     1    0.8130 -1.94 0.927
 SP      2.34   1    0.1264 2.39     2    0.3023 -1.61 0.925

Approximate Estimates after Deleting Factors

            Coef    S.E.     Wald Z   P
Intercept  5.38578 0.163739 32.892   0.000e+00
lnHP      -0.24895 0.048845 -5.097   3.455e-07
WT        -0.02417 0.002498 -9.678   0.000e+00

Factors in Final Model

[1] lnHP WT
```

Model Selection: Best Subsets

```
library(leaps)
stepBS <- regsubsets(x=lnMPG ~
    WT+SP+lnHP+VOL,
    data = gas,
    nbest = 2)
sum.stepBS <- summary(stepBS)
sum.stepBS$which
sum.stepBS$rsq
sum.stepBS$cp
plot(c(1,2,2,3,3,4),
    sum.stepBS$cp[-2],
    main = "Cp by p",
    ylab = "Cp",
    xlab = "p",
    col = "red",
    pch = 16)
abline(a = 1, b = 1, lwd = 2)
# Final model without outlier
which(gas$MAKE.MODEL==
    "Subaru Loyale")
# Record 29 is an outlier
gas2 <- gas1[-29,]
mreg.fin2 <- lm(lnMPG ~
    lnHP+WT,
    data = gas2)
summary(mreg.fin2)
plot(mreg.fin2)
```

```
> sum.stepBS$which
  (Intercept)   WT    SP   lnHP   VOL
1        TRUE  TRUE FALSE FALSE FALSE
1        TRUE FALSE FALSE  TRUE FALSE
2        TRUE  TRUE FALSE  TRUE FALSE
2        TRUE  TRUE  TRUE FALSE FALSE
3        TRUE  TRUE  TRUE  TRUE FALSE
3        TRUE  TRUE FALSE  TRUE  TRUE
4        TRUE  TRUE  TRUE  TRUE  TRUE
> sum.stepBS$rsq
[1] 0.9005306 0.8366288 0.9250532
[4] 0.9178972 0.9272591 0.9256456
[7] 0.9273119
> sum.stepBS$cp
[1] 27.369888 95.062410  3.392653
[4] 10.973080  3.055936  4.765084
[7]  5.000000
```

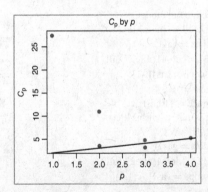

Display final model

```
mreg.fin <- lm(lnMPG ~
        lnHP+WT,
    data = gas1)
summary(mreg.fin)
par(mfrow=c(2,2))
plot(mreg.fin)
```

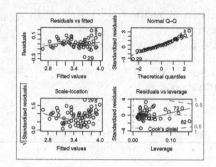

```
# Final model without outlier
which(gas$MAKE.MODEL==
    "Subaru Loyale")
# Record 29 is an outlier
gas2 <- gas1[-29,]
mreg.fin2 <- lm(lnMPG ~
    lnHP+WT,
    data = gas2)
summary(mreg.fin2)
plot(mreg.fin2)
```

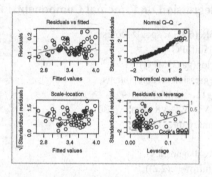

Regression on Principal Components: Preparation Step

```
# Standardize all data
gas$CabSpace_z <- (gas$VOL - mean(gas$VOL))/sd(gas$VOL)
gas$Horsepower_z <- (gas$HP - mean(gas$HP))/sd(gas$HP)
gas$TopSpeed_z <- (gas$SP - mean(gas$SP))/sd(gas$SP)
gas$Weight_z <- (gas$WT - mean(gas$WT))/sd(gas$WT)
# Create new dataset
gas3 <- gas[,-c(1:3,5:8)]
names(gas3)
```

Regression on Principal Components: PCA Step

```
# Run PCA on predictors
library(psych)
pca1 <- principal(gas3[,-1],
    rotate="varimax",
    nfactors = 3)
pca1$loadings
```

```
Loadings:
              RC1    RC2    RC3
CabSpace_z           0.988  0.152
Horsepower_z  0.892         0.449
TopSpeed_z    0.969         0.236
weight_z      0.518  0.279  0.809

                 RC1   RC2   RC3
SS loadings    2.003 1.058 0.934
Proportion Var 0.501 0.265 0.234
Cumulative Var 0.501 0.765 0.999
```

Regression on Principal Components: Regression Step

```
gas3[,c(6:8)] <- pca1$scores
gas3$lnMPG <-
    log(gas3$MPG)
# Regression on components
mreg11 <- lm(lnMPG ~
    V6+V7+V8, data = gas3)
summary(mreg11)

# Plot diagnostics
par(mfrow=c(2,2))
plot(mreg11)
```

```
call:
lm(formula = lnMPG ~ v6 + v7 + v8, data = gas3)

Residuals:
     Min       1Q   Median       3Q      Max
-0.28477 -0.05303 -0.01717  0.03899  0.27432

coefficients:
            Estimate Std. Error t value Pr(>|t|)
(Intercept)  3.475713  0.009918 350.451  < 2e-16 ***
v6          -0.184021  0.009979 -18.441  < 2e-16 ***
v7          -0.075567  0.009979  -7.573  6.3e-11 ***
v8          -0.212837  0.009979 -21.329  < 2e-16 ***
---
Signif. codes:  0 '***' 0.001 '**' 0.01 '*' 0.05 '.' 0.1 ' ' 1

Residual standard error: 0.08981 on 78 degrees of freedom
Multiple R-squared: 0.9162, Adjusted R-squared: 0.9129
F-statistic: 284.1 on 3 and 78 DF,  p-value: < 2.2e-16
```

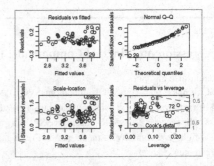

R REFERENCES

1. Harrell FE Jr. 2014. rms: Regression modeling strategies. R package version 4.1-3. http://CRAN
   .R-project.org/package=rms.
2. Fox J, Weisberg S. *An {R} Companion to Applied Regression*. 2nd ed. Thousand Oaks, CA: Sage; 2011.
   http://socserv.socsci.mcmaster.ca/jfox/Books/Companion.
3. Ligges U, Mächler M. Scatterplot3d – an R Package for visualizing multivariate data. *Journal of Statistical Software* 2003;8(11):1–20.
4. R Core Team. *R: A Language and Environment for Statistical Computing*. Vienna, Austria: R Foundation for Statistical Computing; 2012. ISBN: 3-900051-07-0,http://www.R-project.org/.
5. Revelle W. *psych: Procedures for Personality and Psychological Research*. Evanston, Illinois, USA: Northwestern University; 2013. . http://CRAN.R-project.org/package=psych Version=1.4.2.

6. Thomas Lumley using Fortran code by Alan Miller. 2009. leaps: regression subset selection. R package version 2.9. http://CRAN.R-project.org/package=leaps.
7. Venables WN, Ripley BD. *Modern Applied Statistics with S*. 4th ed. New York: Springer; 2002. ISBN: 0-387-95457-0.

EXERCISES

CLARIFYING THE CONCEPTS

1. Indicate whether the following statements are true or false. If the statement is false, alter it so that the statement becomes true.

   a. If we would like to approximate the relationship between a response and two continuous predictors, we would need a plane.

   b. In linear regression, while the response variable is typically continuous, it may be categorical as well.

   c. In general, for a multiple regression with m predictor variables, we would interpret coefficient b_i as follows: "the estimated change in the response variable for a unit increase in variable x_i is b_i."

   d. In multiple regression, the residual is represented by the vertical distance between the data point and the regression plane or hyperplane.

   e. Whenever a new predictor variable is added to the model, the value of R^2 always goes up.

   f. The alternative hypothesis in the *F-test* for the overall regression asserts that the regression coefficients all differ from zero.

   g. The standard error of the estimate is a valid measure of the usefulness of the regression, without reference to an inferential model (i.e., the assumptions need not be relevant).

   h. If we were to use only the categorical variables as predictors, then we would have to use *analysis of variance* and could not use linear regression.

   i. For use in regression, a categorical variable with k categories must be transformed into a set of k indicator variables.

   j. The first sequential sum of squares is exactly the value for SSR from the simple linear regression of the response on the first predictor.

   k. The VIF has a minimum of zero, but no upper limit.

   l. A variable that has been entered into the model early in the forward selection process will remain significant, once other variables have been entered into the model.

   m. The variable selection criteria for choosing the best model account for the multicollinearity among the predictors.

   n. The VIFs for principal components using varimax rotation always equal 1.0.

2. Clearly explain why s and R^2_{adj} are preferable to R^2 as measures for model building.

3. Explain the difference between the *t-test* and the *F-test* for assessing the significance of the predictors.

4. Construct indicator variables for the categorical variable *class*, which takes four values, freshman, sophomore, junior, and senior.

5. When using indicator variables, explain the meaning and interpretation of the indicator variable coefficients, graphically and numerically.

6. Discuss the concept of the level of significance (α). At what value should it be set? Who should decide the value of α? What if the observed p-value is close to α? Describe a situation where a particular p-value will lead to two different conclusions, given two different values for α.

7. Explain what it means when R^2_{adj} is much less than R^2.

8. Explain the difference between the sequential sums of squares and the partial sums of squares. For which procedures do we need these statistics?

9. Explain some of the drawbacks of a set of predictors with high multicollinearity.

10. Which statistics report the presence of multicollinearity in a set of predictors? Explain, using the formula, how this statistic works. Also explain the effect that large and small values of this statistic will have on the standard error of the coefficient.

11. Compare and contrast the effects that multicollinearity has on the point and intervals estimates of the response versus the values of the predictor coefficients.

12. Describe the differences and similarities among the forward selection procedure, the backward elimination procedure, and the stepwise procedure.

13. Describe how the best subsets procedure works. Why not always use the best subsets procedure?

14. Describe the behavior of Mallows' C_p statistic, including the heuristic for choosing the best model.

15. Suppose we wished to limit the number of predictors in the regression model to a lesser number than those obtained using the default settings in the variable selection criteria. How should we alter each of the selection criteria? Now, suppose we wished to increase the number of predictors. How then should we alter each of the selection criteria?

16. Explain the circumstances under which the value for R^2 would reach 100%. Now explain how the p-value for any test statistic could reach zero.

WORKING WITH THE DATA

For Exercises 17–27, consider the multiple regression output from *SPSS* in Table 9.25, using the *nutrition* data set, found on the book web site, www.DataMiningConsultant.com.

17. What is the response? What are the predictors?

18. What is the conclusion regarding the significance of the overall regression? How do you know? Does this mean that all of the predictors are important? Explain.

19. What is the typical error in prediction? (Hint: This may take a bit of digging.)

20. How many foods are included in the sample?

21. How are we to interpret the value of b_0, the coefficient for the constant term? Is this coefficient significantly different from zero? Explain how this makes sense.

TABLE 9.25 **Regression results for Exercises 17–27**

ANOVA[b]

Model		Sum of Squares	df	Mean Square	F	Sig.
1	Regression	2.83E+08	6	47,104,854.46	132,263.1	.000[a]
	Residual	339,762.5	954	356.145		
	Total	2.83E+08	960			

[a] Predictors: (Constant), SODIUM, CHOLEST, IRON, FAT, PROTEIN, CARBO.

[b] Dependent variable: CALORIES.

Coefficients[a]

Model		Unstandardized Coefficients		Standardized Coefficients			Collinearity Statistics	
		B	Std. Error	Beta	t	Sig.	Tolerance	VIF
1	(Constant)	−0.323	0.768		−0.421	0.674		
	PROTEIN	4.274	0.088	0.080	48.330	0.000	0.463	2.160
	FAT	8.769	0.023	0.535	375.923	0.000	0.621	1.611
	CHOLEST	0.006	0.007	0.001	0.897	0.370	0.535	1.868
	CARBO	3.858	0.013	0.558	293.754	0.000	0.349	2.864
	IRON	−1.584	0.305	−0.009	−5.187	0.000	0.404	2.475
	SODIUM	0.005	0.001	0.006	4.032	0.000	0.557	1.796

[a] Dependent variable: CALORIES.

22. Which of the predictors probably does not belong in the model? Explain how you know this. What might be your next step after viewing these results?

23. Suppose we omit cholesterol from the model and rerun the regression. Explain what will happen to the value of R^2.

24. Which predictor is negatively associated with the response? Explain how you know this.

25. Discuss the presence of multicollinearity. Evaluate the strength of evidence for the presence of multicollinearity. On the basis of this, should we turn to principal components analysis?

26. Clearly and completely express the interpretation for the coefficient for *sodium*.

27. Suppose a certain food was predicted to have 60 calories fewer than it actually has, based on its content of the predictor variables. Would this be considered unusual? Explain specifically how you would determine this.

For Exercises 28–29, next consider the multiple regression output from *SPSS* in Table 9.26. Three predictor variables have been added to the analysis in Exercises 17–27: saturated fat, monounsaturated fat, and polyunsaturated fat.

28. Evaluate the strength of evidence for the presence of multicollinearity.

29. On the basis of this, should we turn to principal components analysis?

TABLE 9.26 **Regression results for Exercises 28–29**

Coefficients[a]

Model	Unstandardized coefficients		Standardized Coefficients			Collinearity Statistics	
	B	Std. Error	Beta	t	Sig.	Tolerance	VIF
1 (Constant)	−0.158	0.772		−0.205	0.838		
PROTEIN	4.278	0.088	0.080	48.359	0.000	0.457	2.191
FAT	9.576	1.061	0.585	9.023	0.000	0.000	3379.867
CHOLEST	1.539E−02	0.008	0.003	1.977	0.048	0.420	2.382
CARBO	3.860	0.014	0.558	285.669	0.000	0.325	3.073
IRON	−1.672	0.314	−0.010	−5.328	0.000	0.377	2.649
SODIUM	5.183E−03	0.001	0.006	3.992	0.000	0.555	1.803
SAT_FAT	−1.011	1.143	−0.020	−0.884	0.377	0.002	412.066
MONUNSAT	−0.974	1.106	−0.025	−0.881	0.379	0.002	660.375
POLUNSAT	−0.600	1.111	−0.013	−0.541	0.589	0.002	448.447

[a]Dependent variable: CALORIES.

For Exercises 30–37, consider the multiple regression output from *SPSS* in Table 9.27, using the *New York* data set, found on the book web site, www.DataMiningConsultant.com. The data set contains demographic information about a set of towns in New York state. The response "MALE_FEM" is the number of males in the town for every 100 females. The predictors are the percentage under the age of 18, the percentage between 18 and 64, and the percentage over 64 living in the town (all expressed in percents such as "57.0"), along with the town's total population.

30. Note that the variable PCT_O64 was excluded. Explain why this variable was automatically excluded from the analysis by the software. (Hint: Consider the analogous case of using too many indicator variables to define a particular categorical variable.)

31. What is the conclusion regarding the significance of the overall regression?

32. What is the typical error in prediction?

33. How many towns are included in the sample?

34. Which of the predictors probably does not belong in the model? Explain how you know this. What might be your next step after viewing these results?

35. Suppose we omit TOT_POP from the model and rerun the regression. Explain what will happen to the value of R^2.

36. Discuss the presence of multicollinearity. Evaluate the strength of evidence for the presence of multicollinearity. On the basis of this, should we turn to principal components analysis?

37. Clearly and completely express the interpretation for the coefficient for PCT_U18. Discuss whether this makes sense.

TABLE 9.27 Regression results for Exercises 30–37

ANOVA[b]

Model		Sum of Squares	df	Mean Square	F	Sig.
1	Regression	100,298.8	3	33,432.919	44.213	0.000[a]
	Residual	594,361.3	786	756.185		
	Total	694,660.1	789			

[a] Predictors: (Constant), PC_18_64, TOT_POP, PCT_U18.
[b] Dependent variable: MALE_FEM.

Coefficients[a]

Model		Unstandardized Coefficients		Standardized Coefficients			Collinearity Statistics	
		B	Std. Error	Beta	t	Sig.	Tolerance	VIF
1	(Constant)	−63.790	16.855		−3.785	0.000		
	TOT_POP	−1.90E-06	0.000	−0.017	−0.506	0.613	1.000	1.000
	PCT_U18	0.660	0.249	0.105	2.657	0.008	0.700	1.428
	PC_18_64	2.250	0.208	0.427	10.830	0.000	0.700	1.428

[a] Dependent variable: MALE_FEM.

Excluded Variables[b]

Model		Beta In	t	Sig.	Partial Correlation	Collinearity Statistics		Minimum Tolerance
						Tolerance	VIF	
1	PCT_O64	−0.338[a]	−0.103	0.918	−0.004	1.009E-04	9907.839	7.906E-05

[a] Predictors in the Model: (Constant), PC_18_64, TOT_POP, PCT_U18.
[b] Dependent variable: MALE_FEM.

HANDS-ON ANALYSIS

For Exercises 38–41, use the *nutrition* data set, found on the book web site, www.DataMining-Consultant.com.

38. Build the best multiple regression model you can for the purposes of predicting calories, using all the other variables as the predictors. Do not worry about whether the predictor coefficients are stable or not. Compare and contrast the results from the forward selection, backward elimination, and stepwise variable selection procedures.

39. Apply the best subsets procedure, and compare against the previous methods.

40. (Extra credit). Write a script that will perform all possible regressions. Did the variable selection algorithms find the best regression?

41. Next, build the best multiple regression model you can for the purposes both of predicting the response and of profiling the predictors' individual relationship with the response. Make sure you account for multicollinearity.

For Exercises 42–44, use the *New York* data set, found on the book web site.

42. Build the best multiple regression model you can for the purposes of predicting the response, using the gender ratio as the response, and all the other variables as the predictors. Compare and contrast the results from the forward selection, backward elimination, and stepwise variable selection procedures.

43. Apply the best subsets procedure, and compare against the previous methods.

44. Perform all possible regressions. Did the variable selection algorithms find the best regression?

For Exercises 45–49, use the *crash* data set, found on the book web site.

45. Build the best multiple regression model you can for the purposes of predicting head injury severity, using all the other variables as the predictors.

46. Determine which variables must be made into indicator variables.

47. Determine which variables might be superfluous.

48. Build two parallel models, one where we account for multicollinearity, and another where we do not. For which purposes may each of these models be used?

49. Continuing with the *crash* data set, combine the four injury measurement variables into a single variable, defending your choice of combination function. Build the best multiple regression model you can for the purposes of predicting injury severity, using all the other variables as the predictors. Build two parallel models, one where we account for multicollinearity, and another where we do not. For which purposes may each of these models be used?

For Exercises 50–51, see if you can improve on the regression model of *ln MPG* on *ln HP* and *weight*.

50. Use a Box–Cox transformation to try to eliminate the skewness in the normal probability plot.

51. Do you see some curvature in the residuals versus fitted values plot? Produce a plot of the residuals against each of the predictors. Any curvature? Add a quadratic term of one of the predictors (e.g., weight^2) to the model, and see if this helps.

52. Using the four criteria from Chapter 5, determine the best number of principal components to extract for the gas mileage data.

53. Take a shot at improving the regression of $MPG_{BC\ 0.75}$ on the principal components. For example, you may wish to tweak the Box–Cox transformation, or you may wish to use an indicator variable for the luxury cars. Using whatever means you can bring to bear, obtain your best model that deals with multicollinearity and validates the regression assumptions.

PART III

CLASSIFICATION

k-NEAREST NEIGHBOR ALGORITHM

10.1 CLASSIFICATION TASK

Perhaps the most common data mining task is that of *classification*. Examples of classification tasks may be found in nearly every field of endeavor:

- *Banking*: Determining whether a mortgage application is a good or bad credit risk, or whether a particular credit card transaction is fraudulent.
- *Education*: Placing a new student into a particular track with regard to special needs.
- *Medicine*: Diagnosing whether a particular disease is present.
- *Law*: Determining whether a will was written by the actual person deceased or fraudulently by someone else.
- *Homeland security*: Identifying whether or not certain financial or personal behavior indicates a possible terrorist threat.

In classification, there is a target categorical variable, (e.g., *income bracket*), which is partitioned into predetermined classes or categories, such as high income, middle income, and low income. The data mining model examines a large set of records, each record containing information on the target variable as well as a set of input or predictor variables. For example, consider the excerpt from a data set shown in Table 10.1. Suppose that the researcher would like to be able to *classify* the income bracket of persons not currently in the database, based on the other characteristics associated with that person, such as age, gender, and occupation. This task is a classification task, very nicely suited to data mining methods and techniques.

The algorithm would proceed roughly as follows. First, examine the data set containing both the predictor variables and the (already classified) target variable, *income bracket*. In this way, the algorithm (software) "learns about" which combinations of variables are associated with which income brackets. For example, older females may be associated with the high-income bracket. This data set is called *the training set*. Then the algorithm would look at new records for which no information

Data Mining and Predictive Analytics, First Edition. Daniel T. Larose and Chantal D. Larose.
© 2015 John Wiley & Sons, Inc. Published 2015 by John Wiley & Sons, Inc.

TABLE 10.1   Excerpt from data set for classifying income

Subject	Age	Gender	Occupation	Income Bracket
001	47	F	Software engineer	High
002	28	M	Marketing consultant	Middle
003	35	M	Unemployed	Low
⋮				

about income bracket is available. Based on the classifications in the training set, the algorithm would assign classifications to the new records. For example, a 63-year-old female professor might be classified in the high-income bracket.

10.2   *k*-NEAREST NEIGHBOR ALGORITHM

The first algorithm we shall investigate is the *k-nearest neighbor* algorithm, which is most often used for classification, although it can also be used for estimation and prediction. *k*-Nearest neighbor is an example of *instance-based learning*, in which the training data set is stored, so that a classification for a new unclassified record may be found simply by comparing it to the most similar records in the training set. Let us consider an example.

Recall the example from Chapter 1 where we were interested in classifying the type of drug a patient should be prescribed, based on certain patient characteristics, such as the age of the patient and the patient's sodium/potassium ratio. For a sample of 200 patients, Figure 10.1 presents a scatter plot of the patients' sodium/potassium (Na/K) ratio against the patients' ages. The particular drug prescribed is symbolized by the shade of the points. Light gray points indicate drug Y; medium gray points indicate drug A or X; dark gray points indicate drug B or C.

Now suppose that we have a new patient record, without a drug classification, and would like to classify which drug should be prescribed for the patient based on which drug was prescribed for other patients with similar attributes. Identified as "new patient 1," this patient is 40 years old and has a Na/K ratio of 29, placing her at the center of the circle indicated for new patient 1 in Figure 10.1. Which drug classification should be made for new patient 1? Since her patient profile places her deep into a section of the scatter plot where all patients are prescribed drug Y, we would thereby classify new patient 1 as drug Y. All of the points nearest to this point, that is, all of the patients with a similar profile (with respect to age and Na/K ratio) have been prescribed the same drug, making this an easy classification.

Next, we move to new patient 2, who is 17 years old with a Na/K ratio of 12.5. Figure 10.2 provides a close-up view of the training data points in the local neighborhood of and centered at new patient 2. Suppose we let $k = 1$ for our *k*-nearest neighbor algorithm, so that new patient 2 would be classified according to whichever *single* (one) observation it was closest to. In this case, new patient 2 would be classified for drugs B and C (dark gray), since that is the classification of the point closest to the point on the scatter plot for new patient 2.

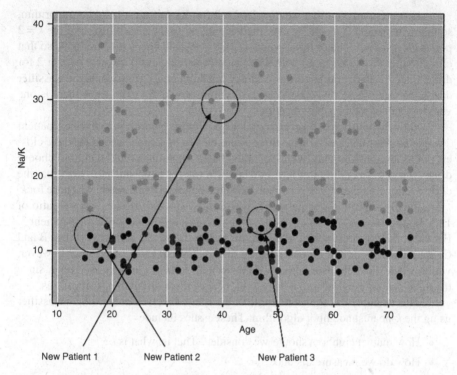

Figure 10.1   Scatter plot of sodium/potassium ratio against age, with drug overlay.

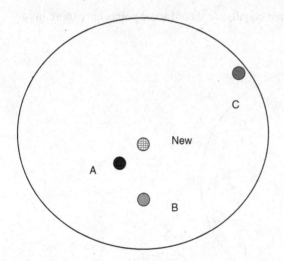

Figure 10.2   Close-up of three nearest neighbors to new patient 2.

However, suppose that we now let $k = 2$ for our k-nearest neighbor algorithm, so that new patient 2 would be classified according to the classification of the $k = 2$ points closest to it. One of these points is dark gray, and one is medium gray, so that our classifier would be faced with a decision between classifying new patient 2 for drugs B and C (dark gray) or drugs A and X (medium gray). How would the classifier decide between these two classifications? Voting would not help, since there is one vote for each of the two classifications.

Voting would help, however, if we let $k = 3$ for the algorithm, so that new patient 2 would be classified based on the three points closest to it. Since two of the three closest points are medium gray, a classification based on voting would therefore choose drugs A and X (medium gray) as the classification for new patient 2. Note that the classification assigned for new patient 2 differed based on which value we chose for k.

Finally, consider new patient 3, who is 47 years old and has a Na/K ratio of 13.5. Figure 10.3 presents a close-up of the three nearest neighbors to new patient 3. For $k = 1$, the k-nearest neighbor algorithm would choose the dark gray (drugs B and C) classification for new patient 3, based on a distance measure. For $k = 2$, however, voting would not help. But voting would not help for $k = 3$ in this case either, since the three nearest neighbors to new patient 3 are of three different classifications.

This example has shown us some of the issues involved in building a classifier using the k-nearest neighbor algorithm. These issues include

- How many neighbors should we consider? That is, what is k?
- How do we measure distance?
- How do we combine the information from more than one observation?

Later we consider other questions, such as

- Should all points be weighted equally, or should some points have more influence than others?

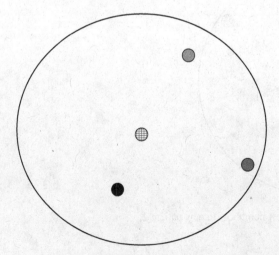

Figure 10.3   Close-up of three nearest neighbors to new patient 3.

10.3   DISTANCE FUNCTION

We have seen above how, for a new record, the k-nearest neighbor algorithm assigns the classification of the most similar record or records. But just how do we define *similar*? For example, suppose that we have a new patient who is a 50-year-old male. Which patient is more similar, a 20-year-old male or a 50-year-old female?

Data analysts define distance metrics to measure similarity. A *distance metric* or *distance function* is a real-valued function d, such that for any coordinates x, y, and z:

1. $d(x,y) \geq 0$, and $d(x,y) = 0$ if and only if $x = y$;
2. $d(x,y) = d(y,x)$;
3. $d(x,z) \leq d(x,y) + d(y,z)$.

Property 1 assures us that distance is always nonnegative, and the only way for distance to be zero is for the coordinates (e.g., in the scatter plot) to be the same. Property 2 indicates commutativity, so that, for example, the distance from New York to Los Angeles is the same as the distance from Los Angeles to New York. Finally, property 3 is the *triangle inequality*, which states that introducing a third point can never shorten the distance between two other points.

The most common distance function is *Euclidean distance*, which represents the usual manner in which humans think of distance in the real world:

$$d_{\text{Euclidean}}(x, y) = \sqrt{\sum_i (x_i - y_i)^2}$$

where $x = x_1, x_2, \ldots, x_m$ and $y = y_1, y_2, \ldots, y_m$ represent the m attribute values of two records. For example, suppose that patient A is $x_1 = 20$ years old and has a Na/K ratio of $x_2 = 12$, while patient B is $y_1 = 30$ years old and has a Na/K ratio of $y_2 = 8$. Then the Euclidean distance between these points, as shown in Figure 10.4, is

$$d_{\text{Euclidean}}(x, y) = \sqrt{\sum_i (x_i - y_i)^2} = \sqrt{(20 - 30)^2 + (12 - 8)^2}$$

$$= \sqrt{100 + 16} = 10.77$$

When measuring distance, however, certain attributes that have large values, such as income, can overwhelm the influence of other attributes that are measured on a smaller scale, such as years of service. To avoid this, the data analyst should make sure to *normalize* the attribute values.

For continuous variables, the *min−max normalization* or *Z-score standardization*, discussed in Chapter 2, may be used:

Min−max normalization:

$$X^* = \frac{X - \min(X)}{\text{range}(X)} = \frac{X - \min(X)}{\max(X) - \min(X)}$$

Z-score standardization:

$$X^* = \frac{X - \text{mean}(X)}{\text{SD}(X)}$$

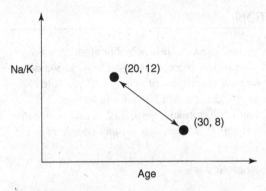

Figure 10.4 Euclidean distance.

For categorical variables, the Euclidean distance metric is not appropriate. Instead, we may define a function, "different from," used to compare the *i*th attribute values of a pair of records, as follows:

$$\text{Different}(x_i, y_i) = \begin{cases} 0 & \text{if } x_i = y_i \\ 1 & \text{otherwise} \end{cases}$$

where x_i and y_i are categorical values. We may then substitute different (x_i, y_i) for the *i*th term in the Euclidean distance metric above.

For example, let us find an answer to our earlier question: Which patient is more similar to a 50-year-old male: a 20-year-old male or a 50-year-old female? Suppose that for the *age* variable, the range is 50, the minimum is 10, the mean is 45, and the standard deviation is 15. Let patient A be our 50-year-old male, patient B the 20-year-old male, and patient C the 50-year-old female. The original variable values, along with the min–max normalization (age$_{\text{MMN}}$) and Z-score standardization (age$_{\text{Zscore}}$), are listed in Table 10.2.

TABLE 10.2 Variable values for age and gender

Patient	Age	Age$_{\text{MMN}}$	Age$_{\text{Zscore}}$	Gender
A	50	$\dfrac{50-10}{50} = 0.8$	$\dfrac{50-45}{15} = 0.33$	Male
B	20	$\dfrac{20-10}{50} = 0.2$	$\dfrac{20-45}{15} = -1.67$	Male
C	50	$\dfrac{50-10}{50} = 0.8$	$\dfrac{50-45}{15} = 0.33$	Female

We have one continuous variable (age, x_1) and one categorical variable (gender, x_2). When comparing patients A and B, we have different $(x_2, y_2) = 0$, with different $(x_2, y_2) = 1$ for the other combinations of patients. First, let us see what happens when we forget to normalize the age variable. Then, the distance between patients A and B is $d(A, B) = \sqrt{(50-20)^2 + 0^2} = 30$, and the distance between patients A and C is $d(A, C) = \sqrt{(20-20)^2 + 1^2} = 1$. We would thus conclude that the 20-year-old male is 30 times more "distant" from the 50-year-old male than the 50-year-old female is. In other words, the 50-year-old female is 30 times more "similar" to the 50-year-old male than the 20-year-old male is. Does this seem justified to you? Well, in certain circumstances, it may be justified, as in certain age-related illnesses. But, in general, one may judge that the two men are just as similar as are the two 50-year-olds. The problem is that the *age* variable is measured on a larger scale than the different(x_2, y_2) variable. Therefore, we proceed to account for this discrepancy by normalizing and standardizing the age values, as shown in Table 10.2.

Next, we use the min−max normalization values to find which patient is more similar to patient A. We have $d_{\text{MMN}}(A, B) = \sqrt{(0.8 - 0.2)^2 + 0^2} = 0.6$ and $d_{\text{MMN}}(A, C) = \sqrt{(0.8 - 0.8)^2 + 1^2} = 1$, which means that patient B is now considered to be more similar to patient A.

Finally, we use the Z-score standardization values to determine which patient is more similar to patient A. We have $d_{\text{Zscore}}(A, B) = \sqrt{[0.33 - (-1.67)]^2 + 0^2} = 2.0$ and $d_{\text{Zscore}}(A, C) = \sqrt{(0.33 - 0.33)^2 + 1^2} = 1.0$, which means that patient C is closer. Using the Z-score standardization rather than the min−max standardization has reversed our conclusion about which patient is considered to be more similar to patient A. This underscores the importance of understanding which type of normalization one is using. The min−max normalization will almost always lie between zero and 1 just like the "identical" function. The Z-score standardization, however, usually takes values $-3 < z < 3$, representing a wider scale than that of the min−max normalization. Therefore, perhaps, when mixing categorical and continuous variables, the min−max normalization may be preferred.

10.4 COMBINATION FUNCTION

Now that we have a method of determining which records are most similar to the new, unclassified record, we need to establish how these similar records will combine to provide a classification decision for the new record. That is, we need a *combination function*. The most basic combination function is simple unweighted voting.

10.4.1 Simple Unweighted Voting

1. Before running the algorithm, decide on the value of k, that is, how many records will have a voice in classifying the new record.

2. Then, compare the new record to the *k nearest neighbors*, that is, to the k records that are of minimum distance from the new record in terms of the Euclidean distance or whichever metric the user prefers.

3. Once the k records have been chosen, then for simple unweighted voting, their distance from the new record no longer matters. It is simple one record, one vote.

We observed simple unweighted voting in the examples for Figures 10.2 and 10.3. In Figure 10.2, for $k = 3$, a classification based on simple voting would choose drugs A and X (medium gray) as the classification for new patient 2, as two of the three closest points are medium gray. The classification would then be made for drugs A and X, with *confidence* 66.67%, where the confidence level represents the count of records, with the winning classification divided by k.

However, in Figure 10.3, for $k = 3$, simple voting would fail to choose a clear winner as each of the three categories receives one vote. There would be a tie among the three classifications represented by the records in Figure 10.3, and a tie may not be a preferred result.

10.4.2 Weighted Voting

One may feel that neighbors that are closer or more similar to the new record should be weighted more heavily than more distant neighbors. For example, in Figure 10.3, does it seem fair that the light gray record farther away gets the same vote as the dark gray vote that is closer to the new record? Perhaps not. Instead, the analyst may choose to apply *weighted voting*, where closer neighbors have a larger voice in the classification decision than do more distant neighbors. Weighted voting also makes it much less likely for ties to arise.

In weighted voting, the influence of a particular record is inversely proportional to the distance of the record from the new record to be classified. Let us look at an example. Consider Figure 10.2, where we are interested in finding the drug classification for a new record, using the $k = 3$ nearest neighbors. Earlier, when using simple unweighted voting, we saw that there were two votes for the medium gray classification, and one vote for the dark gray. However, the dark gray record is closer than the other two records. Will this greater proximity be enough for the influence of the dark gray record to overcome that of the more numerous medium gray records?

Assume that the records in question have the values for age and Na/K ratio given in Table 10.3, which also shows the min–max normalizations for these values. Then the distances of records A, B, and C from the new record are as follows:

$$d(\text{new}, A) = \sqrt{(0.05 - 0.0467)^2 + (0.25 - 0.2471)^2} = 0.004393$$

$$d(\text{new}, B) = \sqrt{(0.05 - 0.0533)^2 + (0.25 - 0.1912)^2} = 0.58893$$

$$d(\text{new}, C) = \sqrt{(0.05 - 0.0917)^2 + (0.25 - 0.2794)^2} = 0.051022$$

The votes of these records are then weighted according to the inverse square of their distances.

One record (A) votes to classify the new record as dark gray (drugs B and C), so the weighted vote for this classification is

$$\text{Votes(dark gray)} = \frac{1}{d(\text{new}, A)^2} = \frac{1}{0.004393^2} \cong 51,818$$

Two records (B and C) vote to classify the new record as medium gray (drugs A and X), so the weighted vote for this classification is

$$\text{Votes(medium gray)} = \frac{1}{d(\text{new}, B)^2} + \frac{1}{d(\text{new}, C)^2} = \frac{1}{0.058893^2} + \frac{1}{0.051022^2} \cong 672$$

TABLE 10.3   Age and Na/K ratios for records from Figure 5.4

Record	Age	Na/K	Age$_{MMN}$	Na/K$_{MMN}$
New	17	12.5	0.05	0.25
A (dark gray)	16.8	12.4	0.0467	0.2471
B (medium gray)	17.2	10.5	0.0533	0.1912
C (medium gray)	19.5	13.5	0.0917	0.2794

Therefore, by the convincing total of 51,818 to 672, the weighted voting procedure would choose dark gray (drugs B and C) as the classification for a new 17-year-old patient with a sodium/potassium ratio of 12.5. Note that this conclusion reverses the earlier classification for the unweighted $k = 3$ case, which chose the medium gray classification.

When the distance is zero, the inverse would be undefined. In this case, the algorithm should choose the majority classification of all records whose distance is zero from the new record.

Consider for a moment that once we begin weighting the records, there is no theoretical reason why we could not increase k arbitrarily so that all existing records are included in the weighting. However, this runs up against the practical consideration of very slow computation times for calculating the weights of all of the records every time a new record needs to be classified.

10.5   QUANTIFYING ATTRIBUTE RELEVANCE: STRETCHING THE AXES

Consider that not all attributes may be relevant to the classification. In decision trees (Chapter 11), for example, only those attributes that are helpful to the classification are considered. In the k-nearest neighbor algorithm, the distances are by default calculated on all the attributes. It is possible, therefore, for relevant records that are proximate to the new record in all the important variables, but are distant from the new record in unimportant ways, to have a moderately large distance from the new record, and therefore not be considered for the classification decision. Analysts may therefore consider restricting the algorithm to fields known to be important for classifying new records, or at least to blind the algorithm to known irrelevant fields.

Alternatively, rather than restricting fields a priori, the data analyst may prefer to indicate which fields are of more or less importance for classifying the target variable. This can be accomplished using a *cross-validation approach* or one based on domain expert knowledge. First, note that the problem of determining which fields are more or less important is equivalent to finding a coefficient z_j by which to multiply the jth axis, with larger values of z_j associated with more important variable axes. This process is therefore termed *stretching the axes*.

The cross-validation approach then selects a random subset of the data to be used as a training set and finds the set of values $z_1, z_2, \ldots, z_m$ that minimize the classification error on the test data set. Repeating the process will lead to a more accurate set of values $z_1, z_2, \ldots, z_m$. Otherwise, domain experts may be called on to recommend a set of values for $z_1, z_2, \ldots, z_m$. In this way, the *k*-nearest neighbor algorithm may be made more precise.

For example, suppose that either through cross-validation or expert knowledge, the Na/K ratio was determined to be three times as important as age for drug classification. Then we would have $z_{Na/K} = 3$ and $z_{age} = 1$. For the example above, the new distances of records A, B, and C from the new record would be as follows:

$$d(\text{new, A}) = \sqrt{(0.05 - 0.0467)^2 + [3(0.25 - 0.2471)]^2} = 0.009305$$

$$d(\text{new, B}) = \sqrt{(0.05 - 0.0533)^2 + [3(0.25 - 0.1912)]^2} = 0.17643$$

$$d(\text{new, C}) = \sqrt{(0.05 - 0.0917)^2 + [3(0.25 - 0.2794)]^2} = 0.09756$$

In this case, the classification would not change with the stretched axis for Na/K, remaining dark gray. In real-world problems, however, axis stretching can lead to more accurate classifications, as it represents a method for quantifying the relevance of each variable in the classification decision.

10.6 DATABASE CONSIDERATIONS

For instance-based learning methods such as the *k*-nearest neighbor algorithm, it is vitally important to have access to a rich database full of as many different combinations of attribute values as possible. It is especially important that rare classifications be represented sufficiently, so that the algorithm does not only predict common classifications. Therefore, the data set would need to be *balanced*, with a sufficiently large percentage of the less common classifications. One method to perform balancing is to reduce the proportion of records with more common classifications.

Maintaining this rich database for easy access may become problematic if there are restrictions on main memory space. Main memory may fill up, and access to auxiliary storage is slow. Therefore, if the database is to be used for *k*-nearest neighbor methods only, it may be helpful to retain only those data points that are near a classification "boundary." For example, in Figure 10.1, all records with Na/K ratio value greater than, say, 19 could be omitted from the database without loss of classification accuracy, as all records in this region are classified as light gray. New records with Na/K ratio >19 would therefore be classified similarly.

10.7 *k*-NEAREST NEIGHBOR ALGORITHM FOR ESTIMATION AND PREDICTION

So far we have considered how to use the *k*-nearest neighbor algorithm for classification. However, it may be used for estimation and prediction as well as for continuous-valued target variables. One method for accomplishing this is called *locally weighted averaging*. Assume that we have the same data set as the example above, but this time rather than attempting to classify the drug prescription, we are trying to estimate the systolic blood pressure reading (BP, the target variable) of the patient, based on that patient's *age* and *Na/K ratio* (the predictor variables). Assume that BP has a range of 80 with a minimum of 90 in the patient records.

In this example, we are interested in estimating the systolic BP reading for a 17-year-old patient with a Na/K ratio of 12.5, the same new patient record for which we earlier performed drug classification. If we let $k = 3$, we have the same three nearest neighbors as earlier, shown here in Table 10.4. Assume that we are using the $z_{Na/K}$ = three-axis-stretching to reflect the greater importance of the Na/K ratio.

TABLE 10.4 $k = 3$ nearest neighbors of the new record

Record	Age	Na/K	BP	Age$_{MMN}$	Na/K$_{MMN}$	Distance
New	17	12.5	?	0.05	0.25	—
A	16.8	12.4	120	0.0467	0.2471	0.009305
B	17.2	10.5	122	0.0533	0.1912	0.17643
C	19.5	13.5	130	0.0917	0.2794	0.26737

Locally weighted averaging would then estimate BP as the weighted average of BP for the $k = 3$ nearest neighbors, using the same inverse square of the distances for the weights that we used earlier. That is, the estimated target value $\hat{y}$ is calculated as

$$\hat{y}_{new} = \frac{\sum_i w_i y_i}{\sum_i w_i}$$

where $w_i = 1/d(new, x_i)^2$ for existing records $x_1, x_2, \ldots, x_k$. Thus, in this example, the estimated systolic BP reading for the new record would be

$$\hat{y}_{new} = \frac{\sum_i w_i y_i}{\sum_i w_i} = \frac{(120/0.009305^2) + (122/0.17643^2) + (130/0.09756^2)}{(1/0.009305^2) + (1/0.17643^2) + (1/0.09756^2)} = 120.0954.$$

As expected, the estimated BP value is quite close to the BP value in the present data set that is much closer (in the stretched attribute space) to the new record. In other words, as record A is closer to the new record, its BP value of 120 contributes greatly to the estimation of the BP reading for the new record.

10.8   CHOOSING k

How should one go about choosing the value of k? In fact, there may not be an obvious best solution. Consider choosing a small value for k. Then it is possible that the classification or estimation may be unduly affected by outliers or unusual observations ("noise"). With small k (e.g., $k = 1$), the algorithm will simply return the target value of the nearest observation, a process that may lead the algorithm toward overfitting, tending to memorize the training data set at the expense of generalizability.

However, choosing a value of k that is not too small will tend to smooth out any idiosyncratic behavior learned from the training set. However, if we take this too far and choose a value of k that is too large, locally interesting behavior will be overlooked. The data analyst needs to balance these considerations when choosing the value of k.

It is possible to allow the data itself to help resolve this problem, by following a cross-validation procedure similar to the earlier method for finding the optimal values $z_1, z_2, \ldots, z_m$ for axis stretching. Here, we would try various values of k with different randomly selected training sets and choose the value of k that minimizes the classification or estimation error.

10.9 APPLICATION OF *k*-NEAREST NEIGHBOR ALGORITHM USING IBM/SPSS MODELER

Table 10.5 contains a small data set of 10 records excerpted from the *ClassifyRisk* data set, with predictors' *age*, *marital status*, and *income*, and target variable *risk*. We seek the *k*-nearest neighbor for record 10, using $k = 2$. Modeler's results are shown in Figure 10.5. (Note that Modeler automatically normalizes the data.) Records 8 and 9 are the two nearest neighbors to Record 10, with the same marital status, and somewhat similar ages. As both Records 8 and 9 and classified as Good risk, the prediction for Record 10 would be Good risk as well.

TABLE 10.5 Find the *k*-nearest neighbor for Record #10

Record	Age	Marital	Income	Risk
1	22	Single	$46,156.98	Bad loss
2	33	Married	$24,188.10	Bad loss
3	28	Other	$28,787.34	Bad loss
4	51	Other	$23,886.72	Bad loss
5	25	Single	$47,281.44	Bad loss
6	39	Single	$33,994.90	Good risk
7	54	Single	$28,716.50	Good risk
8	55	Married	$49,186.75	Good risk
9	50	Married	$46,726.50	Good risk
10	66	Married	$36,120.34	Good risk

THE R ZONE

Create the data set using Table 10.3

```
new <- c(0.05,0.25)
A <- c(0.0467, 0.2471)
B <- c(0.0533, 0.1912)
C <- c(0.0917, 0.2794)
data <- rbind(A, B, C)
dimnames(data) <- list(c("Dark", "Medium", "Light"),
    c("Age (MMN)", "Na/K (MMN)"))
# Declare true classifications of A, B, and C.
trueclass <- c("Dark", "Medium", "Light")
```

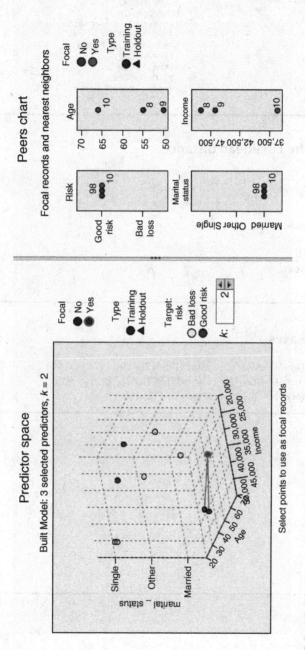

Figure 10.5 Modeler *k*-nearest neighbor results.

Run KNN

```
# Requires package "class"
library(class)
knn <- knn(data,
    new,
    cl = trueclass,
    k = 3,
    prob = TRUE)
knn
```

```
> knn(data,
+      new,
+      cl = trueclass,
+      k = 3,
+      prob = TRUE)
[1] Medium
attr(,"prob")
[1] 0.6666667
Levels: Dark Medium
```

Calculate the Euclidean distance

```
# Requires
    package "fields"
library(fields)
together <- rbind(new,
    data)
# The top row has the
# distances from New
rdist(together)
```

```
> rdist(together)
           [,1]          [,2]          [,3]          [,4]
[1,] 0.0000000001 0.0043931765 0.0588925292 0.0510220541
[2,] 0.0043931765 0.0000000001 0.0562882759 0.0553921475
[3,] 0.0588925292 0.0562882759 0.0000000001 0.0961966735
[4,] 0.0510220541 0.0553921475 0.0961966735 0.0000000001
```

Stretch the axes

```
ds_newA <- sqrt((new[1] -A[1])^2 + (3*(new[2]-A[2]))^2)
ds_newB <- sqrt((new[1] -B[1])^2 + (3*(new[2]-B[2]))^2)
ds_newC <- sqrt((new[1] -C[1])^2 + (3*(new[2]-C[2]))^2)
```

Table 10.4

```
distance <- c(ds_newA,
    ds_newB,
    ds_newC)
BP <- c(120, 122, 130)
data <- cbind(BP,
    data,
    distance)
data
```

```
> data
        BP  Age (MMN) Na/K (MMN)    distance
Dark   120    0.0467     0.2471 0.009304837
Medium 122    0.0533     0.1912 0.176430865
Medium 130    0.0917     0.2794 0.097560904
```

Locally Weighted Averaging

```
weights <- (1/(distance^2))
sum_wi <- sum(weights)
sum_wiyi <- sum(weights*data[,1])
yhat_new <- sum_wiyi/sum_wi
yhat_new
```

```
> yhat_new
[1] 120.0954
```

ClassifyRisk example: Prep the data

```
# Read in the ClassifyRisk dataset
risk <- read.csv(file = "C:/ ... /classifyrisk.txt", stringsAsFactors=FALSE, header=TRUE,
    sep="\t")
# Table 10.5 contains Records 51, 65, 79, 87, 124, 141, 150, 162, 163
risk2 <- risk[c(51, 65, 79, 87, 124, 141, 150, 162), c(5, 1, 4, 6)]
risk2$married.I <- ifelse(risk2$marital_status=="married",1,0)
risk2$single.I <- ifelse(risk2$marital_status=="single", 1, 0)
risk2 <- risk2[,-2]; new2 <- risk[163, c(5, 1, 4)]
new2$married.I <- 1; new2$single.I <- 0
new2 <- new2[,-2]; cll <- c(risk2[,3])
```

ClassifyRisk example: KNN

```
knn2 <- knn(train = risk2[,c(1,2,4,5)],
    test = new2,
    cl = cll,
    k = 3)
```

```
> knn2
[1] good risk
Levels: bad loss good risk
```

R REFERENCES

R Core Team (2012). *R: A Language and Environment for Statistical Computing*. R Foundation for Statistical Computing, Vienna, Austria. 3-900051-07-0, http://www.R-project.org/.
Venables WN, Ripley BD. *Modern Applied Statistics with S*. 4th ed. New York: Springer; 2002. ISBN: 0-387-95457-0.

EXERCISES

1. Clearly describe what is meant by classification.

2. What is meant by the term *instance-based learning*?

3. Make up a set of three records, each with two numeric predictor variables and one categorical target variable, so that the classification would not change regardless of the value of k.

4. Refer to Exercise 3. Alter your data set so that the classification changes for different values of *k*.

5. Refer to Exercise 4. Find the Euclidean distance between each pair of points. Using these points, verify that Euclidean distance is a true distance metric.

6. Compare the advantages and drawbacks of unweighted versus weighted voting.

7. Why does the database need to be balanced?

8. The example in the text regarding using the *k*-nearest neighbor algorithm for estimation has the closest record, overwhelming the other records in influencing the estimation. Suggest two creative ways that we could use to dilute this strong influence of the closest record.

9. Discuss the advantages and drawbacks of using a small value versus a large value for *k*.

10. Why would one consider stretching the axes?

11. What is locally weighted averaging, and how does it help in estimation?

HANDS-ON ANALYSIS

12. Using the data in table 10.5, find the *k*-nearest neighbor for Record #10, using *k* = 3.

13. Using the *ClassifyRisk* data set with predictors *age*, *marital status*, and *income*, and target variable *risk*, find the *k*-nearest neighbor for Record #1, using *k* = 2 and Euclidean distance.

14. Using the *ClassifyRisk* data set with predictors *age*, *marital status*, and *income*, and target variable *risk*, find the *k*-nearest neighbor for Record #1, using *k* = 2 and Minkowski (city-block) distance (Chapter 19).

## CHAPTER 11

DECISION TREES

11.1 WHAT IS A DECISION TREE?

In this chapter, we continue our examination of classification methods for data mining. One attractive classification method involves the construction of a *decision tree*, a collection of *decision nodes*, connected by *branches*, extending downward from the *root node* until terminating in *leaf nodes*. Beginning at the root node, which by convention is placed at the top of the decision tree diagram, attributes are tested at the decision nodes, with each possible outcome resulting in a branch. Each branch then leads either to another decision node or to a terminating leaf node. Figure 11.1 provides an example of a simple decision tree.

The target variable for the decision tree in Figure 11.1 is *credit risk*, with potential customers being classified as either good or bad credit risks. The predictor variables are *savings* (low, medium, and high), *assets* (low or not low), and *income* (≤$30,000 or >$30,000). Here, the root node represents a decision node, testing whether each record has a low, medium, or high savings level (as defined by the analyst or domain expert). The data set is partitioned, or *split*, according to the values of this attribute. Those records with low savings are sent via the leftmost branch (*savings = low*) to another decision node. The records with high savings are sent via the rightmost branch to a different decision node.

The records with medium savings are sent via the middle branch directly to a leaf node, indicating the termination of this branch. Why a leaf node and not another decision node? Because, in the data set (not shown), all of the records with medium savings levels have been classified as good credit risks. There is no need for another decision node, because our knowledge that the customer has medium savings predicts good credit with 100% accuracy in the data set.

For customers with low savings, the next decision node tests whether the customer has low assets. Those with low assets are then classified as bad credit risks; the others are classified as good credit risks. For customers with high savings, the next decision node tests whether the customer has an income of at most $30,000. Customers with incomes of $30,000 or less are then classified as bad credit risks, with the others classified as good credit risks.

Data Mining and Predictive Analytics, First Edition. Daniel T. Larose and Chantal D. Larose.
© 2015 John Wiley & Sons, Inc. Published 2015 by John Wiley & Sons, Inc.

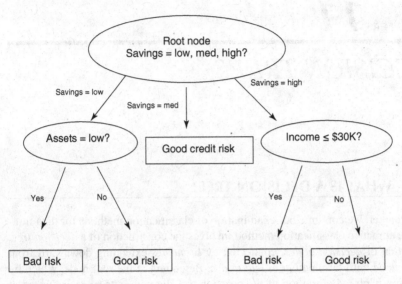

Figure 11.1 Simple decision tree.

When no further splits can be made, the decision tree algorithm stops growing new nodes. For example, suppose that all of the branches terminate in "pure" leaf nodes, where the target variable is unary for the records in that node (e.g., each record in the leaf node is a good credit risk). Then no further splits are necessary, so no further nodes are grown.

However, there are instances when a particular node contains "diverse" attributes (with non-unary values for the target attribute), and yet the decision tree cannot make a split. For example, suppose that we consider the records from Figure 11.1 with high savings and low income (≤$30,000). Suppose that there are five records with these values, all of which also have low assets. Finally, suppose that three of these five customers have been classified as bad credit risks and two as good credit risks, as shown in Table 11.1. In the real world, one often encounters situations such as this, with varied values for the response variable, even for exactly the same values for the predictor variables.

Here, as all customers have the same predictor values, there is no possible way to split the records according to the predictor variables that will lead to a pure leaf

TABLE 11.1 Sample of records that cannot lead to pure leaf node

Customer	Savings	Assets	Income	Credit Risk
004	High	Low	≤$30,000	Good
009	High	Low	≤$30,000	Good
027	High	Low	≤$30,000	Bad
031	High	Low	≤$30,000	Bad
104	High	Low	≤$30,000	Bad

node. Therefore, such nodes become diverse leaf nodes, with mixed values for the target attribute. In this case, the decision tree may report that the classification for such customers is "bad," with 60% confidence, as determined by the three-fifths of customers in this node who are bad credit risks. Note that not all attributes are tested for all records. Customers with low savings and low assets, for example, are not tested with regard to income in this example.

11.2   REQUIREMENTS FOR USING DECISION TREES

Following requirements must be met before decision tree algorithms may be applied:

1. Decision tree algorithms represent supervised learning, and as such require preclassified target variables. A training data set must be supplied, which provides the algorithm with the values of the target variable.

2. This training data set should be rich and varied, providing the algorithm with a healthy cross section of the types of records for which classification may be needed in the future. Decision trees learn by example, and if examples are systematically lacking for a definable subset of records, classification and prediction for this subset will be problematic or impossible.

3. The target attribute classes must be discrete. That is, one cannot apply decision tree analysis to a continuous target variable. Rather, the target variable must take on values that are clearly demarcated as either belonging to a particular class or not belonging.

Why, in the example above, did the decision tree choose the *savings* attribute for the root node split? Why did it not choose *assets* or *income* instead? Decision trees seek to create a set of leaf nodes that are as "pure" as possible; that is, where each of the records in a particular leaf node has the same classification. In this way, the decision tree may provide classification assignments with the highest measure of confidence available.

However, how does one measure uniformity, or conversely, how does one measure heterogeneity? We shall examine two of the many methods for measuring leaf node purity, which lead to the following two leading algorithms for constructing decision trees:

- Classification and regression trees (CART) algorithm;
- C4.5 algorithm.

11.3   CLASSIFICATION AND REGRESSION TREES

The CART method was suggested by Breiman *et al.*[1] in 1984. The decision trees produced by CART are strictly binary, containing exactly two branches for each decision

[1]Leo Breiman, Jerome Friedman, Richard Olshen, and Charles Stone, *Classification and Regression Trees*, Chapman & Hall/CRC Press, Boca Raton, FL, 1984.

node. CART recursively partitions the records in the training data set into subsets of records with similar values for the target attribute. The CART algorithm grows the tree by conducting for each decision node, an exhaustive search of all available variables and all possible splitting values, selecting the optimal split according to the following criteria (from Kennedy et al.[2]).

Let $\Phi(s|t)$ be a measure of the "goodness" of a candidate split s at node t, where

$$\Phi(s|t) = 2P_L P_R \sum_{j=1}^{\#\text{classes}} |P(j|t_L) - P(j|t_R)| \tag{11.1}$$

and where

$$t_L = \text{left child node of node } t$$

$$t_R = \text{right child node of node } t$$

$$P_L = \frac{\text{number of records at } t_L}{\text{number of records in training set}}$$

$$P_R = \frac{\text{number of records at } t_R}{\text{number of records in training set}}$$

$$P(j|t_L) = \frac{\text{number of class } j \text{ records at } t_L}{\text{number of records at } t}$$

$$P(j|t_R) = \frac{\text{number of class } j \text{ records at } t_R}{\text{number of records at } t}$$

Then the optimal split is whichever split maximizes this measure $\Phi(s|t)$ over all possible splits at node t.

Let us look at an example. Suppose that we have the training data set shown in Table 11.2 and are interested in using CART to build a decision tree for predicting whether a particular customer should be classified as being a good or a bad credit risk.

[2]Ruby L. Kennedy, Yuchun Lee, Benjamin Van Roy, Christopher D. Reed, and Richard P. Lippman, *Solving Data Mining Problems through Pattern Recognition*, Pearson Education, Upper Saddle River, NJ, 1995.

TABLE 11.2 Training set of records for classifying credit risk

Customer	Savings	Assets	Income ($1000s)	Credit Risk
1	Medium	High	75	Good
2	Low	Low	50	Bad
3	High	Medium	25	Bad
4	Medium	Medium	50	Good
5	Low	Medium	100	Good
6	High	High	25	Good
7	Low	Low	25	Bad
8	Medium	Medium	75	Good

In this small example, all eight training records enter into the root node. As CART is restricted to binary splits, the candidate splits that the CART algorithm would evaluate for the initial partition at the root node are shown in Table 11.3. Although *income* is a continuous variable, CART may still identify a finite list of possible splits based on the number of different values that the variable actually takes in the data set. Alternatively, the analyst may choose to categorize the continuous variable into a smaller number of classes.

TABLE 11.3   Candidate splits for t = root node

Candidate Split	Left Child Node, t_L	Right Child Node, t_R
1	*Savings = low*	*Savings ∈ {medium, high}*
2	*Savings = medium*	*Savings ∈ {low, high}*
3	*Savings = high*	*Savings ∈ {low, medium}*
4	*Assets = low*	*Assets ∈ {medium, high}*
5	*Assets = medium*	*Assets ∈ {low, high}*
6	*Assets = high*	*Assets ∈ {low, medium}*
7	*Income ≤ \$25,000*	*Income > \$25,000*
8	*Income ≤ \$50,000*	*Income > \$50,000*
9	*Income ≤ \$75,000*	*Income > \$75,000*

For each candidate split, let us examine the values of the various components of the optimality measure $\Phi(s|t)$ in Table 11.4. Using these observed values, we may investigate the behavior of the optimality measure under various conditions. For example, when is $\Phi(s|t)$ large? We see that $\Phi(s|t)$ is large when both of its main components are large: $2P_L P_R$ and $\sum_{j=1}^{\#classes} |P(j|t_L) - P(j|t_R)|$.

Consider $Q(s|t) = \sum_{j=1}^{\#classes} |P(j|t_L) - P(j|t_R)|$. When is the component $Q(s|t)$ large? $Q(s|t)$ is large when the distance between $P(j|t_L)$ and $P(j|t_R)$ is maximized across each class (value of the target variable). In other words, this component is maximized when the proportions of records in the child nodes for each particular value of the target variable are as different as possible. The maximum value would therefore occur when for each class the child nodes are completely uniform (pure). The theoretical maximum value for $Q(s|t)$ is k, where k is the number of classes for the target variable. As our output variable *credit risk* takes two values, *good* and *bad*, $k = 2$ is the maximum for this component.

The component $2P_L P_R$ is maximized when P_L and P_R are large, which occurs when the proportions of records in the left and right child nodes are equal. Therefore, $\Phi(s|t)$ will tend to favor balanced splits that partition the data into child nodes containing roughly equal numbers of records. Hence, the optimality measure $\Phi(s|t)$ prefers splits that will provide child nodes that are homogeneous for all classes and have roughly equal numbers of records. The theoretical maximum for $2P_L P_R$ is $2(0.5)(0.5) = 0.5$.

In this example, only candidate split 5 has an observed value for $2P_L P_R$ that reaches the theoretical maximum for this statistic, 0.5, because the records are

TABLE 11.4 Values of the components of the optimality measure Φ(s|t) for each candidate split, for the root node (best performance highlighted)

Split	P_L	P_R	$P(j|t_L)$	$P(j|t_R)$	$2P_L P_R$	$Q(s|t)$	$\Phi(s|t)$
1	0.375	0.625	G: 0.333	G: 0.8	0.46875	0.934	0.4378
			B: 0.667	B: 0.2			
2	0.375	0.625	G: 1	G: 0.4	0.46875	1.2	0.5625
			B: 0	B: 0.6			
3	0.25	0.75	G: 0.5	G: 0.667	0.375	0.334	0.1253
			B: 0.5	B: 0.333			
4	0.25	0.75	G: 0	G: 0.833	0.375	1.667	**0.6248**
			B: 1	B: 0.167			
5	0.5	0.5	G: 0.75	G: 0.5	0.5	0.5	0.25
			B: 0.25	B: 0.5			
6	0.25	0.75	G: 1	G: 0.5	0.375	1	0.375
			B: 0	B: 0.5			
7	0.375	0.625	G: 0.333	G: 0.8	0.46875	0.934	0.4378
			B: 0.667	B: 0.2			
8	0.625	0.375	G: 0.4	G: 1	0.46875	1.2	0.5625
			B: 0.6	B: 0			
9	0.875	0.125	G: 0.571	G: 1	0.21875	0.858	0.1877
			B: 0.429	B: 0			

partitioned equally into two groups of four. The theoretical maximum for $Q(s|t)$ is obtained only when each resulting child node is pure, and thus is not achieved for this data set.

The maximum observed value for $\Phi(s|t)$ among the candidate splits is therefore attained by split 4, with $\Phi(s|t) = 0.6248$. CART therefore chooses to make the initial partition of the data set using candidate split 4, assets = low versus assets ∈ {medium, high}, as shown in Figure 11.2.

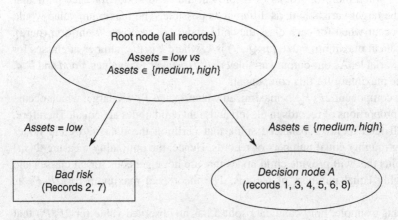

Figure 11.2 CART decision tree after initial split.

The left child node turns out to be a terminal leaf node, because both of the records that were passed to this node had *bad* credit risk. The right child node, however, is diverse and calls for further partitioning.

We again compile a table of the candidate splits (all are available except split 4), along with the values for the optimality measure (Table 11.5). Here two candidate splits (3 and 7) share the highest value for $\Phi(s|t)$, 0.4444. We arbitrarily select the first split encountered, split 3, savings = high versus savings $\in$ {low, medium}, for decision node A, with the resulting tree shown in Figure 11.3.

TABLE 11.5 **Values of the components of the optimality measure $\Phi(s|t)$ for each candidate split, for decision node A (best performance highlighted)**

Split	P_L	P_R	$P(j|t_L)$	$P(j|t_R)$	$2P_LP_R$	$Q(s|t)$	$\Phi(s|t)$
1	0.167	0.833	G: 1	G: 0.8	0.2782	0.4	0.1113
			B: 0	B: 0.2			
2	0.5	0.5	G: 1	G: 0.667	0.5	0.6666	0.3333
			B: 0	B: 0.333			
3	0.333	0.667	G: 0.5	G: 1	0.4444	1	**0.4444**
			B: 0.5	B: 0			
5	0.667	0.333	G: 0.75	G: 1	0.4444	0.5	0.2222
			B: 0.25	B: 0			
6	0.333	0.667	G: 1	G: 0.75	0.4444	0.5	0.2222
			B: 0	B: 0.25			
7	0.333	0.667	G: 0.5	G: 1	0.4444	1	**0.4444**
			B: 0.5	B: 0			
8	0.5	0.5	G: 0.667	G: 1	0.5	0.6666	0.3333
			B: 0.333	B: 0			
9	0.833	0.167	G: 0.8	G: 1	0.2782	0.4	0.1113
			B: 0.2	B: 0			

As decision node B is diverse, we again need to seek the optimal split. Only two records remain in this decision node, each with the same value for savings (high) and income (25). Therefore, the only possible split is assets = high versus assets = medium, providing us with the final form of the CART decision tree for this example, in Figure 11.4. Compare Figure 11.4 with Figure 11.5, the decision tree generated by *Modeler's* CART algorithm.

Let us leave aside this example now, and consider how CART would operate on an arbitrary data set. In general, CART would recursively proceed to visit each remaining decision node and apply the procedure above to find the optimal split at each node. Eventually, no decision nodes remain, and the "full tree" has been grown. However, as we have seen in Table 11.1, not all leaf nodes are necessarily homogeneous, which leads to a certain level of *classification error*.

For example, suppose that, as we cannot further partition the records in Table 11.1, we classify the records contained in this leaf node as *bad credit risk*. Then the probability that a randomly chosen record from this leaf node would

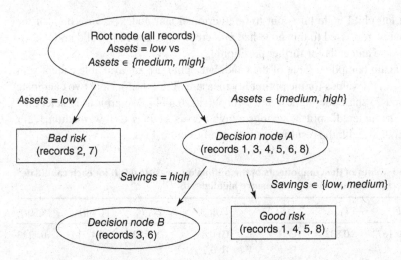

Figure 11.3 CART decision tree after decision node *A* split.

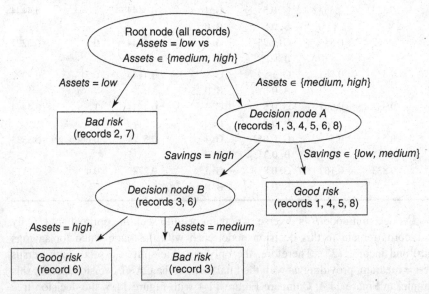

Figure 11.4 CART decision tree, fully grown form.

be classified correctly is 0.6, because three of the five records (60%) are actually classified as bad credit risks. Hence, our *classification error rate* for this particular leaf would be 0.4 or 40%, because two of the five records are actually classified as good credit risks. CART would then calculate the error rate for the entire decision tree to be the weighted average of the individual leaf error rates, with the weights equal to the proportion of records in each leaf.

To avoid memorizing the training set, the CART algorithm needs to begin pruning nodes and branches that would otherwise reduce the generalizability of the

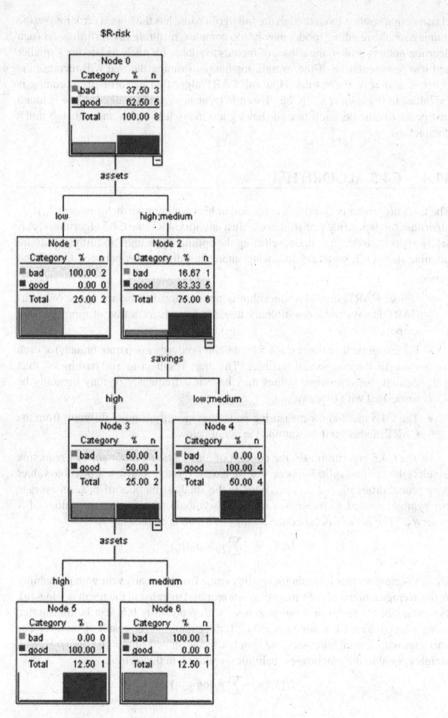

Figure 11.5   Modeler's CART decision tree.

classification results. Even though the fully grown tree has the lowest error rate on the training set, the resulting model may be too complex, resulting in overfitting. As each decision node is grown, the subset of records available for analysis becomes smaller and less representative of the overall population. Pruning the tree will increase the generalizability of the results. How the CART algorithm performs tree pruning is explained in Breiman *et al.* [p. 66]. Essentially, an adjusted overall error rate is found that penalizes the decision tree for having too many leaf nodes and thus too much complexity.

11.4   C4.5 ALGORITHM

The C4.5 *algorithm* is Quinlan's extension of his own iterative dichotomizer 3 (ID3) algorithm for generating decision trees.[3] Just as with CART, the C4.5 algorithm recursively visits each decision node, selecting the optimal split, until no further splits are possible. However, there are following interesting differences between CART and C4.5:

- Unlike CART, the C4.5 algorithm is not restricted to binary splits. Whereas CART always produces a binary tree, C4.5 produces a tree of more variable shape.

- For categorical attributes, C4.5 by default produces a separate branch for each value of the categorical attribute. This may result in more "bushiness" than desired, because some values may have low frequency or may naturally be associated with other values.

- The C4.5 method for measuring node homogeneity is quite different from the CART method and is examined in detail below.

The C4.5 algorithm uses the concept of *information gain* or *entropy reduction* to select the optimal split. Suppose that we have a variable X whose k possible values have probabilities $p_1, p_2, \ldots, p_k$. What is the smallest number of bits, on average per symbol, needed to transmit a stream of symbols representing the values of X observed? The answer is called the *entropy of X* and is defined as

$$H(X) = -\sum_j p_j \log_2(p_j)$$

Where does this formula for entropy come from? For an event with probability p, the average amount of information in bits required to transmit the result is $-\log_2(p)$. For example, the result of a fair coin toss, with probability 0.5, can be transmitted using $-\log_2(0.5) = 1$ bit, which is a 0 or 1, depending on the result of the toss. For variables with several outcomes, we simply use a weighted sum of the $\log_2(p_j)$s, with weights equal to the outcome probabilities, resulting in the formula

$$H(X) = -\sum_j p_j \log_2(p_j)$$

[3] J. Ross Quinlan, *C4.5: Programs for Machine Learning*, Morgan Kaufmann, San Francisco, CA, 1992.

C4.5 uses this concept of entropy as follows. Suppose that we have a candidate split S, which partitions the training data set T into several subsets, $T_1, T_2, \ldots, T_k$. The mean information requirement can then be calculated as the weighted sum of the entropies for the individual subsets, as follows:

$$H_S(T) = -\sum_{i=1}^{k} p_i H_S(T_i) \tag{11.2}$$

where P_i represents the proportion of records in subset i. We may then define our *information gain* to be $\text{gain}(S) = H(T) - H_S(T)$, that is, the increase in information produced by partitioning the training data T according to this candidate split S. At each decision node, C4.5 chooses the optimal split to be the split that has the greatest information gain, $\text{gain}(S)$.

To illustrate the C4.5 algorithm at work, let us return to the data set in Table 11.2 and apply the C4.5 algorithm to build a decision tree for classifying credit risk, just as we did earlier using CART. Once again, we are at the root node and are considering all possible splits using all the data (Table 11.6).

Now, because five of the eight records are classified as *good credit risk*, with the remaining three records classified as *bad credit risk*, the entropy before splitting is

$$H(T) = -\sum_{j} p_j \log_2(p_j) = -\frac{5}{8}\log_2\left(\frac{5}{8}\right) - \frac{3}{8}\log_2\left(\frac{3}{8}\right) = 0.9544$$

We shall compare the entropy of each candidate split against this $H(T) = 0.9544$, to see which split results in the greatest reduction in entropy (or gain in information).

For candidate split 1 (*savings*), two of the records have *high* savings, three of the records have *medium* savings, and three of the records have *low* savings, so we have $P_{\text{high}} = 2/8$, $P_{\text{medium}} = 3/8$, $P_{\text{low}} = 3/8$. Of the records with *high* savings, one is a good credit risk and one is bad, giving a probability of 0.5 of choosing the record with a good credit risk. Thus, the entropy for *high* savings is $-1/2\log_2(1/2) - 1/2\log_2(1/2) = 1$, which is similar to the flip of a fair coin. All three of the records with *medium* savings are good credit risks, so that the entropy for *medium* is $-3/3\log_2(3/3) - 0/3\log_2(0/3) = 0$, where by convention we define $\log_2(0) = 0$.

In engineering applications, *information* is analogous to *signal*, and *entropy* is analogous to *noise*, so it makes sense that the entropy for medium savings is zero, because the signal is crystal clear and there is no noise: If the customer has medium

TABLE 11.6   Candidate splits at root node for C4.5 algorithm

Candidate Split		Child Nodes	
1	Savings = low	Savings = medium	Savings = high
2	Assets = low	Assets = medium	Assets = high
3	Income ≤ \$25,000		Income > \$25,000
4	Income ≤ \$50,000		Income > \$50,000
5	Income ≤ \$75,000		Income > \$75,000

savings, he or she is a good credit risk, with 100% confidence. The amount of information required to transmit the credit rating of these customers is zero, as long as we know that they have medium savings.

One of the records with *low* savings is a good credit risk, and two records with *low* savings are bad credit risks, giving us our entropy for *low* credit risk as $-1/3 \log_2(1/3) - 2/3 \log_2(2/3) = 0.9183$. We combine the entropies of these three subsets, using equation (11.2) and the proportions of the subsets P_i, so that $H_{\text{savings}}(T) = (2/8)(1) + (3/8)(0) + (3/8)(0.9183) = 0.5944$. Then the information gain represented by the split on the *savings* attribute is calculated as $H(T) - H_{\text{savings}}(T) = 0.9544 - 0.5944 = 0.36$ bits.

How are we to interpret these measures? First, $H(T) = 0.9544$ means that, on average, one would need 0.9544 bits (0's or 1's) to transmit the credit risk of the eight customers in the data set. Now, $H_{\text{savings}}(T) = 0.5944$ means that the partitioning of the customers into three subsets has lowered the average bit requirement for transmitting the credit risk status of the customers to 0.5944 bits. Lower entropy is good. This *entropy reduction* can be viewed as *information gain*, so that we have gained on average $H(T) - H_{\text{savings}}(T) = 0.9544 - 0.5944 = 0.36$ bits of information by using the *savings* partition. We will compare this to the information gained by the other candidate splits, and choose the split with the largest information gain as the optimal split for the root node.

For candidate split 2 (*assets*), two of the records have *high* assets, four of the records have *medium* assets, and two of the records have *low* assets, so we have $P_{\text{high}} = 2/8$, $P_{\text{medium}} = 4/8$, $P_{\text{low}} = 2/8$. Both of the records with *high* assets are classified as good credit risks, which means that the entropy for *high* assets will be zero, just as it was for *medium savings* above.

Three of the records with *medium* assets are good credit risks and one is a bad credit risk, giving us entropy $-3/4 \log_2(3/4) - 1/4 \log_2(1/4) = 0.8113$. And both of the records with *low* assets are bad credit risks, which results in the entropy for *low* assets equaling zero. Combining the entropies of these three subsets, using equation (11.2) and the proportions of the subsets P_i, we have $H_{\text{assets}}(T) = (2/8)(0) + (4/8)(0.8113) + (2/8)(0) = 0.4057$. The entropy for the *assets* split is lower than the entropy (0.5944) for the *savings* split, which indicates that the *assets* split contains less noise and is to be preferred over the *savings* split. This is measured directly using the information gain, as follows: $H(T) - H_{\text{assets}}(T) = 0.9544 - 0.4057 = 0.5487$ bits. This information gain of 0.5487 bits is larger than that for the *savings* split of 0.36 bits, verifying that the *assets* split is preferable.

While C4.5 partitions the categorical variables differently from CART, the partitions for the numerical variables are similar. Here we have four observed values for *income*: 25,000, 50,000, 75,000, and 100,000, which provide us with three thresholds for partitions, as shown in Table 11.6. For candidate split 3 from Table 11.6, *income* ≤ \$25,000 versus *income* > \$25,000, three of the records have *income* ≤ \$25,000, with the other five records having *income* > \$25,000, giving us $P_{\text{income} \leq \$25,000} = 3/8$, $P_{\text{income} > \$25,000} = 5/8$. Of the records with *income* ≤ \$25,000, one is a good credit risk and two are bad, giving us the entropy for *income* ≤ \$25,000 as $-1/3 \log_2(1/3) - 2/3 \log_2(2/3) = 0.9483$. Four of the five records with *income* > \$25,000 are good credit risks, so that the entropy for *income* > \$25,000 is $-4/5 \log_2(4/5) - 1/5 \log_2(1/5) = 0.7219$. Combining, we find the entropy for candidate split 3 to be $H_{\text{income} \leq \$25,000}(T) = (3/8)(0.9183) + (5/8)(0.7219) = 0.7956$. Then the information gain for this split is $H(T) - H_{\text{income} \leq \$25,000}(T) = 0.9544 - 0.7956 = 0.1588$ bits, which is our poorest choice yet.

For candidate split 4, *income* ≤ \$50,000 versus *income* > \$50,000, two of the five records with *income* ≤ \$50,000 are good credit risks, and three are bad, while all three of the records with *income* > \$50,000 are good credit risks. This gives us the entropy for candidate split 4 as

$$H_{\text{income} \leq \$50,000}(T) = \frac{5}{8}\left(-\frac{2}{5}\log_2\frac{2}{5} - \frac{3}{5}\log_2\frac{3}{5}\right)$$
$$+ \frac{3}{8}\left(-\frac{3}{3}\log_2\frac{3}{3} - \frac{0}{3}\log_2\frac{0}{3}\right) = 0.6069$$

The information gain for this split is thus $H(T) - H_{\text{income} \leq \$50,000}(T) = 0.9544 - 0.6069 = 0.3475$, which is not as good as for *assets*. Finally, for candidate split 5, *income* ≤ \$75,000 versus *income* > \$75,000, four of the seven records with *income* ≤ \$75,000 are good credit risks, and three are bad, while the single record with *income* > \$75,000 is a good credit risk. Thus, the entropy for candidate split 4 is

$$H_{\text{income} \leq \$75,000}(T) = \frac{7}{8}\left(-\frac{4}{7}\log_2\frac{4}{7} - \frac{3}{7}\log_2\frac{3}{7}\right) + \frac{1}{8}\left(-\frac{1}{1}\log_2\frac{1}{1} - \frac{0}{1}\log_2\frac{0}{1}\right)$$
$$= 0.8621$$

The information gain for this split is $H(T) - H_{\text{income} \leq \$75,000}(T) = 0.9544 - 0.8621 = 0.0923$, making this split the poorest of the five candidate splits.

Table 11.7 summarizes the information gain for each candidate split at the root node. Candidate split 2, *assets*, has the largest information gain, and so is chosen for the initial split by the C4.5 algorithm. Note that this choice for an optimal split concurs with the partition preferred by CART, which split on *assets* = *low* versus *assets* = {*medium*, *high*}. The partial decision tree resulting from C4.5's initial split is shown in Figure 11.6.

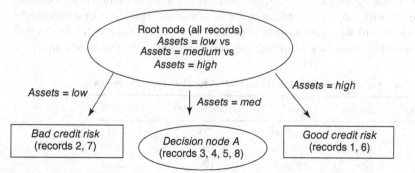

Figure 11.6   C4.5 concurs with CART in choosing *assets* for the initial partition.

TABLE 11.7 Information gain for each candidate split at the root node

Candidate Split	Child Nodes	Information Gain (Entropy Reduction)
1	*Savings = low* *Savings = medium* *Savings = high*	0.36 bits
2	*Assets = low* *Assets = medium* *Assets = high*	0.5487 bits
3	*Income ≤ $25,000* *Income > $25,000*	0.1588 bits
4	*Income ≤ $50,000* *Income > $50,000*	0.3475 bits
5	*Income ≤ $75,000* *Income > $75,000*	0.0923 bits

The initial split has resulted in the creation of two terminal leaf nodes and one new decision node. As both records with *low assets* have bad credit risk, this classification has 100% confidence, and no further splits are required. It is similar for the two records with *high assets*. However, the four records at decision node *A* (*assets = medium*) contain both *good* and *bad* credit risks, so that further splitting is called for.

We proceed to determine the optimal split for decision node *A*, containing records 3, 4, 5, and 8, as indicated in Table 11.8. Because three of the four records are classified as *good credit risks*, with the remaining record classified as a *bad credit risk*, the entropy before splitting is

$$H(A) = -\sum_j p_j \log_2(p_j) = -\frac{3}{4} \log_2\left(\frac{3}{4}\right) - \frac{1}{4} \log_2\left(\frac{1}{4}\right) = 0.8113$$

The candidate splits for decision node A are shown in Table 11.9.

For candidate split 1, *savings*, the single record with *low* savings is a good credit risk, along with the two records with *medium* savings. Perhaps counterintuitively, the single record with *high* savings is a *bad* credit risk. So the entropy for each of these three classes equals zero, because the level of savings determines the credit

TABLE 11.8 Records available at decision node A for classifying credit risk

Customer	Savings	Assets	Income ($1000s)	Credit Risk
3	High	Medium	25	Bad
4	Medium	Medium	50	Good
5	Low	Medium	100	Good
8	Medium	Medium	75	Good

TABLE 11.9   Candidate splits at decision node A

Candidate Split		Child Nodes	
1	*Savings = low*	*Savings = medium*	*Savings = high*
3	*Income* ≤ $25,000		*Income* > $25,000
4	*Income* ≤ $50,000		*Income* > $50,000
5	*Income* ≤ $75,000		*Income* > $75,000

risk completely. This also results in a combined entropy of zero for the *assets* split, $H_{assets}(A) = 0$, which is optimal for decision node A. The information gain for this split is thus $H(A) - H_{assets}(A) = 0.8113 - 0.0 = 0.8113$. This is, of course, the maximum information gain possible for decision node A. We therefore need not continue our calculations, because no other split can result in a greater information gain. As it happens, candidate split 3, *income* ≤ $25,000 versus *income* > $25,000, also results in the maximal information gain, but again we arbitrarily select the first such split encountered, the *savings* split.

Figure 11.7 shows the form of the decision tree after the *savings* split. Note that this is the fully grown form, because all nodes are now leaf nodes, and C4.5 will grow no further nodes. Comparing the C4.5 tree in Figure 11.7 with the CART tree in Figure 11.4, we see that the C4.5 tree is "bushier," providing a greater breadth, while the CART tree is one level deeper. Both algorithms concur that *assets* is the most important variable (the root split) and that *savings* is also important. Finally, once the decision tree is fully grown, C4.5 engages in *pessimistic postpruning*. Interested readers may consult Kantardzic.[4]

[4]Mehmed Kantardzic, *Data Mining: Concepts, Models, Methods, and Algorithms*, Wiley-Interscience, Hoboken, NJ, second edition.

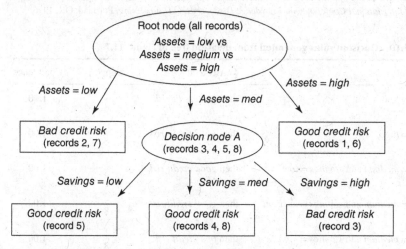

Figure 11.7   C4.5 Decision tree: fully grown form.

11.5 DECISION RULES

One of the most attractive aspects of decision trees lies in their interpretability, especially with respect to the construction of *decision rules*. Decision rules can be constructed from a decision tree simply by traversing any given path from the root node to any leaf. The complete set of decision rules generated by a decision tree is equivalent (for classification purposes) to the decision tree itself. For example, from the decision tree in Figure 11.7, we may construct the decision rules given in Table 11.10.

Decision rules come in the form *if antecedent, then consequent*, as shown in Table 11.10. For decision rules, the antecedent consists of the attribute values from the branches taken by the particular path through the tree, while the consequent consists of the classification value for the target variable given by the particular leaf node.

The *support* of the decision rule refers to the proportion of records in the data set that rest in that particular terminal leaf node. The *confidence* of the rule refers to the proportion of records in the leaf node for which the decision rule is true. In this small example, all of our leaf nodes are pure, resulting in perfect confidence levels of $100\% = 1.00$. In real-world examples, such as in the next section, one cannot expect such high confidence levels.

11.6 COMPARISON OF THE C5.0 AND CART ALGORITHMS APPLIED TO REAL DATA

Next, we apply decision tree analysis using IBM/SPSS Modeler on a real-world data set. We use a subset of the data set *adult*, which was drawn from US census data by Kohavi.[5] You may download the data set used here from the book series website, www.dataminingconsultant.com. Here we are interested in classifying whether

[5]Ronny Kohavi, Scaling up the accuracy of naive Bayes classifiers: A decision tree hybrid, *Proceedings of the 2nd International Conference on Knowledge Discovery and Data Mining*, Portland, OR, 1996.

TABLE 11.10 Decision rules generated from decision tree in Figure 11.7

Antecedent	Consequent	Support	Confidence
If *assets = low*	then *bad credit risk*	$\frac{2}{8}$	1.00
If *assets = high*	then *good credit risk*	$\frac{2}{8}$	1.00
If *assets = medium* and *savings = low*	then *good credit risk*	$\frac{1}{8}$	1.00
If *assets = medium* and *savings = medium*	then *good credit risk*	$\frac{2}{8}$	1.00
If *assets = medium* and *savings = high*	then *bad credit risk*	$\frac{1}{8}$	1.00

or not a person's income is less than $50,000, based on the following set of predictor fields.

- Numerical variables
  Age
  Years of education
  Capital gains
  Capital losses
  Hours worked per week.
- Categorical variables
  Race
  Gender
  Work class
  Marital status.

The numerical variables were normalized so that all values ranged between 0 and 1. Some collapsing of low-frequency classes was carried out on the *work class* and *marital status* categories. Modeler was used to compare the C5.0 algorithm (an update of the C4.5 algorithm) with CART. The decision tree produced by the CART algorithm is shown in Figure 11.8.

Here, the tree structure is displayed horizontally, with the root node at the left and the leaf nodes on the right. For the CART algorithm, the root node split is on *marital status*, with a binary split separating married persons from all others (*Marital_Status in* ["*Divorced*" "*Never-married*" "*Separated*" "*Widowed*"]). That is, this particular split on *marital status* maximized the CART split selection criterion [equation (11.1)]:

$$\Phi(s|t) = 2P_L P_R \sum_{j=1}^{\#\text{classes}} |P(j|t_L) - P(j|t_R)|$$

Note that the mode classification for each branch is less than or equal to $50,000. The married branch leads to a decision node, with several further splits downstream.

```
⊟  Marital status in [ "Married" ] [ Mode: <=50K ] (8,247)
   ⊟  Years of education_mm <= 0.700 [ Mode: <=50K ] (5,508)
      ⸺ Capital gains_mm <= 0.051 [ Mode: <=50K ]  ⇨ <=50K (5,242; 0.713)
      ⸺ Capital gains_mm > 0.051 [ Mode: >50K ]  ⇨ >50K (266; 0.974)
   ⊟  Years of education_mm > 0.700 [ Mode: >50K ] (2,739)
      ⊟  Capital gains_mm <= 0.051 [ Mode: >50K ] (2,357)
         ⊟  Capital losses_mm <= 0.412 [ Mode: >50K ] (2,126)
            ⸺ Hours_mm <= 0.342 [ Mode: <=50K ]  ⇨ <=50K (211; 0.611)
            ⸺ Hours_mm > 0.342 [ Mode: >50K ]  ⇨ >50K (1,915; 0.628)
         ⸺ Capital losses_mm > 0.412 [ Mode: >50K ]  ⇨ >50K (231; 0.952)
      ⸺ Capital gains_mm > 0.051 [ Mode: >50K ]  ⇨ >50K (382; 0.995)
⸺ Marital status in [ "Divorced" "Never-married" "Separated" "Widowed" ] [ Mode: <=50K ]  ⇨ <=50K (9,228; 0.937)
```

Figure 11.8   CART decision tree for the adult data set.

However, the nonmarried branch is a leaf node, with a classification of less than or equal to $50,000 for the 9228 such records, with 93.7% confidence. In other words, of the 9228 persons in the data set who are not presently married, 93.7% of them have incomes of at most $50,000.

The root node split is considered to indicate the most important single variable for classifying income. Note that the split on the *Marital_Status* attribute is binary, as are all CART splits on categorical variables. All the other splits in the full CART decision tree shown in Figure 11.8 are on numerical variables. The next decision node is *Years of education_mm*, representing the min−max normalized number of years of education. The split occurs at *Years of education_mm* ≤ 0.700 (mode $\leq \$50,000$) versus *Years of education_mm* > 0.700 (mode $> \$50,000$). However, your client may not understand what the normalized value of 0.700 represents. So, when reporting results, the analyst should always *denormalize*, to identify the original field values. The min−max normalization was of the form $X^* = \frac{X-\min(X)}{\text{range}(X)} = \frac{X-\min(X)}{\max(X)-\min(X)}$. Years of education ranged from 16 (maximum) to 1 (minimum), for a range of 15. Therefore, denormalizing, we have $X = X^* \times \text{range}(X) + \min(X) = 0.700 \times 15 + 1 = 11.5$. Thus, the split occurs at 11.5 years of education. It seems that those who have graduated high school tend to have higher incomes than those who have not.

Interestingly, for both education groups, *Capital gains* represents the next most important decision node. For the branch with more years of education, there are two further splits, on *Capital loss*, and then *Hours* (worked per week).

Now, will the information-gain splitting criterion and the other characteristics of the C5.0 algorithm lead to a decision tree that is substantially different from or largely similar to the tree derived using CART's splitting criteria? Compare the CART decision tree above with Modeler's C5.0 decision tree of the same data displayed in Figure 11.9. (We needed to specify only three levels of splits. *Modeler* gave us eight levels of splits, which would not have fit on the page.)

Differences emerge immediately at the root node. Here, the root split is on the *Capital gains_mm* attribute, with the split occurring at the relatively low normalized level of 0.068. As the range of capital gains in this data set is $99,999 (maximum = 99,999, minimum = 0), this is denormalized as $X = X^* \times \text{range}(X) + \min(X) = 0.0685 \times 99,999 + 0 = \$6850$. More than half of those with capital gains greater than $6850 have incomes above $50,000, whereas more than half of those with capital gains of less than $6850 have incomes below $50,000. This is the split that was chosen by the information-gain criterion as the optimal split among all possible splits over all fields. Note, however, that there are 23 times more records in the low-capital-gains category than in the high-capital-gains category (23,935 vs 1065 records).

For records with lower capital gains, the second split occurs on *capital loss*, with a pattern similar to the earlier split on capital gains. Most people (23,179 records) had low capital loss, and most of these have incomes below $50,000. Most of the few (756 records) who had higher capital loss had incomes above $50,000.

For records with low capital gains and low capital loss, consider the next split, which is made on *marital status*. Note that C5.0 provides a separate branch for each categorical field value, whereas CART was restricted to binary splits. A possible

```
⊟ Capital gains_mm <= 0.068 [ Mode: <=50K ] (23,935)
   ⊟ Capital losses_mm <= 0.417 [ Mode: <=50K ] (23,179)
      ⊟ Marital status = Divorced [ Mode: <=50K ] (3,288)
         — Years of education_mm <= 0.733 [ Mode: <=50K ] ⇨ <=50K (2,715; 0.957)
         ⊞ Years of education_mm > 0.733 [ Mode: <=50K ] (573)
      ⊟ Marital status = Married [ Mode: <=50K ] (10,369)
         ⊞ Capital gains_mm <= 0.050 [ Mode: <=50K ] (10,284)
         ⊞ Capital gains_mm > 0.050 [ Mode: >50K ] (85)
      ⊟ Marital status = Never-married [ Mode: <=50K ] (8,025)
         — Years of education_mm <= 0.733 [ Mode: <=50K ] ⇨ <=50K (6,279; 0.989)
         ⊞ Years of education_mm > 0.733 [ Mode: <=50K ] (1,746)
      ⊟ Marital status = Separated [ Mode: <=50K ] (761)
         — Years of education_mm <= 0.733 [ Mode: <=50K ] ⇨ <=50K (668; 0.979)
         ⊞ Years of education_mm > 0.733 [ Mode: <=50K ] (93)
         — Marital status = Widowed [ Mode: <=50K ] ⇨ <=50K (736; 0.948)
   ⊟ Capital losses_mm > 0.417 [ Mode: >50K ] (756)
      ⊟ Capital losses_mm <= 0.454 [ Mode: >50K ] (487)
         — Marital status in [ "Divorced" "Never-married" "Separated" "Widowed" ] [ Mode: <=50K ] ⇨ <=50K (48; 1.0)
         — Marital status in [ "Married" ] [ Mode: >50K ] ⇨ >50K (439; 0.977)
      ⊟ Capital losses_mm > 0.454 [ Mode: <=50K ] (269)
         ⊞ Capital losses_mm <= 0.540 [ Mode: <=50K ] (168)
         ⊞ Capital losses_mm > 0.540 [ Mode: >50K ] (101)
⊟ Capital gains_mm > 0.068 [ Mode: >50K ] (1,065)
   ⊟ Hours_mm <= 0.347 [ Mode: >50K ] (92)
      — Age_mm <= 0.137 [ Mode: <=50K ] ⇨ <=50K (6; 0.833)
      — Age_mm > 0.137 [ Mode: >50K ] ⇨ >50K (86; 0.965)
   — Hours_mm > 0.347 [ Mode: >50K ] ⇨ >50K (973; 0.99)
```

Figure 11.9   C5.0 decision tree for the adult data set.

drawback of C5.0's strategy for splitting categorical variables is that it may lead to an overly bushy tree, with many leaf nodes containing few records.

Although the CART and C5.0 decision trees do not agree in the details, we may nevertheless glean useful information from the broad areas of agreement between them. For example, the most important variables are clearly marital status, education, capital gains, capital losses, and perhaps hours per week. Both models agree that these fields are important, but disagree as to the ordering of their importance. Much more modeling analysis may be called for.

For a soup-to-nuts application of decision trees to a real-world data set, from data preparation through model building and decision rule generation, see the Case Study in Chapter 29–32.

THE R ZONE

Read in and prepare the data

```
adult <- read.csv(file = "C:/ ... /adult.txt", stringsAsFactors=TRUE)
# Collapse some of the categories by giving them the same factor label
levels(adult$marital.status); levels(adult$workclass)
levels(adult$marital.status)[2:4] <- "Married"
levels(adult$workclass)[c(2,3,8)] <- "Gov"
levels(adult$workclass)[c(5, 6)] <- "Self"
levels(adult$marital.status); levels(adult$workclass)
```

Standardize the numeric variables

```
adult$age.z <- (adult$age - mean(adult$age))/sd(adult$age)
adult$education.num.z <- (adult$education.num-
    mean(adult$education.num))/sd(adult$education.num)
adult$capital.gain.z <- (adult$capital.gain - mean(adult$capital.gain))/sd(adult$capital.gain)
adult$capital.loss.z <- (adult$capital.loss - mean(adult$capital.loss))/sd(adult$capital.loss)
adult$hours.per.week.z <- (adult$hours.per.week-
    mean(adult$hours.per.week))/sd(adult$hours.per.week)
```

Use predictors to classify whether or not a person's income is less than $50K

```
# Requires package "rpart"
library("rpart")
cartfit <- rpart(income ~ age.z + education.num.z + capital.gain.z + capital.loss.z +
    hours.per.week.z + race + sex + workclass + marital.status,
    data = adult,
    method = "class")
print(cartfit)
```

Plot the decision tree

```
# Requires package "rpart.plot"
library("rpart.plot")
rpart.plot(cartfit, main =
    "Classification Tree")
```

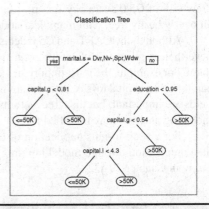

C5.0

```
# Requires package "C50"
library("C50")
names(adult)
x <- adult[,c(2,6, 9, 10, 16, 17, 18, 19, 20)]
y <- adult$income
c50fit1 <- C5.0(x, y)
summary(c50fit1)
```

```
> c50fit1

Call:
C5.0.default(x = x, y = y)

Classification Tree
Number of samples: 25000
Number of predictors: 9

Tree size: 78

Non-standard options: attempt to group attributes
```

C5.0 - Pruned

```
c50fit2 <- C5.0(x, y, control =
    C5.0Control(CF=.1))
summary(c50fit2)
```

```
> c50fit2

Call:
C5.0.default(x = x, y = y, control = C5.0Control(CF = 0.1))

Classification Tree
Number of samples: 25000
Number of predictors: 9

Tree size: 30

Non-standard options: attempt to group
    attributes, confidence level: 0.1
```

R REFERENCES

1. Kuhn M, Weston S, Coulter N. 2013. C code for C5.0 by R. Quinlan. C50: C5.0 decision trees and rule-based models. R package version 0.1.0-15. http://CRAN.R-project.org/package=C50.
2. Milborrow S. 2012. rpart.plot: Plot rpart models. An enhanced version of plot.rpart. R package version 1.4-3. http://CRAN.R-project.org/package=rpart.plot.
3. Therneau T, Atkinson B, Ripley B. 2013. rpart: Recursive partitioning. R package version 4.1-3. http://CRAN.R-project.org/package=rpart.
4. R Core Team. *R: A Language and Environment for Statistical Computing*. Vienna, Austria: R Foundation for Statistical Computing; 2012. ISBN: 3-900051-07-0, http://www.R-project.org/.

EXERCISES

CLARIFYING THE CONCEPTS

1. Describe the possible situations when no further splits can be made at a decision node.

2. Suppose that our target variable is continuous numeric. Can we apply decision trees directly to classify it? How can we work around this?

3. True or false: Decision trees seek to form leaf nodes to maximize heterogeneity in each node.

4. Discuss the benefits and drawbacks of a binary tree versus a bushier tree.

WORKING WITH THE DATA

Consider the data in Table 11.11. The target variable is salary. Start by discretizing salary as follows:

- Less than $35,000, Level 1
- $35,000 to less than $45,000, Level 2
- $45,000 to less than $55,000, Level 3
- Above $55,000, Level 4.

5. Construct a classification and regression tree to classify *salary* based on the other variables. Do as much as you can by hand, before turning to the software.

6. Construct a C4.5 decision tree to classify *salary* based on the other variables. Do as much as you can by hand, before turning to the software.

TABLE 11.11 Decision tree data

Occupation	Gender	Age	Salary
Service	Female	45	$48,000
	Male	25	$25,000
	Male	33	$35,000
Management	Male	25	$45,000
	Female	35	$65,000
	Male	26	$45,000
	Female	45	$70,000
Sales	Female	40	$50,000
	Male	30	$40,000
Staff	Female	50	$40,000
	Male	25	$25,000

7. Compare the two decision trees and discuss the benefits and drawbacks of each.

8. Generate the full set of decision rules for the CART decision tree.

9. Generate the full set of decision rules for the C4.5 decision tree.

10. Compare the two sets of decision rules and discuss the benefits and drawbacks of each.

HANDS-ON ANALYSIS

For the following exercises, use the *churn* data set available at the book series web site. Normalize the numerical data and deal with the correlated variables.

11. Generate a CART decision tree.

12. Generate a C4.5-type decision tree.

13. Compare the two decision trees and discuss the benefits and drawbacks of each.

14. Generate the full set of decision rules for the CART decision tree.

15. Generate the full set of decision rules for the C4.5 decision tree.

16. Compare the two sets of decision rules and discuss the benefits and drawbacks of each.

## CHAPTER 12

NEURAL NETWORKS

The inspiration for neural networks was the recognition that complex learning systems in the animal brains consisted of closely interconnected sets of neurons. Although a particular neuron may be relatively simple in structure, dense networks of interconnected neurons could perform complex learning tasks such as classification and pattern recognition. The human brain, for example, contains approximately 10^{11} neurons, each connected on average to 10,000 other neurons, making a total of $1,000,000,000,000,000 = 10^{15}$ synaptic connections. *Artificial neural networks* (hereafter, *neural networks*) represent an attempt at a very basic level to imitate the type of nonlinear learning that occurs in the networks of neurons found in nature.

As shown in Figure 12.1, a real neuron uses dendrites to gather inputs from other neurons and combines the input information, generating a nonlinear response ("firing") when some threshold is reached, which it sends to other neurons using the axon. Figure 12.1 also shows an artificial neuron model used in most neural networks. The inputs (x_i) are collected from upstream neurons (or the data set) and combined through a combination function such as summation $(\sum)$, which is then input into (usually nonlinear) activation function to produce an output response (y), which is then channeled downstream to other neurons.

What types of problems are appropriate for neural networks? One of the advantages of using neural networks is that they are quite robust with respect to noisy data. Because the network contains many nodes (artificial neurons), with weights assigned to each connection, the network can learn to work around these uninformative (or even erroneous) examples in the data set. However, unlike decision trees, which produce intuitive rules that are understandable to nonspecialists, neural networks are relatively opaque to human interpretation, as we shall see. Also, neural networks usually require longer training times than decision trees, often extending into several hours.

12.1 INPUT AND OUTPUT ENCODING

One possible drawback of neural networks is that all attribute values must be encoded in a standardized manner, taking values between 0 and 1, even for categorical variables. Later, when we examine the details of the back-propagation algorithm,

Data Mining and Predictive Analytics, First Edition. Daniel T. Larose and Chantal D. Larose.
© 2015 John Wiley & Sons, Inc. Published 2015 by John Wiley & Sons, Inc.

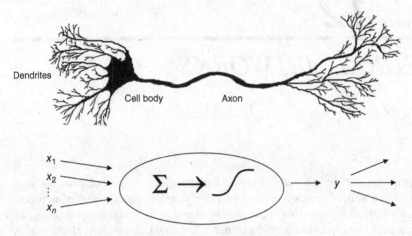

Figure 12.1   Real neuron and artificial neuron model.

we shall understand why this is necessary. For now, however, how does one go about standardizing all the attribute values?

For continuous variables, this is not a problem, as we discussed in Chapter 2. We may simply apply the *min−max normalization*:

$$X^* = \frac{X - \min(X)}{\text{range}(X)} = \frac{X - \min(X)}{\max(X) - \min(X)}$$

This works well as long as the minimum and maximum values are known and all potential new data are bounded between them. Neural networks are somewhat robust to minor violations of these boundaries. If more serious violations are expected, certain *ad hoc* solutions may be adopted, such as rejecting values that are outside the boundaries, or assigning such values to either the minimum or the maximum value.

Categorical variables are more problematical, as might be expected. If the number of possible categories is not too large, one may use *indicator (flag) variables*. For example, many data sets contain a *gender attribute*, containing values *female, male*, and *unknown*. As the neural network could not handle these attribute values in their present form, we could, instead, create indicator variables for *female* and *male*. Each record would contain values for each of these two indicator variables. Records for females would have values of 1 for *female* and 0 for *male*, while records for males would have values of 0 for *female* and 1 for *male*. Records for persons of unknown gender would have values of 0 for *female* and 0 for *male*. In general, categorical variables with k classes may be translated into $k - 1$ indicator variables, as long as the definition of the indicators is clearly defined.

Be wary of recoding unordered categorical variables into a single variable with a range between 0 and 1. For example, suppose that the data set contains information on a *marital status* attribute. Suppose that we code the attribute values *divorced, married, separated, single, widowed*, and *unknown*, as 0.0, 0.2, 0.4, 0.6, 0.8, and 1.0, respectively. Then this coding implies, for example, that *divorced* is "closer" to *married* than it is to *separated*, and so on. The neural network would be aware only of the numerical values in the *marital status* field, not of their preencoded meanings, and would thus be naive of their true meaning. Spurious and meaningless findings may result.

With respect to output, we shall see that neural network output nodes always return a continuous value between 0 and 1 as output. How can we use such continuous output for classification?

Many classification problems have a dichotomous result, an up-or-down decision, with only two possible outcomes. For example, "Is this customer about to leave our company's service?" For dichotomous classification problems, one option is to use a single output node (such as in Figure 12.2), with a threshold value set a priori that would separate the classes, such as "leave" or "stay." For example, with the threshold of "leave if *output* ≥ 0.67," an output of 0.72 from the output node would classify that record as likely to leave the company's service.

Single output nodes may also be used when the classes are clearly ordered. For example, suppose that we would like to classify elementary school reading prowess based on a certain set of student attributes. Then, we may be able to define the thresholds as follows:

- If $0 \leq output < 0.25$, classify *first-grade reading level*.
- If $0.25 \leq output < 0.50$, classify *second-grade reading level*.
- If $0.50 \leq output < 0.75$, classify *third-grade reading level*.
- If $output \geq 0.75$, classify *fourth-grade reading level*.

Fine-tuning of the thresholds may be required, tempered by the experience and the judgment of domain experts.

Not all classification problems, however, are soluble using a single output node only. For instance, suppose that we have several unordered categories in our target variable, as, for example, with the *marital status* variable mentioned above. In this case, we would choose to adopt *1-of-n output encoding*, where one output node is used for each possible category of the target variable. For example, if *marital status* was our target variable, the network would have six output nodes in the output layer, one for each of the six classes *divorced*, *married*, *separated*, *single*, *widowed*, and

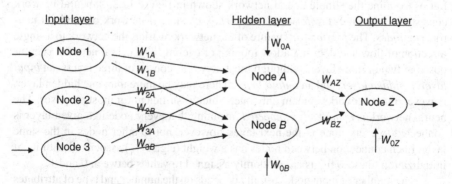

Figure 12.2   Simple neural network.

unknown. The output node with the highest value is then chosen as the classification for that particular record.

One benefit of using 1-of-*n* output encoding is that it provides a measure of confidence in the classification, in the form of the difference between the highest-value output node and the second-highest-value output node. Classifications with low confidence (small difference in node output values) can be flagged for further clarification.

12.2 NEURAL NETWORKS FOR ESTIMATION AND PREDICTION

Clearly, as neural networks produce continuous output, they may quite naturally be used for estimation and prediction. Suppose, for example, that we are interested in predicting the price of a particular stock 3 months in the future. Presumably, we would have encoded price information using the min–max normalization above. However, the neural network would output a value between 0 and 1, which (one would hope) does not represent the predicted price of the stock.

Rather, the min–max normalization needs to be inverted, so that the neural network output can be understood on the scale of the stock prices. In general, this denormalization is as follows:

$$\text{Prediction} = \text{output(data range)} + \text{minimum}$$

where *output* represents the neural network output in the (0,1) range, *data range* represents the range of the original attribute values on the nonnormalized scale, and *minimum* represents the smallest attribute value on the nonnormalized scale. For example, suppose that the stock prices ranged from \$20 to \$30 and that the network output was 0.69. Then the predicted stock price in 3 months is

$$\text{Prediction} = \text{output(data range)} + \text{minimum} = 0.69(\$10) + \$20 = \$26.90$$

12.3 SIMPLE EXAMPLE OF A NEURAL NETWORK

Let us examine the simple neural network shown in Figure 12.2. A neural network consists of a *layered, feedforward, completely connected* network of artificial neurons, or *nodes.* The *feedforward* nature of the network restricts the network to a single direction of flow and does not allow looping or cycling. The neural network is composed of two or more layers, although most networks consist of three layers: an *input layer*, a *hidden layer*, and an *output layer*. There may be more than one hidden layer, however, most networks contain only one, which is sufficient for most purposes. The neural network is *completely connected*, meaning that every node in a given layer is connected to every node in the next layer, however, not to other nodes in the same layer. Each connection between nodes has a weight (e.g., W_{1A}) associated with it. At initialization, these weights are randomly assigned to values between 0 and 1.

The number of input nodes usually depends on the number and type of attributes in the data set. The number of hidden layers and the number of nodes in each hidden layer are both configurable by the user. One may have more than one node in the output layer, depending on the particular classification task at hand.

How many nodes should one have in the hidden layer? As more nodes in the hidden layer increases the power and flexibility of the network for identifying complex patterns, one might be tempted to have a large number of nodes in the hidden layer. However, an overly large hidden layer leads to overfitting, memorizing the training set at the expense of generalizability to the validation set. If overfitting is occurring, one may consider reducing the number of nodes in the hidden layer; conversely, if the training accuracy is unacceptably low, one may consider increasing the number of nodes in the hidden layer.

The input layer accepts inputs from the data set, such as attribute values, and simply passes these values along to the hidden layer without further processing. Thus, the nodes in the input layer do not share the detailed node structure that the hidden layer nodes and the output layer nodes share.

We will investigate the structure of hidden layer nodes and output layer nodes using the sample data provided in Table 12.1. First, a *combination function* (usually summation, $\sum$) produces a linear combination of the node inputs and the connection weights into a single scalar value, which we will term as *net*. Thus, for a given node j,

$$\text{Net}_j = \sum_i W_{ij} x_{ij} = W_{0j} x_{0j} + W_{1j} x_{1j} + \cdots + W_{Ij} x_{Ij}$$

where x_{ij} represents the ith input to node j, W_{ij} represents the weight associated with the ith input to node j, and there are $I + 1$ inputs to node j. Note that $x_1, x_2, \ldots, x_I$ represent inputs from upstream nodes, while x_0 represents a *constant* input, analogous to the constant factor in regression models, which by convention uniquely takes the value $x_{0j} = 1$. Thus, each hidden layer or output layer node j contains an "extra" input equal to a particular weight $W_{0j} x_{0j} = W_{0j}$, such as W_{0B} for node B.

For example, for node A in the hidden layer, we have

$$\text{Net}_A = \sum_i W_{iA} x_{iA} = W_{0A}(1) + W_{1A} x_{1A} + W_{2A} x_{2A} + W_{3A} x_{3A}$$

$$= 0.5 + 0.6(0.4) + 0.80(0.2) + 0.6(0.7) = 1.32$$

Within node A, this combination function $\text{net}_A = 1.32$ is then used as an input to an activation function. In biological neurons, signals are sent between neurons when the combination of inputs to a particular neuron crosses a certain threshold, and the neuron "fires." This is nonlinear behavior, as the firing response is not necessarily linearly related to the increment in input stimulation. Artificial neural networks model this behavior through a nonlinear activation function.

TABLE 12.1   Data inputs and initial values for neural network weights

$x_0 = 1.0$	$W_{0A} = 0.5$	$W_{0B} = 0.7$	$W_{0Z} = 0.5$
$x_1 = 0.4$	$W_{1A} = 0.6$	$W_{1B} = 0.9$	$W_{AZ} = 0.9$
$x_2 = 0.2$	$W_{2A} = 0.8$	$W_{2B} = 0.8$	$W_{BZ} = 0.9$
$x_3 = 0.7$	$W_{3A} = 0.6$	$W_{3B} = 0.4$	

The most common activation function is the sigmoid function:

$$y = \frac{1}{1 + e^{-x}}$$

where e is base of natural logarithms, equal to about 2.718281828. Thus, within node A, the activation would take $net_A = 1.32$ as input to the sigmoid activation function, and produce an output value of $y = 1/(1 + e^{-1.32}) = 0.7892$. Node A's work is done (for the moment), and this output value would then be passed along the connection to the output node Z, where it would form (via another linear combination) a component of net_Z.

But before we can compute net_Z, we need to find the contribution of node B. From the values in Table 12.1, we have

$$Net_B = \sum_i W_{iB}x_{iB} = W_{0B}(1) + W_{1B}x_{1B} + W_{2B}x_{2B} + W_{3B}x_{3B}$$

$$= 0.7 + 0.9(0.4) + 0.80(0.2) + 0.4(0.7) = 1.5$$

Then,

$$f(net_B) = \frac{1}{1 + e^{-1.5}} = 0.8176$$

Node Z then combines these outputs from nodes A and B, through net_Z, a weighted sum, using the weights associated with the connections between these nodes. Note that the inputs x_i to node Z are not data attribute values but the outputs from the sigmoid functions from upstream nodes:

$$Net_Z = \sum_i W_{iZ}x_{iZ} = W_{0Z}(1) + W_{AZ}x_{AZ} + W_{BZ}x_{BZ}$$

$$= 0.5 + 0.9(0.7892) + 0.9(0.8176) = 1.9461$$

Finally, net_Z is input into the sigmoid activation function in node Z, resulting in

$$f(net_Z) = \frac{1}{1 + e^{-1.9461}} = 0.8750$$

This value of 0.8750 is the *output* from the neural network for this first pass through the network, and represents the value predicted for the target variable for the first observation.

12.4 SIGMOID ACTIVATION FUNCTION

Why use the sigmoid function? Because it combines nearly linear behavior, curvilinear behavior, and nearly constant behavior, depending on the value of the input. Figure 12.3 shows the graph of the sigmoid function $y = f(x) = 1/(1 + e^{-x})$, for $-5 < x < 5$ (although $f(x)$ may theoretically take any real-valued input). Through much of the center of the domain of the input x (e.g., $-1 < x < 1$), the behavior of $f(x)$ is nearly linear. As the input moves away from the center, $f(x)$ becomes curvilinear. By the time the input reaches extreme values, $f(x)$ becomes nearly constant.

Moderate increments in the value of x produce varying increments in the value of $f(x)$, depending on the location of x. Near the center, moderate increments in

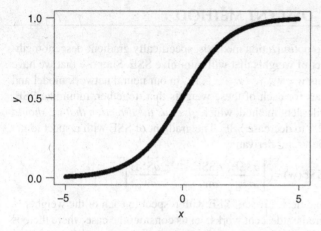

Figure 12.3   Graph of the sigmoid function $y = f(x) = 1/(1 + e^{-x})$.

the value of x produce moderate increments in the value of $f(x)$; however, near the extremes, moderate increments in the value of x produce tiny increments in the value of $f(x)$. The sigmoid function is sometimes called a *squashing function,* as it takes any real-valued input and returns an output bounded between 0 and 1.

12.5   BACK-PROPAGATION

How does the neural network learn? Neural networks represent a supervised learning method, requiring a large training set of complete records, including the target variable. As each observation from the training set is processed through the network, an output value is produced from the output node (assuming that we have only one output node, as in Figure 12.2). This output value is then compared to the actual value of the target variable for this training set observation, and the error (actual − output) is calculated. This prediction error is analogous to the residuals in regression models. To measure how well the output predictions fit the actual target values, most neural network models use the sum of squared errors (SSE):

$$\text{SSE} = \sum_{\text{records}} \sum_{\text{output nodes}} (\text{actual} - \text{output})^2$$

where the squared prediction errors are summed over all the output nodes and over all the records in the training set.

The problem is therefore to construct a set of model weights that will minimize the SSE. In this way, the weights are analogous to the parameters of a regression model. The "true" values for the weights that will minimize SSE are unknown, and our task is to estimate them, given the data. However, due to the nonlinear nature of the sigmoid functions permeating the network, there exists no closed-form solution for minimizing SSE as exists for least-squares regression.

12.6 GRADIENT-DESCENT METHOD

We must therefore turn to optimization methods, specifically gradient-descent methods, to help us find the set of weights that will minimize SSE. Suppose that we have a set (vector) of m weights $\mathbf{w} = w_0, w_1, w_2, \ldots, w_m$ in our neural network model and we wish to find the values for each of these weights that, together, minimize SSE. We can use the gradient-descent method, which *gives us the direction that we should adjust the weights* in order to decrease SSE. The gradient of SSE with respect to the vector of weights $\mathbf{w}$ is the vector derivative:

$$\nabla \text{SSE}(\mathbf{w}) = \left[\frac{\partial \text{SSE}}{\partial w_0}, \frac{\partial \text{SSE}}{\partial w_1}, \ldots, \frac{\partial \text{SSE}}{\partial w_m} \right]$$

that is, the vector of partial derivatives of SSE with respect to each of the weights.

To illustrate how gradientdescent works, let us consider the case where there is only a single weight w_1. Consider Figure 12.4, which plots the error SSE against the range of values for w_1. We would prefer values of w_1 that would minimize the SSE. The optimal value for the weight w_1 is indicated as w_1^*. We would like to develop a rule that would help us move our current value of w_1 closer to the optimal value w_1^* as follows: $w_{\text{new}} = w_{\text{current}} + \Delta w_{\text{current}}$, where $\Delta w_{\text{current}}$ is the "change in the current location of w."

Now, suppose that our current weight value w_{current} is near w_{1L}. Then we would like to *increase* our current weight value to bring it closer to the optimal value w_1^*. However, if our current weight value w_{current} were near w_{1R}, we would instead prefer to *decrease* its value, to bring it closer to the optimal value w_1^*. Now the derivative $\partial \text{SSE}/\partial w_1$ is simply the slope of the SSE curve at w_1. For values of w_1 close to w_{1L}, this slope is negative, and for values of w_1 close to w_{1R}, this slope is positive. Hence, the direction for adjusting w_{current} is the negative of the sign of the derivative of SSE at w_{current}, that is, $-\text{sign}(\partial \text{SSE}/\partial w_{\text{current}})$.

Now, how far should w_{current} be adjusted in the direction of $-\text{sign}(\partial \text{SSE}/\partial w_{\text{current}})$? Suppose that we use the magnitude of the derivative of SSE at w_{current}. When the curve is steep, the adjustment will be large, as the slope is greater in magnitude at those points. When the curve is nearly flat, the adjustment will be

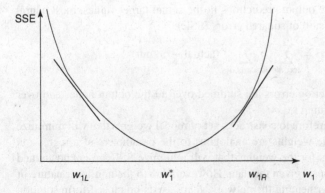

Figure 12.4 Using the slope of SSE with respect to w_1 to find weight adjustment direction.

smaller, due to less slope. Finally, the derivative is multiplied by a positive constant η (Greek lowercase eta), called the *learning rate*, with values ranging between 0 and 1. (We discuss the role of η in more detail below.) The resulting form of $\Delta w_{\text{current}}$ is as follows: $\Delta w_{\text{current}} = -\eta(\partial \text{SSE}/\partial w_{\text{current}})$, meaning that the change in the current weight value equals negative a small constant times the slope of the error function at w_{current}.

12.7 BACK-PROPAGATION RULES

The back-propagation algorithm takes the prediction error (actual − output) for a particular record and percolates the error back through the network, assigning partitioned responsibility for the error to the various connections. The weights on these connections are then adjusted to decrease the error using gradient descent.

Using the sigmoid activation function and gradient descent, Mitchell[1] derives the back-propagation rules as follows:

$$w_{ij,\text{new}} = w_{ij,\text{current}} + \Delta w_{ij}, \quad \text{where} \quad \Delta w_{ij} = \eta \delta_j x_{ij}$$

Now we know that η represents the learning rate and x_{ij} signifies the ith input to node j, but what does δ_j represent? The component δ_j represents the *responsibility* for a particular error belonging to node j. The error responsibility is computed using the partial derivative of the sigmoid function with respect to net_j and takes the following forms, depending on whether the node in question lies in the output layer or the hidden layer:

$$\delta_j = \begin{cases} \text{output}_j \left(1 - \text{output}_j\right) \left(\text{actual}_j - \text{output}_j\right) & \text{for output layernode} \\ \text{output}_j(1 - \text{output}_j) \displaystyle\sum_{\text{downstream}} W_{jk}\delta_j & \text{for hidden layer nodes} \end{cases}$$

where $\sum_{\text{downstream}} W_{jk}\delta_j$ refers to the weighted sum of the error responsibilities for the nodes downstream from the particular hidden layer node. (For the full derivation, see Mitchell.)

Also, note that the back-propagation rules illustrate why the attribute values need to be normalized to between 0 and 1. For example, if income data, with values ranging into six figures, were not normalized, the weight adjustment $\Delta w_{ij} = \eta \delta_j x_{ij}$ would be dominated by the data value x_{ij}. Hence, the error propagation (in the form of δ_j) through the network would be overwhelmed, and learning (weight adjustment) would be stifled.

12.8 EXAMPLE OF BACK-PROPAGATION

Recall from our introductory example that the output from the first pass through the network was $output = 0.8750$. Assume that the actual value of the target attribute is

---

[1] Tom M. Mitchell, *Machine Learning*, McGraw-Hill, New York, 1997.

actual = 0.8 and that we will use a learning rate of $\eta = 0.1$. Then the *prediction error* equals $0.8 - 0.8750 = -0.075$, and we may apply the foregoing rules to illustrate how the back-propagation algorithm works to adjust the weights by portioning out responsibility for this error to the various nodes. Although it is possible to update the weights only after all records have been read, neural networks use *stochastic* (or *online*) back-propagation, which updates the weights after each record.

First, the error responsibility δ_Z for node Z is found. As node Z is an output node, we have

$$\delta_Z = \text{output}_Z(1 - \text{output}_Z)(\text{actual}_Z - \text{output}_Z)$$
$$= 0.8751(1 - 0.875)(0.8 - 0.875) = -0.0082$$

We may now adjust the "constant" weight W_{0Z} (which transmits an "input" of 1) using the back-propagation rules as follows:

$$\Delta W_{0Z} = \eta \delta_Z(1) = 0.1(-0.0082)(1) = -0.00082$$

$$w_{0Z,\text{new}} = w_{0Z,\text{current}} + \Delta w_{0Z} = 0.5 - 0.00082 = 0.49918$$

Next, we move upstream to node A. As node A is a hidden layer node, its error responsibility is

$$\delta_A = \text{output}_A(1 - \text{output}_A) \sum_{\text{downstream}} W_{Ak}\delta_k$$

The only node downstream from node A is node Z. The weight associated with this connection is $W_{AZ} = 0.9$, and the error responsibility at node Z is -0.0082, so that $\delta_A = 0.7892(1 - 0.7892)(0.9)(-0.0082) = -0.00123$.

We may now update weight W_{AZ} using the back-propagation rules as follows:

$$\Delta W_{AZ} = \eta \delta_Z \cdot \text{output}_A = 0.1(-0.0082)(0.7892) = -0.000647$$

$$w_{AZ,\text{new}} = w_{AZ,\text{current}} + \Delta w_{AZ} = 0.9 - 0.000647 = 0.899353$$

The weight for the connection between hidden layer node A and output layer node Z has been adjusted from its initial value of 0.9 to its new value of 0.899353.

Next, we turn to node B, a hidden layer node, with error responsibility

$$\delta_B = \text{output}_B(1 - \text{output}_B) \sum_{\text{downstream}} W_{Bk}\delta_k$$

Again, the only node downstream from node B is node Z, giving us $\delta_B = 0.8176(1 - 0.8176)(0.9)(-0.0082) = -0.0011$.

Weight W_{BZ} may then be adjusted using the back-propagation rules as follows:

$$\Delta W_{BZ} = \eta \delta_Z \cdot \text{output}_B = 0.1(-0.0082)(0.8176) = -0.00067$$

$$w_{BZ,\text{new}} = w_{BZ,\text{current}} + \Delta w_{BZ} = 0.9 - 0.00067 = 0.89933$$

We move upstream to the connections being used as inputs to node A. For weight W_{1A} we have

$$\Delta W_{1A} = \eta \delta_A x_1 = 0.1(-0.00123)(0.4) = -0.0000492$$

$$w_{1A,\text{new}} = w_{1A,\text{current}} + \Delta w_{1A} = 0.6 - 0.000492 = 0.5999508$$

For weight W_{2A} we have

$$\Delta W_{2A} = \eta \delta_A x_2 = 0.1(-0.00123)(0.2) = -0.0000246$$

$$w_{2A,\text{new}} = w_{2A,\text{current}} + \Delta w_{2A} = 0.8 - 0.0000246 = 0.7999754$$

For weight W_{3A} we have

$$\Delta W_{3A} = \eta \delta_A x_3 = 0.1(-0.00123)(0.7) = -0.0000861$$

$$w_{3A,\text{new}} = w_{3A,\text{current}} + \Delta w_{3A} = 0.6 - 0.0000861 = 0.5999139.$$

Finally, for weight W_{0A} we have

$$\Delta W_{0A} = \eta \delta_A (1) = 0.1(-0.00123) = -0.000123$$

$$w_{0A,\text{new}} = w_{0A,\text{current}} + \Delta w_{0A} = 0.5 - 0.000123 = 0.499877.$$

Adjusting weights W_{0B}, W_{1B}, W_{2B}, and W_{3B} is left as an exercise.

Note that the weight adjustments have been made based on only a single perusal of a single record. The network calculated a predicted value for the target variable, compared this output value to the actual target value, and then percolated the error in prediction throughout the network, adjusting the weights to provide a smaller prediction error. Showing that the adjusted weights result in a smaller prediction error is left as an exercise.

12.9 TERMINATION CRITERIA

The neural network algorithm would then proceed to work through the training data set, record by record, adjusting the weights constantly to reduce the prediction error. It may take many passes through the data set before the algorithm's termination criterion is met. What, then, serves as the termination criterion, or stopping criterion? If training time is an issue, one may simply set the number of passes through the data, or the amount of real time the algorithm may consume, as termination criteria. However, what one gains in short training time is probably bought with degradation in model efficacy.

Alternatively, one may be tempted to use a termination criterion that assesses when the SSE on the training data has been reduced to some low threshold level. Unfortunately, because of their flexibility, neural networks are prone to overfitting, memorizing the idiosyncratic patterns in the training set instead of retaining generalizability to unseen data.

Therefore, most neural network implementations adopt the following cross-validation termination procedure:

1. Retain part of the original data set as a holdout validation set.
2. Proceed to train the neural network as above on the remaining training data.
3. Apply the weights learned from the training data on the validation data.
4. Monitor *two sets of weights*, one "current" set of weights produced by the training data, and one "best" set of weights, as measured by the lowest SSE so far on the validation data.
5. When the current set of weights has significantly greater SSE than the best set of weights, then terminate the algorithm.

Regardless of the stopping criterion used, the neural network is not guaranteed to arrive at the optimal solution, known as *the global minimum* for the SSE. Rather, the algorithm may become stuck in a local minimum, which represents a good, if not optimal solution. In practice, this has not presented an insuperable problem.

- For example, multiple networks may be trained using different initialized weights, with the best-performing model being chosen as the "final" model.
- Second, the *online* or *stochastic* back-propagation method itself acts as a guard against getting stuck in a local minimum, as it introduces a random element to the gradient descent (see Reed and Marks[2]).
- Alternatively, a *momentum* term may be added to the back-propagation algorithm, with effects discussed below.

12.10   LEARNING RATE

Recall that the learning rate η, $0 < \eta < 1$, is a constant chosen to help us move the network weights toward a global minimum for SSE. However, what value should η take? How large should the weight adjustments be?

When the learning rate is very small, the weight adjustments tend to be very small. Thus, if η is small when the algorithm is initialized, the network will probably take an unacceptably long time to converge. Is the solution therefore to use large values for η? Not necessarily. Suppose that the algorithm is close to the optimal solution and we have a large value for η. This large η will tend to make the algorithm overshoot the optimal solution.

Consider Figure 12.5, where W^* is the optimum value for weight W, which has current value $W_{current}$. According to the gradient-descent rule, $\Delta w_{current} = -\eta(\partial SSE/\partial w_{current})$, $W_{current}$ will be adjusted in the direction of W^*. But if the learning rate η, which acts as a multiplier in the formula for $\Delta w_{current}$, is too large, the new weight value W_{new} will jump right past the optimal value W^*, and may in fact end up farther away from W^* than $W_{current}$.

---

[2]Russell D. Reed and Robert J. Marks II, *Neural Smithing: Supervised Learning in Feedforward Artificial Neural Networks*, MIT Press, Cambridge, MA, 1999.

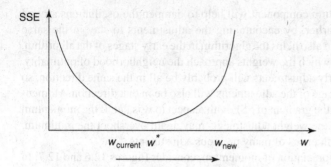

Figure 12.5   Large η may cause algorithm to overshoot global minimum.

In fact, as the new weight value will then be on the opposite side of W^*, the next adjustment will again overshoot W^*, leading to an unfortunate oscillation between the two "slopes" of the valley and never settling down in the ravine (the minimum). One solution is to allow the learning rate η to change values as the training moves forward. At the start of training, η should be initialized to a relatively large value to allow the network to quickly approach the general neighborhood of the optimal solution. Then, when the network is beginning to approach convergence, the learning rate should gradually be reduced, thereby avoiding overshooting the minimum.

12.11   MOMENTUM TERM

The back-propagation algorithm is made more powerful through the addition of a *momentum term* α, as follows:

$$\Delta w_{\text{current}} = -\eta \frac{\partial \text{SSE}}{\partial w_{\text{current}}} + \alpha \Delta w_{\text{previous}}$$

where $\Delta w_{\text{previous}}$ represents the previous weight adjustment, and $0 \leq \alpha < 1$. Thus, the new component $\alpha \Delta w_{\text{previous}}$ represents a fraction of the previous weight adjustment for a given weight.

Essentially, the momentum term represents *inertia*. Large values of α will influence the adjustment in the current weight, $\Delta w_{\text{current}}$, to move in the same direction as previous adjustments. It has been shown (e.g., Reed and Marks) that including momentum in the back-propagation algorithm results in the adjustment becoming an exponential average of *all* previous adjustments:

$$\Delta w_{\text{current}} = -\eta \sum_{k=0}^{\infty} \alpha^k \frac{\partial \text{SSE}}{\partial w_{\text{current}-k}}$$

The α^k term indicates that the more recent adjustments exert a larger influence. Large values of α allow the algorithm to "remember" more terms in the adjustment history. Small values of α reduce the inertial effects as well as the influence of previous adjustments, until, with $\alpha = 0$, the component disappears entirely.

Clearly, a momentum component will help to dampen the oscillations around optimality mentioned earlier, by encouraging the adjustments to stay in the same direction. But momentum also helps the algorithm in the early stages of the algorithm, by increasing the rate at which the weights approach the neighborhood of optimality. This is because these early adjustments will probably be all in the same direction, so that the exponential average of the adjustments will also be in that direction. Momentum is also helpful when the gradient of SSE with respect to **w** is flat. If the momentum term α is too large, then the weight adjustments may again overshoot the minimum, due to the cumulative influences of many previous adjustments.

For an informal appreciation of momentum, consider Figures 12.6 and 12.7. In both figures, the weight is initialized at location I, local minima exist at locations A and C, with the optimal global minimum at B. In Figure 12.6, suppose that we have a small value for the momentum term α, symbolized by the small mass of the "ball" on the curve. If we roll this small ball down the curve, it may never make it over the first hill, and remain stuck in the first valley. That is, the small value for α enables the algorithm to easily find the first trough at location A, representing a local minimum, but does not allow it to find the global minimum at B.

Next, in Figure 12.7, suppose that we have a large value for the momentum term α, symbolized by the large mass of the "ball" on the curve. If we roll this large ball down the curve, it may well make it over the first hill but may then have so much momentum that it overshoots the global minimum at location B and settles for the local minimum at location C.

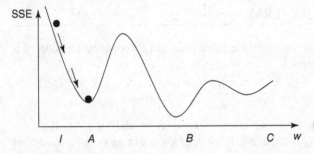

Figure 12.6   Small momentum α may cause algorithm to undershoot global minimum.

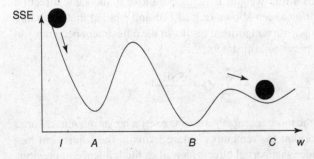

Figure 12.7   Large momentum α may cause algorithm to overshoot global minimum.

Thus, one needs to consider carefully what values to set for both the learning rate η and the momentum term α. Experimentation with various values of η and α may be necessary before the best results are obtained.

12.12   SENSITIVITY ANALYSIS

One of the drawbacks of neural networks is their opacity. The same wonderful flexibility that allows neural networks to model a wide range of nonlinear behavior also limits our ability to interpret the results using easily formulated rules. Unlike decision trees, no straightforward procedure exists for translating the weights of a neural network into a compact set of decision rules.

However, a procedure is available, called *sensitivity analysis*, which does allow us to measure the relative influence each attribute has on the output result. Using the test data set mentioned above, the sensitivity analysis proceeds as follows:

1. Generate a new observation x_{mean}, with each attribute value in x_{mean} equal to the mean of the various attribute values for all records in the test set.
2. Find the network output for input x_{mean}. Call it output$_{mean}$.
3. Attribute by attribute, vary x_{mean} to reflect the attribute minimum and maximum. Find the network output for each variation and compare it to output$_{mean}$.

The sensitivity analysis will find that varying certain attributes from their minimum to their maximum will have a greater effect on the resulting network output than it has for other attributes. For example, suppose that we are interested in predicting stock price based on *price to earnings ratio*, *dividend yield*, and other attributes. Also, suppose that varying *price to earnings ratio* from its minimum to its maximum results in an increase of 0.20 in the network output, while varying *dividend yield* from its minimum to its maximum results in an increase of 0.30 in the network output when the other attributes are held constant at their mean value. We conclude that the network is more *sensitive* to variations in dividend yield and that therefore dividend yield is a more important factor for predicting stock prices than is price to earnings ratio.

12.13   APPLICATION OF NEURAL NETWORK MODELING

Next, we apply a neural network model using Insightful Miner on the *adult* data set from the UCal Irvine Machine Learning Repository. The Insightful Miner neural network software was applied to a training set of 25,000 cases, using a single hidden layer with eight hidden nodes. The algorithm iterated 47 epochs (runs through the data set) before termination. The resulting neural network is shown in Figure 12.8. The squares on the left represent the input nodes. For the categorical variables, there is one input node per class. The eight dark circles represent the hidden layer. The light gray circles represent the constant inputs. There is only a single output node, indicating whether or not the record is classified as having income less than or equal to $50,000.

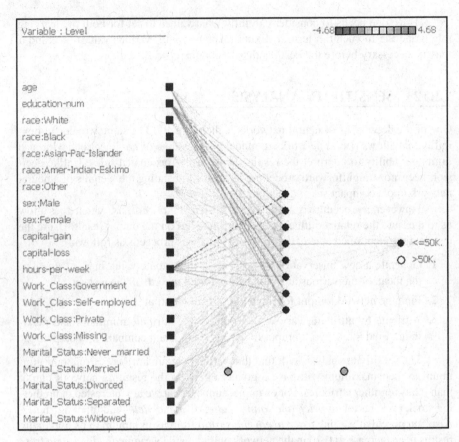

Figure 12.8   Neural network for the adult data set generated by Insightful Miner.

In this algorithm, the weights are centered at 0. An excerpt of the computer output showing the weight values is provided in Figure 12.9. The columns in the first table represent the input nodes: 1 = *age*, 2 = *education-num*, and so on, while the rows represent the hidden layer nodes: 22 = first (top) hidden node, 23 = second hidden node, and so on. For example, the weight on the connection from *age* to the topmost hidden node is −0.97, while the weight on the connection from *Race: American Indian/Eskimo* (the sixth input node) to the last (bottom) hidden node is −0.75. The lower section of Figure 12.9 displays the weights from the hidden nodes to the output node.

The estimated prediction accuracy using this very basic model is 82%, which is in the ballpark of the accuracies reported by Kohavi.[3] As over 75% of the subjects have incomes at or below $50,000, simply predicted "less than or equal to $50,000" for every person would provide a baseline accuracy of about 75%.

[3]Ronny Kohavi, Scaling up the accuracy of naïve Bayes classifiers: A decision tree hybrid, *Proceedings of the 2nd International Conference on Knowledge Discovery and Data Mining*, Portland, OR, 1996.

Weights

To/From	1	2	3	4	5	6	7	8	9
22	-0.97	-1.32	-0.18	-0.51	0.69	0.13	-0.25	-0.33	0.30
23	-0.70	-2.97	-0.12	0.34	0.43	0.50	1.03	-0.29	-0.10
24	-0.70	-2.96	-0.24	0.05	0.16	0.46	1.15	-0.16	-0.07
25	0.74	2.86	0.22	0.41	-0.03	-0.59	-1.05	0.18	0.14
26	-0.84	-2.82	-0.23	0.02	-0.16	0.62	1.06	-0.22	-0.20
27	-0.68	-2.89	-0.18	-0.03	-0.03	0.50	1.07	-0.24	-0.12
28	-1.68	-2.54	-0.43	-0.09	0.04	0.54	0.88	-0.18	-0.26
29	-2.11	-1.95	0.01	0.34	0.04	-0.75	-1.16	-0.03	0.38

Weights

To/From	22	23	24	25	26	27	28	29	0
30	0.18	0.59	0.69	-1.40	0.77	0.76	0.74	1.06	-0.08

Figure 12.9   Some of the neural network weights for the income example.

However, we would like to know which variables are most important for predicting (classifying) income. We therefore perform a sensitivity analysis using Modeler, with results shown in Figure 12.10. Clearly, the amount of capital gains is the best predictor of whether a person has income less than or equal to $50,000, followed by the number of years of education. Other important variables include the number of hours worked per week and marital status. A person's gender does not seem to be highly predictive of income.

Of course, there is much more involved in developing a neural network classification model. For example, further data preprocessing may be called for; the model

Relative Importance of Inputs

capital-gain	0.719519
education-num	0.486229
hours-per-week	0.289301
Marital_Status	0.27691
age	0.237282
capital-loss	0.228844
race	0.183006
Work_Class	0.119079
sex	0.0641384

Figure 12.10   Most important variables: results from sensitivity analysis.

would need to be validated using a holdout validation data set, and so on. For a start-to-finish application of neural networks to a real-world data set, from data preparation through model building and sensitivity analysis, see the Case Study in Chapters 29–32.

The R Zone

Read in and prepare the data

```
adult <- read.csv(file = "C:/ ... /adult.txt";
    stringsAsFactors=TRUE)
# Collapse categories as in Chapter 11
# We will work with a small sample of data
adult <- adult[1:500,]
```

Determine how many Indicator variables are needed

```
unique(adult$income)          # One variable for income
unique(adult$sex)             # One variable for sex
unique(adult$race)            # Four variables for race
unique(adult$workclass)       # Three variables for workclass
unique(adult$marital.status)  # Four variables for marital.status
```

Create indicator variables

```
adult$race_white <- adult$race_black <- adult$race_as.pac.is <-
    adult$race_am.in.esk <- adult$wc_gov <- adult$wc_self <- adult$wc_priv <-
    adult$ms_marr <- adult$ms_div <- adult$ms_sep <- adult$ms_wid <-
    adult$income_g50K <- adult$sex2 <- c(rep(0, length(adult$income)))
for (i in 1:length(adult$income)) {
    if(adult$income[i]==">50K.")
        adult$income_g50K[i]<-1
    if(adult$sex[i] == "Male")
        adult$sex2[i] <- 1
    if(adult$race[i] == "White") adult$race_white[i] <- 1
    if(adult$race[i] == "Amer-Indian-Eskimo") adult$race_am.in.esk[i] <- 1

if(adult$race[i] == "Asian-Pac-Islander") adult$race_as.pac.is[i] <- 1
    if(adult$race[i] == "Black") adult$race_black[i] <- 1
    if(adult$workclass[i] == "Gov") adult$wc_gov[i] <- 1
    if(adult$workclass[i] == "Self") adult$wc_self[i] <- 1
    if(adult$workclass[i] == "Private") adult$wc_priv[i] <- 1
    if(adult$marital.status[i] == "Married") adult$ms_marr[i] <- 1
    if(adult$marital.status[i] == "Divorced" ) adult$ms_div[i] <- 1
    if(adult$marital.status[i] == "Separated" ) adult$ms_sep[i] <- 1
    if(adult$marital.status[i] == "Widowed" ) adult$ms_wid[i] <- 1
}
```

Minimax transform the continuous variables

```
adult$age_mm <- (adult$age - min(adult$age))/(max(adult$age)-min(adult$age))
adult$edu.num_mm <- (adult$education.num - min(adult$education.num))/
    (max(adult$education.num)-min(adult$education.num))
adult$capital.gain_mm <- (adult$capital.gain - min(adult$capital.gain))/
    (max(adult$capital.gain)- min(adult$capital.gain))
adult$capital.loss_mm <- (adult$capital.loss - min(adult$capital.loss))/
    (max(adult$capital.loss)- min(adult$capital.loss))
adult$hours.p.w_mm <- (adult$hours.per.week - min(adult$hours.per.week))/
(max(adult$hours.per.week)-min(adult$hours.per.week))
newdat <- as.data.frame(adult[,-c(1:15)]) # Get rid of the variables we no longer need
```

Run the neural net

```
library(nnet) # Requires package nnet
net.dat <- nnet(income_g50K ~ ., data = newdat, size = 8)
table(round(net.dat$fitted.values, 1))   # If fitted values are all the same, rerun nnet
net.dat$wts # Weights
hist(net.dat$wts)
```

R REFERENCES

1. R Core Team. *R: A Language and Environment for Statistical Computing*. Vienna, Austria: R Foundation for Statistical Computing; 2012. ISBN: 3-900051-07-0, http://www.R-project.org/.
2. Venables WN, Ripley BD. *Modern Applied Statistics with S*. 4th ed. New York: Springer; 2002. ISBN: 0-387-95457-0.

EXERCISES

1. Suppose that you need to prepare the data in Table 6.10 for a neural network algorithm. Define the indicator variables for the *occupation* attribute.

2. Clearly describe each of these characteristics of a neural network:

   a. Layered

   b. Feedforward

   c. Completely connected

3. What is the sole function of the nodes in the input layer?

4. Should we prefer a large hidden layer or a small one? Describe the benefits and drawbacks of each.

5. Describe how neural networks function nonlinearly.

6. Explain why the updating term for the current weight includes the *negative* of the sign of the derivative (slope).

7. Adjust the weights W_{0B}, W_{1B}, W_{2B}, and W_{3B} from the example on back-propagation in the text.

8. Refer to Exercise 7. Show that the adjusted weights result in a smaller prediction error.

9. True or false: Neural networks are valuable because of their capacity for always finding the global minimum of the SSE.

10. Describe the benefits and drawbacks of using large or small values for the learning rate.

11. Describe the benefits and drawbacks of using large or small values for the momentum term.

HANDS-ON ANALYSIS

For Exercises 12–14, use the data set *churn*. Normalize the numerical data, recode the categorical variables, and deal with the correlated variables.

12. Generate a neural network model for classifying *churn* based on the other variables. Describe the topology of the model.

13. Which variables, in order of importance, are identified as most important for classifying *churn?*

14. Compare the neural network model with the classification and regression tree (CART) and C4.5 models for this task in Chapter 11. Describe the benefits and drawbacks of the neural network model compared to the others. Is there convergence or divergence of results among the models?

For Exercises 15–17, use the *ClassifyRisk* data set.

15. Run a NN model predicting income based only on age. Use the default settings and make sure there is one hidden layer with one neuron.

16. Consider the following quantity: (weight for Age-to-Neuron1) + (weight for Bias-to-Neuron1)*(weight for Neuron 1-to-Output node). Explain whether this makes sense, given the data, and why.

17. Make sure the target variable takes the flag type. Compare the sign of (weight for Age-to-Neuron1) + (weight for Bias-to-Neuron1)*(weight for Neuron 1-to-Output node) for the good risk output node, as compared to the bad loss output node. Explain whether this makes sense, given the data, and why.

IBM/SPSS Modeler Analysis. For Exercises 18, 19, use the *nn1* data set.

18. Set your neural network build options as follows: Use a Multilayer Perceptron and customize number of units in Hidden Layer 1 to be 1 and Hidden Layer 2 to be 0. For Stopping Rules, select ONLY Customize number of maximum training cycles. Start at 1 and go to about 20. For Advanced, de-select Replicate Results.

19. Browse your model. In the Network window of the Model tab, select the Style: Coefficients. Record the Pred1-to-Neuron1 weight and the Pred2-to-Neuron1 weight for each run. Describe the behavior of these weights. Explain why this is happening.

## CHAPTER 13

LOGISTIC REGRESSION

Linear regression is used to approximate the relationship between a continuous response variable and a set of predictor variables. However, for many data applications, the response variable is categorical rather than continuous. For such cases, linear regression is not appropriate. Fortunately, the analyst can turn to an analogous method, logistic regression, which is similar to linear regression in many ways.

Logistic regression refers to methods for describing the relationship between a categorical response variable and a set of predictor variables. In this chapter, we explore the use of logistic regression for binary or dichotomous variables; those interested in using logistic regression for response variables with more than two categories may refer to Hosmer and Lemeshow.[1] To motivate logistic regression, and to illustrate its similarities to linear regression, consider the following example.

13.1 SIMPLE EXAMPLE OF LOGISTIC REGRESSION

Suppose that medical researchers are interested in exploring the relationship between patient *age* (x) and the presence (1) or absence (0) of a particular *disease* (y). The data collected from 20 patients is shown in Table 13.1, and a plot of the data is shown in Figure 13.1. The plot shows the least-squares regression line (dotted straight line), and the logistic regression line (solid curved line), along with the estimation error for patient 11 (*age* = 50, *disease* = 0) for both lines.

Note that the least-squares regression line is linear, which means that linear regression assumes that the relationship between the predictor and the response is linear. Contrast this with the logistic regression line that is nonlinear, meaning that logistic regression assumes the relationship between the predictor and the response is nonlinear. The scatter plot makes plain the discontinuity in the response variable; scatter plots that look like this should alert the analyst not to apply linear regression.

Consider the prediction errors for patient 11, indicated in Figure 13.1. The distance between the data point for patient 11 ($x = 50$, $y = 0$) and the linear regression line is indicated by the dotted vertical line, while the distance between the data point and the logistic regression line is shown by the solid vertical line. Clearly, the distance

---

[1] Hosmer and Lemeshow, *Applied Logistic Regression*, 3rd edition, John Wiley and Sons, 2013.

Data Mining and Predictive Analytics, First Edition. Daniel T. Larose and Chantal D. Larose.
© 2015 John Wiley & Sons, Inc. Published 2015 by John Wiley & Sons, Inc.

TABLE 13.1 Age of 20 patients, with indicator of disease

Patient ID	1	2	3	4	5	6	7	8	9	10
Age (x)	25	29	30	31	32	41	41	42	44	49
Disease (y)	0	0	0	0	0	0	0	0	1	1
Patient ID	11	12	13	14	15	16	17	18	19	20
Age (x)	50	59	60	62	68	72	79	80	81	84
Disease (y)	0	1	0	0	1	0	1	0	1	1

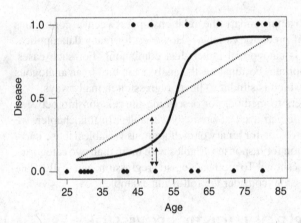

Figure 13.1 Plot of disease versus age, with least squares and logistic regression lines.

is greater for the linear regression line, which means that linear regression does a poorer job of estimating the presence of disease as compared to logistic regression for patient 11. Similarly, this observation is also true for most of the other patients.

Where does the logistic regression curve come from? Consider the *conditional mean of Y given X = x,* denoted as $E(Y|x)$. This is the expected value of the response variable for a given value of the predictor. Recall that, in linear regression, the response variable is considered to be a random variable defined as $Y = \beta_0 + \beta_1 x + \varepsilon$. Now, as the error term ε has mean zero, we then obtain $E(Y|x) = \beta_0 + \beta_1 x$ for linear regression, with possible values extending over the entire real number line.

For simplicity, denote the conditional mean $E(Y|x)$ as $\pi(x)$. Then, the conditional mean for logistic regression takes on a different form from that of linear regression. Specifically,

$$\pi(x) = \frac{e^{\beta_0 + \beta_1 x}}{1 + e^{\beta_0 + \beta_1 x}} \tag{13.1}$$

Curves of the form in equation (13.1) are called *sigmoidal* because they are S-shaped, and therefore nonlinear. Statisticians have chosen the logistic distribution to model dichotomous data because of its flexibility and interpretability. The minimum for $\pi(x)$ is obtained at $\lim_{a \to -\infty} \left[\frac{e^a}{1+e^a} \right] = 0$, and the maximum for $\pi(x)$ is obtained at $\lim_{a \to \infty} \left[\frac{e^a}{1+e^a} \right] = 1$. Thus, $\pi(x)$ is of a form that may be interpreted as a probability, with $0 \leq \pi(x) \leq 1$. That is, $\pi(x)$ may be interpreted as the probability that the positive outcome (e.g., disease) is present for records with $X = x$, and $1 - \pi(x)$ may be interpreted as the probability that the positive outcome is absent for such records.

Linear regression models assume that $Y = \beta_0 + \beta_1 x + \varepsilon$, where the error term ε is normally distributed with mean zero and constant variance. The model assumption for logistic regression is different. As the response is dichotomous, the errors can take only one of two possible forms: If $Y = 1$ (e.g., disease is present), which occurs with probability $\pi(x)$ (the probability that the response is positive), then $\varepsilon = 1 - \pi(x)$, the vertical distance between the data point $Y = 1$ and the curve $\pi(x) = \frac{e^{\beta_0 + \beta_1 x}}{1 + e^{\beta_0 + \beta_1 x}}$ directly below it, for $X = x$. However, if $Y = 0$ (e.g., disease is absent), which occurs with probability $1 - \pi(x)$ (the probability that the response is negative), then $\varepsilon = 0 - \pi(x) = -\pi(x)$, the vertical distance between the data point $Y = 0$ and the curve $\pi(x)$ directly above it, for $X = x$. Thus, the variance of ε is $\pi(x)[1 - \pi(x)]$, which is the variance for a binomial distribution, and the response variable in logistic regression $Y = \pi(x) + \varepsilon$ is assumed to follow a binomial distribution with probability of success $\pi(x)$.

A useful transformation for logistic regression is the *logit transformation,* and it is given as follows:

$$g(x) = \ln \left[\frac{\pi(x)}{1 - \pi(x)} \right] = \beta_0 + \beta_1 x$$

The logit transformation $g(x)$ exhibits several attractive properties of the linear regression model, such as its linearity, its continuity, and its range from negative to positive infinity.

13.2   MAXIMUM LIKELIHOOD ESTIMATION

One of the most attractive properties of linear regression is that closed-form solutions for the optimal values of the regression coefficients may be obtained, courtesy of the least-squares method. Unfortunately, no such closed-form solution exists for estimating logistic regression coefficients. Thus, we must turn to *maximum-likelihood estimation,* which finds estimates of the parameters for which the likelihood of observing the observed data is maximized.

The *likelihood function* $l(\boldsymbol{\beta}|x)$ is a function of the parameters $\boldsymbol{\beta} = \beta_0, \beta_1, \dots, \beta_m$ that expresses the probability of the observed data, x. By finding the values of $\boldsymbol{\beta} = \beta_0, \beta_1, \dots, \beta_m$, which maximize $l(\boldsymbol{\beta}|x)$, we thereby uncover the *maximum-likelihood estimators,* the parameter values most favored by the observed data.

The probability of a positive response given the data is $\pi(x) = P(Y = 1|x)$, and the probability of a negative response given the data is given by $1 - \pi(x) = P(Y = 0|x)$. Then, observations where the response is positive, $(X_i = x_i, \ Y_i = 1)$, will contribute probability $\pi(x)$ to the likelihood, while observations where the response is negative, $(X_i = x_i, \ Y_i = 0)$, will contribute probability $1 - \pi(x)$ to the likelihood. Thus, as $Y_i = 0$ or 1, the contribution to the likelihood of the ith observation may be expressed as $[\pi(x_i)]^{y_i}[1 - \pi(x_i)]^{1-y_i}$. The assumption that the observations are independent allows us to express the likelihood function $l(\boldsymbol{\beta}|x)$ as the product of the individual terms:

$$l(\boldsymbol{\beta}|x) = \prod_{i=1}^{n} [\pi(x_i)]^{y_i} [1 - \pi(x_i)]^{1-y_i}$$

The log-likelihood $L(\boldsymbol{\beta}|x) = \ln[l(\boldsymbol{\beta}|x)]$ is computationally more tractable:

$$L(\boldsymbol{\beta}|x) = \ln[l(\boldsymbol{\beta}|x)] = \sum_{i=1}^{n} \{y_i \ln[\pi(x_i)] + (1 - y_i) \ln[1 - \pi(x_i)]\} \qquad (13.2)$$

The maximum-likelihood estimators may be found by differentiating $L(\boldsymbol{\beta}|x)$ with respect to each parameter, and setting the resulting forms equal to zero. Unfortunately, unlike linear regression, closed-form solutions for these differentiations are not available. Therefore, other methods must be applied, such as iterative weighted least squares (see McCullagh and Nelder[2]).

13.3 INTERPRETING LOGISTIC REGRESSION OUTPUT

Let us examine the results of the logistic regression of *disease* on *age*, shown in Table 13.2. The coefficients, that is, the maximum-likelihood estimates of the unknown parameters β_0 and β_1, are given as $b_0 = -4.372$ and $b_1 = 0.06696$. Thus, $\pi(x) = \frac{e^{\beta_0 + \beta_1 x}}{1 + e^{\beta_0 + \beta_1 x}}$ is estimated as

$$\widehat{\pi}(x) = \frac{e^{\widehat{g}(x)}}{1 + e^{\widehat{g}(x)}} = \frac{e^{-4.372 + 0.06696(\text{age})}}{1 + e^{-4.372 + 0.06696(\text{age})}},$$

with the estimated logit

$$\widehat{g}(x) = -4.372 + 0.06696(\text{age}).$$

These equations may then be used to estimate the probability that the disease is present in a particular patient, given the patient's age. For example, for a 50-year-old patient, we have

$$\widehat{g}(x) = -4.372 + 0.06696(50) = -1.024$$

and

$$\widehat{\pi}(x) = \frac{e^{\widehat{g}(x)}}{1 + e^{\widehat{g}(x)}} = \frac{e^{-1.024}}{1 + e^{-1.024}} = 0.26$$

Thus, the estimated probability that a 50-year-old patient has the disease is 26%, and the estimated probability that the disease is not present is $100\% - 26\% = 74\%$.

However, for a 72-year-old patient, we have

$$\widehat{g}(x) = -4.372 + 0.06696(72) = 0.449$$

and

$$\widehat{\pi}(x) = \frac{e^{\widehat{g}(x)}}{1 + e^{\widehat{g}(x)}} = \frac{e^{0.449}}{1 + e^{0.449}} = 0.61$$

[2]McCullagh and Nelder, *Generalized Linear Models*, 2nd edition, Chapman and Hall, London, 1989.

TABLE 13.2 Logistic regression of *disease* on *age*, results from *minitab*

```
Logistic Regression Table
                                          Odds       95% CI
Predictor      Coef      StDev      Z    P  Ratio  Lower   Upper
Constant     -4.372     1.966   -2.22 0.026
Age           0.06696   0.03223   2.08 0.038  1.07   1.00    1.14

Log-Likelihood = -10.101
Test that all slopes are zero: G = 5.696, DF = 1, P-Value = 0.017
```

The estimated probability that a 72-year-old patient has the disease is 61%, and the estimated probability that the disease is not present is 39%.

13.4 INFERENCE: ARE THE PREDICTORS SIGNIFICANT?

Recall from simple linear regression that the regression model was considered significant if mean square regression (MSR) was large compared to mean squared error (MSE). The MSR is a measure of the improvement in estimating the response when we include the predictor, as compared to ignoring the predictor. If the predictor variable is helpful for estimating the value of the response variable, then MSR will be large, the test statistic $F = \frac{\text{MSR}}{\text{MSE}}$ will also be large, and the linear regression model will be considered significant.

Significance of the coefficients in logistic regression is determined analogously. Essentially, we examine whether the model that includes a particular predictor provides a substantially better fit to the response variable than a model that does not include this predictor.

Define the *saturated model* to be the model that contains as many parameters as data points, such as a simple linear regression model with only two data points. Clearly, the saturated model predicts the response variable perfectly, and there is no prediction error. We may then look on the *observed* values of the response variable to be the predicted values from the saturated model. To compare the values predicted by our fitted model (with fewer parameters than data points) to predicted by the saturated the values model, we use the *deviance* (McCullagh and Nelder[3]), as defined here:

$$\text{Deviance} = D = -2 \ln \left[\frac{\text{likelihood of the fitted model}}{\text{likelihood of the saturated model}} \right]$$

Here we have a ratio of two likelihoods, so that the resulting hypothesis test is called a *likelihood ratio test*. In order to generate a measure whose distribution is known, we must take $-2 \ln[\text{likelihood ratio}]$. Denote the estimate of $\pi(x_i)$ from the fitted model to be $\hat{\pi}_i$. Then, for the logistic regression case, and using equation (13.2), we have

---

[3]McCullagh and Nelder, *Generalized Linear Models*, 2nd edition, Chapman and Hall, London, 1989.

deviance equal to:

$$\text{Deviance} = D = -2\ln\sum_{i=1}^{n}\left\{y_i\ln\left[\frac{\hat{\pi}_i}{y_i}\right] + (1-y_i)\ln\left[\frac{1-\hat{\pi}_i}{1-y_i}\right]\right\}$$

The deviance represents the error left over in the model, after the predictors have been accounted for. As such it is analogous to the sum of squares error in linear regression.

The procedure for determining whether a particular predictor is significant is to find the deviance of the model without the predictor and subtract the deviance of the model with the predictor, thus:

$$G = \text{deviance(model without predictor)} - \text{deviance(model with predictor)}$$

$$= -2\ln\left[\frac{\text{likelihood without predictor}}{\text{likelihood with predictor}}\right]$$

Let $n_1 = \sum y_i$ and $n_0 = \sum(1-y_i)$. Then, for the case of a single predictor only, we have:

$$G = 2\left\{\sum_{i=1}^{n}\left[y_i\ln\left[\hat{\pi}_i\right] + (1-y_i)\ln[1-\hat{\pi}_i]\right] - [n_1\ln(n_1) + n_0\ln(n_0) - n\ln(n)]\right\}$$

For the *disease* example, note from Table 13.2 that the log-likelihood is given as -10.101. Then,

$$G = 2\{-10.101 - [7\ln(7) + 13\ln(13) - 20\ln(20)]\} = 5.696$$

as indicated in Table 13.2.

The test statistic G follows a chi-square distribution with 1 degree of freedom (i.e., $\chi^2_{v=1}$), assuming that the null hypothesis is true that $\beta_1 = 0$. The resulting p-value for this hypothesis test is therefore $P(\chi^2_1) > G_{\text{observed}} = P(\chi^2_1) > 5.696 = 0.017$, as shown in Table 13.2. This fairly small p-value indicates that there is evidence that *age* is useful in predicting the presence of *disease*.

Another hypothesis test used to determine whether a particular predictor is significant is the Wald test (e.g., Rao[4]). Under the null hypothesis that $\beta_1 = 0$, the ratio

$$Z_{\text{Wald}} = \frac{b_1}{SE(b_1)}$$

follows a standard normal distribution, where SE refers to the standard error of the coefficient, as estimated from the data and reported by the software. Table 13.2 provides the coefficient estimate and the standard error as follows: $b_1 = 0.06696$ and $SE(b_1) = 0.03223$, giving us:

$$Z_{\text{Wald}} = \frac{0.06696}{0.03223} = 2.08$$

as reported under z for the coefficient *age* in Table 13.2. The p-value is then reported as $P(|z| > 2.08) = 0.038$. This p-value is also fairly small, although not as small as

---

[4]Rao, *Linear Statistical Inference and Its Application*, 2nd edition, John Wiley and Sons, Inc., 1973.

the likelihood ratio test, and therefore concurs in the significance of *age* for predicting *disease*.

We may construct $100(1 - \alpha)\%$ confidence intervals for the logistic regression coefficients, as follows.

$$b_0 \pm z \cdot \text{SE}(b_0)$$
$$b_1 \pm z \cdot \text{SE}(b_1)$$

where z represents the z-critical value associated with $100(1 - \alpha)\%$ confidence.

In our example, a 95% confidence interval for the slope β_1 could be found thus:

$$b_1 \pm z \cdot \text{SE}(b_1) = 0.06696 \pm (1.96)(0.03223)$$
$$= 0.06696 \pm 0.06317$$
$$= (0.00379, 0.13013)$$

As zero is not included in this interval, we can conclude with 95% confidence that $\beta_1 \neq 0$, and that therefore the variable *age* is significant.

The above results may be extended from the simple (one predictor) logistic regression model to the multiple (many predictors) logistic regression model. (See Hosmer and Lemeshow[5] for details.)

13.5   ODDS RATIO AND RELATIVE RISK

Recall from simple linear regression that the slope coefficient β_1 was interpreted as the change in the response variable for every unit increase in the predictor. The slope coefficient β_1 is interpreted analogously in logistic regression, but through the logit function. That is, the slope coefficient β_1 may be interpreted as the change in the value of the logit for a unit increase in the value of the predictor. In other words,

$$\beta_1 = g(x + 1) - g(x)$$

In this section, we discuss the interpretation of β_1 in simple logistic regression for the following three cases:

1. A dichotomous predictor
2. A polychotomous predictor
3. A continuous predictor.

To facilitate our interpretation, we need to consider the concept of *odds*. Odds may be defined as the probability that an event occurs divided by the probability that the event does not occur. For example, earlier we found that the estimated probability that a 72-year-old patient has the disease is 61%, and the estimated probability that the 72-year-old patient does not have the disease is 39%. Thus, the odds of a 72-year-old patient having the disease equal odds $= \frac{0.61}{0.39} = 1.56$. We also found that the estimated probabilities of a 50-year-old patient having or not having the disease are 26% and

---

[5] Hosmer and Lemeshow, *Applied Logistic Regression*, 3rd edition, John Wiley and Sons, 2013.

74%, respectively, providing odds for the 50-year-old patient to be odds $= \frac{0.26}{0.74} = 0.35$.

Note that when the event is more likely than not to occur, then odds > 1; when the event is less likely than not to occur, then odds < 1; and when the event is just as likely as not to occur, then odds $= 1$. Note also that the concept of odds differs from the concept of probability, because probability ranges from zero to one while odds can range from zero to infinity. Odds indicate how much more likely it is that an event occurred compared to it is not occurring.

In binary logistic regression with a dichotomous predictor, the odds that the response variable occurred ($y = 1$) for records with $x = 1$ can be denoted as:

$$\frac{\pi(1)}{1 - \pi(1)} = \frac{\frac{e^{\beta_0 + \beta_1}}{1 + e^{\beta_0 + \beta_1}}}{\frac{1}{1 + e^{\beta_0 + \beta_1}}} = e^{\beta_0 + \beta_1}$$

Correspondingly, the odds that the response variable occurred for records with $x = 0$ can be denoted as:

$$\frac{\pi(0)}{1 - \pi(0)} = \frac{\frac{e^{\beta_0}}{1 + e^{\beta_0}}}{\frac{1}{1 + e^{\beta_0}}} = e^{\beta_0}$$

The *odds ratio* (OR) is defined as the odds that the response variable occurred for records with $x = 1$ divided by the odds that the response variable occurred for records with $x = 0$. That is,

$$\begin{aligned}
\text{Odds ratio} = \text{OR} &= \frac{\pi(1)/[1 - \pi(1)]}{\pi(0)/[1 - \pi(0)]} \\
&= \frac{e^{\beta_0 + \beta_1}}{e^{\beta_0}} \\
&= e^{\beta_1}
\end{aligned} \qquad (13.3)$$

The OR is sometimes used to estimate the *relative risk*, defined as the probability that the response occurs for $x = 1$ divided by the probability that the response occurs for $x = 0$. That is,

$$\text{Relative risk} = \frac{\pi(1)}{\pi(0)}$$

For the OR to be an accurate estimate of the relative risk, we must have $\frac{[1 - \pi(0)]}{[1 - \pi(1)]} \approx 1$, which we obtain when the probability that the response occurs is small, for both $x = 1$ and $x = 0$.

The OR has come into widespread use in the research community, because of the above simply expressed relationship between the OR and the slope coefficient. For example, if a clinical trial reports that the OR for endometrial cancer among ever-users and never-users of estrogen replacement therapy is 5.0, then this may be interpreted as meaning that ever-users of estrogen replacement therapy are five times more likely to develop endometrial cancer than are never-users. However, this interpretation is valid only when $\frac{[1 - \pi(0)]}{[1 - \pi(1)]} \approx 1$.

13.6 INTERPRETING LOGISTIC REGRESSION FOR A DICHOTOMOUS PREDICTOR

Recall the *churn* data set, where we were interested in predicting whether a customer would leave the cell phone company's service (churn), based on a set of predictor variables. For this simple logistic regression example, assume that the only predictor available is *Voice Mail Plan,* a flag variable indicating membership in the plan.

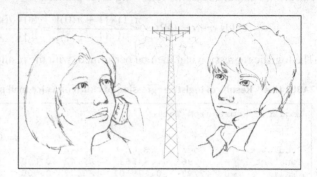

The cross-tabulation of *churn* by *Voice Mail Plan* membership is shown in Table 13.3.

The likelihood function is then given by:

$$l(\boldsymbol{\beta}|x) = [\pi(0)]^{403} \times [1 - \pi(0)]^{2008} \times [\pi(1)]^{80} \times [1 - \pi(1)]^{842}$$

Note that we may use the entries from Table 13.3 to construct the odds and the OR directly.

- Odds of those with *Voice Mail Plan* churning $= \dfrac{\pi(1)}{[1 - \pi(1)]} = \dfrac{80}{842} = 0.0950$

- Odds of those without *Voice Mail Plan* churning $= \dfrac{\pi(0)}{[1 - \pi(0)]} = \dfrac{403}{2008} = 0.2007$, and

$$\text{Odds ratio} = \text{OR} = \frac{\pi(1)/[1 - \pi(1)]}{\pi(0)/[1 - \pi(0)]} = \frac{80/842}{403/2008} = 0.47$$

TABLE 13.3 Cross-tabulation of *churn* by membership in the *voice mail plan*

	VMail = No $x = 0$	VMail = Yes $x = 1$	Total
Churn = False $y = 0$	2008	842	2850
Churn = True $y = 1$	403	80	483
Total	2411	922	3333

That is, the odds of churning for those with the *Voice Mail Plan* is only 0.47 as large as the odds of churning for those without the *Voice Mail Plan*. Note that the OR can also be calculated as the following cross product:

$$\text{Odds ratio} = \text{OR} = \frac{\pi(1) \cdot [1 - \pi(0)]}{\pi(0) \cdot [1 - \pi(1)]} = \frac{80 \cdot 2008}{403 \cdot 842} = 0.47$$

The logistic regression can then be performed, with the results shown in Table 13.4.

TABLE 13.4 Results of logistic regression of churn on voice mail plan

```
Logistic Regression Table

                                            Odds       95% CI
Predictor      Coef      SE Coef      Z        P   Ratio  Lower  Upper
Constant    -1.60596   0.0545839  -29.42   0.000
VMail       -0.747795  0.129101    -5.79   0.000   0.47   0.37   0.61


Log-Likelihood = -1360.165
Test that all slopes are zero: G = 37.964, DF = 1, P-Value = 0.000
```

First, note that the OR reported by *Minitab* equals 0.47, the same value we found using the cell counts directly. Next, equation (13.3) tells us that OR $= e^{\beta_1}$. We verify this by noting that $b_1 = -0.747795$, so that $e^{b_1} = 0.47$.

Here we have $b_0 = -1.60596$ and $b_1 = -0.747795$. So, the probability of churning for a customer belonging ($x = 1$) or not belonging ($x = 0$) to the voice mail plan is estimated as:

$$\hat{\pi}(x) = \frac{e^{\hat{g}(x)}}{1 + e^{\hat{g}(x)}} = \frac{e^{-1.60596+-0.747795(x)}}{1 + e^{-1.60596+-0.747795(x)}},$$

with the estimated logit:

$$\hat{g}(x) = -1.60596 - 0.747795(x).$$

For a customer belonging to the plan, we estimate his or her probability of churning:

$$\hat{g}(1) = -1.60596 - 0.747795(1) = -2.3538$$

and

$$\hat{\pi}(1) = \frac{e^{\hat{g}(x)}}{1 + e^{\hat{g}(x)}} = \frac{e^{-2.3538}}{1 + e^{-2.3538}} = 0.0868$$

So, the estimated probability that a customer who belongs to the voice mail plan will churn is only 8.68%, which is less than the overall proportion of churners in the data set, 14.5%, indicating that belonging to the voice mail plan protects against churn. Also, this probability could have been found directly from Table 13.3, $P(\text{churn}|\text{voice mail plan}) = \frac{80}{922} = 0.0868$.

For a customer not belonging to the voice mail plan, we estimate the probability of churning:

$$\hat{g}(0) = -1.60596 - 0.747795(0) = -1.60596$$

and

$$\widehat{\pi}(0) = \frac{e^{\widehat{g}(x)}}{1 + e^{\widehat{g}(x)}} = \frac{e^{-1.60596}}{1 + e^{-1.60596}} = 0.16715$$

This probability is slightly higher than the overall proportion of churners in the data set, 14.5%, indicating that not belonging to the voice mail may be slightly indicative of churning. This probability could also have been found directly from Table 13.3, $P(\text{churn}|\text{not voice mail plan}) = \frac{403}{2411} = 0.16715$.

Next, we apply the Wald test for the significance of the parameter for voice mail plan. We have $b_1 = -0.747795$, and $SE(b_1) = 0.129101$, giving us:

$$Z_{\text{Wald}} = \frac{-0.747795}{0.129101} = -5.79,$$

as reported under z for the coefficient *Voice Mail Plan* in Table 13.4. The p-value is $P(|z| > 5.79) \cong 0.000$, which is strongly significant. There is strong evidence that the *Voice Mail Plan* variable is useful for predicting the churn.

A $100(1 - \alpha)\%$ confidence interval for the OR may be found thus:

$$\exp[b_1 \pm z \cdot \widehat{SE}(b_1)]$$

where $\exp[a]$ represents e^a.

Thus, here we have a 95% confidence interval for the OR given by:

$$\begin{aligned}
\exp[b_1 \pm z \cdot \widehat{SE}(b_1)] &= \exp[-0.747795 \pm (1.96) \cdot (0.129101)] \\
&= (e^{-1.0008}, e^{-0.4948}) \\
&= (0.37, 0.61)
\end{aligned}$$

as reported in Table 13.4. Thus, we are 95% confident that the OR for churning among voice mail plan members and nonmembers lies between 0.37 and 0.61. As the interval does not include $e^0 = 1$, the relationship is significant with 95% confidence.

We can use the cell entries to estimate the standard error of the coefficients directly, as follows (result from Bishop, Feinberg, and Holland[6]). The standard error for the logistic regression coefficient b_1 for *Voice Mail Plan* is estimated as follows:

$$\widehat{SE}(b_1) = \sqrt{\frac{1}{403} + \frac{1}{2008} + \frac{1}{80} + \frac{1}{842}} = 0.129101$$

In this *churn* example, the voice mail members were coded as 1 and the non-members coded as 0. This is an example of *reference cell coding*, where the reference cell refers to the category coded as zero. ORs are then calculated as the comparison of the members *relative to* the nonmembers, that is, with reference to the nonmembers.

In general, for variables coded as a and b rather than 0 and 1, we have:

$$\begin{aligned}
\ln[OR(a, b)] &= \widehat{g}(x = a) - \widehat{g}(x = b) \\
&= (b_0 + b_1 \cdot a) - (b_0 + b_1 \cdot b) \\
&= b_1(a - b) \qquad\qquad (13.4)
\end{aligned}$$

---

[6]Bishop, Feinberg, and Holland, *Discrete Multivariate Analysis: Theory and Practice*, MIT Press, 1975.

So an estimate of the OR in this case is given by:

$$\exp(b_1(a - b))$$

which becomes e^{b_1} when $a = 1$ and $b = 0$.

13.7 INTERPRETING LOGISTIC REGRESSION FOR A POLYCHOTOMOUS PREDICTOR

For the *churn* data set, suppose we categorize the *customer service calls* variable into a new variable *CSC* as follows:

- Zero or one customer service calls: *CSC = Low*
- Two or three customer service calls: *CSC = Medium*
- Four or more customer service calls: *CSC = High.*

Then, *CSC* is a trichotomous predictor. How will logistic regression handle this? First, the analyst will need to code the data set using indicator (dummy) variables and reference cell coding. Suppose we choose *CSC = Low* to be our reference cell. Then we assign the indicator variable values to two new indicator variables *CSC_Med* and *CSC_Hi*, given in Table 13.5. Each record will have assigned to it a value of zero or one for each of *CSC_Med* and *CSC_Hi*. For example, a customer with 1 customer service call will have values *CSC_Med = 0* and *CSC_Hi = 0*, a customer with three customer service calls will have *CSC_Med = 1* and *CSC_Hi = 0*, and a customer with seven customer service calls will have *CSC_Med = 0* and *CSC_Hi = 1*.

Table 13.6 shows a cross-tabulation of churn by *CSC*.

Using *CSC = Low* as the reference class, we can calculate the ORs using the cross products as follows:

- For *CSC = Medium*, we have OR $= \dfrac{131 \cdot 1664}{214 \cdot 1057} = 0.963687 \approx 0.96$;

TABLE 13.5 Reference cell encoding for *customer service calls* indicator variables

	CSC_Med	CSC_Hi
Low (0–1 calls)	0	0
Medium (2–3 calls)	1	0
High (≥ 4 calls)	0	1

TABLE 13.6 Cross-tabulation of *churn* by *CSC*

	CSC = Low	CSC = Medium	CSC = High	Total
Churn = False y = 0	1664	1057	129	2850
Churn = True y = 1	214	131	138	483
Total	1878	1188	267	3333

- For $CSC = High$, we have $OR = \dfrac{138 \cdot 1664}{214 \cdot 129} = 8.31819 \approx 8.32$.

The logistic regression is then performed, with the results shown in Table 13.7.

TABLE 13.7   Results of logistic regression of _churn_ on _CSC_

```
Logistic Regression Table

                                              Odds     95% CI
Predictor      Coef    SE Coef      Z      P  Ratio  Lower  Upper
Constant   -2.05100  0.0726213  -28.24  0.000
CSC-Med   -0.0369891  0.117701   -0.31  0.753   0.96   0.77   1.21
CSC-Hi      2.11844   0.142380   14.88  0.000   8.32   6.29  11.00


Log-Likelihood = -1263.368
Test that all slopes are zero: G = 231.557, DF = 2, P-Value = 0.000
```

Note that the ORs reported by *Minitab* are the same that we found using the cell counts directly. We verify the ORs given in Table 13.7 using equation (13.3):

- CSC_Med: $\widehat{OR} = e^{b_1} = e^{-0.0369891} = 0.96$
- CSC_Hi: $\widehat{OR} = e^{b_2} = e^{2.11844} = 8.32$

Here we have $b_0 = -2.051$, $b_1 = -0.0369891$, and $b_2 = 2.11844$. So, the probability of churning is estimated as:

$$\hat{\pi}(x) = \frac{e^{\hat{g}(x)}}{1 + e^{\hat{g}(x)}} = \frac{e^{-2.051 - 0.0369891(CSC\_Med) + 2.11844(CSC\_Hi)}}{1 + e^{-2.051 - 0.0369891(CSC\_Med) + 2.11844(CSC\_Hi)}}$$

with the estimated logit:

$$\hat{g}(x) = -2.051 - 0.0369891 \ (CSC\_Med) + 2.11844(CSC\_Hi)$$

For a customer with low customer service calls, we estimate his or her probability of churning:

$$\hat{g}(0,0) = -2.051 - 0.0369891(0) + 2.11844(0) = -2.051$$

and

$$\hat{\pi}(0,0) = \frac{e^{\hat{g}(0,0)}}{1 + e^{\hat{g}(0,0)}} = \frac{e^{-2.051}}{1 + e^{-2.051}} = 0.114$$

So, the estimated probability that a customer with low numbers of customer service calls will churn is 11.4%, which is less than the overall proportion of churners in the data set, 14.5%, indicating that such customers churn somewhat less frequently than the overall group. Also, this probability could have been found directly from Table 13.6, $P(\text{churn}|CSC = \text{low}) = \frac{214}{1878} = 0.114$.

For a customer with medium customer service calls, the probability of churn is estimated as:

$$\hat{g}(1,0) = -2.051 - 0.0369891(1) + 2.11844(0) = -2.088$$

and

$$\hat{\pi}(1,0) = \frac{e^{\hat{g}(1,0)}}{1 + e^{\hat{g}(1,0)}} = \frac{e^{-2.088}}{1 + e^{-2.088}} = 0.110$$

The estimated probability that a customer with medium numbers of customer service calls will churn is 11.0%, which is about the same as that for customers with low numbers of customer service calls. The analyst may consider collapsing the distinction between *CSC_Med* and *CSC_Low*. This probability could have been found directly from Table 13.6, $P(\text{churn}|CSC = \text{medium}) = \frac{131}{1188} = 0.110$.

For a customer with high customer service calls, the probability of churn is estimated as:

$$\hat{g}(0,1) = -2.051 - 0.0369891(0) + 2.11844(1) = 0.06744$$

and

$$\hat{\pi}(0,1) = \frac{e^{\hat{g}(0,1)}}{1 + e^{\hat{g}(0,1)}} = \frac{e^{0.06744}}{1 + e^{0.06744}} = 0.5169$$

Thus, customers with high levels of customer service calls have a much higher estimated probability of churn, over 51%, which is more than triple the overall churn rate. Clearly, the company needs to flag customers who make four or more customer service calls, and intervene with them before they leave the company's service. This probability could also have been found directly from Table 13.6, $P(\text{churn}|CSC = \text{high}) = \frac{138}{267} = 0.5169$.

Applying the Wald test for the significance of the *CSC_Med* parameter, we have $b_1 = -0.0369891$, and $\text{SE}(b_1) = 0.117701$, giving us:

$$Z_{\text{Wald}} = \frac{-0.0369891}{0.117701} = -0.31426,$$

as reported under z for the coefficient *CSC_Med* in Table 13.7. The p-value is $P(|z| > 0.31426) = 0.753$, which is not significant. There is no evidence that the *CSC_Med* versus *CSC_Low* distinction is useful for predicting the churn.

For the *CSC_Hi* parameter, we have $b_1 = 2.11844$, and $\text{SE}(b_1) = 0.142380$, giving us:

$$Z_{\text{Wald}} = \frac{2.11844}{0.142380} = 14.88$$

as shown for the coefficient *CSC_Hi* in Table 13.7. The p-value, $P(|z| > 14.88) \cong 0.000$, indicates that there is strong evidence that the distinction *CSC_Hi* versus *CSC_Low* is useful for predicting the churn.

Examining Table 13.7, note that the ORs for both *CSC = Medium* and *CSC = High* are equal to those we calculated using the cell counts directly. Also note that the logistic regression coefficients for the indicator variables are equal to the natural log of their respective ORs:

$$b_{\text{CSC-Med}} = \ln(0.96) \approx \ln(0.963687) = -0.0369891$$
$$b_{\text{CSC-High}} = \ln(8.32) \approx \ln(8.31819) = 2.11844$$

For example, the natural log of the OR of *CSC_High* to *CSC_Low* can be derived using equation (13.4) as follows:

$$\ln[\text{OR}(\text{High}, \text{Low})] = \hat{g}(\text{High}) - \hat{g}(\text{Low})$$
$$= [b_0 + b_1 \cdot (\text{CSC\_Med} = 0) + b_2 \cdot (\text{CSC\_Hi} = 1)]$$
$$- [b_0 + b_1 \cdot (\text{CSC\_Med} = 0) + b_2 \cdot (\text{CSC\_Hi} = 0)]$$
$$= b_2 = 2.11844$$

Similarly, the natural log of the OR of *CSC_Medium* to *CSC_Low* is given by:

$$\ln[\text{OR}(\text{Medium}, \text{Low})] = \hat{g}(\text{Medium}) - \hat{g}(\text{Low})$$
$$= [b_0 + b_1 \cdot (\text{CSC\_Med} = 1) + b_2 \cdot (\text{CSC\_Hi} = 0)]$$
$$- [b_0 + b_1 \cdot (\text{CSC\_Med} = 0) + b_2 \cdot (\text{CSC\_Hi} = 0)]$$
$$= b_1 = -0.0369891$$

Just as for the dichotomous case, we may use the cell entries to estimate the standard error of the coefficients directly. For example, the standard error for the logistic regression coefficient b_1 for *CSC_Med* is estimated as follows:

$$\widehat{\text{SE}}(b_1) = \sqrt{\frac{1}{131} + \frac{1}{1664} + \frac{1}{214} + \frac{1}{1057}} = 0.117701$$

Also similar to the dichotomous case, we may calculate $100(1 - \alpha)\%$ confidence intervals for the ORs, for the ith predictor, as follows:

$$\exp[b_i \pm z \cdot \widehat{\text{SE}}(b_i)]$$

For example, a 95% confidence interval for the OR between *CSC_Hi* and *CSC_Low* is given by:

$$\exp[b_2 \pm z \cdot \widehat{\text{SE}}(b_2)] = \exp[2.11844 \pm (1.96) \cdot (0.142380)]$$
$$= (e^{1.8394}, e^{2.3975})$$
$$= (6.29, 11.0),$$

as reported in Table 13.7. We are 95% confident that the OR for churning for customers with high customer service calls compared to customers with low customer service calls lies between 6.29 and 11.0. As the interval does not include $e^0 = 1$, the relationship is significant with 95% confidence.

However, consider the 95% confidence interval for the OR between *CSC_Med* and *CSC_Low*:

$$\exp[b_1 \pm z \cdot \widehat{\text{SE}}(b_1)] = \exp[-0.0369891 \pm (1.96) \cdot (0.117701)]$$
$$= (e^{-0.2677}, e^{0.1937})$$
$$= (0.77, 1.21),$$

as reported in Table 13.7. We are 95% confident that the OR for churning for customers with medium customer service calls compared to customers with low customer service calls lies between 0.77 and 1.21. As this interval does include $e^0 = 1$, then the relationship is not significant with 95% confidence. Depending on other modeling factors, the analyst may consider collapsing *CSC_Med* and *CSC_Low* into a single category.

13.8 INTERPRETING LOGISTIC REGRESSION FOR A CONTINUOUS PREDICTOR

Our first example of predicting the presence of disease based on age was an instance of using a continuous predictor in logistic regression. Here we present another example, based on the *churn* data set. Suppose we are interested in predicting churn based on a single continuous variable, *Day Minutes*.

We first examine an individual value plot of the day minute usage among churners and non-churners, provided in Figure 13.2.

The plot seems to indicate that churners have slightly higher mean day minute usage than non-churners, meaning that heavier usage may be a predictor of churn. We verify this using the descriptive statistics given in Table 13.8. The mean and five-number-summary for the *churn = true* customers indicates higher day minutes usage than for the *churn = false* customers, supporting the observation from Figure 13.2.

Is this difference significant? A two-sample *t*-test is carried out, with the null hypothesis being that there is no difference in true mean day minute usage between churners and non-churners. The results are shown in Table 13.9.

The resulting *t*-statistic is -9.68, with a *p*-value rounding to zero, representing strong significance. That is, the null hypothesis that there is no difference in true mean day minute usage between churners and non-churners is strongly rejected.

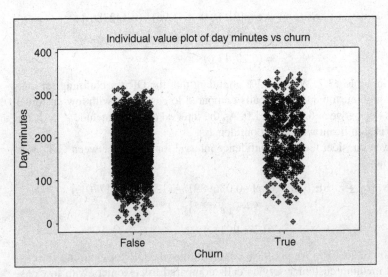

Figure 13.2 Churners have slightly higher mean *day minutes* usage.

TABLE 13.8 Descriptive statistics for *day minutes* by *churn*

Descriptive Statistics: Day Mins								
						Five – Number - Summary		
Variable	Churn	N	Mean	StDev	Min	Q1	Median	Q3	Max
Day Mins	False	2850	175.18	50.18	0.00	142.75	177.20	210.30	315.60
	True	483	206.91	69.00	0.00	153.10	217.60	266.00	350.80

TABLE 13.9 Results of two-sample *t*-test for *day minutes* by *churn*

```
Two-Sample T-Test and CI: Day Mins, Churn

Two-sample T for Day Mins

Churn     N    Mean   StDev   SE Mean
False   2850   175.2   50.2     0.94
True     483   206.9   69.0     3.1


Difference = mu (False) - mu (True)
Estimate for difference:  -31.7383
95% CI for difference:  (-38.1752, -25.3015)
T-Test of difference = 0 (vs not =): T-Value = -9.68  P-Value = 0.000  DF = 571
```

Let us reiterate our word of caution about carrying out inference in data mining problems, or indeed in any problem where the sample size is very large. Most statistical tests become very sensitive at very large sample sizes, rejecting the null hypothesis for tiny effects. The analyst needs to understand that, just because the effect is found to be statistically significant because of the huge sample size, it does not necessarily follow that the effect is of practical significance. The analyst should keep in mind the constraints and desiderata of the business or research problem, seek confluence of results from a variety of models, and always retain a clear eye for the interpretability of the model and the applicability of the model to the original problem.

Note that the *t*-test does not give us an idea of how an increase in *Day Minutes* affects the odds that a customer will churn. Neither does the *t*-test provide a method for finding the probability that a particular customer will churn, based on the customer's day minutes usage. To learn this, we must turn to logistic regression, which we now carry out, with the results given in Table 13.10.

First, we verify the relationship between the OR for *Day Minutes* and its coefficient. $\widehat{OR} = e^{b_1} = e^{0.0112717} = 1.011335 \cong 1.01$, as shown in Table 13.10. We discuss interpreting this value a bit later. In this example we have $b_0 = -3.92929$ and $b_1 = 0.0112717$. Thus, the probability of churning $\pi(x) = \frac{e^{\beta_0+\beta_1 x}}{1+e^{\beta_0+\beta_1 x}}$ for a customer with a given number of day minutes is estimated as:

$$\widehat{\pi}(x) = \frac{e^{\widehat{g}(x)}}{1 + e^{\widehat{g}(x)}} = \frac{e^{-3.92929+0.0112717(\text{day minutes})}}{1 + e^{-3.92929+0.0112717(\text{day minutes})}}$$

TABLE 13.10   Results of logistic regression of *churn* on *day minutes*

```
Logistic Regression Table

                                                  Odds      95% CI
Predictor       Coef      SE Coef       Z      P  Ratio  Lower  Upper
Constant     -3.92929    0.202822   -19.37  0.000
Day Mins    0.0112717   0.0009750    11.56  0.000  1.01   1.01   1.01


Log-Likelihood = -1307.129
Test that all slopes are zero: G = 144.035, DF = 1, P-Value = 0.000
```

with the estimated logit:

$$\hat{g}(x) = -3.92929 + 0.0112717(\text{day minutes}).$$

For a customer with 100 day minutes, we can estimate his or her probability of churning:

$$\hat{g}(100) = -3.92929 + 0.0112717(100) = -2.80212$$

and

$$\hat{\pi}(100) = \frac{e^{\hat{g}(100)}}{1 + e^{\hat{g}(100)}} = \frac{e^{-2.80212}}{1 + e^{-2.80212}} = 0.0572$$

Thus, the estimated probability that a customer with 100 day minutes will churn is less than 6%. This is less than the overall proportion of churners in the data set, 14.5%, indicating that low day minutes somehow protects against churn.

However, for a customer with 300 day minutes, we have

$$\hat{g}(300) = -3.92929 + 0.0112717(300) = -0.54778$$

and

$$\hat{\pi}(300) = \frac{e^{\hat{g}(300)}}{1 + e^{\hat{g}(300)}} = \frac{e^{-0.54778}}{1 + e^{-0.54778}} = 0.3664$$

The estimated probability that a customer with 300 day minutes will churn is over 36%, which is more than twice the overall proportion of churners in the data set, indicating that heavy-use customers have a higher propensity to churn.

The deviance difference G for this example is given by:

$$G = \text{deviance(model without predictor)} - \text{deviance(model with predictor)}$$

$$= -2\ln\left[\frac{\text{likelihood without predictor}}{\text{likelihood with predictor}}\right]$$

$$= 2\left\{\sum_{i=1}^{n}\left[y_i \ln\left[\hat{\pi}_i\right] + (1 - y_i)\ln[1 - \hat{\pi}_i]\right] - [n_1 \ln(n_1) + n_0 \ln(n_0) - n \ln(n)]\right\}$$

$$= 2\{-1307.129 - [483\ln(483) + 2850\ln(2850) - 3333\ln(3333)]\}$$

$$= 144.035$$

as indicated in Table 13.10.

The p-value for the chi-square test for G, under the assumption that the null hypothesis is true $(\beta_1 = 0)$, is given by $P(\chi_1^2) > G_{observed} = P(\chi_1^2) > 144.035 \cong 0.000$, as shown in Table 13.10. Thus, the logistic regression concludes that there is strong evidence that *Day Minutes* is useful in predicting *churn*.

Applying the Wald test for the significance of the *Day Minutes* parameter, we have $b_1 = 0.0112717$, and $SE(b_1) = 0.0009750$, giving us:

$$Z_{Wald} = \frac{0.0112717}{0.0009750} = 11.56,$$

as shown in Table 13.10. The associated p-value of $P(|z| > 11.56) \cong 0.000$, using $\alpha = 0.05$, indicates strong evidence for the usefulness of the *Day Minutes* variable for predicting churn.

Examining Table 13.10, note that the coefficient for D*ay Minutes* is equal to the natural log of its OR:

$$b_{\text{day minutes}} = \ln(1.01) \approx \ln(1.011335) = 0.0112717$$

Also, this coefficient may be derived as follows, similarly to equation (13.4), as follows:

$$
\begin{aligned}
\ln[\text{OR(day minutes)}] &= \hat{g}(x+1) - \hat{g}(x) \\
&= [b_0 + b_1 \cdot (x+1)] \\
&\quad - [b_0 + b_1 \cdot (x)] \\
&= b_1 = 0.0112717 \quad\quad (13.5)
\end{aligned}
$$

This derivation provides us with the interpretation of the value for b_1. That is, b_1 *represents the estimated change in the log OR, for a unit increase in the predictor.* In this example, $b_1 = 0.0112717$, which means that, for every additional day minute that the customer uses, the log OR for churning increases by 0.0112717.

The value for the OR we found above, $\widehat{OR} = e^{b_1} = e^{0.0112717} = 1.011335 \cong 1.01$, may be interpreted as the odds of a customer with $x + 1$ minutes churning compared to the odds of a customer with x minutes churning. For example, a customer with 201 minutes is about 1.01 times as likely to churn as compared to a customer with 200 minutes.

This unit-increase interpretation may be of limited usefulness, because the analyst may prefer to interpret the results using a different scale, such as 10 or 60 min, or even (conceivably) 1 s. We therefore generalize the interpretation of the logistic regression coefficient as follows:

INTERPRETING THE LOGISTIC REGRESSION COEFFICIENT FOR A CONTINUOUS PREDICTOR

For a constant c, the quantity $c \cdot b_1$ represents the estimated change in the log OR, for an increase of c units in the predictor.

This result can be seen to follow from the substitution of $\hat{g}(x+c) - \hat{g}(x)$ for $\hat{g}(x+1) - \hat{g}(x)$ in equation (13.5):

$$\hat{g}(x+c) - \hat{g}(x) = [b_0 + b_1 \cdot (x+c)]$$
$$= [b_0 + b_1 \cdot (x)]$$
$$= c \cdot b_1$$

For example, let $c = 60$, so that we are interested in the change in the log OR for an increase of 60 day minutes of cell phone usage. This increase would be estimated as $c \cdot b_1 = 60 \cdot (0.0112717) = 0.676302$. Consider a customer A, who had 60 more day minutes than customer B. Then we would estimate the OR for customer A to churn compared to customer B to be $e^{0.676302} = 1.97$. That is, an increase of 60 day minutes nearly doubles the odds that a customer will churn.

Similar to the categorical predictor case, we may calculate $100(1 - \alpha)\%$ confidence intervals for the ORs, as follows:

$$\exp[b_i \pm z \cdot \widehat{SE}(b_i)]$$

For example, a 95% confidence interval for the OR for *Day Minutes* is given by:

$$\exp[b_1 \pm z \cdot \widehat{SE}(b_1)] = \exp[0.0112717 \pm (1.96) \cdot (0.0009750)]$$
$$= (e^{0.0093607}, e^{0.0131827})$$
$$= (1.0094, 1.0133)$$
$$\cong (1.01, 1.01),$$

as reported in Table 13.10. We are 95% confident that the OR for churning for customers with one additional day minute lies between 1.0094 and 1.0133. As the interval does not include $e^0 = 1$, the relationship is significant with 95% confidence.

Confidence intervals may also be found for the OR for the ith predictor, when there is a change in c units in the predictor, as follows:

$$\exp[c \cdot b_i \pm z \cdot c \cdot \widehat{SE}(b_i)]$$

For example, earlier we estimated the increase in the OR, when the day minutes increased by $c = 60$ minutes, to be 1.97. The 99% confidence interval associated with this estimate is given by:

$$\exp[c \cdot b_i \pm z \cdot c \cdot \widehat{SE}(b_i)] = \exp[60 \cdot (0.0112717) \pm 2.576 \cdot (60) \cdot (0.0009750)]$$
$$= \exp[0.6763 \pm 0.1507]$$
$$= (1.69, 2.29)$$

So, we are 99% confident that an increase of 60 day minutes will increase the OR of churning by a factor of between 1.69 and 2.29.

13.9 ASSUMPTION OF LINEARITY

Now, if the logit is not linear in the continuous variables, then there may be problems with the application of estimates and confidence intervals for the OR. The reason is that the estimated OR is constant across the range of the predictor. For example, the estimated OR of 1.01 is the same for every unit increase of *Day Minutes*, whether it is the 23rd minute or the 323rd minute. The same is true of the estimated OR for the increase of 60 day minutes; the estimated OR of 1.97 is the same whether we are referring to the 0–60 min timeframe or the 55–115 min timeframe, and so on.

Such an assumption of constant OR is not always warranted. For example, suppose we performed a logistic regression of *churn* on *Customer Service Calls* (the original variable, not the set of indicator variables), which takes values 0–9. The results are shown in Table 13.11.

TABLE 13.11   Questionable results of logistic regression of *churn* on *customer service calls*

```
Logistic Regression Table

                                                    Odds      95% CI
Predictor          Coef     SE Coef       Z      P  Ratio  Lower  Upper
Constant        -2.49016   0.0863180  -28.85  0.000
CustServ Calls   0.396169  0.0345617   11.46  0.000  1.49   1.39   1.59


Log-Likelihood = -1313.618
Test that all slopes are zero: G = 131.058, DF = 1, P-Value = 0.000
```

The estimated OR of 1.49 indicates that the OR for churning increases by this factor for every additional customer service call that is made. We would therefore expect that a plot of *Customer Service Calls* with a *churn* overlay would form a fairly regular steplike pattern. However, consider Figure 13.3, which shows a normalized histogram of *Customer Service Calls* with a *churn* overlay. (The normalization makes

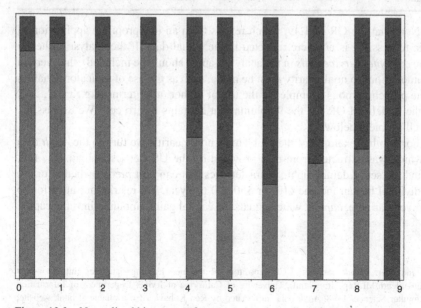

Figure 13.3   Normalized histogram of *customer service calls* with *churn* overlay.

each rectangle the same length, thereby increasing the contrast, at the expense of information about bin size.) Darker portions indicate the proportion of customers who churn.

Note that we do not encounter a gradual step-down pattern as we proceed left to right. Instead, there is a single rather dramatic discontinuity at four customer service calls. This is the pattern we uncovered earlier when we performed binning on *customer service calls*, and found that those with three or fewer calls had a much different propensity to churn than did customers with four or more.

Specifically, the results in Table 13.11 assert that, for example, moving from zero to one customer service calls increases the OR by a factor of 1.49. This is not the case, as fewer customers with one call churn than do those with zero calls. For example, Table 13.12 shows the counts of customers churning and not churning for the 10 values of *Customer Service Calls*, along with the estimated OR for the one additional customer service call. For example, the estimated OR for moving from zero to one call is 0.76, which means that churning is less likely for those making one call than it is for those making none. The discontinuity at the fourth call is represented by the OR of 7.39, meaning that a customer making his or her fourth call is more than seven times as likely to churn as a customer who has made three calls.

TABLE 13.12 *Customer service calls by churn,* with estimated odds ratios

	Customer Service Calls									
	0	1	2	3	4	5	6	7	8	9
Churn = False	605	1059	672	385	90	26	8	4	1	0
Churn = True	92	122	87	44	76	40	14	5	1	2
Odds ratio	—	0.76	1.12	0.88	7.39	1.82	1.14	0.71	0.8	Undefined

Note that the OR of 1.49, which results from an inappropriate application of logistic regression, is nowhere reflected in the actual data. If the analyst wishes to include *customer service calls* in the analysis (and it should be included), then certain accommodations to nonlinearity must be made, such as the use of indicator variables (see the polychotomous example) or the use of higher order terms (e.g., $x^2, x^3, \ldots$). Note the undefined OR for the 9 column that contains a zero cell. We discuss the zero-cell problem below.

For another example of the problem of nonlinearity, we turn to the *Adult* data set,[7] which was extracted from data provided by the US Census Bureau. The task is to find the set of demographic characteristics that can best predict whether or not the individual has an income of over \$50,000 per year. We restrict our attention to the derived variable, *capnet*, which equals the capital gains amount minus the capital

---

[7]Blake and Merz, *Adult* data set, UCI Repository of machine learning databases (http://www.ics .udi.edu/~mlearn/MLRepository.html), University of California at Irvine, Department of Information and Computer Science, 1998. *Adult* data set donated by Ron Kohavi. Also available at book website, www.DataMiningConsultant.com.

losses, expressed in dollars. The naïve application of logistic regression of *income* on *capnet* provides the results shown in Table 13.13.

TABLE 13.13   Results of questionable logistic regression of income on capnet

```
Logistic Regression Table


                                                   Odds      95% CI
Predictor        Coef     SE Coef       Z       P  Ratio  Lower  Upper
Constant      -1.32926  0.0159903  -83.13   0.000
capnet       0.0002561  0.0000079   32.58   0.000   1.00   1.00   1.00


Log-Likelihood = -12727.406
Test that all slopes are zero: G = 2062.242, DF = 1, P-Value = 0.000
```

The OR for the *capnet* variable is reported as 1.00, with both endpoints of the confidence interval also reported as 1.00. Do we conclude from this that *capnet* is not significant? And if so, then how do we resolve the apparent contradiction with the strongly significant Z-test p-value of approximately zero?

Actually, of course, there is no contradiction. The problem lies in the fact that the OR results are reported only to two decimal places. More detailed 95% confidence intervals are provided here:

$$\text{CI}(\text{OR}_{capnet}) = \exp[b_1 \pm z \cdot \widehat{\text{SE}}(b_1)]$$
$$= \exp[0.0002561 \pm (1.96) \cdot (0.0000079)]$$
$$= (e^{0.0002406}, e^{0.0002716})$$
$$= (1.000241, 1.000272),$$

Thus, the 95% confidence interval for the *capnet* variable does not include the null value of $e^0 = 1$, indicating that this variable is in fact significant. Why is such precision needed? Because *capnet* is measured in dollars. One additional dollar in capital gains, for example, would presumably not increase the probability of a high income very dramatically. Hence, the tiny but significant OR. (Of course, requesting more decimal points in the output would have uncovered similar results.)

However, nearly 87% of the records have zero *capnet* (neither capital gains nor capital losses). What effect would this have on the linearity assumption? Table 13.14 provides the income level counts for a possible categorization of the *capnet* variable.

TABLE 13.14   *Income* level counts for categories of *capnet*

Income	Capnet Categories							
	Loss		None		Gain <$3000		Gain ≥$3000	
≤$50,000	574	49.7%	17,635	81.0%	370	100%	437	25.6%
>$50,000	582	50.3%	4133	19.0%	0	0%	1269	74.4%
Total	1156		21,768		370		1706	

Note that high income is associated with either *capnet loss* or *capnet gain* ≥$3000, while low income is associated with *capnet none* or *capnet gain* <$3000. Such relationships are incompatible with the assumption of linearity. We would therefore like to rerun the logistic regression analysis, this time using the *capnet* categorization shown in Table 13.14.

13.10 ZERO-CELL PROBLEM

Unfortunately, we are now faced with a new problem, the presence of a zero-count cell in the cross-classification table. There are no records of individuals in the data set with income greater than $50,000 and capnet gain less than $3000. Zero cells play havoc with the logistic regression solution, causing instability in the analysis and leading to possibly unreliable results.

Rather than omitting the "gain < $3000" category, we may try to collapse the categories or redefine them somehow, in order to find some records for the zero cell. In this example, we will try to redefine the class limits for the two capnet gains categories, which will have the added benefit of finding a better balance of records in these categories. The new class boundaries and cross-classification is shown in Table 13.15.

The logistic regression of *income* on the newly categorized *capnet* has results that are shown in Table 13.16.

TABLE 13.15 *Income* level counts for categories of *capnet*, new categorization

Income	Capnet Categories							
	Loss		None		Gain < $5000		Gain ≥$5000	
≤$50,000	574	49.7%	17,635	81.0%	685	83.0%	122	9.8%
>$50,000	582	50.3%	4133	19.0%	140	17.0%	1129	90.2%
Total	1156		21,768		370		1706	

TABLE 13.16 Results from logistic regression of income on categorized capnet

```
Logistic Regression Table

                                                  Odds      95% CI
Predictor         Coef     SE Coef      Z      P  Ratio  Lower  Upper
Constant       -1.45088  0.0172818  -83.95  0.000
capnet-cat
  gain < $5,000  -0.136894  0.0943471   -1.45  0.147   0.87   0.72   1.05
  gain >= $5,000  3.67595  0.0968562   37.95  0.000  39.49  32.66  47.74
  loss            1.46472  0.0613110   23.89  0.000   4.33   3.84   4.88


Log-Likelihood = -12156.651
Test that all slopes are zero: G = 3203.753, DF = 3, P-Value = 0.000
```

The reference category is *zero capnet*. The category of gain <$5000 is not significant, because its proportions of high and low income are quite similar to those of *zero capnet*, as shown in Table 13.15. The categories of *loss* and *gain* ≥$5000 are both significant, but at different orders of magnitude. Individuals showing a capital loss are 4.33 times as likely to have high income than zero capnet individuals, while people showing a capnet gain of at least $5000 are nearly 40 times more likely to have high income than the reference category.

The variability among these results reinforces the assertion that the relationship between *income* and *capnet* is nonlinear, and that naïve insertion of the *capnet* variable into a logistic regression would be faulty.

For a person showing a capnet loss, we can estimate his or her probability of having an income above $50,000. First the logit:

$$\hat{g}(0,1) = -1.45088 + 3.67595(0) + 1.46472(1) = 0.01384$$

with probability:

$$\hat{\pi}(0,1) = \frac{e^{\hat{g}(0,1)}}{1 + e^{\hat{g}(0,1)}} = \frac{e^{0.01384}}{1 + e^{0.01384}} = 0.5035$$

So, the probability that a person with a capnet loss has an income above $50,000 is about 50–50. Also, we can estimate the probability that a person showing a capnet gain of at least $5000 will have an income above $50,000. The logit is:

$$\hat{g}(1,0) = -1.45088 + 3.67595(1) + 1.46472(0) = 2.22507$$

and the probability is:

$$\hat{\pi}(1,0) = \frac{e^{\hat{g}(1,0)}}{1 + e^{\hat{g}(1,0)}} = \frac{e^{2.22507}}{1 + e^{2.22507}} = 0.9025$$

Note that these probabilities are the same as could be found using the cell counts in Table 13.15. It is similar for a person with a capnet gain of under $5000. However, this category was found to be not significant. What, then, should be our estimate of the probability that a person with a small capnet gain will have high income?

Should we use the estimate provided by the cell counts and the logistic regression (probability = 17%), even though it was found to be not significant? The answer is no, not for formal estimation. To use nonsignificant variables for estimation increases the chances that the estimation will not be generalizable. That is, the generalizability (and hence, usefulness) of the estimation will be reduced.

Now, under certain circumstances, such as a cross-validated (see validating the logistic regression, below) analysis, where all subsamples concur that the variable is nearly significant, then the analyst may annotate the estimation with a note that there may be some evidence for using this variable in the estimation. However, in general, retain for estimation and prediction purposes only those variables that are significant. Thus, in this case, we would estimate the probability that a person with a small capnet gain will have high income as follows:

$$\hat{g}(0,0) = -1.45088$$

with probability:

$$\hat{\pi}(0,0) = \frac{e^{\hat{g}(0,0)}}{1 + e^{\hat{g}(0,0)}} = \frac{e^{-1.45088}}{1 + e^{-1.45088}} = 0.1899$$

which is the same as the probability that a person with zero capnet will have high income.

13.11 MULTIPLE LOGISTIC REGRESSION

Thus far, we have examined logistic regression using only one variable at a time. However, very few data mining data sets are restricted to one variable! We therefore turn to multiple logistic regression, in which more than one predictor variable is used to classify the binary response variable.

Returning to the *churn* data set, we examine whether a relationship exists between *churn* and the following set of predictors.

- International Plan, a flag variable
- Voice Mail Plan, a flag variable
- CSC-Hi, a flag variable indicating whether or not a customer had high (≥ 4) level of customer services calls
- Account length, continuous
- Day Minutes, continuous
- Evening Minutes, continuous
- Night Minutes, continuous
- International Minutes, continuous.

The results are provided in Table 13.17.

First, note that the overall regression is significant, as shown by the *p*-value of approximately zero for the *G*-statistic. Therefore, the overall model is useful for classifying *churn*.

However, not all variables contained in the model need necessarily be useful. Examine the *p*-values for the (Wald) *z*-statistics for each of the predictors. All *p*-values are small except one, indicating that there is evidence that each predictor belongs in the model, except *Account Length*, the standardized customer account length. The Wald *z*-statistic for account length is 0.56, with a large *p*-value of 0.578, indicating that this variable is not useful for classifying *churn*. Further, the 95% confidence interval for the OR includes 1.0, reinforcing the conclusion that *Account Length* does not belong in the model.

Therefore, we now omit *Account Length* from the model, and proceed to run the logistic regression again with the remaining variables. The results are shown in Table 13.18. Comparing Table 13.18 to Table 13.17, we see that the omission of *Account Length* has barely affected the remaining analysis. All remaining variables are considered significant, and retained in the model.

The positive coefficients indicate predictors for which an increase in the value of the predictor is associated with an increase in the probability of churning. Similarly,

TABLE 13.17   Results of multiple logistic regression of *churn* on several variables

```
Logistic Regression Table

                                                      Odds     95% CI
Predictor            Coef     SE Coef      Z      P   Ratio  Lower  Upper
Constant          -8.15980   0.536092  -15.22  0.000
Account Length     0.0008006 0.0014408    0.56  0.578  1.00   1.00   1.00
Day Mins           0.0134755 0.0011192   12.04  0.000  1.01   1.01   1.02
Eve Mins           0.0073029 0.0011695    6.24  0.000  1.01   1.01   1.01
Night Mins         0.0042378 0.0011474    3.69  0.000  1.00   1.00   1.01
Intl Mins          0.0853508 0.0210217    4.06  0.000  1.09   1.05   1.13
Int_l Plan
 yes               2.03287   0.146894    13.84  0.000  7.64   5.73  10.18
VMail Plan
 yes              -1.04435   0.150087    -6.96  0.000  0.35   0.26   0.47
CSC-Hi
 1                 2.67683   0.159224    16.81  0.000 14.54  10.64  19.86

Log-Likelihood = -1036.038
Test that all slopes are zero: G = 686.218, DF = 8, P-Value = 0.000
```

TABLE 13.18   Results of multiple logistic regression after omitting *account length*

```
Logistic Regression Table

                                                      Odds     95% CI
Predictor            Coef     SE Coef      Z      P   Ratio  Lower  Upper
Constant          -8.07374   0.512446  -15.76  0.000
Day Mins           0.0134735 0.0011190   12.04  0.000  1.01   1.01   1.02
Eve Mins           0.0072939 0.0011694    6.24  0.000  1.01   1.01   1.01
Night Mins         0.0042223 0.0011470    3.68  0.000  1.00   1.00   1.01
Intl Mins          0.0853509 0.0210212    4.06  0.000  1.09   1.05   1.13
Int_l Plan
 yes               2.03548   0.146822    13.86  0.000  7.66   5.74  10.21
VMail Plan
 yes              -1.04356   0.150064    -6.95  0.000  0.35   0.26   0.47
CSC-Hi


Log-Likelihood = -1036.192
Test that all slopes are zero: G = 685.910, DF = 7, P-Value = 0.000
```

negative coefficients indicate predictors associated with reducing the probability of churn. Unit increases for each of the *minutes* variables are associated with an increase in the probability of churn, as well as membership in the *International Plan*, and customers with high levels of customer service calls. Only membership in the *Voice Mail Plan* reduces the probability of churn.

Table 13.18 provides the estimated logit:

$$\hat{g}(x) = -8.07374 + 0.0134735(\text{DayMins}) + 0.0072939(\text{EveMins})$$
$$+ 0.0042223(\text{NightMins}) + 0.0853509(\text{IntlMins})$$
$$+ 2.03548(\text{Int\_l Plan} = \text{Yes}) - 1.04356(\text{VMail Plan} = \text{Yes})$$
$$+ 2.67697(\text{CSC} - \text{Hi} = 1)$$

where *Intl Plan = Yes*, *VMail Plan = Yes*, and *CSC-Hi = 1* represent indicator (dummy) variables. Then, using

$$\hat{\pi}(x) = \frac{e^{\hat{g}(x)}}{1 + e^{\hat{g}(x)}},$$

we may estimate the probability that a particular customer will churn, given various values for the predictor variables. We will estimate the probability of churn for the following customers:

1. A low usage customer belonging to no plans with few calls to customer service.
2. A moderate usage customer belonging to no plans with few calls to customer service.
3. A high usage customer belonging to the International Plan but not the Voice Mail Plan, with many calls to customer service.
4. A high usage customer belonging to the Voice Mail Plan but not the International Plan, with few calls to customer service.

   o A low usage customer belonging to no plans with few calls to customer service. This customer has 100 minutes for each of day, evening, and night minutes, and no international minutes. The logit looks like:

$$\hat{g}(x) = -8.07374 + 0.0134735(100) + 0.0072939(100)$$
$$+ 0.0042223(100) + 0.0853509(0)$$
$$+ 2.03548(0) - 1.04356(0) + 2.67697(0)$$
$$= -5.57477$$

The probability that customer (1) will churn is therefore:

$$\hat{\pi}(x) = \frac{e^{\hat{g}(x)}}{1 + e^{\hat{g}(x)}} = \frac{e^{-5.57477}}{1 + e^{-5.57477}} = 0.003778$$

That is, a customer with low usage, belonging to no plans, and making few customer service calls has less than a 1% chance of churning.

   o A moderate usage customer belonging to no plans with few calls to customer service. This customer has 180 day minutes, 200 evening and night minutes, and 10 international minutes, each number near the average for the category.

Here is the logit:

$$\hat{g}(x) = -8.07374 + 0.0134735(180) + 0.0072939(200)$$
$$+ 0.0042223(200) + 0.0853509(10)$$
$$+ 2.03548(0) - 1.04356(0) + 2.67697(0)$$
$$= -2.491761$$

The probability that customer (2) will churn is:

$$\hat{\pi}(x) = \frac{e^{\hat{g}(x)}}{1 + e^{\hat{g}(x)}} = \frac{e^{-2.491761}}{1 + e^{-2.491761}} = 0.076435$$

A customer with moderate usage, belonging to no plans, and making few customer service calls still has less than an 8% probability of churning.

- A high usage customer belonging to the International Plan but not the Voice Mail Plan, with many calls to customer service. This customer has 300 day, evening, and night minutes, and 20 international minutes. The logit is:

$$\hat{g}(x) = -8.07374 + 0.0134735(300) + 0.0072939(300)$$
$$+ 0.0042223(300) + 0.0853509(20)$$
$$+ 2.03548(1) - 1.04356(0) + 2.67697(1)$$
$$= 5.842638$$

Thus, the probability that customer (3) will churn is:

$$\hat{\pi}(x) = \frac{e^{\hat{g}(x)}}{1 + e^{\hat{g}(x)}} = \frac{e^{5.842638}}{1 + e^{5.842638}} = 0.997107$$

High usage customers, belonging to the International Plan but not the Voice Mail Plan, and with many calls to customer service, have as astonishing 99.71% probability of churning. The company needs to deploy interventions for these types of customers as soon as possible, to avoid the loss of these customers to other carriers.

- A high usage customer belonging to the Voice Mail Plan but not the International Plan, with few calls to customer service. This customer also has 300 day, evening, and night minutes, and 20 international minutes. The logit is:

$$\hat{g}(x) = -8.07374 + 0.0134735(300) + 0.0072939(300)$$
$$+ 0.0042223(300) + 0.0853509(20)$$
$$+ 2.03548(0) - 1.04356(1) + 2.67697(0)$$
$$= 0.086628$$

Hence, the probability that customer (4) will churn is:

$$\hat{\pi}(x) = \frac{e^{\hat{g}(x)}}{1 + e^{\hat{g}(x)}} = \frac{e^{0.086628}}{1 + e^{0.086628}} = 0.5216$$

This type of customer has over a 50% probability of churning, which is more than three times the 14.5% overall churn rate.

For data that are missing one or more indicator variable values, it would not be appropriate to simply ignore these missing variables when making an estimation. For example, suppose for customer (4), we had no information regarding membership in the Voice Mail Plan. If we then ignored the Voice Mail Plan variable when forming the estimate, then we would get the following logit:

$$
\begin{aligned}
\hat{g}(x) = {} & -8.07374 + 0.0134735(300) + 0.0072939(300) \\
& + 0.0042223(300) + 0.0853509(20) \\
& + 2.03548(0) + 2.67697(0) \\
= {} & 1.130188
\end{aligned}
$$

Note that this is the same value for $\hat{g}(x)$ that we would obtain for a customer who was known to not be a member of the Voice Mail Plan. To estimate the probability of a customer whose Voice Mail Plan membership was unknown using this logit would be incorrect. This logit would instead provide the probability of a customer who did not have the Voice Mail Plan, but was otherwise similar to customer (4), as follows:

$$
\hat{\pi}(x) = \frac{e^{\hat{g}(x)}}{1 + e^{\hat{g}(x)}} = \frac{e^{1.130188}}{1 + e^{1.130188}} = 0.7559
$$

Such a customer would have a churn probability of about 76%.

13.12 INTRODUCING HIGHER ORDER TERMS TO HANDLE NONLINEARITY

We illustrate how to check the assumption of linearity in multiple logistic regression by returning to the *Adult* data set. For this example, we shall use only the following variables:

- *Age*
- *Education-num*
- *Hours-per-week*
- *Capnet* (=*capital gain – capital loss*)
- *Marital-status*
- *Sex*
- *Income*: the target variable, binary, either ≤$50,000 or >$50,000.

The three "Married" categories in *marital-status* in the raw data were collapsed into a single "Married" category. A normalized histogram of *age* with an overlay of the target variable *income* is shown in Figure 13.4.

The darker bands indicate the proportion of high incomes. Clearly, this proportion increases until about age 52, after which it begins to drop again. This behavior is nonlinear and should not be naively modeled as such in the logistic regression. Suppose, for example, that we went ahead and performed a logistic regression of *income* on the singleton predictor *age*. The results are shown in Table 13.19.

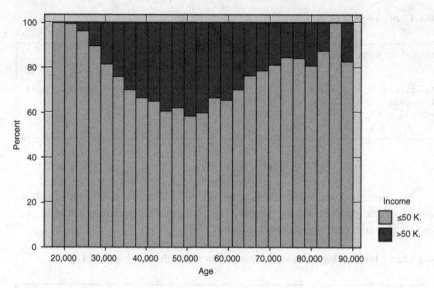

Figure 13.4   Normalized histogram of *Age* with *Income* overlay shows quadratic relationship.

TABLE 13.19   Results of naïve application of logistic regression of *income* on *age*

```
Logistic Regression Table

                                               Odds      95% CI
Predictor      Coef      SE Coef        Z     P  Ratio Lower  Upper
Constant   -2.72401   0.0486021   -56.05  0.000
age         0.0388221  0.0010994    35.31  0.000   1.04  1.04   1.04
```

Table 13.19 shows that the predictor *age* is significant, with an estimated OR of 1.04. Recall that the interpretation of this OR is as follows: that the odds of having high income for someone of age $x + 1$ are 1.04 times higher than for someone of age x.

Now consider this interpretation in light of Figure 13.4. The OR of 1.04 is clearly inappropriate for the subset of subjects older than 50 or so. This is because the logistic regression assumes linearity, while the actual relationship is nonlinear.

There are a couple of approaches we could take to alleviate this problem. First, we could use indicator variables as we did earlier. Here, we use an indicator variable *age* 33–65, where all records falling in this range are coded as 1 and all other records coded as 0. This coding was used because the higher incomes were found in the histogram to fall within this range. The resulting logistic regression is shown in Table 13.20. The OR is 5.01, indicating that persons between 33 and 65 years of age are about five times more likely to have high income than persons outside this age range.

TABLE 13.20 Logistic regression of *income* on *age* 33–65

```
Logistic Regression Table

                                          Odds    95% CI
Predictor       Coef    SE Coef     Z    P  Ratio  Lower  Upper
Constant     -2.26542  0.0336811  -67.26  0.000
age 33 - 65   1.61103  0.0379170   42.49  0.000   5.01   4.65   5.39
```

An alternative modeling method would be to directly model the quadratic behavior of the relationship by introducing an age^2 (age-squared) variable. The logistic regression results are shown in Table 13.21.

TABLE 13.21 Introducing a quadratic term age^2 to model the nonlinearity of *age*

```
Logistic Regression Table

                                             Odds    95% CI
Predictor          Coef     SE Coef     Z    P  Ratio  Lower  Upper
Constant        -9.08016   0.194526  -46.68  0.000
age              0.347807  0.0089465  38.88  0.000   1.42   1.39   1.44
age-squared     -0.0034504 0.0000992 -34.77  0.000   1.00   1.00   1.00
```

The OR for the *age* variable has increased from the value of 1.04, previously determined, to 1.42. For the age^2 term, the OR and the endpoints of the confidence interval are reported as 1.00, but this is only due to rounding. We use the fact that OR = e^{b_2} to find the more accurate estimate of the OR as OR = $e^{b_2} = e^{-0.0034504} = 0.99656$. Also, the 95% confidence interval is given by

$$CI(OR) = \exp[b_2 \pm z \cdot \widehat{SE}(b_2)]$$
$$= \exp[-0.0034504 \pm (1.96) \cdot (0.0000992)]$$
$$= (e^{-0.003645}, e^{-0.003256})$$
$$= (0.9964, 0.9967),$$

which concurs with the *p*-value regarding the significance of the term.

The age^2 term acts as a kind of penalty function, reducing the probability of high income for records with high age. We examine the behavior of the *age* and age^2 terms working together by estimating the probability that each of the following people will have incomes greater than $50,000:

1. A 30-year-old person
2. A 50-year-old person
3. A 70-year-old person.

We have the estimated logit:

$$\hat{g}(age, age^2) = -9.08016 + 0.347807(age) - 0.0034504(age^2)$$

which has the following values for our three individuals:

1. $\hat{g}(30, 30^2) = -9.08016 + 0.347807(30) - 0.0034504(30^2) = -1.75131$
2. $\hat{g}(50, 50^2) = -9.08016 + 0.347807(50) - 0.0034504(50^2) = -0.31581$
3. $\hat{g}(70, 70^2) = -9.08016 + 0.347807(70) - 0.0034504(70^2) = -1.64063$

Note that the logit is greatest for the 50-year-old, which models the behavior seen in Figure 13.4. Then, the estimated probability of having an income greater than \$50,000 is then found for our three people:

$$\hat{\pi}(x) = \frac{e^{\hat{g}(x)}}{1 + e^{\hat{g}(x)}}$$

$$\begin{cases} (1) = \dfrac{e^{-1.75131}}{1 + e^{-1.75131}} = 0.1479 \\[3mm] (2) = \dfrac{e^{-0.31581}}{1 + e^{-0.31581}} = 0.4217 \\[3mm] (3) = \dfrac{e^{-1.64063}}{1 + e^{-1.64063}} = 0.1624 \end{cases}$$

The probabilities that the 30-year-old, 50-year-old, and 70-year-old have an income greater than \$50,000 are 14.79%, 42.17%, and 16.24%, respectively. This is compared to the overall proportion of the 25,000 records in the training set that have income greater than \$50,000, which is $\frac{5984}{25,000} = 23.94\%$.

One benefit of using the quadratic term (together with the original *age* variable) rather than the indicator variable is that the quadratic term is continuous, and can presumably provide tighter estimates for a variety of ages. For example, the indicator variable *age* 33–65 categorizes all records into two classes, so that a 20-year-old is binned together with a 32-year-old, and the model (all other factors held constant) generates the same probability of high income for the 20-year-old as the 32-year-old. The quadratic term, however, will provide a higher probability of high income for the 32-year-old than the 20-year-old (see exercises).

Next, we turn to the *education-num* variable, which indicates the number of years of education the subject has had. The relationship between *income* and *education-num* is shown in Figure 13.5.

The pattern shown in Figure 13.5 is also quadratic, although perhaps not as manifestly so as in Figure 13.4. As education increases, the proportion of subjects having high income also increases, but not at a linear rate. Until eighth grade or so, the proportion increases slowly, and then more quickly as education level increases. Therefore, modeling the relationship between income and education level as strictly linear would be an error; we again need to introduce a quadratic term.

Note that, for *age*, the coefficient of the quadratic term age^2 was negative, representing a downward influence for very high ages. For *education-num*, however, the proportion of high incomes is highest for the highest levels of income, so that we

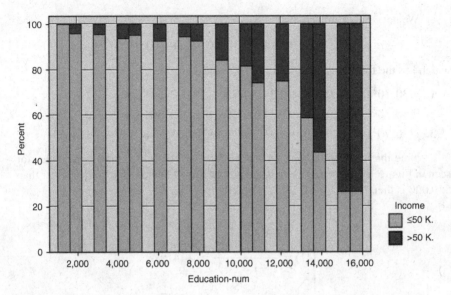

Figure 13.5   Normalized histogram of *education-num* with *income* overlay.

would expect a positive coefficient for the quadratic term $education^2$. The results of a logistic regression run on education-num and $education^2$ are shown in Table 13.22.

TABLE 13.22   Results from logistic regression of *income* on *education-num* and *education*^{2}

```
Logistic Regression Table

                                                    Odds     95% CI
Predictor           Coef    SE Coef      Z      P  Ratio  Lower  Upper
Constant         -3.10217  0.235336  -13.18  0.000
education-num    -0.0058715 0.0443558   -0.13  0.895   0.99   0.91   1.08
educ-squared      0.0170305 0.0020557    8.28  0.000   1.02   1.01   1.02
```

As expected, the coefficient for $education^2$ is positive. However, note that the variable *education-num* is not significant, because it has a large *p*-value, and the confidence interval contains 1.0. We therefore omit *education-num* from the analysis and perform a logistic regression of income on $education^2$ alone, with results shown in Table 13.23.

Here, the $education^2$ term is significant, and we have $\text{OR} = e^{b_1} = e^{0.0167617} = 1.0169$, with the 95% confidence interval given by:

$$\text{CI(OR)} = \exp[b_1 \pm z \cdot \widehat{\text{SE}}(b_1)]$$
$$= \exp[0.0167617 \pm (1.96) \cdot (0.0003193)]$$
$$= (e^{0.01614}, e^{0.01739})$$
$$= (1.01627, 1.01754)$$

TABLE 13.23   Results from logistic regression of *income* on *education*² alone

```
Logistic Regression Table

                                                    Odds     95% CI
Predictor           Coef    SE Coef       Z     P  Ratio  Lower  Upper
Constant        -3.13280  0.0431422  -72.62  0.000
educ-squared   0.0167617  0.0003193   52.50  0.000  1.02   1.02   1.02
```

We estimate the probability that persons with the following years of education will have incomes greater than $50,000:

1. 12 years of education
2. 16 years of education.

The estimated logit:

$$\hat{g}(x) = -3.1328 + 0.0167617\,(education^2)$$

has the following values:

1. $\hat{g}(x) = -3.1328 + 0.0167617\,(12^2) = -0.719115$
2. $\hat{g}(x) = -3.1328 + 0.0167617\,(16^2) = 1.1582$

Then, we can find the estimated probability of having an income greater than $50,000 as:

$$\hat{\pi}(x) = \frac{e^{\hat{g}(x)}}{1 + e^{\hat{g}(x)}}$$

$$\begin{cases} (1) = \dfrac{e^{-0.719115}}{1 + e^{-0.719115}} = 0.3276 \\[3mm] (2) = \dfrac{e^{1.1582}}{1 + e^{1.1582}} = 0.7610 \end{cases}$$

The probabilities that people with 12 years and 16 years of education will have an income greater than $50,000 are 32.76% and 76.10%, respectively. Evidently, for this population, it pays to stay in school.

Finally, we examine the variable *hours-per-week*, which represents the number of hours worked per week for the subject. The normalized histogram is shown in Figure 13.6.

In Figure 13.6, we certainly find nonlinearity. A quadratic term would seem indicated by the records up to 50 h per week. However, at about 50 h per week, the pattern changes, so that the overall curvature is that of a backwards S-curve. Such a pattern is indicative of the need for a *cubic* term, where the cube of the original variable is introduced. We therefore do so here, introducing *hours*³, and performing the logistic regression of *income* on *hours-per-week*, *hours*², and *hours*³, with the results shown in Table 13.24.

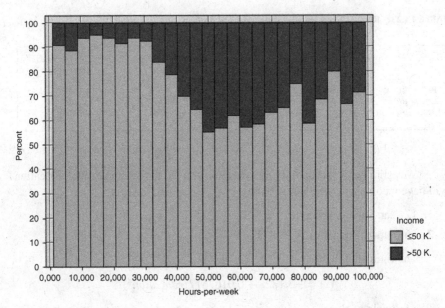

Figure 13.6 Normalized histogram of *hours-per-week* with *income* overlay.

TABLE 13.24 **Results from logistic regression of *income* on *hours-per-week*, *hours²*, and *hours³***

```
Logistic Regression Table

                                                        Odds      95% CI
Predictor           Coef     SE Coef       Z       P   Ratio  Lower  Upper
Constant         -3.04582   0.232238  -13.12   0.000
hours-per-week   -0.0226237 0.0155537   -1.45   0.146   0.98   0.95   1.01
hours squared     0.0026616 0.0003438    7.74   0.000   1.00   1.00   1.00
hours cubed      -0.0000244 0.0000024  -10.14   0.000   1.00   1.00   1.00
```

Note that the original variable, *hours-per-week*, is no longer significant. We therefore rerun the analysis, including only *hours²* and *hours³*, with the results shown in Table 13.25. Both the *hours²* and *hours³* terms are significant. Analysis and interpretation of these results is left to the exercises.

Putting all the previous results from this section together, we construct a logistic regression model for predicting *income* based on the following variables:

- *Age*
- *Age²*
- *Education²*
- *Hours²*
- *Hours³*

TABLE 13.25   Results from logistic regression of *income* on *hours*^{2} and *hours*^{3}

```
Logistic Regression Table

                                                   Odds      95% CI
Predictor           Coef    SE Coef       Z      P Ratio  Lower  Upper
Constant         -3.37144  0.0708973  -47.55  0.000
hours squared     0.0021793 0.0000780   27.96  0.000  1.00   1.00   1.00
hours cubed      -0.0000212 0.0000009  -22.64  0.000  1.00   1.00   1.00
```

- *Capnet-cat*
- *Marital-status*
- *Sex.*

The results, provided in Table 13.26, are analyzed and interpreted in the exercises.

TABLE 13.26   Results from multiple logistic regression of *income*

```
Logistic Regression Table

                                                     Odds      95% CI
Predictor            Coef     SE Coef       Z      P Ratio  Lower  Upper
Constant          -11.5508  0.282276  -40.92  0.000
age                 0.235060 0.0115234   20.40  0.000  1.26   1.24   1.29
age-squared        -0.0023038 0.0001253 -18.38  0.000  1.00   1.00   1.00
educ-squared        0.0163723 0.0004017   40.76  0.000  1.02   1.02   1.02
hours squared       0.0012647 0.0000888   14.25  0.000  1.00   1.00   1.00
hours cubed        -0.0000127 0.0000010  -12.35  0.000  1.00   1.00   1.00
capnet-cat
 gain < $5,000     -0.189060  0.109220   -1.73  0.083  0.83   0.67   1.03
 gain >= $5,000     3.46054   0.114327   30.27  0.000 31.83  25.44  39.83
 loss               1.15582   0.0793780  14.56  0.000  3.18   2.72   3.71
marital-status
 Married            2.15226   0.0749850  28.70  0.000  8.60   7.43   9.97
 Never-married     -0.124760  0.0931762  -1.34  0.181  0.88   0.74   1.06
 Separated         -0.0212868 0.175555   -0.12  0.903  0.98   0.69   1.38
 Widowed            0.372877  0.169419    2.20  0.028  1.45   1.04   2.02
sex
 Male               0.209341  0.0554578   3.77  0.000  1.23   1.11   1.37


Log-Likelihood = -8238.566
Test that all slopes are zero: G = 11039.923, DF = 13, P-Value = 0.000
```

13.13   VALIDATING THE LOGISTIC REGRESSION MODEL

Hosmer and Lebeshow[8] provide details for assessing the fit of a logistic regression model, including goodness-of-fit statistics and model diagnostics. Here, however, we

---

[8]Hosmer and Lemeshow, *Applied Logistic Regression*, 3rd edition, John Wiley and Sons, 2013.

investigate validation of the logistic regression model through the traditional method of a hold-out sample.

The training data set of 25,000 records was partitioned randomly into two data sets, training set A of 12,450 records and training set B of 12,550 records. Training set A has 2953 records (23.72%) with income greater than $50,000, while training set B has 3031 (24.15%) such records. Therefore, we cannot expect that the parameter estimates and ORs for the two data sets will be exactly the same. Indicator variables are provided for *marital status* and *sex*. The reference categories (where all indicators equal zero) are *divorced* and *female*, respectively. The logistic regression results for training sets A and B are provided in Tables 13.27 and 13.28, respectively.

TABLE 13.27 Logistic regression results for training set A

```
Logistic Regression Table

                                                     Odds     95% CI
Predictor            Coef     SE Coef       Z     P  Ratio  Lower  Upper
Constant          -9.06305   0.232199  -39.03  0.000
age                0.0278994 0.0023420   11.91  0.000  1.03   1.02   1.03
education-num      0.374356  0.0120668   31.02  0.000  1.45   1.42   1.49
marital-status
 Married           2.02743   0.103258    19.63  0.000  7.59   6.20   9.30
 Never-married    -0.489140  0.127005    -3.85  0.000  0.61   0.48   0.79
 Separated        -0.369533  0.278258    -1.33  0.184  0.69   0.40   1.19
 Widowed          -0.0760889 0.233292    -0.33  0.744  0.93   0.59   1.46
sex
 Male              0.166622  0.0757310    2.20  0.028  1.18   1.02   1.37
hours-per-week     0.0309548 0.0023358   13.25  0.000  1.03   1.03   1.04
capnet             0.0002292 0.0000127   17.98  0.000  1.00   1.00   1.00


Log-Likelihood = -4358.063
Test that all slopes are zero: G = 4924.536, DF = 9, P-Value = 0.000
```

Note that, for both data sets, all parameters are significant (as shown by the *Wald-Z p*-values) except the *separated* and *widowed* indicator variables for *marital status*. Overall, the coefficient values are fairly close to each other, except those with high variability, such as *male* and *separated*.

The estimated logit for training sets A and B are:

$$\hat{g}_A(x) = -9.06305 + 0.0278994(Age) + 0.374356(Education\_num)$$
$$+ 2.02743(Married) - 0.489140(Never\_married)$$
$$- 0.369533(Separated) - 0.0760889(Widowed) + 0.166622(Male)$$
$$+ 0.0309548(Hours\_per\_week) + 0.0002292(Capnet)$$

$$\hat{g}_B(x) = -8.85216 + 0.0224645(Age) + 0.368721(Education\_num)$$
$$+ 2.02076(Married) - 0.587585(Never\_married)$$
$$- 0.094394(Separated) - 0.181349(Widowed) + 0.311218(Male)$$
$$+ 0.0316433(Hours\_per\_week) + 0.0002455(Capnet)$$

TABLE 13.28   Logistic regression results for training set B

```
Logistic Regression Table
                                        Odds      95% CI
Predictor         Coef    SE Coef    Z      P    Ratio  Lower  Upper
Constant       -8.85216  0.230298 -38.44  0.000
age             0.0224645 0.0023381  9.61  0.000  1.02   1.02   1.03
education-num   0.368721  0.0121961 30.23  0.000  1.45   1.41   1.48
marital-status
 Married        2.02076   0.100676  20.07  0.000  7.54   6.19   9.19
 Never-married -0.587585  0.126032  -4.66  0.000  0.56   0.43   0.71
 Separated      0.0943940 0.222559   0.42  0.671  1.10   0.71   1.70
 Widowed       -0.181349  0.246958  -0.73  0.463  0.83   0.51   1.35
sex
 Male           0.311218  0.0745234  4.18  0.000  1.37   1.18   1.58
hours-per-week  0.0316433 0.0023875 13.25  0.000  1.03   1.03   1.04
capnet          0.0002455 0.0000135 18.16  0.000  1.00   1.00   1.00


Log-Likelihood = -4401.957
Test that all slopes are zero: G = 5071.837, DF = 9, P-Value = 0.000
```

For each of these logits, we will estimate the probability that each of the following types of people have incomes over $50,000:

1. A 50-year-old married male with 20 years of education working 40 hours per week with a capnet of $500.

2. A 50-year-old married male with 16 years of education working 40 hours per week with no capital gains or losses.

3. A 35-year-old divorced female with 12 years of education working 30 hours per week with no capital gains or losses.

1. For the 50-year-old married male with 20 years of education working 40 hours per week with a capnet of $500, we have the following logits for training sets A and B:

$$\hat{g}_A(x) = -9.06305 + 0.0278994(50) + 0.374356(20)$$
$$+ 2.02743(1) - 0.489140(0)$$
$$- 0.369533(0) - 0.0760889(0) + 0.166622(1)$$
$$+ 0.0309548(40) + 0.0002292(500)$$
$$= 3.365884$$

$$\hat{g}_B(x) = -8.85216 + 0.0224645(50) + 0.368721(20)$$
$$+ 2.02076(1) - 0.587585(0)$$
$$- 0.094394(0) - 0.181349(0) + 0.311218(1)$$
$$+ 0.0316433(40) + 0.0002455(500)$$
$$= 3.365945$$

Thus, the estimated probability that this type of person will have an income exceeding $50,000 is for each data set:

$$\hat{\pi}_A(x) = \frac{e^{\hat{g}(x)}}{1 + e^{\hat{g}(x)}} = \frac{e^{3.365884}}{1 + e^{3.365884}} = 0.966621$$

$$\hat{\pi}_B(x) = \frac{e^{\hat{g}(x)}}{1 + e^{\hat{g}(x)}} = \frac{e^{3.365945}}{1 + e^{3.365945}} = 0.966623$$

That is, the estimated probability that a 50-year-old married male with 20 years of education working 40 hours per week with a capnet of $500 will have an income exceeding $50,000 is 96.66%, as reported by both data sets with a difference of only 0.000002 between them. If sound, then the similarity of these estimated probabilities shows strong evidence for the validation of the logistic regression.

Unfortunately, these estimates are not sound, because they represent extrapolation on the education variable, whose maximum value in this data set is only 16 years. Therefore, these estimates should not be used in general, and should certainly not be used for model validation.

2. For the 50-year-old married male with 16 years of education working 40 hours per week with a capnet of $500, the logits look like this:

$$\begin{aligned}
\hat{g}_A(x) = &-9.06305 + 0.0278994(50) + 0.374356(16) \\
&+ 2.02743(1) - 0.489140(0) \\
&- 0.369533(0) - 0.0760889(0) + 0.166622(1) \\
&+ 0.0309548(40) + 0.0002292(500) \\
= &\; 1.86846
\end{aligned}$$

$$\begin{aligned}
\hat{g}_B(x) = &-8.85216 + 0.0224645(50) + 0.368721(16) \\
&+ 2.02076(1) - 0.587585(0) \\
&- 0.094394(0) - 0.181349(0) + 0.311218(1) \\
&+ 0.0316433(40) + 0.0002455(500) \\
= &\; 1.891061
\end{aligned}$$

The estimated probability that a 50-year-old married male with 16 years of education working 40 hours per week with a capnet of $500 will have an income exceeding $50,000 is therefore for each data set:

$$\hat{\pi}_A(x) = \frac{e^{\hat{g}(x)}}{1 + e^{\hat{g}(x)}} = \frac{e^{1.86846}}{1 + e^{1.86846}} = 0.8663$$

$$\hat{\pi}_B(x) = \frac{e^{\hat{g}(x)}}{1 + e^{\hat{g}(x)}} = \frac{e^{1.891061}}{1 + e^{1.891061}} = 0.8689$$

That is, the estimated probability that such a person will have an income greater than $50,000 is reported by models based on both data sets to be about 87%. There is a difference of only 0.0026 between the point estimates, which may be considered small, although, of course, what constitutes small depends on the particular research problem, and other factors.

3. For the 35-year-old divorced female with 12 years of education working 30 hours per week with no capital gains or losses, we have the following logits:

$$\hat{g}_A(x) = -9.06305 + 0.0278994(35) + 0.374356(12)$$
$$+ 2.02743(0) - 0.489140(0)$$
$$- 0.369533(0) - 0.0760889(0) + 0.166622(0)$$
$$+ 0.0309548(30) + 0.0002292(0)$$
$$= -2.66566$$

$$\hat{g}_B(x) = -8.85216 + 0.0224645(35) + 0.368721(12)$$
$$+ 2.02076(0) - 0.587585(0)$$
$$- 0.094394(0) - 0.181349(0) + 0.311218(0)$$
$$+ 0.0316433(30) + 0.0002455(0)$$
$$= -2.69195$$

Therefore, for each data set, the estimated probability that this type of person will have an income exceeding \$50,000 is:

$$\hat{\pi}_A(x) = \frac{e^{\hat{g}(x)}}{1 + e^{\hat{g}(x)}} = \frac{e^{-2.66566}}{1 + e^{-2.66566}} = 0.06503$$
$$\hat{\pi}_B(x) = \frac{e^{\hat{g}(x)}}{1 + e^{\hat{g}(x)}} = \frac{e^{-2.69195}}{1 + e^{-2.69195}} = 0.06345$$

That is, the estimated probability that a 35-year-old divorced female with 12 years of education working 30 hours per week with no capital gains or losses will have an income greater than \$50,000 is reported by models based on both data sets to be between 6.3% and 6.5%. There is a difference of only 0.00158 between the point estimates, which is slightly better (i.e., smaller) than the estimate for the 50-year-old male.

13.14 WEKA: HANDS-ON ANALYSIS USING LOGISTIC REGRESSION

In this exercise, a logistic regression model is built using Waikato Environment for Knowledge Analysis (WEKA's) Logistic class. A modified version of the cereals data set is used as input, where the RATING field is discretized by mapping records with values greater than 42 to "High," while those less than or equal to 42 become "Low." This way, our model is used to classify a cereal as having either a "High" or "Low" nutritional rating. Our data set consists of the three numeric predictor fields *PROTEIN*, *SODIUM*, and *FIBER*.

The data set is split into separate training and test files. The training file *cereals_train.arff* consists of 24 instances and is used to train our logistic regression model. The file is balanced 50–50 where half the instances take on class value "High," while the other half have the value "Low." The mean values for the predictor fields *PROTEIN*, *SODIUM*, and *FIBER* are 2.667, 146.875, and 2.458, respectively. The complete training file is shown in Table 13.29.

TABLE 13.29 ARFFTraining File*cereals_train.arff*

```
        @relation cereals_train.arff

        @attribute PROTEIN numeric
        @attribute SODIUM numeric
        @attribute FIBER numeric
        @attribute RATING {High,Low}

        @data
        3,200,3.000000,High
        3,230,3.000000,High
        3,200,3.000000,High
        3,0,4.000000,High
        4,150,2.000000,High
        3,0,3.000000,High
        4,260,9.000000,High
        3,140,3.000000,High
        2,0,3.000000,High
        2,0,2.000000,High
        3,80,1.000000,High
        2,200,4.000000,High
        2,180,1.500000,Low
        4,150,3.000000,Low
        2,140,2.000000,Low
        4,95,3.000000,Low
        1,220,0.000000,Low
        2,180,0.000000,Low
        3,140,4.000000,Low
        3,170,2.000000,Low
        2,200,1.000000,Low
        3,250,1.500000,Low
        2,200,1.000000,Low
        1,140,0.000000,Low
```

Our training and test files are both represented in ARFF format, which is WEKA's standard method of representing the instances and attributes found in data sets. The keyword *relation* indicates the name for the file, which is followed by a block defining each *attribute* in the data set. Notice that the three predictor fields are defined as type *numeric*, whereas the target variable *RATING* is categorical. The *data* section lists each instance, which corresponds to a specific cereal. For example, the first line in the data section describes a cereal having *PROTEIN* = 3, *SODIUM* = 200, *FIBER* = 3.0, and *RATING* = High.

Let us load the training file and build the Logistic model.

1. Click Explorer from the WEKA GUI Chooser dialog.
2. On the Preprocess tab, press Open file and specify the path to the training file, *cereals_train.arff*.

The WEKA Explorer Panel displays several characteristics of the training file as shown in Figure 13.7. The three predictor attributes and class variable are shown on the attributes pane (left). Statistics for *PROTEIN*, including range (1–4), mean (2.667), and standard deviation (0.868) are shown on the selected attribute pane (right). The status bar at the bottom of the panel tells us WEKA loaded the file successfully.

1. Next, select the Classify tab.
2. Under Classifier, press the Choose button.
3. Select Classifiers → Functions → Logistic from the navigation hierarchy.
4. In our modeling experiment, we have separate training and test sets; therefore, under Test options, choose the Use training set option.
5. Click Start to build the model.

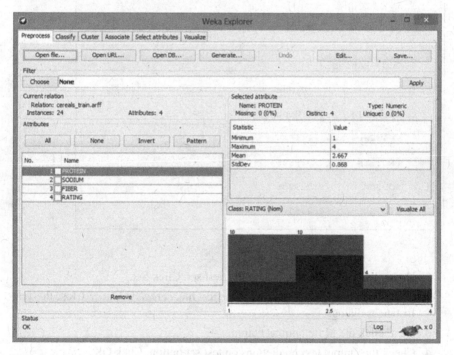

Figure 13.7   WEKA explorer panel: preprocess tab.

WEKA creates the logistic regression model and reports results in the Classifier output window. Although the results (not shown) indicate that the classification accuracy of the model, as measured against the training set, is 75% $\left(\frac{18}{24}\right)$, we are interested in using the model to classify the unseen data found in the test set. The ORs and values for the regression coefficients β_0, β_1, β_2, and β_3 are also reported by the model as shown in Table 13.30. We will revisit these values shortly, but first let us evaluate our model against the test set.

TABLE 13.30   Logistic regression coefficients

```
                       Class
     Variable          High

     ====================

     PROTEIN        -0.0423

     SODIUM         -0.0107

     FIBER           0.9476

     Intercept      -0.5478




     Odds Ratios...

                       Class
     Variable          High

     ====================

     PROTEIN         0.9586

     SODIUM          0.9893

     FIBER           2.5795
```

1. Under Test options, choose Supplied test set. Click Set.
2. Click Open file, specify the path to the test file, *cereals_test.arff*. Close the Test Instances dialog.
3. Next, click the More options button.
4. Check the Output text predictions on test set option. Click OK.
5. Click the Start button to evaluate the model against the test set.

Again, the results appear in the Classifier output window; however, now the output shows that the logistic regression model has classified 62.5% $\left(\frac{5}{8}\right)$ of the instances in the test set correctly. In addition, the model now reports the actual predictions, and probabilities by which it classified each instance, as shown in Table 13.31.

For example, the first instance is incorrectly predicted (classified) to be "Low" with probability 0.567. The plus (+) symbol in error column indicates this classification is incorrect according to the maximum (*0.567) probability. Let us compute the estimated logit $\hat{g}(x)$ for this instance according to the coefficients found in Table 13.30.

However, we first examine the test file *cereals_test.arff* and determine the first record contains the attribute-value pairs *PROTEIN* = 4, *SODIUM* = 135, *FIBER* = 2.0, and *RATING* = High. Therefore, the estimated logit equals:

$$\hat{g}(x) = -0.5478 - 0.0423(4) - 0.0107(135) + 0.9476(2) = -0.2663$$

It follows that,

$$\hat{\pi}(x) = \frac{e^{-0.2663}}{1 + e^{-0.2663}} = 0.43382$$

Therefore, the estimated probability equals about 43.4% that a cereal with protein (4 g), sodium (135 mg), and fiber (2 g) is of high nutritional value. Note that WEKA reports this same probability (except for slight rounding variations) for the first instance in Table 13.31. It follows that the model estimates a probability equal to $1 - \hat{\pi}(x) = 56.6\%$ that this cereal has a low nutritional rating. Therefore, based on the higher probability, the model incorrectly classified the record as "Low."

Table 13.31 also shows reports of the ORs for the three continuous predictors. For example, the OR for *PROTEIN* is $\widehat{OR} = e^{b_1} = e^{-0.0423} = 0.9586$. This is interpreted as the odds of a cereal with $x + 1$ grams of protein being of high nutritional value, as compared to a cereal with x grams of protein being highly nutritious.

TABLE 13.31   Logistic regression test set predictions

```
=== Predictions on test split ===

inst#,    actual, predicted, error, probability distribution

   1      1:High      2:Low        +     0.433 *0.567

   2      1:High      2:Low        +     0.357 *0.643

   3      1:High      1:High            *0.586  0.414

   4      1:High      1:High            *0.578  0.422

   5      2:Low       2:Low              0.431 *0.569

   6      2:Low       2:Low              0.075 *0.925

   7      2:Low       2:Low              0.251 *0.749

   8      2:Low       1:High        +   *0.86   0.14
```

THE R ZONE

Logistic Regression

```
patients <- data.frame(age = c(25, ..., 84),
    disease = c(0, ..., 1)) # Input the data
lm1 <- lm(disease ~ age, data = patients)
lr1 <- glm(disease ~ age, data = patients,
    family=binomial)
plot(patients$age, patients$disease,
    xlab = "Age", ylab = "Disease",
    main = "Disease vs. Age",
    xlim = c(20, 90), pch = 16)
abline(lm1; lty = 3)
curve(predict(lr1, data.frame(age=x),
        type = "resp"),
    add = TRUE, lwd = 2)
legend("topleft",
    legend=c("LS", "Log."),
    lty = c(3, 1), cex = .9)
```

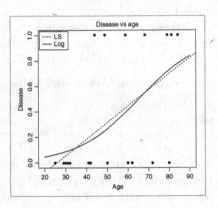

Inference on parameters

```
with(lr1, null.deviance - deviance)
with(lr1, df.null - df.residual)
with(lr1, pchisq(null.deviance -
    deviance,
    df.null - df.residual,
    lower.tail = FALSE))
```

```
> with(lr1, null.deviance - deviance)
[1] 5.696407324
> with(lr1, df.null - df.residual)
[1] 1
> with(lr1, pchisq(null.deviance - deviance,
+                  df.null - df.residual,
+                  lower.tail = FALSE))
[1] 0.01699967537
```

Make predictions

```
newd <- with(patients,
    data.frame(age =
    c(50, 72)))
predict.glm(lr1,
    newdata = newd)
    # log odds
predict.glm(lr1,
    newdata = newd,
    type="resp") # prob.
```

```
> newd <- with(patients, data.frame(age = c(50, 72)))
> predict.glm(lr1, newdata = newd) # log odds
            1             2
-1.0242944778 0.4487387796
> predict.glm(lr1, newdata = newd, type="resp") # prob.
            1            2
0.2641917329 0.6103393257
```

Odds Ratios

```
round(exp(coef(lr1)), 3)
```

```
> round(exp(coef(lr1)), 3)
(Intercept)           age
      0.013         1.069
```

Dichotomous example

```
churn <- read.csv(file =
    "C:/ .../churn.txt",
    stringsAsFactors=TRUE)
table(churn$Churn,
    churn$VMail.Plan)
churn$VMP.ind <-
    ifelse(churn$VMail.Plan==
        "yes",
    1, 0)
lr2 <- glm(Churn ~ VMP.ind,
    data = churn,
    family = "binomial")
summary(lr2)
```

```
> table(churn$Churn, churn$VMail.Plan)

          no   yes
 False  2008   842
 True    403    80

> summary(lr2)

Call:
glm(formula = Churn ~ VMP.ind, family = "binomial",
data = churn)

Deviance Residuals:
    Min      1Q   Median      3Q      Max
-0.6048  -0.6048  -0.6048  -0.4261   2.2111

Coefficients:
            Estimate Std. Error z value Pr(>|z|)
(Intercept) -1.60596    0.05458 -29.422  < 2e-16 ***
VMP.ind     -0.74780    0.12910  -5.792 6.94e-09 ***
---
Signif. codes:  0 '***' 0.001 '**' 0.01 '*' 0.05 '.'
0.1 ' ' 1
```

Dichotomous example: Odds Ratios and Predictions

```
# Odds ratio
round(exp(coef(lr2)), 3)
# Make predictions
newd <- with(churn,
    data.frame(VMP.ind = c(0,
        1)))
predict.glm(lr2, newdata = newd)
predict.glm(lr2, newdata = newd,
    type="resp")
```

```
> round(exp(coef(lr2)), 3)
(Intercept)      VMP.ind
      0.201        0.473

> predict.glm(lr2, newdata = newd)
          1            2
-1.605957919 -2.353753380
> predict.glm(lr2, newdata = newd, type="resp")
          1            2
0.16715055993 0.08676789588
```

Polychotomous example

```
# Redefine Customer Service
# Calls
churn$CSC <-
    factor(churn$CustServ.Calls)
levels(churn$CSC)
levels(churn$CSC)[1:2] <- "Low"
levels(churn$CSC)[2:3] <-
    "Medium"
levels(churn$CSC)[3:8] <- "High"
churn$CSC_Med <-
    ifelse(churn$CSC ==
        "Medium", 1, 0)
churn$CSC_Hi <-
    ifelse(churn$CSC == "High",
    1, 0)
table(churn$Churn, churn$CSC)
lr3 <- glm(Churn ~ CSC_Med +
    CSC_Hi, data = churn,
    family = "binomial")
summary(lr3)
```

```
> summary(lr3)

Call:
glm(formula = Churn ~ CSC_Med + CSC_Hi, family =
"binomial",
    data = churn)

Deviance Residuals:
    Min       1Q   Median       3Q      Max
-1.2062  -0.4919  -0.4919  -0.4834   2.0999

Coefficients:
            Estimate Std. Error z value Pr(>|z|)
(Intercept) -2.05100    0.07262 -28.243   <2e-16 ***
CSC_Med     -0.03699    0.11770  -0.314    0.753
CSC_Hi       2.11844    0.14238  14.879   <2e-16 ***
---
Signif. codes:  0 '***' 0.001 '**' 0.01 '*' 0.05 '.'
0.1 ' ' 1
```

Continuous example

```
lr4 <- glm(Churn ~ Day.Mins,
    data = churn,
    family = "binomial")
summary(lr4)
```

```
> summary(lr4)

Call:
glm(formula = Churn ~ Day.Mins, family = "binomial",
data = churn)

Deviance Residuals:
    Min       1Q   Median       3Q      Max
-1.0241  -0.6001  -0.4902  -0.3738   2.8102

Coefficients:
            Estimate Std. Error z value Pr(>|z|)
(Intercept) -3.929289   0.202823  -19.37   <2e-16 ***
Day.Mins     0.011272   0.000975   11.56   <2e-16 ***
---
Signif. codes:  0 '***' 0.001 '**' 0.01 '*' 0.05 '.'
0.1 ' ' 1
```

Adult data example

```
# Read in data using stringsAs
    Factors = TRUE
adult$over50K <-
    ifelse(adult$income== ">50K.", 1, 0)
adult$"capnet"<- adult$capital.gain-
    adult$capital.loss
lr5 <- glm(over50K ~ capnet,
    data = adult,
    family = "binomial")
summary(lr5)
```

```
> summary(lr5)

Call:
glm(formula = over50K ~ capnet, family = "binomial",
data = adult)

Deviance Residuals:
    Min       1Q   Median       3Q      Max
-4.3015  -0.6853  -0.6853  -0.5596   2.1775

Coefficients:
              Estimate Std. Error z value Pr(>|z|)
(Intercept) -1.329e+00  1.599e-02  -83.13   <2e-16
capnet       2.561e-04  7.871e-06   32.54   <2e-16

(Intercept) ***
capnet      ***
---
Signif. codes:  0 '***' 0.001 '**' 0.01 '*' 0.05 '.'
0.1 ' ' 1
```

Adult data example: Categorize capnet

```
adult$cap_lvl <- factor(adult$capnet)
levels(adult$cap_lvl)
levels(adult$cap_lvl)[1:88] <- "Loss"
levels(adult$cap_lvl)[2] <- "None"
levels(adult$cap_lvl)[3:77] <- "Gain < $5000"
levels(adult$cap_lvl)[4:44] <- "Gain >= $5000"
adult$cap_loss <- ifelse(adult$cap_lvl == "Loss", 1, 0)
adult$cap_l5K <- ifelse(adult$cap_lvl == "Gain < $5000", 1, 0)
adult$cap_ge5K <- ifelse(adult$cap_lvl == "Gain >= $5000", 1, 0)
```

Adult data example: Regression model

```
lr6 <- glm(over50K ~ cap_loss +
    cap_l5K + cap_ge5K,
    data = adult,
    family = "binomial")
summary(lr6)
```

```
> summary(lr6)

Call:
glm(formula = over50K ~ cap_loss + cap_l5K + cap_ge5K,
family = "binomial",
    data = adult)

Deviance Residuals:
    Min       1Q   Median       3Q      Max
-2.1576  -0.6489  -0.6489  -0.6099   1.8835

Coefficients:
              Estimate Std. Error z value Pr(>|z|)
(Intercept) -1.45088    0.01728  -83.954   <2e-16 ***
cap_loss     1.46472    0.06131   23.890   <2e-16 ***
cap_l5K     -0.13689    0.09435   -1.451    0.147
cap_ge5K     3.67595    0.09685   37.957   <2e-16 ***
---
Signif. codes:  0 '***' 0.001 '**' 0.01 '*' 0.05 '.'
0.1 ' ' 1
```

Multiple Logistic Regression

```
churn$IntlP.ind <-
    ifelse(churn$Int.l.Plan ==
        "yes",
    1, 0)
churn$VMP.ind <-
    ifelse(churn$VMail.Plan ==
        "yes",
    1, 0)
lr7 <- glm(Churn ~
    IntlP.ind+VMP.ind+CSC_Hi+
    Day.Mins+Eve.Mins+
    Night.Mins+ Intl.Mins,
    data = churn,
    family = "binomial")
summary(lr7)
```

```
> summary(lr7)

Call:
glm(formula = Churn ~ IntlP.ind + VMP.ind + CSC_Hi +
Day.Mins +
    Eve.Mins + Night.Mins + Intl.Mins, family =
"binomial", data = churn)

Deviance Residuals:
    Min      1Q   Median       3Q      Max
-2.5992  -0.4708  -0.3330  -0.1993   3.0945

Coefficients:
             Estimate Std. Error z value Pr(>|z|)
(Intercept) -8.073740   0.512453 -15.755  < 2e-16 ***
IntlP.ind    2.035480   0.146823  13.863  < 2e-16 ***
VMP.ind     -1.043561   0.150067  -6.954 3.55e-12 ***
CSC_Hi       2.676966   0.159152  16.820  < 2e-16 ***
Day.Mins     0.013474   0.001119  12.041  < 2e-16 ***
Eve.Mins     0.007294   0.001169   6.237 4.46e-10 ***
Night.Mins   0.004222   0.001147   3.681 0.000232 ***
Intl.Mins    0.085351   0.021021   4.060 4.90e-05 ***
---
Signif. codes:  0 '***' 0.001 '**' 0.01 '*' 0.05 '.'
0.1 ' ' 1
```

Higher order terms

```
adult$age.sq <- adult$age^2
lr8 <- glm(over50K ~ age +
    age.sq,
    data = adult,
    family = "binomial")
summary(lr8)
```

```
> summary(lr8)

Call:
glm(formula = over50K ~ age + age.sq, family =
"binomial", data = adult)

Deviance Residuals:
    Min      1Q   Median       3Q      Max
-1.0466  -0.8746  -0.4929  -0.1756   3.3850

Coefficients:
             Estimate Std. Error z value Pr(>|z|)
(Intercept) -9.080e+00  1.945e-01  -46.68   <2e-16
age          3.478e-01  8.946e-03   38.88   <2e-16
age.sq      -3.450e-03  9.922e-05  -34.77   <2e-16

(Intercept) ***
age         ***
age.sq      ***
---
Signif. codes:  0 '***' 0.001 '**' 0.01 '*' 0.05 '.'
0.1 ' ' 1
```

Validating the model: Preparing the data

```
# Prepare the data
levels(adult$marital.status)
levels(adult$marital.status)[2:4] <- "Married"
levels(adult$marital.status)
adult$ms.married <- ifelse(adult$marital.status == "Married", 1, 0)
adult$ms.neverm <- ifelse(adult$marital.status == "Never-married", 1, 0)
```

```
adult$ms.sep <- ifelse(adult$marital.status == "Separated", 1, 0)
adult$ms.widowed <- ifelse(adult$marital.status == "Widowed", 1, 0)
adult$capnet <- adult$capital.gain-adult$capital.loss
levels(adult$sex)
adult$male <- ifelse(adult$sex == "Male", 1, 0)
# Create hold-out sample
hold <- runif(dim(adult)[1], 0, 1)
trainA <- adult[which(hold < .5),]
trainB <- adult[which(hold >= .5),]
dim(trainA); dim(trainB)
```

Validating the model: Run the models

```
lr11A <- glm(over50K ~ age + education.num + ms.married + ms.neverm + ms.sep +
    ms.widowed + male + hours.per.week + capnet,
    data = trainA,
    family = "binomial")
lr11B <- glm(over50K ~ age + education.num + ms.married + ms.neverm + ms.sep +
    ms.widowed + male + hours.per.week + capnet,
    data = trainB,
    family = "binomial")
summary(lr11A)
summary(lr11B)
```

R REFERENCES

R Core Team. *R: A Language and Environment for Statistical Computing*. Vienna, Austria: R Foundation for Statistical Computing; 2012. 3-900051-07-0, http://www.R-project.org/. Accessed 2014 Oct 5.

EXERCISES

CLARIFYING THE CONCEPTS

1. Indicate whether the following statements are true or false. If the statement is false, alter it so that the statement becomes true.

   a. Logistic regression refers to methods for describing the relationship between a categorical response variable and a set of categorical predictor variables.

   b. Logistic regression assumes the relationship between the predictor and the response is nonlinear.

   c. $\pi(x)$ may be interpreted as a probability.

   d. Logistic regression models assume that the error term ε is normally distributed with mean zero and constant variance.

 e. In logistic regression, closed-form solutions for the optimal values of the regression coefficients may be obtained.

 f. The saturated model predicts the response variable perfectly.

 g. The deviance represents the total variability in the response.

 h. Encoding a trichotomous predictor requires only two indicator variables.

 i. The t-test provides a method for finding the response probabilities.

 j. The interpretation of the logistic regression coefficient for a continuous predictor may be extended from the usual unit increase to an increase of any arbitrary amount.

 k. The estimated OR is constant across the range of the predictor.

2. By hand, derive the logit result $g(x) = \beta_0 + \beta_1 x$.

3. Explain what is meant by maximum-likelihood estimation and maximum-likelihood estimators.

4. Explain clearly how the slope coefficient β_1, and its estimate b_1, may be interpreted in logistic regression. Provide at least two examples, using both a categorical and a continuous predictor.

5. What are odds? What is the difference between odds and probability?

6. What is the definition of the odds ratio? What is the relationship between the odds ratio and the slope coefficient β_1? For what quantity is the odds ratio sometimes used as an estimate?

7. Describe how we determine the statistical significance of the odds ratio, using a confidence interval.

8. If the difference between a particular indicator variable and the reference category is not significant, then what should the analyst consider doing?

9. Discuss the role of statistical inference with respect to the huge sample sizes prevalent in data mining.

10. Discuss the assumption that the odds ratio is constant across the range of the predictor, with respect to various types of relationships between the predictor and the response. Provide modeling options for when this assumption may not be reflected in the data.

11. Discuss the use of predictors that turn out to be nonsignificant in estimating the response. When might this be appropriate, if at all? Why would this not be appropriate in general?

12. Explain why, for data that are missing one or more indicator variable values, it would not be appropriate to simply ignore these missing variables when making an estimation. Provide options for the data analyst in this case.

WORKING WITH THE DATA

For Exercises 13–18, use the following information. The logistic regression output shown in Table 13.32 refers to the *breast cancer* data set. This data set was collected by Dr. William H. Wohlberg from the University of Wisconsin Hospitals, Madison. Ten numeric predictors are used to predict the class of malignant breast cancer tumor (class = 1), as opposed to a benign tumor (class = 0).

TABLE 13.32   Logistic regression results for Exercises 13

```
Logistic Regression Table
                                                              Odds
Predictor                     Coef     SE Coef       Z      P  Ratio
Constant                  -10.1039     1.17490   -8.60  0.000
Clump Thickness             0.535014   0.142018    3.77  0.000   1.71
Cell Size Uniformity       -0.0062797  0.209079   -0.03  0.976   0.99
Cell Shape Uniformity       0.322706   0.230602    1.40  0.162   1.38
Marginal Adhesion           0.330637   0.123451    2.68  0.007   1.39
Single Epithelial Cell Size 0.0966354  0.156593    0.62  0.537   1.10
Bare Nuclei                 0.383025   0.0938437   4.08  0.000   1.47
Bland Chromatin             0.447188   0.171383    2.61  0.009   1.56
Normal Nucleoli             0.213031   0.112874    1.89  0.059   1.24
Mitoses                     0.534836   0.328777    1.63  0.104   1.71

Log-Likelihood = -51.444
Test that all slopes are zero: G = 781.462, DF = 9, P-Value = 0.000
```

13. What is the value of the deviance difference? Is the overall logistic regression significant? How can you tell? What does it mean to say that the overall logistic regression is significant?

14. Without reference to inferential significance, express the form of the logit.

15. Which variables do not appear to be significant predictors of breast tumor class? How can you tell?

16. Discuss whether the variables you cited in Exercise 15 should be used in predicting the class of tumor with a new unseen data set.

17. Discuss how you should handle the variables with p-values around 0.05, 0.10, or 0.15.

18. Explain what will happen to the deviance difference if we rerun the model, dropping the nonsignificant variables. Work by analogy with the linear regression case.

For Exercises 19–24, use the following information. Continuing from the previous exercises, the logistic regression for the breast cancer data set was run again, this time dropping the *cell size uniformity* and *single epithelial cell size* variables, but retaining all the others. The logistic regression output shown in Table 13.33 contains the results.

TABLE 13.33   Logistic regression results for Exercises 19–24

```
Logistic Regression Table
                                                        Odds    95% CI
Predictor              Coef     SE Coef      Z      P  Ratio  Lower  Upper
Constant            -9.98278    1.12607  -8.87  0.000
Clump Thickness      0.534002   0.140788   3.79  0.000   1.71   1.29   2.25
Cell Shape Uniformity 0.345286  0.171640   2.01  0.044   1.41   1.01   1.98
Marginal Adhesion    0.342491   0.119217   2.87  0.004   1.41   1.11   1.78
Bare Nuclei          0.388296   0.0935616   4.15  0.000   1.47   1.23   1.77
Bland Chromatin      0.461943   0.168195   2.75  0.006   1.59   1.14   2.21
Normal Nucleoli      0.226055   0.110970   2.04  0.042   1.25   1.01   1.56
Mitoses              0.531192   0.324454   1.64  0.102   1.70   0.90   3.21

Log-Likelihood = -51.633
Test that all slopes are zero: G = 781.083, DF = 7, P-Value = 0.000
```

19. Explain why the deviance difference fell, but only by a small amount.

20. Did you drop *cell shape uniformity* in the previous exercise? Are you surprised that the variable is now a significant predictor? Discuss the importance of retaining variables of borderline significance in the early stages of model building.

21. Assume that our level of significance is 0.11. Express the logit, using all significant variables.

22. Find the probability that a tumor is malignant, given the following:
    a. The values for all predictors are at the minimum (1).
    b. The values for all predictors are at a moderate level (5).
    c. The values for all predictors are at the maximum (10).

23. Calculate the 95% confidence intervals for the following predictor coefficients.
    a. Clump thickness
    b. Mitoses
    c. Comment as to the evidence provided by the confidence interval for the mitoses coefficient regarding its significance.

24. Clearly interpret the value of the coefficients for the following predictors:
    a. Bland chromatin
    b. Normal nucleoli

HANDS-ON ANALYSIS

For Exercises 25–37, use the *adult* data set.

25. Construct the logistic regression model developed in the text, with the age^2 term and the indicator variable age 33–65.
    Verify that using the quadratic term provides a higher estimate of the probability of high income for the 32-year-old than the 20-year-old.

Use Table 13.25 for Exercises 26–28.

26. Find the form of the estimated logit.

27. Find the probability of high income for someone working 30, 40, 50, and 60 hours per week.

28. Construct and interpret a 95% confidence interval for each coefficient.

Use Table 13.26 for Exercises 29–31.

29. Consider the results from Table 13.26. Construct the logistic regression model that produced these results.

30. For indicator categories that are not significant, collapse the categories with the reference category. (How are you handling the category with the 0.083 *p*-value?) Rerun the logistic regression with these collapsed categories.

Use the results from your rerunning of the logistic regression for Exercises 31–34.

31. Find the estimated logit.

32. Construct and interpret 95% confidence intervals for the coefficients for age, sex-male, and educ-squared. Verify that these predictors belong in the model.

33. Find the probability of high income for a 20-year-old single female with 12 years education working 20 hours per week with no capital gains or losses.

34. Find the probability of high income for a 50-year-old married male with 16 years education working 40 hours per week with capital gains of $6000.

35. Open the data set, *German*, which is provided on the textbook website. The data set consists of 20 predictors, both continuous and categorical, and a single response variable, indicating whether the individual record represents a good or bad credit risk. The predictors are as follows, with amounts in Deutsche marks (DM):

    o Status of existing checking account
    o Duration in months
    o Credit history
    o Loan purpose
    o Credit amount
    o Savings account/bonds
    o Presently employed since
    o Payment as percentage of disposable income
    o Personal status and gender
    o Other debtors/guarantors
    o Present residence since
    o Property
    o Age
    o Other installment plans
    o Housing
    o Number of existing credits at this bank
    o Job
    o Number of people being liable to provide maintenance for
    o Telephone
    o Foreign worker.

    More information is available about this data set from the textbook website. Construct the best logistic regression model you can, using as many of the methods we learned in this chapter as possible. Provide strong interpretive support for your model, including explanations of derived variables, indicator variables, and so on.

36. Open the *breast cancer* data set. Investigate, for each significant predictor, whether the linearity assumption is warranted. If not, ameliorate the situation using the methods discussed in this chapter.

37. Recall the WEKA Logistic example for classifying cereals as either high or low. Compute the probability that the fourth instance from the test set is classified either high or low. Does your probability match that produced by WEKA?

## CHAPTER 14

NAÏVE BAYES AND BAYESIAN NETWORKS

14.1 BAYESIAN APPROACH

In the field of statistics, there are two main approaches to probability. The usual way probability is taught, for example in most typical introductory statistics courses, represents the *frequentist* or *classical* approach. In the frequentist approach to probability, the population parameters are fixed constants whose values are unknown. These probabilities are defined to be the relative frequencies of the various categories, where the experiment is repeated an indefinitely large number of times. For example, if we toss a fair coin 10 times, it may not be very unusual to observe 80% heads; but if we toss the fair coin 10 trillion times, we can be fairly certain that the proportion of heads will be near 50%. It is this "long-run" behavior that defines probability for the frequentist approach.

However, there are situations for which the classical definition of probability is unclear. For example, what is the probability that terrorists will strike New York City with a dirty bomb? As such an occurrence has never occurred, it is difficult to conceive what the long-run behavior of this gruesome experiment might be. In the frequentist approach to probability, the parameters are fixed, and the randomness lies in the data, which are viewed as a random sample from a given distribution with unknown but fixed parameters.

The *Bayesian* approach to probability turns these assumptions around. In Bayesian statistics, the parameters are considered to be random variables, and the data are considered to be known. The parameters are regarded as coming from a distribution of possible values, and Bayesians look to the observed data to provide information on likely parameter values.

Let θ represent the parameters of the unknown distribution. Bayesian analysis requires elicitation of a prior distribution for θ, called the *prior distribution, $p(\theta)$*. This prior distribution can model extant expert knowledge, if any, regarding the distribution of θ. For example, churn[1] modeling experts may be aware that a customer

---

[1]Churn represents customers leaving one company in favor of another company's products or services.

Data Mining and Predictive Analytics, First Edition. Daniel T. Larose and Chantal D. Larose.

exceeding a certain threshold number of calls to customer service may indicate a likelihood to churn. This knowledge can be distilled into prior assumptions about the distribution of customer service calls, including its mean and standard deviation. If no expert knowledge regarding the prior distribution is available, Bayesian analysts may posit a so-called *non-informative* prior, which assigns equal probability to all values of the parameter. For example, the prior probability of both churners and non-churners could be set at 0.5, using a non-informative prior. (Note, if in this case, this assumption does not seem reasonable, then you must be applying your expert knowledge about churn modeling!) Regardless, because the field of data mining often encounters huge datasets, the prior distribution should be dominated by the overwhelming amount of information to be found in the observed data.

Once the data have been observed, prior information about the distribution of θ can be *updated,* by factoring in the information about θ contained in the observed data. This modification leads to the *posterior distribution, $p(\theta|\mathbf{X})$,* where $\mathbf{X}$ represents the entire array of data.

This updating of our knowledge about θ from prior distribution to posterior distribution was first performed by the Reverend Thomas Bayes, in his *Essay Towards Solving a Problem in the Doctrine of Chances,*[2] published posthumously in 1763.

The posterior distribution is found as follows: $p(\theta|\mathbf{X}) = \frac{p(\mathbf{X}|\theta)p(\theta)}{p(\mathbf{X})}$, where $p(\mathbf{X}|\theta)$ represents the likelihood function, $p(\theta)$ is the prior distribution, and $p(\mathbf{X})$ is a normalizing factor called the marginal distribution of the data. As the posterior is a distribution rather than a single value, we can conceivably examine any possible statistic of this distribution that we are interested in, such as the first quartile, or the mean absolute deviation (Figure 14.1).

However, it is common to choose the posterior mode, the value of θ which maximizes $p(\theta|\mathbf{X})$, for an estimate, in which case we call this estimation method

Figure 14.1   The Reverend Thomas Bayes (1702–1761).

[2]Thomas Bayes, *Essay Towards Solving a Problem in the Doctrine of Chances, Philosophical Transactions of the Royal Society of London*, 1763.

the *maximum a posteriori* (*MAP*) method. For non-informative priors, the *MAP* estimate and the frequentist maximum-likelihood estimate often coincide, because the data dominate the prior. The likelihood function $p(\mathbf{X}|\theta)$ derives from the assumption that the observations are independently and identically distributed according to a particular distribution $f(\mathbf{X}|\theta)$, so that $p(\mathbf{X}|\theta) = \prod_{i=1}^{n} f(X_i|\theta)$.

The normalizing factor $p(\mathbf{X})$ is essentially a constant, for a given data set and model, so that we may express the posterior distribution such as this: $p(\theta|\mathbf{X}) \propto p(\mathbf{X}|\theta)p(\theta)$. That is, the posterior distribution of θ, given the data, is proportional to the product of the likelihood and the prior. Thus, when we have a great deal of information coming from the likelihood, as we do in most data mining applications, the likelihood will overwhelm the prior.

Criticism of the Bayesian framework has mostly focused on two potential drawbacks. First, elicitation of a prior distribution may be subjective. That is, two different subject matter experts may provide two different prior distributions, which will presumably percolate through to result in two different posterior distributions. The solution to this problem is (i) to select non-informative priors if the choice of priors is controversial, and (ii) apply lots of data so that the relative importance of the prior is diminished. Failing this, model selection can be performed on the two different posterior distributions, using model adequacy and efficacy criteria, resulting in the choice of the better model. Is reporting more than one model a bad thing?

The second criticism has been that Bayesian computation has been intractable for most interesting problems, in data mining terms, where the approach suffered from scalability issues. The curse of dimensionality hits Bayesian analysis rather hard, because the normalizing factor requires integrating (or summing) over all possible values of the parameter vector, which may be computationally infeasible when applied directly. However, the introduction of Markov chain Monte Carlo (MCMC) methods such as Gibbs sampling and the Metropolis algorithm has greatly expanded the range of problems and dimensions that Bayesian analysis can handle.

14.2 MAXIMUM A POSTERIORI (MAP) CLASSIFICATION

How do we find the *MAP* estimate of θ? Well, we need the value of θ that will maximize $p(\theta|\mathbf{X})$; this value is expressed as $\theta_{\text{MAP}} = \arg\max_{\theta} p(\theta|\mathbf{X})$, because it is the argument (value) that maximizes $p(\theta|\mathbf{X})$ over all θ. Then, using the formula for the posterior distribution, we have, because $p(\mathbf{X})$ has no θ term:

$$\theta_{\text{MAP}} = \arg\max_{\theta} p(\theta|\mathbf{X}) = \arg\max_{\theta} \frac{p(\mathbf{X}|\theta)p(\theta)}{p(\mathbf{X})} = \arg\max_{\theta} p(\mathbf{X}|\theta)p(\theta) \qquad (14.1)$$

The Bayesian *MAP* classification is optimal; that is, it achieves the minimum error rate for all possible classifiers (Mitchell,[3] page 174). Next, we apply these formulas

---

[3] Optimal, that is, for the (0, 1) loss function. Mitchell, *Machine Learning*, WGB-McGraw-Hill, Boston, 1997.

to a subset of the *churn* data set,[4] specifically, so that we may find the *MAP* estimate of churn for this subset.

First, however, let us step back for a moment and derive Bayes' theorem for simple events. Let A and B be events in a sample space. Then the *conditional probability* $P(A|B)$ is defined as:

$$P(A|B) = \frac{P(A \cap B)}{P(B)} = \frac{\#\text{of outcomes in both } A \text{ and } B}{\#\text{of outcomes in } B}.$$

Also, $P(B|A) = \frac{P(A \cap B)}{P(A)}$. Now, re-expressing the intersection, we have $P(A \cap B) = P(B|A) \cdot P(A)$, and substituting, we obtain

$$P(A|B) = \frac{P(B|A) \cdot P(A)}{P(B)}, \tag{14.2}$$

which is Bayes' theorem for simple events.

We shall restrict our example to only two categorical predictor variables, *International Plan* and *Voice Mail Plan*, and the categorical target variable, *churn*. The business problem is to classify new records as either churners or non-churners, based on the associations of churn with the two predictor variables learned in the training set. Now, how are we to think about this churn classification problem in the Bayesian terms addressed above? First, we let the parameter vector θ represent the dichotomous variable *churn*, taking on the two values *true* and *false*. For clarity, we denote θ as C for *churn*. The 3333×2 matrix $\mathbf{X}$ consists of the 3333 records in the data set, each with two fields, specifying either *yes* or *no* for the two predictor variables.

Thus, equation (14.1) can be reexpressed as:

$$\theta_{\text{MAP}} = C_{\text{MAP}} = \arg\max_{c,\bar{c}} p(I \cap V|C)p(C), \tag{14.3}$$

where I represents the *International Plan* and V represents the *Voice Mail Plan*. Denote:

- I to mean *International Plan = yes*
- $\bar{I}$ to mean *International Plan = no*
- V to mean *Voice Mail Plan = yes*
- $\bar{V}$ to mean *Voice Mail Plan = no*
- C to mean *Churn = true*
- $\bar{C}$ to mean *Churn = false*.

For example, for a new record containing $(I \cap V)$, we seek to calculate the following probabilities, using equation (14.3):

---

[4]Churn data set. Blake, C.L. & Merz, C.J. UCI Repository of machine learning databases [http://www.ics.uci.edu/~mlearn/MLRepository.html]. Irvine, CA: University of California, Department of Information and Computer Science, 1998. Also available at textbook website, www.DataMiningConsultant.com.

For customers who churn (churners):

$$P(International\ Plan = yes,\ Voice\ Mail\ Plan = yes|Churn = true)$$
$$\cdot P(Churn = true) = P(I \cap V|C) \cdot P(C),\ \text{and}$$

For customers who do not churn (non-churners):

$$P(International\ Plan = yes,\ Voice\ Mail\ Plan = yes|Churn = false)$$
$$\cdot P(Churn = false) = P(I \cap V|\overline{C}) \cdot P(\overline{C}).$$

We will then determine which value for *churn* produces the larger probability, and select it as C_{MAP}, the *MAP* estimate of *churn*.

We begin by finding a series of marginal and conditional probabilities, all of which we shall use as we build toward our *MAP* estimates. Also, as we may examine the entire training data set of 3333 records, we may calculate the posterior probabilities directly, as given in Table 14.2.

Note that, using the probabilities given in Tables 14.1 and 14.2, we can easily find the complement of these probabilities by subtracting from 1. For completeness, we present these complement probabilities in Table 14.3.

TABLE 14.1 Marginal and conditional probabilities for the *churn* data set

	Count	Count	Probability
International Plan	No 3010	Yes 323	$P(I) = \dfrac{323}{(323 + 3010)} = 0.0969$
Voice Mail Plan	No 2411	Yes 922	$P(V) = \dfrac{922}{(922 + 2411)} = 0.2766$
Churn	False 2850	True 483	$P(C) = \dfrac{483}{(483 + 2850)} = 0.1449$
International Plan, given churn = false	No 2664	Yes 186	$P(I|\overline{C}) = \dfrac{186}{(186 + 2664)} = 0.0653$
Voice Mail Plan, given churn = false	No 2008	Yes 842	$P(V|\overline{C}) = \dfrac{842}{(842 + 2008)} = 0.2954$
International Plan, given churn = true	No 346	Yes 137	$P(I|C) = \dfrac{137}{(137 + 346)} = 0.2836$
Voice Mail Plan, given churn = true	No 403	Yes 80	$P(V|C) = \dfrac{80}{(80 + 403)} = 0.1656$

TABLE 14.2 Posterior probabilities for the *churn* training data set

	Count	Count	Probability
Churn = true, given International Plan = yes	False 186	True 137	$P(C|I) = \dfrac{137}{(137 + 186)} = 0.4241$
Churn = true, given Voice Mail Plan = Yes	False 842	True 80	$P(C|V) = \dfrac{80}{(80 + 842)} = 0.0868$

TABLE 14.3   Complement probabilities for the *churn* training data set

Complement Probabilities

$P(\bar{I}) = 1 - P(I) = 1 - 0.0969 = 0.9031$	$P(\bar{V}) = 1 - 0.2766 = 0.7234$
$P(\bar{C}) = 1 - 0.1449 = 0.8551$	$P(\bar{I}\mid\bar{C}) = 1 - 0.0653 = 0.9347$
$P(\bar{V}\mid\bar{C}) = 1 - 0.2954 = 0.7046$	$P(\bar{I}\mid C) = 1 - 0.2836 = 0.7164$
$P(\bar{V}\mid C) = 1 - 0.1656 = 0.8344$	$P(\bar{C}\mid I) = 1 - 0.4241 = 0.5759$
$P(\bar{C}\mid V) = 1 - 0.0868 = 0.9132$	

Let us verify Bayes' theorem for this data set, using the probabilities in Table 14.1. $P(C\mid V) = \frac{P(V\mid C)\cdot P(C)}{P(V)} = \frac{(0.1656)\cdot(0.1449)}{0.2766} = 0.0868$, which is the value for this posterior probability given in Table 14.2.

We are still not in a position to calculate the *MAP* estimate of *churn*. We must first find *joint conditional probabilities* of the form $P(I, V\mid C)$. The contingency tables are shown in Table 14.4, allowing us to calculate joint conditional probabilities, by counting the records for which the respective joint conditions are held.

TABLE 14.4   Joint conditional probabilities for the *churn* training data set

		Churn	
		False	True
$I \cap V$	No	2794	447
	Yes	56	36

$p(I \cap V \mid C) = 36/(36+447) = 0.0745$

$p(I \cap V \mid \bar{C}) = 56/(56+2794) = 0.0196$

		Churn	
		False	True
$I \cap \bar{V}$	No	2720	382
	Yes	130	101

$p(I \cap \bar{V} \mid C) = 101/(101+382) = 0.2091$

$p(I \cap \bar{V} \mid \bar{C}) = 130/(130+2720) = 0.0456$

		Churn	
		False	True
$\bar{I} \cap V$	No	2064	439
	Yes	786	44

$p(\bar{I} \cap V \mid C) = 44/(44+439) = 0.0911$

$p(\bar{I} \cap V \mid \bar{C}) = 786/(786+2064) = 0.2758$

		Churn	
		False	True
$\bar{I} \cap \bar{V}$	No	972	181
	Yes	1878	302

$p(\bar{I} \cap \bar{V} \mid C) = 302/(302+181) = 0.6253$

$p(\bar{I} \cap \bar{V} \mid \bar{C}) = 1878/(1878+972) = 0.6589$

Now we can find the *MAP* estimate of *churn* for the four combinations of *International Plan* and *Voice Mail Plan* membership, using equation (14.3):

$$\theta_{\text{MAP}} = C_{\text{MAP}} = \arg\max_{c,\bar{c}} p(I, V|C)p(C)$$

Suppose we have a new record, where the customer belongs to the *International Plan* and *Voice Mail Plan*. Do we expect that this new customer will churn or not? That is, what will be the *MAP* estimate of *churn* for this new customer? We will apply equation (14.3) for each of the *churn* or *non-churn* cases, and select the classification that provides the larger value.

Here, we have:

For churners:

$$P(International\ Plan = yes,\ \ Voice\ Mail\ Plan = yes|Churn = true)$$
$$\cdot P(Churn = true) = P(I \cap V|C) \cdot P(C) = (0.0745) \cdot (0.1449) = 0.0108,\ \text{and}$$

For non-churners:

$$P(International\ Plan = yes,\ \ Voice\ Mail\ Plan = yes|Churn = false)$$
$$\cdot P(Churn = false) = P(I \cap V|\overline{C}) \cdot P(\overline{C}) = (0.0196)$$
$$\cdot (0.8551) = 0.0168.$$

As 0.0167 for *churn = false* is the maximum of the two cases, then $\theta_{\text{MAP}} = C_{\text{MAP}}$, the *MAP* estimate of *churn* for this new customer, is *churn = false*. For customers belonging to both plans, this MAP estimate of "Churn = false" becomes our prediction; that is, we would predict that they would not churn.

Suppose a new customer belongs to the *International Plan*, but not the *Voice Mail Plan*. Then $P(I \cap \overline{V}|C) \cdot P(C) = (0.2091) \cdot (0.1449) = 0.0303$, and

$$P(I \cap \overline{V}|\overline{C}) \cdot P(\overline{C}) = (0.0456) \cdot (0.8551) = 0.0390.$$

So that $\theta_{\text{MAP}} = C_{\text{MAP}}$ is *churn = false*.

What if a new customer belongs to the *Voice Mail Plan*, but not the *International Plan?* Then $P(\overline{I} \cap V|C) \cdot P(C) = (0.0911) \cdot (0.1449) = 0.0132$, and

$$P(\overline{I} \cap V|\overline{C}) \cdot P(\overline{C}) = (0.2758) \cdot (0.8551) = 0.2358.$$

Here again $\theta_{\text{MAP}} = C_{\text{MAP}}$ is *churn = false*.

Finally, suppose a new customer belongs to neither the *International Plan*, nor the *Voice Mail Plan*. Then $P(\overline{I} \cap \overline{V}|C) \cdot P(C) = (0.6253) \cdot (0.1449) = 0.0906$, and

$$P(\overline{I} \cap \overline{V}|\overline{C}) \cdot P(\overline{C}) = (0.6589) \cdot (0.8551) = 0.5634.$$

So that, yet again, $\theta_{\text{MAP}} = C_{\text{MAP}}$ is *churn = false*.

14.3   POSTERIOR ODDS RATIO

Therefore, the *MAP* estimate for *churn* is *false* for each combination of *International Plan* and *Voice Mail Plan* membership. This result does not appear to be very helpful, because we will predict the same outcome for all customers regardless of their membership in the plans. However, not all of the classifications have the same strength of evidence. Next, we consider the level of evidence in each case, as defined by the *posterior odds ratio*. The posterior odds ratio represents a measure of the strength of evidence in favor of a particular classification, and is calculated as follows:

POSTERIOR ODDS RATIO

$$\frac{p(\theta_c|\mathbf{X})}{p(\overline{\theta}_c|\mathbf{X})} = \frac{p(\mathbf{X}|\theta_c) \cdot p(\theta_c)}{p(\mathbf{X}|\overline{\theta}_c) \cdot p(\overline{\theta}_c)}$$

where θ_c represents a particular classification of the unknown target variable.

A posterior odds ratio of exactly 1.0 would mean that the evidence from the posterior distribution supports both classifications equally. That is, the combination of information from the data and the prior distributions does not favor one category over the other. A value greater than 1.0 indicates that the posterior distribution favors the positive classification, while a value less than 1.0 represents evidence against the positive classification (e.g., *churn = true*). The value of the posterior odds ratio may be interpreted as indicating roughly the proportion or ratio of evidence provided by the posterior distribution in favor of the positive classification against the negative classification.

In our example, the posterior odds ratio for a new customer who belongs to both plans is

$$\frac{P(I \cap V|C) \cdot P(C)}{P(I \cap V|\overline{C}) \cdot P(\overline{C})} = \frac{0.0108}{0.0168} = 0.6467$$

This means that there is 64.67% as much evidence from the posterior distribution in support of *churn = true* as there is in support of *churn = false* for this customer.

For a new customer who belongs to the *International Plan* only, the posterior odds ratio is

$$\frac{P(I \cap \overline{V}|C) \cdot P(C)}{P(I \cap \overline{V}|\overline{C}) \cdot P(\overline{C})} = \frac{0.0303}{0.0390} = 0.7769$$

indicating that there is 77.69% as much evidence from the posterior distribution in support of *churn = true* as there is in support of *churn = false* for such a customer.

New customers who belong to the *Voice Mail Plan* only have a posterior odds ratio of

$$\frac{P(\overline{I} \cap V|C) \cdot P(C)}{P(\overline{I} \cap V|\overline{C}) \cdot P(\overline{C})} = \frac{0.0132}{0.2358} = 0.0560$$

indicating that there is only 5.6% as much evidence from the posterior distribution in support of *churn = true* as there is in support of *churn = false* for these customers.

Finally, for customers who belong to neither plan, the posterior odds ratio is

$$\frac{P(\overline{I} \cap \overline{V}|C) \cdot P(C)}{P(\overline{I} \cap \overline{V}|\overline{C}) \cdot P(\overline{C})} = \frac{0.0906}{0.5634} = 0.1608$$

indicating that there is only 16.08% as much evidence from the posterior distribution in support of *churn* = *true* as there is in support of *churn* = *false* for customers who belong to neither plan.

Thus, although the *MAP* classification is *churn* = *false* in each case, the "confidence" in the classification varies greatly, with the evidence for *churn* = *true* ranging from 5.6% up to 77.69% of the evidence for *churn* = *false*. For the customers who belong to the *International Plan*, the evidence for churn is much stronger. In fact, note from the *MAP* calculations above that the joint conditional probabilities for customers belonging to the *International Plan* (with or without the *Voice Mail Plan*) favored *churn* = *true*, but were overwhelmed by the preponderance of non-churners in the data set, from 85.51% to 14.49%, so that the *MAP* classification turned out to be *churn* = *false*. Thus, the posterior odds ratio allows us to assess the strength of evidence for our MAP classifications, which is more helpful to the analyst than a simple up-or-down decision.

14.4 BALANCING THE DATA

However, as the classification decision was influenced by the preponderance of non-churners in the data set, we may consider what might happen if we balanced the data set. Some data mining algorithms operate best when the relative frequencies of classes in the target variable are not extreme. For example, in fraud investigation, such a small percentage of transactions are fraudulent, that an algorithm could simply ignore such transactions, classify only *non-fraudulent*, and be correct 99.99% of the time. Therefore, balanced sampling methods are used to reduce the disparity among the proportions of target classes appearing in the training data.

In our case, we have 14.49% of the records representing churners, which may be considered somewhat uncommon, although one could argue otherwise. Nevertheless, let us balance the training data set, so that we have approximately 25% of the records representing churners. In Chapter 4, we learned two methods for balancing the data.

1. Resample a number of rare records.
2. Set aside a number of non-rare records.

Here we will balance the data by setting aside a number of the more common, non-churn records. This may be accomplished if we (i) accept all of the *churn* = *true* records, and (ii) take a random sample of 50% of our *churn* = *false* records. As the original data set had 483 churners and 2850 non-churners, this balancing procedure would provide us with $\frac{483}{(483+1425)} = 25.3\%$ *churn* = *true* records, as desired.

Hence, using the balanced *churn* data set, we once again compute the *MAP* estimate for *churn*, for our four types of customers. Our updated probability of churning is

$$P(C_{\text{Bal}}) = \frac{483}{(483 + 1425)} = 0.2531$$

and for not churning is

$$P(\overline{C}_{\text{Bal}}) = 1 - 0.2531 = 0.7469$$

For new customers who belong to the *International Plan* and *Voice Mail Plan,* we have

$$P(I \cap V | C_{\text{Bal}}) \cdot P(C_{\text{Bal}}) = (0.0745) \cdot (0.2531) = 0.0189$$

and

$$P(I \cap V | \overline{C}_{\text{Bal}}) \cdot P(\overline{C}_{\text{Bal}}) = (0.0196) \cdot (0.7469) = 0.0146$$

Thus, after balancing, C_{MAP}, the *MAP* estimate of *churn* is *churn = true,* because 0.0189 is the greater value. Balancing has reversed the classification decision for this category of customers.

For customers who belong to the *International Plan* only, we have

$$P(I \cap \overline{V} | C_{\text{Bal}}) \cdot P(C_{\text{Bal}}) = (0.2091) \cdot (0.2531) = 0.0529$$

and

$$P(I \cap \overline{V} | \overline{C}_{\text{Bal}}) \cdot P(\overline{C}_{\text{Bal}}) = (0.0456) \cdot (0.7469) = 0.0341$$

The *MAP* estimate C_{MAP} is now *churn = true,* because 0.0529 is the greater value. Once again, balancing has reversed the original classification decision for this category of customers.

For new customers belonging only to the *Voice Mail Plan,* we have

$$P(\overline{I} \cap V | C_{\text{Bal}}) \cdot P(C_{\text{Bal}}) = (0.0911) \cdot (0.2531) = 0.0231$$

and

$$P(\overline{I} \cap V | \overline{C}_{\text{Bal}}) \cdot P(\overline{C}_{\text{Bal}}) = (0.2758) \cdot (0.7469) = 0.2060$$

The *MAP* estimate has not changed from the original C_{MAP}: *churn = false* for members of the *Voice Mail Plan* only.

Finally, for new customers belonging to neither plan, we have

$$P(\overline{I} \cap \overline{V} | C_{\text{Bal}}) \cdot P(C_{\text{Bal}}) = (0.6253) \cdot (0.2531) = 0.1583$$

and

$$P(\overline{I} \cap \overline{V} | \overline{C}_{\text{Bal}}) \cdot P(\overline{C}_{\text{Bal}}) = (0.6589) \cdot (0.7469) = 0.4921$$

Again, the *MAP* estimate has not changed from the original C_{MAP}: *churn = false* for customers belonging to neither plan.

In the original data, *MAP* estimates were *churn = false* for all customers, a finding of limited actionability. Balancing the data set has provided different *MAP* estimates for different categories of new customers, providing executives with simple and actionable results. We may of course proceed to compute the posterior odds ratio for each of these classification decisions, if we are interested in assessing the strength of evidence for the classifications. The reader is invited to do so in the exercises.

14.5 NAÏVE BAYES CLASSIFICATION

For our simplified example using two dichotomous predictors and one dichotomous target variable, finding the *MAP* classification posed no computational difficulties.

However, Hand, Mannila, and Smyth[5] (page 354) state that, in general, the number of probabilities that would need to be calculated to find the *MAP* classification would be on the order of k^m, where k is the number of classes for the target variable, and m is the number of predictor variables. In our example, we had $k = 2$ classes in *churn*, and $m = 2$ predictors, meaning that we had to find four probabilities to render a classification decision, for example, $P(I \cap V | C)$, $P(C)$, $P(I \cap V | \overline{C})$, and $P(\overline{C})$.

However, suppose we are trying to predict the marital status ($k = 5$: single, married, divorced, widowed, separated) of individuals based on a set of $m = 10$ demographic predictors. Then, the number of probabilities to calculate would be on the order of $k^m = 5^{10} = 9,765,625$ probabilities. Note further that each of these 9,765,625 probabilities would need to be calculated based on relative frequencies of the appropriate cells in the 10-dimensional array. Using a minimum of 10 records per cell to estimate the relative frequencies, and on the unlikely assumption that the records are distributed uniformly across the array, the minimum requirement would be nearly 100 million records.

Thus, *MAP* classification is impractical to apply directly to any interesting real-world data mining scenarios. What, then, can be done?

MAP classification requires that we find:

$$\arg \max_{\theta} p(\mathbf{X}|\theta)p(\theta) = \arg \max_{\theta} p(X_1 = x_1, X_2 = x_2, \ldots, X_m = x_m | \theta)p(\theta).$$

The problem is not calculating $p(\theta)$, for which there is usually a small number of classes. Rather, the problem is the curse of dimensionality; that is, finding $p(X_1 = x_1, X_2 = x_2, \ldots, X_m = x_m | \theta)$ for all the possible combinations of the X-variables (the predictors). Here is where the search space explodes, so, if there is a way to cut down on the search space for this problem, then it is to be found right here.

Here is the key: Suppose we make the simplifying assumption that the predictor variables are conditionally independent, given the target value (e.g., *churn = false*). Two events A and B are said to be *conditionally independent* if, for a given event C, $p(A \cap B | C) = p(A|C) \cdot p(B|C)$. For example, conditional independence would state that, for customers who churn, membership in one of the two plans (I or V) would not affect the probability of membership in the other plan. Similarly, the idea extends to customers who do not churn.

In general, the assumption of conditional independence may be expressed as follows:

$$p(X_1 = x_1, X_2 = x_2, \ldots, X_m = x_m | \theta) = \prod_{i=1}^{m} p(X_i = x_i | \theta).$$

The *naïve Bayes classification* is therefore $\theta_{\text{NB}} = \arg \max_{\theta} \prod_{i=1}^{m} p(X_i = x_i | \theta)p(\theta)$.

When the conditional independence assumption is valid, the naïve Bayes classification is the same as the *MAP* classification. Therefore, we investigate whether

[5]David Hand, Heiki Mannila and Padhraic Smyth, *Principles of Data Mining*, MIT Press, Cambridge, Mass, 2001.

the assumption of conditional independence holds for our *churn* data set example, as shown in Table 14.5. In each case, note that the approximation for the non-churners is several times closer than for the churners. This may indicate that the assumption of conditional independence assumption is best validated for non-rare categories, another argument in support of balancing when necessary.

TABLE 14.5 **Checking the conditional independence assumption for** *churn* **data set**

$(I \cap V)|C$	$(I \cap \overline{V})|C$
$p(I \cap V|C) = 0.0745$	$p(I \cap \overline{V}|C) = 0.2091$
$p(I|C) \cdot p(V|C)$ $= (0.2836) \cdot (0.1656) = 0.0470$	$p(I|C) \cdot p(\overline{V}|C)$ $\cap (0.2836) \cdot (0.8344) = 0.2366$
Difference $= |0.0745 - 0.0470| = 0.0275$	Difference $= |0.2091 - 0.2366| = 0.0275$
$(I \cap V)|\overline{C}$	$(I \cap \overline{V})|\overline{C}$
$p(I \cap V|\overline{C}) = 0.0196$ $p(I|\overline{C}) \cdot p(V|\overline{C}) = (0.0653) \cdot (0.2954)$ $= 0.0193$ Difference $= |0.0196 - 0.0193|$ $= 0.0003$	$p(I \cap \overline{V}|\overline{C}) = 0.0456$ $p(I|\overline{C}) \cdot p(V|\overline{C}) = (0.0653) \cdot (0.7046)$ $= 0.0460$ Difference $= |0.0456 - 0.0460|$ $= 0.0004$
$(\overline{I} \cap V)|C$	$(\overline{I} \cap \overline{V})|C$
$p(\overline{I} \cap V|C) = 0.0911$ $p(\overline{I}|C) \cdot p(V|C) = (0.7164) \cdot (0.1656)$ $= 0.1186$ Difference $= |0.0911 - 0.1186|$ $= 0.0275$	$p(\overline{I} \cap \overline{V}|C) = 0.6253$ $p(\overline{I}|C) \cdot p(\overline{V}|C) = (0.7164) \cdot (0.8344)$ $= 0.5978$ Difference $= |0.6253 - 0.5978| = 0.0275$
$(\overline{I} \cap V)|\overline{C}$	$(\overline{I} \cap \overline{V})|\overline{C}$
$p(\overline{I} \cap V|\overline{C}) = 0.2758$ $p(\overline{I}|\overline{C}) \cdot p(V|\overline{C}) = (0.9347) \cdot (0.2954)$ $= 0.2761$ Difference $= |0.2758 - 0.2761|$ $= 0.0003$	$p(\overline{I} \cap \overline{V}|\overline{C}) = 0.6589$ $p(\overline{I}|\overline{C}) \cdot p(\overline{V}|\overline{C}) = (0.9347) \cdot (0.7046)$ $= 0.6586$ Difference $= |0.6589 - 0.6586| = 0.0003$

We now proceed to calculate naïve Bayes classifications for the *churn* data set. For a new customer belonging to both plans, we have for churners,

$$p(I|C) \cdot p(V|C) \cdot p(C) = (0.0470) \cdot (0.1449) = (0.0068)$$

and for non-churners,

$$p(I|\overline{C}) \cdot p(V|\overline{C}) \cdot p(\overline{C}) = (0.0193) \cdot (0.8551) = (0.0165)$$

The naïve Bayes classification for new customers who belong to both plans is therefore *churn = false* because 0.0165 is the larger of the two values. It turns out that, just as for the *MAP* classifier, all four cases return a naïve Bayes classification of *churn = false*. Also, after $\frac{25.31\%}{74.69\%}$ balancing, new customers who belong to the *International Plan* are classified by naïve Bayes as churners, regardless of *Voice Mail Plan* membership, just as for the *MAP* classifier. These results are left to the exercises for verification.

When using naïve Bayes classification, far fewer probabilities need to be estimated, just $k \cdot m$ probabilities rather than k^m for the *MAP* classifier; in other words, just the number of predictor variables times the number of distinct values of the target variable. In the marital status example, where we had $k = 5$ distinct marital statuses and $m = 10$ predictor variables, we would need to compute only $k \cdot m = 5 \cdot 10 = 50$ probabilities, rather than the 9.7 million needed for the *MAP* classifier. At 10 records per cell, that would mean that only 500 records would be needed, compared to the nearly 100 million calculated earlier. Clearly, the conditional independence assumption, when valid, makes our computational life much easier. Further, as the naïve Bayes classification is the same as the *MAP* classification when the conditional independence assumption is met, then the naïve Bayes classification is also optimal, in the sense of minimizing the error rate over all classifiers. In practice, however, departures from the conditional independence assumption tend to inhibit the optimality of the naïve Bayes classifier.

The conditional independence assumption should not be made blindly. Correlated predictors, for example, violate the assumption. For example, in classifying risk for credit default, total assets and annual income would probably be correlated. However, naïve Bayes would, for each classification (default, no default), consider total assets and annual income to be independent and uncorrelated. Of course, careful data mining practice includes dealing with correlated variables at the exploratory data analysis (EDA) stage anyway, because the correlation can cause problems for several different data methods. Principal components analysis can be used to handle correlated variables. Another option is to construct a user-defined composite, a linear combination of a small set of highly correlated variables. (See Chapter 1 for more information on handling correlated variables.)

14.6 INTERPRETING THE LOG POSTERIOR ODDS RATIO

Next, we examine the log of the posterior odds ratio, which can provide us with an intuitive measure of the amount that each variable contributes toward the classification decision. The posterior odds ratio takes the form:

$$\frac{p(\theta_c|\mathbf{X})}{p(\theta_{\bar{c}}|\mathbf{X})} = \frac{p(\mathbf{X}|\theta_c) \cdot p(\theta_c)}{p(\mathbf{X}|\theta_{\bar{c}}) \cdot p(\theta_{\bar{c}})}$$

$$= \frac{p(X_1 = x_1, X_2 = x_2, \ldots, X_m = x_m|\theta) \cdot p(\theta_c)}{p(X_1 = x_1, X_2 = x_2, \ldots, X_m = x_m|\theta) \cdot p(\theta_{\bar{c}})}$$

$$\underset{=}{\overset{\text{conditional}}{\underset{\text{assumption}}{\text{independence}}}} \frac{\prod\limits_{i=1}^{m} p(X_i = x_i|\theta) \cdot p(\theta_c)}{\prod\limits_{i=1}^{m} p(X_i = x_i|\theta) \cdot p(\theta_{\bar{c}})},$$

which is the form of the posterior odds ratio for naïve Bayes.

Next, consider the log of the posterior odds ratio. As the log of a product is the sum of the logs, we have:

$$\log\left(\frac{\prod\limits_{i=1}^{m} p\left(X_i = x_i|\theta\right) \cdot p(\theta_c)}{\prod\limits_{i=1}^{m} p(X_i = x_i|\bar{\theta}) \cdot p(\bar{\theta}_c)}\right)$$

$$= \log\left(\prod\limits_{i=1}^{m} p\left(X_i = x_i|\theta\right)\right) + m \log p(\theta_c) - \log\left(\prod\limits_{i=1}^{m} p\left(X_i = x_i|\bar{\theta}\right)\right)$$

$$- m \log p(\bar{\theta}_c)$$

$$= m \log \frac{p(\theta_c)}{p(\bar{\theta}_c)} + \sum\limits_{i=1}^{m} \log\left(\frac{p\left(X_i = x_i|\theta\right)}{p(X_i = x_i|\bar{\theta})}\right).$$

This form of the log posterior odds ratio is useful from an interpretive point of view, because each term,

$$\log\left(\frac{p\left(X_i = x_i|\theta\right)}{p(X_i = x_i|\bar{\theta})}\right)$$

relates to the additive contribution, either positive or negative, of each attribute.

For example, consider the log posterior odds ratio for a new customer who belongs to both the *International Plan* and *Voice Mail Plan*. Then, for the *International Plan*, we have

$$\log\left(\frac{p(I|C)}{p(I|\bar{C})}\right) = \log\left(\frac{0.2836}{0.0653}\right) = 0.6378$$

and for the *Voice Mail Plan*, we have

$$\log\left(\frac{p(V|C)}{p(V|\bar{C})}\right) = \log\left(\frac{0.1656}{0.2954}\right) = -0.2514$$

Thus, we see that membership in the International Plan contributes in a positive way to the likelihood that a particular customer will churn, while membership in the Voice Mail Plan decreases the churn probability. These findings concur with our exploratory results from Chapter 3, *Exploratory Data Analysis*.

14.7 ZERO-CELL PROBLEM

As we saw in Chapter 13, *Logistic Regression,* a cell with frequency zero can pose difficulties for the analysis. Now, for naïve Bayes estimation, what if a particular cell (combination of attribution values) has a zero frequency? For example, of the 483 customers who churned, 80 had the *Voice Mail Plan,* so that $p(V|C) = \frac{80}{483} = 0.1656$. However, suppose none of the churners had the *Voice Mail Plan.* Then $p(V|C)$ would equal $\frac{0}{483} = 0.0$. The real problem with this is that, because the conditional independence assumption means that we take the product of the marginal probabilities, this zero value for $p(V|C)$ will percolate through and dominate the result. As the naïve Bayes classification contains $\prod_{i=1}^{m} p(X_i = x_i|\theta)$, a single zero probability in this product will render the entire product to be zero, which will also make $\prod_{i=1}^{m} p(X_i = x_i|\theta) \cdot p(\theta)$ equal to zero, thereby effectively eliminating this class (*churn = true*) from consideration for any future probability involving the *Voice Mail Plan.*

To avoid this problem, we posit an additional number of "virtual" samples, which provides the following adjusted probability estimate for zero-frequency cells:

ADJUSTED PROBABILITY ESTIMATE FOR ZERO-FREQUENCY CELLS

$$\frac{n_c + n_{equiv} \cdot p}{n + n_{equiv}}$$

where n represents the total number of records for this target class, n_c represents the number of these n records that also have the attribute value of interest, p is the prior estimate of the probability being estimated, and n_{equiv} is a constant representing the *equivalent sample size.*

The constant n_{equiv} represents the additional number of virtual samples used to find the adjusted probability, and controls how heavily the adjustment is weighted. The prior probability estimate p may be assigned, in the absence of other information, to be the non-informative uniform prior $p = \frac{1}{k}$, where k is the number of classes for the target variable. Thus, n_{equiv} additional samples, distributed according to p, are contributed to the calculation of the probability.

In our example, we have $n = 483$, $n_c = 0$, and $p = \frac{1}{2}$. We choose $n_{equiv} = 1$ to minimize the effect of the intervention. The adjusted probability estimate for the zero probability cell for $p(V|C)$ is therefore: $\frac{n_c + n_{equiv} \cdot p}{n + n_{equiv}} = \frac{0 + 1 \cdot (1/2)}{483 + 1} = 0.0010$.

14.8 NUMERIC PREDICTORS FOR NAÏVE BAYES CLASSIFICATION

Bayesian classification can be extended from categorical to continuous predictor variables, provided we know the relevant probability distribution. Suppose that, in addition to *International Plan* and *Voice Mail Plan*, we also had access to *Total Minutes*, the total number of minutes used by the cell-phone customer, along with evidence that the distribution of *Total Minutes* is normal, for both churners and non-churners. The mean *Total Minutes* for churners is $\mu_{churn} = 635$ minutes, with a standard deviation of $\sigma_{churn} = 111$ minutes. The mean *Total Minutes* for non-churners is $\mu_{non-churn} = 585$ with a standard deviation of $\sigma_{non-churn} = 84$ minutes. Thus, we assume that the distribution of *Total Minutes* for churners is Normal(635, 111) and for non-churners is Normal(585, 84).

Let T_{churn} represent the random variable *Total Minutes* for churners. Then,

$$p(T_{churn} = t) \cong f_{T|C}$$

$$= \frac{1}{\sqrt{2\pi}\sigma_{churn}} \exp\left(\frac{-1}{2\sigma^2_{churn}}\left(t - \mu_{churn}\right)^2\right)$$

$$= \frac{1}{\sqrt{2\pi}(111)} \exp\left(\frac{-1}{2(111)^2}(t - 635)^2\right),$$

with an analogous form for non-churners. (Here, $\exp(y)$ represents e^y.)

Also, $f_{T|C}(t)$ is substituted for $p(T = t|C)$, because, for continuous random variables, $p(T = t) = 0, \forall t$.

Next, suppose we are interested in classifying new customers who have 800 *Total Minutes*, and belong to both plans, using naïve Bayes classification. We have:

For churners:

$$p(I \cap V \cap T = 800|C) \cdot P(C) = P(I|C) \cdot P(V|C) \cdot f_{T|C}(800) \cdot P(C)$$

$$= (0.2836) \cdot (0.1656) \cdot (0.001191) \cdot (0.1449)$$

$$= 0.000008105$$

and for non-churners:

$$p(I \cap V \cap T = 800|\overline{C}) \cdot P(\overline{C}) = P(I|\overline{C}) \cdot P(V|\overline{C}) \cdot f_{T|\overline{C}}(800) \cdot P(\overline{C})$$

$$= (0.0653) \cdot (0.2954) \cdot (0.0001795) \cdot (0.8551)$$

$$= 0.000002961$$

Hence, the naïve Bayes classification for new customers who have 800 *Total Minutes* and belong to both plans is *churn = true*, by a posterior odds ratio of

$$\frac{0.000008105}{0.000002961} = 2.74$$

In other words, the additional information that the new customer had 800 *Total Minutes* was enough to *reverse the classification* from *churn = false* (previously, without *Total Minutes*) to *churn = true*. This is due to the somewhat heavier cell-phone usage of the churners group, with a higher mean *Total Minutes*.

Now, assumptions of normality should not be made without supporting evidence. Consider Figure 14.2, a comparison dot plot of the two distributions. Immediately we can see that indeed there are many more non-churner records than churners. We also note that the balancing point (the mean, indicated by the triangle) for churners is greater than for non-churners, supporting the above statistics. Finally, we notice that the normality assumption for non-churners looks quite solid, while the normality assumption for the churners looks a little shaky.

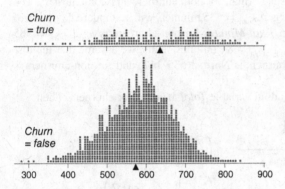

Figure 14.2   Comparison dot plot of *Total Minutes* for churners and non-churners.

Normal probability plots are then constructed for the two distributions just described, and shown in Figure 14.3. In a normal probability plot, there should be no systematic deviations from linearity; otherwise, the normality assumption is called

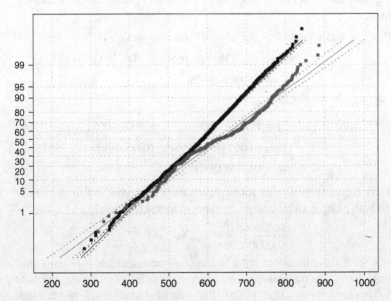

Figure 14.3   Normal probability plots of *Total Minutes* for churners and non-churners.

into question. In Figure 14.3, the bulk of the points for the non-churners line up nearly perfectly on a straight line, indicating that the normality assumption is validated for non-churners' *Total Minutes*. However, there does appear to be systematic curvature in the churners' data points, in a slight backwards S-curve, indicating that the normality assumption for churners' *Total Minutes* is not validated. As the assumption is not validated, then all subsequent inference applying this assumption must be flagged as such for the end-user. For example, the naïve Bayes classification of *churn = true* may or may not be valid, and the end-user should be informed of this uncertainty.

Often, non-normal distribution can be transformed to normality, using, for example, the *Box–Cox* transformation $T(y) = \frac{(y^\lambda - 1)}{\lambda}$. However, Figure 14.2 shows that *Total Minutes* for churners actually looks like a mixture of two normal distributions, which will prove resistant to monotonic transformations to normality. The mixture idea is intriguing and deserves further investigation, which we do not have space for here. Data transformations were investigated more fully in Chapters 8 and 9.

Alternatively, one may dispense with the normality assumption altogether, and choose to work directly with the observed empirical distribution of *Total Minutes* for churners and non-churners. We are interested in comparing the $p(T = 800)$ for each distribution; why not estimate this probability by directly estimating $p(798 \le T \le 802)$ for each distribution? It turns out that three of the churner customers had between 798 and 802 total minutes, compared to one for the non-churner customers. So, the probability estimates would be $p(T = 800|C) \cong \frac{3}{483} = 0.006211$ for the churners, and $p(T = 800|\overline{C}) \cong \frac{1}{2850} = 0.0003509$ for the non-churners.

Thus, to find the naïve Bayes classification for churners,

$$p(I \cap V \cap T = 800|C) \cdot P(C) = P(I|C) \cdot P(V|C) \cdot \hat{f}_{T|C}(800) \cdot P(C)$$

$$= (0.2836) \cdot (0.1656) \cdot (0.006211) \cdot (0.1449)$$

$$= 0.00004227,$$

and for non-churners,

$$p(I \cap V \cap T = 800|\overline{C}) \cdot P(\overline{C}) = P(I|\overline{C}) \cdot P(V|\overline{C}) \cdot \hat{f}_{T|\overline{C}}(800) \cdot P(\overline{C})$$

$$= (0.0653) \cdot (0.2954) \cdot (0.0003509) \cdot (0.8551)$$

$$= 0.000005788.$$

(Here, $\hat{f}_{T|C}(800)$ represents our empirical estimate of $f_{T|C}(800)$.)

Thus, once again, the naïve Bayes classification for new customers who have 800 *Total Minutes* and belong to both plans is *churn = true,* this time by a posterior odds ratio of $\frac{0.00004227}{0.000005788} = 7.30$. The evidence is even more solid in favor of a classification of *churn = true* for these customers, and we did not have to burden ourselves with an assumption about normality.

The empirical probability estimation method shown here should be verified over a range of margins of error. Above, we found the numbers of records within a margin of error of 2 records ($798 \le T \le 802$). The reader may verify that that there are 8 churn records and 3 non-churn records within 5 minutes of the desired 800 minutes;

and that there are 15 churn records and 5 non-churn records within 10 minutes of the desired 800 minutes. So the approximate $3:1$ ratio of churn records to non-churn records in this area of the distribution seems fairly stable.

14.9 WEKA: HANDS-ON ANALYSIS USING NAÏVE BAYES

In this exercise, Waikato Environment for Knowledge Analysis's (WEKA's) naïve Bayes classifier is used to classify a small set of movie reviews as either positive (pos) or negative (neg). First, the text from 20 actual reviews is preprocessed to create a training file *movies_train.arff* containing three Boolean attributes and a target variable. This file is used to train our naïve Bayes model and contains a set of 20 individual review instances, where 10 reviews have the class value "pos," and the remaining 10 reviews take on the class value "neg." Similarly, a second file is created to test our model. In this case, *movies_test.arff* only contains four review instances, where two are positive and the remaining two are negative.

During the preprocessing stage, the unigrams (specifically adjectives) are extracted from the reviews and a list of adjectives is derived. The three most frequently occurring adjectives are chosen from the list and form the set of attributes used by each review instance. Specifically, each instance is represented as a Boolean document vector of length three, where each attribute's value is either 1 or 0, corresponding to whether the review contains or does not contain the particular adjective, respectively. The Attribute-Relation File Format (ARFF)-based training file *movies_train.arff* is shown in Table 14.6.

All attributes in the ARFF file are nominal and take on one of two values; inputs are either "0" or "1," and the target variable *CLASS* is either "pos" or "neg." The *data* section lists each instance, which corresponds to a specific movie review record. For example, the third line in the data section corresponds to a review where *more* = 1, *much* = 1, *other* = 0, and *CLASS* = neg.

Now, we load the training file and build the naïve Bayes classification model.

1. Click Explorer from the WEKA GUI Chooser dialog.
2. On the Preprocess tab, press Open file and specify the path to the training file, *movies_train.arff*.
3. Select the Classify tab.
4. Under Classifier, press the Choose button
5. Select Classifiers → Bayes → Naïve Bayes from the navigation hierarchy.
6. In our modeling experiment, we have separate training and test sets; therefore, under Test options, choose the Use training set option.
7. Click Start to build the model.

WEKA creates the naïve Bayes model and produces the results in the Classifier output window as shown in Figure 14.4. In general, the results indicate that the classification accuracy of the model, as measured against the training set, is 65% $\left(\frac{13}{20}\right)$.

TABLE 14.6   ARFF Movies Training File *movies_train.arff*.

```
@relation movies_train.arff

@attribute more          {0, 1}
@attribute much          {0, 1}
@attribute other         {0, 1}
@attribute CLASS         {neg, pos}

@data
1, 0, 0, neg
1, 1, 0, neg

1, 1, 0, neg

0, 1, 1, neg

1, 1, 1, neg

1, 1, 0, neg

1, 0, 0, neg

1, 0, 1, neg

1, 1, 1, neg

1, 1, 1, neg

1, 1, 1, pos

1, 0, 1, pos

1, 1, 1, pos

1, 1, 1, pos

1, 0, 0, pos

1, 1, 0, pos

0, 1, 1, pos

1, 0, 1, pos

0, 0, 0, pos

1, 1, 1, pos
```

Next, our model is evaluated against the unseen data found in the test set, *movies_test.arff*.

1. Under Test options, choose Supplied test set. Click Set.
2. Click Open file, specify the path to the test file, *movies_test.arff*. Close the Test Instances dialog.
3. Check the Output text predictions on test set option. Click OK.

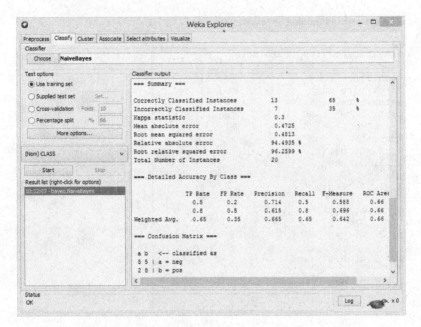

Figure 14.4   WEKA Explorer: naïve Bayes training results.

Click the Start button to evaluate the model against the test set.

Surprisingly, the Explorer Panel shows that our naïve Bayes model has classified all four movie reviews in the test set correctly. Although these results are encouraging, from a real-world perspective, the training set lacks a sufficient number of both attributes and examples to be considered practical in any real sense. We continue with the objective of becoming familiar with the naïve Bayes classifier. Let us explore how naïve Bayes arrived at the decision to classify the fourth record in the test set correctly. First, however, we examine the probabilities reported by the naïve Bayes classifier.

The naïve Bayes model reports the actual probabilities it used to classify each review instance from the test set as either "pos" or "neg." For example, Table 14.7 shows that naïve Bayes has classified the fourth instance from the test set as "pos" with a probability equal to 0.60.

In Table 14.8, the conditional probabilities are calculated that correspond to the data found in *movies_train.arff*. For example, given that the review is negative, the conditional probability of the word "more" occurring is $p(more = 1 | CLASS = neg) = \frac{9}{10}$. In addition, we also know the prior probabilities of $p(CLASS = pos) = p(CLASS = neg) = \frac{10}{20} = 0.5$. These simply correspond with the fact that our training set is balanced $\frac{50}{50}$.

Recall the method of adjusting the probability estimate to avoid zero-frequency cells, as described earlier in the chapter. In this particular case, naïve Bayes produces an internal adjustment, where $n_{equiv} = 2$ and $p = 0.5$, to produce $\frac{(n_c+1)}{n+2}$. Therefore,

TABLE 14.7   Naive bayes test set predictions

```
=== Predictions on test split ===

inst#,    actual, predicted, error, probability distribution
```

inst#	actual	predicted	error	probability distribution	
1	1:neg	1:neg		*0.533	0.467
2	1:neg	1:neg		*0.533	0.467
3	2:pos	2:pos		0.444	*0.556
4	2:pos	2:pos		0.4	*0.6

TABLE 14.8   Conditional probabilities derived from *movies_training.arff*

more		much		other	
neg					
1	0	1	0	1	0
9/10	1/10	7/10	3/10	5/10	5/10
pos					
1	0	1	0	1	0
8/10	2/10	6/10	4/10	7/10	3/10

we now calculate the probably of the fourth review from the test as set being either "pos" or "neg":

$$\prod_{i=1}^{3} p(X_i = x_i | CLASS = pos)p(CLASS = pos)$$

$$= \left(\frac{8+1}{10+2}\right) \cdot \left(\frac{4+1}{10+2}\right) \cdot \left(\frac{7+1}{10+2}\right) \cdot (0.5)$$

$$= \left(\frac{9}{12}\right) \cdot \left(\frac{5}{12}\right) \cdot \left(\frac{8}{12}\right) \cdot (0.5) \approx 0.1042$$

$$\prod_{i=1}^{3} p(X_i = x_i | CLASS)p(CLASS = neg)$$

$$= \left(\frac{9+1}{10+2}\right) \cdot \left(\frac{3+1}{10+2}\right) \cdot \left(\frac{5+1}{10+2}\right) \cdot (0.5)$$

$$= \left(\frac{10}{12}\right) \cdot \left(\frac{4}{12}\right) \cdot \left(\frac{6}{12}\right) \cdot (0.5) \approx 0.0694$$

Finally, we normalize the probabilities and determine:

$$p(pos) = \frac{0.1042}{0.1042 + 0.0694} \approx 0.6002$$

$$p(neg) = \frac{0.0694}{0.1042 + 0.0694} \approx 0.3998$$

Here, the review is classified as positive with a 0.60 probability. These results agree with those reported by WEKA in Table 14.7, which also classified the review as positive. In fact, our hand-calculated probabilities match those reported by WEKA. Although the data set used for this example is rather small, it demonstrates the use of the naïve Bayes classifier in WEKA when using separate training and test files. More importantly, our general understanding of the algorithm has increased, as a result of computing the probabilities that led to an actual classification by the model.

14.10 BAYESIAN BELIEF NETWORKS

Naïve Bayes classification assumes that the attributes are conditionally independent, given the value of the target variable. This assumption may in fact be too strong for environments where dependence exists among the predictor variables. *Bayesian belief networks (BBNs)* are designed to allow joint conditional independencies to be defined among subsets of variables. *BBNs,* also called *Bayesian networks* or *Bayes nets,* take the form of a directed acyclic graph (DAG), where *directed* means that the arcs are traversed in one direction only, and *acyclic* means that no child node cycles backup to any progenitor.

An example of a Bayesian network in the form of a DAG is shown in Figure 14.5. The nodes represent variables, and the arcs represent the (directed) dependence among the variables. In general, Node A is a *parent* or *immediate predecessor* of Node X, and Node X is a *descendant* of Node A, if there exists a directed arc from A to X. The intrinsic relationship among the variables in a Bayesian network is as follows:

Each variable in a Bayesian network is conditionally independent of its non-descendants in the network, given its parents.

Thus, we have:

$$p(X_1 = x_1, X_2 = x_2, \dots, X_m = x_m) = \prod_{i=1}^{m} p(X_i = x_i | parents(X_i)). \quad (14.4)$$

Note that the child node probability depends only on its parents.

14.11 CLOTHING PURCHASE EXAMPLE

To introduce Bayesian networks, we shall use the clothing purchase example, illustrated by the Bayes net in Figure 14.5. Suppose a clothes retailer operates two outlets, one in New York and one in Los Angeles, each producing sales throughout the four seasons. The retailer is interested in probabilities concerning three articles of clothing, in particular, warm coats, business shirts, and Bermuda shorts. Questions of interest include the fabric weight of the article of clothing (light, medium, or heavy), and the color of the article (bright, neutral, or dark).

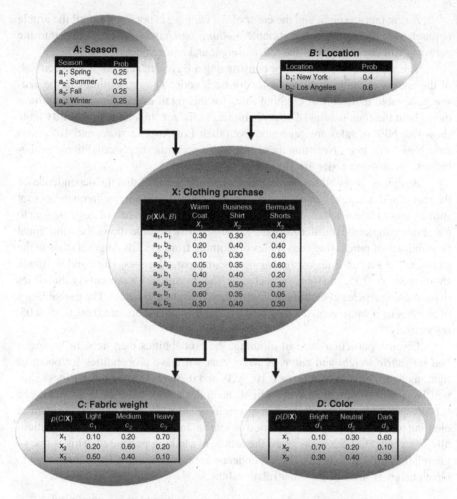

A: Season

Season	Prob
a_1: Spring	0.25
a_2: Summer	0.25
a_3: Fall	0.25
a_4: Winter	0.25

B: Location

Location	Prob
b_1: New York	0.4
b_2: Los Angeles	0.6

X: Clothing purchase

$p(X|A, B)$	Warm Coat X_1	Business Shirt X_2	Bermuda Shorts X_3
a_1, b_1	0.30	0.30	0.40
a_1, b_2	0.20	0.40	0.40
a_2, b_1	0.10	0.30	0.60
a_2, b_2	0.05	0.35	0.60
a_3, b_1	0.40	0.40	0.20
a_3, b_2	0.20	0.50	0.30
a_4, b_1	0.60	0.35	0.05
a_4, b_2	0.30	0.40	0.30

C: Fabric weight

$p(C|X)$	Light c_1	Medium c_2	Heavy c_3
X_1	0.10	0.20	0.70
X_2	0.20	0.60	0.20
X_3	0.50	0.40	0.10

D: Color

$p(D|X)$	Bright d_1	Neutral d_2	Dark d_3
X_1	0.10	0.30	0.60
X_2	0.70	0.20	0.10
X_3	0.30	0.40	0.30

Figure 14.5   A Bayesian network for the clothing purchase example.

To build a Bayesian network, there are two main considerations:

1. What is the dependence relationship among the variables of interest?
2. What are the associated "local" probabilities?

The retailer has five variables: *season, location, clothing purchase, fabric weight,* and *color.* What is the dependence relationship among these variables? For example, does the season of the year depend on the color of the clothes purchased? Certainly not, because a customer's purchase of some bright clothing does not mean that spring is here, for example, although the customer may wish it so. In fact, the season of the year does not depend on any of the other variables, and so we place the node for the variable *season* at the top of the Bayes network, which indicates that it does not depend on the other variables. Similarly, *location* does not depend on the other variables, and is therefore placed at the top of the network.

As the fabric weight and the color of the clothing is not known until the article is purchased, the node for the variable *clothing purchase* is inserted next into the network, with arcs to each of the *fabric weight* and *color* nodes.

The second consideration for constructing a Bayesian network is to specify all of the entries in the probability tables for each node. The probabilities in the *season* node table indicate that clothing sales for this retail establishment are uniform throughout the four seasons. The probabilities in the *location* node probability table show that 60% of sales are generated from their Los Angeles store, and 40% from their New York store. Note that these two tables need not supply conditional probabilities, because the nodes are at the top of the network.

Assigning probabilities for *clothing purchase* requires that the dependence on the parent nodes be taken into account. Expert knowledge or relative frequencies (not shown) should be consulted. Note that the probabilities in each row of the table sum to one. For example, the fourth row of the *clothing purchase* table shows the conditional probabilities of purchasing the articles of clothing from the Los Angeles store in the summer. The probabilities of purchasing a warm coat, a business shirt, and Bermuda shorts are 0.05, 0.35, and 0.60, respectively. The seventh row represents probabilities of purchasing articles of clothing from the New York store in winter. The probabilities of purchasing a warm coat, a business shirt, and Bermuda shorts are 0.60, 0.35, 0.05, respectively.

Given a particular item of clothing, the probabilities then need to be specified for *fabric weight* and *color*. A warm coat will have probabilities for being of light, medium, or heavy fabric or 0.10, 0.20, and 0.70, respectively. A business shirt will have probabilities of having bright, neutral, or dark color of 0.70, 0.20, and 0.10, respectively. Note that the fabric weight or color depends only on the item of clothing purchased, and not the location or season. In other words, *color* is conditionally independent of *location*, given the article of clothing purchased. This is one of the relationships of conditional independence to be found in this Bayesian network. Given below is some of the other relationships:

- *Color* is conditionally independent of *season*, given clothing purchased.
- *Color* is conditionally independent of *fabric weight*, given clothing purchased.
- *Fabric weight* is conditionally independent of *color*, given clothing purchased.
- *Fabric weight* is conditionally independent of *location*, given clothing purchased.
- *Fabric weight* is conditionally independent of *season*, given clothing purchased.

Note that we could say that *season* is conditionally independent of *location*, given its parents. But as *season* has no parents in the Bayes net, this means that *season* and *location* are (unconditionally) independent.

Be careful when inserting arcs into the Bayesian network, because these represent strong assertions of conditional independence.

14.12   USING THE BAYESIAN NETWORK TO FIND PROBABILITIES

Next, suppose we would like to find the probability that a given purchase involved light-fabric, neutral-colored Bermuda shorts were purchased in New York in the winter. Using equation (14.4), we may express what we seek as:

$$
\begin{aligned}
p(A = a_4, B &= b_1, C = c_1, D = d_2, X = x_3) \\
&= p(A = a_4) \cdot p(B = b_1) \cdot p(X = x_3 | A = a_4 \cap B = b_1) \\
&\quad \cdot p(C = c_1 | X = x_3) \cdot p(D = d_2 | X = x_3) \\
&= p(season = winter) \cdot p(location = New\ York) \\
&\quad \cdot p(clothing = shorts | season = winter\ and\ location = New\ York) \\
&\quad \cdot p(fabric = light | clothing = shorts) \cdot p(color = neutral | clothing = shorts) \\
&= (0.25) \cdot (0.4) \cdot (0.05) \cdot (0.50) \cdot (0.40) = 0.001.
\end{aligned}
$$

Evidently, there is not much demand for light-fabric, neutral-colored Bermuda shorts in New York in the winter.

Similarly, probabilities may be found in this way for any combinations of season, location, article of clothing, fabric weight, and color. Using the Bayesian network structure, we can also calculate prior probabilities for each node. For example, the prior probability of a warm coat is found as follows:

$$
\begin{aligned}
p(coat) &= p(X = x_1) \\
&= p(X = x_1 | A = a_1 \cap B = b_1) \cdot p(A = a_1 \cap B = b_1) \\
&\quad + p(X = x_1 | A = a_1 \cap B = b_2) \cdot p(A = a_1 \cap B = b_2) \\
&\quad + p(X = x_1 | A = a_2 \cap B = b_1) \cdot p(A = a_2 \cap B = b_1) \\
&\quad + p(X = x_1 | A = a_2 \cap B = b_2) \cdot p(A = a_2 \cap B = b_2) \\
&\quad + p(X = x_1 | A = a_3 \cap B = b_1) \cdot p(A = a_3 \cap B = b_1) \\
&\quad + p(X = x_1 | A = a_3 \cap B = b_2) \cdot p(A = a_3 \cap B = b_2) \\
&\quad + p(X = x_1 | A = a_4 \cap B = b_1) \cdot p(A = a_4 \cap B = b_1) \\
&\quad + p(X = x_1 | A = a_4 \cap B = b_2) \cdot p(A = a_4 \cap B = b_2) \\
&= (0.30) \cdot (0.10) + (0.20) \cdot (0.15) + (0.10) \cdot (0.10) + (0.05) \cdot (0.15) \\
&\quad + (0.40) \cdot (0.10) + (0.20) \cdot (0.15) + (0.60) \cdot (0.10) + (0.30) \cdot (0.15) \\
&= 0.2525.
\end{aligned}
$$

So the prior probability of purchasing a warm coat is 0.2525. Note that we used the information that *season* and *location* are independent, so that $p(A \cap B) = p(A) \cdot p(B)$. For example, the probability that a sale is made in the spring in New York is $p(A = a_1 \cap B = b_1) = p(A = a_1) \cdot p(B = b_1) = (0.25) \cdot (0.4) = 0.10$.

Posterior probabilities may also be found. For example,

$$
p(winter | coat) = \frac{p(winter \cap coat)}{p(coat)}.
$$

To find $p(winter \cap coat)$, we must first find $p(winter \cap New\ York \cap coat)$ and $p(winter \cap Los\ Angeles \cap coat)$. Using the conditional probability structure of the Bayesian network in Figure 14.5, we have

$p(winter \cap New\ York \cap coat)$

$= p(winter) \cdot p(New\ York) \cdot p(coat|winter \cap New\ York)$

$= (0.25) \cdot (0.4) \cdot (0.6) = 0.06,$

$p(winter \cap Los\ Angeles \cap coat)$

$= p(winter) \cdot p(Los\ Angeles) \cdot p(coat|winter \cap Los\ Angeles)$

$= (0.25) \cdot (0.6) \cdot (0.3) = 0.045.$

So, $p(winter \cap coat) = 0.06 + 0.045 = 0.105$.

Thus, we have $p(winter|coat) = p(winter \cap coat)/p(coat) = 0.105 / 0.2525 = 0.4158$. Then the Bayes net could provide a classification decision using the highest posterior probability, among $p(winter|coat)$, $p(spring|coat)$, $p(summer|coat)$, and $p(fall|coat)$ (see Exercises).

A Bayesian network represents the joint probability distribution for a given set of variables. What is a joint probability distribution? Let $X_1, X_2, \ldots, X_m$ represent a set of m random variables, with each random variable X_i defined on space S_{X_i}. For example, a normal random variable X is defined on space S_X, where S_X is the real number line. Then the joint space of $X_1, X_2, \ldots, X_m$ is defined as the Cartesian product $S_{X_1} \times S_{X_2} \times \cdots \times S_{X_m}$. That is, each joint observation consists of the vector of length m of observed field values $\langle x_1, x_2, \ldots, x_m \rangle$. The distribution of these observations over the joint space is called the *joint probability distribution*.

The Bayesian network represents the joint probability distribution by providing (i) a specified set of assumptions regarding the conditional independence of the variables, and (ii) the probability tables for each variable, given its direct predecessors. For each variable, information regarding both (i) and (ii) are provided.

For a subset of variables, $X_1, X_2, \ldots, X_m$, the joint probability may be found thus:

$$p(X_1 = x_1, X_2 = x_2, \ldots, X_m = x_m) = \prod_{i=1}^{m} p(X_i = x_i | parents(X_i)),$$

where we define $parents(X_i)$ to be the set of immediate predecessors of X_i in the network. The probabilities $p(X_i = x_i | parents(X_i)p(X_i = x_i | parents(X_i))$ are the probabilities that have been specified in the probability table associated with the node for X_i.

How does learning take place in a Bayesian network? When the structure of the network is known, and the field values have all been observed, then learning in Bayesian nets is straightforward. The local (node-specific) probability tables are fully specified, and any desired joint, conditional, prior, or posterior probability may be calculated.

However, when some of the field values are hidden or unknown, then we need to turn to other methods, with the goal of filling in all the entries in the local probability distribution table. Russell *et al.*[6] suggest a gradient descent method for learning in Bayesian networks. In this paradigm, the unknown entries in the probability distribution tables are considered to be unknown weights, and gradient descent methods, analogous to the neural network learning case (Chapter 12 of this book, or Chapter 4 of Mitchell[7]), can be applied to find the optimal set of weights (probability values), given the data.

Bayes nets were originally designed to aid subject matter experts to graphically specify the conditional independence structure among variables. However, analysts may also attempt to discern the unknown structure of Bayes nets by studying the dependence and independence relationships among the observed variable values. Sprites, Glymour, and Scheines[8] and Ramoni and Sebastian[9] provide further information about learning both the content and structure of Bayesian networks.

14.12.1 WEKA: Hands-On Analysis Using Bayes Net

Let us revisit the movies data set; however, this time, classification of the data is explored using WEKA's Bayes net classifier. Similarly to our last experiment, the 20 instances in *movies_train.arff* are used to train our model, whereas it is tested using the four reviews in *movies_test.arff*. Let us begin by loading the training file.

1. Click Explorer from the WEKA GUI Chooser dialog.
2. On the Preprocess tab, press Open file and specify the path to the training file, *movies_train.arff*.
3. If successful, the Explorer Panel looks similar to Figure 14.6, and indicates the relation *movies_train.arff* consists of 20 instances with four attributes. It also shows, by default, that *CLASS* is specified as the class variable for the data set. Next, select the Classify tab.
4. Under Classifier, press the Choose button.
5. Select Classifiers → Bayes → BayesNet from the navigation hierarchy.
6. Under Test options, specify Supplied training set.
7. Click Start.

The results are reported in the Classifier output window. The classification accuracy for Bayes net is 65% (13/20), which is identical to the results reported by naïve Bayes. Again, let us evaluate our classification model using the data from

---

[6]Russell, Binder, Koller, and Kanazawa, 1995. Local learning in probabilistic networks with hidden variables. In *Proceedings of the Fourteenth International Joint Conference on Artificial Intelligence*, pages 1146–1152. San Francisco: Morgan Kaufmann, 1995.

[7]Tom Mitchell, 1997. *Machine Learning*, WCB-McGraw-Hill, Boston.

[8]Sprites, Glymour, and Scheines, *Causation, Prediction, and Search*. Springer Verlag, New York, 1993.

[9]Ramoni and Sebastian, Bayesian Methods, in *Intelligent Data Analysis*, Michael Berthold and David J. Hand, editors, Springer, Berlin, 1999.

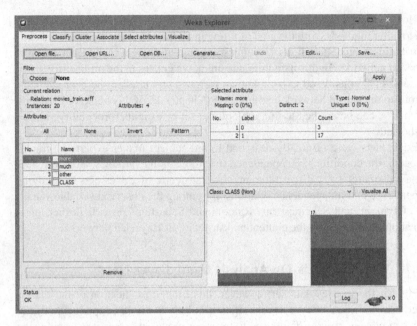

Figure 14.6   WEKA explorer panel: preprocess tab.

movies_test.arff, with the goal of determining the probabilities by which Bayes net classifies these instances.

1. Under Test options, choose Supplied test set. Click Set.
2. Click Open file, specify the path to the test file, *movies_test.arff.* Close the Test Instances dialog.
3. Next, click the More options button.
4. Check the Output text predictions on test set option. Click OK.
5. Click the Start button to evaluate the model against the test set.

Now, the predictions for each instance, including their associated probability, are reported in the Classifier output window. For example, Bayes net correctly classified instance three as "pos," with probability 0.577, as shown in Table 14.9. Next, let us evaluate how Bayes net made its classification decision for the third instance.

First, recall the data set used to build our model, as shown in Table 14.6. From here the prior probabilities for the attributes *more, much,* and *other* can be derived; for example, $p(more = 1) = \frac{17}{20}$ and $p(more = 0) = \frac{3}{20}$. In addition, to avoid zero-probability cells, Bayes net uses a simple estimation method that adds 0.5 to each cell count. Using this information, the prior probability tables for the three parent nodes used in the network are shown in Table 14.10.

Now, according to the model built from the training set data, we calculate the probability of classifying the third record from the test set as "pos" using the formula:

TABLE 14.9 Bayes net test set predictions

```
=== Predictions on test split ===

inst#,    actual, predicted, error, probability distribution

   1        1:neg      1:neg       *0.521  0.479

   2        1:neg      1:neg       *0.521  0.479

   3        2:pos      2:pos        0.423 *0.577

   4        2:pos      2:pos        0.389 *0.611
```

TABLE 14.10   Prior probabilities derived from *movies_training.arff*.

more		much		other	
1	0	1	0	1	0
17.5/20	3.5/20	13.5/20	7.5/20	12.5/20	8.5/20

$$p(more = 0, much = 0, after = 0, CLASS = pos)$$
$$= p(more = 0) \cdot (much = 0) \cdot (after = 0)$$
$$\cdot p(CLASS = pos|more = 0) \cdot p(CLASS = pos|much = 0)$$
$$\cdot p(CLASS = pos|after = 0)$$

As described above, Bayes net also adds 0.5 to the conditional probability table cell counts to prevent zero-based probabilities from occurring. For example, the conditional probability $p(CLASS = pos|more = 0) = \frac{2}{10}$ becomes $\frac{2.5}{10}$ using this internal adjustment. Therefore, the probability of a positive classification, given the values for *more, much,* and *other* found in the third instance, is computed as follows:

$$p(more = 0, much = 0, after = 0, CLASS = pos)$$
$$= \left(\frac{3.5}{20}\right) \cdot \left(\frac{7.5}{20}\right) \cdot \left(\frac{8.5}{20}\right) \cdot \left(\frac{2.5}{10}\right) \cdot \left(\frac{4.5}{10}\right) \cdot \left(\frac{3.5}{10}\right)$$
$$= (0.175) \cdot (0.375) \cdot (0.425) \cdot (0.25) \cdot (0.45) \cdot (0.35)$$
$$\approx 0.001098$$

Likewise, the probability of a negative classification is derived using a similar approach:

$$p(more = 0, much = 0, after = 0, CLASS = neg)$$
$$= \left(\frac{3.5}{20}\right) \cdot \left(\frac{7.5}{20}\right) \cdot \left(\frac{8.5}{20}\right) \cdot \left(\frac{1.5}{10}\right) \cdot \left(\frac{3.5}{10}\right) \cdot \left(\frac{5.5}{10}\right)$$
$$= (0.175) \cdot (0.375) \cdot (0.425) \cdot (0.15) \cdot (0.35) \cdot (0.55)$$
$$\approx 0.000805$$

Our last step is to normalize the probabilities as follows:

$$p(pos) = \frac{0.001098}{0.001098 + 0.000805} \approx 0.57698$$

$$p(neg) = \frac{0.000805}{0.001098 + 0.000805} \approx 0.42302$$

Our calculations have determined that, according to the Bayes net model built from the training set, instance three is classified as positive with probability 0.577. Again, our hand-calculated probabilities agree with those produced by the WEKA model, as shown in Table 14.9. Clearly, our results indicate that "hand-computing" the probability values for a network of moderate size is a nontrivial task.

THE R ZONE

Read in Churn data, calculate marginal probabilities

```
churn <- read.csv(file = "C:/ ... /churn.txt",
    stringsAsFactors=TRUE)
n <- dim(churn)[1] # Total sample size
p.IntlPlan <- sum(churn$Int.l.Plan=="yes")/n
p.VMailPlan <- sum(churn$VMail.Plan=="yes")/n
p.Churn  <- sum(churn$Churn=="True")/n
```

```
> p.IntlPlan
[1] 0.09690969
> p.VMailPlan
[1] 0.2766277
> p.Churn
[1] 0.1449145
```

Calculate conditional probabilities

```
n.ChurnT <- length(churn$Churn[which(churn$Churn=="True")])
# Number of  Churn = True
n.ChurnF <- length(churn$Churn[which(churn$Churn=="False")])
p.Intl.g.ChurnF <-
    sum(churn$Int.l.Plan[which(churn$Churn=="False")]=="yes")/n.ChurnF
p.VMP.g.ChurnF <-
    sum(churn$VMail.Plan[which(churn$Churn=="False")]=="yes")/n.ChurnF
p.Intl.g.ChurnT <-
    sum(churn$Int.l.Plan[which(churn$Churn=="True")]=="yes")/n.ChurnT
p.VMP.g.ChurnT <-
    sum(churn$VMail.Plan[which(churn$Churn=="True")]=="yes")/n.ChurnT
```

Posterior Probabilities using previous calculations

```
p.Churn.g.Intl <- p.Intl.g.ChurnT*p.Churn/p.IntlPlan
p.Churn.g.VMP <- p.VMP.g.ChurnT*p.Churn/p.VMailPlan
```

```
> p.Churn.g.Intl
[1] 0.4241486
> p.Churn.g.VMP
[1] 0.0867679
```

Posterior Probabilities calculated directly

```
# Sample size of Int'l Plan = "yes"
n.Intl <- length(churn$Int.l.Plan[which(churn$Int.l.Plan=="yes")])
# Sample size of Voicemail Plan = "yes"
n.VMP <- length(churn$Int.l.Plan[which(churn$VMail.Plan=="yes")])
p2.Churn.g.Intl <- sum(churn$Churn[which(churn$Int.l.Plan=="yes")]=="True")/n.Intl
p2.Churn.g.VMP <- sum(churn$Churn[which(churn$VMail.Plan=="yes")]=="True")/n.VMP
```

Joint Conditional Probabilities

```
i.v <- i.vbar <- ibar.v <- ibar.vbar <- rep("no", n)
for(i in 1:n){
    if(churn$Int.l.Plan[i]=="yes" &&
    churn$VMail.Plan[i]=="yes") i.v[i] <- "yes"
    if(churn$Int.l.Plan[i]=="yes" &&
    churn$VMail.Plan[i]=="no") i.vbar[i] <-
        "yes"
    if(churn$Int.l.Plan[i]=="no" &&
    churn$VMail.Plan[i]=="yes")
```

```
> p.i.v.ChurnT*p.Churn
[1] 0.01080108
> p.i.v.ChurnF*(1-p.Churn)
[1] 0.01680168
```

```
ibar.v[i] <- "yes"
    if(churn$Int.l.Plan[i]=="no" &&
    churn$VMail.Plan[i]=="no")
        ibar.vbar[i] <- "yes"
}
tiv <- table(i.v, churn$Churn); tivbar <- table(i.vbar, churn$Churn)
tibarv <- table(ibar.v, churn$Churn); tibarvbar <- table(ibar.vbar, churn$Churn)
p.i.v.ChurnT <- tiv[4]/sum(tiv[4], tiv[3])
p.i.v.ChurnF <- tiv[2]/sum(tiv[2], tiv[1])
p.i.v.ChurnT*p.Churn
p.i.v.ChurnF*(1-p.Churn)
# And so on for the other tables
```

Posterior Odds Ratio

```
(p.i.v.ChurnT*p.Churn)/
    (p.i.v.ChurnF*(1-p.Churn))
```

```
> (p.i.v.ChurnT*p.Churn)/
+    (p.i.v.ChurnF*(1-p.Churn))
[1] 0.6428571
```

Balance the data

```
b.churn <- churn[which(churn$Churn=="True"),]
notchurn <- churn[which(churn$Churn=="False"),]
choose <- runif(dim(notchurn)[1], 0,1)
halfnotchurn <- notchurn[which(choose<.5),]
b.churn <- rbind(b.churn, halfnotchurn)
# Updated probabilities
n <- dim(b.churn)[1]
p.Churn  <- sum(b.churn$Churn=="True")/n
```

Joint probability distribution

```
i.v <- rep("no", n)
for(i in 1:n){
    if(b.churn$Int.l.Plan[i]=="yes" &&
    b.churn$VMail.Plan[i]=="yes")
        i.v[i] <- "yes"
}
tiv <- table(i.v, b.churn$Churn)
p.i.v.ChurnT <- tiv[4]/sum(tiv[4], tiv[3])
p.i.v.ChurnF <- tiv[2]/sum(tiv[2], tiv[1])
p.i.v.ChurnT*p.Churn
p.i.v.ChurnF*(1-p.Churn)
```

```
> p.i.v.ChurnT*p.Churn
[1] 0.01909814
> p.i.v.ChurnF*(1-p.Churn)
[1] 0.01167109
```

Naïve Bayes Classification, using original Churn data

```
N <- dim(churn)[1]
p.Churn  <- sum(churn$Churn=="True")/n
n.ChurnTrue <- length(churn$Churn[which(churn$Churn=="True")])
n.ChurnFalse <- length(churn$Churn[which(churn$Churn=="False")])
p.Intl.given.ChurnF <-
    sum(churn$Int.l.Plan[which(churn$Churn=="False")]=="yes")/n.ChurnFalse
p.VMP.given.ChurnF <-
    sum(churn$VMail.Plan[which(churn$Churn=="False")]=="yes")/n.ChurnFalse
p.Intl.given.ChurnT <-
    sum(churn$Int.l.Plan[which(churn$Churn=="True")]=="yes")/n.ChurnTrue
p.VMP.given.ChurnT <-
    sum(churn$VMail.Plan[which(churn$Churn=="True")]=="yes")/n.ChurnTrue
p.Intl.given.ChurnT*p.VMP.given.ChurnT*p.Churn
p.Intl.given.ChurnF*p.VMP.given.ChurnF*(1-p.Churn)
```

Log Posterior Odds Ratio

```
log((p.Intl.given.ChurnT)/
    (p.Intl.given.ChurnF))
log((p.VMP.given.ChurnT)/
    (p.VMP.given.ChurnF))
```

```
> log((p.Intl.given.churnT)/
+    (p.Intl.given.churnF))
[1] 1.469292
> log((p.VMP.given.churnT)/
+    (p.VMP.given.churnF))
[1] -0.5786958
```

Numeric Predictors for Naïve Bayes Classification

```
p.ChurnT.t800 <- dnorm(800, mean = 635,
    sd = 111)
p.ChurnF.t800 <- dnorm(800, mean = 585,
    sd = 84)
p.i.v.t800.givenChurnT <- p.Intl.given.ChurnT*
p.VMP.given.ChurnT*p.ChurnT.t800*p.Churn
p.i.v.t800.givenChurnF <- p.Intl.given.ChurnF*
p.VMP.given.ChurnF*p.ChurnF.t800*(1-p.Churn)
p.i.v.t800.givenChurnT/p.i.v.t800.givenChurnF
```

```
> p.i.v.t800.givenChurnT/
+  p.i.v.t800.givenChurnF
[1] 2.738979
```

R REFERENCES

R Core Team. *R: A Language and Environment for Statistical Computing*. Vienna, Austria: R Foundation for Statistical Computing; 2012. 3-900051-07-0, http://www.R-project.org/. Accessed 2014 Oct 07.

EXERCISES

CLARIFYING THE CONCEPTS

1. Describe the differences between the frequentist and Bayesian approaches to probability.

2. Explain the difference between the prior and posterior distributions.

3. Why would we expect, in most data mining applications, the *maximum a posteriori* estimate to be close to the maximum-likelihood estimate?

4. Explain in plain English what is meant by the *maximum a posteriori* classification.

5. Explain the interpretation of the posterior odds ratio. Also, why do we need it?

6. Describe what balancing is, and when and why it may be needed. Also, describe two techniques for achieving a balanced data set, and explain why one method is preferred.

7. Explain why we cannot avoid altering, even slightly, the character of the data set, when we apply balancing.

8. Explain why the *MAP* classification is impractical to apply directly for any interesting real-world data mining application.

9. What is meant by conditional independence? Provide an example of events that are conditionally independent. Now provide an example of events that are not conditionally independent.

10. When is the naïve Bayes classification the same as the *MAP* classification? What does this mean for the naïve Bayes classifier, in terms of optimality?

11. Explain why the log posterior odds ratio is useful. Provide an example.

12. Describe the process for using continuous predictors in Bayesian classification, using the concept of distribution.

13. Extra credit: Investigate the mixture idea for the continuous predictor mentioned in the text.

14. Explain what is meant by working with the empirical distribution. Describe how this can be used to estimate the true probabilities.

15. Explain the difference in assumptions between naïve Bayes classification and Bayesian networks.

16. Describe the intrinsic relationship among the variables in a Bayesian network.

17. What are the two main considerations when building a Bayesian network?

WORKING WITH THE DATA

18. Compute the posterior odds ratio for each of the combinations of *International Plan* and *Voice Mail Plan* membership, using the balanced data set.

19. Calculate the naïve Bayes classification for all four possible combinations of *International Plan* and *Voice Mail Plan* membership, using the $\frac{25.31\%}{74.69\%}$ balancing.

20. Verify the empirical distribution results referred to in the text, of the numbers of records within the certain margins of error of 800 minutes, for each of churners and non-churners.

21. Find the naïve Bayes classifier for the following customers. Use the empirical distribution where necessary.

   a. Belongs to neither plan, with 400 day minutes.

   b. Belongs to the International Plan only, with 400 minutes.

   c. Belongs to both plans, with 400 minutes.

   d. Belongs to both plans, with zero minutes. Comment.

22. Provide the *MAP* classification for *season* given that a warm coat was purchased, in the clothing purchase example in the Bayesian network section.

23. Revisit the WEKA naïve Bayes example. Calculate the probability that the first instance in *movies_test.arff* is "pos" and "neg." Do your calculations agree with those reported by WEKA leading to a negative classification?

24. Compute the probabilities by which the Bayes net model classifies the fourth instance from the test file *movies_test.arff*. Do your calculations result in a positive classification as reported by WEKA?

HANDS-ON ANALYSIS

For Exercises 25–35, use the *breast cancer* data set.[10] This data set was collected by Dr. William H. Wohlberg from the University of Wisconsin Hospitals, Madison. Ten numeric predictors are used to predict the class of malignant breast cancer tumor (class = 1), as opposed to a benign tumor (class = 0).

25. Consider using only two predictors, *mitoses* and *clump thickness,* to predict tumor class. Categorize the values for *mitoses* as follows: Low = 1 and High = 2–10. Categorize the values for *clump thickness* as follows: Low = 1–5 and High = 6–10. Discard the original variables and use these categorized predictors.

26. Find the prior probabilities for each of the predictors and the target variable. Find the complement probabilities of each.

27. Find the conditional probabilities for each of the predictors, given that the tumor is malignant. Then find the conditional probabilities for each of the predictors, given that the tumor is benign.

---

[10]Breast cancer data set. Dr. William H. Wohlberg, University of Wisconsin Hospitals, Madison, Wisconsin. Cited in: Mangasarian and Wohlberg, Cancer diagnosis via linear programming, *SIAM News*, **23**, 5, September, 1990.

28. Find the posterior probability that the tumor is malignant, given that *mitoses* is (i) high and (ii) low.

29. Find the posterior probability that the tumor is malignant, given that *clump thickness* is (i) high and (ii) low.

30. Construct the joint conditional probabilities, similarly to Table 14.4.

31. Using your results from the previous exercise, find the *maximum a posteriori* classification of tumor class, for each of the following combinations:

    a. *Mitoses* = low and *Clump Thickness* = low.

    b. *Mitoses* = low and *Clump Thickness* = high.

    c. *Mitoses* = high and *Clump Thickness* = low.

    d. *Mitoses* = high and *Clump Thickness* = high.

32. For each of the combinations in the previous exercise, find the posterior odds ratio.

33. (Optional) Assess the validity of the conditional independence assumption, using calculations similarly to Table 14.5.

34. Find the naïve Bayes classifications for each of the combinations in Exercise 31.

35. For each of the predictors, find the log posterior odds ratio, and explain the contribution of this predictor to the probability of a malignant tumor.

## CHAPTER 15

MODEL EVALUATION TECHNIQUES

As you may recall from Chapter 1, the cross-industry standard process (CRISP) for data mining consists of the following six phases to be applied in an iterative cycle:

1. Business understanding phase
2. Data understanding phase
3. Data preparation phase
4. Modeling phase
5. Evaluation phase
6. Deployment phase.

Nestled between the modeling and deployment phases comes the crucial evaluation phase, the techniques for which are discussed in this chapter. By the time we arrive at the evaluation phase, the modeling phase has already generated one or more candidate models. It is of critical importance that these models be evaluated for quality and effectiveness *before* they are deployed for use in the field. Deployment of data mining models usually represents a capital expenditure and investment on the part of the company. If the models in question are invalid, then the company's time and money are wasted. In this chapter, we examine model evaluation techniques for each of the six main tasks of data mining: description, estimation, prediction, classification, clustering, and association.

15.1 MODEL EVALUATION TECHNIQUES FOR THE DESCRIPTION TASK

In Chapter 3, we learned how to apply exploratory data analysis (EDA) to learn about the salient characteristics of a data set. EDA represents a popular and powerful technique for applying the descriptive task of data mining. However, because descriptive techniques make no classifications, predictions, or estimates, an objective method for evaluating the efficacy of these techniques can be elusive. The watchword is common sense. Remember that the data mining models should be as *transparent* as possible. That is, the results of the data mining model should describe clear patterns that are amenable to intuitive interpretation and explanation. The effectiveness of your EDA is best evaluated by the clarity of understanding elicited in your target audience, whether a group of managers evaluating your new initiative or the evaluation board of the US Food and Drug Administration is assessing the efficacy of a new pharmaceutical submission.

If one insists on using a quantifiable measure to assess description, then one may apply the *minimum descriptive length principle*. Other things being equal, *Occam's razor* (a principle named after the medieval philosopher William of Occam) states that simple representations are preferable to complex ones. The minimum descriptive length principle quantifies this, saying that the best representation (or description) of a model or body of data is the one that minimizes the information required (in bits) to encode (i) the model and (ii) the exceptions to the model.

15.2 MODEL EVALUATION TECHNIQUES FOR THE ESTIMATION AND PREDICTION TASKS

For estimation and prediction models, we are provided with both the estimated (or predicted) value $\hat{y}$ of the numeric target variable and the actual value y. Therefore, a natural measure to assess model adequacy is to examine the *estimation error*, or *residual*, $(y - \hat{y})$. As the average residual is always equal to zero, we cannot use it for model evaluation; some other measure is needed.

The usual measure used to evaluate estimation or prediction models is the *mean square error* (MSE):

$$\text{MSE} = \frac{\sum_i (y_i - \hat{y}_i)^2}{n - p - 1}$$

where p represents the number of model variables. Models that minimize MSE are preferred. The square root of MSE can be regarded as an estimate of the typical error in estimation or prediction when using the particular model. In context, this is *known as* the *standard error of the estimate* and denoted by $s = \sqrt{\text{MSE}}$.

For example, consider Figure 15.1 (excerpted from Chapter 8), which provides the Minitab regression output for the estimated nutritional rating based on sugar content for the 76 breakfast cereals with nonmissing sugar values. Both MSE = 84.0 and $s = 9.16616$ are circled on the output. The value of 9.16616 for s indicates that the estimated prediction error from using this regression model to predict nutrition rating based on sugar content alone is 9.16616 rating points.

Is this good enough to proceed to model deployment? That depends on the objectives of the business or research problem. Certainly the model is simplicity itself, with only one predictor and one response; however, perhaps the prediction error is too large to consider for deployment. Compare this estimated prediction error with the value of s obtained by the multiple regression in Table 9.1: $s = 6.12733$. The estimated error in prediction for the multiple regression is smaller, but more information is required to achieve this, in the form of a second predictor: fiber. As with so much else

```
Regression Analysis: Rating versus Sugars

The regression equation is
Rating = 59.9 - 2.46 Sugars


76 cases used, 1 cases contain missing values


Predictor      Coef   SE Coef        T      P
Constant     59.853     1.998    29.96  0.000
Sugars      -2.4614    0.2417   -10.18  0.000


S = 9.16616    R-sq = 58.4%    R-sq(adj) = 57.8%


Analysis of Variance

Source            DF       SS       MS       F      P
Regression         1   8711.9   8711.9  103.69  0.000
Residual Error    74   6217.4     84.0
Total             75  14929.3
```

Figure 15.1   Regression results, with MSE and *s* indicated.

in statistical analysis and data mining, there is a trade-off between model complexity and prediction error. The domain experts for the business or research problem in question need to determine where the point of diminishing returns lies.

In Chapter 12, we examined an evaluation measure that was related to MSE:

$$\text{SSE} = \sum_{\text{Records}} \sum_{\text{Output nodes}} (\text{actual output})^2$$

which represents roughly the numerator of MSE above. Again, the goal is to minimize the sum of squared errors over all output nodes. In Chapter 8, we learned another measure of the goodness of a regression model that is the *coefficient of determination*:

$$R^2 = \frac{\text{SSR}}{\text{SST}}$$

Where R^2 represents the proportion of the variability in the response that is accounted for by the linear relationship between the predictor (or predictors) and the response. For example, in Figure 15.1, we see that $R^2 = 58.4\%$, which means that 58.4% of the variability in cereal ratings is accounted for by the linear relationship between ratings and sugar content. This is actually quite a chunk of the variability, as it leaves only 41.6% of the variability left for all other factors.

One of the drawbacks of the above evaluation measures is that outliers may have an undue influence on the value of the evaluation measure. This is because the above measures are based on the *squared error*, which is much larger for outliers than for the bulk of the data. Thus, the analyst may prefer to use the *mean absolute error* (*MAE*). The MAE is defined as follows:

$$\text{Mean absolute error} = \text{MAE} = \frac{\sum |y_i - \widehat{y}_i|}{n}$$

where $|x|$ represents the absolute value of x. The *MAE* will treat all errors equally, whether outliers or not, and thereby avoid the problem of undue influence of outliers. Unfortunately, not all statistical packages report this evaluation statistic. Thus, to find the MAE, the analyst may perform the following steps:

CALCULATING THE MEAN ABSOLUTE ERROR (MAE)

---

1. Calculate the estimated target values, $\widehat{y}_i$.
2. Find the absolute value between each estimated value, and its associated actual target value, y_i, giving you $|y_i - \widehat{y}_i|$.
3. Find the mean of the absolute values from step 2. This is *MAE*.

15.3 MODEL EVALUATION MEASURES FOR THE CLASSIFICATION TASK

How do we assess how well our classification algorithm is functioning? Classification assignments could conceivably be made based on coin flips, tea leaves, goat entrails, or a crystal ball. Which evaluative methods should we use to assure ourselves that the classifications made by our data mining algorithm are efficacious and accurate? Are we outperforming the coin flips?

In the context of a C5.0 model for classifying income, we examine the following evaluative concepts, methods, and tools in this chapter[1]:

- Model accuracy
- Overall error rate
- Sensitivity and specificity
- False-positive rate and false-negative rate
- Proportions of true positives and true negatives
- Proportions of false positives and false negatives
- Misclassification costs and overall model cost

---

[1]The models considered in this chapter relate to a binary target variable. For discussion of classification of trinary or *k*-nary target variables, see Chapter 17. Also, further graphical evaluation measures, such as profits charts, are discussed in Chapter 18.

- Cost-benefit table
- Lift charts
- Gains charts.

Recall the *adult* data set from Chapter 11 that we applied a C5.0 model for classifying whether a person's income was low ($\leq$\$50,000) or high ($>$\$50,000), based on a set of predictor variables which included capital gain, capital loss, marital status, and so on. Let us evaluate the performance of that decision tree classification model (with all levels retained, not just three, as in Figure 11.9), using the notions of error rate, false positives, and false negatives.

The general form of the matrix of the correct and incorrect classifications made by a classification algorithm, termed the *contingency table*,[2] is shown in Table 15.1. Table 15.2 contains the statistics from the C5.0 model, with "$\geq 50\,K$" denoted as the positive classification. The columns represent the predicted classifications, and the rows represent the actual (true) classifications, for each of the 25,000 records. There

TABLE 15.1   General form of the contingency table of correct and incorrect classifications

		Predicted Category		
		0	1	Total
Actual category	0	Truenegatives: Predicted 0 Actually 0	Falsepositives: Predicted 1 Actually 0	Totalactuallynegative
	1	Falsenegatives: Predicted 0 Actually 1	Truepositives: Predicted1 Actually1	Totalactuallypositive
	Total	Total Predictednegative	Total Predictedpositive	Grandtotal

TABLE 15.2   Contingency table for the C5.0 model

		Predicted Category		
		50 K	> 50 K	Total
Actual category	50 K	18,197	819	19,016
	> 50 K	2561	3423	5984
	Total	20,758	4242	25,000

are 19,016 records whose actual value for the target variable *income* is less than or equal to 50,000, and there are 5984 records whose actual value *income* is greater than 50,000. The C5.0 algorithm classified 20,758 of the records as having *income* less than or equal to 50,000, and 4242 records as having *income* greater than 50,000.

---

[2] Also referred to as the *confusion matrix* or the *error matrix*.

Of the 20,758 records whose income is predicted by the algorithm to be less than or equal to 50,000, 18,197 of these records actually do have low income. However, the algorithm incorrectly classified 2561 of these 20,758 records as having *income* $\leq 50,000$, when their income is actually greater than 50,000.

Now, suppose that this analysis is being carried out for a financial lending firm, which is interested in determining whether or not a loan applicant's income is greater than 50,000. A classification of *income* greater than 50,000 is considered to be *positive*, as the lending firm would then proceed to extend the loan to the person in question. A classification of *income* less than or equal to 50,000 is considered to be *negative*, as the firm would proceed to deny the loan application to the person, based on low income (in this simplified scenario). Assume that in the absence of other information, the default decision would be to deny the loan due to low income.

Thus, the 20,758 classifications (predictions) of *income* less than or equal to 50,000 are said to be *negatives*, and the 4242 classifications of *income* greater than 50,000 are said to be *positives*. The 2561 negative classifications that were made in error are said to be *false negatives*. That is, a false negative represents a record that is classified as negative but is actually positive. Of the 4242 positive classifications, 819 actually had low incomes so that there are 819 false positives. A *false positive* represents a record that is classified as positive but is actually negative.

Let TN, FN, FP, and TP represent the numbers of true negatives, false negatives, false positives, and true positives, respectively, in our contingency table. Also, let

$$TAN = \text{Total actually negative} = TN + FP$$
$$TAP = \text{Total actually positive} = FN + TP$$
$$TPN = \text{Total predicted negative} = TN + FN$$
$$TPN = \text{Total predicted positive} = FP + TP$$

Further, let $N = TN + FN + FP + TP$ represent the grand total of the counts in the four cells.

15.4 ACCURACY AND OVERALL ERROR RATE

Using this notation we begin our discussion of classification evaluation measures with *accuracy* and *overall error rate* (or simply *error rate*):

$$\text{Accuracy} = \frac{TN + TP}{TN + FN + FP + TP} = \frac{TN + TP}{N}$$

$$\text{Overall error rate} = 1 - \text{Accuracy} = \frac{FN + FP}{TN + FN + FP + TP} = \frac{FN + FP}{N}$$

Accuracy represents an overall measure of the proportion of correct classifications being made by the model, while overall error rate measures the proportion of incorrect classifications, across all cells in the contingency table. For this example, we have:

$$\text{Accuracy} = \frac{TN + TP}{N} = \frac{18,197 + 3423}{25,000} = 0.8648$$

$$\text{Overall error rate} = 1 - \text{Accuracy} = \frac{\text{FN} + \text{FP}}{N} = \frac{2561 + 819}{25,000} = 0.1352$$

That is, 86.48% of the classifications made by this model are correct, while 13.52% are wrong.

15.5   SENSITIVITY AND SPECIFICITY

Next, we turn to *sensitivity* and *specificity*, defined as follows:

$$\text{Sensitivity} = \frac{\text{Number of true positives}}{\text{Total actually positive}} = \frac{\text{TP}}{\text{TAP}} = \frac{\text{TP}}{\text{TP} + \text{FN}}$$

$$\text{Specificity} = \frac{\text{Number of true negatives}}{\text{Total actually negative}} = \frac{\text{TN}}{\text{TAN}} = \frac{\text{TN}}{\text{FP} + \text{TN}}$$

Sensitivity measures the ability of the model to classify a record positively, while specificity measures the ability to classify a record negatively. For this example, we have

$$\text{Sensitivity} = \frac{\text{Number of true positives}}{\text{Total actually positive}} = \frac{\text{TP}}{\text{TAP}} = \frac{3423}{5984} = 0.5720$$

$$\text{Specificity} = \frac{\text{Number of true negatives}}{\text{Total actually negative}} = \frac{\text{TN}}{\text{TAN}} = \frac{18,197}{19,016} = 0.9569$$

In some fields, such as information retrieval,[3] sensitivity is referred to as *recall*. A good classification model should be *sensitive*, meaning that it should identify a high proportion of the customers who are positive (have high income). However, this model seems to struggle to do this, correctly classifying only 57.20% of the actual high-income records as having high income.

Of course, a perfect classification model would have sensitivity = 1.0 = 100%. However, a null model which simply classified all customers as positive would also have sensitivity = 1.0. Clearly, it is not sufficient to identify the positive responses alone. A classification model also needs to be *specific*, meaning that it should identify a high proportion of the customers who are negative (have low income). In this example, our classification model has correctly classified 95.69% of the actual low-income customers as having low income.

Of course, a perfect classification model would have specificity = 1.0. But so would a model which classifies all customers as low income. A good classification model should have acceptable levels of both sensitivity and specificity, but what constitutes acceptable varies greatly from domain to domain. Our model specificity of 0.9569 is higher than our model sensitivity of 0.5720, which is probably okay in this instance. In the credit application domain, it may be more important to correctly identify the customers who will default rather than those who will not default, as we shall discuss later in this chapter.

---

[3]Zdravko Markov and Daniel Larose, *Data Mining the Web, Uncovering Patterns in Web Content, Structure, and Usage*, John Wiley and Sons, New York, 2007.

15.6   FALSE-POSITIVE RATE AND FALSE-NEGATIVE RATE

Our next evaluation measures are *false-positive rate* and *false-negative rate*. These are additive inverses of sensitivity and specificity, as we see in their formulas:

$$\text{False positive rate} = 1 - \text{specificity} = \frac{FP}{TAN} = \frac{FP}{FP + TN}$$

$$\text{False negative rate} = 1 - \text{sensitivity} = \frac{FN}{TAP} = \frac{FN}{TP + FN}$$

For our example, we have

$$\text{False positive rate} = 1 - \text{specificity} = \frac{FP}{TAN} = \frac{819}{19,016} = 0.0431$$

$$\text{False negative rate} = 1 - \text{sensitivity} = \frac{FN}{TAP} = \frac{2561}{5984} = 0.4280$$

Our low false-positive rate of 4.31% indicates that we incorrectly identify actual low-income customers as high income only 4.31% of the time. The much higher false-negative rate indicates that we incorrectly classify actual high-income customers as low income 42.80% of the time.

15.7   PROPORTIONS OF TRUE POSITIVES, TRUE NEGATIVES, FALSE POSITIVES, AND FALSE NEGATIVES

Our next evaluation measures are the *proportion of true positives*[4] and the *proportion of true negatives*,[5] and are defined as follows:

$$\text{Proportion of true positives} = PTP = \frac{TP}{TPP} = \frac{TP}{FP + TP}$$

$$\text{Proportion of true negatives} = PTN = \frac{TN}{TPN} = \frac{TN}{FN + TN}$$

For our income example, we have

$$\text{Proportion of true positives} = PTP = \frac{TP}{TPP} = \frac{3423}{4242} = 0.8069$$

$$\text{Proportion of true negatives} = PTN = \frac{TN}{TPN} = \frac{18,197}{20,758} = 0.8766$$

That is, the probability is 80.69% that a customer actually has high income, given that our model has classified it as high income, while the probability is 87.66% that a customer actually has low income, given that we have classified it as low income.

---

[4]In the field of information retrieval, the proportion of true positives is called *precision*.

[5]The medical literature calls these measures the *positive predictive value* and the *negative predictive value*, respectively. For this book, we prefer to avoid the term *predictive value* for an evaluation measure, since we think the phrase *predictive value* should be reserved for the estimated value or predicted value from an estimation or prediction model such as linear regression or CART.

Unfortunately, the proportion of true positives in the medical world has been demonstrated to be dependent on the *prevalence* of the disease.[6] In fact, as disease prevalence increases, PTP also increases. In the exercises, we provide a simple example to show that this relationship holds. Outside of the medical world, we would say that, for example, as the actual proportion of records classified as positive increases, so does the proportion of true positives. Nevertheless, the data analyst will still find these measures useful, as we usually use them to compare the efficacy of competing models, and these models are usually based on the same actual class proportions in the test data set.

Finally, we turn to the *proportion of false positives* and the *proportion of false negatives*, which, unsurprisingly, are additive inverses of the proportion of true positives and the proportion of true negatives, respectively.

$$\text{Proportion of false positives} = 1 - \text{PTP} = \frac{\text{FP}}{\text{TPP}} = \frac{\text{FP}}{\text{FP} + \text{TP}}$$

$$\text{Proportion of false negatives} = 1 - \text{PTN} = \frac{\text{FN}}{\text{TPN}} = \frac{\text{FN}}{\text{FN} + \text{TN}}$$

Note the difference between the proportion of false-positives and the false-positive rate. The denominator for the false-positive rate is the total number of actual negative records, while the denominator for the proportion of false positives is the total number of records predicted positive. For our example, we have

$$\text{Proportion of false positives} = 1 - \text{PTP} = \frac{\text{FP}}{\text{TPP}} = \frac{819}{4242} = 0.1931$$

$$\text{Proportion of false negatives} = 1 - \text{PTN} = \frac{\text{FN}}{\text{TPN}} = \frac{2561}{20,758} = 0.1234$$

In other words, there is a 19.31% likelihood that a customer actually has low income, given that our model has classified it as high income, and there is 12.34% likelihood that a customer actually has high income, given that we have classified it as low income.

Using these classification model evaluation measures, the analyst may compare the accuracy of various models. For example, a C5.0 decision tree model may be compared against a classification and regression tree (CART) decision tree model or a neural network model. Model choice decisions can then be rendered based on the relative model performance based on these evaluation measures.

As an aside, in the parlance of hypothesis testing, as the default decision is to find that the applicant has low income, we would have the following hypotheses:

H_0: *income* $\leq 50,000$

H_a: *income* $> 50,000$

where H_0 represents the default, or null, hypothesis, and H_a represents the alternative hypothesis, which requires evidence to support it. A false positive would be considered a *type I error* in this setting, incorrectly rejecting the null hypothesis, while

---

[6]For example, see Understanding and using sensitivity, specificity, and predictive values, by Parikh, Mathai, Parikh, Sekhar, and Thomas, *Indian Journal of Opthamology*, **Volume 56**, 1, pages 45–50, 2008.

a false negative would be considered a *type II error*, incorrectly accepting the null hypothesis.

15.8 MISCLASSIFICATION COST ADJUSTMENT TO REFLECT REAL-WORLD CONCERNS

Consider this situation from the standpoint of the lending institution. Which error, a false negative or a false positive, would be considered more damaging from the lender's point of view? If the lender commits a false negative, an applicant who had high income gets turned down for a loan: an unfortunate but not very expensive mistake.

However, if the lender commits a false positive, an applicant who had low income would be awarded the loan. This error greatly increases the chances that the applicant will default on the loan, which is very expensive for the lender. Therefore, the lender would consider the false positive to be the more damaging type of error and would prefer to minimize the proportion of false positives. The analyst would therefore adjust the C5.0 algorithm's misclassification cost matrix to reflect the lender's concerns. Suppose, for example, that the analyst increased the false positive cost from 1 to 2, while the false negative cost remains at 1. Thus, a false positive would be considered twice as damaging as a false negative. The analyst may wish to experiment with various cost values for the two types of errors, to find the combination best suited to the task and business problem at hand.

How would you expect the misclassification cost adjustment to affect the performance of the algorithm? Which evaluation measures would you expect to increase or decrease? We might expect the following:

EXPECTED CONSEQUENCES OF INCREASING THE FALSE POSITIVE COST

- **Proportion of false positives** should decrease, since the cost of making such an error has been doubled.
- **Proportion of false negatives** should increase, because fewer false positives usually means more false negatives.
- **Sensitivity** should decrease. The denominator in the formula TP/TAP stays the same, but there will be fewer true positives, because the model will shy away from making positive predictions in general, due to the higher cost of the false positive.
- **Specificity** should increase, because the total actually negative stays the same, while there should be more true negatives due to the model being more inclined toward a negative classification.

The C5.0 algorithm was rerun, this time including the misclassification cost adjustment. The resulting contingency table is shown in Table 15.3. The classification model evaluation measures are presented in Table 15.4, with each cell containing its additive inverse. As expected, the proportion of false positives has increased,

TABLE 15.3 Contingency table after misclassification cost adjustment

		Predicted Category		Total
		≤ 50 K	> 50 K	
Actual category	≤ 50 K	18,711	305	19,016
	> 50 K	3307	2677	5984
	Total	22,018	2982	25,000

TABLE 15.4 Comparison of evaluation measures for CART models with and without misclassification costs (better performance in bold)

Evaluation Measure	CART Model	
	Model 1: Without Misclassification Costs	Model 2: With Misclassification Costs
Accuracy	**0.8648**	0.8552
Overall error rate	**0.1352**	0.1448
Sensitivity	**0.5720**	0.4474
False-positive rate	**0.4280**	0.5526
Specificity	0.9569	**0.9840**
False-negative rate	0.0431	**0.0160**
Proportion of true positives	0.8069	**0.8977**
Proportion of false positives	0.1931	**0.1023**
Proportion of true negatives	**0.8766**	0.8498
Proportion of false negatives	**0.1234**	0.1502

while the proportion of false negatives has decreased. Whereas previously, false positives were more likely to occur, this time the proportion of false positives is lower than the proportion of false negatives. As desired, the proportion of false positives has decreased. However, this has come at a cost. The algorithm, hesitant to classify records as positive due to the higher cost, instead made many more negative classifications, and therefore more false negatives. As expected, sensitivity has decreased while specificity has increased, for the reasons mentioned above.

Unfortunately, the overall error rate has climbed as well:

$$\text{Overall error rate} = \frac{3307 + 305}{25,000} = 0.14448, \quad \text{up from } 0.1352 \text{ previously.}$$

Nevertheless, a higher overall error rate and a higher proportion of false negatives considered a "good trade" by this lender, who is eager to reduce the loan default rate, which is very costly to the firm. The decrease in the proportion of false positives from 19.31% to 10.23% will surely result in significant savings to the financial lending firm, as fewer applicants who cannot afford to repay the loan will be awarded the loan. Data analysts should note an important lesson here: that we should not be wed to the overall error rate as the best indicator of a good model.

15.9 DECISION COST/BENEFIT ANALYSIS

Company managers may require that model comparisons be made in terms of cost/benefit analysis. For example, in comparing the original C5.0 model before the misclassification cost adjustment (call this *model 1*) against the C5.0 model using the misclassification cost adjustment (call this *model 2*), managers may prefer to have the respective error rates, false negatives and false positives, translated into dollars and cents.

Analysts can provide model comparison in terms of anticipated profit or loss by associating a cost or benefit with each of the four possible combinations of correct and incorrect classifications. For example, suppose that the analyst makes the cost/benefit value assignments shown in Table 15.5. The "−$300" cost is actually the anticipated average interest revenue to be collected from applicants whose income is actually greater than 50,000. The $500 reflects the average cost of loan defaults, averaged over all loans to applicants whose income level is low. Of course, the specific numbers assigned here are subject to discussion and are meant for illustration only.

Using the costs from Table 15.5, we can then compare models 1 and 2:

Cost of model 1 (false positive cost not doubled):

$$18,197(\$0) + 3423(-\$300) + 2561(\$0) + 819(\$500) = -\$275,100$$

Cost of model 2 (false positive cost doubled):

$$18,711(\$0) + 2677(-\$300) + 3307(\$0) + 305(\$500) = -\$382,900$$

Negative costs represent profits. Thus, the *estimated cost savings* from deploying model 2, which doubles the cost of a false positive error, is

$$-\$275,100 - (-\$382,900) = \$107,800$$

In other words, the simple data mining step of doubling the false positive cost has resulted in the deployment of a model greatly increasing the company's profit. Is it not amazing what a simple misclassification cost adjustment can mean to the company's bottom line? Thus, even though model 2 suffered from a higher overall error rate and a higher proportion of false negatives, it outperformed model 1 "where it counted," with a lower proportion of false positives, which led directly to a six-figure increase

TABLE 15.5 Cost/benefit table for each combination of correct/incorrect decision

Outcome	Classification	Actual Value	Cost	Rationale
True negative	≤50,000	≤50,000	$0	No money gained or lost
True positive	>50,000	>50,000	−$300	Anticipated average interest revenue from loans
False negative	≤50,000	>50,000	$0	No money gained or lost
False positive	>50,000	≤50,000	$500	Cost of loan default averaged over all loans to ≤50,000 group

in the company's estimated profit. When misclassification costs are involved, the best model evaluation measure is the overall cost of the model.

15.10   LIFT CHARTS AND GAINS CHARTS

For classification models, lift is a concept, originally from the marketing field, which seeks to compare the response rates with and without using the classification model. Lift charts and gains charts are graphical evaluative methods for assessing and comparing the usefulness of classification models. We shall explore these concepts by continuing our examination of the C5.0 models for classifying income.

Suppose that the financial lending firm is interested in identifying high-income persons to put together a targeted marketing campaign for a new platinum credit card. In the past, marketers may have simply canvassed an entire list of contacts without regard to clues about the contact's income. Such blanket initiatives are expensive and tend to have low response rates. It is much better to apply demographic information that the company may have about the list of contacts, build a model to predict which contacts will have high income, and restrict the canvassing to these contacts classified as high income. The cost of the marketing program will then be much reduced and the response rate may be higher.

A good classification model should identify in its positive classifications (the >50,000 column in Tables 15.2 and 15.3), a group that has a higher proportion of positive "hits" than the database as a whole. The concept of *lift* quantifies this. We define *lift* as the proportion of true positives, divided by the proportion of positive hits in the data set overall:

$$\text{Lift} = \frac{\text{Proportion of true positives}}{\text{Proportion of positive hits}} = \frac{\text{TP}/\text{TPP}}{\text{TAP}/N}$$

Now, earlier we saw that, for model 1,

$$\text{Proportion of true positives} = \text{PTP} = \frac{\text{TP}}{\text{TPP}} = \frac{3423}{4242} = 0.8069$$

And we have

$$\text{Proportion of positive hits} = \frac{\text{TAP}}{N} = \frac{5984}{25,000} = 0.23936$$

Thus, the lift, measured at the 4242 positively predicted records, is

$$\text{Lift} = \frac{0.8069}{0.23936} = 3.37$$

Lift is a function of sample size, which is why we had to specify that the lift of 3.37 for model 1 was measured at $n = 4242$ records. When calculating lift, the software will first sort the records by the probability of being classified positive. The lift is then calculated for every sample size from $n = 1$ to $n = $ the size of the data set. A chart is then produced that graphs lift against the percentile of the data set.

Consider Figure 15.2, which represents the lift chart for model 1. Note that lift is highest at the lowest percentiles, which makes sense as the data are sorted according to the most likely positive hits. The lowest percentiles have the highest proportion of positive hits. As the plot moves from left to right, the positive hits tend to get "used up," so that the proportion steadily decreases until the lift finally equals exactly 1, when the entire data set is considered the sample. Therefore, for any lift chart, the highest lift is always obtained with the smallest sample sizes.

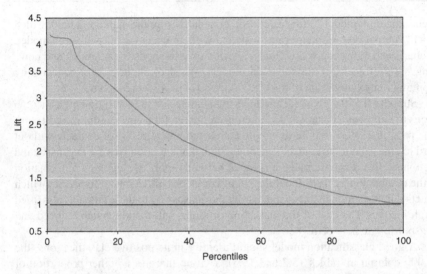

Figure 15.2   Lift chart for model 1: strong lift early, then falls away rapidly.

Now, 4242 records represents about the 17th percentile of the 25,000 total records. Note in Figure 15.2 that the lift at about the 17th percentile would be near 3.37, as we calculated above. If our market research project required merely the most likely 5% of records, the lift would have been higher, about 4.1, as shown in Figure 15.2. However, if the project required 60% of all records, the lift would have fallen off to about 1.6. As the data are sorted by positive propensity, the further we reach into the data set, the lower our overall proportion of positive hits becomes. Another balancing act is required: between reaching lots of contacts and having a high expectation of success per contact.

Lift charts are often presented in their cumulative form, where they are denoted as *cumulative lift charts*, or *gains charts*. The gains chart associated with the lift chart in Figure 15.2 is presented in Figure 15.3. The diagonal on the gains chart is analogous to the horizontal axis at *lift* = 1 on the lift chart. Analysts would like to see gains charts where the upper curve rises steeply as one moves from left to right and then gradually flattens out. In other words, one prefers a deeper "bowl" to a shallower bowl. How do you read a gains chart? Suppose that we canvassed the top 20% of our contact list (percentile = 20). By doing so, we could expect to reach about 62% of the total number of high-income persons on the list. Would doubling our effort also double our results? No. Canvassing the top 40% on the list would enable us to reach approximately 85% of the high-income persons on the list. Past this point, the law of diminishing returns is strongly in effect.

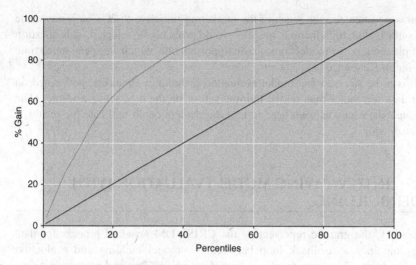

Figure 15.3   Gains chart for model 1.

Lift charts and gains charts can also be used to compare model performance. Figure 15.4 shows the combined lift chart for models 1 and 2. The figure shows that when it comes to model selection, a particular model may not be uniformly preferable. For example, up to about the 6th percentile, there appears to be no apparent difference in model lift. Then, up to approximately the 17th percentile, model 2 is preferable, providing slightly higher lift. Thereafter, model 1 is preferable.

Hence, if the goal were to canvass up to the top 17% or so of the people on the contact list with high incomes, model 2 would probably be selected. However, if

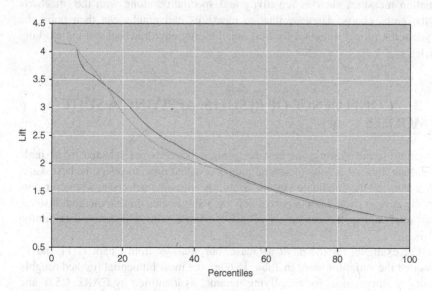

Figure 15.4   Combined lift chart for models 1 and 2.

the goal were to extend the reach of the marketing initiative to 20% or more of the likely contacts with high income, model 1 would probably be selected. This question of multiple models and model choice is an important one, which we spend much time discussing in Reference [1].

It is to be stressed that model evaluation techniques should be performed on the test data set, rather than on the training set, or on the data set as a whole. (The entire *adult* data set was used here so that the readers could replicate the results if they choose so.)

15.11 INTERWEAVING MODEL EVALUATION WITH MODEL BUILDING

In Chapter 1, the graphic representing the CRISP-DM standard process for data mining contained a feedback loop between the model building and evaluation phases. In Chapter 7, we presented a *methodology for building and evaluating a data model*. Where do the methods for model evaluation from Chapter 15 fit into these processes?

We would recommend that model evaluation become a nearly "automatic" process, performed to a certain degree whenever a new model is generated. Therefore, at any point in the process, we may have an accurate measure of the quality of the current or working model. Therefore, it is suggested that model evaluation be interwoven seamlessly into the *methodology for building and evaluating a data model* presented in Chapter 7, being performed on the models generated from each of the training set and the test set. For example, when we adjust the provisional model to minimize the error rate on the test set, we may have at our fingertips the evaluation measures such as sensitivity and specificity, along with the lift charts and the gains charts. These evaluative measures and graphs can then point the analyst in the proper direction for best ameliorating any drawbacks of the working model.

15.12 CONFLUENCE OF RESULTS: APPLYING A SUITE OF MODELS

In Olympic figure skating, the best-performing skater is not selected by a single judge alone. Instead, a suite of several judges is called upon to select the best skater from among all the candidate skaters. Similarly in model selection, whenever possible, the analyst should not depend solely on a single data mining method. Instead, he or she should seek a *confluence of results* from a suite of different data mining models.

For example, for the *adult* database, our analysis from Chapters 11 and 12 shows that the variables listed in Table 15.6 are the most influential (ranked roughly in order of importance) for classifying income, as identified by CART, C5.0, and the neural network algorithm, respectively. Although there is not a perfect match in the ordering of the important variables, there is still much that these three separate classification algorithms have uncovered, including the following:

- All three algorithms identify *Marital_Status*, *education-num*, *capital-gain*, *capital-loss*, and *hours-per-week* as the most important variables, except for the neural network, where *age* snuck in past *capital-loss*.
- None of the algorithms identified either *work-class* or *sex* as important variables, and only the neural network identified *age* as important.
- The algorithms agree on various ordering trends, such as *education-num* is more important than *hours-per-week*.

TABLE 15.6 **Most important variables for classifying income, as identified by CART, C5.0, and the neural network algorithm**

CART	C5.0	Neural Network
Marital_Status	*Capital-gain*	*Capital-gain*
Education-num	*Capital-loss*	*Education-num*
Capital-gain	*Marital_Status*	*Hours-per-week*
Capital-loss	*Education-num*	*Marital_Status*
Hours-per-week	*Hours-per-week*	*Age*
		Capital-loss

When we recall the strongly differing mathematical bases on which these three data mining methods are built, it may be considered remarkable that such convincing concurrence prevails among them with respect to classifying income. Remember that CART bases its decisions on the "goodness of split" criterion $\Phi(s|t)$, that C5.0 applies an information-theoretic approach, and that neural networks base their learning on back propagation. Yet these three different algorithms represent streams that broadly speaking, have come together, forming a *confluence* of results. In this way, the models act as validation for each other.

THE R ZONE

The confusion matrix

After using the C5.0 package, the confusion matrix is included in the output of summary()
See Chapter 11 for data preparation and code to implement the C5.0 package

Add costs to the model

```
library("C50")
#After data preparation from Chapter 11
x <- adult[,c(2,6, 9, 10, 16, 17, 18, 19, 20)]
y <- adult$income
# Without weights:
c50fit <- C5.0(x,
    y,
        control = C5.0Control(CF=.1))
summary(c50fit)
```

```
         Decision Tree
         -----------------
         size       Errors

         30 3462(13.8%)   <<


         (a)   (b)    <-classified as
         ----  ----
         18132  884   (a): class <=50K.
         2578  3406   (b): class >50K.
```

```
# With weights:
costm <- matrix(c(1, 2, 1, 1),
    byrow = FALSE,
    2, 2)
c50cost <- C5.0(x,
    y,
        costs = costm,
        control = C5.0Control(CF=.1))
summary(c50cost)
```

```
         Decision Tree
         ------------------------
         size       Errors   Cost

         42 3669(14.7%)   0.16   <<


         (a)   (b)    <-classified as
         ----  ----
         18768  248   (a): class <=50K.
         3421  2563   (b): class >50K.
```

R REFERENCES

Kuhn, M, Weston, S, Coulter, N. 2013. C code for C5.0 by R. Quinlan. C50: C5.0 decision trees and rule-based models. R package version 0.1.0-15. http://CRAN.R-project.org/package= C50.

R Core Team. *R: A Language and Environment for Statistical Computing*. Vienna, Austria: R Foundation for Statistical Computing; 2012. ISBN: 3-900051-07-0, http://www.R-project.org/.

EXERCISES

CLARIFYING THE CONCEPTS

1. Why do we need to evaluate our models before model deployment?

2. What is the minimum descriptive length principle, and how does it represent the principle of Occam's razor?

3. Why do we not use the average deviation as a model evaluation measure?

4. How is the square root of the MSE interpreted?

5. Describe the trade-off between model complexity and prediction error.

6. What might be a drawback of evaluation measures based on squared error? How might we avoid this?

7. Describe the general form of a contingency table.

8. What is a false positive? A false negative?

9. What is the difference between the total predicted negative and the total actually negative?

10. What is the relationship between accuracy and overall error rate?

11. True or false: If model A has better accuracy than model B, then model A has fewer false negatives than model B. If false, give a counterexample.

12. Suppose our model has perfect sensitivity. Why is that insufficient for us to conclude that we have a good model?

13. Suppose our model has perfect sensitivity and perfect specificity. What then is our accuracy and overall error rate?

14. What is the relationship between false positive rate and sensitivity?

15. What is the term used for the proportion of true positives in the medical literature? Why do we prefer to avoid this term in this book?

16. Describe the difference between the proportion of false-positives and the false-positive rate.

17. If we use a hypothesis testing framework, explain what represents a type I error and a type II error.

18. The text describes a situation where a false positive is worse than a false negative. Describe a situation from the medical field, say from screen testing for a virus, where a false negative would be worse than a false positive. Explain why it would be worse.

19. In your situation from the previous exercise, describe the expected consequences of increasing the false negative cost. Why would these be beneficial?

20. Are accuracy and overall error rate always the best indicators of a good model?

21. When misclassification costs are involved, what is the best model evaluation measure?

22. Explain in your own words what is meant by *lift*.

23. Describe the trade-off between reaching out to a large number of customers and having a high expectation of success per contact.

24. What should one look for when evaluating a gains chart?

25. For model selection, should model evaluation be performed on the training data set or the test data set, and why?

26. What is meant by a *confluence of results*?

HANDS-ON ANALYSIS

Use the *churn* data set at the book series website for the following exercises. Make sure that the correlated variables have been accounted for.

27. Apply a CART model for predicting *churn*. Use default misclassification costs. Construct a table containing the following measures:

   a. Accuracy and overall error rate

   b. Sensitivity and false-positive rate

   c. Specificity and false-negative rate

   d. Proportion of true positives and proportion of false positives

   e. Proportion of true negatives and proportion of false negatives

   f. Overall model cost.

28. In a typical churn model, in which interceding with a potential churner is relatively cheap but losing a customer is expensive, which error is more costly, a false negative or a false positive (where positive = customer predicted to churn)? Explain.

29. Based on your answer to the previous exercise, adjust the misclassification costs for your CART model to reduce the prevalence of the more costly type of error. Rerun the CART algorithm. Compare the false positive, false negative, sensitivity, specificity, and overall error rate with the previous model. Discuss the trade-off between the various rates in terms of cost for the company.

30. Perform a cost/benefit analysis for the default CART model from Exercise 1 as follows. Assign a cost or benefit in dollar terms for each combination of false and true positives and negatives, similarly to Table 15.5. Then, using the contingency table, find the overall anticipated cost.

31. Perform a cost/benefit analysis for the CART model with the adjusted misclassification costs. Use the same cost/benefits assignments as for the default model. Find the overall anticipated cost. Compare with the default model, and formulate a recommendation as to which model is preferable.

32. Construct a lift chart for the default CART model. What is the estimated lift at 20%? 33%? 40%? 50%?

33. Construct a gains chart for the default CART model. Explain the relationship between this chart and the lift chart.

34. Construct a lift chart for the CART model with the adjusted misclassification costs. What is the estimated lift at 20%? 33%? 40%? 50%?

35. Construct a single lift chart for both of the CART models. Which model is preferable over which regions?

36. Now turn to a C4.5 decision tree model, and redo Exercises 17–35. Compare the results. Which model is preferable?

37. Next, apply a neural network model to predict churn. Construct a table containing the same measures as in Exercise 27.

38. Construct a lift chart for the neural network model. What is the estimated lift at 20%? 33%? 40%? 50%?

39. Construct a single lift chart which includes the better of the two CART models, the better of the two C4.5 models, and the neural network model. Which model is preferable over which regions?

40. In view of the results obtained above, discuss the overall quality and adequacy of our *churn* classification models.

## CHAPTER 16

COST-BENEFIT ANALYSIS USING DATA-DRIVEN COSTS

In Chapter 15, we were introduced to cost-benefit analysis and misclassification costs. Our goal in this chapter is to derive a methodology whereby the data itself teaches us what the misclassification costs should be; that is, *cost-benefit analysis using data-driven misclassification costs*. Before we can perform that, however, we must turn to a more systematic treatment of misclassification costs and cost-benefit tables, deriving the following three important results regarding misclassification costs and cost-benefit tables[1]:

- *Decision invariance under row adjustment*
- *Positive classification criterion*
- *Decision invariance under scaling.*

16.1 DECISION INVARIANCE UNDER ROW ADJUSTMENT

For a binary classifier, define $P(i|x)$ to be the confidence (to be defined later) of the model for classifying a data record as $i = 0$ or $i = 1$. For example, $P(1|x)$ represents the confidence that a given classification algorithm has in classifying a record as positive (1), given the data. $P(i|x)$ is also called the posterior probability of a given classification. By way of contrast, $P(i)$ would represent the prior probability of a given classification; that is, the proportion of 1's or 0's in the training data set. Also, let $\text{Cost}_{\text{TN}}, \text{Cost}_{\text{FP}}, \text{Cost}_{\text{FN}}$, and Cost_{TP} represent the cost of a true negative, a false positive, a false negative, and a true positive, respectively, for the cost matrix shown in Table 16.1.

---

[1]Following Charles X. Ling and Victor S. Sheng, Cost-Sensitive Learning and the Class Imbalance Problem, *Encyclopedia of Machine Learning*, C. Sammut (Ed.), Springer, 2008.

Data Mining and Predictive Analytics, First Edition. Daniel T. Larose and Chantal D. Larose.
© 2015 John Wiley & Sons, Inc. Published 2015 by John Wiley & Sons, Inc.

TABLE 16.1 **Cost matrix for binary classifier**

		Predicted Category	
		0	1
Actual category	0	$Cost_{TN}$	$Cost_{FP}$
	1	$Cost_{FN}$	$Cost_{TP}$

Then, the expected cost of a positive or negative classification may be written as follows:

Expected cost of positive classification $= P(0|x) \cdot Cost_{FP} + P(1|x) \cdot Cost_{TP}$

Expected cost of negative classification $= P(0|x) \cdot Cost_{TN} + P(1|x) \cdot Cost_{FN}$

For a positive classification, this represents the weighted average of the costs in the positive predicted column, weighted by the confidence for classifying the records as negative and positive, respectively. It is similar for a negative classification. The *minimum expected cost principle* is then applied, as described here.

MINIMUM EXPECTED COST PRINCIPLE

Given a cost matrix, a data record should be classified into the class that has the minimum expected cost.

Thus, a data record will be classified as positive if and only if the expected cost of the positive classification is no greater than the expected cost of the negative classification. That is, we will make a positive classification if and only if:

$$P(0|x) \cdot Cost_{FP} + P(1|x) \cdot Cost_{TP} \le P(0|x) \cdot Cost_{TN} + P(1|x) \cdot Cost_{FN}$$

That is, if and only if:

$$P(0|x) \cdot (Cost_{FP} - Cost_{TN}) \le P(1|x) \cdot (Cost_{FN} - Cost_{TP}) \qquad (16.1)$$

Now, suppose we subtract a constant a from each cell in the top row of the cost matrix (Table 16.1), and we subtract a constant b from each cell in the bottom row. Then equation (16.1) becomes

$$P(0|x) \cdot [(Cost_{FP} - a) - (Cost_{TN} - a)] \le P(1|x) \cdot [(Cost_{FN} - b) - (Cost_{TP} - b)]$$

which simplifies to equation (16.1). Thus, we have *Result 1*.

RESULT 1: DECISION INVARIANCE UNDER ROW ADJUSTMENT

A classification decision is not changed by the addition or subtraction of a constant from the cells in the same *row* of a cost matrix.

16.2 POSITIVE CLASSIFICATION CRITERION

We use Result 1 to develop a criterion for making positive classification decisions, as follows. First, subtract $a = \text{Cost}_{TN}$ from each cell in the top row of the cost matrix, and subtract $b = \text{Cost}_{TP}$ from each cell in the bottom row of the cost matrix. This gives us the *adjusted cost matrix* shown in Table 16.2.

Result 1 means that we can always adjust the costs in our cost matrix so that the two cells representing correct decisions have zero cost. Thus, the adjusted costs are

$$\text{Cost}_{FP,\text{Adjusted}} = \text{Cost}_{FP,\text{Adj}} = \text{Cost}_{FP} - \text{Cost}_{TN}$$
$$\text{Cost}_{FN,\text{Adjusted}} = \text{Cost}_{FN,\text{Adj}} = \text{Cost}_{FN} - \text{Cost}_{TP}$$
$$\text{Cost}_{TP,\text{Adjusted}} = \text{Cost}_{TP,\text{Adj}} = 0$$
$$\text{Cost}_{TN,\text{Adjusted}} = \text{Cost}_{TN,\text{Adj}} = 0$$

Rewriting equation (16.1), we will then make a positive classification if and only if:

$$P(0|x) \cdot \text{Cost}_{FP,\text{Adj}} \leq P(1|x) \cdot \text{Cost}_{FN,\text{Adj}} \tag{16.2}$$

As $P(0|x) = 1 - P(1|x)$, we can re-express equation (16.2) as

$$[1 - P(1|x)] \cdot \text{Cost}_{FP,\text{Adj}} \leq P(1|x) \cdot \text{Cost}_{FN,\text{Adj}}$$

which, after some algebraic modifications, becomes:

$$\text{Cost}_{FP,\text{Adj}} \leq P(1|x) \cdot [\text{Cost}_{FN,\text{Adj}} + \text{Cost}_{FP,\text{Adj}}]$$

This leads us to Result 2.

RESULT 2: POSITIVE CLASSIFICATION CRITERION

Let $P(1|x) = PC$ represent a model's *positive confidence*; that is, the model's confidence in making a positive classification. And let the *positive confidence threshold* (*PCT*) be defined as

$$PCT = \text{Positive Confidence Threshold} = \frac{\text{Cost}_{FP,\text{Adj}}}{\text{Cost}_{FN,\text{Adj}} + \text{Cost}_{FP,\text{Adj}}}$$

Then, a positive classification is made if and only if

$$PC \geq PCT.$$

TABLE 16.2 Adjusted cost matrix

		Predicted Category	
		0	1
Actual category	0	0	$\text{Cost}_{FP} - \text{Cost}_{TN}$
	1	$\text{Cost}_{FN} - \text{Cost}_{TP}$	0

16.3 DEMONSTRATION OF THE POSITIVE CLASSIFICATION CRITERION

For C5.0 models, the model's confidence in making a positive *or* negative classification is given as

$$\text{Confidence} = \frac{\text{Number correct in leaf} + 1}{\text{Total number in leaf} + 2}$$

The model's positive confidence PC is then calculated as

> If classification is positive, then $PC = \text{confidence}$,
>
> Else, $PC = 1 - \text{confidence}$.

We demonstrate the positive classification criterion using the *Adult2_training* data set and the *Adult2_test* data set, as follows. First, three C5.0 classification models are trained on the training data set:

- Model A, with no misclassification costs. Here, $\text{Cost}_{FP} = \text{Cost}_{FN} = 1$ and $\text{Cost}_{TP} = \text{Cost}_{TN} = 0$, so that $\text{Cost}_{FP,Adj} = \text{Cost}_{FP} - \text{Cost}_{TN} = 1, \text{Cost}_{FN,Adj} = \text{Cost}_{FN} - \text{Cost}_{TP} = 1$ and the positive confidence threshold is $PCT = \frac{\text{Cost}_{FP,Adj}}{\text{Cost}_{FP,Adj} + \text{Cost}_{FP,Adj}} = \frac{1}{2} = 0.5$. Thus, Model A should make positive classifications when $PC \geq 0.5$.

- Model B, with $\text{Cost}_{FP} = 2, \text{Cost}_{FN} = 1$, and $\text{Cost}_{TP} = \text{Cost}_{TN} = 0$. Here, $\text{Cost}_{FP,Adj} = 2, \text{Cost}_{FN,Adj} = 1$ and the positive confidence threshold is $PCT = \frac{2}{3} = 0.67$. Thus, Model B should make positive classifications when $PC \geq 0.67$.

- Model C, with $\text{Cost}_{FP} = 4, \text{Cost}_{FN} = 1$, and $\text{Cost}_{TP} = \text{Cost}_{TN} = 0$. Here, $\text{Cost}_{FP,Adj} = 4, \text{Cost}_{FN,Adj} = 1$ and the positive confidence threshold is $PCT = \frac{4}{5} = 0.8$. Thus, Model C should make positive classifications when $PC \geq 0.8$.

Each model is evaluated on the test data set. For each record for each model, the model's positive confidence PC is calculated. Then, for each model, a histogram of the values of PC is constructed, with an overlay of the target classification. These histograms are shown in Figures 16.1a–c for Models A, B, and C, respectively. Note that, as expected:

- For Model A, the model makes positive classifications, whenever $PC \geq 0.5$.

- For Model B, the model makes positive classifications, whenever $PC \geq 0.67$.

- For Model C, the model makes positive classifications, whenever $PC \geq 0.8$.

16.4 CONSTRUCTING THE COST MATRIX

Suppose that our client is a retailer seeking to maximize revenue from a direct marketing mailing of coupons to likely customers for an upcoming sale. A positive response

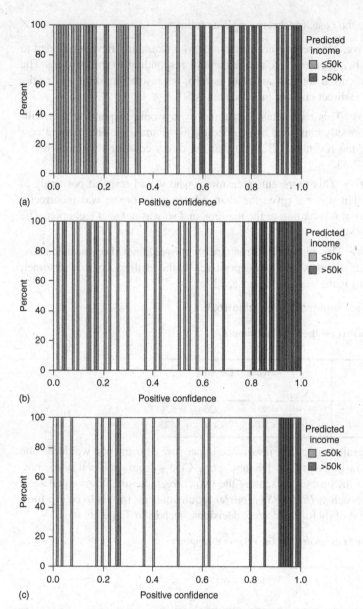

Figure 16.1   (a) Model A: Positive classification when PC $\geq$ 0.5. (b) Model B: Positive classification when PC $\geq$ 0.67. (c) Model C: Positive classification when PC $\geq$ 0.8.

represents a customer who will shop the sale and spend money. A negative response represents a customer who will not shop the sale and spend money. Suppose that mailing a coupon to a customer costs \$2, and that previous experience suggests that those who shopped similar sales spent an average of \$25.

We calculate the costs for this example as follows:

- **True Negative**. This represents a customer who would not have responded to the mailing being correctly classified as not responding to the mailing. The actual cost incurred for this customer is zero, because no mailing was made. Therefore, the direct cost for this decision is $0.

- **True Positive**. This represents a customer who would respond to the mailing being correctly classified as responding to the mailing. The mailing cost is $2, while the revenue is $25, so that the direct cost for this customer is $2 - $25 = -$23.

- **False Negative**. This represents a customer who would respond positively to the mailing, but was not given the chance because he or she was incorrectly classified as not responding to the mailing, and so was not sent a coupon. The direct cost is $0.

- **False Positive**. This represents a customer who would not shop the sale being incorrectly classified as responding positively to the mailing. For this customer, the direct cost is the mailing expense, $2.

These costs are summarized in Table 16.3.

TABLE 16.3 Cost matrix for the retailer example

		Predicted Category	
		0	1
Actual category	0	$Cost_{TN} = \$0$	$Cost_{FP} = \$2$
	1	$Cost_{FN} = \$0$	$Cost_{TP} = \$23$

Then, by Result 1 (decision invariance under row adjustment), we derive the adjusted cost matrix in Table 16.4 by subtracting $Cost_{TP}$ from each cell in the bottom row. Note that the costs representing the two correct classifications equal zero. Software packages such as *IBM/SPSS Modeler* require the cost matrix to be in a form where there are zero costs for the correct decisions, such as in Table 16.4.

TABLE 16.4 Adjusted cost matrix for the retailer example

		Predicted Category	
		0	1
Actual category	0	0	$Cost_{FP,Adj} = \$2$
	1	$Cost_{FN,Adj} = \$23$	0

16.5 DECISION INVARIANCE UNDER SCALING

Now, Result 2 states that we will make a positive classification when a model's PC is not less than the following:

$$\frac{Cost_{FP,Adj}}{Cost_{FN,Adj} + Cost_{FP,Adj}} = \frac{2}{2+23} = \frac{2}{25} = \frac{1}{12.5} = \frac{0.08}{1} = 0.08 \qquad (16.3)$$

Examining equation (16.3), we can see that the new adjusted cost matrices in Tables 16.5 and 16.6 are equivalent to the adjusted cost matrix in Table 16.4 for the purposes of rendering a classification decision. If it is important, say for interpretation purposes, for one of the adjusted costs to be expressed as a unit (e.g., $1), then this can be done – for either adjusted cost – by dividing through by the appropriate adjusted cost. For example, we can tell our client that, for every dollar that a false positive costs us, a false negative costs us $11.50 (Table 16.5); or conversely, for every dollar that a false negative costs us, a false positive costs us only eight cents (Table 16.6).

What we are doing here is scaling (dividing) by one of the adjusted costs; hence, we have Result 3.

RESULT 3: DECISION INVARIANCE UNDER SCALING

A classification decision is not changed by scaling by a constant in all cells of the cost matrix.

For example, the pairs of adjusted costs in Table 16.7 are equivalent for the purposes of rendering a classification decision:

Important note: When calculating the total cost of a classification model, or when comparing the total cost of a set of models, the analyst should use the original unadjusted cost matrix as shown in Table 16.3, and without applying any matrix

TABLE 16.5 **Adjusted cost matrix, where the false positive adjusted cost equals 1**

		Predicted Category	
		0	1
Actual category	0	0	$Cost_{FP,Adj\_3} = \$1$
	1	$Cost_{FN,Adj\_3} = \$11.5$	0

TABLE 16.6 **Adjusted cost matrix, where the false negative adjusted cost equals 1**

		Predicted Category	
		0	1
Actual category	0	0	$Cost_{FP,Adj\_4} = \$0.08$
	1	$Cost_{FN,Adj\_4} = \$1$	0

TABLE 16.7   Pairs of equivalent adjusted costs

Adjusted Cost Matrix	Adjusted False Positive Cost	Adjusted False Negative Cost
Original	$\text{Cost}_{FP,Adj}$	$\text{Cost}_{FN,Adj}$
Scaled by $\text{Cost}_{FP,Adj}$	$\dfrac{\text{Cost}_{FP,Adj}}{\text{Cost}_{FP,Adj}} = 1$	$\dfrac{\text{Cost}_{FN,Adj}}{\text{Cost}_{FP,Adj}}$
Scaled by $\text{Cost}_{FN,Adj}$	$\dfrac{\text{Cost}_{FP,Adj}}{\text{Cost}_{FN,Adj}}$	$\dfrac{\text{Cost}_{FN,Adj}}{\text{Cost}_{FN,Adj}} = 1$

row adjustment or scaling. The row adjustment and scaling leads to equivalent classification decisions, but it changes the reported costs of the final model. Therefore, use the unadjusted cost matrix when calculating the total cost of a classification model.

16.6   DIRECT COSTS AND OPPORTUNITY COSTS

Direct cost represents the actual expense of the class chosen by the classification model, while *direct gain* is the actual revenue obtained by choosing that class. Our cost matrix above was built using direct costs only. However, *opportunity cost* represents the lost benefit of the class that was *not* chosen by the classification model. *Opportunity gain* represents the unincurred cost of the class that was *not* chosen by the classification model. We illustrate how to combine direct costs and opportunity costs into total costs, which can then be used in a cost-benefit analysis, using the following example. For example, for the false negative situation, the *opportunity gain* is $2, in that the client saved the cost of the coupon, but the *opportunity cost* is $25, in that the client did not receive the benefit of the $25 in revenue this customer would have spent. So, the opportunity cost is $25 − $2 = $23. Why then, do not we use opportunity costs when constructing the cost matrix? Because doing so would double count the costs. For example, a switch of a single customer from a false negative to a true positive would result in an decrease in model cost of $46 if we counted both the false negative opportunity cost and the true positive direct cost, which is twice as much as a single customer spends, on average.[2]

16.7   CASE STUDY: COST-BENEFIT ANALYSIS USING DATA-DRIVEN MISCLASSIFICATION COSTS

Many of the concepts presented in this chapter are now brought together in the following case study application of cost-benefit analysis using data-driven misclassification

[2]Thanks to Frank Bensics, PhD, FSA, and to Iain Pardoe, PhD, for valuable discussions regarding these issues.

costs. In this era of big data, businesses should leverage the information in their existing databases in order to help uncover the optimal predictive models. In other words, as an alternative to assigning misclassification costs because "these cost values seem right to our consultant" or "that is how we have always modeled them," we would instead be well advised to listen to the data, and learn from the data itself what the misclassification costs should be. The following case study illustrates this process.

The *Loans* data set represents a set of bank loan applications for a 3-year term. Predictors include *debt-to-income ratio*, *request amount*, and *FICO score*. The target variable is *approval*; that is, whether or not the loan application is approved, based on the predictor information. The interest represents a flat rate of 15% times the request amount, times 3 years, and should not be used to build prediction models. The bank would like to maximize its revenue by funding the loan applications that are likely to be repaid, and not funding those loans that will default. (We make the simplifying assumption that all who are approved for the loan actually take the loan.)

Our strategy for deriving and applying data-driven misclassification costs is as follows.

STRATEGY FOR APPLYING DATA-DRIVEN MISCLASSIFICATION COSTS

1. Calculate the mean request amount per applicant. (Assume approved loans are fully funded.) This represents what the bank stands to lose if the applicant defaults on the loan.

2. Find the mean amount of loan interest per applicant. This represents the bank's revenue.

3. Use the information in Steps (1) and (2) to construct data-driven misclassification costs. Construct the cost matrix.

4. Adjust the cost matrix from Step (3) into a form conducive to the software, in this case, *IBM/SPSS Modeler*.

5. Using the *Loans_training* data set, develop a classification and regression trees (CART) model that does not use misclassification costs for predicting *approval*, based on *debt-to-income ratio*, *request amount*, and *FICO score*. Assume that this naïve model has been in use by the bank until now.

6. Using the *Loans_training* data set, develop a CART model that uses the adjusted cost matrix from (4), for predicting *approval*, based on *debt-to-income ratio*, *request amount*, and *FICO score*.

7. Using the *Loans_test* data set, evaluate each model from (5) and (6) using the model comparison cost matrix (similarly to Table 16.9). For each model, report the usual model evaluation measures, such as overall error rate. Most importantly, however, report *total model revenue* (i.e., negative model cost) and the *revenue per applicant*. Report the absolute difference in total model revenue and the percentage difference in revenue per applicant harvested by the model using misclassification costs and compare the naïve model the bank used previously.

Note that our misclassification costs are *data-driven*, meaning that the data set itself is providing all of the information needed to assign the values of the misclassification costs. Using the *Loans_training* data set, we find that the mean amount requested is $13,427, and the mean amount of loan interest is $6042. A positive decision represents loan approval. We make a set of simplifying assumptions, to allow us to concentrate on the process at hand, as follows.

SIMPLIFYING ASSUMPTIONS

- The only costs and gains that we model are principal and interest. Other types of costs such as clerical costs are ignored.
- If a customer defaults on a loan, the default is assumed to occur essentially immediately, so that no interest is accrued to the bank from such loans.

We proceed to develop the cost matrix, as follows.

- **True Negative**. This represents an applicant who would not have been able to repay the loan (i.e., defaulted) being correctly classified for non-approval. The cost incurred for this applicant is $0, because no loan was proffered, no interest was accrued, and no principal was lost.
- **True Positive**. This represents an applicant who would reliably repay the loan being correctly classified for loan approval. The bank stands to make $6042 (the mean amount of loan interest) from customers such as this. So the cost for this applicant is −$6042.
- **False Negative**. This represents an applicant who would have reliably paid off the loan, but was not given the chance because he or she was incorrectly classified for non-approval. The cost incurred for this applicant is $0, because no loan was proffered, no interest was accrued, and no principal was lost.
- **False Positive**. This represents an applicant who will default being incorrectly classified for loan approval. This is a very costly error for the bank, directly costing the bank the mean loan amount requested, $13,427.

We summarize the costs in Table 16.8.

Table 16.8 will be used to calculate the total cost of any classification models built using these misclassification costs.

TABLE 16.8 Matrix of direct costs for the bank loan case study

		Predicted Category	
		0	1
Actual category	0	$\text{Cost}_{TN} = \$0$	$\text{Cost}_{FP} = \$13,427$
	1	$\text{Cost}_{FN} = \$0$	$\text{Cost}_{TP} = -\$6042$

We adjust the cost matrix in Table 16.8 to make it conducive to the software, by subtracting $\text{Cost}_{TP} = -\$6042$ from the bottom row, giving us the adjusted cost matrix in Table 16.9.

TABLE 16.9   Adjusted cost matrix for the bank loan case study

		Predicted Category	
		0	1
Actual category	0	0	$\text{Cost}_{FP,Adj} = \$13,427$
	1	$\text{Cost}_{FN,Adj} = \$6042$	0

For simplicity, we apply Result 3, scaling each of the non-zero costs by $\text{Cost}_{FN,Adj} = \$6042$, to arrive at the cost matrix shown in Table 16.10.

TABLE 16.10   Simplified cost matrix for the bank loan case study

		Predicted Category	
		0	1
Actual category	0	0	$\text{Cost}_{FP,Adj} = 2.222277$
	1	$\text{Cost}_{FN,Adj} = 1$	0

Using the *Loans_training* data set, two CART models are constructed:

- Model 1: The naïve CART model with no misclassification costs, used by the bank until now.
- Model 2: The CART model with misclassification costs specified in Table 16.10.

These models are then evaluated using the *Loans_test* data set. The resulting contingency tables for Model 1 and Model 2 are shown in Tables 16.11 and 16.12, respectively. These counts were evaluated using the matrix of total costs in Table 16.8.

TABLE 16.11   Contingency table for Model 1 with no misclassification costs

		Predicted Category	
		0	1
Actual category	0	18,314	6620
	1	1171	23,593

Table 16.13 contains the evaluation measures for Models 1 and 2, with the better performing model's results in bold. Note that Model 1 performs better with the following measures: accuracy, overall error rate, sensitivity, false positive rate, proportion of true negatives, and proportion of false negatives. Model 2 performs

TABLE 16.12 Contingency table for Model 2, with data-driven misclassification costs

		Predicted Category	
		0	1
Actual category	0	21,595	3339
	1	6004	18,760

TABLE 16.13 Evaluation measures. Model 2, with data-driven misclassification costs, has increased revenue by nearly $15 million (better performance in bold)

	CART Model	
Evaluation Measure	Model 1: Without Misclassification Costs	Model 2: With Misclassification Costs
Accuracy	**0.8432**	0.8120
Overall error rate	**0.1568**	0.1880
Sensitivity	**0.9527**	0.7576
False positive rate	**0.0473**	0.2424
Specificity	0.7345	**0.8661**
False negative rate	0.2655	**0.1339**
Proportion of true positives	0.7809	**0.8489**
Proportion of false positives	0.2191	**0.1511**
Proportion of true negatives	**0.9399**	0.7825
Proportion of false negatives	**0.0601**	0.2175
Overall model cost	−$53,662,166	**−$68,515,167**
Revenue per applicant	$1080	**$1379**

better with respect to specificity, false negative rate, proportion of true positives, and proportion of false positives. Recall that, for the bank, the false positive error is the more costly mistake. Thus, Model 2, with its heavier penalty for making the false positive error, delivers a lower proportion of false positives (0.1511 vs 0.2191). But most importantly, Model 2 delivers where it counts: in the bottom line. The overall model cost is −$53,662,166 for Model 1 and −$68,515,167 for Model 2, meaning that the increase in revenue for the model using misclassification costs compared to the model not using misclassification costs is

$$\text{Increase in Revenue} = \$68,515,167 - \$53,662,166 = \$14,853,001$$

That is, the simple step of applying data-driven misclassification costs has led to an increase in revenue of nearly $15 million. This represents a per-applicant increase in revenues of $1379 − $1080 = $299.

16.8 REBALANCING AS A SURROGATE FOR MISCLASSIFICATION COSTS

Not all algorithms have an explicit method for applying misclassification costs. For example, the *IBM/SPSS Modeler* implementation of neural network modeling does not allow for misclassification costs. Fortunately, data analysts may use rebalancing as a surrogate for misclassification costs. *Rebalancing* refers to the practice of oversampling either the positive or negative responses, in order to mirror the effects of misclassification costs. The formula for the rebalancing, due to Elkan,[3] is as follows.

REBALANCING AS A SURROGATE FOR MISCLASSIFICATION COSTS

- If $Cost_{FP,Adj} > Cost_{FN,Adj}$, then multiply the number of records with negative responses in the training data by a, before applying the classification algorithm, where a is the *resampling ratio*, $a = Cost_{FP,Adj}/Cost_{FN,Adj}$.

- If $Cost_{FN,Adj} > Cost_{FP,Adj}$, then multiply the number of records with positive responses in the training data by b, before applying the classification algorithm, where b is the *resampling ratio*, $b = Cost_{FN,Adj}/Cost_{FP,Adj}$.

For the bank loan case study, we have $Cost_{FP,Adj} = \$13,427 > Cost_{FN,Adj} = \$6042$, so that our resampling ratio is $a = 13,427/6042 = 2.22$. We therefore multiply the number of records with negative responses (Approval $= F$) in the training data set by 2.22. This is accomplished by resampling the records with negative responses with replacement.

We then provide the following four network models:

- Model 3: The naïve neural network model, constructed on a training set with no rebalancing.

- Model 4: A neural network model constructed on a training set with $a = 2.0$ times as many negative records as positive records.

- Model 5: The neural network model constructed on a training set with $a = 2.22$ times as many negative records as positive records.

- Model 6: A neural network model constructed on a training set with $a = 2.5$ times as many negative records as positive records.

Table 16.14 contains the counts of positive and negative responses in the training data set, along with the achieved resampling ratio for each of Models 3–6. Note that the higher counts for the negative responses were accomplished through resampling with replacement.

. The four models were then evaluated using the test data set. Table 16.15 contains the evaluation measures for these models.

---

[3]Charles Elkan, The Foundations of Cost-Sensitive Learning, in *Proceedings of the Seventeenth International Joint Conference of Artificial Intelligence*, 973–978, Seattle, WA, Morgan Kaufmann, 2001.

TABLE 16.14   Counts of negative and positive responses, and achieved resampling ratios

	Negative Responses	Positive Responses	Desired Resampling Ratio	Achieved Resampling Ratio
Model 3	75,066	75,236	N/A	N/A
Model 4	150,132	75,236	2.0	$150,132/75,236 = 1.996$
Model 5	166,932	75,236	2.22	$166,932/75,236 = 2.219$
Model 6	187,789	75,236	2.5	$187,789/75,236 = 2.496$

TABLE 16.15   Evaluation measures for resampled models. The resampled neural network model with the data-driven resampling ratio, is the highest performing model of all (best performing model highlighted)

	CART Model			
Evaluation Measure	Model 3: None	Model 4: $a=2.0$	Model 5: $a=2.22$	Model 6: $a=2.5$
Accuracy	**0.8512**	0.8361	0.8356	0.8348
Overall error rate	**0.1488**	0.1639	0.1644	0.1652
Sensitivity	**0.9408**	0.8432	0.8335	0.8476
False positive rate	**0.0592**	0.1568	0.1665	0.1526
Specificity	0.7622	0.8291	**0.8376**	0.8221
False negative rate	0.2378	0.1709	**0.1624**	0.1779
Proportion of true positives	0.7971	0.8305	**0.8360**	0.8256
Proportion of false positives	0.2029	0.1695	**0.1640**	0.1744
Proportion of true negatives	**0.9284**	0.8418	0.8351	0.8446
Proportion of false negatives	**0.0716**	0.1582	0.1649	0.1554
Overall model cost	−$61,163,875	−$68,944,513	**−$70,346,999**	−$67,278,877
Revenue per applicant	$1231	$1387	**$1415**	$1354

Note that Model 5, whose resampling ratio of 2.22 is data-driven, being entirely specified by the data-driven adjusted misclassification costs, is the highest performing model of all, with model cost of $-\$70,346,999$, and a per-applicant revenue of $1415. In fact, the neural network model with 2.22 rebalancing outperformed our previous best model, the CART model with misclassification costs, by

$$\text{Increase in Revenue} = \$70,346,999 - \$68,515,167 = \$1,831,832$$

This $1.83 million may have been lost had the bank's data analyst not had recourse to the technique of using rebalancing as a surrogate for misclassification costs.

Why does rebalancing work? Take the case where $\text{Cost}_{FP,Adj} > \text{Cost}_{FN,Adj}$. Here, the false positive is the more expensive error. The only way a false positive error can arise is if the response should be negative. Rebalancing provides the algorithm with a greater number of records with a negative response, so that the algorithm can have a richer set of examples from which to learn about records with negative responses. This preponderance of information about records with negative responses is taken into account by the algorithm, just as if the weight of these records was greater. This diminishes the propensity of the algorithm to classify a record as positive, and therefore decreases the proportion of false positives.

For example, suppose we have a decision tree algorithm that defined confidence and PC as follows:

$$\text{Confidence} = \frac{\text{Number correct in leaf} + 1}{\text{Total number in leaf} + 2}$$

If classification is positive, then positive confidence = confidence,

Else, positive confidence = 1 − confidence.

And suppose (for illustration) that this decision tree algorithm did not have a way to define the misclassification costs, $\text{Cost}_{FP,Adj} > \text{Cost}_{FN,Adj}$. Consider Result 2, which states that a model will make a positive classification if and only if its positive confidence is greater than the positive confidence threshold; that is, if and only if

$$PC \geq PCT$$

where

$$PCT = \text{Positive Confidence Threshold} = \frac{\text{Cost}_{FP,Adj}}{\text{Cost}_{FN,Adj} + \text{Cost}_{FP,Adj}}$$

The algorithm does not have recourse to the misclassification costs on the right-hand side of the inequality $PC \geq PCT$. However, equivalent behavior may be obtained by manipulating the PC on the left-hand side. Because $\text{Cost}_{FP,Adj} > \text{Cost}_{FN,Adj}$, we add extra negative-response records, which has the effect of increasing the typical number of records in each leaf across the tree, which, because the new records are negative, typically reduces the PC. Thus, on average, it becomes more difficult for the algorithm to make positive predictions, and therefore fewer false positive errors will be made.

The R Zone

Load and prepare the data, and load the required package

```
adult <- read.csv(file = "C:/ ... /adult.txt",
    stringsAsFactors=TRUE)
library("C50")

# After collapsing categories and standardize variables in Chapter 11:
x <- adult[,c(2,6, 9, 10, 16, 17, 18, 19, 20)]
y <- adult$income
xydat <- cbind(x, y)
# Create Training and Testing Adult datasets
choose <- runif(dim(xydat)[1], 0, 1)
a.train <- xydat[which(choose <= 0.75),]
a.test<- xydat[which(choose > 0.75),]
```

Run the models

```
# Model A: Cost FP = 1, FN = 1, TP = 0, TN = 0
costA <- matrix(c(0, 1, 1, 0),  2, 2)
rownames(costA) <- colnames(costA) <- levels(y)
c50fitA <- C5.0(x=a.train[,1:9], a.train$y, costs = costA)

# Model B: Cost FP = 2, FN = 1, TP = 0, TN = 0
costB <- matrix(c(0, 2, 1, 0),  2, 2)
rownames(costB) <- colnames(costB) <- levels(y)
c50fitB <- C5.0(x=a.train[,1:9], a.train$y, costs = costB)

# Model C: Cost FP = 4, FN = 1, TP = 0, TN = 0
costC <- matrix(c(0, 4, 1, 0), 2, 2)
rownames(costC) <- colnames(costC) <- levels(y)
c50fitC <- C5.0(x=a.train[,1:9], a.train$y, costs = costC)
```

Evaluate each model on the test data set

```
pA.prob <- predict(c50fitA, newdata=a.test[,1:9], type = "prob")
pA.class <- predict(c50fitA, newdata=a.test[,1:9], type = "class" )
# Model A
modelA.class <- ifelse(pA.class==">50K.", 2, 1)
dotchart(pA.prob[,2], color = modelA.class, pch = 16, bg = "white",
    lcolor = "white",ylab = "", labels="", xlab = "Positive Confidence",
    main = "Plot of Positive Confidence for Model A")
# NOTE:  As of May 2014, the C5.0 package does not supply confidence values for
# models built using costs.  Therefore, Model B and Model C
    cannot have their PC plots made.
# For more detail, type: ?C5.0
```

Read in and prepare Loans data sets, and display mean request amount

```
loan.train <- read.csv(file="C:/ ... /Loans_Training.csv",
    header = TRUE)
choose <- sample(dim(loan.train)[1], size = 1000)
train <- loan.train[choose,-5]
test <- read.csv(file="C:/ ... /Loans_Test.csv",
    header = TRUE)
train$DtIR.z <- (train$Debt.to.Income.Ratio-
    mean(train$Debt.to.Income.Ratio))/sd(train$Debt.to.Income.Ratio)
train$FICOs.z <- (train$FICO.Score - mean(train$FICO.Score))/sd(train$FICO.Score)
train$ReqAmt.z <- (train$Request.Amount-
    mean(train$Request.Amount))/sd(train$Request.Amount)
mean(train$Request.Amount)  # Mean request amount
mean(train$Request.Amount*0.15)*3 # Mean interest
train <- train[,-c(2:4)]
test$DtIR.z <- (test$Debt.to.Income.Ratio-
    mean(test$Debt.to.Income.Ratio))/sd(test$Debt.to.Income.Ratio)
test$FICOs.z <- (test$FICO.Score - mean(test$FICO.Score))/sd(test$FICO.Score)
test$ReqAmt.z <- (test$Request.Amount-
    mean(test$Request.Amount))/sd(test$Request.Amount)
test <- test[,-c(2:4)]
```

Run the models and evaluate on Test data

```
# Declare cost matrix
costs <- matrix(c(0, 2.22, 1, 0), ncol=2, byrow=FALSE)
rownames(costs) <- colnames(costs) <- levels(as.factor(train[,1]))
# Run the models
m.nocost <- C5.0(x=train[,-1], as.factor(train[,1]))
m.cost <- C5.0(x=train[,-1], as.factor(train[,1]), costs = costs)
# Predict Test data
m.nocost.pred <- predict(object=m.nocost, newdata=test)
m.cost.pred <- predict(object=m.cost, newdata=test)
```

Evaluate results

```
test[,1] # Actual categories
m.nocost.pred # Predicted categories
sum(test[,1]==m.nocost.pred)/dim(test)[1] # Accuracy
1 - sum(test[,1]==m.nocost.pred)/dim(test)[1] # Overall Error Rate
# And so on
```

R REFERENCES

1. Kuhn M, Weston S, Coulter N. 2013. C code for C5.0 by R. Quinlan. C50: C5.0 decision trees and rule-based models. R package version 0.1.0-15. http://CRAN.R-project.org/package=C50.
2. R Core Team. *R: A Language and Environment for Statistical Computing*. Vienna, Austria: R Foundation for Statistical Computing; 2012. ISBN: 3-900051-07-0, http://www.R-project.org/.

EXERCISES

For Exercises 1–8, state what you would expect to happen to the indicated classification evaluation measure, if we increase the false negative misclassification cost, while not increasing the false positive cost. Explain your reasoning.

1. Sensitivity.
2. False positive rate.
3. Specificity.
4. False negative rate.
5. Proportion of true positives.
6. Proportion of false positives.
7. Proportion of true negatives
8. Proportion of false negatives.
9. True or false: The overall error rate is always the best indicator of a good model.

10. Describe what is meant by the minimum expected cost principle.

11. Explain decision invariance under row adjustment.

12. True or false: We can always adjust the costs in our cost matrix so that the two cells representing correct decisions have zero cost.

13. What is the difference between confidence and positive confidence?

14. What is the adjusted false positive cost? The adjusted false negative cost?

15. What is the positive confidence threshold?

16. Explain the positive classification criterion.

17. Clearly explain how Figure 16.1 demonstrates the positive classification criterion for a C5.0 binary classifier.

18. Explain what is meant by decision invariance under scaling.

19. How might Result 3 be of use to an analyst making a presentation to a client?

20. What are direct costs? Opportunity costs? Why should we not include both when constructing our cost matrix?

21. What do we mean when we say that the misclassification costs in the case study are data-driven?

22. In the case study, explain why Model 1 has better sensitivity, lower proportion of false negatives, and lower overall error rate. Then explain why Model 2 is better.

23. Why might we need rebalancing as a surrogate for misclassification costs?

24. Explain how we do such rebalancing when the adjusted false positive cost is greater than the adjusted false negative cost.

25. What does it mean to say that the resampling ratio is data-driven?

26. Why does rebalancing work as a surrogate for misclassification costs?

Use the following information for Exercises 27–44.

Suppose that our client is a retailer seeking to maximize revenue from a direct marketing mailing of coupons to likely customers for an upcoming sale. A positive response represents a customer who will shop the sale and spend money. A negative response represents a customer who will not shop the sale and spend money. Suppose that mailing a coupon to a customer costs $5, and that previous experience suggests that those who shopped similar sales spent an average of $100.

27. Explain why (i) misclassification costs are needed in this scenario, and (ii) the overall error rate is not the best measure of a good model.

28. Construct the cost matrix. Provide rationales for each cost.

29. Use Result 1 to construct the adjusted cost matrix. Interpret the adjusted costs.

30. Calculate the positive confidence threshold. Use Result 2 to state when the model will make a positive classification.

31. Use Result 3 to readjust the adjusted misclassification costs, so that the readjusted false positive cost is $1. Interpret the readjusted false positive and false negative costs.

32. Use Result 3 to readjust the adjusted misclassification costs, so that the readjusted false negative cost is $1. Interpret the readjusted false positive and false negative costs.

For Exercises 33–42, consider two classification models: Model 1 is a naïve model with no misclassification costs, and Model 2 uses the cost matrix you constructed earlier. Which model do you expect to perform better according to the following measures, and why?

33. Sensitivity.

34. False positive rate.

35. Specificity.

36. False negative rate.

37. Proportion of true positives.

38. Proportion of false positives.

39. Proportion of true negatives.

40. Proportion of false negatives.

41. Model cost.

42. Revenue per customer.

43. Suppose the classification algorithm of choice had no method of applying misclassification costs.

    a. What would be the resampling ratio for using rebalancing as a surrogate for misclassification costs?

    b. How should the training set be rebalanced?

44. Why don't we rebalance the test data set?

HANDS-ON EXERCISES

Use the *Churn* data set for Exercises 45–52. A positive response represents a churner (customer who will leave the company's service). A negative response represents a non-churner. Suppose that intervening with a customer in danger of churning costs $100, and that a customer who churns represents $2000 in lost revenue. Now, suppose the company's intervention strategy is useless, and that everyone the company intervenes with to stop churning will churn anyway.

45. Construct the cost matrix. Provide rationales for each cost.

46. Partition the *Churn* data set into a training data set and a test data set.

47. Using the training set, develop a CART model for predicting *Churn*. Do not use misclassification costs. Call this Model 1.

48. Using the training set, and the cost matrix, develop a CART model for predicting *Churn*. Call this Model 2.

49. Construct a table of evaluation measures for the two models, similarly to Table 16.13.

50. Report the increase or decrease in revenue, and the percentage increase or decrease in revenue per customer, obtained from using Model 2.

51. Next, assume the company's intervention strategy is perfect, and that everyone the company intervenes with to stop churning will not churn. Redo Exercises 45–50 under this assumption.

52. Finally, assume that 50% of those customers who are in danger of churning, and with whom the company intervenes, will stay with the company, and 50% will churn anyway. Redo Exercises 45–50 under this assumption.

## CHAPTER 17

COST-BENEFIT ANALYSIS FOR TRINARY AND *k*-NARY CLASSIFICATION MODELS

Not all classification problems involve binary targets. For example, color researchers may be interested in user classification of colors such as red, blue, yellow, green, and so on. In earlier chapters, we dealt with cost-benefit analysis for classification models having a binary target variable only. In this chapter, we extend our analytic framework to encompass classification evaluation measures and data-driven misclassification costs, first for trinary targets, and then for *k*-nary targets in general.

17.1 CLASSIFICATION EVALUATION MEASURES FOR A GENERIC TRINARY TARGET

For the classification problem with a generic trinary target variable taking values A, B, and C, there are nine possible combinations of predicted/actual categories, as shown in Table 17.1. The contingency table for this generic trinary problem is as shown in Table 17.2.

Decision$_{A|A}$ may be considered a *true A*, analogous to a true positive or true negative decision in the binary case. Similarly, Decision$_{B|B}$ and Decision$_{C|C}$ may be viewed as a *true B* and a *true C*, respectively. *Note, however, that the true positive/false positive/true negative/false negative usage is no longer applicable here for this trinary target variable. Thus, we need to define new classification evaluation measures.*

We denote the marginal totals as follows. Let the total number of records predicted to belong to category A be denoted as

$$\text{Count}_{A|\Sigma} = \text{Count}_{A|A} + \text{Count}_{A|B} + \text{Count}_{A|C}$$

Data Mining and Predictive Analytics, First Edition. Daniel T. Larose and Chantal D. Larose.
© 2015 John Wiley & Sons, Inc. Published 2015 by John Wiley & Sons, Inc.

TABLE 17.1   Definition and notation for the nine possible decision combinations, generic trinary variable

	Decision	Predicted	Actual
A|A	$Decision_{A\|A}$	A	A
B|B	$Decision_{B\|B}$	B	B
C|C	$Decision_{C\|C}$	C	C
A|B	$Decision_{A\|B}$	A	B
A|C	$Decision_{A\|C}$	A	C
B|A	$Decision_{B\|A}$	B	A
B|C	$Decision_{B\|C}$	B	C
C|A	$Decision_{C\|A}$	C	A
C|B	$Decision_{C\|B}$	C	B

TABLE 17.2   Contingency table for generic trinary problem

		Predicted Category			
		A	B	C	Actual Totals
Actual category	A	$Count_{A\|A}$	$Count_{B\|A}$	$Count_{C\|A}$	$Count_{\Sigma\|A}$
	B	$Count_{A\|B}$	$Count_{B\|B}$	$Count_{C\|B}$	$Count_{\Sigma\|B}$
	C	$Count_{A\|C}$	$Count_{B\|C}$	$Count_{C\|C}$	$Count_{\Sigma\|C}$
	Predicted totals	$Count_{A\|\Sigma}$	$Count_{B\|\Sigma}$	$Count_{C\|\Sigma}$	$Count_{\Sigma\|\Sigma}$

Similarly, the number of records predicted to belong to category B is given as

$$Count_{B\|\Sigma} = Count_{B\|A} + Count_{B\|B} + Count_{B\|C}$$

and the number of records predicted to belong to category C is given as

$$Count_{C\|\Sigma} = Count_{C\|A} + Count_{C\|B} + Count_{C\|C}$$

Also, let the total number of records actually belonging to category A be denoted as

$$Count_{\Sigma\|A} = Count_{A\|A} + Count_{B\|A} + Count_{C\|A}$$

Similarly, the number of actual category B records is given as

$$Count_{\Sigma\|B} = Count_{A\|B} + Count_{B\|B} + Count_{C\|B}$$

and the number of actual category C records is given as

$$Count_{\Sigma\|C} = Count_{A\|C} + Count_{B\|C} + Count_{C\|C}$$

The grand total $N = Count_{\Sigma\|\Sigma}$ represents the sum of all the cells in the contingency table.

Next, we define classification evaluation measures for the trinary case, extending and amending the similar well-known binary classification evaluation measures.

For the binary case, *sensitivity* and *specificity* are defined as follows:

$$\text{Sensitivity} = \frac{TP}{TP + FN}$$

$$\text{Specificity} = \frac{TN}{FP + TN}$$

In the binary case, sensitivity is defined as the ratio of the number of true positives to the number of actual positives in the data set. Specificity is defined as the ratio of the number of true negatives to the number of actual negatives. For the trinary case, we analogously define the following measures:

$$\text{A-sensitivity} = \frac{Count_{A|A}}{Count_{\Sigma|A}}$$

$$\text{B-sensitivity} = \frac{Count_{B|B}}{Count_{\Sigma|B}}$$

$$\text{C-sensitivity} = \frac{Count_{C|C}}{Count_{\Sigma|C}}$$

For example, A-*sensitivity* is the ratio of correctly predicted A-records to the total number of A-records. It is interpreted as the probability that a record is correctly classified as A, given that the record is actually belongs to the A class; similarly for B-*sensitivity* and C-*sensitivity*. No specificity measure is needed, because specificity in the binary case is essentially a type of sensitivity measure for the negative category.

Next, in the binary case, we have the following measures:

$$\text{False-positive rate} = 1 - \text{specificity} = \frac{FP}{FP + TN}$$

$$\text{False-negative rate} = 1 - \text{sensitivity} = \frac{FN}{TP + FN}$$

We extend these measures for the trinary case as follows:

$$\text{False A rate} = 1 - \text{A-sensitivity} = \frac{Count_{B|A} + Count_{C|A}}{Count_{\Sigma|A}}$$

$$\text{False B rate} = 1 - \text{B-sensitivity} = \frac{Count_{A|B} + Count_{C|B}}{Count_{\Sigma|B}}$$

$$\text{False C rate} = 1 - \text{C-sensitivity} = \frac{Count_{A|C} + Count_{B|C}}{Count_{\Sigma|C}}$$

For example, the *false A rate* is interpreted as the ratio of *incorrectly* classified A-records to the total number of A-records. For the binary case, the *proportion of true positives* and the *proportion of true negatives* are given as follows:

$$\text{Proportion of true positives} = PTP = \frac{TP}{TP + FP}$$

$$\text{Proportion of true negatives} = PTN = \frac{TN}{TN + FN}$$

In the binary case, PTP is interpreted as the likelihood that the record is actually positive, given that it is classified as positive. Similarly, PTN is interpreted as the likelihood that the record is actually negative, given that it is classified as negative. For the trinary case, we have the following evaluation measures, analogously defined from the binary case:

$$\text{Proportion of true As} = \frac{\text{Count}_{A|A}}{\text{Count}_{A|\Sigma}}$$

$$\text{Proportion of true Bs} = \frac{\text{Count}_{B|B}}{\text{Count}_{B|\Sigma}}$$

$$\text{Proportion of true Cs} = \frac{\text{Count}_{C|C}}{\text{Count}_{C|\Sigma}}$$

For example, the interpretation of the proportion of true As is the likelihood that a particular record actually belongs to class A, given that it is classified as A. Next we turn to the proportions of false positives and negatives, defined in the binary case as

$$\text{Proportion of false positives} = \frac{\text{FP}}{\text{FP} + \text{TP}}$$

$$\text{Proportion of false negatives} = \frac{\text{FN}}{\text{FN} + \text{TN}}$$

We extend these measures for the trinary case as follows:

$$\text{Proportion of false As} = 1 - \text{proportion of true As} = \frac{\text{Count}_{A|B} + \text{Count}_{A|C}}{\text{Count}_{A|\Sigma}}$$

$$\text{Proportion of false Bs} = 1 - \text{proportion of true Bs} = \frac{\text{Count}_{B|A} + \text{Count}_{B|C}}{\text{Count}_{B|\Sigma}}$$

$$\text{Proportion of false Cs} = 1 - \text{proportion of true Cs} = \frac{\text{Count}_{C|A} + \text{Count}_{C|B}}{\text{Count}_{C|\Sigma}}$$

Finally, we have *accuracy* and the *overall error rate*, defined as follows:

$$\text{Accuracy} = \frac{\sum_{i=j}\text{Count}_{i|j}}{N} = \frac{\text{Count}_{A|A} + \text{Count}_{B|B} + \text{Count}_{C|C}}{N}$$

$$\text{Overall error rate} = 1 - \text{accuracy} = \frac{\sum_j \sum_{i \neq j}\text{Count}_{i|j}}{N}$$

$$= \frac{(\text{Count}_{A|B} + \text{Count}_{A|C} + \text{Count}_{B|A} + \text{Count}_{B|C} + \text{Count}_{C|A} + \text{Count}_{C|B})}{N}$$

17.2 APPLICATION OF EVALUATION MEASURES FOR TRINARY CLASSIFICATION TO THE LOAN APPROVAL PROBLEM

For the trinary target variable approval, there are nine combinations of predicted/actual categories as shown in Table 17.3.

TABLE 17.3   Definition and notation for the nine possible loan decision combinations

	Decision	Predicted	Actual
D|D	$Decision_{D\|D}$	Denied	Denied
AH|AH	$Decision_{AH\|AH}$	Approved half	Approved half
AW|AW	$Decision_{AW\|AW}$	Approved whole	Approved whole
D|AH	$Decision_{D\|AH}$	Denied	Approved half
D|AW	$Decision_{D\|AW}$	Denied	Approved whole
AH|D	$Decision_{AH\|D}$	Approved half	Denied
AH|AW	$Decision_{AH\|AW}$	Approved half	Approved whole
AW|D	$Decision_{AW\|D}$	Approved whole	Denied
AW|AH	$Decision_{AW\|AH}$	Approved whole	Approved half

Table 17.4 presents the contingency table for a classification and regression trees (CART) model without misclassification costs applied to the *Loans3_training* data set and evaluated on the *Loans3_test* data set. Note that the *Loans3* data sets are similar to the *Loans* data sets except for record distribution between the two data sets, and the change from a binary target to a trinary target. We denote the marginal totals as follows. Let the total number of records predicted to be denied as

TABLE 17.4   Contingency table of CART model without misclassification costs ("model 1"), evaluated on *Loans3_test* data set

		Predicted Category			
		Denied	Approved Half	Approved Whole	Actual Totals
Actual category	Denied	$Count_{D\|D}$ 14,739	$Count_{AH\|D}$ 919	$Count_{AW\|D}$ 29	$Count_{\Sigma\|D}$ 15,687
	Approved half	$Count_{D\|AH}$ 1,098	$Count_{AH\|AH}$ 11,519	$Count_{AW\|AH}$ 1,518	$Count_{\Sigma\|AH}$ 14,135
	Approved whole	$Count_{D\|AW}$ 5	$Count_{AH\|AW}$ 1,169	$Count_{AW\|AW}$ 18,702	$Count_{\Sigma\|AW}$ 19,876
Predicted totals		$Count_{D\|\Sigma}$ 15,842	$Count_{AH\|\Sigma}$ 13,607	$Count_{AW\|\Sigma}$ 20,249	$Count_{\Sigma\|\Sigma}$ 49,698

$$Count_{D|\Sigma} = Count_{D|D} + Count_{D|AH} + Count_{D|AW}$$
$$= 14,701 + 1098 + 5 = 15,842$$

Similarly, let the number of customers predicted to be approved for funding at half the requested loan amount as

$$Count_{AH|\Sigma} = Count_{AH|D} + Count_{AH|AH} + Count_{AH|AW}$$
$$= 919 + 11,519 + 1169 = 13,607$$

and let the number of customers predicted to be approved for funding at the whole requested loan amount as

$$\text{Count}_{AW|\Sigma} = \text{Count}_{AW|D} + \text{Count}_{AW|AH} + \text{Count}_{AW|AW}$$
$$= 29 + 1518 + 18,702 = 20,249$$

Also, let the total number of customers who are actually financially insecure and should have been denied a loan as

$$\text{Count}_{\Sigma|D} = \text{Count}_{D|D} + \text{Count}_{AH|D} + \text{Count}_{AW|D}$$
$$= 14,739 + 919 + 29 = 15,687$$

Similarly, the number of customers who are actually somewhat financially secure and should have been approved for a loan at half the requested amount as

$$\text{Count}_{\Sigma|AH} = \text{Count}_{D|AH} + \text{Count}_{AH|AH} + \text{Count}_{AW|AH}$$
$$= 1098 + 11,519 + 1518 = 14,135$$

and let the number of customers who are actually quite financially secure and should have been approved for a loan at the whole requested amount as

$$\text{Count}_{\Sigma|AW} = \text{Count}_{D|AW} + \text{Count}_{AH|AW} + \text{Count}_{AW|AW}$$
$$= 5 + 1169 + 18,702 = 19,876$$

Let the grand total $N = \text{Count}_{\Sigma|\Sigma} = 49,698$ represent the sum of all the cells in the contingency table.

We are interested in evaluating our contingency tables using the trinary classification evaluation measures developed earlier. These are adapted to the trinary loan classification problem as follows:

$$\text{D-sensitivity} = \frac{\text{Count}_{D|D}}{\text{Count}_{\Sigma|D}} = \frac{14,739}{15,687} = 0.94$$

$$\text{AH-sensitivity} = \frac{\text{Count}_{AH|AH}}{\text{Count}_{\Sigma|AH}} = \frac{11,519}{14,135} = 0.81$$

$$\text{AW-sensitivity} = \frac{\text{Count}_{AW|AW}}{\text{Count}_{\Sigma|AW}} = \frac{18,702}{19,876} = 0.94$$

For example, D-*sensitivity* is the ratio of the number of applicants correctly denied a loan to the total number of applicants who were denied a loan. This is interpreted as the probability that an applicant is correctly classified as *Denied*, given that the applicant actually belongs to the *denied* class. The CART model is less sensitive to the presence of *approved half* applicants than the other classes. For example, *AH-sensitivity* = 0.81 indicates that the ratio of the number of applicants correctly denied a loan to the total number of applicants who were denied a loan. In other words, the probability is 0.81 that an applicant is correctly classified as *approved half*, given that the applicant actually belongs to the *approved half* class.

Next, we have the following:

False D rate = 1 − D-sensitivity

$$= \frac{Count_{AH|D} + Count_{AW|D}}{Count_{\Sigma|D}} = \frac{919 + 29}{15,687} = 0.06$$

False AH rate = 1 − AH-sensitivity

$$= \frac{Count_{D|AH} + Count_{AW|AH}}{Count_{\Sigma|AH}} = \frac{1098 + 1518}{14,135} = 0.19$$

False AW rate = 1 − AW-sensitivity

$$= \frac{Count_{D|AW} + Count_{AH|AW}}{Count_{\Sigma|AW}} = \frac{5 + 1169}{19,876} = 0.06$$

For example, as the complement of D-*sensitivity*, the *false D rate* is interpreted as the probability that an applicant is not classified as *denied*, even though the applicant actually belongs to the *denied* class. In this case, this probability is 0.06. Note that the false AH rate is three times that of the other rates, indicating that we can be less confident in the classifications our model makes of the *approved half* category.

For the three classes, the proportions of true classifications are specified as follows:

$$\text{Proportion of true Ds} = \frac{Count_{D|D}}{Count_{D|\Sigma}} = \frac{14,739}{15,842} = 0.93$$

$$\text{Proportion of true AHs} = \frac{Count_{AH|AH}}{Count_{AH|\Sigma}} = \frac{11,519}{13,607} = 0.85$$

$$\text{Proportion of true AWs} = \frac{Count_{AW|AW}}{Count_{AW|\Sigma}} = \frac{18,702}{20,249} = 0.92$$

For example, if a particular applicant is classified as *denied*, then the probability that this customer actually belongs to the *denied* class is 0.93. This is higher than the analogous measures for the other classes, especially AH.

Next, we find the additive inverses of these measures as follows:

Proportion of false Ds = 1 − proportion of true Ds

$$= \frac{Count_{D|AH} + Count_{D|AW}}{Count_{D|\Sigma}} = \frac{1098 + 5}{15,842} = 0.07$$

Proportion of false AHs = 1 − proportion of true AHs

$$= \frac{Count_{AH|D} + Count_{AH|AW}}{Count_{AH|\Sigma}} = \frac{919 + 1169}{13,607} = 0.15$$

Proportion of false AWs = 1 − proportion of true AWs

$$= \frac{Count_{AW|D} + Count_{AW|AH}}{Count_{AW|\Sigma}} = \frac{29 + 1518}{20,249} = 0.08$$

For instance, if an applicant is classified as *approved half*, there is a 15% chance that the applicant actually belongs to a different class.

Finally, the accuracy is given as follows:

$$\text{Accuracy} = \frac{\sum_{i=j} \text{Count}_{i|j}}{N} = \frac{\text{Count}_{D|D} + \text{Count}_{AH|AH} + \text{Count}_{AW|AW}}{N}$$
$$= \frac{14,739 + 11,519 + 18,702}{49,698} = 0.90$$

and the overall error rate is as follows:

Overall error rate

$$= 1 - \text{accuracy} = \frac{\sum_{i \neq j} \text{Count}_{i|j}}{N}$$
$$= \frac{\text{Count}_{D|AH} + \text{Count}_{D|AW} + \text{Count}_{AH|D} + \text{Count}_{AH|AW}}{N}$$
$$\qquad\qquad +\text{Count}_{AW|D} + \text{Count}_{AW|AH}$$
$$= \frac{1098 + 5 + 919 + 1169 + 29 + 1518}{49,698} = 0.10$$

That is, across all classes, our model classifies 90% of the applicants correctly, and misclassifies only 10% of all applicants.

17.3   DATA-DRIVEN COST-BENEFIT ANALYSIS FOR TRINARY LOAN CLASSIFICATION PROBLEM

To conduct a data-driven cost-benefit analysis, we look to the data to tell us what the costs and benefits of the various decisions will be.

- **Principal.** Using the *Loans3_training* data set, we find that the mean amount requested is $13,427.
  - Thus, for loans approved for the entire amount, the loan principal will be modeled as $13,427.
  - For loans approved for only half the amount, the loan principal will be set as half of $13,427, which is $6713.50.
- **Interest.** From the *Loans3_training* data set, the mean amount of loan interest is $6042.
  - Thus, for loans approved for the whole amount, the loan interest is set to $6042.
  - For loans approved for only half the amount, the loan interest is modeled as half of $6042; that is, $3021.
- **Simplifying Assumptions.** For simplicity, we make the following assumptions:
  - The only costs and gains that we model are principal and interest. Other types of costs such as clerical costs are ignored.

- ○ If a customer defaults on a loan, the default is assumed to occur essentially immediately, so that no interest is accrued to the bank from such loans.

On the basis of these data-driven specifications and simplifying assumptions, we proceed to calculate the costs as follows.

- **Decision$_{D|D}$**: Correctly predict that an applicant should be denied. This represents an applicant who would not have been able to repay the loan (i.e., defaulted) being correctly classified for non-approval. The direct cost incurred for this applicant is zero. As no loan was proffered, there could be neither interest incurred nor any default made. Thus, the cost is $0.

- **Decision$_{AH|D}$**: Predict loan approval at half the requested amount, when the applicant should have been denied the loan. The customer will default immediately, so that the bank receives no interest. Plus the bank will lose the entire amount loaned, which equals on average $6713.50, or half the average requested amount in the data set. Thus, the cost for this error is $6713.50.

- **Decision$_{AW|D}$**: Predict loan approval at the whole requested amount, when the applicant should have been denied the loan. This is the most expensive error the bank can make. On average, the bank will lose $13,427, or the average loan request amount, for each of these errors, so the cost is $13,427.

- **Decision$_{D|AH}$**: Predict loan denial when the applicant should have been approved for half the requested loan amount. As no loan was proffered, there could be neither interest incurred nor any default made. Thus, the cost is $0.

- **Decision$_{AH|AH}$**: Correctly predict than an applicant should be approved for funding half of the requested loan amount. This represents an applicant who would reliably repay the loan at half the requested amount being correctly classified for loan approval at this level. The bank stands to make $3021 (half the mean amount of loan interest) from customers such as this. So the cost for this applicant −$3021.

- **Decision$_{AW|AH}$**: Predict loan approval at the whole requested amount, when the applicant should have been approved at only half the requested amount. The assumption is that the applicant will pay off half the loan, the bank will receive the interest for half of the loan (cost = −$3021), and then the applicant will immediately default for the remainder of the loan (cost = $6713.50). Thus, the cost of this error is $3692.50 ($6713.50 − $3021).

- **Decision$_{D|AW}$**: Predict loan denial when the applicant should have been approved for the whole loan amount. Again, no loan was proffered, so the cost is $0.

- **Decision$_{AH|AW}$**: Predict loan approval at half the requested amount, when the applicant should have been approved for the entire requested loan amount. This financially secure customer will presumably be able to pay off this smaller loan, so that the bank will earn $3021 (half the mean amount of loan interest from the data set). Thus, the cost is −$3021.

- **Decision$_{AW|AW}$**: Correctly predict than an applicant should be approved for funding the whole requested loan amount. This represents an applicant who would reliably repay the entire loan being correctly classified for loan approval at this level. The bank stands to make $6042 (the mean amount of loan interest) from customers such as this. So the cost for this applicant −$6042.

We assemble these costs into the cost matrix shown in Table 17.5.

TABLE 17.5 Cost matrix for the trinary loan classification problem. Use this matrix form for calculating the *total cost* of the model

		Predicted Category		
		Denied	Approved Half	Approved Whole
Actual category	Denied	$\text{Cost}_{D|D} = \$0$	$\text{Cost}_{AH|D} = \$6713.50$	$\text{Cost}_{AW|D} = \$13,427$
	Approved half	$\text{Cost}_{D|AH} = \$0$	$\text{Cost}_{AH|AH} = -\$3021$	$\text{Cost}_{AW|AH} = \$3692.50$
	Approved whole	$\text{Cost}_{D|AW} = \$0$	$\text{Cost}_{AH|AW} = -\$3021$	$\text{Cost}_{AW|AW} = -\$6042$

17.4 COMPARING CART MODELS WITH AND WITHOUT DATA-DRIVEN MISCLASSIFICATION COSTS

Let us see what the effects are of using the data-driven misclassification costs for our CART model. We would like the diagonal elements of the total cost matrix to contain zeroes, because software such as *IBM SPSS Modeler* requires such a structure when setting the misclassification costs. By decision invariance under cost matrix row adjustment (Chapter 16), a classification decision is not changed by the addition or subtraction of a constant from the cells in the same row of a cost matrix. Thus, we can obtain our desired cost matrix with zeroes on the diagonal by

1. not altering the first row;
2. adding $3021 to each cell in the second row;
3. adding $6042 to each cell in the third row.

We then obtain the direct cost matrix with zeroes on the diagonal as shown in Table 17.6. For simplicity and perspective, the costs in Table 17.6 were scaled by the minimum nonzero entry $3021, giving us the scaled cost matrix in Table 17.7. The scaled costs in Table 17.7 were then used as the software misclassification costs to construct a CART model for predicting loan approval, based on the *Loans3_training* data set. The resulting contingency table obtained by evaluating this model with the *Loans3_test* data set is provided in Table 17.8.

Table 17.9 contains a comparison of the classification evaluation measures we have examined in this chapter for the two models. (Calculations for the model with misclassification costs are not shown, to save space.) Denote the model without misclassification costs as model 1 and the model with misclassification costs as model

TABLE 17.6 Cost matrix with zeroes on the diagonal

		Predicted Category		
		Denied	Approved Half	Approved Whole
Actual category	Denied	$\text{Cost}_{D|D} = \$0$	$\text{Cost}_{AH|D} = \$6713.50$	$\text{Cost}_{AW|D} = \$13,427$
	Approved half	$\text{Cost}_{D|AH} = \$3021$	$\text{Cost}_{AH|AH} = \$0$	$\text{Cost}_{AW|AH} = \$6713.50$
	Approved whole	$\text{Cost}_{D|AW} = \$6042$	$\text{Cost}_{AH|AW} = \$3021$	$\text{Cost}_{AW|AW} = \$0$

TABLE 17.7 Scaled cost matrix

		Predicted Category		
		Denied	Approved Half	Approved Whole
Actual category	Denied	0	2.222277	4.444555
	Approved half	1	0	2.222277
	Approved whole	2	1	0

TABLE 17.8 Contingency table of CART model with misclassification costs ("model 2")

		Predicted Category			
		Denied	Approved Half	Approved Whole	Actual Totals
Actual category	Denied	$\text{Count}_{D|D}$ 14,739	$\text{Count}_{AH|D}$ 948	$\text{Count}_{AW|D}$ 0	$\text{Count}_{\Sigma|D}$ 15,687
	Approved half	$\text{Count}_{D|AH}$ 1,098	$\text{Count}_{AH|AH}$ 12,616	$\text{Count}_{AW|AH}$ 421	$\text{Count}_{\Sigma|AH}$ 14,135
	Approved whole	$\text{Count}_{D|AW}$ 5	$\text{Count}_{AH|AW}$ 2,965	$\text{Count}_{AW|AW}$ 16,906	$\text{Count}_{\Sigma|AW}$ 19,876
	Predicted totals	$\text{Count}_{D|\Sigma}$ 15,842	$\text{Count}_{AH|\Sigma}$ 16,529	$\text{Count}_{AW|\Sigma}$ 17,327	$\text{Count}_{\Sigma|\Sigma}$ 49,698

2. Note that the measures within a cell sum to 1, indicating that the measures are additive inverses. For each metric, the better performing model is indicated in bold.

We may observe the following points of interest from the comparison provided in Table 17.9.

- Interestingly, the counts in the leftmost column of the contingency table for both models are the same, indicating that there is no difference in the models

TABLE 17.9 Comparison of evaluation measures for CART models with and without misclassification costs (better performance highlighted)

Evaluation Measure	CART Model	
	Model 1: Without Misclassification Costs	Model 2: With Misclassification Costs
D-sensitivity	0.94	0.94
False D rate	0.06	0.06
AH-sensitivity	0.81	**0.89**
False AH rate	0.19	**0.11**
AW-sensitivity	**0.94**	0.85
False AW rate	**0.06**	0.15
Proportion of true Ds	0.93	0.93
Proportion of false Ds	0.07	0.07
Proportion of true AHs	**0.85**	0.77
Proportion of false AHs	**0.15**	0.23
Proportion of true AWs	0.92	**0.98**
Proportion of false AWs	0.08	**0.02**
Accuracy	**0.90**	0.89
Overall error rate	**0.10**	0.11

with respect to predicting the *denied* category. This is supported by the exact same values for proportion of true Ds and proportion of false Ds. (The values for D-sensitivity and false D rate are similar, but not exactly the same, apart from rounding.)

- The AH-sensitivity of model 2 is superior, because it makes fewer errors of the form Decision$_{AW|AH}$. This is presumably because of the misclassification cost associated with this decision.

- The AW-sensitivity of model 1 is superior, because it makes fewer errors of the form Decision$_{AH|AW}$. One may speculate that this is because the generally high misclassification costs associated with classifying an applicant as *approved whole* have tended to make our model shy about making such a classification, thereby pushing some AW|AW decisions into the AH|AW cell.

- The proportion of true AHs of model 1 is superior, again because it makes fewer errors of the form Decision$_{AH|AW}$, and perhaps for the same reason as mentioned above.

- The proportion of true AWs of model 2 is superior, because model 2 makes fewer errors of the form Decision$_{AW|AH}$ and of the form Decision$_{AW|D}$.

- The accuracy and overall error rate of model 1 is slightly better. Does this mean that model 1 is superior overall?

When the business or research problem calls for misclassification costs, then the best metric for comparing the performance of two or models is *overall cost* of the model. Using the cost matrix from Table 17.5, we find the overall cost of model

1 (from Table 17.4) to be −$139, 163, 628, for a per-applicant profit of $2800.19. The overall cost for model 1 (from Table 17.8) is −$141, 138, 534, with a profit of $2839.92 per applicant.

Thus, the estimated revenue increase from using model 2 rather than model 1 is given as follows:

$$\text{Revenue increase} = \$141, 138, 534 - \$139, 163, 628 = \$1, 974, 906$$

Thus, model 2 is superior, in the way that counts the most, on the bottom line. In fact, simply by applying data-driven misclassification costs to our CART model, we have enhanced our estimated revenue by nearly $2 million. Now, that should be enough to earn the hardworking data analyst a nice holiday bonus.

17.5 CLASSIFICATION EVALUATION MEASURES FOR A GENERIC *k*-NARY TARGET

For the classification problem with a generic *k*-nary target variable taking values $A_1, A_2, \dots, A_k$, there are k^2 possible combinations of predicted/actual categories, as shown in Table 17.10.

The contingency table for this generic *k*-nary problem is shown in Table 17.11.

The marginal totals are defined analogously to the trinary case, and again we let the grand total $N = \text{Count}_{\Sigma|\Sigma}$ represent the sum of all the cells in the contingency table.

Next, we define classification evaluation measures for the *k*-nary case, extending the trinary case. For the *i*th class, we define sensitivity as follows:

$$A_i\text{-sensitivity} = \frac{\text{Count}_{A_i|A_i}}{\text{Count}_{\Sigma|A_i}}, \quad i = 1, 2, \dots, k$$

TABLE 17.10 The k^2 possible decision combinations, generic *k*-nary variable

	Decision	Predicted	Actual
$A_1|A_1$	$\text{Decision}_{A_1|A_1}$	A_1	A_1
$A_1|A_2$	$\text{Decision}_{A_1|A_2}$	A_1	A_2
$\vdots$	$\vdots$	$\vdots$	$\vdots$
$A_1|A_k$	$\text{Decision}_{A_1|A_k}$	A_1	A_k
$A_2|A_1$	$\text{Decision}_{A_2|A_1}$	A_2	A_1
$\vdots$	$\vdots$	$\vdots$	$\vdots$
$A_2|A_k$	$\text{Decision}_{A_2|A_k}$	A_2	A_k
$\vdots$	$\vdots$	$\vdots$	$\vdots$
$A_k|A_1$	$\text{Decision}_{A_k|A_1}$	A_k	A_1
$\vdots$	$\vdots$	$\vdots$	$\vdots$
$A_k|A_k$	$\text{Decision}_{A_k|A_k}$	A_k	A_k

TABLE 17.11 Contingency table for generic *k*-nary problem

		Predicted Category				
		A_1	A_2	$\cdots$	A_k	Actual totals
Actual category	A_1	$\text{Count}_{A_1|A_1}$	$\text{Count}_{A_2|A_1}$	$\cdots$	$\text{Count}_{A_k|A_1}$	$\text{Count}_{\Sigma|A_1}$
	A_2	$\text{Count}_{A_1|A_2}$	$\text{Count}_{A_2|A_2}$	$\cdots$	$\text{Count}_{A_k|A_2}$	$\text{Count}_{\Sigma|A_2}$
	$\vdots$	$\vdots$	$\vdots$	$\vdots$	$\vdots$	$\vdots$
	A_k	$\text{Count}_{A_1|A_k}$	$\text{Count}_{A_2|A_k}$	$\cdots$	$\text{Count}_{A_k|A_k}$	$\text{Count}_{\Sigma|A_k}$
Predicted totals		$\text{Count}_{A_1|\Sigma}$	$\text{Count}_{A_2|\Sigma}$	$\cdots$	$\text{Count}_{A_k|\Sigma}$	$\text{Count}_{\Sigma|\Sigma}$

Here A_i-sensitivity is the ratio of correctly predicted A_i-records to the total number of A_i-records. It is interpreted as the probability that a record is correctly classified A_i, given that the record actually belongs to the A_i class. Next, the *false* A_i *rate* is given by the following equation:

$$\text{False } A_i \text{ rate} = 1 - A_i\text{-}sensitivity = \frac{\sum_{i \neq j}\text{Count}_{A_j|A_i}}{\text{Count }_{\Sigma|A_i}}$$

The *false* A_i *rate* is interpreted as the ratio of *incorrectly* classified A_i-records to the total number of A_i-records. Next, we have

$$\text{Proportion of true } A_i s = \frac{\text{Count }_{A_i|A_i}}{\text{Count }_{A_i|\Sigma}}$$

and

$$\text{Proportion of false } A_i's = 1 - \text{proportion of true } A_i's = \frac{\sum_{j \neq i}\text{Count}_{A_i|A_j}}{\text{Count }_{A_i|\Sigma}}$$

Finally, the accuracy and the overall error rate are defined as

$$\text{Accuracy} = \frac{\sum_{i=j}\text{Count}_{i|j}}{N}$$

$$\text{Overall error rate} = \frac{\sum_{i \neq j}\text{Count}_{i|j}}{N}$$

17.6 EXAMPLE OF EVALUATION MEASURES AND DATA-DRIVEN MISCLASSIFICATION COSTS FOR *k*-NARY CLASSIFICATION

The *Loans4_training* and *Loans4_test* data sets are used to illustrate classification evaluation measures for a target with four classes. Note that the *Loans4* data sets are similar to the *Loans* data sets except for record distribution between the two data sets, and the change from a binary target to a quaternary (*k*-nary with $k = 4$) target. In this case, the target classes are *denied, approved 1/3, approved 2/3,* and *approved whole*. *Approved* 1/3 (denoted as A1 below) indicates that the applicant was approved for only one-third of the loan request amount, and *Approved* 2/3 (denoted A2) indicates approval of two-thirds of the request amount. A CART model was trained on the *Loans4_training* data set without misclassification costs, and fit to the data in the *Loans4_test* data set, with the resulting contingency table provided in Table 17.12.

TABLE 17.12 **Contingency table of CART model without misclassification costs, for the *Loans4* target with four classes**

		Predicted Category				
		Denied	Approved 1/3	Approved 2/3	Approved Whole	Actual Totals
Actual category	Denied	$\text{Count}_{D\mid D}$ 12,095	$\text{Count}_{A1\mid D}$ 1,018	$\text{Count}_{A2\mid D}$ 6	$\text{Count}_{AW\mid D}$ 0	$\text{Count}_{\Sigma\mid D}$ 13,119
	Approved 1/3	$\text{Count}_{D\mid A1}$ 763	$\text{Count}_{A1\mid A1}$ 7,697	$\text{Count}_{A2\mid A1}$ 1,152	$\text{Count}_{AW\mid A1}$ 13	$\text{Count}_{\Sigma\mid A1}$ 9,625
	Approved 2/3	$\text{Count}_{D\mid A2}$ 3	$\text{Count}_{A1\mid A2}$ 1,708	$\text{Count}_{A2\mid A2}$ 8,242	$\text{Count}_{AW\mid A2}$ 1,675	$\text{Count}_{\Sigma\mid A2}$ 11,628
	Approved whole	$\text{Count}_{D\mid AW}$ 0	$\text{Count}_{A1\mid AW}$ 158	$\text{Count}_{A2\mid AW}$ 1,072	$\text{Count}_{AW\mid AW}$ 14,096	$\text{Count}_{\Sigma\mid AW}$ 15,326
Predicted totals		$\text{Count}_{D\mid\Sigma}$ 12,861	$\text{Count}_{A1\mid\Sigma}$ 10,581	$\text{Count}_{A2\mid\Sigma}$ 10,472	$\text{Count}_{AW\mid\Sigma}$ 15,784	$\text{Count}_{\Sigma\mid\Sigma}$ 49,698

Again, to conduct a data-driven cost-benefit analysis, we look to the data to tell us what the costs and benefits of the various decisions will be. The mean amount of the principal for the training set is still \$13,427, so that loans approved for only one-third or two-thirds of the full amount will have principal set as \$13,427/3 = \$4475.67 and $2 \cdot \$13,427/3 = \$8951.33$, respectively. The mean amount of interest for the training set is still \$6042, so that loans approved for only one-third or two-thirds of the whole amount will have interest set as \$6042/3 = \$2014 and $2 \cdot \$6042/3 = \$4028$, respectively. The assumptions are the same as for the trinary case.

The cost matrix for this quaternary classification framework is given in Table 17.13. The reader is asked to justify these costs in the exercises. Here is a sample justification for the direct costs for $\text{Decision}_{AW\mid A2}$.

- **$\text{Decision}_{AW\mid A2}$**: Predict loan approval at the whole requested amount, when the applicant should have been approved at only two-thirds the requested amount. The assumption is that the applicant will pay off two-thirds of the loan, the bank will receive the interest for two-thirds of the loan (Cost = −\$4028), and then the applicant will immediately default for the remainder of the loan (Cost = \$4475.67). Thus, the cost of this error is \$447.67 (\$4475.67 − \$4028).

In the exercises, the reader is asked to adjust the cost matrix into a form amenable to software analysis.

TABLE 17.13   Cost matrix for quaternary classification framework

			Predicted Category		
		Denied	Approved 1/3	Approved 2/3	Approved Whole
Actual category	Denied	$\text{Cost}_{D\mid D}$ $0	$\text{Cost}_{A1\mid D}$ $4475.67	$\text{Cost}_{A2\mid D}$ $8951.33	$\text{Cost}_{AW\mid D}$ $13,427
	Approved 1/3	$\text{Cost}_{D\mid A1}$ $0	$\text{Cost}_{A1\mid A1}$ −$2014	$\text{Cost}_{A2\mid A1}$ $2461.67	$\text{Cost}_{AW\mid A1}$ $6937.33
	Approved 2/3	$\text{Cost}_{D\mid A2}$ $0	$\text{Cost}_{A1\mid A2}$ −$2014	$\text{Cost}_{A2\mid A2}$ −$4028	$\text{Cost}_{AW\mid A2}$ $447.67
	Approved whole	$\text{Cost}_{D\mid AW}$ $0	$\text{Cost}_{A1\mid AW}$ −$2014	$\text{Cost}_{A2\mid AW}$ −$4028	$\text{Cost}_{AW\mid AW}$ −$6042

Misclassification costs supplied by the adjusted cost matrix from Table 17.13 (and constructed in the exercises) were applied to a CART model, with the resulting contingency table shown in Table 17.14.

TABLE 17.14   Contingency table of CART model with misclassification costs, for the *Loans4* target with four classes

		Predicted Category				
		Denied	Approved 1/3	Approved 2/3	Approved Whole	Actual Totals
Actual category	Denied	$\text{Count}_{D\mid D}$ 12,044	$\text{Count}_{A1\mid D}$ 1,073	$\text{Count}_{A2\mid D}$ 2	$\text{Count}_{AW\mid D}$ 0	$\text{Count}_{\Sigma\mid D}$ 13,119
	Approved 1/3	$\text{Count}_{D\mid A1}$ 729	$\text{Count}_{A1\mid A1}$ 7,737	$\text{Count}_{A2\mid A1}$ 1,158	$\text{Count}_{AW\mid A1}$ 1	$\text{Count}_{\Sigma\mid A1}$ 9,625
	Approved 2/3	$\text{Count}_{D\mid A2}$ 3	$\text{Count}_{A1\mid A2}$ 1,372	$\text{Count}_{A2\mid A2}$ 9,664	$\text{Count}_{AW\mid A2}$ 589	$\text{Count}_{\Sigma\mid A2}$ 11,628
	Approved whole	$\text{Count}_{D\mid AW}$ 1	$\text{Count}_{A1\mid AW}$ 110	$\text{Count}_{A2\mid AW}$ 1,922	$\text{Count}_{AW\mid AW}$ 13,293	$\text{Count}_{\Sigma\mid AW}$ 15,326
	Predicted totals	$\text{Count}_{D\mid \Sigma}$ 12,777	$\text{Count}_{A1\mid \Sigma}$ 10,292	$\text{Count}_{A2\mid \Sigma}$ 12,746	$\text{Count}_{AW\mid \Sigma}$ 13,883	$\text{Count}_{\Sigma\mid \Sigma}$ 49,698

Table 17.15 contains a comparison of the classification evaluation measures for the models with and without misclassification costs. Denote the model without misclassification costs as model 3 and the model with misclassification costs as model 4. For each metric, the better performing model is indicated in bold. The evaluation metrics are mixed, with some metrics favoring each model. However, for the most important metric, that of total model cost, model 4 is superior.

The overall cost of model 3 is −$133, 658, 890, with a per-applicant cost of −$2689, while the overall cost of model 4 is −$137, 610, 255, with a per-applicant cost of −$2769. The increase in revenue per applicant from using misclassification

TABLE 17.15   Comparison of evaluation measures for quaternary CART models with and without misclassification costs (better performance highlighted)

Evaluation Measure	CART Model	
	Model 3: Without Misclassification Costs	Model 4: With Misclassification Costs
D-sensitivity	**0.92**	0.91
False D rate	**0.08**	0.09
A1-sensitivity	0.80	**0.84**
False A1 rate	0.20	**0.16**
A2-sensitivity	**0.83**	0.77
False AW rate	**0.17**	0.23
AW-sensitivity	0.87	**0.92**
False AW rate	0.13	**0.08**
Proportion of true Ds	0.94	**0.96**
Proportion of false Ds	0.06	**0.04**
Proportion of true A1s	**0.75**	0.74
Proportion of false A1s	**0.25**	0.26
Proportion of true A2s	0.76	**0.81**
Proportion of false A2s	0.24	**0.19**
Proportion of true AW's	**0.96**	0.92
Proportion of false AWs	**0.04**	0.08
Accuracy	0.86	**0.87**
Overall error rate	0.14	**0.13**

costs is \$80, with a total revenue increase of

$$\text{Revenue increase} = \$137,610,255 - \$133,658,890 = \$3,951,365$$

Thus, the model constructed using data-driven misclassification costs increases the bank's revenue by nearly \$4 million. However, the trinary models (models 1 and 2) outperformed the quaternary models (models 3 and 4) in terms of overall cost.

THE R ZONE

Load the required package and the data

```
library(rpart)
train3 <− read.csv(file="C:/ ... /Loans3_training.txt",
    header = TRUE)
test3 <− read.csv(file="C:/ ... /Loans3_test.txt",
    header = TRUE)
```

Run the model

```
cart3 <- rpart(Approval3 ~ Debt.to.Income.Ratio_z+ FICO.Score_z+Request.Amount_z,
    data = train3,
    method = "class")
```

Evaluate the model

```
pred3.class <- predict(object=cart3, newdata=test3[,3:5], type="class")
pred3.prob <- predict(object=cart3, newdata=test3[,3:5], type="prob")
c.table <- t(table(pred3.class, test3[,7]))
c.table[1,1]/sum(c.table[1,]) # D-sensitivity
# And so on
```

R REFERENCES

Therneau T, Atkinson B, Ripley B. 2013. rpart: Recursive partitioning. R package version 4.1-3. http://CRAN.R-project.org/package=rpart.

R Core Team. *R: A Language and Environment for Statistical Computing*. Vienna, Austria: R Foundation for Statistical Computing; 2012. ISBN: 3-900051-07-0, http://www.R-project.org/.

EXERCISES

CLARIFYING THE CONCEPTS

1. Explain why the true positive/false positive/true negative/false negative usage is not applicable to classification models with trinary targets.

2. Explain the Σ notation used in the notation in this chapter, for the marginal totals and the grand total of the contingency tables.

3. Explain why we do not use a specificity measure for a trinary classification problem.

4. What is the relationship between false A rate and A-sensitivity?

5. How are A-sensitivity and false A rate interpreted?

6. Why do we avoid the term *positive predictive value* in this book?

7. What is the relationship between the proportion of true As and the proportion of false As?

8. Interpret the proportion of true As and the proportion of false As.

9. Use the term "diagonal elements of the contingency table" to define (i) accuracy and (ii) overall error rate.

10. Express in your own words how we interpret the following measures:
    a. D-sensitivity, where D represents the *denied* class in the *Loans* problem
    b. False D rate
    c. Proportion of true Ds
    d. Proportion of false Ds.

11. Explain how we determine the principal and interest amounts for the *Loans* problem.

12. Why do we adjust our cost matrix so that there are zeroes on the diagonal?

13. Which cost matrix should we use when comparing models?

14. When misclassification costs are involved, what is the best metric for comparing model performance?

WORKING WITH THE DATA

15. Provide justifications for each of the direct costs given in Table 17.5.

16. Adjust Table 17.13 so that there are zeroes on the diagonal and the matrix is scaled, similarly to Table 17.7.

17. Using the results in Tables 17.12 and 17.14, confirm the values for the evaluation measures in Table 17.15.

HANDS-ON ANALYSIS

18. On your own, recapitulate the trinary classification analysis undertaken in this chapter using the *Loans3* data sets. (Note that the results may differ slightly due to different settings in the CART models.) Report all salient results, including a summary table, similarly to Table 17.9.

19. On your own, recapitulate the trinary classification analysis undertaken in this chapter using the *Loans4* data sets. (Note that the results may differ slightly due to different settings in the CART models.) Report all salient results, including a summary table, similarly to Table 17.15.

## CHAPTER 18

GRAPHICAL EVALUATION OF CLASSIFICATION MODELS

18.1   REVIEW OF LIFT CHARTS AND GAINS CHARTS

In Chapter 15, we learned about lift charts and gains charts. Recall that *lift* is defined as the proportion of positive hits in the set of the model's positive classifications, divided by the proportion of positive hits in the data set overall:

$$\text{Lift} = \frac{\text{Proportion of positive hits in set of positive classifications}}{\text{Proportion of positive hits in data set as a whole}}$$

where a *hit* is defined as a positive response that was predicted to be positive. To construct a lift chart, the software sorts the records by propensity to respond positively, and then calculates the lift at each percentile. For example, a lift value of 2.0 at the 20th percentile means that the 20% of records that contain the most likely responders have twice as many responders as a similarly sized random sample of records. Gains charts represent the cumulative form of lift charts. For more on lift charts and gains charts, see Chapter 15.

18.2   LIFT CHARTS AND GAINS CHARTS USING MISCLASSIFICATION COSTS

Lift charts and gains charts may be used in the presence of misclassification costs. This works because the software ranks the records by propensity to respond, and the misclassification costs directly affect the propensity to respond for a given classification model. Recall the *Loans* data set, where a bank would like to predict loan approval for a training data set of about 150,000 loan applicants, based on the predictors *debt-to-income ratio*, *FICO score*, and *request amount*. In Chapter 16, we found the data-driven misclassification costs to be as shown in the cost matrix in Table 18.1.

For illustration, classification and regression tree (CART) models were developed with and without these misclassification costs, and the resulting comparison lift chart is shown in Figure 18.1. The lift for the model with misclassification costs is shown to be superior to that of the model without misclassification costs, until about

Data Mining and Predictive Analytics, First Edition. Daniel T. Larose and Chantal D. Larose.
© 2015 John Wiley & Sons, Inc. Published 2015 by John Wiley & Sons, Inc.

TABLE 18.1   Cost matrix for the bank loan example

		Predicted Category	
		0	1
Actual category	0	$Cost_{TN} = -\$13,427$	$Cost_{FP} = \$13,427$
	1	$Cost_{FN} = \$6042$	$Cost_{TP} = -\$6042$

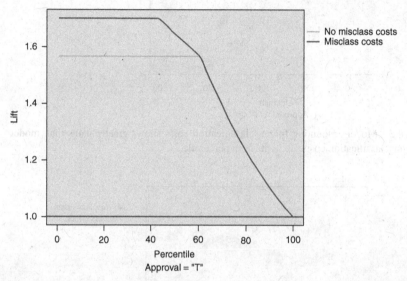

Figure 18.1   Model accounting for misclassification costs has greater lift than model without misclassification costs.

the 60th percentile. This reflects the superiority of the model with misclassification costs. This superiority is also reflected when accounting for cumulative lift, that is, in the gains chart shown in Figure 18.2.

18.3   RESPONSE CHARTS

Response charts are almost identical to lift charts, with the only difference being the vertical axis. Instead of measuring lift, the vertical axis indicates the proportion of positive hits in the given quantile (Figure 18.3). For example, at the 40th percentile, 84.8% of the most likely responder records for the model with misclassification costs are positive hits, compared to 78.1% of the most likely responder records for the model without misclassification costs. The analyst may choose when to use a lift chart or a response chart, based on the needs or quantitative sophistication of the client.

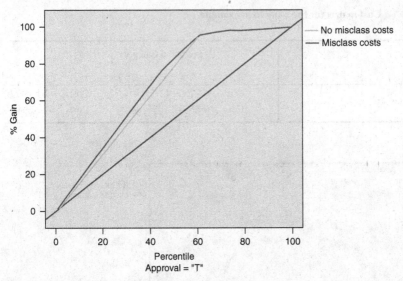

Figure 18.2 Model accounting for misclassification costs shows greater gains than model without misclassification costs, up to the 60th percentile.

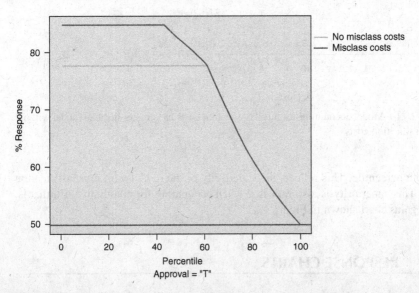

Figure 18.3 Response chart is same as lift chart, except for the vertical axis.

18.4 PROFITS CHARTS

Thus far, the model evaluation charts have dealt with positive hits, as measured by lift, gains, and response proportion. However, clients may be interested in a graphical display of the profitability of the candidate models, in order to better communicate within the corporation in terms that manager best understands: money. In such a case, the analyst may turn to *profits charts* or *return-on-investment* (*ROI*) *charts*.

Let *profits* be defined as follows:

$$\text{Profits} = \text{Revenue} - \text{Costs}$$

To construct a profits chart in modeler, the analyst must specify the cost or revenue for each cell in the cost matrix. Figures 18.4 and 18.5 show how this may be done for the *Loans* data set, using derive nodes, and in Figure 18.6, using the evaluation node.

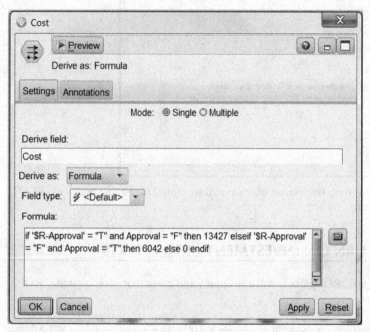

Figure 18.4   Specifying the cost of a false positive ($13,427) and a false negative ($6042) for the profits chart.

A profits chart expresses the cumulative profits that a company can expect, as we scan from the most likely hits to the less likely hits. A good profits chart increases to a peak near the center, and thereafter decreases. This peak is an important point, for it represents the point of maximum profitability.

For example, consider Figure 18.7, the profits chart for the *Loans* data set. For the model with misclassification costs, profits rise fairly steeply as the model makes its way through the most likely hits, and maxes out at the 44th percentile, with an estimated profit of $66,550,919. For the model without misclassification costs, profits rise less steeply, and do not max out until the 61st percentile, with an estimated profit of $53,583,427 (not shown). Thus, not only does the model with misclassification costs produce an extra $13 million, this increased profit is realized from processing only the top 44% of applicants, thereby saving the bank's further time and expense.

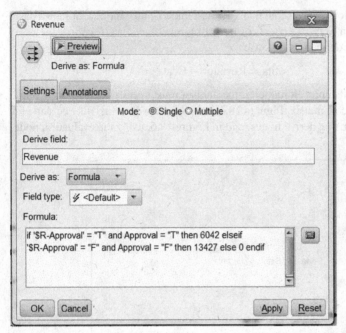

Figure 18.5   Specifying the revenue of a true positive ($6042) and a true negative ($13,427) for the profits chart.

18.5   RETURN ON INVESTMENT (ROI) CHARTS

Like profits charts, ROI plots involve revenues and costs. For each quantile, ROI is defined as follows:

$$\text{ROI} = \text{Return on investment} = \frac{\text{Profits}}{\text{Costs}} \times 100\% = \frac{\text{Revenue} - \text{Costs}}{\text{Costs}} \times 100\%$$

That is, ROI is the *ratio of profits to costs*, expressed as a percentage.

The ROI chart for the bank loans data set is shown in Figure 18.8. The model without misclassification costs shows ROI of about 60% through the 60th percentile, which indicates what would normally be a fairly respectable ROI. However, the model with misclassification costs provides a very strong 150% ROI through the 60th percentile, two-and-a-half times greater than the model without misclassification costs.

Note that all of these graphical evaluations, like all model evaluation techniques, need to be carried out on the test data set, not the training data set. Finally, although our examples in this chapter have dealt with the misclassification costs/no misclassification costs dichotomy, combined evaluation charts can also be used to compare classification models from different algorithms. For example, the profits from a CART model could be graphically evaluated against those from a C5.0 model, a neural network model, and a logistic regression model.

To summarize, in this chapter we have explored some charts that the analyst may consider useful for graphically evaluating his or her classification models.

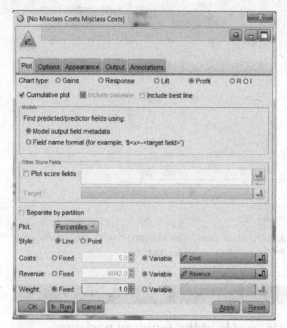

Figure 18.6   Constructing a profits chart in IBM Modeler, specifying the variable cost and revenue.

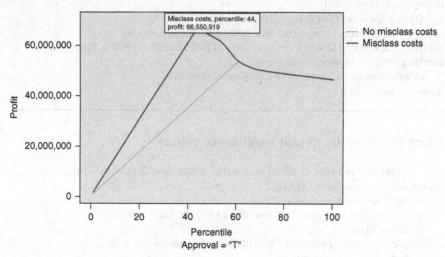

Figure 18.7   Profits chart for the *Loans* data set. Profits are maximized from processing only 44% of the applicants.

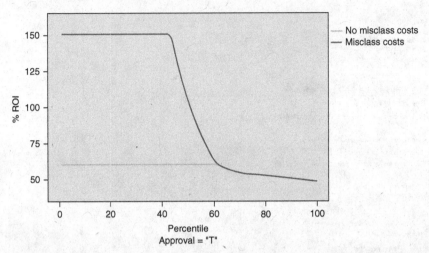

Figure 18.8 Return on investment (ROI) chart shows that the model with misclassification costs provides a very strong 150% ROI through the 60th percentile.

THE R ZONE

Load and prepare the data, and load the required packages

```
loan.train <- read.csv(file="C:/ ... /Loans_Training.csv",
    header = TRUE)
choose <- sample(dim(loan.train)[1], size = 1000)
train <- loan.train[choose,-5]
library(rpart);  library(caret)
train$DtIR.z <- (train$Debt.to.Income.Ratio-
    mean(train$Debt.to.Income.Ratio))/sd(train$Debt.to.Income.Ratio)
train$FICOs.z <- (train$FICO.Score - mean(train$FICO.Score))/sd(train$FICO.Score)
train$ReqAmt.z <- (train$Request.Amount-
    mean(train$Request.Amount))/sd(train$Request.Amount)
 train <- train[,-c(2:4)]
```

Run the models, obtain confidence values

```
costs <- list(loss = matrix(c(-13427, 13427, 6042, -6042), ncol=2, byrow=TRUE))
costs$loss[1,] <- costs$loss[1,]+13427
costs$loss[2,] <- costs$loss[2,]+6042
cart.woCost <- rpart(Approval ~ DtIR.z+FICOs.z+ReqAmt.z,data = train,
    method = "class")
cart.withCost <- rpart(Approval ~ DtIR.z+FICOs.z+ReqAmt.z,data = train,
    method = "class", parms = costs)
conf <- predict(cart.woCost, newdata = train, type = "prob")
conf.cost <- predict(cart.withCost, newdata = train, type = "prob")
```

Make the Lift chart

```
m <- data.frame(NoCost = conf[,2],
    Cost = conf.cost[,2])
our.lift <- lift(as.factor(train[,1]) ~
    NoCost + Cost, data = m)
xyplot(our.lift, plot = "lift",
    auto.key = list(columns = 2),
    main = "Lift for Models With
    and Without Cost")
```

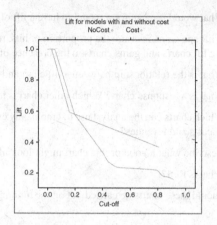

Make the Gains chart

```
xyplot(our.lift, plot = "gain",
    auto.key = list(columns = 2),
    main = "Gain for Models With
    and Without Cost")
```

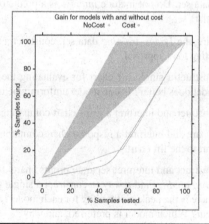

R REFERENCES

Kuhn M. Contributions from Jed Wing, Steve Weston, Andre Williams, Chris Keefer, Allan Engelhardt, Tony Cooper, Zachary Mayer and the R Core Team. 2014. caret: Classification and regression training. R package version 6.0-24. http://CRAN.R-project.org/package= caret.

Therneau T, Atkinson B, Ripley B. 2013. rpart: Recursive partitioning. R package version 4.1-3. http://CRAN.R-project.org/package=rpart.

R Core Team. *R: A Language and Environment for Statistical Computing.* Vienna, Austria: R Foundation for Statistical Computing; 2012. ISBN: 3-900051-07-0, http://www.R-project.org/. Accessed 2014 Sep 30.

EXERCISES

1. What would it mean for a model to have a lift of 2.5 at the 15th percentile?

2. If lift and gains measure the proportion of hits, regardless of the cost matrix, why can we use lift charts and gains charts in the presence of misclassification costs?

3. What is the relationship between a lift chart and a gains chart?

4. What is a response chart? Which other chart is it similar to?

5. Which charts can the analyst use to graphically evaluate the classification models in terms of costs and revenues?

6. Describe what a good profits chart might look like.

7. What is ROI?

8. Should these charts be carried out on the training data set or the test data set? Why?

HANDS-ON EXERCISES

For Exercises 9–14, provide graphical evaluations of a set of classification models for the *Loans* data set. Do not include *interest* as a predictor. Make sure to develop the charts using the test data set.

9. Using the *Loans_training* data set, construct a CART model and a C5.0 model for predicting loan approval.

10. Construct a single lift chart for evaluating the two models. Interpret the chart. Which model does better? Is one model uniformly better?

11. Construct and interpret a gains chart comparing the two models.

12. Prepare and interpret a response chart comparing the two models. Compare the response chart to the lift chart.

13. Construct and interpret separate profits charts for the CART model and the C5.0 model. (*Extra credit*: Find a way to construct a single profits chart comparing the two models.) Where is the peak profitability for each model? At what percentile does peak profitability occur? Which model is preferred, and why?

14. Construct and interpret separate ROI charts for the two models. (*Extra credit*: Find a way to construct a single ROI chart comparing the two models.) Which model is preferred, and why?

   For Exercises 15–18 we use rebalancing as a surrogate for misclassification costs, in order to add neural networks and logistic regression to our candidate models.

15. Neural networks and logistic regression in modeler do not admit explicit misclassification costs. Therefore undertake rebalancing of the data set as a surrogate for the misclassification costs used in this chapter.

16. Using the *Loans_training* data set, construct a neural networks model and a logistic regression model for predicting loan approval, using the rebalanced data.

17. Construct a single lift chart for evaluating the four models: CART, C5.0, neural networks, and logistic regression. Interpret the chart. Which model does better? Is one model uniformly better?

18. Construct and interpret a gains chart comparing the four models.

19. Prepare and interpret a response chart comparing four two models.

20. Construct and interpret separate profits charts for each of the four models. (*Extra credit*: Find a way to construct a single profits chart comparing the four models.) Where is the peak profitability for each model? At what percentile does peak profitability occur? Which model is preferred, and why?

21. Construct and interpret separate ROI charts for the four models. (*Extra credit*: Find a way to construct a single ROI chart comparing the four models.) Which model is preferred, and why?

PART IV

CLUSTERING

## CHAPTER 19

HIERARCHICAL AND k-MEANS CLUSTERING

19.1 THE CLUSTERING TASK

Clustering refers to the grouping of records, observations, or cases into classes of similar objects. A *cluster* is a collection of records that are similar to one another and dissimilar to records in other clusters. Clustering differs from classification in that there is no target variable for clustering. The clustering task does not try to classify, estimate, or predict the value of a target variable. Instead, clustering algorithms seek to segment the entire data set into relatively homogeneous subgroups or clusters, where the similarity of the records within the cluster is maximized, and the similarity to records outside this cluster is minimized.

For example, the Nielsen PRIZM segments, developed by Claritas Inc., represent demographic profiles of each geographic area in the United States, in terms of distinct lifestyle types, as defined by zip code. For example, the clusters identified for zip code 90210, Beverly Hills, California, are as follows:

- Cluster # 01: Upper Crust Estates
- Cluster # 03: Movers and Shakers
- Cluster # 04: Young Digerati
- Cluster # 07: Money and Brains
- Cluster # 16: Bohemian Mix.

The description for Cluster # 01: Upper Crust is "The nation's most exclusive address, Upper Crust is the wealthiest lifestyle in America, a haven for empty-nesting couples between the ages of 45 and 64. No segment has a higher concentration of residents earning over $100,000 a year and possessing a postgraduate degree. And none has a more opulent standard of living."

Examples of clustering tasks in business and research include the following:

- Target marketing of a niche product for a small-capitalization business that does not have a large marketing budget.

Data Mining and Predictive Analytics, First Edition. Daniel T. Larose and Chantal D. Larose.
© 2015 John Wiley & Sons, Inc. Published 2015 by John Wiley & Sons, Inc.

- For accounting auditing purposes, to segment financial behavior into benign and suspicious categories.
- As a dimension-reduction tool when a data set has hundreds of attributes.
- For gene expression clustering, where very large quantities of genes may exhibit similar behavior.

Clustering is often performed as a preliminary step in a data mining process, with the resulting clusters being used as further inputs into a different technique downstream, such as neural networks. Owing to the enormous size of many present-day databases, it is often helpful to apply clustering analysis first, to reduce the search space for the downstream algorithms. In this chapter, after a brief look at hierarchical clustering methods, we discuss in detail *k*-means clustering; in Chapter 20, we examine clustering using Kohonen networks, a structure related to neural networks.

Cluster analysis encounters many of the same issues that we dealt with in the chapters on classification. For example, we shall need to determine

- how to measure similarity;
- how to recode categorical variables;
- how to standardize or normalize numerical variables;
- how many clusters we expect to uncover.

For simplicity, in this book, we concentrate on Euclidean distance between records:

$$d_{\text{Euclidean}}(x, y) = \sqrt{\sum_i (x_i - y_i)^2}$$

where $x = x_1, x_2, \ldots, x_m$, and $y = y_1, y_2, \ldots, y_m$ represent the m attribute values of two records. Of course, many other metrics exist, such as *city-block distance:*

$$d_{\text{city-block}}(x, y) = \sum_i |x_i - y_i|$$

or *Minkowski distance*, which represents the general case of the foregoing two metrics for a general exponent q:

$$d_{\text{Minkowski}}(x, y) = \left(\sum_i |x_i - y_i|^q \right)^{1/q}$$

For categorical variables, we may again define the "different from" function for comparing the ith attribute values of a pair of records:

$$\text{different}(x_i, y_i) = \begin{cases} 0 & \text{if } x_i = y_i \\ 1 & \text{otherwise} \end{cases}$$

where x_i and y_i are categorical values. We may then substitute different (x_i, y_i) for the ith term in the Euclidean distance metric above.

For optimal performance, clustering algorithms, just like algorithms for classification, require the data to be normalized so that no particular variable or subset of variables dominates the analysis. Analysts may use either the *min–max normalization* or *Z-score standardization*, discussed in earlier chapters:

$$\text{Min} - \text{max normalization: } X^* = \frac{X - \min(X)}{\text{Range}(X)}$$

$$\text{Z-score standardization: } X^* = \frac{X - \text{mean}(X)}{\text{SD}(X)}$$

All clustering methods have as their goal the identification of groups of records such that similarity within a group is very high while the similarity to records in other groups is very low. In other words, as shown in Figure 19.1, clustering algorithms seek to construct clusters of records such that the *between-cluster variation* is large compared to the *within-cluster variation*. This is somewhat analogous to the concept behind analysis of variance.

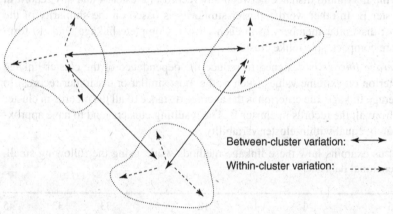

Between-cluster variation: ←——→

Within-cluster variation: - - - - →

Figure 19.1   Clusters should have small within-cluster variation compared to the between–cluster variation.

19.2   HIERARCHICAL CLUSTERING METHODS

Clustering algorithms are either hierarchical or nonhierarchical. In *hierarchical clustering*, a treelike cluster structure (*dendrogram*) is created through recursive partitioning (divisive methods) or combining (agglomerative) of existing clusters. *Agglomerative clustering methods* initialize each observation to be a tiny cluster of its own. Then, in succeeding steps, the two closest clusters are aggregated into a new combined cluster. In this way, the number of clusters in the data set is reduced by one at each step. Eventually, all records are combined into a single huge cluster. *Divisive clustering methods* begin with all the records in one big cluster, with the most dissimilar records being split off recursively, into a separate cluster, until each record represents its own cluster. Because most computer programs that apply hierarchical clustering use agglomerative methods, we focus on those.

Distance between records is rather straightforward once appropriate recoding and normalization has taken place. But how do we determine *distance between clusters* of records? Should we consider two clusters to be close if their nearest neighbors are close or if their farthest neighbors are close? How about criteria that average out these extremes?

We examine several criteria for determining distance between arbitrary clusters A and B:

- *Single linkage*, sometimes termed the *nearest-neighbor approach*, is based on the minimum distance between any record in cluster A and any record in cluster B. In other words, cluster similarity is based on the similarity of the most similar members from each cluster. Single linkage tends to form long, slender clusters, which may sometimes lead to heterogeneous records being clustered together.

- *Complete linkage*, sometimes termed the *farthest-neighbor approach*, is based on the maximum distance between any record in cluster A and any record in cluster B. In other words, cluster similarity is based on the similarity of the most dissimilar members from each cluster. Complete linkage tends to form more compact, spherelike clusters.

- *Average linkage* is designed to reduce the dependence of the cluster-linkage criterion on extreme values, such as the most similar or dissimilar records. In average linkage, the criterion is the average distance of all the records in cluster A from all the records in cluster B. The resulting clusters tend to have approximately equal within-cluster variability.

Let us examine how these linkage methods work, using the following small, one-dimensional data set:

2	5	9	15	16	18	25	33	33	45

19.3 SINGLE-LINKAGE CLUSTERING

Suppose that we are interested in using *single-linkage* agglomerative clustering on this data set. Agglomerative methods start by assigning each record to its own cluster. Then, single linkage seeks the minimum distance between any records in two clusters. Figure 19.2 illustrates how this is accomplished for this data set. The minimum cluster distance is clearly between the single-record clusters where each contains the value 33, for which the distance must be 0 for any valid metric. Thus, these two clusters are combined into a new cluster of two records, both of value 33, as shown in Figure 19.2. Note that, after step 1, only nine $(n - 1)$ clusters remain. Next, in step 2, the clusters containing values 15 and 16 are combined into a new cluster, because their distance of 1 is the minimum between any two clusters remaining.

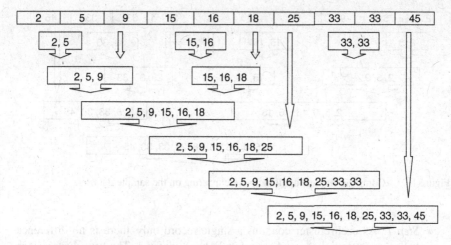

Figure 19.2   Single-linkage agglomerative clustering on the sample data set.

Here are the remaining steps:

- *Step 3:* The cluster containing values 15 and 16 (cluster {15,16}) is combined with cluster {18}, because the distance between 16 and 18 (the closest records in each cluster) is 2, the minimum among remaining clusters.
- *Step 4:* Clusters {2} and {5} are combined.
- *Step 5:* Cluster {2,5} is combined with cluster {9}, because the distance between 5 and 9 (the closest records in each cluster) is 4, the minimum among remaining clusters.
- *Step 6:* Cluster {2,5,9} is combined with cluster {15,16,18}, because the distance between 9 and 15 is 6, the minimum among remaining clusters.
- *Step 7:* Cluster {2,5,9,15,16,18} is combined with cluster {25}, because the distance between 18 and 25 is 7, the minimum among remaining clusters.
- *Step 8:* Cluster {2,5,9,15,16,18,25} is combined with cluster {33,33}, because the distance between 25 and 33 is 8, the minimum among remaining clusters.
- *Step 9:* Cluster {2,5,9,15,16,18,25,33,33} is combined with cluster {45}. This last cluster now contains all the records in the data set.

19.4   COMPLETE-LINKAGE CLUSTERING

Next, let us examine whether using the complete-linkage criterion would result in a different clustering of this sample data set. Complete linkage seeks to minimize the distance among the records in two clusters that are farthest from each other. Figure 19.3 illustrates complete-linkage clustering for this data set.

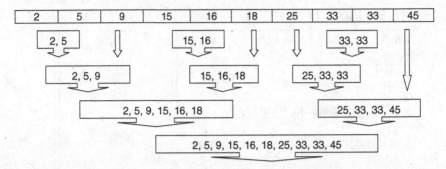

Figure 19.3 Complete-linkage agglomerative clustering on the sample data set.

- *Step 1:* As each cluster contains a single record only, there is no difference between single linkage and complete linkage at step 1. The two clusters each containing 33 are again combined.

- *Step 2:* Just as for single linkage, the clusters containing values 15 and 16 are combined into a new cluster. Again, this is because there is no difference in the two criteria for single-record clusters.

- *Step 3:* At this point, complete linkage begins to diverge from its predecessor. In single linkage, cluster {15,16} was at this point combined with cluster {18}. But complete linkage looks at the farthest neighbors, not the nearest neighbors. The farthest neighbors for these two clusters are 15 and 18, for a distance of 3. This is the same distance separating clusters {2} and {5}. The complete-linkage criterion is silent regarding ties, so we arbitrarily select the first such combination found, therefore combining the clusters {2} and {5} into a new cluster.

- *Step 4:* Now cluster {15,16} is combined with cluster {18}.

- *Step 5:* Cluster {2,5} is combined with cluster {9}, because the complete-linkage distance is 7, the smallest among remaining clusters.

- *Step 6:* Cluster {25} is combined with cluster {33,33}, with a complete-linkage distance of 8.

- *Step 7:* Cluster {2,5,9} is combined with cluster {15,16,18}, with a complete-linkage distance of 16.

- *Step 8:* Cluster {25,33,33} is combined with cluster {45}, with a complete-linkage distance of 20.

- *Step 9:* Cluster {2,5,9,15,16,18} is combined with cluster {25,33,33,45}. All records are now contained in this last large cluster.

Finally, with average linkage, the criterion is the average distance of all the records in cluster A from all the records in cluster B. As the average of a single record is the record's value itself, this method does not differ from the earlier methods in the early stages, where single-record clusters are being combined. At step 3, average linkage would be faced with the choice of combining clusters {2} and {5}, or combining the {15,16} cluster with the single-record {18} cluster. The average distance between the {15,16} cluster and the {18} cluster is the average of |18 − 15| and |18 − 16|, which is 2.5, while the average distance between clusters {2} and {5} is of course 3. Therefore, average linkage would combine the {15,16} cluster with cluster {18} at this step, followed by combining cluster {2} with cluster {5}. The reader may verify that the average-linkage criterion leads to the same hierarchical structure for this example as the complete-linkage criterion. In general, average linkage leads to clusters more similar in shape to complete linkage than does single linkage.

19.5   *k*-MEANS CLUSTERING

The *k*-means clustering algorithm[1] is a straightforward and effective algorithm for finding clusters in data. The algorithm proceeds as follows:

- *Step 1:* Ask the user how many clusters *k* the data set should be partitioned into.
- *Step 2:* Randomly assign *k* records to be the initial cluster center locations.
- *Step 3:* For each record, find the nearest cluster center. Thus, in a sense, each cluster center "owns" a subset of the records, thereby representing a partition of the data set. We therefore have *k* clusters, $C_1, C_2, \ldots, C_k$.
- *Step 4:* For each of the *k* clusters, find the cluster *centroid*, and update the location of each cluster center to the new value of the centroid.
- *Step 5:* Repeat steps 3–5 until convergence or termination.

The "nearest" criterion in step 3 is usually Euclidean distance, although other criteria may be applied as well. The cluster centroid in step 4 is found as follows. Suppose that we have n data points $(a_1, b_1, c_1), (a_2, b_2, c_2), \ldots, (a_n, b_n, c_n)$, the *centroid* of these points is the center of gravity of these points and is located at point $\left(\sum a_i/n, \sum b_i/n, \sum c_i/n, \right)$. For example, the points (1,1,1), (1,2,1), (1,3,1), and (2,1,1) would have centroid

$$\left(\frac{1+1+1+2}{4}, \frac{1+2+3+1}{4}, \frac{1+1+1+1}{4} \right) = (1.25, 1.75, 1.00)$$

The algorithm terminates when the centroids no longer change. In other words, the algorithm terminates when for all clusters $C_1, C_2, \ldots, C_k$, all the records "owned" by each cluster center remain in that cluster. Alternatively, the algorithm may terminate when some convergence criterion is met, such as no significant shrinkage in the *mean squared error* (MSE):

$$\text{MSE} = \frac{\text{SSE}}{N - k} = \frac{\sum_{i=1}^{k} \sum_{p \in C_i} d(p, m_i)^2}{N - k}$$

where SSE represents the *sum of squares error*, $p \in C_i$ represents each data point in cluster *i*, m_i represents the centroid (cluster center) of cluster *i*, *N* is the total sample

---

[1] J. MacQueen, Some methods for classification and analysis of multivariate observations, *Proceedings of the 5th Berkeley Symposium on Mathematical Statistics and Probability*, Vol. 1, pp. 281–297, University of California Press, Berkeley, CA, 1967.

size, and k is the number of clusters. Recall that clustering algorithms seek to construct clusters of records such that the between-cluster variation is large compared to the within-cluster variation. Because this concept is analogous to the analysis of variance, we may define a *pseudo-F statistic* as follows:

$$F_{k-1,N-k} = \frac{\text{MSB}}{\text{MSE}} = \frac{\text{SSB}/k - 1}{\text{SSE}/N - k}$$

where SSE is defined as above, MSB is the *mean square between*, and SSB is the *sum of squares between* clusters, defined as

$$\text{SSB} = \sum_{i=1}^{k} n_i \cdot d(m_i, M)^2$$

where n_i is the number of records in cluster i, m_i is the centroid (cluster center) for cluster i, and M is the grand mean of all the data.

MSB represents the between-cluster variation and MSE represents the within-cluster variation. Thus, a "good" cluster would have a large value of the pseudo-F statistic, representing a situation where the between-cluster variation is large compared to the within-cluster variation. Hence, as the k-means algorithm proceeds, and the quality of the clusters increases, we would expect MSB to increase, MSE to decrease, and F to increase.

19.6 EXAMPLE OF *k*-MEANS CLUSTERING AT WORK

Let us examine an example of how the k-means algorithm works. Suppose that we have the eight data points in two-dimensional space shown in Table 19.1 and plotted in Figure 19.4 and are interested in uncovering $k = 2$ clusters.

Let us apply the k-means algorithm step by step.

- *Step 1*: Ask the user how many clusters k the data set should be partitioned into. We have already indicated that we are interested in $k = 2$ clusters.
- *Step 2*: Randomly assign k records to be the initial cluster center locations. For this example, we assign the cluster centers to be $m_1 = (1,1)$ and $m_2 = (2,1)$.
- *Step 3 (first pass)*: For each record, find the nearest cluster center. Table 19.2 contains the (rounded) Euclidean distances between each point and each cluster center $m_1 = (1,1)$ and $m_2 = (2,1)$, along with an indication of which cluster center the point is nearest to. Therefore, cluster 1 contains points $\{a,e,g\}$, and cluster 2 contains points $\{b,c,d,f,h\}$.
- *Step 4 (first pass)*: For each of the k clusters find the cluster *centroid* and update the location of each cluster center to the new value of the centroid. The centroid

TABLE 19.1 Data points for *k*-means example

a	b	c	d	e	f	g	h
(1,3)	(3,3)	(4,3)	(5,3)	(1,2)	(4,2)	(1,1)	(2,1)

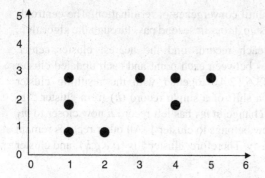

Figure 19.4   How will *k*-means partition this data into $k = 2$ clusters?

TABLE 19.2   Finding the nearest cluster center for each record (first pass)

Point	Distance from m_1	Distance from m_2	Cluster Membership
a	2.00	2.24	C_1
b	2.83	2.24	C_2
c	3.61	2.83	C_2
d	4.47	3.61	C_2
e	1.00	1.41	C_1
f	3.16	2.24	C_2
g	0.00	1.00	C_1
h	1.00	0.00	C_2

for cluster 1 is $[(1 + 1 + 1)/3, (3 + 2 + 1)/3] = (1,2)$. The centroid for cluster 2 is $[(3 + 4 + 5 + 4 + 2)/5, (3 + 3 + 3 + 2 + 1)/5] = (3.6, 2.4)$. The clusters and centroids (triangles) at the end of the first pass are shown in Figure 19.5. Note that m_1 has moved up to the center of the three points in cluster 1, while m_2 has moved up and to the right a considerable distance, to the center of the five points in cluster 2.

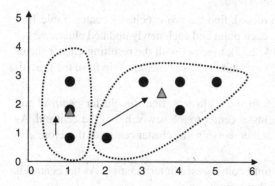

Figure 19.5   Clusters and centroids Δ after first pass through *k*-means algorithm.

- *Step 5:* Repeat steps 3 and 4 until convergence or termination. The centroids have moved, so we go back to step 3 for our second pass through the algorithm.
- *Step 3 (second pass):* For each record, find the nearest cluster center. Table 19.3 shows the distances between each point and each updated cluster center $m_1 = (1,2)$ and $m_2 = (3.6, 2.4)$, together with the resulting cluster membership. There has been a shift of a single record (h) from cluster 2 to cluster 1. The relatively large change in m_2 has left record h now closer to m_1 than to m_2, so that record h now belongs to cluster 1. All other records remain in the same clusters as previously. Therefore, cluster 1 is $\{a,e,g,h\}$, and cluster 2 is $\{b,c,d,f\}$.

TABLE 19.3 Finding the nearest cluster center for each record (second pass)

Point	Distance from m_1	Distance from m_2	Cluster Membership
a	1.00	2.67	C_1
b	2.24	0.85	C_2
c	3.16	0.72	C_2
d	4.12	1.52	C_2
e	0.00	2.63	C_1
f	3.00	0.57	C_2
g	1.00	2.95	C_1
h	1.41	2.13	C_1

- *Step 4 (second pass):* For each of the k clusters, find the cluster *centroid* and update the location of each cluster center to the new value of the centroid. The new centroid for cluster 1 is $[(1+1+1+2)/4, (3+2+1+1)/4] = (1.25, 1.75)$. The new centroid for cluster 2 is $[(3+4+5+4)/4, (3+3+3+2)/4] = (4, 2.75)$. The clusters and centroids at the end of the second pass are shown in Figure 19.6. Centroids m_1 and m_2 have both moved slightly.
- *Step 5:* Repeat steps 3 and 4 until convergence or termination. As the centroids have moved, we once again return to step 3 for our third (and as it turns out, final) pass through the algorithm.
- *Step 3 (third pass):* For each record, find the nearest cluster center. Table 19.4 shows the distances between each point and each newly updated cluster center $m_1 = (1.25, 1.75)$ and $m_2 = (4, 2.75)$, together with the resulting cluster membership. Note that no records have shifted cluster membership from the preceding pass.
- *Step 4 (third pass):* For each of the k clusters, find the cluster *centroid* and update the location of each cluster center to the new value of the centroid. As no records have shifted cluster membership, the cluster centroids therefore also remain unchanged.
- *Step 5:* Repeat steps 3 and 4 until convergence or termination. As the centroids remain unchanged, the algorithm terminates.

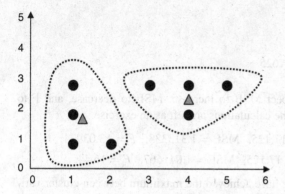

Figure 19.6   Clusters and centroids Δ after second pass through k-means algorithm.

TABLE 19.4   Finding the nearest cluster center for each record (third pass)

Point	Distance from m_1	Distance from m_2	Cluster Membership
a	1.27	3.01	C_1
b	2.15	1.03	C_2
c	3.02	0.25	C_2
d	3.95	1.03	C_2
e	0.35	3.09	C_1
f	2.76	0.75	C_2
g	0.79	3.47	C_1
h	1.06	2.66	C_1

19.7   BEHAVIOR OF MSB, MSE, AND PSEUDO-F AS THE k-MEANS ALGORITHM PROCEEDS

Let us observe the behavior of these statistics after step 4 of each pass.
First pass:

- $$\text{SSB} = \sum_{i=1}^{k} n_i \cdot d(m_i, M)^2 =$$
$3 \cdot d((1,2), (2.625, 2.25))^2 + 5 \cdot d((3.6, 2.4), (2.625, 2.25))^2 = 12.975$

- $$\text{MSB} = \frac{\text{SSB}}{k-1} = \frac{12.975}{2-1} = 12.975$$

- $$\text{SSE} = \sum_{i=1}^{k} \sum_{p \epsilon C_i} d(p, m_i)^2$$
$$= 2^2 + 2.24^2 + 2.83^2 + 3.61^2 + 1^2 + 2.24^2 + 0^2 + 0^2 = 36$$

- $\text{MSE} = \dfrac{\text{SSE}}{N - k} = \dfrac{36}{6} = 6$

- $F = \dfrac{\text{MSB}}{\text{MSE}} = \dfrac{12.975}{6} = 2.1625$

In general, we would expect MSB to increase, MSE to decrease, and F to increase, and such is the case. The calculations are left as an exercise.

$$\text{Second pass : MSB} = 17.125, \quad \text{MSE} = 1.313333, \quad F = 13.03934.$$

$$\text{Third pass : MSB} = 17.125, \quad \text{MSE} = 1.041667, \quad F = 16.44.$$

These statistics indicate that we have achieved the maximum between-cluster variation (as measured by MSB), compared to the within-cluster variation (as measured by MSE).

Note that the k-means algorithm cannot guarantee finding the global maximum pseudo-F statistic, instead often settling at a local maximum. To improve the probability of achieving a global minimum, the analyst may consider using a variety of initial cluster centers. Moore[2] suggests (i) placing the first cluster center on a random data point, and (ii) placing the subsequent cluster centers on points as far away from previous centers as possible.

One potential problem for applying the k-means algorithm is: Who decides how many clusters to search for? That is, who decides k? Unless the analyst has a priori knowledge of the number of underlying clusters; therefore, an "outer loop" should be added to the algorithm, which cycles through various promising values of k. Clustering solutions for each value of k can therefore be compared, with the value of k resulting in the largest F statistic being selected. Alternatively, some clustering algorithms, such as the BIRCH clustering algorithm, can select the optimal number of clusters.[3]

What if some attributes are more relevant than others to the problem formulation? As cluster membership is determined by distance, we may apply the same axis-stretching methods for quantifying attribute relevance that we discussed in Chapter 10. In Chapter 20, we examine another common clustering method, Kohonen networks, which are related to artificial neural networks in structure.

19.8   APPLICATION OF k-MEANS CLUSTERING USING SAS ENTERPRISE MINER

Next, we turn to the powerful SAS Enterpriser Miner[4] software for an application of the k-means algorithm on the *churn* data set (available at the book series web site; also

---

[2] Andrew Moore, *k-Means and Hierarchical Clustering*, Course Notes, http://www.autonlab.org/tutorials/kmeans11.pdf.

[3] For more on BIRCH clustering, see Chapter 21.

[4] The SAS Institute, Cary, NC, www.sas.com.

available from http://www.sgi.com/tech/mlc/db/). Recall that the data set contains 20 variables' worth of information about 3333 customers, along with an indication of whether or not that customer churned (left the company).

The following variables were passed to the Enterprise Miner clustering node:

- Flag (0/1) variables
  - International Plan and VoiceMail Plan
- Numerical variables
  - *Account length, voice mail messages, day minutes, evening minutes, night minutes, international minutes,* and *customer service calls*
  - After applying min–max normalization to all numerical variables.

The *Enterprise Miner* clustering node uses SAS's FASTCLUS procedure, a version of the *k*-means algorithm. The number of clusters was set to $k = 3$. The three clusters uncovered by the algorithm varied greatly in size, with tiny cluster 1 containing 92 records, large cluster 2 containing 2411 records, and medium-sized cluster 3 containing 830 records.

Some basic cluster profiling will help us to learn about the types of records falling into each cluster. Figure 19.7 provides a look at the clustering results window of *Enterprise Miner*, containing a pie chart profile of the *International Plan* membership across the three clusters. All members of cluster 1, a fraction of the members of cluster 2, and no members of cluster 3 have adopted the *International Plan*. Note that the leftmost pie chart represents all records, and is similar to cluster 2.

Next, Figure 19.8 illustrates the proportion of VoiceMail Plan adopters in each cluster. (Note the confusing color reversal for *yes/no* responses.) Remarkably, clusters 1 and 3 contain only VoiceMail Plan adopters, while cluster 2 contains only non-adopters of the plan. In other words, this field was used by the *k*-means algorithm to create a "perfect" discrimination, dividing the data set perfectly among adopters and nonadopters of the International Plan.

It is clear from these results that the algorithm is relying heavily on the categorical variables to form clusters. The comparison of the means of the numerical variables across the clusters in Table 19.5 shows relatively little variation, indicating that the clusters are similar across these dimensions. Figure 19.9, for example, illustrates that the distribution of *customer service calls* (normalized) is relatively similar

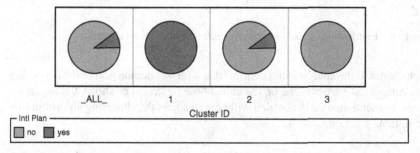

Figure 19.7   Enterprise Miner profile of International Plan adopters across clusters.

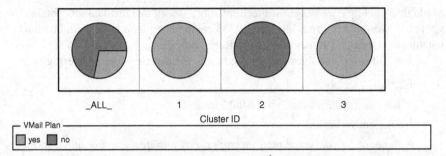

Figure 19.8 VoiceMail Plan adopters and nonadopters are mutually exclusive.

TABLE 19.5 **Comparison of variable means across clusters shows little variation**

Cluster	Frequency	AcctLength_m	VMailMessage	DayMins_mm
1	92	0.4340639598	0.5826939471	0.5360015616
2	2411	0.4131940041	0	0.5126334451
3	830	0.4120730857	0.5731159934	0.5093940185
Cluster	EveMins_mm	NightMins_mm	IntMins_mm	CustServCalls
1	0.5669029659	0.4764366069	0.5467934783	0.1630434783
2	0.5507417372	0.4773586813	0.5119784322	0.1752615328
3	0.5564095259	0.4795138596	0.5076626506	0.1701472557

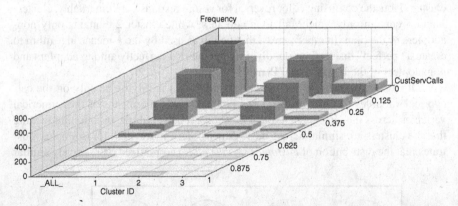

Figure 19.9 Distribution of *customer service calls* is similar across clusters.

in each cluster. If the analyst is not comfortable with this domination of the clustering by the categorical variables, he or she can choose to stretch or shrink the appropriate axes, as mentioned earlier, which will help to adjust the clustering algorithm to a more suitable solution.

The clusters may therefore be summarized, using only the categorical variables, as follows:

- **Cluster 1: Sophisticated Users**. A small group of customers who have adopted both the International Plan and the VoiceMail Plan.
- **Cluster 2: The Average Majority**. The largest segment of the customer base, some of whom have adopted the VoiceMail Plan but none of whom have adopted the International Plan.
- **Cluster 3: Voice Mail Users**. A medium-sized group of customers who have all adopted the VoiceMail Plan but not the International Plan.

19.9   USING CLUSTER MEMBERSHIP TO PREDICT CHURN

Suppose, however, that we would like to apply these clusters to assist us in the *churn classification* task. We may compare the proportions of churners directly among the various clusters, using graphs such as Figure 19.10. Here we see that overall (the leftmost column of pie charts), the proportion of churners is much higher among those who have adopted the International Plan than among those who have not. This

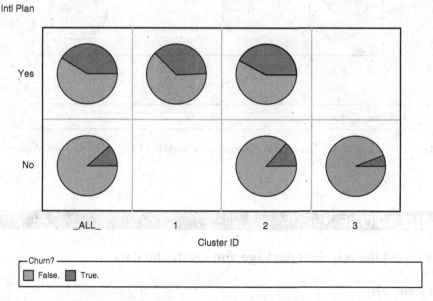

Figure 19.10   Churn behavior across clusters for International Plan adopters and nonadopters.

finding was uncovered in Chapter 3. Note that the churn proportion is higher in cluster 1, which contains International Plan adopters, than in cluster 2, which contains a mixture of adopters and nonadopters, and higher still than cluster 3, which contains no such adopters of the International Plan. Clearly, the company should look at the plan to see why the customers who have it are leaving the company at a higher rate.

Now, as we know from Chapter 3 that the proportion of churners is lower among adopters of the VoiceMail Plan, we would expect that the churn rate for cluster 3 would be lower than for the other clusters. This expectation is confirmed in Figure 19.11.

In Chapter 20, we explore using cluster membership as input to downstream data mining models.

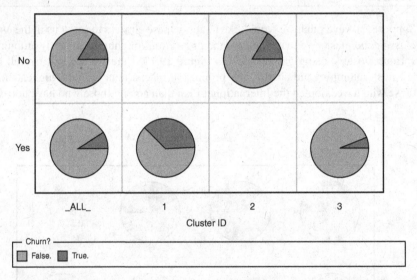

Figure 19.11   Churn behavior across clusters for VoiceMail Plan adopters and nonadopters.

THE R ZONE

Install the required package and create the data

```
library(cluster)
data <- c(2, 5, 9, 15, 16, 18, 25, 33, 33, 45)
```

Single-Linkage Clustering

```
agn <- agnes(data,
    diss = FALSE,
    stand = FALSE,
    method = "single")
# Make and plot the dendrogram
dend_agn <- as.dendrogram(agn)
plot(dend_agn,
    xlab = "Index of Data Points",
    ylab = "Steps",
    main = "Single-Linkage Clustering")
```

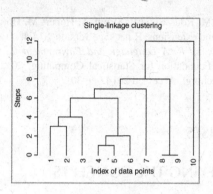

Complete-Linkage Clustering

```
agn_complete <- agnes(data,
    diss = FALSE,
    stand = FALSE,
    method = "complete")
# Make and plot the dendrogram
dend_agn_complete <-
    as.dendrogram(agn_complete)
plot(dend_agn_complete,
    xlab = "Index of Data Points",
    ylab = "Steps",
    main = "Complete-Linkage
    Clustering")
```

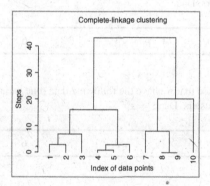

K-Means clustering

```
# Create the data matrix
# from Table 10.1
m <- matrix(c(1,3,3,3,4,3,5,3,
    1,2,4,2,1,1,2,1),
    byrow=TRUE,
    ncol = 2)
km <- kmeans(m,
    centers = 2)
km
```

```
> km
K-means clustering with 2 clusters of sizes 4, 4

Cluster means:
    [,1] [,2]
1 1.25 1.75
2 4.00 2.75

Clustering vector:
a b c d e f g h
1 2 2 2 1 2 1 1

within cluster sum of squares by cluster:
[1] 3.50 2.75
 (between_SS / total_SS =  73.3 %)

Available components:

[1] "cluster"    "centers"      "totss"
[4] "withinss"   "tot.withinss" "betweenss"
[7] "size"
```

R REFERENCES

Maechler M, Rousseeuw P, Struyf A, Hubert M, Hornik K. 2013. cluster: Cluster analysis basics and extensions. R package version 1.14.4.

R Core Team. *R: A Language and Environment for Statistical Computing*. Vienna, Austria: R Foundation for Statistical Computing; 2012. ISBN: 3-900051-07-0, http://www.R-project.org/. Accessed 2014 Sep 30.

EXERCISES

CLARIFYING THE CONCEPTS

1. To which cluster for the 90210 zip code would you prefer to belong?

2. Describe the goal of all clustering methods.

3. Suppose that we have the following data (one variable). Use single linkage to identify the clusters. Data:

0	0	1	3	3	6	7	9	10	10

4. Suppose that we have the following data (one variable). Use complete linkage to identify the clusters. Data:

0	0	1	3	3	6	7	9	10	10

5. What is an intuitive idea for the meaning of the *centroid* of a cluster?

6. Suppose that we have the following data:

a	b	c	d	e	f	g	h	i	j
(2,0)	(1,2)	(2,2)	(3,2)	(2,3)	(3,3)	(2,4)	(3,4)	(4,4)	(3,5)

Identify the cluster by applying the *k*-means algorithm, with $k = 2$. Try using initial cluster centers as far apart as possible.

7. Refer to Exercise 6. Show that the ratio of the between-cluster variation to the within-cluster variation increases with each pass of the algorithm.

8. Once again identify the clusters in Exercise 6 data, this time by applying the *k*-means algorithm, with $k = 3$. Try using initial cluster centers as far apart as possible.

9. Refer to Exercise 8. Show that the ratio of the between-cluster variation to the within-cluster variation increases with each pass of the algorithm.

10. Which clustering solution do you think is preferable? Why?

11. Confirm the calculations for the second pass and third pass for MSB, MSE, and pseudo-F for step 4 of the example given in the chapter.

HANDS-ON ANALYSIS

Use the *cereals* data set, included at the book series web site, for the following exercises. Make sure that the data are normalized.

12. Using all of the variables, except *name* and *rating,* run the k-means algorithm with $k = 5$ to identify clusters within the data.

13. Develop clustering profiles that clearly describe the characteristics of the cereals within the cluster.

14. Rerun the k-means algorithm with $k = 3$.

15. Which clustering solution do you prefer, and why?

16. Develop clustering profiles that clearly describe the characteristics of the cereals within the cluster.

17. Use cluster membership to predict *rating.* One way to do this would be to construct a histogram of *rating* based on cluster membership alone. Describe how the relationship you uncovered makes sense, based on your earlier profiles.

## CHAPTER 20

KOHONEN NETWORKS

20.1 SELF-ORGANIZING MAPS

Kohonen networks were introduced in 1982 by Finnish researcher Tuevo Kohonen.[1] Although applied initially to image and sound analyses, Kohonen networks are nevertheless an effective mechanism for clustering analysis. Kohonen networks represent a type of *self-organizing map* (SOM), which itself represents a special class of neural networks, which we studied in Chapter 12.

The goal of SOMs is to convert a complex high-dimensional input signal into a simpler low-dimensional discrete map.[2] Thus, SOMs are nicely appropriate for cluster analysis, where underlying hidden patterns among records and fields are sought. SOMs structure the output nodes into clusters of nodes, where nodes in closer proximity are more similar to each other than to other nodes that are farther apart. Ritter[3] has shown that SOMs represent a nonlinear generalization of principal components analysis, another dimension-reduction technique.

SOMs are based on *competitive learning,* where the output nodes compete among themselves to be the winning node (or neuron), the only node to be activated by a particular input observation. As Haykin describes it: "The neurons become *selectively tuned* to various input patterns (stimuli) or classes of input patterns in the course of a competitive learning process." A typical SOM architecture is shown in Figure 20.1. The input layer is shown at the bottom of the figure, with one input node for each field. Just as with neural networks, these input nodes perform no processing themselves, but simply pass the field input values along downstream.

Like neural networks, SOMs are *feedforward* and *completely connected. Feedforward* networks do not allow looping or cycling. *Completely connected* means that every node in a given layer is connected to every node in the next layer, although not to

---

[1] Tuevo Kohonen, Self-organized formation of topologically correct feature maps, *Biological Cybernetics*, Vol. 43, pp. 59–69, 1982.

[2] Simon Haykin, *Neural Networks: A Comprehensive Foundation*, Prentice Hall, Upper Saddle River, NJ, 1990.

[3] Helge Ritter, Self-organizing feature maps: Kohonen maps, in M.A. Arbib, ed., *The Handbook of Brain Theory and Neural Networks*, pp. 846–851, MIT Press, Cambridge, MA, 1995.

Data Mining and Predictive Analytics, First Edition. Daniel T. Larose and Chantal D. Larose.
© 2015 John Wiley & Sons, Inc. Published 2015 by John Wiley & Sons, Inc.

other nodes in the same layer. Like neural networks, each connection between nodes has a weight associated with it, which at initialization is assigned randomly to a value between 0 and 1. Adjusting these weights represents the key for the learning mechanism in both neural networks and SOMs. Variable values need to be normalized or standardized, just as for neural networks, so that certain variables do not overwhelm others in the learning algorithm.

Unlike most neural networks, however, SOMs have no hidden layer. The data from the input layer is passed along directly to the output layer. The output layer is represented in the form of a lattice, usually in one or two dimensions, and typically in the shape of a rectangle, although other shapes, such as hexagons, may be used. The output layer shown in Figure 20.1 is a 3×3 square.

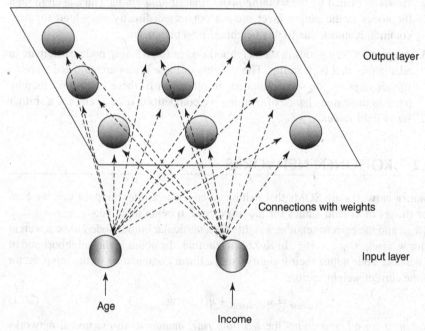

Figure 20.1   Topology of a simple self-organizing map for clustering records by age and income.

For a given record (instance), a particular field value is forwarded from a particular input node to every node in the output layer. For example, suppose that the normalized age and income values for the first record in the data set are 0.69 and 0.88, respectively. The 0.69 value would enter the SOM through the input node associated with *age*, and this node would pass this value of 0.69 to every node in the output layer. Similarly, the 0.88 value would be distributed through the *income* input node to every node in the output layer. These values, together with the weights assigned to each of the connections, would determine the values of a *scoring function* (such as Euclidean distance) for each output node. The output node with the "best" outcome from the scoring function would then be designated as the *winning node*.

SOMs exhibit three characteristic processes:

1. *Competition*. As mentioned above, the output nodes compete with each other to produce the best value for a particular scoring function, most commonly the Euclidean distance. In this case, the output node that has the smallest Euclidean distance between the field inputs and the connection weights would be declared the winner. Later, we examine in detail an example of how this works.

2. *Cooperation*. The winning node therefore becomes the center of a neighborhood of excited neurons. This emulates the behavior of human neurons, which are sensitive to the output of other neurons in their immediate neighborhood. In SOMs, all the nodes in this neighborhood share in the "excitement" or "reward" earned by the winning nodes, that of *adaptation*. Thus, even though the nodes in the output layer are not connected directly, they tend to share common features, due to this neighborliness parameter.

3. *Adaptation*. The nodes in the neighborhood of the winning node participate in adaptation, that is, learning. The weights of these nodes are adjusted so as to further improve the score function. In other words, these nodes will thereby have an increased chance of winning the competition once again, for a similar set of field values.

20.2 KOHONEN NETWORKS

Kohonen networks are SOMs that exhibit *Kohonen learning*. Suppose that we consider the set of m field values for the nth record to be an input vector $\mathbf{x}_n = x_{n1}, x_{n2}, \ldots, x_{nm}$, and the current set of m weights for a particular output node j to be a weight vector $\mathbf{w}_j = w_{1j}, w_{2j}, \ldots, w_{mj}$. In Kohonen learning, the nodes in the neighborhood of the winning node adjust their weights using a linear combination of the input vector and the current weight vector:

$$w_{ij,\text{new}} = w_{ij,\text{current}} + \eta(x_{ni} - w_{ij,\text{current}}) \tag{20.1}$$

where η, $0 < \eta < 1$, represents the *learning rate*, analogous to the neural networks case. Kohonen[4] indicates that the learning rate should be a decreasing function of training epochs (runs through the data set) and that a linearly or geometrically decreasing η is satisfactory for most purposes.

The algorithm for Kohonen networks (after Fausett[5]) is shown in the accompanying box. At initialization, the weights are randomly assigned, unless firm a priori knowledge exists regarding the proper value for the weight vectors. Also at initialization, the learning rate η and neighborhood size R are assigned. The value of R may start out moderately large but should decrease as the algorithm progresses. Note that nodes that do not attract a sufficient number of hits may be pruned, thereby improving algorithm efficiency.

[4] Tuevo Kohonen, *Self-Organization and Associative Memory*, 3rd ed., Springer-Verlag, Berlin, 1989.
[5] Laurene Fausett, *Fundamentals of Neural Networks*, Prentice Hall, Upper Saddle River, NJ, 1994.

KOHONEN NETWORKS ALGORITHM

For each input vector **x**, perform the following steps:

- *Competition.* For each output node j, calculate the value $D(w_j, x_n)$ of the scoring function. For example, for Euclidean distance, $D(w_j, x_n) = \sqrt{\sum_i (w_{ij} - x_{ni})^2}$. Find the winning node J that minimizes $D(w_j, x_n)$ over all output nodes.

- *Cooperation.* Identify all output nodes j within the neighborhood of J defined by the neighborhood size R. For these nodes, perform the following for all input record fields:

  - *Adaptation.* Adjust the weights:

$$w_{ij,\text{new}} = w_{ij,\text{current}} + \eta(x_{ni} - w_{ij,\text{current}})$$

- Adjust the learning rate and neighborhood size, as needed.

- Stop when the termination criteria are met.

20.3   EXAMPLE OF A KOHONEN NETWORK STUDY

Consider the following simple example. Suppose that we have a data set with two attributes, *age* and *income*, which have already been normalized, and suppose that we would like to use a 2×2 Kohonen network to uncover hidden clusters in the data set. We would thus have the topology shown in Figure 20.2.

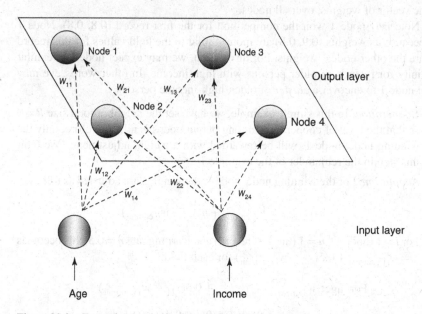

Figure 20.2   Example: topology of the 2×2 Kohonen network.

A set of four records is ready to be input, with a thumbnail description of each record provided. With such a small network, we set the neighborhood size to be $R = 0$, so that only the winning node will be awarded the opportunity to adjust its weight. Also, we set the learning rate η to be 0.5. Finally, assume that the weights have been randomly initialized as follows:

$$
\begin{array}{llll}
w_{11} = 0.9 & w_{21} = 0.8 & w_{12} = 0.9 & w_{22} = 0.2 \\
w_{13} = 0.1 & w_{23} = 0.8 & w_{14} = 0.1 & w_{24} = 0.2
\end{array}
$$

For the first input vector, $\mathbf{x}_1 = (0.8, 0.8)$, we perform the following competition, cooperation, and adaptation sequence.

- *Competition.* We compute the Euclidean distance between this input vector and the weight vectors for each of the four output nodes:

$$\text{Node } 1: D(w_1, x_1) = \sqrt{\sum_i (w_{i1} - x_{1i})^2} = \sqrt{(0.9 - 0.8)^2 + (0.8 - 0.8)^2} = 0.1$$

$$\text{Node } 2: D(w_2, x_1) = \sqrt{(0.9 - 0.8)^2 + (0.2 - 0.8)^2} = 0.61$$

$$\text{Node } 3: D(w_3, x_1) = \sqrt{(0.1 - 0.8)^2 + (0.8 - 0.8)^2} = 0.70$$

$$\text{Node } 4: D(w_4, x_1) = \sqrt{(0.1 - 0.8)^2 + (0.2 - 0.8)^2} = 0.92$$

The winning node for this first input record is therefore node 1, as it minimizes the score function D, the Euclidean distance between the input vector for this record, and the vector of weights, over all nodes.

Note *why* node 1 won the competition for the first record (0.8, 0.8). Node 1 won because its weights (0.9, 0.8) are more similar to the field values for this record than are the other nodes' weights. For this reason, we may expect node 1 to exhibit an affinity for records of older persons with high income. In other words, we may expect node 1 to uncover a *cluster* of older, high-income persons.

- *Cooperation.* In this simple example, we have set the neighborhood size $R = 0$ so that the level of cooperation among output nodes is nil! Therefore, only the winning node, node 1, will be rewarded with a weight adjustment. (We omit this step in the remainder of the example.)

- *Adaptation.* For the winning node, node 1, the weights are adjusted as follows:

$$w_{ij,\text{new}} = w_{ij,\text{current}} + \eta(x_{ni} - w_{ij,\text{current}})$$

For $j = 1$ (node 1), $n = 1$ (the first record) and learning rate $\eta = 0.5$, this becomes $w_{i1,\text{new}} = w_{i1,\text{current}} + 0.5(x_{1i} - w_{i1,\text{current}})$ for each field:

For age: $w_{11,\text{new}} = w_{11,\text{current}} + 0.5(x_{11} - w_{11,\text{current}})$

$$= 0.9 + 0.5(0.8 - 0.9) = 0.85$$

For income: $w_{21,new} = w_{21,current} + 0.5(x_{12} - w_{21,current})$

$$= 0.8 + 0.5(0.8 - 0.8) = 0.8$$

Note the type of adjustment that takes place. The weights are nudged in the direction of the fields' values of the input record. That is, w_{11}, the weight on the *age* connection for the winning node, was originally 0.9, but was adjusted in the direction of the normalized value for *age* in the first record, 0.8. As the learning rate $\eta = 0.5$, this adjustment is half (0.5) of the distance between the current weight and the field value. This adjustment will help node 1 to become even more proficient at capturing the records of older, high-income persons.

Next, for the second input vector, $\mathbf{x}_2 = (0.8, 0.1)$, we have the following sequence:

- *Competition*

Node 1: $D(w_1, x_2) = \sqrt{(0.85 - 0.8)^2 + (0.8 - 0.1)^2} = 0.78$

Node 2: $D(w_2, x_2) = \sqrt{(0.9 - 0.8)^2 + (0.2 - 0.1)^2} = 0.14$

Node 3: $D(w_3, x_2) = \sqrt{(0.1 - 0.8)^2 + (0.8 - 0.1)^2} = 0.99$

Node 4: $D(w_4, x_2) = \sqrt{(0.1 - 0.8)^2 + (0.2 - 0.1)^2} = 0.71$

Winning node: node 2. Note that node 2 won the competition for the second record (0.8, 0.1), because its weights (0.9, 0.2) are more similar to the field values for this record than are the other nodes' weights. Thus, we may expect node 2 to "collect" records of older persons with low income. That is, node 2 will represent a cluster of older, low-income persons.

- *Adaptation.* For the winning node, node 2, the weights are adjusted as follows: For $j = 2$ (node 2), $n = 2$ (the first record), and learning rate $\eta = 0.5$, we have $w_{i2, new} = w_{i2, current} + 0.5(x_{2i} - w_{i2, current})$ for each field:

For age: $w_{12,new} = w_{12,current} + 0.5(x_{21} - w_{12,current})$

$$= 0.9 + 0.5(0.8 - 0.9) = 0.85$$

For income: $w_{22,new} = w_{22,current} + 0.5(x_{22} - w_{22,current})$

$$= 0.2 + 0.5(0.1 - 0.2) = 0.15$$

Again, the weights are updated in the direction of the field values of the input record. Weight w_{12} undergoes the same adjustment w_{11} above, as the current weights and *age* field values were the same. Weight w_{22} for income is adjusted downward, as the *income* level of the second record was lower than the current *income* weight for the winning node. Because of this adjustment, node 2 will be even better at catching records of older, low-income persons.

Next, for the third input vector, $\mathbf{x}_3 = (0.2, 0.9)$, we have the following sequence:

- *Competition*

$$\text{Node 1: } D(w_1, x_3) = \sqrt{\sum_i (w_{i1} - x_{3i})^2} = \sqrt{(0.85 - 0.2)^2 + (0.8 - 0.9)^2}$$
$$= 0.66$$

$$\text{Node 2: } D(w_2, x_3) = \sqrt{(0.85 - 0.2)^2 + (0.15 - 0.9)^2} = 0.99$$

$$\text{Node 3: } D(w_3, x_3) = \sqrt{(0.1 - 0.2)^2 + (0.8 - 0.9)^2} = 0.14$$

$$\text{Node 4: } D(w_4, x_3) = \sqrt{(0.1 - 0.2)^2 + (0.2 - 0.9)^2} = 0.71$$

The winning node is node 3 because its weights (0.1, 0.8) are the closest to the third record's field values. Hence, we may expect node 3 to represent a cluster of younger, high-income persons.

- *Adaptation.* For the winning node, node 3, the weights are adjusted as follows: $w_{i3,\text{new}} = w_{i3,\text{current}} + 0.5(x_{3i} - w_{i3,\text{current}})$, for each field:

$$\text{For age: } w_{13,\text{new}} = w_{13,\text{current}} + 0.5(x_{31} - w_{13,\text{current}})$$
$$= 0.1 + 0.5(0.2 - 0.1) = 0.15$$

$$\text{For income: } w_{23,\text{new}} = w_{23,\text{current}} + 0.5(x_{32} - w_{23,\text{current}})$$
$$= 0.8 + 0.5(0.9 - 0.8) = 0.85$$

Finally, for the fourth input vector, $\mathbf{x}_4 = (0.1, 0.1)$, we have the following sequence:

- *Competition*

$$\text{Node 1: } D(w_1, x_4) = \sqrt{\sum_i (w_{i1} - x_{4i})^2} = \sqrt{(0.85 - 0.1)^2 + (0.8 - 0.1)^2}$$
$$= 1.03$$

$$\text{Node 2: } D(w_2, x_4) = \sqrt{(0.85 - 0.1)^2 + (0.15 - 0.1)^2} = 0.75$$

$$\text{Node 3: } D(w_3, x_4) = \sqrt{(0.15 - 0.1)^2 + (0.85 - 0.1)^2} = 0.75$$

$$\text{Node 4: } D(w_4, x_4) = \sqrt{(0.1 - 0.1)^2 + (0.2 - 0.1)^2} = 0.10$$

The winning node is node 4 because its weights (0.1, 0.2) have the smallest Euclidean distance to the fourth record's field values. We may therefore expect node 4 to represent a cluster of younger, low-income persons.

TABLE 20.1   Four clusters uncovered by Kohonen network

Cluster	Associated with	Description
1	Node 1	Older person with high income
2	Node 2	Older person with low income
3	Node 3	Younger person with high income
4	Node 4	Younger person with low income

- *Adaptation.* For the winning node, node 4, the weights are adjusted as follows: $w_{i4,\text{new}} = w_{i4,\text{current}} + 0.5(x_{4i} - w_{i4,\text{current}})$, for each field:

$$\text{For age: } w_{14,\text{new}} = w_{14,\text{current}} + 0.5(x_{41} - w_{14,\text{current}})$$
$$= 0.1 + 0.5(0.1 - 0.1) = 0.10$$
$$\text{For income: } w_{24,\text{new}} = w_{24,\text{current}} + 0.5(x_{42} - w_{24,\text{current}})$$
$$= 0.2 + 0.5(0.1 - 0.2) = 0.15$$

Thus, we have seen that the four output nodes will represent four distinct clusters if the network continues to be fed data similar to the four records shown in Figure 20.2. These clusters are summarized in Table 20.1.

Clearly, the clusters uncovered by the Kohonen network in this simple example are fairly obvious. However, this example does serve to illustrate how the network operates at a basic level, using competition and Kohonen learning.

20.4   CLUSTER VALIDITY

To avoid spurious results, and to assure that the resulting clusters are reflective of the general population, the clustering solution should be validated. One common validation method is to split the original sample randomly into two groups, develop cluster solutions for each group, and then compare their profiles using the methods below or other summarization methods.

Now, suppose that a researcher is interested in performing further inference, prediction, or other analysis downstream on a particular field, and wishes to use the clusters as predictors. Then, it is important that the researcher do not include the field of interest as one of the fields used to build the clusters. For example, in the example below, clusters are constructed using the *churn* data set. We would like to use these clusters as predictors for later assistance in classifying customers as churners or not. Therefore, we must be careful not to include the *churn* field among the variables used to build the clusters.

20.5   APPLICATION OF CLUSTERING USING KOHONEN NETWORKS

Next, we apply the Kohonen network algorithm to the *churn* data set from Chapter 3 (available at the book series web site; also available from http://www.sgi.com/tech/mlc

/db/). Recall that the data set contains 20 variables worth of information about 3333 customers, along with an indication of whether that customer churned (left the company) or not. The following variables were passed to the Kohonen network algorithm, using IBM/SPSS Modeler:

- Flag (0/1) variables
  - International Plan and VoiceMail Plan
- Numerical variables
  - *Account length, voice mail messages, day minutes, evening minutes, night minutes, international minutes*, and *customer service calls*
  - After applying Z-score standardization to all numerical variables.

The topology of the network was as in Figure 20.3, with every node in the input layer being connected with weights (not shown) to every node in the output layer, which is labeled in accordance with their use in the Modeler results. The Kohonen learning parameters were set in Modeler as follows. For the first 20 cycles (passes through the data set), the neighborhood size was set at $R = 2$, and the learning rate was set to decay linearly starting at $\eta = 0.3$. Then, for the next 150 cycles, the neighborhood size was reset to $R = 1$, while the learning rate was allowed to decay linearly from $\eta = 0.3$ to $\eta = 0$.

As it turned out, the Modeler Kohonen algorithm used only six of the nine available output nodes, as shown in Figure 20.4, with output nodes 01, 11, and 21 being pruned. (Note that each of the six clusters is actually of constant value in this plot, such as (0,0) and (1,2). A random shock (*x, y agitation*, artificial noise) was introduced to illustrate the size of the cluster membership.)

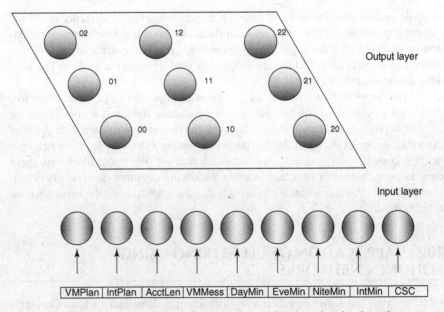

Figure 20.3 Topology of 3 × 3 Kohonen network used for clustering the churn data set.

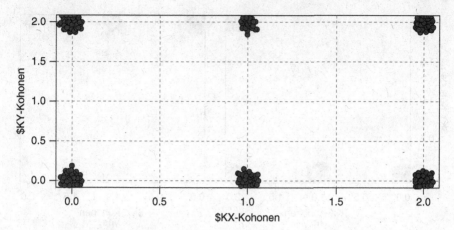

Figure 20.4   Modeler uncovered six clusters.

20.6   INTERPRETING THE CLUSTERS

How are we to interpret these clusters? How can we develop cluster profiles? Consider Figure 20.5, which plots the clusters similar to Figure 20.4, but with panels for whether a customer is an adopter of the International Plan. Figure 20.5 shows that International Plan adopters reside exclusively in Clusters 12 and 22, with the other clusters containing only non-adopters of the International Plan. The Kohonen clustering algorithm has found a high-quality discrimination along this dimension, dividing the data set neatly among adopters and non-adopters of the International Plan.

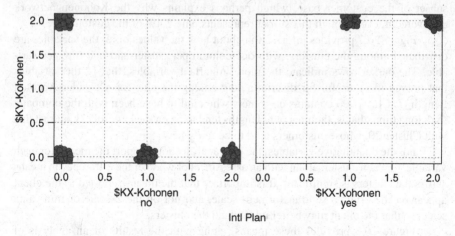

Figure 20.5   International Plan adopters reside exclusively in Clusters 12 and 22.

Figure 20.6 shows the VoiceMail Plan adoption status of the cluster members. The three clusters along the bottom row (i.e., Cluster 00, Cluster 10, and Cluster 20) contain only non-adopters of the VoiceMail Plan. Clusters 02 and 12 contain only

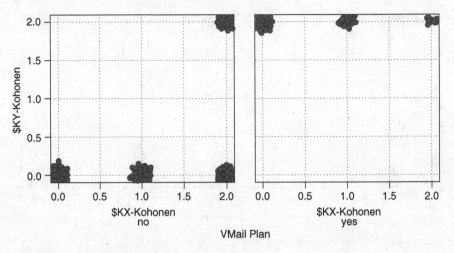

Figure 20.6 Similar clusters are closer to each other.

adopters of the VoiceMail Plan. Cluster 22 contains mostly non-adopters and also some adopters of the VoiceMail Plan.

Recall that because of the neighborliness parameter, clusters that are closer together should be more similar than clusters that are farther apart. Note in Figure 20.5 that all International Plan adopters reside in contiguous (neighboring) clusters, as do all non-adopters. Similarly for Figure 20.6, except that Cluster 22 contains a mixture.

We see that Cluster 12 represents a special subset of customers, those who have adopted both the International Plan and the VoiceMail Plan. This is a well-defined subset of the customer base, which perhaps explains why the Kohonen network uncovered it, even though this subset represents only 2.4% of the customers.

Figure 20.7 provides information about how the values of all the variables are distributed among the clusters, with one column per cluster and one row per variable. The darker rows indicate the more important variables, that is, the variables that proved more useful for discriminating among the clusters. Consider Account Length_Z. Cluster 00 contains customers who tend to have been with the company for a long time, that is, their account lengths tend to be on the large side. Contrast this with Cluster 20, whose customers tend to be fairly new.

For the quantitative variables, the data analyst should report the means for each variable, for each cluster, along with an assessment of whether the difference in means across the clusters is significant. It is important that the means reported to the client appear on the original (untransformed) scale, and not on the Z scale or min–max scale, so that the client may better understand the clusters.

Figure 20.8 provides these means, along with the results of an analysis of variance (see Chapter 5) for assessing whether the difference in means across clusters is significant. Each row contains the information for one numerical variable, with one analysis of variance for each row. Each cell contains the cluster mean, standard deviation, standard error (standard deviation$/\sqrt{\text{cluster count}}$), and cluster count. The degrees of freedom are $\text{df}_1 = k - 1 = 6 - 1 = 5$ and

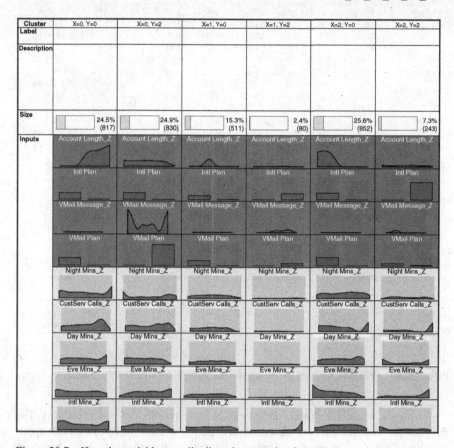

Figure 20.7 How the variables are distributed among the clusters.

$df_2 = N - k = 3333 - 6 = 3327$. The F-test statistic is the value of $F = MSTR/MSE$ for the analysis of variance for that particular variable, and the Importance statistic is simply $1 - p$-value, where p-value $= P(F > F \text{ test statistic})$.

Note that both Figures 20.7 and 11.8 concur in identifying account length and the number of voice mail messages as the two most important numerical variables for discriminating among clusters. Next, Figure 20.7 showed graphically that the account length for Cluster 00 is greater than that of Cluster 20. This is supported by the statistics in Figure 20.8, which shows that the mean account length of 141.508 days for Cluster 00 and 61.707 days for Cluster 20. Also, tiny Cluster 12 has the highest mean number of voice mail messages (31.662), with Cluster 02 also having a large amount (29.229). Finally, note that the neighborliness of Kohonen clusters tends to make neighboring clusters similar. It would have been surprising, for example to find a cluster with 141.508 mean account length right next to a cluster with 61.707 mean account length. In fact, this did not happen.

Grouping field: $KXY-Kohonen

*Cells contain: Mean, Standard Deviation, Standard Error, Count

Field	X=0, Y=0*	X=0, Y=2*	X=1, Y=0*	X=1, Y=2*	X=2, Y=0*	X=2, Y=2*	F-Test	df	Importance
Account Length	141.508	100.722	100.683	106.962	61.707	103.119	674.616	5, 3327	1.000
	23.917	39.075	8.527	36.221	21.163	39.068			⊞ Important
	0.837	1.356	0.377	4.050	0.725	2.506			
	817	830	511	80	852	243			
VMail Message	0.000	29.229	0.000	31.662	0.000	0.827	7101.682	5, 3327	1.000
	0.000	7.542	0.000	6.240	0.000	3.670			⊞ Important
	0.000	0.262	0.000	0.698	0.000	0.235			
	817	830	511	80	852	243			
Night Mins	196.819	201.483	200.988	204.590	205.786	193.717	3.758	5, 3327	0.998
	49.504	51.374	49.476	53.412	50.421	51.803			⊞ Important
	1.732	1.783	2.189	5.972	1.727	3.323			
	817	830	511	80	852	243			
CustServ Calls	1.696	1.531	1.638	1.425	1.458	1.477	3.597	5, 3327	0.997
	1.378	1.292	1.353	1.329	1.232	1.343			⊞ Important
	0.048	0.045	0.060	0.149	0.042	0.086			
	817	830	511	80	852	243			
Day Mins	176.195	178.695	181.266	189.140	180.253	187.607	2.344	5, 3327	0.961
	54.152	53.576	53.688	51.752	54.926	58.528			⊞ Important
	1.895	1.860	2.375	5.786	1.882	3.755			
	817	830	511	80	852	243			
Eve Mins	201.320	202.366	203.940	207.570	196.409	202.741	2.196	5, 3327	0.948
	51.550	50.477	49.588	48.509	49.766	54.283			⊞ Marginal
	1.804	1.752	2.194	5.424	1.705	3.482			
	817	830	511	80	852	243			
Intl Mins	10.098	10.153	10.225	10.861	10.312	10.551	2.098	5, 3327	0.937
	2.805	2.787	2.864	2.956	2.766	2.609			⊞ Marginal
	0.098	0.097	0.127	0.330	0.095	0.167			
	817	830	511	80	852	243			

Figure 20.8   Assessing whether the means across clusters are significantly different.

In general, not all clusters are guaranteed to offer obvious interpretability. The data analyst should team up with a domain expert to discuss the relevance and applicability of the clusters uncovered using Kohonen or other methods. Here, however, most of these clusters appear fairly clear-cut and self-explanatory.

20.6.1   Cluster Profiles

- *Cluster 00*: *Loyal Non-Adopters*. Belonging to neither the VoiceMail Plan nor the International Plan, customers in large Cluster 00 have nevertheless been with the company the longest, with by far the largest mean account length, which may be related to the largest number of calls to customer service. This cluster exhibits the lowest average minutes usage for day minutes and international minutes, and the second lowest evening minutes and night minutes.

- *Cluster 02*: *Voice Mail Users*. This large cluster contains members of the Voice-Mail Plan, with therefore a high mean number of voice mail messages, and no members of the International Plan. Otherwise, the cluster tends toward the middle of the pack for the other variables.

- *Cluster 10*: *Average Customers.* Customers in this medium-sized cluster belong to neither the Voice Mail Plan nor the International Plan. Except for the second-largest mean number of calls to customer service, this cluster otherwise tends toward the average values for the other variables.

- *Cluster 12*: *Power Customers.* This smallest cluster contains customers who belong to both the VoiceMail Plan and the International Plan. These sophisticated customers also lead the pack in usage minutes across three categories and are in second place in the other category. They also have the fewest average calls to customer service. The company should keep a watchful eye on this cluster, as they may represent a highly profitable group.

- *Cluster 20*: *Newbie Non-AdoptersUsers.* Belonging to neither the VoiceMail Plan nor the International Plan, customers in large Cluster 00 represent the company's newest customers, on average, with easily the shortest mean account length. These customers set the pace with the highest mean night minutes usage.

- *Cluster 22*: *International Plan Users.* This small cluster contains members of the International Plan and only a few members of the VoiceMail Plan. The number of calls to customer service is second lowest, which may mean that they need a minimum of hand-holding. Besides the lowest mean night minutes usage, this cluster tends toward average values for the other variables.

Cluster profiles may of themselves be of actionable benefit to companies and researchers. They may, for example, suggest marketing segmentation strategies in an era of shrinking budgets. Rather than targeting the entire customer base for a mass mailing, for example, perhaps only the most profitable customers may be targeted. Another strategy is to identify those customers whose potential loss would be of greater harm to the company, such as the customers in Cluster 12 above. Finally, customer clusters could be identified that exhibit behavior predictive of churning; intervention with these customers could save them for the company.

Suppose, however, that we would like to apply these clusters to assist us in the *churn classification* task. We may compare the proportions of churners among the various clusters, using graphs such as Figure 20.9. From the figure we can see that customers in Clusters 12 (power customers) and 22 (International Plan users) are in greatest danger of leaving the company, as shown by their higher overall churn proportions. Cluster 02 (VoiceMail Plan users) has the lowest churn rate. The company should take a serious look at its International Plan to see why customers do not seem to be happy with it. Also, the company should encourage more customers to adopt its VoiceMail Plan, in order to make switching companies more inconvenient. These results and recommendations reflect our findings from Chapter 3, where we initially examined the relationship between churning and the various fields. Note also that Clusters 12 and 22 are neighboring clusters; even though *churn* was not an input field for cluster formation, the type of customers who are likely to churn are more similar to each other than to customers not likely to churn.

		Churn	
$KXY-Kohonen		False.	True.
X=0, Y=0	Count	692	125
	Row %	84.700	15.300
X=0, Y=2	Count	786	44
	Row %	94.699	5.301
X=1, Y=0	Count	440	71
	Row %	86.106	13.894
X=1, Y=2	Count	49	31
	Row %	61.250	38.750
X=2, Y=0	Count	746	106
	Row %	87.559	12.441
X=2, Y=2	Count	137	106
	Row %	56.379	43.621

Figure 20.9   Proportions of churners among the clusters.

20.7   USING CLUSTER MEMBERSHIP AS INPUT TO DOWNSTREAM DATA MINING MODELS

Cluster membership may be used to enrich the data set and improve model efficacy. Indeed, as data repositories continue to grow and the number of fields continues to increase, clustering has become a common method of dimension reduction.

We will illustrate how cluster membership may be used as input for downstream data mining models, using the *churn* data set and the clusters uncovered above. Each record now has associated with it a cluster membership assigned by the Kohonen networks algorithm. We shall enrich our data set by adding this cluster membership field to the input fields used for classifying churn. A classification and regression tree (CART) decision tree model was run, to classify customers as either churners or non-churners. The resulting decision tree output is shown in Figure 20.10.

The root node split is on whether *DayMin_Z* (the Z-standardized version of day minutes; the analyst should *untransform* these values if this output is meant for the client) is greater than about 1.573. This represents the 142 users who have the

```
Day Mins_Z <= 1.573 [ Mode: False. ] (2,217)
   CustServ Calls_Z <= 1.473 [ Mode: False. ] (2,049)
      Intl Plan in [ "no" ] [ Mode: False. ] (1,866)
         Day Mins_Z <= 0.772 [ Mode: False. ]  ⇒ False. (1,561; 0.974)
         Day Mins_Z > 0.772 [ Mode: False. ] (305)
            Eve Mins_Z <= 1.298 [ Mode: False. ]  ⇒ False. (274; 0.898)
            Eve Mins_Z > 1.298 [ Mode: True. ]  ⇒ True. (31; 0.742)
      Intl Plan in [ "yes" ] [ Mode: False. ] (183)
         Intl Mins_Z <= 1.007 [ Mode: False. ]  ⇒ False. (151; 0.775)
         Intl Mins_Z > 1.007 [ Mode: True. ]  ⇒ True. (32; 1.0)
   CustServ Calls_Z > 1.473 [ Mode: False. ] (168)
      Day Mins_Z <= -0.359 [ Mode: True. ]  ⇒ True. (71; 0.859)
      Day Mins_Z > -0.359 [ Mode: False. ]  ⇒ False. (97; 0.784)
Day Mins_Z > 1.573 [ Mode: True. ] (142)
   $KXY-Kohonen in [ "X=0, Y=2" ] [ Mode: False. ]  ⇒ False. (31; 1.0)
   $KXY-Kohonen in [ "X=0, Y=0" "X=1, Y=0" "X=1, Y=2" "X=2, Y=0" "X=2, Y=2" ] [ Mode: True. ]  ⇒ True. (111; 0.766)
```

Figure 20.10   Output of CART decision tree for data set enriched by cluster membership.

highest day minutes, 1.573 standard deviations above the mean. For this group, the second-level split is by cluster, with Cluster 02 split off from the remaining clusters. Note that for high day minutes, the mode classification is *True* (churner), but that within this subset, membership in Cluster 02 acts to protect from churn, as the 31 customers with high day minutes and membership in Cluster 02 have a 100% probability of *not* churning. Recall that Cluster 02, which is acting as a brake on churn behavior, represents *Voice Mail Users*, who had the lowest churn rate of any cluster.

The R Zone

Open 'kohonen' package. Read in and prepare the data

```
library(kohonen)
churn <- read.csv(file = "C:/ ... /churn.txt", stringsAsFactors=TRUE)
IntPlan <- VMPlan <- Churn <- c(rep(0, length(churn$Int.l.Plan))) # Flag variables
for (i in 1:length(churn$Int.l.Plan)) {
    if (churn$Int.l.Plan[i]=="yes") IntPlan[i] = 1
    if (churn$VMail.Plan[i]=="yes") VMPlan[i] = 1
    if (churn$Churn[i] == "True") Churn[i] = 1
}
AcctLen <- (churn$Account.Length - mean(churn$Account.Length))/sd(churn$Account.Length)
VMMess <- (churn$VMail.Message - mean(churn$VMail.Message)) /
    sd(churn$VMail.Message)
DayMin <- (churn$Day.Mins - mean(churn$Day.Mins))/sd(churn$Day.Mins)
EveMin <- (churn$Eve.Mins - mean(churn$Eve.Mins))/sd(churn$Eve.Mins)
NiteMin <- (churn$Night.Mins - mean(churn$Night.Mins))/sd(churn$Night.Mins)
IntMin <- (churn$Intl.Mins - mean(churn$Intl.Mins))/sd(churn$Intl.Mins)
CSC <- (churn$CustServ.Calls - mean(churn$CustServ.Calls))/sd(churn$CustServ.Calls)
```

Run the algorithm to get a 3x2 Kohonen network

```
# Make the variables into one matrix, and
# make sure the records are the rows
dat <- t(rbind(IntPlan, VMPlan, AcctLen,
    VMMess, DayMin, EveMin, NiteMin,
    IntMin, CSC))
som.6 <- som(dat,
    grid = somgrid(3, 2),
    rlen = 170,
    alpha = c(0.3, 0.00),
    radius = 2)
# Plot the make-up of each cluster
plot(som.6,
    type = c("codes"),
    palette.name = rainbow,
    main = "Cluster Content")
```

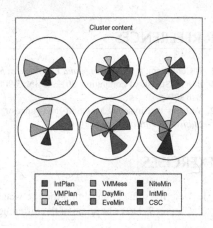

```
# Plot the counts in each cluster
plot(som.6,
    type = c("counts"),
    palette.name = rainbow,
    main = "Cluster Counts")
```

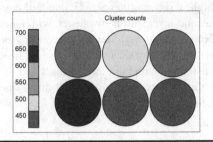

Plot make-up of clusters

```
som.6$unit.classif # Winning Clusters
som.6$grid$pts # Plot locations
coords <- matrix(0, ncol = 2, nrow = dim(dat)[1])
for(i in 1:dim(dat)[1]){
    coords[i,] <-
    som.6$grid$pts[som.6$unit.classif[i],]
}
pchVMPlan <- ifelse(dat[,2]==0 , 1, 16)
colVMPlan <- ifelse(dat[,2]==0 , 1, 2)
plot(jitter(coords), main = "Kohonen Network
    colored by VM Plan",
    col = colVMPlan,
    pch = pchVMPlan)
```

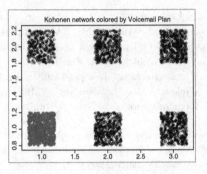

Table of Percent Churn by cluster

```
c.table <- table(Churn, som.6$unit.classif)
round(prop.table(c.table, 2)*100, 2)
```

churn	1	2	3	4	5	6
0	92.56	89.38	93.20	65.44	84.27	80.27
1	7.44	10.62	6.80	34.56	15.73	19.73

R REFERENCES

1. R Core Team. *R: A Language and Environment for Statistical Computing*. Vienna, Austria: R Foundation for Statistical Computing; 2012. ISBN: 3-900051-07-0, http://www.R-project.org/. Accessed 2014 Sep 30.
2. Wehrens R, Buydens LMC. Self- and super-organising paps in R: the Kohonen package *Journal of Statistical Software*, 2007;*21*(5).

EXERCISES

1. Describe some of the similarities between Kohonen networks and the neural networks of Chapter 7. Describe some of the differences.

2. Describe the three characteristic processes exhibited by SOMs such as Kohonen networks. What differentiates Kohonen networks from other SOM models?

3. Using weights and distance, explain clearly why a certain output node will win the competition for the input of a certain record.

4. For larger output layers, what would be the effect of increasing the value of R?

5. Describe what would happen if the learning rate η did not decline?

6. This chapter shows how cluster membership can be used for downstream modeling. Does this apply to the cluster membership obtained by hierarchical and k-means clustering as well?

HANDS-ON ANALYSIS

Use the *adult* data set at the book series Web site for the following exercises.

7. Apply the Kohonen clustering algorithm to the data set, being careful not to include the *income* field. Use a topology that is not too large, such as 3×3.

8. Construct a scatter plot (with x/y agitation) of the cluster membership, with an overlay of *income*. Discuss your findings.

9. Construct a bar chart of the cluster membership, with an overlay of *income*. Discuss your findings. Compare to the scatter plot.

10. Construct a bar chart of the cluster membership, with an overlay of *marital status*. Discuss your findings.

11. If your software supports this, construct a web graph of *income*, *marital status*, and the other categorical variables. Fine-tune the web graph so that it conveys good information.

12. Generate numerical summaries for the clusters. For example, generate a cluster mean summary.

13. Using the information above and any other information you can bring to bear, construct detailed and informative cluster profiles, complete with titles.

14. Use cluster membership as a further input to a CART decision tree model for classifying income. How important is clustering membership in classifying income?

15. Use cluster membership as a further input to a C4.5 decision tree model for classifying income. How important is clustering membership in classifying income? Compare to the CART model.

## CHAPTER 21

BIRCH CLUSTERING

21.1 RATIONALE FOR BIRCH CLUSTERING

BIRCH, which stands for Balanced Iterative Reducing and Clustering using Hierarchies, was developed in 1996 by Tian Zhang, Raghu Ramakrishnan, and Miron Livny.[1] BIRCH is especially appropriate for very large data sets, or for streaming data, because of its ability to find a good clustering solution with only a single scan of the data. Optionally, the algorithm can make further scans through the data to improve the clustering quality. BIRCH handles large data sets with a time complexity and space efficiency that is superior to other algorithms, according to the authors.

The BIRCH clustering algorithm consists of two main phases or steps,[2] as shown here.

BIRCH CLUSTERING ALGORITHM

- **Phase 1: Build the CF Tree.** Load the data into memory by building a *cluster-feature tree* (CF tree, defined below). Optionally, condense this initial CF tree into a smaller CF.
- **Phase 2: Global Clustering.** Apply an existing clustering algorithm on the leaves of the CF tree. Optionally, refine these clusters.

BIRCH is sometimes referred to as *Two-Step Clustering*, because of the two phases shown here. We now consider what constitutes each of these phases.

---

[1] Tian Zhang, Raghu Ramakrishnan, and Miron Livny, BIRCH: an efficient data clustering method for very large databases. In *Proceedings of 1996 ACM-SIGMOD International Conference on Management of Data*, pp. 103–114, Montreal, Quebec, Canada, June 1996, ACM Press.

[2] We have blended the authors' optional phases into their respective required phases.

21.2   CLUSTER FEATURES

BIRCH clustering achieves its high efficiency by clever use of a small set of summary statistics to represent a larger set of data points. For clustering purposes, these summary statistics constitute a CF, and represent a sufficient substitute for the actual data. In their original paper, Zhang *et al.* suggested the following summary statistics for the CF:

CLUSTER FEATURE

A CF is a set of three summary statistics that represent a set of data points in a single cluster. These statistics are as follows:

- *Count.* How many data values in the cluster.
- *Linear Sum.* Sum the individual coordinates. This is a measure of the location of the cluster.
- *Squared Sum.* Sum the squared coordinates. This is a measure of the spread of the cluster.

Note that, together, the linear sum and the squared sum are equivalent to the mean and variance of the data point.

For example, consider Clusters 1 and 2 in Figure 21.1. Cluster 1 contains data values (1, 1), (2, 1), and (1, 2), whereas Cluster 2 contains data values (3, 2), (4, 1), and (4, 2). CF_1, the CF for Cluster 1, consists of the following:

$$CF_1 = \{3, (1+2+1, 1+1+2), (1^2+2^2+1^2, 1^2+1^2+2^2)\}$$
$$= \{3, (4,4), (6,6)\}$$

And for Cluster 2, the CF is

$$CF_2 = \{3, (3+4+4, 2+1+2), (3^2+4^2+4^2, 2^2+1^2+2^2)\}$$
$$= \{3, (11,5), (41,9)\}$$

CF_1 and CF_2 represent the data in Clusters 1 and 2.

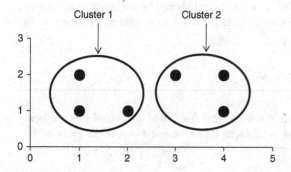

Figure 21.1   Clusters 1 and 2.

One mechanism of the BIRCH algorithm calls for the merging of clusters under certain conditions. The *Additivity Theorem* states that the CFs for two clusters may be merged simply by adding the items in their respective CF trees. Thus, if we needed to merge Clusters 1 and 2, the resulting CF would be

$$CF_{12} = \{3 + 3, (4 + 11, 4 + 5), (6 + 41, 6 + 9)\} = \{6, (15, 9), (47, 15)\}$$

21.3 CLUSTER FEATURE TREE

A CF tree is a tree structure composed of CFs. A CF tree represents a compressed form of the data, preserving any clustering structure in the data. A CF tree has the following parameters:

CLUSTER FEATURE TREE PARAMETERS

- **Branching Factor B.** B determines the maximum children allowed for a non-leaf node.
- **Threshold T.** T is an upper limit to the radius of a cluster in a leaf node.
- **Number of Entries in a Leaf Node L.**

The general structure of a CF tree is shown in Figure 21.2.

For a CF entry in a root node or a non-leaf node, that CF entry equals the sum of the CF entries in the child nodes of that entry. A leaf node CF is referred to simply as a *leaf*.

21.4 PHASE 1: BUILDING THE CF TREE

Phase 1 of the BIRCH algorithm consists of building the CF tree. This is done using a sequential clustering approach, whereby the algorithm scans the data one record at a time, and determines whether a given record should be assigned to an existing cluster, or a new cluster should be constructed. The CF tree building process consists of four steps, as follows:

CF TREE BUILDING PROCESS

1. For each given record, BIRCH compares the location of that record with the location of each CF in the root node, using either the linear sum or the mean of the CF. BIRCH passes the incoming record to the root node CF closest to the incoming record.

2. The record then descends down to the non-leaf child nodes of the root node CF selected in step 1. BIRCH compares the location of the record with the location of each non-leaf CF. BIRCH passes the incoming record to the non-leaf node CF closest to the incoming record.

3. The record then descends down to the leaf child nodes of the non-leaf node CF selected in step 2. BIRCH compares the location of the record with the location of each leaf. BIRCH tentatively passes the incoming record to the leaf closest to the incoming record.

4. Perform one of (a) or (b):

    a. If the radius (defined below) of the chosen leaf including the new record does not exceed the Threshold T, then the incoming record is assigned to that leaf. The leaf and all of its parent CFs are updated to account for the new data point.

    b. If the radius of the chosen leaf including the new record does exceed the Threshold T, then a new leaf is formed, consisting of the incoming record only. The parent CFs are updated to account for the new data point.

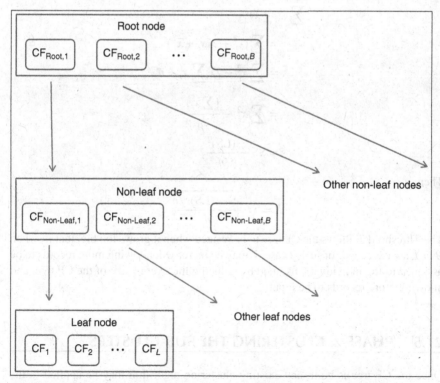

Figure 21.2 General structure of a CF tree, with branching factor B, and L leafs in each leaf node.

Now, if step 4b is executed, and there are already the maximum of L leafs in the leaf node, then the leaf node is split into two leaf nodes. The most distant leaf node CFs are used as leaf node seeds, with the remaining CFs being assigned to whichever leaf node is closer. If the parent node is full, split the parent node, and so on. This process is illustrated in the example below.

Each leaf node CF may be viewed as a sub-cluster. In the cluster step, these sub-clusters will be combined into clusters. For a given cluster, let the cluster centroid be

$$\bar{x} = \frac{\sum x_i}{n}$$

Then the *radius* of the cluster is

$$R = \sqrt{\frac{\sum (x_i - \bar{x})^2}{n}}$$

Note that the radius of a cluster may be calculated even without knowing the data points, as long as we have the count n, the linear sum LS, and the squared sum SS. This allows BIRCH to evaluate whether a given data point belongs to a particular sub-cluster without needing to scan the original data set. The derivation for the sum of squares is as follows:

$$\sum (x_i - \bar{x})^2$$
$$= \sum (x_i^2 - 2\bar{x}x_i + \bar{x}^2)$$
$$= \sum x_i^2 - 2\bar{x} \sum x_i + n\bar{x}^2$$
$$= \sum x_i^2 - \frac{\left(\sum x_i\right)^2}{n}$$
$$= SS - \frac{(LS)^2}{n}$$

Then,

$$R = \sqrt{\frac{SS - (LS)^2/n}{n}}$$

The Threshold T allows the CF tree to be resized when it grows too big, that is, when B or L are exceeded. In such a case, T may be increased, allowing more records to be assigned to the individual CFs, thereby reducing the overall size of the CF tree, and allowing more records to be input.

21.5 PHASE 2: CLUSTERING THE SUB-CLUSTERS

Once the CF tree is built, any existing clustering algorithm may be applied to the sub-clusters (the CF leaf nodes), to combine these sub-clusters into clusters. For example, in their original paper presenting BIRCH clustering, the authors used agglomerative hierarchical clustering[3] for the cluster step, as does IBM/SPSS Modeler. Because there are many fewer sub-clusters than data records, the task becomes much easier for the clustering algorithm in the cluster step.

As mentioned earlier, BIRCH clustering achieves its high efficiency by substituting a small set of summary statistics to represent a larger set of data points. When a new data value is added, these statistics may be easily updated. Because of this, the CF tree is much smaller than the original data set, allowing for more efficient computation.

A detriment of BIRCH clustering is the following. Because of the tree structure inherent in the CF tree, the clustering solution may be dependent on the input ordering of the data records. To avoid this, the data analyst may wish to apply BIRCH clustering on a few different random sortings of the data, and find consensus among the results.

However, a benefit of BIRCH clustering is that the analyst is not required to select the best choice of k, the number of clusters, as is the case with some other clustering methods. Rather, the number of clusters in a BIRCH clustering solution is an outcome of the tree-building process. (See later in the chapter for more on choosing the number of clusters with BIRCH.)

21.6   EXAMPLE OF BIRCH CLUSTERING, PHASE 1: BUILDING THE CF TREE

Let us examine in detail the workings of the BIRCH clustering algorithm as applied to the following one-dimensional toy data set.[4]

$$x_1 = 0.5 \quad x_2 = 0.25 \quad x_3 = 0 \quad x_4 = 0.65 \quad x_5 = 1 \quad x_6 = 1.4 \quad x_7 = 1.1$$

Let us define our CF tree parameters as follows:

- Threshold $T = 0.15$; no leaf may exceed 0.15 in radius.
- Number of entries in a leaf node $L = 2$.
- Branching factor $B = 2$; maximum number of child nodes for each non-leaf node.

The first data value $x_1 = 0.5$ *is entered.* The root node is initialized with the CF values of the first data value. A new leaf *Leaf*1 is created, and BIRCH assigns the first record x_1 to *Leaf*1. Because it contains only one record, the radius of *Leaf*1 is zero, and thus less than $T = 0.15$. The CF tree after one record is shown in Figure 21.3.

The second data value $x_2 = 0.25$ *is entered.* BIRCH tentatively passes $x_2 = 0.25$ to *Leaf*1. The radius of *Leaf*1 is now $R = 0.126 < T = 0.15$, so x_2 is assigned to *Leaf*1. The summary statistics for CF_1 are then updated as shown in Figure 21.4.

The third data value $x_3 = 0$ *is entered.* BIRCH tentatively passes $x_3 = 0$ to *Leaf*1. However, the radius of *Leaf*1 now increases to $R = 0.205 > T = 0.15$. The

---

[3]See Chapter 19.

[4]Thanks to James Cunningham for valuable discussions regarding this example.

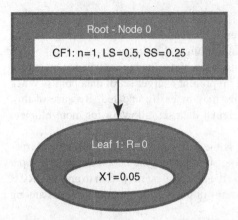

Figure 21.3 CF Tree after the first data value is entered.

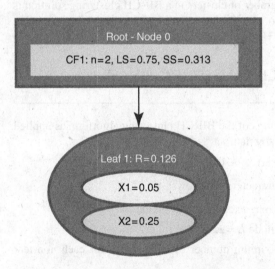

Figure 21.4 Second data value entered: Summary statistics are updated.

Threshold value $T = 0.15$ is exceeded, so x_3 is *not* assigned to *Leaf*1. Instead, a new leaf is initialized, called *Leaf2*, containing x_3 only. The summary statistics for CF_1 and CF_2 are shown in Figure 21.5.

The fourth data value $x_4 = 0.65$ is entered. BIRCH compares x_4 to the locations of CF_1 and CF_2. The location is measured by $\bar{x} = LS/n$. We have $\bar{x}_{CF_1} = 0.75/2 = 0.375$ and $\bar{x}_{CF_2} = 0/1 = 0$. The data point $x_4 = 0.65$ is thus closer to CF_1 than to CF_2. BIRCH tentatively passes x_4 to CF_1. The radius of CF_1 now increases to $R = 0.166 > T = 0.15$. The Threshold value $T = 0.15$ is exceeded, so x_4 is not assigned to CF_1. Instead, we would like to initialize a new leaf. However, $L = 2$ means that we cannot have three leafs in a leaf node. We must therefore split the root node into (i) *Node*1, which has as its children *Leaf*1 and *Leaf2*, and (ii) *Node*2, whose only leaf *Leaf*3

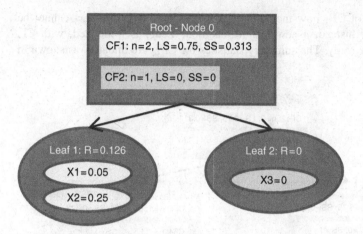

Figure 21.5   Third data value entered: A new leaf is initialized.

contains only x_4, as illustrated in Figure 21.6. The summary statistics for all leafs and nodes are updated, as shown in Figure 21.6. Note that the summary statistics for the parent CFs equal the sum of their children CFs.

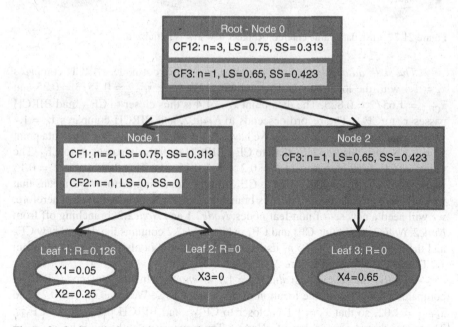

Figure 21.6   Fourth data value entered. The leaf limit $L = 2$ is surpassed, necessitating the creation of new nodes.

The fifth data value $x_5 = 1$ is entered. BIRCH compares $x_5 = 1$ with the location of CF_{12} and CF_3. We have $\bar{x}_{CF_{12}} = 0.75/3 = 0.25$ and $\bar{x}_{CF_4} = 0.65/1 = 0.65$. The data point $x_5 = 1$ is thus closer to CF_3 than to CF_{12}. BIRCH passes x_5 to

CF_3. The radius of CF_3 now increases to $R = 0.175 > T = 0.15$, so x_5 cannot be assigned to CF_3. Instead, a new leaf in leaf node *Leaf4* is initialized, with CF, CF_4, containing x_5 only. The summary statistics for CF_{34} are updated, as shown in Figure 21.7.

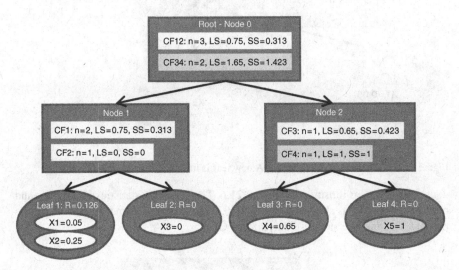

Figure 21.7   Fifth data value entered: Another new leaf is initialized.

The sixth data value $x_6 = 1.4$ is entered. At the root node, BIRCH compares $x_6 = 1.4$ with the location of CF_{12} and CF_{34}. We have $\bar{x}_{CF_{12}} = 0.75/3 = 0.25$ and $\bar{x}_{CF_{34}} = 1.65/2 = 0.825$. The data point $x_6 = 1.4$ is thus closer to CF_{34}, and BIRCH passes x_6 to CF_{34}. The record descends to *Node* 2, and BIRCH compares $x_6 = 1.4$ with the location of CF_3 and CF_4. We have $\bar{x}_{CF_3} = 0.65$ and $\bar{x}_{CF_4} = 1$. The data point $x_6 = 1.4$ is thus closer to CF_4 than to CF_3. BIRCH tentatively passes x_6 to CF_4. The radius of CF_4 now increases to $R = 0.2 > T = 0.15$. The Threshold value $T = 0.15$ is exceeded, so x_6 is not assigned to CF_4. But the branching factor $B = 2$ means that we may have at most two leaf nodes branching off of any non-leaf node. Therefore, we will need a new set of non-leaf nodes, *Node2.1* and *Node2.2*, branching off from *Node2*. *Node2.1* contains CF_3 and CF_4, while *Node2.2* contains the desired new CF_5 and the new leaf node *Leaf 5* as its only child, containing only the information from x_6. This tree is shown in Figure 21.8.

Finally, the last data value $x_7 = 1.1$ is entered. In the root node, BIRCH compares $x_7 = 1.1$ with the location of CF_{12} and CF_{345}. We have $\bar{x}_{CF_{12}} = 0.25$ and $\bar{x}_{CF_{345}} = 1.02$, so that $x_7 = 1.1$ is closer to CF_{345}, and BIRCH passes x_7 to CF_{345}. The record then descends down to *Node* 2. The comparison at this node has $x_7 = 1.1$ closer to CF_{34} than to CF_5. The record then descends down to *Node* 2.1. Here, $x_7 = 1.1$ closer to CF_4 than to CF_3. BIRCH tentatively passes x_7 to CF_4, and to *Leaf* 4. The radius of *Leaf* 4 becomes $R = 0.05$, which does not exceed the radius threshold value of $T = 0.15$. Therefore, BIRCH assigns x_7 to *Leaf* 4. The numerical summaries in all of its parents are updated. The final form of the CF tree is shown in Figure 21.9.

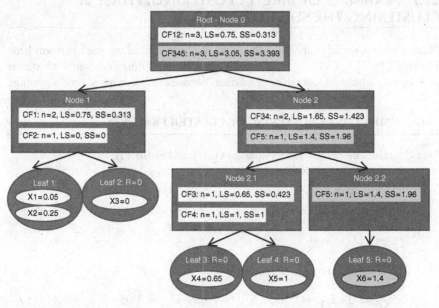

Figure 21.8   Sixth data value entered: A new leaf node is needed, as are a new non-leaf node and a root node.

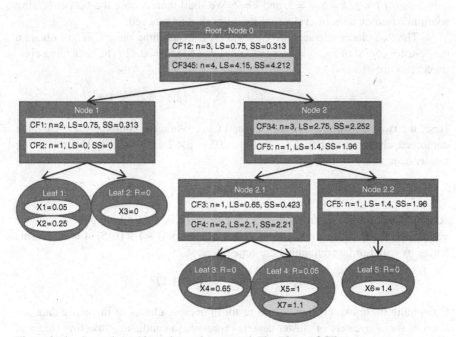

Figure 21.9   Seventh (and last) data value entered: Final form of CF tree.

21.7 EXAMPLE OF BIRCH CLUSTERING, PHASE 2: CLUSTERING THE SUB-CLUSTERS

Phase 2 often uses agglomerative hierarchical clustering, as we shall perform here. The five CFs CF_1, CF_2, ..., CF_5 are the objects that the agglomerative clustering shall be carried out on, not the original data. We use the following simple algorithm:

AGGLOMERATIVE CLUSTERING OF CLUSTER FEATURES

Let k_{max} represent the total number of distinct CFs found by BIRCH.
   For $k = k_{max}$ to 2, perform the following:

- Find the two sub-cluster centers that are closest together.
- Merge the indicated clusters. Update the summary statistics. Report evaluative measures.

The cluster centers are as follows:

$$\bar{x}_{CF_2} = 0 \quad \bar{x}_{CF_1} = 0.375 \quad \bar{x}_{CF_3} = 0.65 \quad \bar{x}_{CF_4} = 1.05 \quad \bar{x}_{CF_5} = 1.4$$

We start with $k = k_{max} = 5$. Now, perhaps $k = 5$ is the optimal cluster solution for this problem. Perhaps not. What we are doing here is forming a set of candidate clustering solutions for $k = 5$, $k = 4$, $k = 3$, and $k = 2$. We shall then choose the best clustering solution based on a set of evaluative measures. Let us proceed.

   The two closest clusters are CF_1 and CF_3. Combining these CFs, we obtain a new cluster center of $\bar{x}_{CF_{1,3}} = (2 \times 0.375 + 1 \times 0.65)/3 = 0.47$. The remaining cluster centers are

$$\bar{x}_{CF_2} = 0 \quad \bar{x}_{CF_{1,3}} = 0.47 \quad \bar{x}_{CF_4} = 1.05 \quad \bar{x}_{CF_5} = 1.4$$

Here, the two nearest clusters are CF_4 and CF_5. When we combine these CFs, the combined cluster center is $\bar{x}_{CF_{4,5}} = (2 \times 1.05 + 1 \times 1.4)/3 = 1.17$. The remaining cluster centers are

$$\bar{x}_{CF_2} = 0 \quad \bar{x}_{CF_{1,3}} = 0.47 \quad \bar{x}_{CF_{4,5}} = 1.17$$

Among these, the two nearest clusters are CF_2 and $CF_{1,3}$. Combining these CFs, we get a new cluster center of $\bar{x}_{CF_{2,1,3}} = (2 \times 0.375 + 1 \times 0 + 1 \times 0.65)/4 = 0.35$. This leaves us with our last remaining cluster centers:

$$\bar{x}_{CF_{2,1,3}} = 0.35 \quad \bar{x}_{CF_{4,5}} = 1.17$$

Combining these two clusters would result in one big cluster of the entire data set. Each of the above sets of cluster centers represents a candidate clustering solution. We turn now to the problem of how to evaluate these candidate clusters, and so to choose the best clustering solution.

21.8   EVALUATING THE CANDIDATE CLUSTER SOLUTIONS

In Chapter 23, we will examine methods for measuring cluster goodness. Here we apply one of the methods, the *pseudo-F statistic*

$$F = \frac{MSB}{MSE} = \frac{SSB/k - 1}{SSE/N - k}$$

in order to select the value of k that delivers the optimal clustering solution for our little data set.

For each of the candidate clustering solutions shown above, the pseudo-F statistic and p-value was calculated, and shown in Table 21.1.

TABLE 21.1   The pseudo-F method selects $k = 2$ as the preferred clustering solution

Value of k	MSB	MSE	Pseudo-F	p-Value
2	**1.1433**	**0.3317**	**17.24**	**0.009**
3	0.6533	0.0408	15.52	0.013
4	0.4628	0.0289	16.02	0.024
5	0.3597	0.0181	19.84	0.049

The smallest p-value occurs when $k = 2$. Thus, the preferred clustering solution is for the following cluster centers:

$$\bar{x}_{CF_{2,1,3}} = 0.35 \quad \bar{x}_{CF_{4,5}} = 1.17$$

This is indeed the clustering solution preferred by IBM/SPSS Modeler's *Two-Step (BIRCH) Algorithm*, as the excerpted results in Figure 21.10 indicate, although it should be noted that Modeler uses a different method to select the best model.

One may wonder whether we may calculate the pseudo-F statistic, without having recourse to the original data, only the summary statistics in the set of CFs. The answer is, yes, we can, and the proof is left as an exercise.

21.9   CASE STUDY: APPLYING BIRCH CLUSTERING TO THE BANK LOANS DATA SET

Recall the *Loans* data sets from Chapter 21. The *Loans_training* data set contains about 150,000 records and the *Loans_test* data set contains about 50,000 records. The task is to classify loan applications as approved or not (the flag response variable), using the following predictors: debt-to-income ratio, FICO score, and request amount. The amount of interest is included as well, but is a mathematical function of the request amount, and so is perfectly correlated with that predictor.

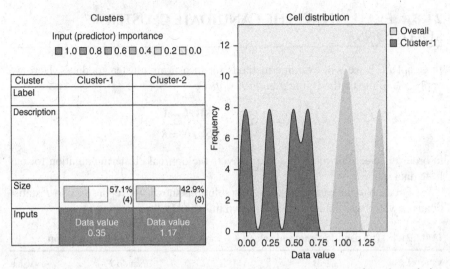

Figure 21.10   Modeler's *Two-Step (BIRCH) Algorithm* selects the same clustering solution that we did.

21.9.1   Case Study Lesson One: Avoid Highly Correlated Inputs to Any Clustering Algorithm

This heading telegraphs our punch line: Analysts should beware of included highly correlated inputs to any clustering algorithm. This section shows just how costly such an error can be.

Define two clustering input collections:

- The *With Interest* input collection wrongly includes *interest* as an input, along with the predictors *debt-to-income ratio*, *FICO score*, and *request amount*.

- The *No Interest* input collection includes only the predictors *debt-to-income ratio*, *FICO score*, and *request amount* as inputs, and does not include *interest*.

BIRCH clustering was applied to both input collections.[5] The *With Interest* clustering model is shown in Figure 21.11. Two clusters are identified, with a reported mean silhouette (MS) value of about 0.6. The *No Interest* clustering model is shown in Figure 21.12. Three clusters are identified, with a reported MS value of about 0.4. Thus, the silhouette measure would lead us to believe that the *With Interest* clustering solution is preferable. However, as we mentioned in Chapter 21, there may be times when the data analyst may have to choose a model that is attuned to the requirements of the client rather than a model that is preferred by a given statistic. Such is the case here.

Figure 21.13 shows how the predictors influenced the composition of the clusters. For the *With Interest* model, Cluster 1 contains those records

---

[5]Criteria selected in IBM Modeler were log-likelihood and BIC.

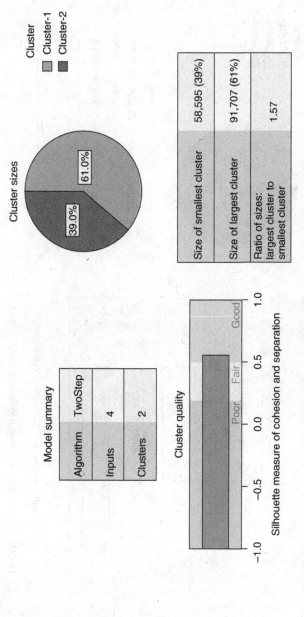

Figure 21.11 The *With Interest* clustering model identifies two clusters, and has a higher silhouette value.

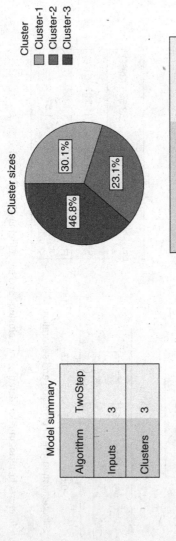

Figure 21.12 The *No Interest* clustering model identifies three clusters.

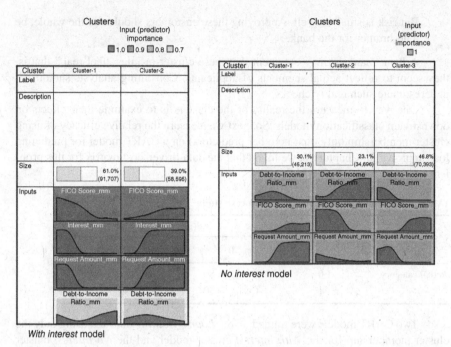

Figure 21.13   Predictor influence on cluster composition. The *With Interest* model is essentially double counting *request amount*.

with low FICO score, low request amount (and therefore low interest), and relatively high debt-to-income ratio. Cluster 2 contains records with the opposite levels. Note that the graphs for interest and request amount are essentially identical. This illustrates that we are essentially *double counting request amount* by including *interest*, which is a function of *request amount*, as an input.

The *No Interest* model, however, shows no such double counting. Let us briefly profile the clusters for the *No Interest* model.

- *Cluster 1: Big Profits, Probably.* Cluster 1 contains those with moderately low debt-to-income ratio, moderately high FICO score, and high request amount. The bank would usually like to lend to these people, since they tend to be fairly financially secure. However, they are not as secure as Cluster 3. Most will likely pay back the loan, and the high request amount means that there is plenty of interest (and therefore profit) to be had. But the occasional default will also be high.

- *Cluster 2: Iffy Propositions.* Cluster 2 consists of applicants with high debt-to-income ratios and low FICO scores. The bank may be advised to tread carefully with this group.

- *Cluster 3: Secure Small Profits.* Cluster 3 contains the most financially secure applicants, with the lowest debt-to-income ratio and the highest FICO scores. Unfortunately for the bank, these customers are looking for small loans only, that is, the request amount is small. Thus profits will be small, per applicant.

But risk is small as well. Approving these customers should, on the whole, be a no-brainer for the bank.

A bank manager may comment that these cluster profiles "feel real," that is, they seem to reflect actual segments of applicants. Consulting analysts should not underestimate such reality checks.

One way to measure the reality of the clusters is to examine their effects on downstream classification models. So, next we measure the relative efficacy of using cluster membership only (and no other predictors) on a CART model for predicting loan approval. In Chapter 16, we found that the data-driven cost matrix for this problem was as shown in Table 21.2.

TABLE 21.2   Cost matrix for the bank loan case study

		Predicted Category	
		0	1
Actual category	0	$Cost_{TN} = \$0$	$Cost_{FP} = \$13,427$
	1	$Cost_{FN} = \$0$	$Cost_{TP} = -\$6,042$

Two CART models were trained on the *Loans_training* data set, using only the cluster membership for the *With Interest* cluster model and the *No Interest* cluster model, respectively. These CART models were then evaluated using the *Loans_test* data set. Table 21.3 shows the contingency table the *With Interest* model, while Table 21.4 shows the contingency table for the *No Interest* model.

The model costs for these models are as follows:

- *With Interest Model*: $(15,624)(\$0) + (9310)(\$13,427) + (14,823)(\$0) + (9941)(-\$6042) = \$64,941,848$, for an average cost of $\$1306.73$ per customer.

TABLE 21.3   Contingency table for *With Interest* model

		Predicted Category	
		Disapprove	Approve
Actual category	Disapprove	15,624	9310
	Approve	14,823	9941

TABLE 21.4   Contingency table for *No Interest* model

		Predicted Category	
		Disapprove	Approve
Actual category	Disapprove	11,350	13,584
	Approve	145	24,619

- *No Interest Model*: $(11,350)(\$0) + (13,584)(\$13,427) + (145)(\$0) + (24,619)(-\$6042) = \$33,644,370$, for an average cost of $676.98 per customer.

Note that the simple step of being careful to remove the perfectly correlated predictor (*interest*) from the clustering algorithm has resulted in an estimated increase in decrease in cost of more than $31 million! Of course, the danger of using correlated inputs is not unique to BIRCH clustering; this warning applies across all clustering algorithms.

21.9.2   Case Study Lesson Two: Different Sortings May Lead to Different Numbers of Clusters

Other clustering algorithms require the user to specify a value of k, that is, the number of clusters in the model. However, for BIRCH, the number of clusters is an implicit outcome of the tree-building process. So, the user need not specify k. However, there is a downside. Because of the tree structure inherent in the CF tree, the clustering solution is dependent on the input ordering of the data records. So, different orderings of the data records may lead to different numbers of BIRCH clusters. We illustrate this phenomenon here.

We produced eight different orderings of the approximately 150,000 records in the *Loans_training* data set. The first ordering was the original ordering of the data used for the *No Interest* model above. The remaining seven orderings were accomplished as follows:

- Step 1. Generate a sort variable consisting of random draws from a Uniform (0,1) distribution.
- Step 2. Sort the records in ascending order, based on the sort variable.
- Step 3. Run BIRCH on the records obtained in step 2.

The clustering solutions obtained by each of the eight different sort orderings are summarized in Figure 21.14. Note the following:

- Sorts 1, 2, and 8 have $k = 3$ clusters.
- Sorts 3, 4, 6, and 7 have $k = 4$ clusters.
- Sort 5 has $k = 6$ clusters.

When different sortings produce varying values of k, the analyst should try to arrive at a consensus as to the best value of k. At first, we would be tempted to declare $k = 4$, because it received the most "votes" among the different sortings. For example, the highest MS values are for $k = 4$ models (see Table 21.5). However, before we declare a winner, it would be helpful to take a closer look at the performance of these cluster models for predicting loan approval.

For each of the eight sortings, we used the training set to construct a CART model using only the cluster memberships as predictors. We then evaluated each model using the test data set. The somewhat surprising results are shown in Table 21.5

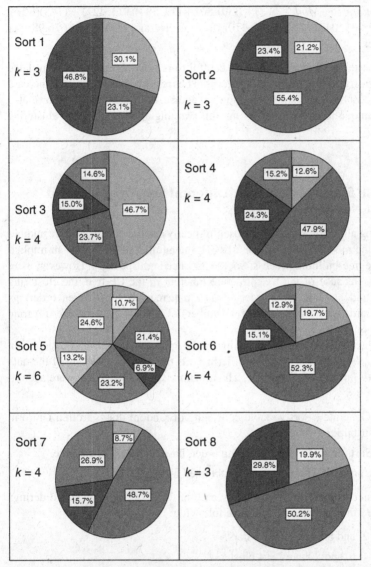

Figure 21.14   Pie chart summaries of the BIRCH clusters resulting from the eight different sortings. Which is the best?

(MS, mean silhouette). The most important column is the "Cost per Customer" column, since these figures affect the bank's bottom line. The three sorts resulting in profit are shown in bold. Note that the three sorts with the highest MS are among the lowest performing models in terms of cost, suggesting that MS may not be a very helpful statistic for our selection of k for this data set.

So, it seems that consensus is eluding us for choice of k with this data set. At this point in the analysis, we are almost beyond the question of choosing k, since

TABLE 21.5   Model summaries for BIRCH clusters as classification predictors: eight different data sorts (best performance highlighted)

	TN	FP	FN	TP	Cost Per Customer	k	MS
Sort 1	11,360	13,584	145	24,619	$676.98	3	0.4
Sort 2	**16,990**	**7,944**	**5,149**	**19,615**	**−$238.43**	**3**	**0.4**
Sort 3	**19,469**	**5,465**	**6,943**	**17,821**	− $ 690.09	**4**	**0.4**
Sort 4	12,444	12,490	1,437	23,327	$538.48	4	0.5
Sort 5	**19,451**	**5,483**	**7,389**	**17,375**	− $ 631.00	**6**	**0.4**
Sort 6	13,538	11,396	380	24,384	$114.41	4	0.4
Sort 7	11,987	12,947	121	24,643	$501.96	4	0.5
Sort 8	9,938	14,996	3	24,619	$1,041.20	3	0.5

the profitability of the models varies considerably for a given value of k. Instead, why not just proceed with the actual clusters obtained with *Sort 3* ($k = 4$) and *Sort 5* ($k = 6$), the two most profitable models? Both of these clustering solutions are remarkably powerful, in that they produce profits using only the cluster memberships as predictors. So the analyst will make a lot of money for the bank if he or she starts with these clusters, and proceeds to enhance these models using the original predictor variables.

In practice, BIRCH is often used to "suggest" a value of k, so that the actual clustering may be performed using some other method, such as k-means clustering. In this case, the analyst may wish to (i) report that BIRCH "suggests" $k = 3$ through 6, and (ii) proceed with these candidate values of k using k-means or some other clustering algorithm.

Finally, close communication with the client is important at all times, but especially in situations like this. Clients often have a good idea of the types of customers they have, and will often have insight into how many of these groups there are. Further, the client may prefer that the number of clusters be small, in order to facilitate in-company dissemination of the cluster results.

THE R ZONE

Open required package, read in the data

```
library(birch)
loan.test <- read.csv(file="C:/ … /Loans_Test.csv",
    header = TRUE)
loan.train <- read.csv(file="C:/ … /Loans_Training.csv",
    header = TRUE)
# Use 5,000 records for a small example
train <- as.matrix(loan.train[1:1000,-c(1,5)])
```

Birch clustering

```
b1 <- birch(x = train, radius=1000) # Create the Birch tree
# Cluster the sub-clusters using kmeans
kb1 <- kmeans.birch(birchObject = b1, centers = 2, nstart = 1)
```

Plot the results

```
par(mfrow=c(2,2))
  plot(b1[,c(2,3)],
  col = kb1$clust$sub)
plot(jitter(train[,c(1,3)], .1),
  col = kb1$clust$sub,
  pch = 16)
plot(jitter(train[,c(1,2)], .1),
  col = kb1$clust$sub,
  pch = 16)
plot(train[,c(2,3)],
  col = kb1$clust$sub,
  pch = 16)
```

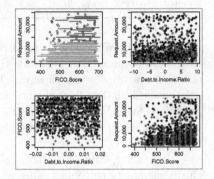

R REFERENCES

R Core Team. *R: A Language and Environment for Statistical Computing*. Vienna, Austria: R Foundation for Statistical Computing; 2012. ISBN: 3-900051-07-0, http://www.
   R-project.org/. Accessed 2014 Sep 30.
Charest L, Harrington J, Salibian-Barrera M. 2012. birch: Dealing with very large data sets
   using BIRCH. R package version 1.2-3. http://CRAN.R-project.org/package=birch.

EXERCISES

1. Why is BIRCH appropriate for streaming data?

2. Describe the two phases of the BIRCH clustering algorithm.

3. What is a CF?

4. How are the CFs for two clusters merged?

5. Describe the parameters of the CF tree.

6. Why is Phase 2 of the BIRCH algorithm efficient?

7. Why is it bad practice to include two highly correlated inputs to a clustering algorithm?

8. Is the MS value always indicative of the best cluster solution?

HANDS-ON EXERCISES

For Exercises 9–12, using the *Loans* data set, demonstrate that it is bad practice to include *interest* with the other predictors, as follows:

9. Follow the methodology in Case Study Lesson One to develop cluster models with and without *interest*.

10. Using the *Loans_training* data set, develop CART models for predicting loan approval, based on cluster membership only, for the two cluster models.

11. Evaluate each CART model using the *Loans_test* data set. Provide contingency tables. Compare the model costs, as in Table 21.4.

12. Based on your work in the previous exercises, what is the lesson we should learn?
    For Exercises 13–16, using the *Loans* data set, demonstrate that different sortings may lead to different numbers of clusters. Make sure you do not include *interest* as an input to the clustering algorithms.

13. Generate four different sortings of the *Loans_training* data set. Together with the original order from the *No Interest* model you generated earlier, this makes five different sortings.

14. Run BIRCH on each of the five different sortings. Report the value of k and the MS for each.

15. Calculate model cost for each of the five different sortings. Which model has the highest profitability or the lowest cost?

16. Briefly profile the clusters for the winning model from the previous exercise.

## CHAPTER 22

MEASURING CLUSTER GOODNESS

22.1 RATIONALE FOR MEASURING CLUSTER GOODNESS

Every modeling technique requires an evaluation phase. For example, we may work hard to develop a multiple regression model for predicting the amount of money to be spent on a new car. But, if the standard error of the estimate s for this regression model is $100,000, then the usefulness of the regression model is questionable. In the classification realm, we would expect that a model predicting who will respond to our direct-mail marketing operation will yield more profitable results than the baseline "send-a-coupon-to-everybody" or "send-out-no-coupons-at-all" models.

In a similar way, clustering models need to be evaluated as well. Some of the questions of interest might be the following:

- Do my clusters actually correspond to reality, or are they simply artifacts of mathematical convenience?
- I am not sure how many clusters there are in the data. What is the optimal number of clusters to identify?
- How do I measure whether one set of clusters is preferable to another?

In this chapter, we introduce two methods for measuring cluster goodness, the *silhouette* method, and the *pseudo-F* statistic. These techniques will help to address these questions by evaluating and measuring the goodness of our cluster solutions. We also examine a method to validate our clusters using cross-validation with graphical and statistical analysis.

Any measure of cluster goodness, or cluster quality, should address the concepts of cluster *separation* as well as cluster *cohesion*. Cluster separation represents how distant the clusters are from each other; cluster cohesion refers to how tightly related the records within the individual clusters are. Good measures of cluster quality need to incorporate both criteria. For example, it has been written elsewhere that the *sum of squares error* (SSE) is a good measure of cluster quality. However, by measuring

Data Mining and Predictive Analytics, First Edition. Daniel T. Larose and Chantal D. Larose.
© 2015 John Wiley & Sons, Inc. Published 2015 by John Wiley & Sons, Inc.

the distance between each record and its cluster center, SSE accounts only for cluster cohesion and does not account for cluster separation. Thus, SSE is monotonically decreasing as the number of clusters increases, which is not a desired property of a valid measure of cluster goodness. Of course, both the silhouette method and the pseudo-F statistic account for both cluster cohesion and cluster separation.

22.2   THE SILHOUETTE METHOD

The silhouette is a characteristic of each data value, and is defined as follows:

SILHOUETTE

For each data value i,

$$\text{Silhouette}_i = s_i = \frac{b_i - a_i}{\max(b_i,\, a_i)}$$

where a_i is the distance between the data value and its cluster center, and b_i is the distance between the data value and the next closest cluster center.

The silhouette value is used to gauge how good the cluster assignment is for that particular point. A positive value indicates that the assignment is good, with higher values being better than lower values. A value that is close to zero is considered to be a weak assignment, as the observation could have been assigned to the next closest cluster with limited negative consequence. A negative silhouette value is considered to be misclassified, as assignment to the next closest cluster would have been better.

Note how the definition of silhouette accounts for both separation and cohesion. The value of a_i represents cohesion, as it measures the distance between the data value and its cluster center, while b_i represents separation, as it measures the distance between the data value and a different cluster. This is illustrated in Figure 22.1. Each of the data values in Cluster 1 have their values of a_i and b_i represented by solid lines and dotted lines, respectively. Clearly, $b_i > a_i$ for each data value, as represented by

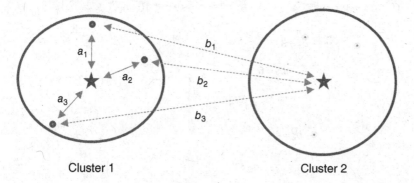

Cluster 1   Cluster 2

Figure 22.1   Illustration of how silhouette accounts for both separation and cohesion.

the longer dotted lines. Thus, each data value's silhouette value is positive, indicating that the data values have not been misclassified. The dotted lines indicate separation, and the solid lines indicate cohesion. (The silhouettes for the data values in Cluster 2 are not represented in Figure 22.1.)

Taking the *average silhouette value* over all records yields a useful measure of how well the cluster solution fits the data. The following thumbnail interpretation of average silhouette is meant as a guideline only, and should bow before the expertise of the domain expert.

INTERPRETATION OF AVERAGE SILHOUETTE VALUE

- 0.5 or better. Good evidence of the reality of the clusters in the data.
- 0.25–0.5. Some evidence of the reality of the clusters in the data. Hopefully, domain-specific knowledge can be brought to bear to support the reality of the clusters.
- Less than 0.25. Scant evidence of cluster reality.

22.3 SILHOUETTE EXAMPLE

Suppose we apply k-means clustering to the following little one-dimensional data set:

$$x_1 = 0 \quad x_2 = 2 \quad x_3 = 4 \quad x_4 = 6 \quad x_5 = 10$$

k-means assigns the first three data values to Cluster 1 and the last two to Cluster 2, as shown in Figure 22.2. The cluster center for Cluster 1 is $m_1 = 2$, and the cluster center

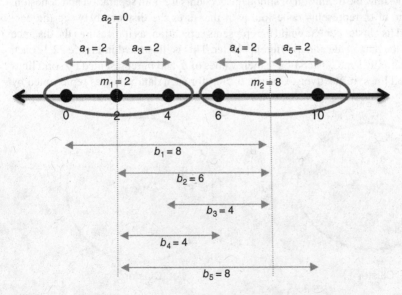

Figure 22.2 Distances between the data values and the cluster centers.

for Cluster 2 is $m_2 = 8$, represented by the dotted vertical lines in Figure 22.2. The values for a_i represent the distance between the data value x_i and the cluster center to which x_i belongs. The values for b_i represent the distance between the data value and the other cluster center. Note that $a_2 = 0$ because $a_2 = m_1 = 2$.

Table 22.1 contains the calculations for the individual data value silhouettes, along with the mean silhouette. Using our rule of thumb, mean silhouette $= 0.7$ represents good evidence of the reality of the clusters in the data. Note that x_2 is perfectly classified as belonging to Cluster 1, as it sits right on the cluster center m_1; thus, its silhouette value is a perfect 1.00. However, x_3 is somewhat farther from its own cluster center, and somewhat closer to the other cluster center; hence, its silhouette value is lower, 0.50.

TABLE 22.1   Calculations for individual data value silhouettes and mean silhouette

x_i	a_i	b_i	$\max(a_i, b_i)$	Silhouette$_i = s_i = \dfrac{b_i - a_i}{\max(b_i, a_i)}$
0	2	8	8	$\dfrac{8-2}{8} = 0.75$
2	0	6	6	$\dfrac{6-0}{6} = 1.00$
4	2	4	4	$\dfrac{4-2}{4} = 0.50$
6	2	4	4	$\dfrac{4-2}{4} = 0.50$
10	2	8	8	$\dfrac{8-2}{8} = 0.75$
				Mean silhouette $= 0.7$

22.4   SILHOUETTE ANALYSIS OF THE *IRIS* DATA SET

Next, we apply the silhouette method to Fisher's well-known *Iris* data set. The data set consists of 150 observations of three species of *Iris*, along with measurements of their petal width, petal length, sepal width, and sepal length. Figure 22.3 shows a scatter plot of petal width versus petal length, with an overlay of *Iris* species. (Note that min–max normalization is used.) Figure 22.3 shows that one species is well separated, but the other two are not, at least in this dimension. So, one question we could ask of these *Irises*: True there are three species in the data set, but are there really three clusters in the data set, or only two?

It makes sense to begin with $k = 3$ clusters. k-means clustering was applied to the *Iris* data, asking for $k = 3$ clusters. A logical question might be: Do the clusters match perfectly with the species? (Of course, the species type was not included as input to the clustering algorithm.) The answer is, not quite. Compare Figure 22.4 with Figure 22.3. For example, most of the *Iris virginica* belong to Cluster 2, but some belong to Cluster 3. And most of the *Iris versicolor* belong to Cluster 3, but some belong to Cluster 2.

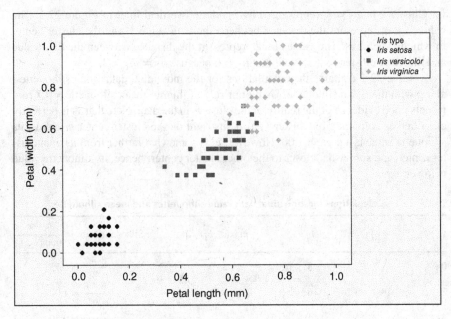

Figure 22.3   Two of the *Iris* species seem to blend into one another.

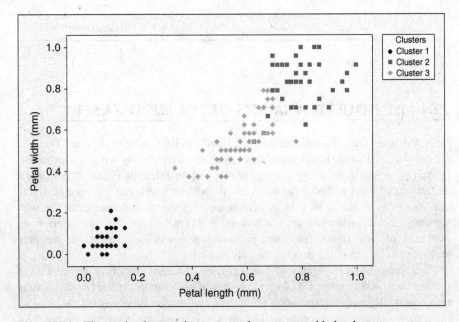

Figure 22.4   The species do not quite correspond one-to-one with the clusters.

So, we proceed with the silhouette analysis. The silhouette values for each flower were calculated, and graphed in the *silhouette plot* in Figure 22.5. This silhouette plot shows the silhouette values, sorted from highest to lowest, for each cluster. Cluster 1 is the best-defined cluster, as most of its silhouette values are rather high. However, Clusters 2 and 3 have some records with high silhouette and some records with low silhouette. However, there are no records with negative silhouette, which would indicate the wrong cluster assignment. The mean silhouette values for each cluster, and the overall mean silhouette, are provided in Table 22.2. These values support our suggestion that, although Cluster 1 is well-defined, Clusters 2 and 3 are not so well-defined. This makes sense, in light of what we learned in Figures 22.3 and 22.4.

TABLE 22.2   Mean silhouette values for $k = 3$ clusters

	Cluster 1	Cluster 2	Cluster 3	Overall
Mean silhouette	0.8002	0.5593	0.5254	0.6258

Many of the low silhouette values for Clusters 2 and 3 come from the boundary area between their respective clusters. Evidence for this is shown in Figure 22.6. The silhouette values were binned (for illustrative purposes): A silhouette value below 0.5 is low; a silhouette value at least 0.5 is high. The lower silhouette values in this boundary area result from the proximity of the "other" cluster center. This holds down the value of b_i, and thus of the silhouette value.

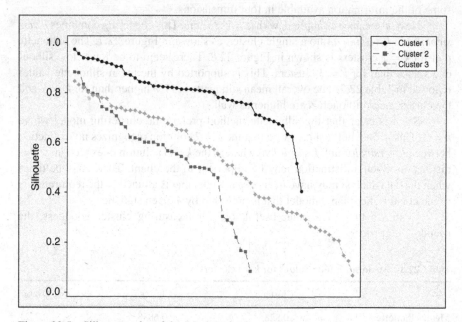

Figure 22.5   Silhouette plot of the *Iris* data, for $k = 3$ clusters.

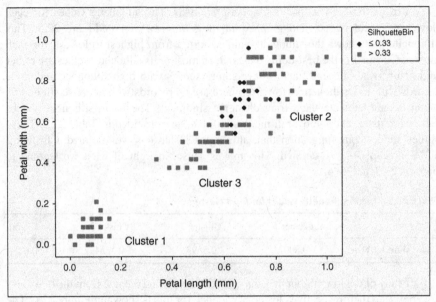

Figure 22.6 The boundary area between Clusters 2 and 3 is where you will find many low silhouette values.

Also, throughout this section, it is worth noting that the clusters were formed using four predictors, but we are examining scatter plots of two predictors only. This represents a projection of the predictor space down to two dimensions, and so loses some of the information available in four dimensions.

Next, k-means was applied, with $k = 2$ clusters. This clustering combines *I. versicolor* and *I. virginica* into a single cluster, as shown in Figure 22.7. The silhouette plot for $k = 2$ clusters is shown in Figure 22.8. There seem to be fewer low silhouette values than for $k = 3$ clusters. This is supported by the mean silhouette values reported in Table 22.3. The overall mean silhouette is 17% higher than for $k = 3$, and the cluster mean silhouettes are higher as well.

So, it is clear that the silhouette method prefers the clustering model where $k = 2$. This is fine, but just be aware that the $k = 2$ solution recognizes no distinction between *I. versicolor* and *I. virginica*, whereas the $k = 3$ solution does recognize this distinction. Such a distinction may be important to the client. There may be times when the data analyst may have to choose a model that is attuned to the requirements of the client rather than a model that is preferred by a given statistic.

Next, we turn to another useful tool for measuring cluster goodness, the pseudo-F statistic.

TABLE 22.3   Mean silhouette values for $k = 3$ clusters

	Cluster 1	Cluster 2	Overall
Mean silhouette	0.8285	0.6838	0.7321

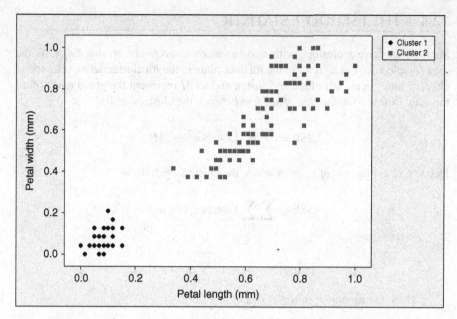

Figure 22.7   *Iris versicolor* and *Iris virginica* are now combined in Cluster 2.

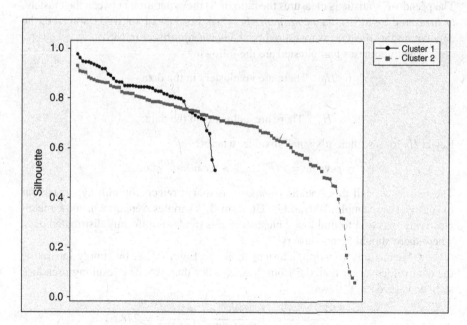

Figure 22.8   Silhouette plot of the *Iris* data, for $k = 2$ clusters.

22.5   THE PSEUDO-F STATISTIC

Suppose we have k clusters, with n_i data values respectively, so that $\Sigma n_i = N$, the total sample size. Let x_{ij} refer to the jth data value in the ith cluster, let m_i refer to the cluster center (centroid) of the ith cluster, and let M represent the grand mean of all the data. Define SSB, the *sum of squares between* the clusters, as follows:

$$SSB = \sum_{i=1}^{k} n_i \cdot \text{Distance}^2(m_i, M)$$

Define SSE or the *sum of squares within* the clusters, as follows:

$$SSE = \sum_{i=1}^{k} \sum_{j=1}^{n_j} \text{Distance}^2(x_{ij}, m_i)$$

where

$$\text{Distance}(a, b) = \sqrt{\sum (a_i - b_i)^2}$$

Then, the *pseudo-F statistic* equals

$$F = \frac{\text{MSB}}{\text{MSE}} = \frac{SSB/k - 1}{SSE/N - k}$$

The pseudo-F statistic is measures the ratio of (i) the separation between the clusters, as measured by MSB, the *mean square between* the clusters, to (ii) the spread of the data within the clusters, as measured by the *mean square error*, MSE.

The hypotheses being tested are the following:

H_0 : There are no clusters in the data.

H_a : There are k clusters in the data.

Reject H_0 for a sufficiently small p-value, where:

$$p\text{-value} = P(F_{k-1,n-k} > \text{pseudo-}F \text{ value})$$

The reason we call this statistic *pseudo-F*, is that it rejects the null hypothesis far too easily. For example, 100 random Uniform(0,1) variates were drawn, and k-means clustering was told to find $k = 2$ clusters in this random uniformly distributed data, where there should be no clusters.

k-Means duly found the clusters shown in Figure 22.9, by simply separating the data values larger than 0.5 from those smaller than 0.5. The resulting pseudo-F statistic is given as follows:

$$F = \frac{SSB/k - 1}{SSE/n - k} = \frac{6.4606/1}{2.2725/98} = \frac{6.4606}{0.0232} = 278.61$$

with a p-value near zero, strongly rejecting the null hypothesis that there are no clusters in the data. But as the data is randomly generated, the presumption must be that there are no true clusters in the data. For this reason, the F statistic should not be

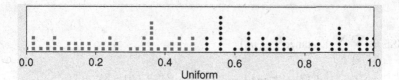

Figure 22.9   The pseudo-*F* statistic found the presence of clusters in randomly generated data.

used to test for the presence of clusters in data, and thereby earns the nomenclature, *pseudo-F*.

However, if we have reason to believe that clusters do exist in the data, but we do not know how many clusters there are, then pseudo-*F* can be helpful. The process is as follows:

USING PSEUDO-F TO SELECT THE OPTIMAL NUMBER OF CLUSTERS

1. Use a clustering algorithm to develop a clustering solution for a variety of values of k.
2. Calculate the pseudo-*F* statistic and *p*-value for each candidate, and select the candidate with the smallest *p*-value as the best clustering solution.

Note: It has been written elsewhere that the best clustering model is the one with the largest value of pseudo-*F*. This is not always correct. One must account for the different degrees of freedom $k - 1$ and $n - k$ for each model. For example, suppose Model A has $k - 1 = 5$, $n - k = 100$, and pseudo-$F = 3.1$, while Model B has $k - 1 = 6$, $n - k = 99$, and pseudo-$F = 3.0$. The larger value of pseudo-*F* is for Model A. However, Model A's *p*-value is 0.0121, while Model B's *p*-value is 0.0098, indicating that Model B is in fact preferred.

22.6   EXAMPLE OF THE PSEUDO-*F* STATISTIC

Recall that we applied k-means clustering to the following data set, and found, for $k = 2$, that k-means assigns the first three data values to Cluster 1 and the last two to Cluster 2.

$$x_1 = 0 \quad x_2 = 2 \quad x_3 = 4 \quad x_4 = 6 \quad x_5 = 10$$

Let us calculate the pseudo-*F* statistic for this clustering.

We have $k = 2$ clusters, with $n_1 = 3$ and $n_2 = 2$ data values, and $N = 5$. The cluster centers are $m_1 = 2$ and $m_2 = 8$, and the grand mean is $\dot{M} = 4.4$. Now, because we are in one dimension, $\text{Distance}(m_i, M) = |m_i - M|$, so that:

$$\text{SSB} = \sum_{i=1}^{k} n_i \cdot \text{Distance}^2(m_i, M)$$

$$= 3 \cdot (2 - 4.4)^2 + 2 \cdot (8 - 4.4)^2 = 43.2$$

Next,

$$SSE = \sum_{i=1}^{k} \sum_{j=1}^{n_j} Distance^2(x_{ij}, m_i)$$

$$= (0-2)^2 + (2-2)^2 + (4-2)^2 + (6-8)^2 + (10-8)^2 = 16$$

Then, the pseudo-F statistic equals

$$F = \frac{MSB}{MSE} = \frac{SSB/k-1}{SSE/N-k} = \frac{43.2/1}{16/3} = \frac{43.2}{5.33} = 8.1$$

Figure 22.10 shows the distribution of the F statistic, with $df_1 = k - 1 = 1$ and $df_2 = N - k = 3$. Note that the p-value is 0.06532, which does not indicate strong evidence in favor of the reality of the clusters. But this is probably due in part to the very small sample size.

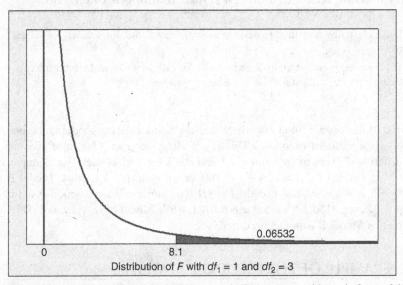

Figure 22.10   The p-value of 0.06532 does not indicate strong evidence in favor of the reality of the clusters.

22.7   PSEUDO-F STATISTIC APPLIED TO THE *IRIS* DATA SET

Next, we see which value of k is favored by the pseudo-F statistic for clustering the *Iris* data set. For the vector (sepal length, sepal width, petal length, petal width), we have $N = 150$ data values, with the grand mean

$$M = (0.4287, \quad 0.4392, \quad 0.4676, \quad 0.4578)$$

For $k = 3$ clusters, we have the following cluster counts and cluster centers:

- Cluster 1: $n_1 = 50$ and $m_1 = (0.1961, \quad 0.5908, \quad 0.0786, \quad 0.06)$
- Cluster 2: $n_2 = 39$ and $m_2 = (0.7073, \quad 0.4509, \quad 0.7970, \quad 0.8248)$
- Cluster 3: $n_2 = 61$ and $m_3 = (0.4413, \quad 0.3074, \quad 0.5757, \quad 0.5492)$

Then we have the following contribution to SSB for each cluster:

- Cluster 1: $50 \times \{(0.1961 - 0.4287)^2 + (0.5908 - 0.4392)^2 + (0.0786 - 0.4676)^2$
  $+ (0.06 - 0.4578)^2\}$
- Cluster 2: $39 \times \{(0.7073 - 0.4287)^2 + (0.4509 - 0.4392)^2 + (0.7970 - 0.4676)^2$
  $+ (0.8248 - 0.4578)^2\}$
- Cluster 3: $61 \times \{(0.4413 - 0.4287)^2 + (0.3074 - 0.4392)^2 + (0.5757 - 0.4676)^2$
  $+ (0.5492 - 0.4578)^2\}$

Summing the three contributions gives us $SSB = \sum_{i=1}^{k} n_i \cdot \text{Distance}^2(m_i, M) = 34.1397$.

The value for $SSE = \sum_{i=1}^{k} \sum_{j=1}^{n_j} \text{Distance}^2(x_{ij}, m_i)$ is obtained by squaring the distance between each observation and its cluster center, and then summing all the entries. Having done this (calculations not shown), we obtain $SSE = 6.9981$. The pseudo-F statistic is then

$$F = \frac{\text{MSB}}{\text{MSE}} = \frac{SSB/k - 1}{SSE/N - k} = \frac{34.1397/2}{6.9981/147} = 358.5$$

with a p-value equal to zero to the 57th (!) decimal place.

For $k = 2$, perform calculations analogous to those above to obtain:

$$F = \frac{28.7319/1}{12.1437/148} = 350.2$$

with a p-value equal to zero only to the 41st decimal place. Thus, the pseudo-F statistic prefers the $k = 3$ solution, in contrast to the silhouette method, which prefers the $k = 2$ solution.

There are other methods for determining the optimal number of clusters. For example, the Bayesian Information Criterion may be used, as demonstrated by Zhao, Xu, and Franti.[1]

Next, we turn to a topic closely associated with measuring cluster goodness: the topic of cluster validation.

22.8   CLUSTER VALIDATION

As with any other data mining modeling technique, the application of cluster analysis should be subject to cross-validation, in order to ensure that the clusters are real, and not just a result of random noise in the training data set. Many sophisticated cluster

---

[1] Qinpei Zhao, Mantao Xu, and Pasi Franti, Knee Point Detection on Bayesian Information Criterion, 20th IEEE Conference on Tools with Artificial Intelligence, 2008.

validation techniques exist, such as the *Prediction Strength*[2] method. However, these methods require data programming beyond the intent of this book.

Instead, we use the following simple, graphical and statistical approach to cluster validation, summarized as follows:

CLUSTER VALIDATION METHODOLOGY

Goal: *Confirm that the clusters found in the test data set match those found in the training data set.*

1. Apply cluster analysis to the training data set.
2. Apply cluster analysis to the test data set.
3. Use graphics and statistics to confirm that the clusters in the training data set match the clusters in the test data set.

This methodology is simply a restatement of the usual cross-validation methodology, in terms of cluster analysis. We now apply this cluster validation methodology to the *Loans* data set.

22.9 CLUSTER VALIDATION APPLIED TO THE LOANS DATA SET

Recall the *Loans* data set, where a bank loan approval analyst is using *debt-to-income ratio (DIR)*, *FICO score*, and *request amount* in order to predict loan *approval*. There are 150,302 records in the training data set and 49,698 records in the test data set. For simplicity, k-means clustering was applied to both the training and the test data sets, with $k = 3$ clusters.

Summary graphics of the clusters generated from the training and test data sets are shown in Figures 22.11 and 22.12. For each partition, Cluster 1 is the smallest and Cluster 3 is the largest, with the percentages involved relatively close. For each partition:

- Cluster 1 contains high debt-to-income applicants, with low FICO scores and low request amounts;
- Cluster 2 contains moderate debt-to-income applicants, with moderate/high FICO scores, and high request amounts;
- Cluster 3 contains low debt-to-income applicants, with high FICO scores, and low request amounts.

Table 22.4 contains the summary statistics (mean, standard deviation, number of records) for the clusters generated by the training and test data sets (DIR).

---

[2] *Cluster Validation by Prediction Strength*, by Robert Tibshirani and Guenther Walther, *Journal of Computational and Graphical Statistics*, Volume 14, Issue 3, 2005.

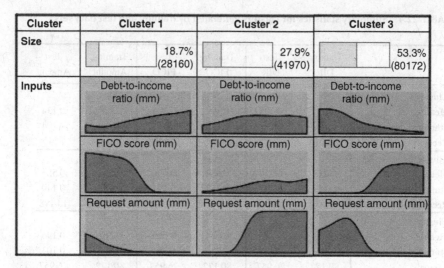

Figure 22.11   Summary graphics of the clusters generated by the training data set.

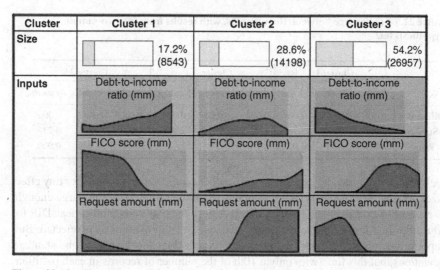

Figure 22.12   Summary graphics of the clusters generated by the test data set.

Table 22.5 contains the difference in variable means for each cluster, along with the t-statistic for the two-sample t-test,[3] and the p-value for this hypothesis test.

Practically all the p-values are small, indicating rejection of the null hypothesis that the true means are equal. In other words, the hypothesis test results suggest that the clusters from the training and test data sets do not match.

However, here we should recall a possible downside to statistical hypothesis tests: *that the null hypothesis is very easily rejected for very large sample sizes.* It is

---

[3] See, for example, Larose, *Discovering Statistics*, second edition, W.H. Freeman and Company Publishers, New York, 2013.

TABLE 22.4 Summary statistics for clusters generated by training and test data sets

	Training DIR	Test DIR	Training FICO	Test FICO	Training Amount	Test Amount
Cluster 1						
Mean	0.200	0.195	0.399	0.385	0.130	0.134
Standard deviation	0.170	0.171	0.120	0.115	0.100	0.104
Records	28,160	8543	28,160	8543	28,160	8543
Cluster 2						
Mean	0.212	0.210	0.628	0.630	0.591	0.587
Standard deviation	0.147	0.147	0.112	0.111	0.139	0.140
Records	41,970	14,198	41,970	14,198	41,970	14,198
Cluster 3						
Mean	0.153	0.156	0.664	0.662	0.202	0.196
Standard deviation	0.102	0.107	0.076	0.077	0.105	0.103
Records	80,172	26,957	80,172	26,957	80,172	26,957

TABLE 22.5 Difference between the variables, with results from the two-sample hypothesis test

	Cluster 1 DIR	Cluster 1 FICO	Cluster 1 Amount	Cluster 2 DIR	Cluster 2 FICO	Cluster 2 Amount	Cluster 3 DIR	Cluster 3 FICO	Cluster 3 Amount
Difference	0.005	0.014	−0.004	0.002	−0.002	0.004	−0.003	0.002	0.006
t-Statistics	2.37	9.76	−3.12	1.40	−1.85	2.95	−4.03	3.70	8.23
p-Value	0.018	0.000	0.002	0.161	0.064	0.003	0.000	0.000	0.000

well known that classical hypothesis tests will reject the null hypothesis for tiny effect sizes, or tiny differences between samples, when the sample sizes are large enough. For example, take the t-test for the difference between partitions for the mean DIR for Cluster 3. In Table 22.5, the p-value is zero, and the null hypothesis is rejected. But, suppose we repeat this t-test with the very same values for the means and standard deviations, but this time with only a 10th of the number of records in each partition: 8017 for the training set and 2696 for the test set. In that case, the p-value becomes 0.203 and the null hypothesis is no longer rejected. So, for the very same difference in means, sufficiently increasing the sample sizes will eventually lead to rejection of most null hypotheses. This makes classical hypothesis testing of limited usefulness for most big data applications.

Instead, consider whether the difference of 0.003 between the partitions for the Cluster 3 DIR means is really of practical significance. Probably not. Instead, the analyst should concentrate on the big picture: We are trying to determine whether there is a match between the clusters uncovered in the training and test data sets. If the clusters are broadly similar, with similar profiles, and variable means close to each other, then they should be confirmed as validated. Based on these criteria, we judge the clusters for the *Loans* data set to be validated.

Why, then, is Table 22.5 included here? First, for small-to-moderate sample sizes, statistical inference is quite helpful in this situation. Second, regardless of the number of records involved, the analyst should report the difference in variable means between the partitions, so that the client (or someone well familiar with the data) can render judgment on whether the difference is of practical significance.

THE R ZONE

Read in and prepare the data

```
i.data <- iris # Iris is a built-in dataset
# Min-max normalization
i.data$SL <- (i.data$Sepal.Length - min(i.data$Sepal.Length))/
    (max(i.data$Sepal.Length) - min(i.data$Sepal.Length))
i.data$SW <- (i.data$Sepal.Width - min(i.data$Sepal.Width))/
    (max(i.data$Sepal.Width) - min(i.data$Sepal.Width))
i.data$PL <- (i.data$Petal.Length - min(i.data$Petal.Length))/
    (max(i.data$Petal.Length) - min(i.data$Petal.Length))
i.data$PW <- (i.data$Petal.Width - min(i.data$Petal.Width))/
    (max(i.data$Petal.Width) - min(i.data$Petal.Width))
```

Silhouette values

```
# Requires package 'cluster'
library(cluster)
# k-means (k=3)
km1 <- kmeans(i.data[,6:9], 3)
dist1 <- dist(i.data[,6:9],
    method = "euclidean")
sil1 <- silhouette(km1$cluster, dist1)
plot(sil1, col = c("black", "red", "green"),
    main = "Silhouette Plot: 3-Cluster
    K-Means Clustering of Iris Data")
# k-means (k=2)
km2 <- kmeans(i.data[,6:9], 2)
dist2 <- dist(i.data[,6:9],
    method = "euclidean")
sil2 <- silhouette(km2$cluster, dist2)
plot(sil2, col = c("black", "red"),
    main = "Silhouette Plot: 2-Cluster
    K-Means Clustering of Iris Data")
```

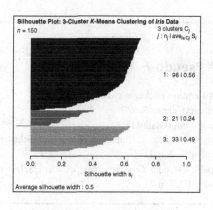

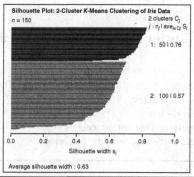

Plot silhouette values

```
silval1 <- ifelse(sil1[,3] <= 0.33, 0, 1)
plot(i.data$PL, i.data$PW, col = silval1+1,
    pch = 16,
    main = "Silhouette Values, K = 3",
    xlab = "Petal Length (min-max)",
    ylab = "Petal Width (min-max)"
legend("topleft", col=c(1,2), pch = 16,
    legend=c("<= 0.33", "> 0.33"))
silval2 <- ifelse(sil2[,3] <= 0.33, 0, 1)
plot(i.data$PL, i.data$PW, col = silval2+1,
    pch = 16,
    main = "Silhouette Values, K = 2",
    xlab = "Petal Length (min-max)",
    ylab = "Petal Width (min-max)")
legend("topleft", col=c(1,2), pch = 16,
    legend=c("<= 0.33", "> 0.33"))
```

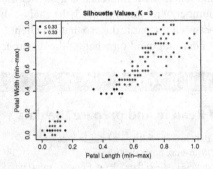

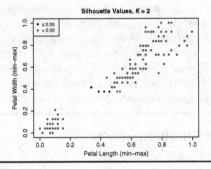

Pseudo-*F*

```
# Requires package 'clusterSim'
library("clusterSim")
n <- dim(i.data)[1]
psF1 <- index.G1(i.data[,6:9], cl = km1$cluster)
pf(psF1, 2, n-2)
psF2 <- index.G1(i.data[,6:9], cl = km2$cluster)
pf(psF2, 1, n-1)
```

Cluster validation — prepare the data

```
loan.test <- read.csv(file="C:/ ... /Loans_Test.csv", header = TRUE)
loan.train <- read.csv(file="C:/ ... /Loans_Training.csv", header = TRUE)
test <- loan.test[,-1]
train <- loan.train[,-1]
kmtest <- kmeans(test, centers = 3)
kmtrain <- kmeans(train, centers = 3)
```

Cluster validation — variable summaries by cluster

```
clust.sum <- matrix(0.0, ncol = 3, nrow = 4)
colnames(clust.sum) <- c("Cluster 1",
    "Cluster 2", "Cluster 3")
rownames(clust.sum) <- c("Test Data Mean",
    "Train Data Mean", "Test Data Std Dev",
    "Test Data Std Dev")
clust.sum[1,] <-
    tapply(test$Debt.to.Income.Ratio,
    kmtest$cluster, mean)
clust.sum[2,] <-
    tapply(train$Debt.to.Income.Ratio,
    kmtrain$cluster, mean)
clust.sum[3,] <-
    tapply(test$Debt.to.Income.Ratio,
    kmtest$cluster, sd)
clust.sum[4,] <-
    tapply(train$Debt.to.Income.Ratio,
    kmtrain$cluster, sd)
```

```
> clust.sum
                  Cluster 1 Cluster 2 Cluster 3
Test Data Mean    0.2131943 0.1847925 0.1674191
Train Data Mean   0.1683801 0.1843572 0.2143234
Test Data Std Dev 0.1519871 0.1312425 0.1343831
Test Data Std Dev 0.1353878 0.1278332 0.1518468
```

R REFERENCES

Maechler, M., Rousseeuw, P., Struyf, A., Hubert, M., Hornik, K.(2013). cluster: Cluster Analysis Basics and Extensions. R package version 1.14.4.

Walesiak, M, Dudek, A <andrzej.dudek@ue.wroc.pl> (2014). clusterSim: Searching for Optimal Clustering Procedure for a Data Set. R package version 0.43-4. http://CRAN.R-project.org/package=clusterSim. Accessed 2014 Sep 30.

R Core Team. *R: A Language and Environment for Statistical Computing.* Vienna, Austria: R Foundation for Statistical Computing; 2012. 3-900051-07-0, http://www.R-project.org/. Accessed 2014 Sep 30.

EXERCISES

1. Why do we need evaluation measures for cluster algorithms?

2. What is cluster separation and cluster cohesion?

3. Why is SSE not necessarily a good measure of cluster quality?

4. What is a silhouette? What is its range? Is it a characteristic of a cluster, a variable, or a data value?

5. How do we interpret a silhouette value?

6. Explain how silhouette accounts for both separation and cohesion.

7. How is average silhouette interpreted?

8. When will a data value have a perfect silhouette value? What is this value?

9. Describe what a silhouette plot is.

10. Should the analyst always choose the cluster solution with the better mean silhouette value? Explain.

11. Explain how the pseudo-F statistic accounts for both separation and cohesion.

12. Why does the pseudo-F statistic have the word *pseudo* in its name?

13. Explain how we can use the pseudo-F statistic to select the optimal number of clusters.

14. True or false: The best clustering model is the one with the largest value of pseudo-F. Explain.

15. What is our cluster validation methodology?

16. Why might statistical hypothesis tests not be very helpful for big data applications?

17. What are the criteria for determining whether there is a match between the clusters uncovered in the training and test data sets?

HANDS-ON EXERCISES

Use the *Loans_training* data set and the *Loans_test* data set for the following exercises. These data sets are available from the textbook web site www.DataMiningConsultant.com.

18. Use k-means with $k = 3$ to generate a cluster model with the training data set.

19. Generate a silhouette plot of your cluster model.

20. Calculate the mean silhouette values for each cluster, as well as the overall mean silhouette for the cluster model.

21. Provide a two-dimensional scatter plot, using variables of your choice, with an overlay of cluster membership. Choose variables that result in an interesting plot. Note where the cluster boundaries are close, and where they are not so close.

22. Using the same variables as the previous exercise, provide a two-dimensional scatter plot, with an overlay of binned silhouette values, as shown in this chapter. Comment on the relationship between your two scatter plots.

23. Repeat Exercises 18–22 using k-means with $k = 4$.

24. Compare the mean silhouette values for the two cluster models. Which model is preferred?

25. Compare the pseudo-F statistics for the two cluster models. Which model is preferred?

26. Develop a good classification model for predicting loan approval, based solely on cluster membership. Apply data-driven misclassification costs as shown in Chapter 16. Compare your results for the $k = 3$ and $k = 4$ cases using overall model cost. Which model is preferred?

27. With the test data set, apply k-means with the value of k from the preferred model above. Perform validation of the clusters you uncovered with the training and test data sets of the preferred model.

PART V

ASSOCIATION RULES

## CHAPTER 23

ASSOCIATION RULES

23.1 AFFINITY ANALYSIS AND MARKET BASKET ANALYSIS

Affinity analysis is the study of attributes or characteristics that "go together." Methods for affinity analysis, also known as *market basket analysis*, seek to uncover *associations* among these attributes; that is, it seeks to uncover rules for quantifying the relationship between two or more attributes. Association rules take the form "If *antecedent*, then *consequent*," along with a measure of the support and confidence associated with the rule. For example, a particular supermarket may find that of the 1000 customers shopping on a Thursday night, 200 bought diapers, and of the 200 who bought diapers, 50 bought beer. Thus, the association rule would be: "If buy diapers, then buy beer," with a *support* of $\frac{50}{1000} = 5\%$ and a *confidence* of $\frac{50}{200} = 25\%$.

Examples of association tasks in business and research include

- investigating the proportion of subscribers to your company's cell phone plan that respond positively to an offer of a service upgrade;
- examining the proportion of children whose parents read to them who are themselves good readers;
- predicting degradation in telecommunications networks;
- finding out which items in a supermarket are purchased together, and which items are never purchased together;
- determining the proportion of cases in which a new drug will exhibit dangerous side effects.

What types of algorithms can we apply to mine association rules from a particular data set? The daunting problem that awaits any such algorithm is the curse of dimensionality: The number of possible association rules grows exponentially in the number of attributes. Specifically, if there are k attributes, we limit ourselves to binary attributes, and we account only for the positive cases (e.g., *buy diapers = yes*), which are on the order of $k \cdot 2^{k-1}$ possible association rules.[1] Consider that a typical

[1] Hand, Mannila, and Smyth, *Principles of Data Mining*, MIT Press, 2001.

Data Mining and Predictive Analytics, First Edition. Daniel T. Larose and Chantal D. Larose.
© 2015 John Wiley & Sons, Inc. Published 2015 by John Wiley & Sons, Inc.

application for association rules is market basket analysis and that there may be *thousands* of binary attributes (*buy beer? buy popcorn? buy milk? buy bread?* etc.), the search problem appears at first glance to be utterly hopeless. For example, suppose that a tiny convenience store has only 100 different items, and a customer could either buy or not buy any combination of those 100 items. Then there are $2^{100} \cong 1.27 \times 10^{30}$ possible association rules that await your intrepid search algorithm.

The *a priori algorithm* for mining association rules, however, takes advantage of structure within the rules themselves to reduce the search problem to a more manageable size. Before we examine the a priori algorithm, however, let us consider some basic concepts and notation for association rule mining. We begin with a simple example.

Suppose that a local farmer has set up a roadside vegetable stand and is offering the following items for sale: {asparagus, beans, broccoli, corn, green peppers, squash, tomatoes}. Denote this set of items as *I*. One by one, customers pull over, pick up a basket, and purchase various combinations of these items, subsets of *I*. (For our purposes, we do not keep track of how much of each item is purchased, just whether or not that particular item is purchased.) Suppose Table 23.1 lists the transactions made during one fine fall afternoon at this roadside vegetable stand.

23.1.1 Data Representation for Market Basket Analysis

There are two principal methods of representing this type of market basket data: using either the transactional data format or the tabular data format. The *transactional data format* requires only two fields, an *ID* field and a *content* field, with each record representing a single item only. For example, the data in Table 23.1 could be represented using transactional data format as shown in Table 23.2.

TABLE 23.1 Transactions made at the roadside vegetable stand

Transaction	Items Purchased
1	Broccoli, green peppers, corn
2	Asparagus, squash, corn
3	Corn, tomatoes, beans, squash
4	Green peppers, corn, tomatoes, beans
5	Beans, asparagus, broccoli
6	Squash, asparagus, beans, tomatoes
7	Tomatoes, corn
8	Broccoli, tomatoes, green peppers
9	Squash, asparagus, beans
10	Beans, corn
11	Green peppers, broccoli, beans, squash
12	Asparagus, beans, squash
13	Squash, corn, asparagus, beans
14	Corn, green peppers, tomatoes, beans, broccoli

TABLE 23.2 Transactional data format for the roadside vegetable stand data

Transaction ID	Items
1	Broccoli
1	Green peppers
1	Corn
2	Asparagus
2	Squash
2	Corn
3	Corn
3	Tomatoes
⋮	⋮

In the *tabular data format*, each record represents a separate transaction, with as many 0/1 flag fields as there are items. The data from Table 23.1 could be represented using the tabular data format, as shown in Table 23.3.

TABLE 23.3 Tabular data format for the roadside vegetable stand data

Transaction	Asparagus	Beans	Broccoli	Corn	Green Peppers	Squash	Tomatoes
1	0	0	1	1	1	0	0
2	1	0	0	1	0	1	0
3	0	1	0	1	0	1	1
4	0	1	0	1	1	0	1
5	1	1	1	0	0	0	0
6	1	1	0	0	0	1	1
7	0	0	0	1	0	0	1
8	0	0	1	0	1	0	1
9	1	1	0	0	0	1	0
10	0	1	0	1	0	0	0
11	0	1	1	0	1	1	0
12	1	1	0	0	0	1	0
13	1	1	0	1	0	1	0
14	0	1	1	1	1	0	1

23.2 SUPPORT, CONFIDENCE, FREQUENT ITEMSETS, AND THE A PRIORI PROPERTY

Let D be the set of transactions represented in Table 23.1, where each transaction T in D represents a set of items contained in I. Suppose that we have a particular set of items A (e.g., beans and squash), and another set of items B (e.g., asparagus). Then an *association rule* takes the form *if A, then B* (i.e., $A \Rightarrow B$), where the *antecedent*

A and the *consequent B* are proper subsets of *I*, and *A* and *B* are mutually exclusive. This definition would exclude, for example, trivial rules such as *if beans and squash, then beans*.

The *support s* for a particular association rule $A \Rightarrow B$ is the proportion of transactions in *D* that contain both *A* and *B*. That is,

$$\text{Support} = P(A \cap B) = \frac{\text{Number of transactions containing both } A \text{ and } B}{\text{Total number of transactions}}.$$

The *confidence c* of the association rule $A \Rightarrow B$ is a measure of the accuracy of the rule, as determined by the percentage of transactions in *D* containing *A* that also contain *B*. In other words,

$$\text{Confidence} = P(B|A) = \frac{P(A \cap B)}{P(A)}$$

$$= \frac{\text{Number of transactions containing both } A \text{ and } B}{\text{Number of transactions containing } A}$$

Analysts may prefer rules that have either high support or high confidence, and usually both. *Strong rules* are those that meet or surpass certain minimum support and confidence criteria. For example, an analyst interested in finding which supermarket items are purchased together may set a minimum support level of 20% and a minimum confidence level of 70%. However, a fraud detection analyst or a terrorism detection analyst would need to reduce the minimum support level to 1% or less, because comparatively few transactions are either fraudulent or terror-related.

An *itemset* is a set of items contained in *I*, and a *k-itemset* is an itemset containing *k* items. For example, {beans, squash} is a 2-itemset, and {broccoli, green peppers, corn} is a 3-itemset, each from the vegetable stand set *I*. The *itemset frequency* is simply the number of transactions that contain the particular itemset. A *frequent itemset* is an itemset that occurs at least a certain minimum number of times, having itemset frequency $\geq \phi$. For example, suppose that we set $\phi = 4$. Then itemsets that occur more than four times are said to be *frequent*. We denote the set of frequent *k*-itemsets as F_k.

MINING ASSOCIATION RULES

The mining of association rules from large databases is a two-step process:

1. Find all frequent itemsets; that is, find all itemsets with frequency $\geq \phi$.
2. From the frequent itemsets, generate association rules satisfying the minimum support and confidence conditions.

The *a priori algorithm* takes advantage of the a priori property to shrink the search space. The *a priori property* states that if an itemset *Z* is not frequent, then adding another item *A* to the itemset *Z* will not make *Z* more frequent. That is, if *Z* is not frequent, $Z \cup A$ will not be frequent. In fact, no *superset* of *Z* (itemset containing *Z*) will be frequent. This helpful property reduces significantly the search space for the a priori algorithm.

A PRIORI PROPERTY

If an itemset Z is not frequent, then for any item A, $Z \cup A$ will not be frequent.

23.3   HOW DOES THE A PRIORI ALGORITHM WORK (PART 1)? GENERATING FREQUENT ITEMSETS

Consider the set of transactions D represented in Table 23.1. How would the a priori algorithm mine association rules from this data set?

Let $\phi = 4$, so that an itemset is frequent if it occurs four or more times in D. We first find F_1, the frequent 1-itemsets, which represent simply the individual vegetable items themselves. To do so, we may turn to Table 23.3 and take the column sums, which give us the number of transactions containing each particular vegetable. As each sum meets or exceeds $\phi = 4$, we conclude that each 1-itemset is frequent. Thus, $F_1 = \{$asparagus, beans, broccoli, corn, green peppers, squash, tomatoes$\}$.

Next, we turn to finding the frequent 2-itemsets. In general, to find F_k, the a priori algorithm first constructs a set C_k of candidate k-itemsets by joining F_{k-1} with itself. Then it prunes C_k using the a priori property. The itemsets in C_k that survive the pruning step then form F_k. Here, C_2 consists of all the combinations of vegetables in Table 23.4.

As $\phi = 4$, we have $F_2 = \{$ {asparagus, beans}, {asparagus, squash}, {beans, corn}, {beans, squash}, {beans, tomatoes}, {broccoli, green peppers}, {corn, tomatoes} $\}$. Next, we use the frequent itemsets in F_2 to generate C_3, the candidate 3-itemsets. To do so, we join F_2 with itself, where *itemsets are joined if they have the first $k - 1$ items in common* (in alphabetical order). For example, {asparagus, beans} and {asparagus, squash} have the first $k - = 1$ item in common, asparagus. Thus, they are joined into the new candidate itemset {asparagus, beans, squash}. Similarly, {beans, corn} and {beans, squash} have the first item, beans, in common, generating

TABLE 23.4   Candidate 2-ItemSets

Combination	Count	Combination	Count
Asparagus, beans	5	Broccoli, corn	2
Asparagus, broccoli	1	Broccoli, green peppers	4
Asparagus, corn	2	Broccoli, squash	1
Asparagus, green peppers	0	Broccoli, tomatoes	2
Asparagus, squash	5	Corn, green peppers	3
Asparagus, tomatoes	1	Corn, squash	3
Beans, broccoli	3	Corn, tomatoes	4
Beans, corn	5	Green peppers, squash	1
Beans, green peppers	3	Green peppers, tomatoes	3
Beans, squash	6	Squash, tomatoes	2
Beans, tomatoes	4		

the candidate 3-itemset {beans, corn, squash}. Finally, candidate 3-itemsets {beans, corn, tomatoes} and {beans, squash, tomatoes} are generated in like manner. Thus, $C_3 = \{$ {asparagus, beans, squash}, {beans, corn, squash}, {beans, corn, tomatoes}, {beans, squash, tomatoes} $\}$.

C_3 is then pruned, using the a priori property. For each itemset s in C_3, its size $k - 1$ subsets are generated and examined. If *any* of these subsets are not frequent, s cannot be frequent and is therefore pruned. For example, consider $s = \{$asparagus, beans, squash$\}$. The subsets of size $k - 1 = 2$ are generated, as follows: {asparagus, beans}, {asparagus, squash}, and {beans, squash}. From Table 23.4, we see that each of these subsets is frequent and that therefore $s = \{$asparagus, beans, squash$\}$ is not pruned. The reader will verify that $s = \{$beans, corn, tomatoes$\}$ will also not be pruned.

However, consider $s = \{$beans, corn, squash$\}$. The subset {corn, squash} has frequency $3 < 4 = \phi$, so that {corn, squash} is not frequent. By the a priori property, therefore, {beans, corn, squash} cannot be frequent, is therefore pruned, and does not appear in F_3. Also consider $s = \{$beans, squash, tomatoes$\}$. The subset {squash, tomatoes} has frequency $2 < 4 = \phi$, and hence is not frequent. Again, by the a priori property, its superset {beans, squash, tomatoes} cannot be frequent and is also pruned, not appearing in F_3.

We still need to check the count for these candidate frequent itemsets. The itemset {asparagus, beans, squash} occurs four times in the transaction list, but {beans, corn, tomatoes} occurs only three times. Therefore, the latter candidate itemset is also pruned, leaving us with a singleton frequent itemset in F_3: {asparagus, beans, squash}. This completes the task of finding the frequent itemsets for the vegetable stand data D.

23.4 HOW DOES THE A PRIORI ALGORITHM WORK (PART 2)? GENERATING ASSOCIATION RULES

Next, we turn to the task of generating association rules using the frequent itemsets. This is accomplished using the following two-step process, for each frequent itemset s:

GENERATING ASSOCIATION RULES

1. First, generate all subsets of s.
2. Then, let ss represent a nonempty subset of s. Consider the association rule $R : ss \Rightarrow (s - ss)$, where $(s - ss)$ indicates the set s without ss. Generate (and output) R if R fulfills the minimum confidence requirement. Do so for every subset ss of s. Note that for simplicity, a single-item consequent is often desired.

For example, consider $s = \{$asparagus, beans, squash$\}$ from F_3. The proper subsets of s are {asparagus}, {beans}, {squash}, {asparagus, beans}, {asparagus, squash}, and {beans, squash}. For the first association rule shown in Table 23.5, we consider $ss = $ {asparagus, beans}, so that $(s - ss) = $ {squash}. We consider the rule R: {asparagus, beans} $\Rightarrow$ {squash}. The support is the proportion of transactions in which both {asparagus, beans} and {squash} occur, which is 4 (or 28.6%) of the 14 total transactions in D. To find the confidence, we note that {asparagus, beans} occurs in 5 of the 14 transactions, four of which also contain {squash}, giving us our confidence of $\frac{4}{5} = 80\%$. The statistics for the second rule in Table 23.5 arise similarly. For the third rule in Table 23.5, the support is still $\frac{4}{14} = 28.6\%$, but the confidence falls to 66.7%. This is because {beans, squash} occurs in six transactions, four of which also contain {asparagus}. Assuming that our minimum confidence criterion is set at 60% and that we desire a single consequent, we therefore have the candidate rules shown in Table 23.5. If our minimum confidence were set at 80%, the third rule would not be reported.

TABLE 23.5   Candidate association rules for vegetable stand data: two antecedents

If *Antecedent*, then *Consequent*	Support	Confidence
If buy asparagus and beans, then buy squash	$\frac{4}{14} = 28.6\%$	$\frac{4}{5} = 80\%$
If buy asparagus and squash, then buy beans	$\frac{4}{14} = 28.6\%$	$\frac{4}{5} = 80\%$
If buy beans and squash, then buy asparagus	$\frac{4}{14} = 28.6\%$	$\frac{4}{6} = 66.7\%$

Finally, we turn to single-antecedent/single-consequent rules. Applying the association rule generation method outlined in the box above, and using the itemsets in F_2, we may generate the candidate association rules shown in Table 23.6.

To provide an overall measure of usefulness for an association rule, analysts sometimes multiply the support times the confidence. This allows the analyst to rank the rules according to a combination of prevalence and accuracy. Table 23.7 provides such a list for our present data set, after first filtering the rules through a minimum confidence level of 80%.

Compare Table 23.7 with Figure 23.1, the association rules reported by Modeler's version of the a priori algorithm, with minimum 80% confidence, and sorted by support × confidence. The third column, which Modeler calls "Support %," is actually not what we defined support to be in this chapter (following Han and Kamber,[2] Hand et al.,[3] and other texts). Instead, what Modeler calls "support" is the proportion of occurrences of the antecedent alone rather than the antecedent and the consequent. To find the actual support for the association rule using the Modeler results, multiply the reported "support" times the reported confidence. For example, Modeler reports 50% support and 85.714% confidence for the first association rule, but this really

---

[2]Jiawei Han and Micheline Kamber, *Data Mining Concepts and Techniques*, Second Edition, Morgan Kaufmann, San Francisco, CA, 2006.

[3]David Hand, Heikki Mannila, and Padhraic Smith, *Principles of Data Mining*, MIT Press, Cambridge, MA, 2001.

TABLE 23.6 **Candidate association rules for vegetable stand data: one antecedent**

If *Antecedent*, then *Consequent*	Support	Confidence
If buy asparagus, then buy beans	$\frac{5}{14} = 35.7\%$	$\frac{5}{6} = 83.3\%$
If buy beans, then buy asparagus	$\frac{5}{14} = 35.7\%$	$\frac{5}{10} = 50\%$
If buy asparagus, then buy squash	$\frac{5}{14} = 35.7\%$	$\frac{5}{6} = 83.3\%$
If buy squash, then buy asparagus	$\frac{5}{14} = 35.7\%$	$\frac{5}{7} = 71.4\%$
If buy beans, then buy corn	$\frac{5}{14} = 35.7\%$	$\frac{5}{10} = 50\%$
If buy corn, then buy beans	$\frac{5}{14} = 35.7\%$	$\frac{5}{8} = 62.5\%$
If buy beans, then buy squash	$\frac{6}{14} = 42.9\%$	$\frac{6}{10} = 60\%$
If buy squash, then buy beans	$\frac{6}{14} = 42.9\%$	$\frac{6}{7} = 85.7\%$
If buy beans, then buy tomatoes	$\frac{4}{14} = 28.6\%$	$\frac{4}{10} = 40\%$
If buy tomatoes, then buy beans	$\frac{4}{14} = 28.6\%$	$\frac{4}{6} = 66.7\%$
If buy broccoli, then buy green peppers	$\frac{4}{14} = 28.6\%$	$\frac{4}{5} = 80\%$
If buy green peppers, then buy broccoli	$\frac{4}{14} = 28.6\%$	$\frac{4}{5} = 80\%$
If buy corn, then buy tomatoes	$\frac{4}{14} = 28.6\%$	$\frac{4}{8} = 50\%$
If buy tomatoes, then buy corn	$\frac{4}{14} = 28.6\%$	$\frac{4}{6} = 66.7\%$

TABLE 23.7 **Final list of association rules for vegetable stand data: ranked by support × confidence, minimum confidence 80%**

If *Antecedent*, then *Consequent*	Support	Confidence	Support × Confidence
If buy squash, then buy beans	$\frac{6}{14} = 42.9\%$	$\frac{6}{7} = 85.7\%$	0.3677
If buy asparagus, then buy beans	$\frac{5}{14} = 35.7\%$	$\frac{5}{6} = 83.3\%$	0.2974
If buy asparagus, then buy squash	$\frac{5}{14} = 35.7\%$	$\frac{5}{6} = 83.3\%$	0.2974
If buy broccoli, then buy green peppers	$\frac{4}{14} = 28.6\%$	$\frac{4}{5} = 80\%$	0.2288
If buy green peppers, then buy broccoli	$\frac{4}{14} = 28.6\%$	$\frac{4}{5} = 80\%$	0.2288
If buy asparagus and beans, then buy squash	$\frac{4}{14} = 28.6\%$	$\frac{4}{5} = 80\%$	0.2288
If buy asparagus and squash, then buy beans	$\frac{4}{14} = 28.6\%$	$\frac{4}{5} = 80\%$	0.2288

Consequent	Antecedent	Support %	Confidence %
Beans	Squash	50.0	85.714
Squash	Asparagus	42.857	83.333
Beans	Asparagus	42.857	83.333
Green Peppers	Broccoli	35.714	80.0
Broccoli	Green Peppers	35.714	80.0
Beans	Asparagus Squash	35.714	80.0
Squash	Asparagus Beans	35.714	80.0
Green Peppers	Broccoli Tomatoes	14.286	100.0
Green Peppers	Broccoli Corn	14.286	100.0
Squash	Asparagus Corn	14.286	100.0
Beans	Tomatoes Squash	14.286	100.0

Figure 23.1   Association rules for vegetable stand data, generated by Modeler.

means 50% × 85.714% = 42.857% support, according to the generally accepted definition of support. Be careful with Figure 23.1, because it reports the consequent before the antecedent. Apart from the "support" anomaly, the software's association rules shown in Figure 23.1 represent the same rules as those we found step by step, and by hand, for the vegetable stand data.

Armed with this knowledge, the vegetable stand entrepreneur can deploy marketing strategies that take advantage of the patterns uncovered above. Why do these particular products co-occur in customers' market baskets? Should the product layout be altered to make it easier for customers to purchase these products together? Should personnel be alerted to remind customers not to forget item B when purchasing associated item A?

23.5   EXTENSION FROM FLAG DATA TO GENERAL CATEGORICAL DATA

Thus far, we have examined association rules using flag data types only. That is, all of the vegetable stand attributes took the form of Boolean 0/1 flags, resulting in the tabular data format found in Table 23.3, reflecting a straightforward market basket analysis problem. However, association rules are not restricted to flag data types. In particular, the a priori algorithm can be applied to categorical data in general. Let us look at an example.

Recall the normalized *adult* data set analyzed in Chapters 8 and 9. Here in Chapter 12, we apply the a priori algorithm, for the predictor variables *marital status, sex, work class,* and the target variable *income* in that same data set, using Modeler. Minimum support of 15%, minimum confidence of 80%, and a maximum of two antecedents are specified, with the resulting association rules shown in Figure 23.2.

Consequent	Antecedent	Support %	Confidence %
Income = <=50K	Marital status = Never-married Work Class = Private	25.184	95.855
Income = <=50K	Marital status = Never-married	32.9	95.319
Income = <=50K	Marital status = Never-married Sex = Male	18.272	94.374
Income = <=50K	Sex = Female Work Class = Private	23.9	90.979
Income = <=50K	Sex = Female	33.164	89.193

Figure 23.2 Association rules for categorical attributes found by the a priori algorithm.

Some of these rules contain the nominal variables *Marital status* and *Work class,* each of which contain several values, so that these attributes are truly non-flag categorical attributes. The a priori algorithm simply finds the frequent itemsets just as before, this time counting the occurrences of the values of the categorical variables rather than simply the occurrence of the flag.

For example, consider the second rule reported in Figure 23.2: "If *Marital status = Never-married,* then *income* <=50K," with confidence 95.319%. There were 8225 instances in the data set where the attribute *Marital status* took the value *Never-married,* which represents 32.9% of the number of records in the data set. (Again, Modeler refers to this as the "support," which is not how most researchers define that term.) The support for this rule is $(0.329)(0.95319) = 0.3136$. That is, 31.362% of the records contained the value *Never-married* for *Marital status* and the value "<=50K" for *income,* thus making this pairing a frequent 2-itemset of categorical attributes.

23.6 INFORMATION-THEORETIC APPROACH: GENERALIZED RULE INDUCTION METHOD

The structure of association rules, where the antecedent and consequent are both Boolean statements, makes them particularly well suited for handling categorical data, as we have seen. However, what happens when we try to extend our association rule mining to a broader range of data, specifically numerical attributes?

Of course, it is always possible to discretize the numerical attributes, for example, by arbitrarily defining income under $30,000 as *low,* income over $70,000 as *high,* and other income as *medium.* Also, we have seen how both C4.5 and CART handle numerical attributes by discretizing the numerical variables at favorable locations. Unfortunately, the a priori algorithm is not well equipped to handle numeric attributes unless they are discretized during preprocessing. Of course, discretization can lead to a loss of information, so if the analyst has numerical inputs and prefers not to discretize them, he or she may choose to apply an alternative method for mining association rules: *generalized rule induction* (GRI). The GRI methodology can handle either categorical or numerical variables as inputs, but still requires categorical variables as outputs.

GRI was introduced by Smyth and Goodman in 1992.[4] Rather than using frequent itemsets, GRI applies an information-theoretic approach (as did the C4.5 decision tree algorithm) to determining the "interestingness" of a candidate association rule.

23.6.1 *J*-Measure

Specifically, GRI applies the *J-measure*:

$$J = p(x) \left[p(y|x) \ln \frac{p(y|x)}{p(y)} + [1 - p(y|x)] \ln \frac{1 - p(y|x)}{1 - p(y)} \right]$$

where

- $p(x)$ represents the probability or confidence of the observed value of x. This is a measure of the coverage of the antecedent. How prevalent is this value of the antecedent attribute? You can calculate $p(x)$ using a frequency distribution for the variable in the antecedent.

- $p(y)$ represents the prior probability or confidence of the value of y. This is a measure of the prevalence of the observed value of y in the consequent. You can calculate $p(y)$ using a frequency distribution for the variable in the consequent.

- $p(y|x)$ represents the conditional probability, or posterior confidence, of y given that x has occurred. This is a measure of the probability of the observed value of y given that this value of x has occurred. That is, $p(y|x)$ represents an updated probability of observing this value of y after taking into account the additional knowledge of the value of x. In association rule terminology, $p(y|x)$ is measured directly by the confidence of the rule.

- ln represents the natural log function (log to the base e).

lsvdvpds
For rules with more than one antecedent, $p(x)$ is considered to be the probability of the conjunction of the variable values in the antecedent.

As usual, the user specifies desired minimum support and confidence criteria. For GRI, however, the user also specifies how many association rules he or she would like to be reported, thereby defining the size of an association rule table referenced by the algorithm. The GRI algorithm then generates single-antecedent association rules, and calculates J, the value of the J-measure for the rule. If the "interestingness" of the new rule, as quantified by the J-measure, is higher than the current minimum J in the

[4]Padhraic Smyth and Rodney M. Goodman, An information theoretic approach to rule induction from databases, *IEEE Transactions on Knowledge and Data Engineering*, Vol. 4, No. 4, August 1992.

rule table, the new rule is inserted into the rule table, which keeps a constant size by eliminating the rule with minimum J. More specialized rules with more antecedents are then considered.

How can the behavior of the J-statistic be described? Clearly (as $p(x)$ sits outside the brackets), higher values of J will be associated with higher values of $p(x)$. That is, the J-measure will tend to favor those rules whose antecedent value is more prevalent, reflecting higher coverage in the data set. Also, the J-measure tends toward higher values when $p(y)$ and $p(y|x)$ are more extreme (near 0 or 1). Hence, the J-measure will also tend to favor those rules whose consequent probability, $p(y)$, is more extreme, or whose rule confidence, $p(y|x)$, is more extreme.

The J-measure favors rules with either very high or very low confidence. Why would we be interested in an association rule with extremely low confidence? For example, suppose that we have a rule R: *If buy beer, then buy fingernail polish*, with confidence $p(y|x) = 0.01\%$, which would presumably be favored by the J-measure, because the confidence is so low. The analyst could then consider the *negative form* of R: *If buy beer, then NOT buy fingernail polish*, with confidence 99.99%. Although such negative rules are often interesting ("I guess we better move that fingernail polish out of the beer section ... "), they are often not directly actionable.

23.7 ASSOCIATION RULES ARE EASY TO DO BADLY

Association rules need to be applied with care, because their results are sometimes deceptive. Let us look at an example. Turning back to the a priori algorithm, we asked Modeler to mine association rules from the *adult* database using 10% minimum support, 60% minimum confidence, and a maximum of two antecedents. One association rule is shown from the results, in Figure 23.3.

The results (not shown) include the following association rule: *If Work_Class = Private, then Sex = Male,* with 65.63% confidence. Marketing analysts interested in small business owners might be tempted to use this association rule in support of a new marketing strategy aimed at males. However, seen in its proper light, this rule may in fact be worse than useless.

One needs to take into account the raw (prior) proportion of males in the data set, which in this case is 66.84%. In other words, applying this association rule actually *reduces* the probability of randomly selecting a male from 0.6684 to 0.6563. You would have been better advised to pull a name out of a hat from the entire data set than apply this rule.

Why, then, if the rule is so useless, did the software report it? The quick answer is that the default ranking mechanism for Modeler's a priori algorithm is confidence. However, it needs to be emphasized here that data miners should never simply believe

Consequent	Antecedent	Support %	Confidence %
sex = Male	workclass = Private	69.54	65.631

Figure 23.3   An association rule that is worse than useless.

the computer output without making the effort to understand the models and mechanisms underlying the results. With the onset of sophisticated point-and-click data mining software, poor analysis costing millions of dollars is more prevalent than ever. In a word, *data mining is easy to do badly*. Insightful human expertise and constant human vigilance are required to translate the nuggets hidden in the database into actionable and profitable results.

With association rules, one needs to keep in mind the prior probabilities involved. To illustrate, we now ask Modeler to provide us with a priori association rules, but this time using the *confidence difference* as the evaluative measure. Here, rules are favored that provide the greatest increase in confidence from the prior to the posterior. One such association rule is shown in Figure 23.4: If *Marital status = Divorced*, then *Sex = Female*. The data set contains 33.16% females, so an association rule that can identify females with 60.029% confidence is useful. The confidence difference for this association rule is $0.60029 - 0.3316 = 0.26869$ between the prior and posterior confidences.

Consequent	Antecedent	Support %	Confidence %
Sex = Female	Marital status = Divorced	13.74	60.029

Figure 23.4 This association rule is useful, because the posterior probability (0.60029) is much greater than the prior probability (0.3316).

Alternatively, analysts may prefer to use the *confidence ratio* to evaluate potential rules. This is defined as

$$\text{Confidence ratio} = 1 - \min\left(\frac{p(y|x)}{p(y)}, \frac{p(y)}{p(y|x)}\right)$$

For example, for the rule: If *Marital status = Divorced*, then *Sex = Female*, we have $p(y) = 0.3316$ and $p(y|x) = 0.60029$, so that

$$\min\left(\frac{p(y|x)}{p(y)}, \frac{p(y)}{p(y|x)}\right) = \frac{p(y)}{p(y|x)} = \frac{0.3316}{0.60029} = 0.5524$$

and the *confidence ratio* equals $1 - 0.5524 = 0.4476$. In the exercises, we explore further the differences among these rule selection criteria.

23.8 HOW CAN WE MEASURE THE USEFULNESS OF ASSOCIATION RULES?

As we have seen, not all association rules are equally useful. Here we are introduced to a measure that can quantify the usefulness of an association rule: *lift*. We define lift as follows:

$$\text{Lift} = \frac{\text{Rule confidence}}{\text{Prior proportion of the consequent}}$$

Recall the supermarket example where, of 1000 customers, 200 bought diapers, and of these 200 customers who bought diapers, 50 also bought beer. The prior proportion of those who bought beer is $\frac{50}{1000} = 5\%$, while the rule confidence is $\frac{50}{200} = 25\%$.

Therefore, the lift for the association rule, "If buy diapers, then buy beer," is

$$\text{Lift} = \frac{0.25}{0.05} = 5$$

This may be interpreted as "Customers who buy diapers are five times as likely to buy beer as customers from the entire data set." Clearly, this association rule would be useful to a store manager wishing to sell more diapers. Next, suppose, of that 40 of the 1000 customers bought expensive makeup, whereas, of the 200 customers who bought diapers, only 5 bought expensive makeup. In this case, the lift for the association rule "If buy diapers, then buy expensive makeup" is

$$\text{Lift} = \frac{5/200}{40/1000} = \frac{0.025}{0.04} = 0.625$$

So, customers who buy diapers are only 62.5% as likely to buy expensive makeup as customers in the entire data set.

In general, association rules with lift values different from 1 will be more interesting and useful than rules with lift values close to 1. Why are rules with lift values close to 1 not useful? Recall the definition of confidence for the association rule "If A then B":

$$\text{Confidence} = P(B|A) = \frac{P(A \cap B)}{P(A)}$$

Then, to obtain lift, we divide by the prior probability of the consequent B, giving us:

$$\text{Lift} = \frac{\text{Rule confidence}}{\text{Prior proportion of the consequent}} = \frac{P(A \cap B)}{P(A)P(B)}$$

Now, events A and B are *independent* when $P(A \cap B) = P(A)P(B)$. Thus, the ratio $\frac{P(A \cap B)}{P(A)P(B)}$ being close to 1 implies that A and B are independent events, meaning that knowledge of the occurrence of A does not alter the probability of the occurrence of B. Such relationships are not useful from a data mining perspective, and thus it makes sense that we prefer our association rules to have a lift value different from 1.

23.9 DO ASSOCIATION RULES REPRESENT SUPERVISED OR UNSUPERVISED LEARNING?

Before we leave the subject of association rules, let us touch on a few topics of interest. First, we may ask whether association rules represent supervised or unsupervised learning. Recall that most data mining methods represent supervised learning, because (i) a target variable is prespecified, and (ii) the algorithm is provided with a rich collection of examples where possible association between the target variable and the predictor variables may be uncovered. Conversely, in unsupervised learning, no target variable is identified explicitly. Rather, the data mining algorithm searches for patterns and structure among all the variables. Clustering is perhaps the most common unsupervised data mining method.

Association rule mining, however, can be applied in either a supervised or an unsupervised manner. In market basket analysis, for example, one may simply be interested in "which items are purchased together," in which case no target variable would be identified. However, some data sets are naturally structured so that a particular variable fulfills the role of a consequent, and not an antecedent (see the *play* example in the exercises). For example, suppose that political pollsters have collected demographic data in their exit polling, along with the subject's voting preference. In this case, association rules could be mined from this data set, where the demographic information could represent possible antecedents, and the voting preference could represent the single consequent of interest. In this way, association rules could be used to help classify the voting preferences of citizens with certain demographic characteristics, in a supervised learning process.

Thus, the answer to the question is that association rules, while generally used for unsupervised learning, may also be applied for supervised learning for a classification task.

23.10 LOCAL PATTERNS VERSUS GLOBAL MODELS

Finally, data analysts need to consider the difference between *models* and *patterns*. A *model* is a global description or explanation of a data set, taking a high-level perspective. Models may be descriptive or inferential. Descriptive models seek to summarize the entire data set in a succinct manner. Inferential models aim to provide a mechanism that enables the analyst to generalize from samples to populations. Either way, the perspective is global, encompassing the entire data set. However, patterns are essentially local features of the data. Recognizable patterns may in fact hold true for only a few variables or a fraction of the records in the data.

Most of the modeling methods we have covered have dealt with global model building. Association rules, however, are particularly well suited to uncovering local patterns in the data. As soon as one applies the *if* clause in an association rule, one is partitioning a data so that, usually, most of the records do not apply. Applying the *if* clause "drills down" deeper into a data set, with the aim of uncovering a hidden local pattern that may or may not be relevant to the bulk of the data.

For example, consider the following association rule from Figure 23.4: If *Marital status = Divorced,* then *Sex = Female,* with confidence 60.029%. We see that this association rule applies to only 13.74% of the records and ignores the remaining 86.24% of the data set. Even among this minority of records, the association rule ignores most of the variables, concentrating on only two. Therefore, this association rule cannot claim to be global and cannot be considered a model in the strict sense. It represents a pattern that is local to these records and variables only.

Then again, finding interesting local patterns is one of the most important goals of data mining. Sometimes, uncovering a pattern within the data can lead to the deployment of new and profitable initiatives. For example, recall from the *churn* data set (Chapter 3) that those customers who belonged to the VoiceMail Plan were at considerably lower risk of churning than other customers (see Figure 23.5). This finding affected only 922 (27.663%) of the 3333 records and only two of the variables, and is thus to be considered a local pattern. Nevertheless, the discovery of this nugget could lead to policy changes that, if properly deployed, could lead to increased profits for the cell phone company.

Consequent	Antecedent	Support %	Confidence %
Churn? = False.	VMail Plan = yes	27.663	91.323

Figure 23.5   Profitable pattern: VoiceMail Plan adopters less likely to churn.

THE R ZONE

Load the data set, load the required package, create a Transaction object

```
adult < – read.csv(file = "C:/ . . . /adult.txt",
    stringsAsFactors = TRUE)
library(arules)
testing < – as(adult[,-c(1, 3, 4, 5, 7, 8, 9, 11, 12, 13, 14)], "transactions")
```

Run the program, view the output sorted by support

```
rules < – apriori(testing,
    parameter = list(supp = 0.15,
    conf = 0.80,
    maxlen = 3))
inspect(sort(rules))
```

```
> inspect(sort(rules))
    lhs                              rhs                                     support confidence      lift
1   {marital.status=Married-civ-spouse} => {sex=Male}                      0.40644 0.8881216677 1.328807331
2   {marital.status=Never-married}       => {income=<=50K.}                0.31360 0.9531914894 1.253144049
3   {sex=Female}                         => {income=<=50K.}                0.29580 0.8919310095 1.172605976
4   {workclass=Private,
    marital.status=Married-civ-spouse}   => {sex=Male}                     0.26300 0.8889940508 1.330112590
5   {workclass=Private,
    marital.status=Never-married}        => {income=<=50K.}                0.24140 0.9585451080 1.260182357
6   {marital.status=Married-civ-spouse,
    income=<=50K.}                       => {sex=Male}                     0.22540 0.8893623737 1.330663675
7   {workclass=Private,
    sex=Female}                          => {income=<=50K.}                0.21744 0.9097907950 1.196085921
8   {income=>50K.}                       => {marital.status=Married-civ-spouse} 0.20420 0.8331082888 1.864147122
9   {income=>50K.}                       => {sex=Male}                     0.20352 0.8502673797 1.272169758
10  {marital.status=Married-civ-spouse,
    income=>50K.}                        => {sex=Male}                     0.18104 0.8865817826 1.326503355
11  {sex=Male,
    income=>50K.}                        => {marital.status=Married-civ-spouse} 0.18104 0.8895440252 1.943763712
12  {marital.status=Never-married,
    sex=Male}                            => {income=<=50K.}                0.17244 0.9437390543 1.240717099
```

R REFERENCES

Hahsler, M, Buchta, C, Gruen, Bettina and Hornik, Kurt (2013). arules: Mining Association
    Rules and Frequent Itemsets. R package version 1.0-15. http://CRAN.R-project.org/package
    =arules. Accessed 2014 Oct 06.
R Core Team. *R: A Language and Environment for Statistical Computing.* Vienna, Austria:
    R Foundation for Statistical Computing; 2012. 3-900051-07-0, http://www.R-project.org/.
    Accessed 2014 Oct 06.

EXERCISES

1. Describe the two main methods of representing market basket data. What are the benefits and drawbacks of each?

2. Describe support and confidence. Express the formula for confidence using support.

3. Restate the a priori property in your own words.

For the following several exercises, consider the following data set from Quinlan[5] shown as Table 23.8. The goal is to develop association rules using the a priori algorithm for trying to predict when a certain (evidently indoor) game may be played. Therefore, unlike the vegetable stand example, we may restrict our itemset search to items that include the attribute *play*.

TABLE 23.8   Weather data set for association rule mining

No.	Outlook	Temperature	Humidity	Windy	Play
1	Sunny	Hot	High	False	No
2	Sunny	Hot	High	True	No
3	Overcast	Hot	High	False	Yes
4	Rain	Mild	High	False	Yes
5	Rain	Cool	Normal	False	Yes
6	Rain	Cool	Normal	True	No
7	Overcast	Cool	Normal	True	Yes
8	Sunny	Mild	High	False	No
9	Sunny	Cool	Normal	False	Yes
10	Rain	Mild	Normal	False	Yes
11	Sunny	Mild	Normal	True	Yes
12	Overcast	Mild	High	True	Yes
13	Overcast	Hot	Normal	False	Yes
14	Rain	Mild	High	True	No

4. Let $\phi = 3$. Generate the frequent 1-itemsets.

5. Let $\phi = 3$. Generate the frequent 2-itemsets.

6. Let $\phi = 3$. Generate the frequent 3-itemsets.

7. Using 75% minimum confidence and 20% minimum support, generate one-antecedent association rules for predicting *play*.

8. Using 75% minimum confidence and 20% minimum support, generate two-antecedent association rules for predicting *play*.

9. Multiply the observed support times the confidence for each of the rules in Exercises 7 and 8, and rank them in a table.

10. Verify your manually found results using association rule software.

[5]J. Ross Quinlan, *C4.5: Programs for Machine Learning*, Morgan Kaufmann, San Francisco, CA, 1993.

11. For each of the association rules found above by the a priori algorithm, find the *J*-measure. Then order the rules by *J*-measure. Compare the ordering with that from the a priori support × confidence ordering.

12. Find the value of the *J*-measure for the sixth rule from Figure 23.5.

HANDS-ON ANALYSIS

Use the *churn* data set, given at the book series web site, for the following exercises. Use the Churn_Training_File. Filter out all variables except the following: VMail Plan, Intl Plan, CustServ Calls, and Churn. Set CustServ Calls to be ordinal. Allow the three predictors to be in either antecedent or consequent, but do not allow Churn to be in the antecedent.

13. Set the minimum antecedent support to 1%, the minimum rule confidence to 5%, and the maximum number of antecedents to 1. Use rule confidence as your evaluation measure.

   a. Find the association rule with the greatest lift.

   b. Report the following for the rule in (a).

   (i) Number of instances

   (ii) Support % (as defined in this chapter)

   (iii) Confidence %

   (iv) Rule support %

   (v) Lift

   (vi) Deployability

   c. Using hand calculations, show how the measures were calculated.

   d. Explain, in terms of this data, what each of the measures in (c) means (you can skip (i)).

14. Set the minimum antecedent support to 1%, the minimum rule confidence to 5%, and the maximum number of antecedents to 1.

   a. Generate rules using confidence difference as your evaluation measure with evaluation measure lower bound = 40. Explain what this evaluation measure means.

   b. For the rules that are generated, use hand calculations to compute the reported evaluation measure, and show that the evaluation measure lower bound has been met.

   c. Generate rules using confidence difference as your evaluation measure with evaluation measure lower bound = 30.

   d. Select the rule with the highest deployability. Explain why the deployability of this rule is greater than the rule we found in Question 13a.

15. Set the minimum antecedent support to 1%, the minimum rule confidence to 5%, and the maximum number of antecedents to 1.

   a. Generate rules using confidence ratio as your evaluation measure with evaluation measure lower bound = 40. Explain what this evaluation measure means.

   b. Select the rule involving Intl Plan. Use hand calculations to compute the reported evaluation measure, and show that the evaluation measure lower bound has been met.

16. Compare the results from Exercise 13 with the results from the EDA and decision tree analysis in Chapters 3 and 6. Discuss similarities and differences. Which analysis format do you prefer? Do you find a confluence of results?

17. Apply the GRI algorithm to uncover association rules for predicting either churn or non-churn behavior. Specify reasonable lower bounds for support and confidence.

18. Compare the results from the a priori algorithm with those of the GRI algorithm. Which algorithm yields a richer set of rules, and why? Which algorithm is probably preferable for this particular data set? Why?

PART VI

ENHANCING MODEL PERFORMANCE

## CHAPTER 24

SEGMENTATION MODELS

In Part 6: Enhancing Model Performance, we examine methods that enable us to enhance the performance of our models. Here in this chapter, we learn about Segmentation Models, where a useful clustering or subdivision of the data set is found, allowing us to develop cluster-specific models for each segment, and thereby enhancing the overall efficacy of the model. In Chapter 25, we learn about ensemble methods, which combine the results from a set of classification models, in order to increase the accuracy and reduce the variability of the classification. Finally, in Chapter 26, we consider other types of ensemble methods, including voting and model averaging.

24.1 THE SEGMENTATION MODELING PROCESS

Thus far, our models have been built to apply to all the records in the test data set, and by extension, to all the observations in the relevant data universe or population. However, in many applications, we can enhance the overall performance of our models, by

a. identifying subsets of the data which differ in predictable ways from other subsets of the data;

b. applying a unique, customized model to each subset.

The resulting set of models is often more efficacious, with a lower overall error rate, say, or a higher overall profit, than a single model applied universally across the population.

The process of identifying useful subsets can be accomplished using exploratory data analysis (EDA), or through clustering analysis. The resulting customized models, unique to each subset of the data, are called *segmentation models*. Segmentation models are well known to be effective in the areas of marketing and customer relationship management, but are a powerful tool that can enhance the performance of predictive models in most applications.

The segmentation modeling process is given as follows and is illustrated in Figure 24.1.

Data Mining and Predictive Analytics, First Edition. Daniel T. Larose and Chantal D. Larose.
© 2015 John Wiley & Sons, Inc. Published 2015 by John Wiley & Sons, Inc.

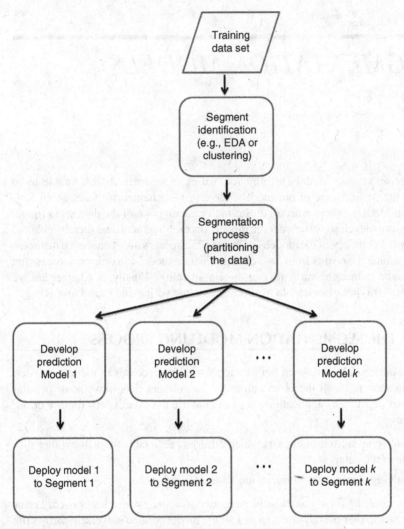

Figure 24.1 Segmentation modeling process.

SEGMENTATION MODELING PROCESS

1. Identify useful segments, using EDA, clustering, or preparatory modeling technique such as regression with dummy variables.

2. Partition the training data set into k segments, based on the segmentation information uncovered in step 1.

3. For each of the k segments, develop a customized prediction model for that segment.

4. For each of the k segments, deploy the customized prediction model for the records in that particular segment.

We provide examples of segmentation modeling, using the following segment identification methods:

- EDA
- Cluster analysis.

24.2 SEGMENTATION MODELING USING EDA TO IDENTIFY THE SEGMENTS

The *Adult* data set seeks to classify income level as greater than $50,000 or not, using a set of predictors, which includes *capital gains* and *capital losses*. We note during the EDA phase that individuals reporting either capital gains or capital losses tend to have higher income than those who do not, as illustrated in the normalized bar graphs of Figures 24.2–24.4. These graphs show the proportions of high-income ($\geq \$50,000$) individuals among those having any capital gains (Figure 24.2), any capital losses (Figure 24.3), or any capital gains or capital losses (Figure 24.4).

Next, we surmise that

a. the EDA in Figures 24.2–24.4 represents a real dichotomy within our population, meaning that the characteristics of those who report capital gains or losses differs systematically from those who do not;

b. we might perform better if we construct models customized to each group, rather than a single global model for all individuals.

To test this supposition, we implement the following *EDA-Driven Segmentation Modeling Process* for the *Adult* data set.

Value ▽	Proportion	%	Count
T		8.3	2076
F		91.7	22924

Figure 24.2 Capital gains.

Value ▽	Proportion	%	Count
T		4.62	1156
F		95.38	23844

Figure 24.3 Capital losses.

Value ▽	Proportion	%	Count
T		12.93	3232
F		87.07	21768

Figure 24.4 Capital gains or capital losses.

EDA-DRIVEN SEGMENTATION MODELING PROCESS

1. Partition the *Adult* data set into a training set and a test set.
2. Train a classification and regression trees (CART) model to predict *Income* using the entire training data set. This is our *Global Model*.
3. Evaluate the Global Model using the entire test data set.
4. Segment the training data set into those who have reported either capital gains or capital losses (Caps), and those who have not (No Caps).
5. Repeat step 4 for the test data set.
6. Train a CART model to predict *Income* using the training set Caps group. This is the *Capital Gains or Losses Model* (*Caps Model*).
7. Train a CART model to predict *Income* using the training set No Caps group. This is the *No Capital Gains or Losses Model* (*No Caps Model*). Together, the Caps Model and the No Caps Model represent our *Segmentation Models*.
8. Evaluate the Caps Model using the Caps group from the test data set.
9. Evaluate the No Caps Model using the No Caps group from the test data set.
10. Compare the contingency tables, error rates, and so on, for the Global Model versus the combined results from the Caps Model and the No Caps Model.

To save space, the output from step 1 to step 9 is not shown here. The contingency tables for each model are shown in Figure 24.5, with the rows representing actual income and the columns representing predicted income.

Comparing the overall error rates,[1] we have

$$\text{Overall error rate}_{\text{Global Model}} = \frac{257 + 787}{6155} = 0.1696$$

Global Model	$R-Income		
	Income	<=50K	>50K
	<=50K	4417	257
	>50K	787	694

Capital Gains or Losses Model	Income	<=50K	>50K
	<=50K	302	10
	>50K	41	406

No Capital Gains or Losses Model	Income	<=50K	>50K
	<=50K	4158	204
	>50K	650	384

Figure 24.5 Contingency tables for Global Model and each Segmented Model.

[1] The reader's results will of course differ somewhat, because of the different training/test set partitions.

$$\text{Overall error rate }_{\text{Caps Model}} = \frac{10 + 41}{759} = 0.0672$$

$$\text{Overall error rate }_{\text{No Caps Model}} = \frac{204 + 650}{5396} = 0.1583$$

$$\text{Overall error rate }_{\text{Combined Caps and No Caps Models}} = \frac{10 + 41 + 204 + 650}{6155} = 0.1470$$

Clearly, our segmentation models easily outperformed the global model. The overall error for the Caps Model was much lower, but the No Caps Model was also slightly lower. The combined model also saw a net 2.26 decrease in the overall error rate, which represents a better than 13% (0.0226/0.1696) decrease relative to the global model's error rate.

24.3 SEGMENTATION MODELING USING CLUSTERING TO IDENTIFY THE SEGMENTS

The *Churn* data set is used to develop models to predict when customers will leave the company's service. We use clustering to develop segmentation models, in the hopes of better understanding the various segments of the company's clientele, using the following *Cluster-Driven Segmentation Modeling Process* for the *Churn* data set.

CLUSTER-DRIVEN SEGMENTATION MODELING PROCESS

1. Partition the *Churn* data set into a training set and a test set.
2. Train a CART model to predict *Churn* using the entire training data set. This is our *Global Model*.
3. Evaluate the Global Model using the entire test data set.
4. Apply k-means clustering to the training data set, and develop a $k = 3$ cluster solution. (Of course, the analyst may apply whatever clustering algorithm and whatever value of k he or she feels is appropriate.)
5. Using the training set, train a customized CART model to predict *Churn* for each of the $k = 3$ clusters. These are models *Cluster1*, *Cluster2*, and *Cluster3*.
6. Evaluate each customized cluster model using the test data set. (When using Modeler, do not train a new cluster model on the test data set. The cluster node will assign each test set record to the appropriate cluster, based on the distance of each record to the cluster centers.)
7. Profile the clusters to better understand the customers.
8. Compare the contingency tables, error rates, costs and benefits, and so on, for the Global Model versus the combined results from the customized cluster models.

The cluster EDA is provided in Figure 24.6. The variables most helpful in discriminating between the clusters are shown at the top, in decreasing order of importance. Here, follow brief cluster profiles.

- **Cluster 1. The No-Plan Majority.** This cluster contains nearly 65% of the training set records (and a similar proportion of the test set). These customers belong to neither the International Plan nor the Voice Mail Plan.
- **Cluster 2. The Voice Mail Plan People.** This cluster contains about 25% of the records, and represents a preponderance of Voice Mail Plan users.
- **Cluster 3. The International Plan People.** This cluster contains only about 10% of the records, and represents those who have opted into the International Plan. Note that this cluster has a spike at the upper end of customer service calls, which does not bode well.

Now, clearly, it is more expensive to get back a customer who has churned rather than to retain an existing customer. For this reason, in our CART models, we shall use a 2-to-1 misclassification cost for false negatives (i.e., predictions that actual churners will not churn).

The contingency tables for the Global Model and each of the cluster models are shown in Figure 24.7.

As we are using misclassification costs, then overall error rate is not as important as the model costs, as calculated here:

$$\text{Model Cost}_{\text{Global Model}} = 26 \times 2 + 58 = 110$$

$$\text{Model Cost}_{\text{Cluster 1 Model}} = 15 \times 2 + 36 = 66$$

$$\text{Model Cost}_{\text{Cluster 2 Model}} = 10 \times 2 + 9 = 29$$

$$\text{Model Cost}_{\text{Cluster 3 Model}} = 5 \times 2 + 0 = 10$$

$$\text{Model Cost}_{\text{Combined Cluster Models}} = 66 + 29 + 10 = 105$$

Thus, the combined costs of the cluster (segmentation) models (105) is about 4.5% less than the cost of the Global Model (110, units not specified), which should please your client. However, a further benefit of using clusters for segmentation is what the clusters reveal to us about the behavior of the customers. Figure 24.8 is a normalized bar graph of the clusters, with an overlay of churn (darker = true). Clearly, Cluster 3, the International Plan People, have a higher churn rate than the other two clusters. The company's managers should look to what is causing the adopters of the International Plan to leave the company's service.

From Figure 24.7 we can calculate the proportions of actual churners for each cluster, and for the entire test data set.

$$\text{Churn proportion}_{\text{Entire test data set}} = \frac{26 + 90}{647 + 58 + 26 + 90} = 0.1413$$

$$\text{Churn proportion}_{\text{Cluster 1}} = \frac{15 + 56}{446 + 36 + 15 + 56} = 0.1284$$

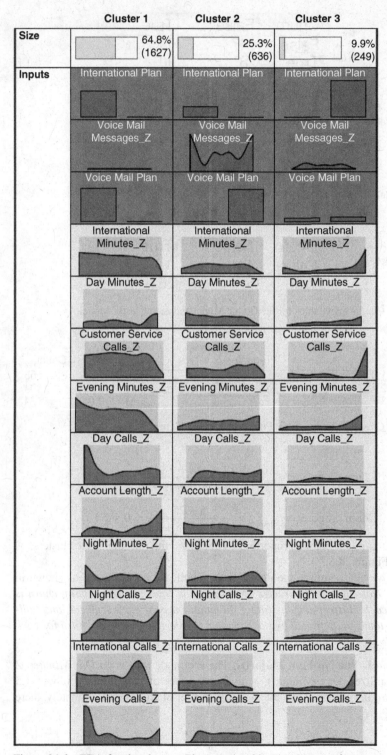

Figure 24.6   EDA for the clusters. Plan memberships are the most important variables for discriminating among the clusters.

Global Model	Churn	False	True
	False	647	58
	True	26	90

Cluster 1 Model	Churn	False	True
	False	446	36
	True	15	56

Cluster 2 Model	Churn	False	True
	False	170	9
	True	10	5

Cluster 3 Model	Churn	False	True
	False	44	0
	True	5	25

Figure 24.7   Contingency tables for the Global Model and each Cluster Model.

Value	Proportion	%	Count
Cluster-1		67.36	553
Cluster-2		23.63	194
Cluster-3		9.01	74

Figure 24.8   Cluster 3 (International Plan People) has a higher churn rate.

$$\text{Churn proportion }_{\text{Cluster 2}} = \frac{10 + 5}{170 + 9 + 10 + 5} = 0.0773$$

$$\text{Churn proportion }_{\text{Cluster 3}} = \frac{5 + 25}{44 + 0 + 5 + 25} = 0.4054$$

Cluster 3 has a much higher proportion of churners, than do the other clusters, as reflected in Figure 24.8.

Next, we can compare the decision trees built for each cluster, as shown in Figure 24.9. *Note that the character of the decision trees for determining churn is distinct for each cluster, demonstrating the uniqueness of each segment, and calling for a customized approach by the company to alleviate customer churn for each segment.*

- **Cluster 1. The No-Plan Majority.** The root node split is on *Day Minutes_Z* (standardized Day Minutes), with heavy users of day minutes (about 1.5 standard deviations above the mean) in danger of churning. Fortunately, there

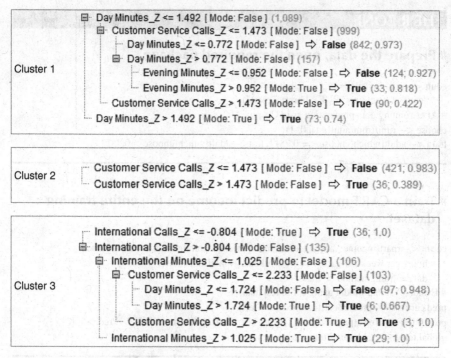

Figure 24.9   CART decision trees for each of the three clusters.

are not many of these. Otherwise, those with a large number of customer service calls (again, about 1.5 or more standard deviations above the mean, which works out to be at least four customer service calls) are at risk of churning.

- **Cluster 2. The Voice Mail Plan People.** Even though Cluster 2 has the lowest churn proportion among the clusters, we still need to be aware of those who are making a high number (at least four) of calls to customer service, for they are at a higher risk of churning. Note that the CART model shows that, even though only 38.9% of the 36 customers have a high number of calls to customer service, the prediction is still for *Churn = True*, because the misclassification cost of making a false negative error is twice as expensive.

- **Cluster 3. The International Plan People.** This is the cluster that is most troublesome to our company, with an over 40% churn rate. Clearly, our International service is driving customers away. The decision tree shows that International Plan members who do not make many International Calls (Calls_Z $\leq$ −0.804) have a 100% churn rate. Among the remaining customers, those with high International Minutes also have a 100% churn rate. Urgent intervention is called for to ameliorate these sad statistics.

THE R ZONE

Prepare the data, open the required package

```
adult <- read.csv(file = "C:/ .../adult.txt",
    stringsAsFactors=TRUE); library("rpart")
# After running data preparation as in Chapter 11
choose <- runif(dim(adult)[1], 0, 1)
train <- adult[which(choose <= 0.75),]; test<- adult[which(choose > 0.75),]
```

Train a CART model to predict income on the entire training dataset

```
cartfit <- rpart(income ~ age.z + education.num.z + capital.gain.z + capital.loss.z +
    hours.per.week.z + race + sex + workclass + marital.status,
    data = train, method = "class")
# Evaluate Global Model using entire test dataset
pred.carttest <- predict(cartfit, newdata = test)
pred.fittest <- ifelse(pred.carttest[,1] > pred.carttest[,2], "Pred: <=50K.", "Pred: >50K.")
global.table <- table(pred.fittest, test$income)
```

Segment the Training and Test data sets

```
train.caps <- train[which(train$capital.gain==0),]
train.nocaps <- train[which(train$capital.gain!=0),]
test.caps <- test[which(test$capital.gain==0),]
test.nocaps <- test[which(test$capital.gain!=0),]
```

Train CART model to predict Income using Caps and No Caps groups

```
cart.caps <- rpart(income ~ age.z + education.num.z + capital.gain.z + capital.loss.z +
    hours.per.week.z + race + sex + workclass + marital.status,
    data = train.caps,
    method = "class")
cart.nocaps <- rpart(income ~ age.z + education.num.z + capital.gain.z +
    capital.loss.z + hours.per.week.z + race + sex + workclass + marital.status,
    data = train.nocaps,
    method = "class")
```

Evaluate Caps and No Caps Model using Caps and No Caps Test data set

```
p.test.caps <- predict(cart.caps, newdata = test.caps)
p.fittest.caps <- ifelse(p.test.caps[,1] > p.test.caps[,2], "Pred: <=50K.", "Pred: >50K.")
caps.table <- table(p.fittest.caps, test.caps$income)
p.test.nocaps <- predict(cart.nocaps, newdata = test.nocaps)
p.fittest.nocaps <- ifelse(p.test.nocaps[,1] > p.test.nocaps[,2], "Pred: <=50K.", "Pred: >50K.")
nocaps.table <- table(p.fittest.nocaps, test.nocaps$income)
```

Compare contingency tables, error rates

```
global.table
caps.table
nocaps.table
(global.table[2]+global.table[3])/ sum(global.table)
(caps.table[2]+caps.table[3])/ sum(caps.table)
(nocaps.table[2]+nocaps.table[3])/ sum(nocaps.table)
(caps.table[2]+caps.table[3]+nocaps.table[2]+nocaps.table[3])/(sum(caps.table)+
    sum(nocaps.table))
```

R REFERENCES

R Core Team. *R: A Language and Environment for Statistical Computing.* Vienna, Austria: R Foundation for Statistical Computing; 2012. ISBN: 3-900051-07-0, http://www.R-project.org/. Accessed 2014 Sep 30.

Therneau T, Atkinson B, Ripley B. 2013. rpart: Recursive partitioning. R package version 4.1-3. http://CRAN.R-project.org/package=rpart.

EXERCISES

1. Give a thumbnail explanation of segmentation modeling.
2. Name two methods for identifying useful segments.
3. Explain the segmentation modeling process.
4. What would you say to a marketing manager who wished to use only one global model across his entire clientele, rather than trying segmentation models?

HANDS-ON ANALYSIS

Use the *WineQuality* data set for Exercises 5–8.

5. Perform Z-standardization. Partition the data set into a training set and a test set.

6. Train a regression model to predict *Quality* using the entire training data set. This is our *Global Model*.

7. Evaluate the Global Model using the entire test data set, by applying the model generated on the training set to the records in the test set. Calculate the standard deviation of the errors (actual values – predicted values), and the mean absolute error. (For IBM/SPSS Modeler you can use the Analysis node to do this.)

8. Segment the training data set into red wines and white wines. Do the same for the test data set.

9. Train a regression model to predict *Quality* using the red wines in the training set. This is the *Red Wines Model*.

10. Train a regression model to predict *Quality* using the white wines in the training set. This is the *White Wines Model*.

11. Evaluate the Red Wines Model using the red wines from the test data set. Calculate the standard deviation of the errors, and the mean absolute error.

12. Evaluate the White Wines Model using the white wines from the test data set. Calculate the standard deviation of the errors, and the mean absolute error.

13. Compare the standard deviations of the errors, and the mean absolute errors, for the Global Model versus the combined results (weighted averages) from the Red Wines Model and the White Wines Model.

14. Contrast the regression models generated for the two types of wines. Discuss any substantive differences.

## CHAPTER 25

ENSEMBLE METHODS: BAGGING AND BOOSTING

Here in Part 6: Enhancing Model Performance, we are learning methods that allow us to improve the performance of our models. In Chapter 24 we learned about Segmentation Models, where a useful clustering or subdivision of the data set is found, allowing us to develop cluster-specific models for each segment, and thereby enhancing the overall efficacy of the classification task. Here in this chapter, we are introduced to *Ensemble Methods*, specifically, bagging and boosting that combine the results from a set of classification models (classifiers), in order to increase the accuracy and reduce the variability of the classification. Next time, in Chapter 26, we consider other types of ensemble methods, including voting and model averaging.

We have become acquainted with a wide range of classification algorithms in this book, including

- *k*-nearest neighbor classification
- Classification and regression trees (CART)
- The C4.5 algorithm
- Neural networks for classification
- Logistic regression
- Naïve Bayes and Bayesian networks.

However, we have so far used our classification algorithms one at a time. Have you wondered what would happen if we were somehow able to combine more than one classification model? Might the resulting combined model be more accurate, or have less variability?

What would be the rationale for using an ensemble of classification models?

25.1 RATIONALE FOR USING AN ENSEMBLE OF CLASSIFICATION MODELS

The benefits of using an ensemble of classification models rather than a single classification model are that

---

Data Mining and Predictive Analytics, First Edition. Daniel T. Larose and Chantal D. Larose.
© 2015 John Wiley & Sons, Inc. Published 2015 by John Wiley & Sons, Inc.

1. the ensemble classifier is likely to have a lower error rate (boosting);
2. the variance of the ensemble classifier will be lower than had we used certain unstable classification models, such as decision trees and neural networks, that have high variability (bagging and boosting);

How does an ensemble classifier succeed in having a lower error rate than the single classifier? Consider the following example.

Suppose we have an ensemble of five binary (0/1, yes/no) classifiers, each of which has an error rate of 0.20. The ensemble classifier will consider the classification (prediction) for each classifier, and the classification with the most votes among the five classifiers will be chosen as the output class for the ensemble classifier. If the individual classifiers classify the cases similarly, then the ensemble classifier will follow suit, in which case the error rate for the ensemble method will be the same as for the individual classifiers, 0.20.

However, if the individual classifiers are independent, that is, if the classification errors of the individual classifiers are uncorrelated, then the voting mechanism ensures that the ensemble classifier will make an error only when the majority of individual classifiers make an error. We may calculate the error rate of the ensemble classifier in this case using the binomial probability distribution formula.

Let ϵ represent the individual classifier error rate. The probability that k of the five individual classifiers will make the wrong prediction is

$$\binom{5}{k} \epsilon^k (1 - \epsilon)^{5-k} = \binom{5}{k} 0.2^k (1 - 0.2)^{5-k}$$

So, the probability that three of the five classifiers will make an error is

$$\binom{5}{3} 0.2^3 (0.8)^2 = 0.0512$$

Similarly, the probability that four of the individual classifiers will make a wrong prediction is

$$\binom{5}{4} 0.2^4 (0.8)^1 = 0.0064$$

And the probability that all five of the classifiers will make an error is

$$\binom{5}{5} 0.2^5 (0.8)^0 = 0.00032$$

Thus, the error rate of the ensemble classifier in this case equals:

$$\text{Error rate}_{\text{Ensemble classifier}} = \sum_{i=3}^{5} \binom{5}{i} \epsilon^i (1 - \epsilon)^{5-i} = \sum_{i=3}^{5} \binom{5}{i} 0.2^i (0.8)^{5-i}$$
$$= 0.0512 + 0.0064 + 0.0003 = 0.05792$$

which is much lower than the base error rate of the individual classification models, 0.20.

When the base error rate is greater than 0.5, however, combining independent models into an ensemble classifier will lead to an even greater error rate. An exercise in this section asks the reader to demonstrate how this is the case. Here in Chapter 25, we examine two ensemble methods for improving classification model performance: *bagging* and *boosting*. But first, we need to consider how the efficacy of a prediction model is measured.

25.2   BIAS, VARIANCE, AND NOISE

We would like our models, either estimation models or classification models, to have low prediction error. That is, we would like the distance $(y - \hat{y})$ between our target y and our prediction $\hat{y}$ to be small. The prediction error for a particular observation can be decomposed as follows:

$$(y - \hat{y}) = \text{Bias} + \text{Variance} + \text{Noise}$$

where

- *Bias* refers to the average distance between the predictions ($\hat{y}$, represented by the lightning darts in Figure 25.1) and the target (y, the bull's eye);
- *Variance* measures the variability in the predictions $\hat{y}$ themselves;
- *Noise* represents the lower bound on the prediction error that the predictor can possibly achieve.

To reduce the prediction error, then, we need to reduce the bias, the variance, or the noise. Unfortunately, there is nothing we can do to reduce the noise: It is an intrinsic characteristic of the prediction problem. Thus, we must try to reduce either the bias or the variance. As we shall see, bagging can reduce the variance of classifier

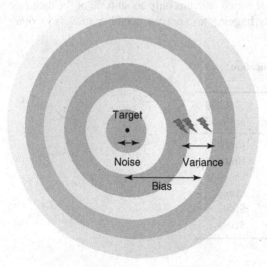

Figure 25.1   Prediction error = Bias + Variance + Noise

models, while boosting can reduce both bias and variance. Thus, boosting offers a way to short-circuit the *bias–variance trade-off*,[1] where efforts to reduce bias will necessarily increase the variance, and vice versa.

25.3 WHEN TO APPLY, AND NOT TO APPLY, BAGGING

Neural networks models can often fit a model to the available training data quite well, so that they have low bias. However, small changes in initial conditions can lead to high variability in predictions, so that neural networks are considered to have low bias but high variance. This high variability would qualify neural networks as an *unstable* classifier. According to Leo Breiman.

> Some classification and regression methods are unstable in the sense that small perturbations in their training sets or in construction may result in large changes in the constructed predictor.
>
> Reference: *Arcing Classifiers*, by Leo Breiman, The Annals of Statistics, Vol 26, No. 3, 801–849, 1998

Table 25.1 contains a listing of the classification algorithms that Breiman states are either stable or unstable.

It would make sense that a method for reducing variance would work best with unstable models, where there is room for improvement in reducing variability. Thus, it is with bagging, which works best with unstable models such as neural networks. It is worthwhile to apply bagging to unstable models, but *applying bagging to stable models can degrade their performance*. This is because bagging works with bootstrap samples of the original data, each of which contains only about 63% of the data (see below). Thus, it is unwise to apply bagging to k-nearest neighbor models or other stable classifiers.

TABLE 25.1 Stable or unstable classification algorithms

Classification Algorithm	Stable or Unstable
Classification and regression trees	Unstable
C4.5	Unstable
Neural networks	Unstable
k-Nearest neighbor	Stable
Discriminant analysis	Stable
Naïve bayes	Stable

[1] See Chapter 7.

25.4   BAGGING

The term *bagging* was coined by Leo Breiman[2] to refer to *Bootstrap Aggregating*; the bagging algorithm is shown here.

THE BAGGING ALGORITHM

Step 1 Samples (with replacement) are repeatedly taken from the training data set, so that each record has an equal probability of being selected, and each sample is the same size as the original training data set. These are the *bootstrap samples*.

Step 2 A classification or estimation model is trained on each bootstrap sample drawn in Step 1, and a prediction is recorded for each sample.

Step 3 The bagging ensemble prediction is then defined to be the class with the most votes in Step 2 (for classification models) or the average of the predictions made in Step 2 (for estimation models).

Thus, the bootstrap samples are drawn in Step 1, the base models are trained in Step 2, and the results are aggregated in Step 3. Note that this process of aggregation, either by voting or by taking the average, has the effect (for unstable models) of reducing the error due to model variance. The reduction in variance accomplished by bagging is in part due to the averaging out of nuisance outliers that will occur in some of the bootstrap samples, but not others.

By way of analogy, consider a normal population with mean μ and variance σ^2. The sample mean $\bar{x}$, representing the aggregation, will then be distributed as normal, with mean μ and variance $\frac{\sigma^2}{n}$, for sample size n. That is, the variance of the aggregated statistic $\bar{x}$ is smaller than that of an individual observation x.

Because sampling with replacement is used, certain observations will occur more than once in a particular bootstrap sample, while others will not occur at all. It can be shown that a bootstrap sample contains about 63% of the records in the original training data set. This is because each observation has the following probability of being selected for a bootstrap sample:

$$1 - \left(1 - \frac{1}{n}\right)^n$$

and, for sufficiently large n, this converges to

$$1 - \frac{1}{e} \cong 0.63$$

This is why the performance of stable classifiers like k-nearest neighbor may be degraded by using bagging, as the bootstrap samples are each missing on average 37% of the original data.

To see how bagging works, consider the data set in Table 25.2. Here, x denotes the variable value and y denotes the classification, either 0 or 1. Suppose we have

---

[2]Leo Breiman, *Bagging Predictors*, Machine Learning, Volume 26, 2, pp. 123–140, 1996.

TABLE 25.2 Data set to be sampled to create the
bootstrap samples

x	0.2	0.4	0.6	0.8	1
y	1	0	0	0	1

a one-level decision tree classifier that chooses a value of k that will minimize leaf
node entropy for the test condition $x \leq k$.

Now, if bagging is not used, then the best that our classifier can do is to split
at $x \leq 0.3$ or $x \leq 0.9$, resulting in either cases with 20% error rate. However, suppose
we now apply the bagging algorithm.

Step 1 Bootstrap samples are taken with replacement for the data set in
Table 25.2. These samples are shown in Table 25.3. (Of course, your
bootstrap samples will differ.)

TABLE 25.3 Bootstrap samples drawn from Table 25.2, with the base classifiers

		Bootstrap Sample					Base Classifier
1	x	0.2	0.2	0.4	0.6	1	$x \leq 0.3 \Rightarrow y = 1$
	y	1	1	0	0	1	Otherwise, $y = 0$
2	x	0.2	0.4	0.4	0.6	0.8	$x \leq 0.3 \Rightarrow y = 1$
	y	1	0	0	0	0	Otherwise, $y = 0$
3	x	0.4	0.4	0.6	0.8	1	$x \leq 0.9 \Rightarrow y = 0$
	y	0	0	0	0	1	Otherwise, $y = 0$
4	x	0.2	0.6	0.8	1	1	$x \leq 0.9 \Rightarrow y = 0$
	y	1	0	0	1	1	Otherwise, $y = 0$
5	x	0.2	0.2	1	1	1	$x \leq 0.1 \Rightarrow y = 0$
	y	1	1	1	1	1	Otherwise, $y = 0$

Step 2 The one-level decision tree classifiers (base classifiers) are trained on
each separate sample, and shown on the right side of Table 25.3.

Step 3 For each record, the votes are tallied, and the majority class is selected
as the decision of the bagging ensemble classifier. As we have a 0/1 classification, this majority equals the average of the individual classifiers, the
proportion of 1's. If the proportion is less than 0.5, then the bagging prediction is 0, otherwise 1. The proportions and bagging predictions are shown
in Table 25.4.

In this case, the bagging prediction classifies each record correctly, so that the
error rate is zero for this toy example. Of course, in most big data applications, this
does not occur.

Breiman states, "The vital element is the instability of the prediction method."
If the base classifier is unstable, then bagging can contribute to a reduction in the

TABLE 25.4   Collection of predictions of base classifiers

Bootstrap Sample	$x = 0.2$	$x = 0.4$	$x = 0.6$	$x = 0.8$	$x = 1$
1	1	0	0	0	0
2	1	0	0	0	0
3	0	0	0	0	1
4	0	0	0	0	1
5	1	1	1	1	1
Proportion	0.6	0.2	0.2	0.2	0.6
Bagging prediction	1	0	0	0	1

Proportion of 1's = average ⇒ majority bagging prediction.

prediction error, because it reduces the classifier variance without affecting the bias, and recall that Prediction error = Bias + Variance + Noise. If, however, the base classifier is stable, then the prediction error stems mainly from the bias in the base classifier; so applying bagging will not help, and may even degrade performance, because each bootstrap sample contains on an average only 63% of the data. Usually, however, bagging is used to reduce the classifier variability for unstable base classifiers, and thus the bagging ensemble model will exhibit enhanced generalizability to the test data.

Bagging does have a downside. The beauty of decision trees, which because of their instability are common candidates for bagging, is their simplicity and interpretability. Clients can understand the flow of a decision tree, and the factors leading to a particular classification. However, aggregating (by voting or averaging) a set of decision trees obfuscates the simple structure of the base decision tree, and loses the easy interpretability.

For stable base classifiers, an alternative strategy is to take bootstrap samples of the predictors rather than the records. This may be especially fruitful when there are sets of highly correlated predictors.[3]

25.5   BOOSTING

Boosting was developed by Freund and Schapire in the 1990s.[4] Boosting differs from bagging in that the algorithm is *adaptive*. The same classification model is applied successively to the training sample, except that, in each iteration, the boosting algorithm applies greater weight to the records that have been misclassified. Boosting has the double benefit of reducing the error due to variance (such as bagging) and also due to bias.

[3]Matthieu Cord and Padraig Cunningham, editors, *Machine Learning Techniques for Multimedia*, Springer-Verlag, Berlin, 2008.
[4]Yoav Freund and Robert E. Schapire, *A decision-theoretic generalization of online learning and an application to boosting*, Journal of Computer and System Sciences, Volume 55 (1), pp. 119 – 139.

THE BOOSTING ALGORITHM

Step 1 All observations have equal weight in the original training data set D_1. An initial "base" classifier h_1 is determined.

Step 2 The observations that were incorrectly classified by the previous base classifier have their weights increased, while the observations that were correctly classified have their weights decreased. This gives us data distribution D_m, $m = 2, \ldots , M$. A new base classifier h_m, $m = 2, \ldots , M$ is determined, based on the new weights. This step is repeated until the desired number of iterations M is achieved.

Step 3 The final boosted classifier is the weighted sum of the M base classifiers.

Here follows a toy example of the ADABoost boosting algorithm, first published in the book *Boosting*: *Foundations and Algorithms*, by Robert E. Schapire and Yoav Freund.[5]

Step 1 The original training data set D_1 consists of a set of 10 dichotomous values, as shown in Figure 25.2. An initial base classifier h_1 is determined to separate the two leftmost values from the others (Figure 25.3). Shaded area represents values classified as "+."

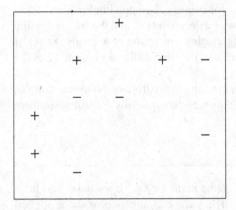

Figure 25.2   Original data.

Step 2 (First pass.) There were three values incorrectly classified by h_1, as shown by the boxed "+" signs in Figure 25.3. These three values have their weights (represented by their relative size in the diagrams) increased, while the other seven values have their weights decreased. This new data distribution D_2 is shown in Figure 25.4. Based on the new weights in D_2, a new base classifier h_2 is determined, as shown in Figure 25.5.

Step 2 (Second pass.) Three values incorrectly classified by h_2, as shown by the boxed "−" signs in Figure 25.5. These three values have their weights

[5]MIT Press, 2012.

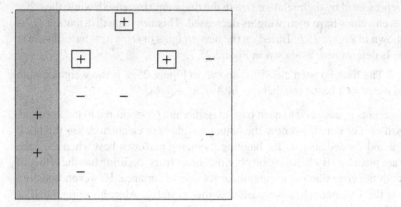

Figure 25.3   Initial base classifier.

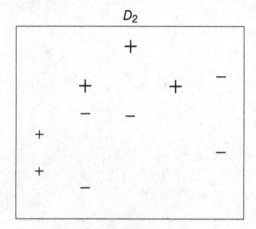

Figure 25.4   First reweighting of the data.

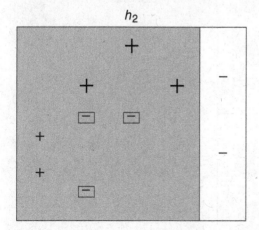

Figure 25.5   Second base classifier.

(represented by their relative size in the diagrams) increased, while the other seven values have their weights decreased. This new data distribution D_3 is shown in Figure 25.6. Based on the new weights in D_3, a new base classifier h_3 is determined, as shown in Figure 25.7.

Step 3 The final boosted classifier, shown in Figure 25.8, is the weighted sum of the $M = 3$ base classifiers: $\alpha_1 h_1 + \alpha_2 h_2 + \alpha_3 h_3$.

The weights α_i assigned to each base classifier are proportional to the accuracy of the classifier. For details on how the actual weights are calculated, see the book by Schapire and Freund. Just as for bagging, boosting performs best when the base classifiers are unstable. By focusing on classification errors, boosting has the effect of reducing both the error due to bias and the error due to variance. However, boosting can increase the variance when the base classifier is stable. Also, boosting, such as bagging, obfuscates the interpretability of the results.

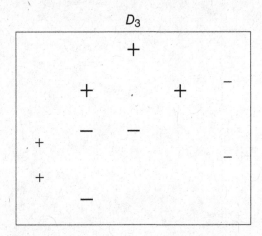

Figure 25.6   Second reweighting of the data.

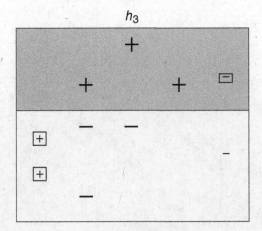

Figure 25.7   Third base classifier.

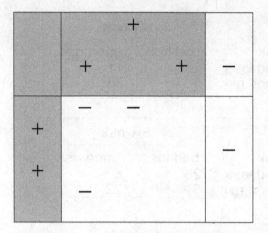

Figure 25.8   Final boosted classifier is a weighted average of the three base classifiers.

25.6   APPLICATION OF BAGGING AND BOOSTING USING IBM/SPSS MODELER

Finally, we offer an example of the efficacy of bagging and boosting for reducing prediction error. The *ClassifyRisk* data set was partitioned into training and test data sets, and three models were developed using the training set: (i) an original CART model for predicting risk, (ii) a bagging model, where five base models were sampled with replacement from the training set, and (iii) a boosting model, where five iterations of the boosting algorithm were applied.

Each of (i), (ii), and (iii) were then applied to the unseen test data set. The resulting contingency tables are shown in Figure 25.9, where the predicted risk ("$R-risk") is given in the columns and the actual risk is given in the rows. A comparison of the error rates shows that the error rates for the bagging and boosting models are lower than that of the original CART model.[6]

$$\text{Error}_{\text{Original CART model}} = \frac{11+5}{59} = 0.27$$

$$\text{Error}_{\text{Bagging model}} = \frac{5+6}{59} = 0.19$$

$$\text{Error}_{\text{Boosting model}} = \frac{5+9}{59} = 0.24$$

Unfortunately, these lower error rates come with a loss of easy interpretability. Figure 25.10 shows the decision tree for the original CART model. From this tree, the client could implement any number of actionable decision rules, such as, for example, "If customer income ≤$37,786.33 and age ≤47.5 and marital status is single or other,

[6]The reader's results will of course differ, because of the different partitions of the data, and different bootstrap samples drawn.

Original CART model

	$R-risk	
risk	bad loss	good risk
bad loss	20	11
good risk	5	23

Bagging ensemble model

	$R-risk	
risk	bad loss	good risk
bad loss	26	5
good risk	6	22

Boosting ensemble model

	$R-risk	
risk	bad loss	good risk
bad loss	26	5
good risk	9	19

Figure 25.9   Ensemble models have lower error rates than the original CART model.

```
⊟ income <= 37786.325 [ Mode: bad loss ] (69)
   ⊟ age <= 47.500 [ Mode: bad loss ] (47)
      ⋯ marital_status in [ "married" ] [ Mode: good risk ]  ⇨ good risk (6; 0.833)
      ⋯ marital_status in [ "other" "single" ] [ Mode: bad loss ]  ⇨ bad loss (41; 0.976)
   ⊟ age > 47.500 [ Mode: bad loss ] (22)
      ⋯ age <= 58 [ Mode: good risk ]  ⇨ good risk (19; 0.579)
      ⋯ age > 58 [ Mode: bad loss ]  ⇨ bad loss (3; 1.0)
   ⋯ income > 37786.325 [ Mode: good risk ]  ⇨ good risk (58; 0.793)
```

Figure 25.10   Decision tree for Original CART model offers greater interpretability.

then we predict a bad loss, with 97.6% confidence." The ensemble methods lose this ease of interpretability by aggregating the results of several decision trees.

REFERENCES

Apart from the sources referenced above, the following books have excellent treatment of ensemble methods, including bagging and boosting.

Introduction to Data Mining, by Pang-Ning Tan, Michael Steinbach, and Vipin Kumar, Pearson Education, 2006.

Data Mining for Statistics and Decision Making, by Stephane Tuffery, John Wiley and Sons, 2011.

THE R ZONE

Prepare the data

```
risk <- read.csv(file = "C:/ ... /classifyrisk.txt",
    stringsAsFactors=FALSE, header=TRUE, sep="\t")
choose <- runif(dim(risk)[1], 0, 1)
train <- risk [which(choose <= 0.75),]
test<- risk [which(choose > 0.75),]
```

Original CART model for predicting risk

```
cart.o <- rpart(risk ~ marital_status+mortgage+loans+income+age,
    data = train,
    method = "class")
p.0 <- predict(cart.o, newdata = test)
pred1 <- ifelse(p.0[,1] > p.0[,2], "Pred: bad loss", "Pred: good risk")
o.t <- table(pred1, test$risk)
```

Bagging model (5 base models)

```
s1 <- train[sample(dim(train)[1], replace = TRUE),]
# Repeat the above for s2 through s5
cart1 <- rpart(risk ~ marital_status+mortgage+loans+income+age,
    data = s1, method = "class")
p1 <- predict(cart1, newdata = test)
pred1 <- ifelse(p1[,1] > p1[,2], "Pred: bad loss", "Pred: good risk")
# Repeat the above for s2, s3, s4, s5
preds <- c(pred1, pred2, pred3, pred4, pred5)
recs <- as.integer(names(preds)); fin.pred <- rep(0, dim(test)[1])
for(i in 1:dim(test)[1]){
    t <- table(preds[which(recs==as.integer(rownames(test))[i])])
    fin.pred[i] <- names(t)[t == max(t)]
}
bag.t <- table(fin.pred, test$risk)  # Contingency table
```

Boosting model (5 iterations)

```
cart6 <- rpart(risk ~ marital_status+mortgage+loans+income+age,
    data = train, method = "class")
p6 <- predict(cart6, newdata = train)
pred6 <- ifelse(p6[,1] > p6[,2], "bad loss", "good risk")
moreweight <- train$risk != pred6
new.weights <- ifelse(moreweight==TRUE, 2, 1)
cart7 <- rpart(risk ~ marital_status+mortgage+loans+income+age,
    weights = new.weights, data = train, method = "class")
```

```
p7 <- predict(cart7, newdata = train)
pred7 <- ifelse(p7[,1] > p7[,2], "bad loss", "good risk")
moreweight <- train$risk != pred7
new.weights <- ifelse(moreweight==TRUE, 2, 1)
# Repeat the above for cart8 and cart9
cart10 <- rpart(risk ~ marital_status+mortgage+loans+income+age,
    weights = new.weights, data = train, method = "class")
p10 <- predict(cart10, newdata = test)
pred10 <- ifelse(p10[,1] > p10[,2], "Pred: bad loss", "Pred: good risk")
boost.t <- table(pred10, test$risk)  # Contingency table
```

Compare models

Compare contingency tables
```
o.t
bag.t
boost.t
```
Compare errors
```
(o.t[2]+o.t[3])/ sum(o.t)
(bag.t[2]+bag.t[3])/ sum(bag.t)
(boost.t[2]+boost.t[3])/ sum(boost.t)
```

```
> o.t

pred1             bad loss good risk
   Pred: bad loss       24         5
   Pred: good risk       7        21
> bag.t

fin.pred          bad loss good risk
   Pred: bad loss       27         7
   Pred: good risk       4        19
> boost.t

pred10            bad loss good risk
   Pred: bad loss       24         6
   Pred: good risk       7        20
```

R REFERENCE

1. R Core Team. *R: A Language and Environment for Statistical Computing.* Vienna, Austria: R Foundation for Statistical Computing; 2012. 3-900051-07-0, http://www.R-project.org/. Accessed 01 Oct 2014.

EXERCISES

1. Describe two benefits of using an ensemble of classification models.

2. Recall the example at the beginning of the chapter, where we show that an ensemble of five independent binary classifiers has a lower error rate than the base error rate of 0.20. Demonstrate that an ensemble of three independent binary classifiers, each of which has a base error rate of 0.10, has a lower error rate than 0.10.

3. Demonstrate that an ensemble of five independent binary classifiers, each with a base error rate of 0.6, has a higher error rate than 0.6.

4. What is the equation for the decomposition of the prediction error?

5. Explain what is meant by the following terms: bias, variance, and noise.

6. True or false: bagging can reduce the variance of classifier models, while boosting can reduce both bias and variance.

7. What does it mean for a classification algorithm to be unstable?

8. Which classification algorithms are considered unstable? Which are considered stable?

9. What can happen if we apply bagging to stable models? Why might this happen?

10. What is a bootstrap sample?

11. State the three steps of the bagging algorithm.

12. How does bagging contribute to a reduction in the prediction error?

13. What is a downside of using bagging?

14. State the three steps of the boosting algorithm.

15. Explain what we mean when we say that the boosting algorithm is adaptive.

16. Does the boosting algorithm use bootstrap samples?

17. The boosting algorithm uses a weighted average of a series of classifiers. On what do the weights in this weighted average depend?

18. True or false: Unlike bagging, boosting does not suffer from a loss of interpretability of the results.

Use the following information for Exercises 19–23. Table 25.5 represents the data set to be sampled to create bootstrap samples. Five bootstrap samples are shown in Table 25.6.

TABLE 25.5 Data set to be sampled to create the bootstrap samples

x	0	0.5	1
y	1	0	1

TABLE 25.6 Bootstrap samples drawn from Table 25.5

		Bootstrap Sample		
1	x	0	0	0.5
	y	1	1	0
2	x	0.5	1	1
	y	0	1	1
3	x	0	0	1
	y	1	1	1
4	x	0.5	0.5	1
	y	0	0	1
5	x	0	0.5	0.5
	y	1	0	0

19. Construct the base classifier for each bootstrap sample, analogous to those found in Table 25.3.

20. Provide a table of the predictions for each base classifier, similarly to those found in Table 25.4.

21. Find the proportion of 1's, and make the majority prediction for each value of x, similarly to that in Table 25.4.

22. Verify that the ensemble classifier correctly predicts the three values of x.

23. Change the fifth bootstrap sample in Table 25.6 to the following:

x	0.5	0.5	1
y	0	0	1

Recalculate the proportion of 1's, and the majority predictions for each value of x. Conclude that the bagging classifier does not always correctly predict all values of x.

HANDS-ON ANALYSIS

Use the *ClassifyRisk* data set for Exercises 24–27.

24. Partition the data set into training and test data sets.

25. Develop three models using the training data set: (i) an original CART model for predicting risk, (ii) a bagging model, where five base models are sampled with replacement from the training set, and (iii) a boosting model, where five iterations of the boosting algorithm are applied.

26. Apply each of (i), (ii), and (iii) to the test data set. Produce the contingency tables for each model. Compare the error rates for the bagging and boosting models against that of the original CART model.

27. Extract a sample interesting decision rule from the original CART model. Comment on the interpretability of the results from the bagging and boosting models.

## CHAPTER 26

MODEL VOTING AND PROPENSITY AVERAGING

In Part 6: Enhancing Model Performance, we are examining methods for improving the performance of our classification and prediction models. In Chapter 24, we learned about segmentation models, where useful segments of the data are leveraged to enhance the overall effectiveness of the model. Then, in Chapter 25, we learned about ensemble methods, which combine the results from a set of classification models, in order to increase the accuracy and reduce the variability of the classification. Now, here in this chapter, we consider methods for combining different types of models, using model voting and propensity averaging.

26.1   SIMPLE MODEL VOTING

In Olympic figure skating, the champion skater is not decided by a single judge alone, but by a panel of judges. The preferences of the individual judges are aggregated using some combination function, which then decides the winner. In data analysis, different classification models (e.g., CART (classification and regression trees) vs logistic regression) may provide different classifications for the same data. Thus, data analysts may also be interested in combining classification models, using model voting or propensity averaging, so that the strengths and weaknesses of each model are smoothed out through combination with the other models. Model voting and propensity averaging are considered to be ensemble methods, because the ultimate classification decision is based, in part, on the input from each of the base classifiers.

One method of combining models is to use simple voting (also called *majority classification*). Consider Table 26.1. Suppose we have a classification task, with a flag target. We develop three independent classification models: (i) a CART model, (ii) a logistic regression model, and (iii) a neural network model. For each record, each model supplies a classification of either response (1) or non-response (0). Table 26.1 shows five records, with the classification supplied by each model, along with the "winning" classification, as tabulated by majority vote among the three classification models.

TABLE 26.1 Example of simple model voting

Records	CART	Logistic Regression	Neural Network	C5.0	Naïve Bayes	Majority Classification
1	0	0	0	0	0	**0**
2	0	1	0	0	0	**0**
3	0	1	0	0	1	**0**
4	1	1	0	0	1	**1**
5	1	1	1	1	1	**1**

In this case, the logistic regression model was more likely to classify the records as 1, while the neural network model was less likely. The simple voting scheme is a way of averaging out these predictions, in the hopes that such a consensus model will provide more stable results. This process is analogous to bootstrap aggregation (bagging). However, in bagging, the classification models are the same while the records are resampled. Here, with simple model voting, the models may be different, as in Table 26.1.

26.2 ALTERNATIVE VOTING METHODS

Note that the majority classification is only one way of counting the votes of the models. Here follows a list of possible ways of combining the votes of binary classification models:

- **Majority Classification**. The classification with more than 50% of the votes is selected.
- **Plurality Classification**. The classification with more votes than any other classification is selected, without having to achieve a majority. For binary classification models, majority classification and plurality classification are equivalent.
- **Single Sufficient Classification**. If at least one model votes positive, then the combination classification is positive.
- **Twofold Sufficient Classification**. If at least two models vote positive, then the combination classification is positive.
- **k-Fold Sufficient Classification**. If at least k models vote positive, then the combination classification is positive, where $k < m$ (total number of models).
- **Positive Unanimity Classification**. The combination classification is positive only if all models vote positive.

(Of course, there are analogous methods for counting the negative votes.) Note that these alternative methods of counting votes often result in different classification decisions for the combination classifier. Table 26.2 shows the classification decisions made for each different method of counting the votes, for the data from Table 26.1.

TABLE 26.2   Alternative voting methods lead to different winners

Records	Plurality Classification	Single Sufficient	Twofold Sufficient	Threefold Sufficient	Fourfold Sufficient	Positive Unanimity
1	0	0	0	0	0	0
2	0	1	0	0	0	0
3	0	1	1	0	0	0
4	1	1	1	1	0	0
5	1	1	1	1	1	1

What are the characteristics of the ensemble models associated with these different voting methods?

- *Single sufficient classification* is highly aggressive in recognizing positive responses. Thus, its sensitivity[1] may be high, but it may also be prone to making a higher number of false positive predictions.

- By contrast, *positive unanimity classification* is resistant to recognizing positive responses. Hence, while its specificity[2] may be high, it may nevertheless be in danger of having too many false negatives.

- We would expect that *majority classification* would fall somewhere between the behaviors in the previous two bullets, having moderate rates of all four statistics cited. Also, for combining m models (where m is odd), we would expect $((m + 1)/2)$-fold *classification* to reflect the behavior of the majority classification strategy.

The downside of ensemble classifiers in general extends to voting models; that is, their lack of interpretability. It may be more difficult to explain to a client how a voting ensemble works, compared to the straightforward interpretability of decision trees.

26.3   MODEL VOTING PROCESS

The model voting process is illustrated in Figure 26.1, and may be summarized as follows:

MODEL VOTING PROCESS

1. Partition the data set into a training data set and a test data set.
2. Train a set of base classifiers using the training data set.

---

[1] Ratio of true positive predictions to actual positive responses.
[2] Ratio of true negative predictions to actual negative responses.

3. Apply the base classifier models from step 2 to the test data set.

4. Combine the classification results from step 3 into voting ensemble models, using whatever voting methods the analyst or client prefers, including the following:

   o Majority classification

   o Single sufficient classification

   o Twofold sufficient classification

   o Positive unanimity classification.

5. Evaluate all base classifier models and all voting ensemble models with respect to overall error rate, sensitivity, specificity, proportion of false positives (PFP), and proportion of false negatives (PFN). Deploy the best performing model.

26.4 AN APPLICATION OF MODEL VOTING

To illustrate the application of simple model voting and alternative voting methods to actual data, the model voting process was applied to the *ClassifyRisk* data set.

1. The data set was partitioned into a training data set and a test data set.

2. The following base classifiers were trained to predict *Risk*, using the training set:

   o Bayesian network

   o Logistic regression

   o Neural network.

3. For the purposes of this example, a random sample of 25 records was taken from the test data set, to be referred to as the working test data set. Each of the three base classifiers from step 2 was applied to the working test data set.

4. The classification results from the three base classifiers were combined into voting ensemble models, using the following voting methods:

   o Majority classification

   o Single sufficient classification

   o Twofold sufficient classification

   o Positive unanimity classification.

5. Each of the base classifiers from step 3 and each of the four voting ensemble models from step 4 were evaluated with respect to overall error rate, sensitivity, specificity, PFP, and PFN.

The working test data set is shown in Table 26.3, along with the classification results from the three base classifiers in step 2 and the four voting ensemble models in step 5. *Risk* represents the actual outcome, and the columns to the right of *Risk* represent the predictions of the base classifiers and the voting ensemble models. (*Good*

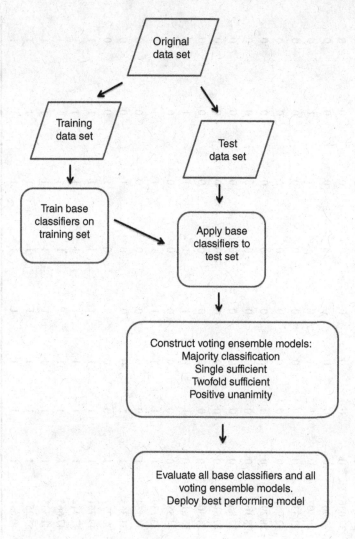

Figure 26.1   Model voting process.

Risk is coded as 1, *Bad Loss* is coded as 0, and *Income* is rounded to the nearest dollar to save space.) Tables 26.4–26.10 represent the contingency tables of each base classifier and voting model.

Table 26.11 contains the model evaluation measures for all of the models. Each of the base classifiers share the same overall error rate, 0.16. However, the positive unanimity ensemble model has a lower overall error rate of 0.12. (The best performance for each of the models is shown in bold.) As expected, the single sufficient model has the best sensitivity and PFN among the ensemble models, but does not perform so well with respect to specificity and PFP. The positive unanimity model does very well in specificity and PFP, and not so well in sensitivity and PFN.

TABLE 26.3 Working test data set

Mort	Loans	Age	Marital Status	Income	Risk	Bayes Net	Log Reg	Neural Net	Majority	Single Sufficient	Twofold Sufficient	Positive Unanimity
Y	2	33	Other	31,287	0	0	0	0	0	0	0	0
Y	2	39	Other	30,954	0	0	0	0	0	0	0	0
Y	1	17	Single	27,948	0	0	0	0	0	0	0	0
Y	2	43	Single	37,036	0	0	0	0	0	0	0	0
Y	2	34	Single	23,905	0	0	0	0	0	1	1	0
Y	1	28	Married	38,407	0	1	1	0	1	1	0	0
N	1	23	Married	23,333	0	0	0	0	0	0	0	0
N	2	38	Other	32,961	0	0	0	0	0	0	0	0
Y	2	26	Other	28,297	0	0	0	0	0	0	0	0
Y	2	43	Other	28,165	0	0	0	0	0	0	0	0
N	2	46	Other	27,869	0	0	0	0	0	0	0	0
Y	2	33	Other	27,615	0	0	0	0	0	0	0	0
Y	3	41	Other	24,308	0	0	0	0	0	0	0	0
Y	1	53	Single	35,816	0	0	0	0	0	0	0	0
Y	2	42	Single	24,534	0	0	0	0	0	0	0	0
Y	1	62	Single	33,139	1	1	0	1	1	1	1	1
N	1	25	Single	34,134	1	0	0	0	0	1	0	0
Y	2	49	Single	31,363	1	1	0	0	1	1	0	0
N	1	35	Single	28,277	1	1	0	0	0	1	1	1
N	1	30	Married	49,751	1	0	0	0	1	1	0	0
N	1	56	Married	47,412	1	1	0	0	1	1	1	1
Y	1	47	Married	47,665	1	1	1	0	1	1	1	1
N	1	48	Married	41,335	1	1	1	0	1	1	1	1
N	0	43	Single	55,251	1	1	1	0	1	1	1	1
Y	1	48	Single	40,631	1	1	1	1	1	1	1	1

TABLE 26.4   Bayesian networks model

		Predicted Risk	
		0	1
Actual Risk	0	13	2
	1	2	8

TABLE 26.5   Logistic regression model

		Predicted Risk	
		0	1
Actual Risk	0	14	1
	1	3	7

TABLE 26.6   Neural networks model

		Predicted Risk	
		0	1
Actual Risk	0	14	1
	1	3	7

TABLE 26.7   Majority voting ensemble model

		Predicted Risk	
		0	1
Actual Risk	0	13	2
	1	3	7

TABLE 26.8   Single sufficient ensemble model

		Predicted Risk	
		0	1
Actual Risk	0	13	2
	1	2	8

TABLE 26.9   Twofold sufficient ensemble model

		Predicted Risk	
		0	1
Actual Risk	0	13	2
	1	3	7

TABLE 26.10 Positive unanimity
ensemble model

		Predicted Risk	
		0	1
Actual Risk	0	15	0
	1	3	7

TABLE 26.11 Model evaluation measures for all base classifiers and voting ensembles (best performance in bold).

Model	Overall Error Rate	Sensitivity	Specificity	PFP	PFN
Bayesian networks	0.16	**0.80**	0.87	0.20	**0.13**
Logistic regression	0.16	0.70	0.93	0.12	0.18
Neural networks	0.16	0.70	0.93	0.12	0.18
Majority vote	0.20	0.70	0.87	0.22	0.19
Single sufficient	0.16	**0.80**	0.87	0.20	**0.13**
Twofold sufficient	0.20	0.70	0.87	0.22	0.19
Positive unanimity	**0.12**	0.70	**1.00**	**0.00**	0.17

This example demonstrates that a well-chosen voting ensemble scheme can sometimes lead to better performance than any of the base classifiers. In effect, voting enables an ensemble classifier to be better than the sum of its parts. Of course, such an improvement in performance is not guaranteed across all data sets. But it is often worth a try.

26.5 WHAT IS PROPENSITY AVERAGING?

Voting is not the only method for combining model results. The voting method represents, for each model, an up-or-down, black-and-white decision without regard for measuring the confidence in the decision. The analyst may prefer a method that takes into account the confidence, or *propensity*, that the models have for a particular classification. This would allow for finer tuning of the decision space.

Fortunately, such propensity measures are available in IBM/SPSS Modeler. For each model's results, Modeler reports not only the decision, but also the confidence of the algorithm in its decision. The reported confidence measure relates to the reported classification. Because we would like to do calculations with this measure, we must first transform the reported confidence into a propensity for a particular class, usually the positive class. For the *ClassifyRisk* data set, we do this as follows:

If predicted class is Good Risk, then Propensity = Reported Confidence

If predicted class is Bad Loss , then Propensity = 1 − Reported Confidence

For an ensemble of m base classifiers, then the *mean propensity*, or *average propensity*, is calculated as follows:

$$\text{Mean Propensity} = \frac{\text{Propensity}_{\text{Model 1}} + \text{Propensity}_{\text{Model 2}} + \cdots + \text{Propensity}_{\text{Model } m}}{m}$$

We may then combine several classification models of various types, such as decision trees, neural networks, and Bayesian networks, and find the mean propensity for a positive response across all these models.

Note that the mean propensity is a field that takes a value *for each record*. Thus, we may examine the *distribution of mean propensities* over all records, and select a particular value that may be useful for partitioning the data set into those for whom we will predict a positive response, and those for whom we will predict a negative response.

26.6   PROPENSITY AVERAGING PROCESS

The propensity averaging process is illustrated in Figure 26.2, and may be summarized as follows:

THE PROPENSITY AVERAGING PROCESS

1. Partition the data set into a training data set and a test data set.
2. Train a set of base classifiers using the training data set.
3. Apply the base classifier models from step 2 to the test data set.
4. For each record in the test data set, calculate the *propensity* of that record toward a positive response for the target variable, for each of the base classifiers. Compute the *mean propensity* for each record across all base classifiers.
5. Construct a normalized histogram of mean propensity, with an overlay of the target variable. (See Figure 26.3 for an illustration.)
6. Scan the histogram from left to right, to identify candidate threshold values of the mean propensity for partitioning the test set into those with positive and negative values for the target variable. The goal is to select a set of candidate threshold values that discriminate well between responders to its right and non-responders to its left.
7. Evaluate all base classifiers, as well as the models defined by the candidate threshold values selected in step 6, using evaluative measures such as overall error rate, sensitivity, specificity, PFP, and PFN. Deploy the best performing model.

26.7   AN APPLICATION OF PROPENSITY AVERAGING

The construction of a propensity-averaged ensemble classification model is illustrated using the *Adult2_training* data set and the *Adult2_test* data set. The binary target

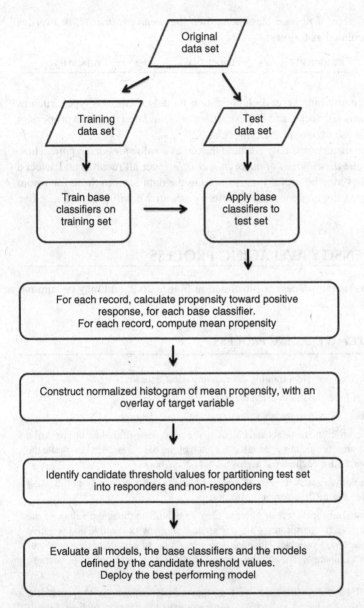

Figure 26.2 Propensity averaging process.

variable *Income* indicates whether income is above $50,000 or not. The propensity averaging process was applied, and is as follows:

1. The *Adult* data set was partitioned into a training data set and a test data set.
2. The following base classifiers were trained to predict *Risk*, using the training set:

- CART
- Logistic regression
- Neural network.

3. Each of the three base classifiers from step 2 was applied to the test data set.

4. For each record in the test data set, the. *propensity* of that record toward a positive response (*Income* > $50,000) was calculated, for each of the base classifiers. The *mean propensity* was then computed for each record.

5. A normalized histogram of the mean propensity, with an overlay of *Income*, was constructed (Figure 26.3).

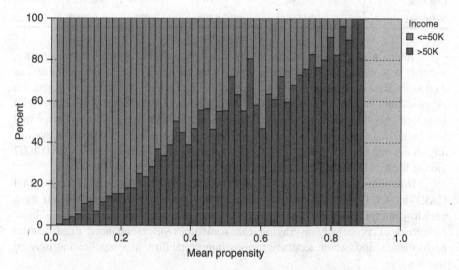

Figure 26.3   Distribution of mean propensity, with *Income* overlay.

6. The histogram in Figure 26.3 was then scanned from left to right, to identify candidate threshold values of the mean propensity for partitioning the test set into those with positive and negative values for the target, *Income*. The goal is to select a set of candidate threshold values that discriminate well between responders to its right and non-responders to its left.

7. A table (Table 26.12) was constructed of the candidate threshold values selected in step 6, together with their evaluative measures such as overall error rate, sensitivity, specificity, PFP, and PFN. The base classifiers are also included in this table.

A threshold value of *t* defines positive and negative response as follows:

If mean propensity $\geq t$,   then target response is classified as positive

If mean propensity is $< t$,   then target response is classified as negative

TABLE 26.12 Candidate mean propensity threshold values, with evaluative measures (best performance in bold).

Threshold Value	Overall Error Rate	Sensitivity	Specificity	PFP	PFN
0.34	0.1672	**0.7346**	0.8639	0.3689	**0.0887**
0.4	0.1610	0.6158	0.9097	0.3163	0.1180
0.6	0.1691	0.4477	**0.9523**	**0.2517**	0.1552
0.4005	0.1608	0.6158	0.9099	0.3158	0.1180
0.4007	**0.1607**	0.6158	0.9101	0.3153	0.1180
0.4009	0.1608	0.6151	0.9101	0.3156	0.1182
CART	0.1608	0.5436	0.9328	0.2806	0.1342
Log Reg	0.1748	0.5105	0.9249	0.3171	0.1436
Neur Net	0.1688	0.5388	0.9238	0.3085	0.1366

Table 26.12 contains the candidate threshold values for the mean propensity, together with evaluative measures for the model defined by the candidate values, as well as the base classifiers. Scanning Figure 26.3, the eye alights on 0.34, 0.4, and 0.6 as good candidate threshold values. Evaluating the models defined by these threshold values reveals that 0.4 is the best of these three, with the lowest overall error rate (assuming that is the preferred measure). Fine-tuning around the value of 0.4 eventually shows that 0.4005, 0.4007, and 0.4009 are the best candidate values, with 0.4007 having the lowest overall error rate of 0.1607.

Note that this overall error rate of 0.1607 barely edges out that of the original CART model, 0.1608. So, bearing in mind that propensity-averaged models have very low interpretability, the original CART model is probably to be preferred here. Nevertheless, propensity averaging can sometimes offer enhanced classification performance, and, when accuracy trumps interpretability, their application may be worth a try.

Table 26.12 helps us describe the expected behavior of the ensemble model, for various mean propensity threshold values.

- *Lower threshold values* are highly aggressive in recognizing positive responses. A model defined by a low threshold value will thus have high sensitivity, but may also be prone to making a higher number of false positive predictions.

- *Higher threshold values* are resistant to recognizing positive responses. A model defined by a higher threshold value will have good specificity, but be in danger of having a high PFN.

Ensembles using voting or propensity averaging can handle base classifiers with misclassification costs. For voting ensembles, the base classifiers' preferences account for any misclassification costs, so that combining these preferences is no different than for models with no misclassification costs. It is similar for the propensity averaging process. Each base classifier will take the misclassification costs into account when calculating propensities, so the process is the same as for models with no misclassification costs. Of course, the models would need to be evaluated using the defined misclassification costs rather than, say, overall error rate.

THE R ZONE

Prepare the data

```
risk <- read.csv(file = "C:/.../classifyrisk.txt",
    stringsAsFactors=FALSE,
    header=TRUE,
    sep="\t")


risk$loans_n <- (risk$loans - min(risk$loans))/(max(risk$loans)-min(risk$loans))
# And so on for the continuous variables
risk$ms_single <- ifelse(risk$marital_status=="single", 1, 0)
# And so on for categorical variables
crisk.n <- risk[,7:13]
# Create 75% Training, 25% Testing dataset
choose <- runif(dim(crisk.n)[1], 0, 1)
train <- crisk.n[which(choose <= .75),]
test <- crisk.n[which(choose > 0.75), ]
```

Build the individual models

```
# Logistic Regression
lr <- glm(risk_good ~ ms_married+ms_single+mortgage_y+loans_n+income_n+age_n,
    data = train,
    family=binomial)
# Neural network
library(nnet)
nn <- nnet(risk_good ~ ms_married+ms_single+mortgage_y+loans_n+income_n+age_n,
    data = train, size = 10)
```

Classify working test set

```
# Create the working test set (n=25)
pick25 <- sample(1:dim(test)[1], size = 25, replace = FALSE)
test.25 <- test[pick25,]
# Classify working test set using models
pred.lr <- ifelse(round(predict(lr, test.25))<.5, 0, 1)
pred.nn <- round(predict(nn, newdata=test.25))
```

Voting ensemble models

```
pred.all <- matrix(c(test.25$risk_good, pred.lr, pred.nn), ncol = 3)
pred.all <- pred.all[order(test.25$risk_good),]
colnames(pred.all) <- c("Risk", "Log Reg", "Neural Net")
sing.s <- pos.un <- rep(0, 25)
for(i in 1:25){
    if(pred.all[i,2]==1 || pred.all[i,3]==1){
        sing.s[i] <- 1# Single Sufficient
    }

if(pred.all[i,2]==1 && pred.all[i,3]==1){
        pos.un[i] <- 1  # Positive Unanimity
    }
}
pred.all <- cbind(pred.all, sing.s, pos.un)
```

Evaluate results

```
lr.t <- table(pred.all[,1], pred.all[,2])
nn.t <- table(pred.all[,1], pred.all[,3])
ss.t <- table(pred.all[,1], pred.all[,4])
pu.t <- table(pred.all[,1], pred.all[,5])
rownames(lr.t) <- rownames(nn.t) <-
    rownames(ss.t) <- rownames(pu.t) <-
    c("Good Risk", "Bad Loss")
colnames(lr.t) <- colnames(nn.t) <-
    colnames(ss.t) <- colnames(pu.t) <-
    c("Pred: Good Risk", "Pred: Bad Loss")
lr.t; nn.t
ss.t; pu.t
```

```
> lr.t
               Pred: Good Risk Pred: Bad Loss
    Good Risk               9              3
    Bad Loss               3             10
> nn.t
               Pred: Good Risk Pred: Bad Loss
    Good Risk               9              3
    Bad Loss               3             10
> ss.t
               Pred: Good Risk Pred: Bad Loss
    Good Risk               9              3
    Bad Loss               2             11
> pu.t
               Pred: Good Risk Pred: Bad Loss
    Good Risk               9              3
    Bad Loss               4              9
```

R REFERENCES

1. R Core Team. *R: A language and environment for statistical computing.* Vienna, Austria: R Foundation for Statistical Computing; 2012. ISBN 3-900051-07-0, URL http://www.R-project.org/. Accessed 2014 Sep 30.
2. Venables WN, Ripley BD. *Modern Applied Statistics with S.* 4th ed. New York: Springer; 2002. ISBN: 0-387-95457-0.

EXERCISES

1. What is another term for simple model voting?

2. What is the difference between majority classification and plurality classification?

3. Explain what single sufficient and twofold sufficient classification represent.

4. Describe what negative unanimity would be.

5. Describe the characteristics of the models associated with the following voting methods:
   a. Single sufficient classification
   b. Positive unanimity classification
   c. Majority classification.

6. What is a detriment of using voting ensemble models?

7. Is a voting ensemble model constructed from the classification results of the training set or the test set?

8. True or false: Voting ensemble models always perform better than any of their constituent classifiers.

9. What is the rationale for using propensity averaging rather than a voting ensemble?

10. For a binary target, how is the propensity for a positive response calculated?

11. For an ensemble of m base classifiers, state in words the formula for mean propensity.

12. True or false: Propensity is a characteristic of a data set rather than a single record.

13. When scanning the normalized histogram of mean propensity values, what should we look for in a candidate threshold value?

14. How does a threshold value of t define positive and negative responses of the target variable?

15. Describe how propensity averaging ensemble models would behave, for the following:
    a. Lower threshold values
    b. Higher threshold values.

16. True or false: Ensemble models using voting or propensity averaging do not perform well with misclassification costs.

HANDS-ON ANALYSIS

Use the *Adult2_training* data set and the *Adult2_test* data set to perform model voting in Exercises 17–21.x2

17. Use the training set to train a CART model, a logistic regression model, and a neural network model to be your set of base classifiers for predicting *Income*.

18. Apply the base classifier models to the test data set.

19. Combine the classification results into voting ensemble models, using the following methods:
    a. Majority classification
    b. Single sufficient classification
    c. Twofold sufficient classification
    d. Positive unanimity classification.

20. Evaluate all base classifier models and all voting ensemble models with respect to overall error rate, sensitivity, specificity, proportion of false positives, and proportion of false negatives. Which model performed the best?

21. Apply a misclassification cost of 2 (rather than the default of 1) for a false negative. Redo Exercises 23–29 using the new misclassification cost. Make sure to evaluate the models using the new misclassification cost rather than the measures mentioned in Exercise 28.

Use the *Churn* data set to perform propensity averaging in Exercises 22–29.

22. Partition the data set into a training data set and a test data set.

23. Use the training set to train a CART model, a logistic regression model, and a neural network model to be your set of base classifiers for predicting *Churn*.

24. Apply the base classifier models to the test data set.

25. For each record in the test data set, calculate the *propensity* of that record toward a positive response for *Churn*, for each of the base classifiers. Compute the *mean propensity* for each record across all base classifiers.

26. Construct a normalized histogram of mean propensity, with an overlay of *Churn*. (See Figure 26.3 for an illustration.)

27. Scan the histogram from left to right, to identify candidate threshold values of the mean propensity for partitioning the test set into churners and non-churners. The goal is to select a set of candidate threshold values that discriminate well between churners to its right and non-churners to its left.

28. Evaluate all base classifiers, as well as the models defined by the candidate threshold values selected in the previous exercise, using overall error rate, sensitivity, specificity, proportion of false positives, and proportion of false negatives. Deploy the best performing model.

29. Apply a misclassification cost of 5 (rather than the default of 1) for a false negative. Redo Exercises 23–29 using the new misclassification cost. Make sure to evaluate the models using the new misclassification cost rather than the measures mentioned in Exercise 28.

PART VII

FURTHER TOPICS

## CHAPTER 27

GENETIC ALGORITHMS

27.1 INTRODUCTION TO GENETIC ALGORITHMS

Genetic algorithms (GAs) attempt to computationally mimic the processes by which natural selection operates, and apply them to solve business and research problems. Developed by John Holland in the 1960s and 1970s (Holland[1]), GAs provide a framework for studying the effects of such biologically inspired factors as mate selection, reproduction, mutation, and crossover of genetic information.

In the natural world, the constraints and stresses of a particular environment force the different species (and different individuals within species) to compete to produce the fittest offspring. In the world of GAs, the fitness of various potential solutions is compared, and the fittest potential solutions evolve to produce ever more optimal solutions.

Not surprisingly, the field of GAs has borrowed heavily from genomic terminology. Each cell in our body contains the same set of *chromosomes*, strings of DNA that function as a blueprint for making one of us. Then, each chromosome can be partitioned into *genes*, which are blocks of DNA designed to encode a particular trait such as eye color. A particular instance of the gene (e.g., brown eyes) is an *allele*. Each gene is to be found at a particular *locus* on the chromosome. Recombination, or *crossover*, occurs during reproduction, where a new chromosome is formed by combining the characteristics of both parents' chromosomes. *Mutation*, the altering of a single gene in a chromosome of the offspring, may occur, randomly and relatively rarely. The offspring's *fitness* is then evaluated, either in terms of viability (living long enough to reproduce) or in the offspring's fertility.

Now, in the field of GAs, a *chromosome* refers to one of the candidate solutions to the problem, a *gene* is a single bit or digit of the candidate solution, and an *allele* is a particular instance of the bit or digit (e.g., 0 for binary-encoded solutions or the number 7 for real-valued solutions). Recall that binary numbers have base two, so that the first "decimal" place represents "ones," the second represents "twos," the third represents "fours," the fourth represents "eights," and so forth. So the binary

---

[1]Holland, *Adaptation in Natural and Artificial Systems*, University of Michigan Press, Second Edition: MIT Press, 1992.

Data Mining and Predictive Analytics, First Edition. Daniel T. Larose and Chantal D. Larose.
© 2015 John Wiley & Sons, Inc. Published 2015 by John Wiley & Sons, Inc.

string 10101010 represents

$$(1 \times 128) + (0 \times 64) + (1 \times 32) + (0 \times 16) + (1 \times 8) + (0 \times 4) + (1 \times 2) + (0 \times 1)$$
$$= 170$$

in decimal notation.

There are three operators used by GAs, *selection*, *crossover*, and *mutation*.

1. **Selection**. The selection operator refers to the method used for selecting which chromosomes will be reproducing. The fitness function evaluates each of the chromosomes (candidate solutions), and the fitter the chromosome, the more likely it will be selected to reproduce.

2. **Crossover**. The crossover operator performs recombination, creating two new offspring by randomly selecting a locus and exchanging subsequences to the left and right of that locus between two chromosomes chosen during selection. For example, in binary representation, two strings 11111111 and 00000000 could be crossed over at the sixth locus in each to generate the two new offspring 11111000 and 00000111.

3. **Mutation**. The mutation operator randomly changes the bits or digits at a particular locus in a chromosome, usually, however with very small probability. For example, after crossover, the 11111000 child string could be mutated at locus two to become 10111000. Mutation introduces new information to the genetic pool, and protects against converging too quickly to a local optimum.

Most GAs function by iteratively updating a collection of potential solutions, called a *population*. Each member of the population is evaluated for fitness on each cycle. A new population then replaces the old population using the above operators, with the fittest members being chosen for reproduction or cloning. The fitness function $f(x)$ is a real-valued function operating on the chromosome (potential solution), not the gene, so that the x in $f(x)$ refers to the numeric value taken by the chromosome at the time of fitness evaluation.

27.2 BASIC FRAMEWORK OF A GENETIC ALGORITHM

The following introductory GA framework is adapted from Mitchell[2] in her interesting book *An Introduction to Genetic Algorithms*.

- **Step 0**. Initialization. Assume that the data are encoded in bit strings (1's and 0's). Specify a *crossover probability* or *crossover rate* p_c, and a *mutation probability* or *mutation rate* p_m. Usually, p_c is chosen to be fairly high (e.g., 0.7), and p_m is chosen to be very low (e.g., 0.001).

- **Step 1**. The population is chosen, consisting of a set of n chromosomes, each of length l.

[2]Melanie Mitchell, *An Introduction to Genetic Algorithms*, MIT Press, Cambridge, Mass, Second edition, 2002.

- **Step 2**. The fitness $f(x)$ for each chromosome in the population is calculated.
- **Step 3**. Iterate through the following steps until n offspring have been generated.

  - **Step 3a. Selection**. Using the values from the fitness function $f(x)$ from step 2, assign a probability of selection to each individual chromosome, with higher fitness providing a higher probability of selection. The usual term for the way these probabilities are assigned is the *roulette wheel* method. For each chromosome x_i, find the proportion of this chromosome's fitness to the total fitness summed over all the chromosomes. That is, find $f(x_i)/\sum_i f(x_i)$, and assign this proportion to be the probability of selecting that chromosome for parenthood. Each chromosome then has a proportional slice of the putative roulette wheel spun to choose the parents. Then select a pair of chromosomes to be parents, based on these probabilities. Allow the same chromosome to be potentially selected to be a parent more than once. Allowing a chromosome to pair with itself will generate three copies of that chromosome to the new generation. If the analyst is concerned about converging too quickly to a local optimum, then perhaps such pairing should not be allowed.

  - **Step 3b. Crossover**. Select a randomly chosen locus (*crossover point*) for where to perform the crossover. Then, with probability p_c, perform crossover with the parents selected in step 3a, thereby forming two new offspring. If the crossover is not performed, clone two exact copies of the parents to be passed on to the new generation.

  - **Step 3c. Mutation**. With probability p_m, perform mutation on each of the two offspring at each locus point. The chromosomes then take their place in the new population. If n is odd, discard one new chromosome at random.

- **Step 4**. The new population of chromosomes replaces the current population.
- **Step 5**. Check whether termination criteria have been met. For example, is the change in mean fitness from generation to generation vanishingly small? If convergence is achieved, then stop and report results; otherwise, go to step 2.

Each cycle through this algorithm is called a *generation*, with most GA applications taking from 50 to 500 generations to reach convergence. Mitchell suggests that researchers try several different runs with different random number seeds, and report the model evaluation statistics (e.g., best overall fitness) averaged over several different runs.

27.3 SIMPLE EXAMPLE OF A GENETIC ALGORITHM AT WORK

Let us examine a simple example of a GA at work. Suppose our task is to find the maximum value of the normal distribution with mean $\mu = 16$ and standard deviation $\sigma = 4$ (Figure 27.1). That is, we would like to find the maximum value of:

$$f(x) = \frac{1}{\sqrt{2\pi}\sigma} \exp\left(\frac{-1}{2\sigma^2}(x - \mu)^2\right) = \frac{1}{\sqrt{2\pi}(4)} \exp\left(\frac{-1}{2(4)^2}(x - 16)^2\right).$$

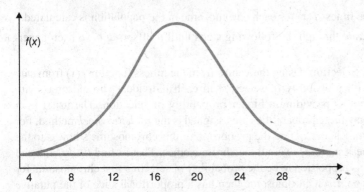

Figure 27.1   Find the maximum value of the normal(16, 4) distribution.

We allow X to take on only the values described by the first five binary digits; that is, 00000 through 11111, or 0–31 in decimal notation.

27.3.1   First Iteration

- **Step 0.** Initialization. We define the *crossover rate* to be $p_c = 0.75$ and the *mutation rate* to be $p_m = 0.002$.
- **Step 1.** Our population will be a set of four chromosomes, randomly chosen from the set 00000–11111. So, $n = 4$ and $l = 5$. These are 00100 (4), 01001 (9), 11011 (27), and 11111 (31).
- **Step 2.** The fitness $f(x)$ for each chromosome in the population is calculated.
- **Step 3.** Iterate through the following steps until n offspring have been generated.
  - **Step 3a. Selection.** We have the sum of the fitness values equal to $\sum_i f(x_i) = 0.001108 + 0.021569 + 0.002273 + 0.000088 = 0.025038$.

    Then, the probability that each of our chromosomes will be selected for parenthood is found by dividing their value for $f(x)$ by the sum 0.025038. These are also shown in Table 27.1. Clearly, chromosome 01001 gets a very large slice of the roulette wheel! The random selection process gets underway. Suppose that chromosomes 01001 and 11011 are selected to be the first pair of parents, because these are the two chromosomes with the highest fitness.
  - **Step 3b. Crossover.** The locus is randomly chosen to be the second position. Suppose the large crossover rate of p_c, 0.75, leads to crossover between 01001 and 11011 occurring at the second position. This is shown in Figure 27.2. Note that the strings are partitioned between the first and the second bits. Each child chromosome receives one segment from each of the parents. The two chromosomes thus formed for the new generation are 01011 (11) and 11001 (25).

TABLE 27.1 Fitness and probability of selection for each chromosome

Chromosome	Decimal Value	Fitness	Selection Probability
00100	4	0.001108	0.04425
01001	9	0.021569	0.86145
11011	27	0.002273	0.09078
11111	31	0.000088	0.00351

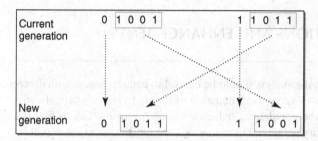

Figure 27.2   Performing crossover at locus two on the first two parents.

- **Step 3c. Mutation**. Because of the low mutation rate, suppose that none of the genes for 01011 or 11001 are mutated. We now have two chromosomes in our new population. We need two more, so we cycle back to step 3a.

- **Step 3a. Selection**. Suppose that this time chromosomes 01001 (9) and 00100 (4) are selected by the roulette wheel method.

- **Step 3b. Crossover**. However, this time suppose that crossover does not take place. Thus, clones of these chromosomes become members of the new generation, 01001 and 00100. We now have $n = 4$ members in our new population.

- **Step 4**. The new population of chromosomes therefore replaces the current population.

- **Step 5**. And we iterate back to Step 2.

27.3.2   Second Iteration

- **Step 2**. The fitness $f(x)$ for each chromosome in the population is calculated, as shown in Table 27.2.

- **Step 3a. Selection**. The sum of the fitness values for the second generation is $\sum_i f(x_i) = 0.076274$, which means that the average fitness among the chromosomes in the second generation is three times that of the first generation. The selection probabilities are calculated, and shown in Table 27.2.

We ask you to continue this example in the exercises.

TABLE 27.2 **Fitness and probability of selection for the second generation**

Chromosome	Decimal Value	Fitness	Selection Probability
00100	4	0.001108	0.014527
01001	9	0.021569	0.282783
01011	11	0.045662	0.598657
11001	25	0.007935	0.104033

27.4 MODIFICATIONS AND ENHANCEMENTS: SELECTION

For the selection operator, the analyst should be careful to balance fitness with diversity. If fitness is favored over variability, then a set of highly fit but suboptimal chromosomes will dominate the population, reducing the ability of the GA to find the global optimum. If diversity is favored over fitness, then model convergence will be too slow.

For example, in the first generation above, one particular gene 01001 (9) dominated the fitness measure, with over 86% of the selection probability. This is an example of *selection pressure*, and a potential example of the *crowding* phenomenon in GAs, where one particular chromosome that is much fitter than the others begins to reproduce, generating too many clones and similar copies of itself in future generations. By reducing the diversity of the population, crowding impairs the ability of the GA to continue to explore new regions of the search space.

A variety of techniques are available to handle crowding. De Jong[3] suggested that new generation chromosomes should replace the individual most similar to itself in the current generation. Goldberg and Richardson[4] posited a *fitness sharing* function, where a particular chromosome's fitness was decreased by the presence of other similar population members, where the more similarity, the greater the decrease. Thus, diversity was rewarded.

Changing the mating conditions can also be used to increase population diversity. Deb and Goldberg[5] showed that if mating can take place only between sufficiently similar chromosomes, then distinct "mating groups" will have a propensity to form. These groups displayed low within-group variation and high between-group

[3] Kenneth De Jong, 1975. *An Analysis of the Behavior of a Class of Genetic Adaptive Systems*, Ph.D. Thesis, University of Michigan, Ann Arbor.

[4] David Goldberg and Jon Richardson, 1987. Genetic algorithms with sharing for multi-modal function optimization, in *Genetic Algorithms and Their Applications: Proceedings of the Second International Conference on Genetic Algorithms*, J. Greffenstette, editor, Erlbaum.

[5] Kalyanmoy Deb and David Goldberg, 1989. An investigation of niche and species formation in genetic function optimization, in *Proceedings of the Third International Conference on Genetic Algorithms*, J. Greffenstette, editor, Morgan Kaufmann.

variation. However, Eshelman[6] and Eshelman and Schaffer[7] investigated the opposite strategy by not allowing matings between chromosomes that were sufficiently alike. The result was to maintain high variability within the population as a whole.

Sigma scaling, proposed by Forrest,[8] maintains the selection pressure at a relatively constant rate, by scaling a chromosome's fitness by the standard deviation of the fitnesses. If a single chromosome dominates at the beginning of the run, then the variability in fitnesses will also be large, and scaling by the variability will reduce the dominance. Later in the run, when populations are typically more homogeneous, scaling by this smaller variability will allow the highly fit chromosomes to reproduce. The sigma-scaled fitness is as follows:

$$f_{\text{sigma-scaled}}(x) = 1 + \frac{f(x) - \mu_f}{\sigma_f}$$

where μ_f and σ_f refer to the mean fitness and standard deviation of the fitnesses for the current generation.

Boltzmann selection varies the selection pressure, depending on how far along in the run the generation is. Early on, it may be better to allow lower selection pressure, allowing the less-fit chromosomes to reproduce at rates similar to the fitter chromosomes, and thereby maintaining a wider exploration of the search space. Later on in the run, increasing the selection pressure will help the GA to converge more quickly to the optimal solution, hopefully the global optimum. In Boltzmann selection, a *temperature* parameter T is gradually reduced from high levels to low levels. A chromosome's adjusted fitness is then found as follows:

$$f_{\text{Boltzmann}}(x) = \frac{\exp(f(x)/T)}{\text{Mean}(\exp(f(x)/T))}$$

As the temperature falls, the difference in expected fitness increases between high-fit and low-fit chromosomes.

Elitism, developed by De Jong, refers to the selection condition requiring that the GA retain a certain number of the fittest chromosomes from one generation to the next, protecting them against destruction through crossover, mutation, or inability to reproduce. Michell, Haupt, and Haupt[9] and others report that elitism greatly improves GA performance.

Rank selection ranks the chromosomes according to fitness. Ranking avoids the selection pressure exerted by the proportional fitness method, but it also ignores the absolute differences among the chromosome fitnesses. Ranking does not take variability into account, and provides a moderate adjusted fitness measure, because

[6]Larry Eschelman, 1991. The CHC adaptive search algorithm: How to have safe search when engaging in nontraditional genetic recombination, in *Foundations of Genetic Algorithms*, G. Rawlins, editor, Morgan Kaufmann.

[7]Larry Eshelman and J. David Schaffer, 1991. Preventing premature convergence in genetic algorithms by preventing incest, in *Proceedings of the Fourth International Conference on Genetic Algorithms*, R. Belew and L. Booker, editors, Morgan Kaufmann.)

[8]Stephanie Forrest, 1985. Scaling fitnesses in the genetic algorithm. In Documentation for PRISONERS DILEMMA and NORMS Programs that Use the Genetic Algorithm. Unpublished manuscript.

[9]Randy Haupt, and Sue Ellen Haupt, *Practical Genetic Algorithms*, John Wiley and Sons, Inc., 1998.

the difference in probability of selection between chromosomes ranked k and $k + 1$ is the same, regardless of the absolute differences in fitness.

Tournament ranking is computationally more efficient than rank selection, while preserving the moderate selection pressure of rank selection. In tournament ranking, two chromosomes are chosen at random and with replacement from the population. Let c be a constant chosen by the user to be between zero and one (e.g., 0.67). A random number r, $0 \leq r \leq 1$, is drawn. If $r < c$, then the fitter chromosome is selected for parenthood; otherwise, the less-fit chromosome is selected.

27.5 MODIFICATIONS AND ENHANCEMENTS: CROSSOVER

27.5.1 Multi-Point Crossover

The single-point crossover operator that we have outlined here suffers from what is known as *positional bias*. That is, the performance of the GA depends, in part, on the order that the variables occur in the chromosome. So, genes in loci 1 and 2 will often be crossed over together, simply because of their proximity to each other, whereas genes in loci 1 and 7 will rarely cross over together. Now, if this positioning reflects natural relationships within the data and among the variables, then this is not such a concern, but such a priori knowledge is relatively rare.

The solution is to perform *multi-point crossover*, as follows. First, randomly select a set of crossover points, and split the parent chromosomes at those points. Then, to form the children, recombine the segments by alternating between the parents, as illustrated in Figure 27.3.

27.5.2 Uniform Crossover

Another alternative crossover operator is *uniform crossover*. In uniform crossover, the first child is generated as follows. Each gene is randomly assigned to be that of either one or the other parent, with 50% probability. The second child would then take

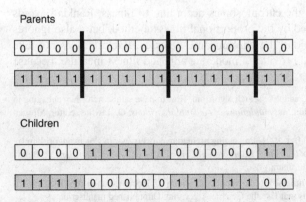

Figure 27.3   Multi-point crossover.

the inverse of the first child. One advantage of uniform crossover is that the inherited genes are independent of position. Uniform crossover is illustrated in Figure 27.4. A modified version of uniform crossover would be to allow the probabilities to depend on the fitness of the respective parents.

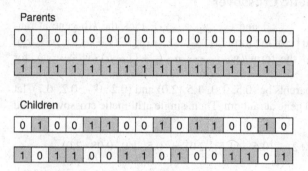

Figure 27.4   Uniform crossover.

Eiben and Smith[10] discuss the roles of crossover and mutation, and the cooperation and competition between them with respect to the search space. They describe crossover as *explorative*, discovering promising new regions in the search space by making a large jump to a region between the two parent areas. And they describe mutation as *exploitative*, optimizing present information within an already discovered promising region, creating small random deviations and thereby not wandering far from the parents. Crossover and mutation complement each other, because only crossover can bring together information from both parents, and only mutation can introduce completely new information.

27.6   GENETIC ALGORITHMS FOR REAL-VALUED VARIABLES

The original framework for GAs was developed for binary-encoded data, because the operations of crossover and mutation worked naturally and well with such data. However, most data mining data come in the form of real numbers, often with many decimals worth of precision.

Some analysts have tried quantizing the real-valued (continuous) data into binary form. However, to re-express the real-valued data in binary terms will necessarily result in a loss of information, due to the degradation in precision caused by rounding to the nearest binary digit. To combat this loss in precision, each binary chromosome would need to be made longer, adding digits that will inevitably impair the speed of the algorithm.

[10]A. E. Eiben, and Jim Smith, 2003. *Introduction to Evolutionary Computing*, Springer, Berlin.

Therefore, methods for applying GAs directly to real-valued data have been investigated. Eiben and Smith suggest the following methods for performing the crossover operation.

27.6.1 Single Arithmetic Crossover

Let the parents be $\langle x_1, x_2, \cdots, x_n \rangle$ and $\langle y_1, y_2, \cdots, y_n \rangle$. Pick the kth gene at random. Then, let the first child be of the form $\langle x_1, x_2, \cdots, \alpha \cdot y_k + (1 - \alpha) \cdot x_k, \cdots, x_n \rangle$, and the second child be of the form $\langle y_1, y_2, \cdots, \alpha \cdot x_k + (1 - \alpha) \cdot y_k, \cdots, y_n \rangle$, for $0 \leq \alpha \leq 1$.

For example, let the parents be $\langle 0.5, 1.0, 1.5, 2.0 \rangle$ and $\langle 0.2, 0.7, 0.2, 0.7 \rangle$, let $\alpha = 0.4$, and select the third gene at random. Then, single arithmetic crossover would produce the first child to be

$$\langle 0.5, 1.0, (0.4) \cdot (0.2) + (0.6) \cdot (1.5), 2.0 \rangle = \langle 0.5, 1.0, 0.98, 2.0 \rangle,$$

and the second child to be

$$\langle 0.2, 0.7, (0.4) \cdot (1.5) + (0.6) \cdot (0.2), 0.7 \rangle = \langle 0.2, 0.7, 0.72, 0.7 \rangle.$$

27.6.2 Simple Arithmetic Crossover

Let the parents be $\langle x_1, x_2, \cdots, x_n \rangle$ and $\langle y_1, y_2, \cdots, y_n \rangle$. Pick the kth gene at random, and mix values for all genes at this point and beyond. That is, let the first child be of the form $\langle x_1, x_2, \cdots, \alpha \cdot y_k + (1 - \alpha) \cdot x_k, \cdots, \alpha \cdot y_n + (1 - \alpha) \cdot x_n \rangle$, and the second child be of the form $\langle y_1, y_2, \cdots, \alpha \cdot x_k + (1 - \alpha) \cdot y_k, \cdots, \alpha \cdot x_n + (1 - \alpha) \cdot y_n \rangle$, for $0 \leq \alpha \leq 1$.

For example, let the parents be $\langle 0.5, 1.0, 1.5, 2.0 \rangle$ and $\langle 0.2, 0.7, 0.2, 0.7 \rangle$, let $\alpha = 0.4$, and select the third gene at random. Then, simple arithmetic crossover would produce the first child to be

$$\langle 0.5, 1.0, (0.4) \cdot (0.2) + (0.6) \cdot (1.5), (0.4) \cdot (0.7) + (0.6) \cdot (2.0) \rangle$$
$$= \langle 0.5, 1.0, 0.98, 1.48 \rangle,$$

and the second child to be

$$\langle 0.2, 0.7, (0.4) \cdot (1.5) + (0.6) \cdot (0.2), (0.4) \cdot (2.0) + (0.6) \cdot (0.7) \rangle$$
$$= \langle 0.2, 0.7, 0.72, 1.22 \rangle$$

27.6.3 Whole Arithmetic Crossover

Let the parents be $\langle x_1, x_2, \cdots, x_n \rangle$ and $\langle y_1, y_2, \cdots, y_n \rangle$. Perform the above mixture to the entire vector for each parent. The calculation of the child vectors is left as an exercise. Note that, for each of these arithmetic crossover techniques, the affected genes represent intermediate points between the parents' values, with $\alpha = 0.5$ generating the mean of the parents' values.

27.6.4   Discrete Crossover

Here, each gene in the child chromosome is chosen with uniform probability to be the gene of one or the other of the parents' chromosomes. For example, let the parents be $\langle 0.5, 1.0, 1.5, 2.0 \rangle$ and $\langle 0.2, 0.7, 0.2, 0.7 \rangle$, one possible child could be $\langle 0.2, 0.7, 1.5, 0.7 \rangle$, with the third gene coming directly from the first parent and the others coming from the second parent.

27.6.5   Normally Distributed Mutation

To avoid converging too quickly toward a local optimum, a normally distributed "random shock" may be added to each variable. The distribution should be normal, with a mean of zero, and a standard deviation of σ, which controls the amount of change (as most random shocks will lie within one σ of the original variable value). If the resulting mutated variable lies outside the allowable range, then its value should be reset so that it lies within the range. If all variables are mutated, then clearly $p_m = 1$ in this case.

For example, suppose the mutation distribution is Normal($\mu = 0$, $\sigma = 0.1$), and that we wish to apply the mutation to the child chromosome from the discrete crossover example, $\langle 0.2, 0.7, 1.5, 0.7 \rangle$. Assume that the four random shocks generated from this distribution are 0.05, -0.17, -0.03, and 0.08. Then, the child chromosome becomes $\langle 0.2 + 0.05, 0.7 - 0.17, 1.5 - 0.03, 0.7 + 0.08 \rangle = \langle 0.25, 0.53, 1.47, 0.78 \rangle$.

27.7   USING GENETIC ALGORITHMS TO TRAIN A NEURAL NETWORK

A neural network consists of a *layered, feed-forward, completely connected* network of artificial neurons, or *nodes*. Neural networks are used for classification or estimation. See Mitchell,[11] Fausett,[12] Haykin,[13] Reed and Marks,[14] or Chapter 12 of this book for details on neural network topology and operation. Figure 27.5 provides a basic diagram of a simple neural network.

The *feed-forward* nature of the network restricts the network to a single direction of flow, and does not allow looping or cycling. The neural network is composed of two or more layers, although most networks consist of three layers, an *input layer*, a *hidden layer*, and an *output layer*. There may be more than one hidden layer, although most networks contain only one, which is sufficient for most purposes. The neural network is *completely connected*, meaning that every node in a given layer is connected to every node in the next layer, although not to other nodes in the same layer. Each

[11] Tom Mitchell, 1997. *Machine Learning*, WCB-McGraw-Hill, Boston.

[12] Laurene Fausett, *Fundamentals of Neural Networks*, Prentice-Hall, New Jersey, 1994.

[13] Simon Haykin, *Neural Networks: A Comprehensive Foundation*, Prentice-Hall, Inc., New Jersey, 1990.

[14] Russell D. Reed and Robert J. Marks II, *Neural Smithing: Supervised Learning in Feedforward Artificial Neural Networks*, MIT Press, Cambridge, 1999.

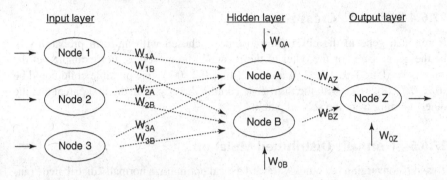

Figure 27.5 A simple neural network.

connection between nodes has a weight (e.g., W_{1A}) associated with it. At initialization, these weights are randomly assigned to values between zero and one.

How does the neural network learn? Neural networks represent a supervised learning method, requiring a large training set of complete records, including the target variable. As each observation from the training set is processed through the network, an output value is produced from the output node (assuming we have only one output node). This output value is then compared to the actual value of the target variable for this training set observation, and the error (actual-output) is calculated. This prediction error is analogous to the residuals in regression models. To measure how well the output predictions are fitting the actual target values, most neural network models use the sum of squared errors:

$$\text{SSE} = \sum_{\text{records}} \sum_{\text{output nodes}} (\text{actual-output})^2,$$

where the squared prediction errors are summed over all the output nodes and over all the records in the training set.

The problem is therefore to construct a set of model weights that will minimize this SSE. In this way, the weights are analogous to the parameters of a regression model. The "true" values for the weights that will minimize SSE are unknown, and our task is to estimate them, given the data. However, due to the nonlinear nature of the sigmoid functions permeating the network, there exists no closed-form solution for minimizing SSE, as there exists for least-squares regression. Most neural network models therefore use *backpropagation*, a gradient-descent optimization method, to help find the set of weights that will minimize SSE. Backpropagation takes the prediction error (actual-output) for a particular record, and percolates the error back through the network, assigning partitioned "responsibility" for the error to the various connections. The weights on these connections are then adjusted to decrease the error, using gradient descent.

However, as finding the best set of weights in a neural network is an optimization task, GAs are wonderfully suited to do so. The drawbacks of backpropagation include the tendency to become stuck at local minima (as it follows a single route through the weight space) and the requirement to calculate derivative or gradient information for each weight. Also, Unnikrishnan *et al.*[15] state that improper selection of initial weights in backpropagation will delay convergence. GAs, however, perform a global search, lessening the chances of becoming caught in a local minimum, although, of course, there can be no guarantees that the global minimum has been obtained. Also, GAs require no derivative or gradient information to be calculated. However, neural networks using GAs for training the weights will run slower than traditional neural networks using backpropagation.

GAs apply a much different search strategy than backpropagation. The gradient-descent methodology in backpropagation moves from one solution vector to another vector that is quite similar. The GA search methodology, however, can shift much more radically, generating a child chromosome that may be completely different than either parent. This behavior decreases the probability that GAs will become stuck in local optima.

Huang, Dorsey, and Boose[16] apply a neural network optimized with a GA to forecast financial distress in life insurance companies. Unnikrishnan, Mahajan, and Chu used GAs to optimize the weights in a neural network, which was used to model a three-dimensional ultrasonic positioning system. They represented the network weights in the form of chromosomes, similarly to Table 27.3 for the neural network weights in Figure 27.5. However, their chromosome was 51 weights long, reflecting their 5-4-4-3 topology of five input nodes, four nodes in each of two hidden layers, and three output nodes. The authors cite the length of the chromosome as the reason the model was outperformed both by a backpropagation neural network and a traditional linear model.

TABLE 27.3   Chromosome representing weights from neural network in Figure 27.5

W_{1A}	W_{1B}	W_{2A}	W_{2B}	W_{3A}	W_{3B}	W_{0A}	W_{0B}	W_{AZ}	W_{BZ}	W_{0Z}

David Montana and Lawrence Davis[17] provide an example of using GAs to optimize the weights in a neural network (adapted here from Mitchell). Their research task was to classify "lofargrams" (underwater sonic spectrograms) as either *interesting* or *not interesting*. Their neural network had a 4-7-10-1 topology, giving a total of 126 weights in their chromosomes. The fitness function used was the usual neural network metric, $\text{SSE} = \sum_{\text{records}} \sum_{\text{output nodes}} (\text{actual-output})^2$, except that the weights being adjusted represented the genes in the chromosome.

For the crossover operator, they used a modified discrete crossover. Here, for each non-input node in the child chromosome, a parent chromosome is selected at

[15]Nishant Unnikrishnan, Ajay Mahajan, and Tsuchin Chu, 2003. Intelligent system modeling of a three-dimensional ultrasonic positioning system using neural networks and genetic algorithms, in *Proceedings of the Institution for Mechanical Engineers*, **Vol 217**, Part I: J. Systems and Control Engineering.

[16]Chin-Sheng Huang, Robert Dorsey, and Mary Ann Boose, 1994. Life Insurer Financial Distress Prediction: A Neural Network Model, *Journal of Insurance Regulation*, Winter 94, **Vol 13**, Issue 2.

[17]David Montana and Lawrence Davis, 1989. Training feedforward networks using genetic algorithms. In *Proceeding of the International Joint Conference on Artificial Intelligence*. Morgan Kaufmann.

random, and the incoming links from the parent are copied to the child for that particular node. Thus, for each pair of parents, only one child is created. For the mutation operator, they used a random shock similar to the normal distribution mutation shown above. Because neural network weights are constrained to lie between −1 and 1, the resulting weights after application of the mutation must be checked that they do not stray outside this range.

The modified discrete crossover is illustrated in Table 27.4 and Figure 27.6. In this example, the weights incoming to Node A are supplied by Parent 1, and the weights incoming to nodes B and Z are supplied by parent 2 (shaded).

TABLE 27.4   Table of neural network weights indicating results of crossover

	W_{1A}	W_{1B}	W_{2A}	W_{2B}	W_{3A}	W_{3B}	W_{0A}	W_{0B}	W_{AZ}	W_{BZ}	W_{0Z}
Parent 1	0.1	−0.2	0.7	−0.6	0.4	0.9	−0.1	0.3	−0.5	0.8	−0.2
Parent 2	0.2	−0.4	0.5	−0.5	0.3	0.7	−0.2	0.1	−0.6	0.9	−0.3
Child	0.1	−0.4	0.7	−0.5	0.4	0.7	−0.1	0.1	−0.6	0.9	−0.3

The random shock mutation is illustrated in Table 27.5 and Figure 27.7. In this example, the mutation was applied to the weights incoming to node B only, for the child generated from the crossover operation. The new weights are not far from the old weights. Montana and Davis' GA-based neural network outperformed a back-propagation neural network, despite a total of 126 weights in their chromosomes.

27.8   WEKA: HANDS-ON ANALYSIS USING GENETIC ALGORITHMS

This exercise explores the use of WEKA's Genetic Search class to optimize (choose) a subset of inputs used to classify patients as having either benign or malignant forms of breast cancer. The input file *breast_cancer.arff* used in our experiment is adapted from the Wisconsin Breast Cancer Database. *Breast_cancer.arff* contains 683 instances after deleting 16 records containing one or more missing values. In addition, it contains nine numeric inputs ("sample code number" attribute deleted) and a target attribute *class* that takes on values 2 (benign) and 4 (malignant). Table 27.6 shows the ARFF header and first 10 instances from *breast_cancer.arff*:

Next, we load the input file and become familiar with the *class* distribution.

1. Click Explorer from the WEKA GUI Chooser dialog.
2. On the Preprocess tab, press Open file and specify the path to the input file, *breast_cancer.arff*.
3. Under Attributes (lower left), select the *class* attribute from the list.

The WEKA Preprocess tab displays the distribution for *class*, and indicates that 65% (444/683) of the records have value 2 (benign), while the remaining 35% (239/683) have value 4 (malignant), as shown in Figure 27.8.

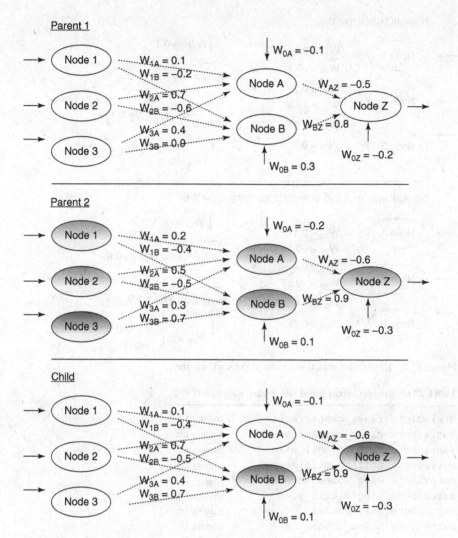

Figure 27.6   Illustrating crossover in neural network weights.

TABLE 27.5   Weights before and after mutation

	W_{1A}	W_{1B}	W_{2A}	W_{2B}	W_{3A}	W_{3B}	W_{0A}	W_{0B}	W_{AZ}	W_{BZ}	W_{0Z}
Before	0.1	−0.4	0.7	−0.5	0.4	0.7	−0.1	0.1	−0.6	0.9	−0.3
Shock	None	−0.05	None	−0.07	None	0.02	None	None	None	None	none
After	0.1	−0.45	0.7	−0.57	0.4	0.72	−0.1	0.1	−0.6	0.9	−0.3

Network before mutation

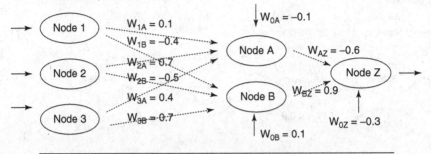

Network after mutation of weights incoming to node B

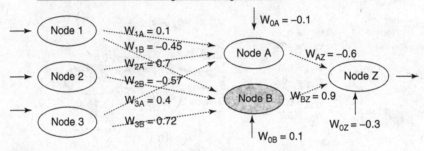

Figure 27.7 Illustrating mutation in neural network weights.

TABLE 27.6 Breast Cancer Input File *breast_cancer.arff*

```
@relation breast_cancer.arff        numeric
@attribute clump_thickness          numeric
@attribute uniform_cell_size        numeric
@attribute uniform_cell_shape       numeric
@attribute marg_adhesion            numeric
@attribute single_cell_size         numeric
@attribute bare_nuclei              numeric
@attribute bland_chromatin          numeric
@attribute normal_nucleoli          numeric
@attribute mitoses                  numeric
@attribute class                    {2,4}
@data
5,1,1,1,2,1,3,1,1,2
5,4,4,5,7,10,3,2,1,2
3,1,1,1,2,2,3,1,1,2
6,8,8,1,3,4,3,7,1,2
4,1,1,3,2,1,3,1,1,2
8,10,10,8,7,10,9,7,1,4
1,1,1,1,2,10,3,1,1,2
2,1,2,1,2,1,3,1,1,2
2,1,1,1,2,1,1,1,5,2
4,2,1,1,2,1,2,1,1,2
...
```

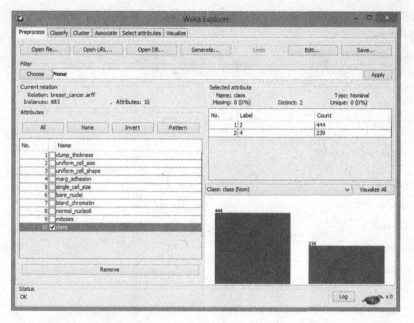

Figure 27.8   WEKA Explorer: *class* distribution.

Next, let us establish a baseline and classify the records using naïve Bayes with 10-fold cross-validation, where *all* nine attributes are input to the classifier.

1. Select the Classify tab.

2. Under Classifier, press the Choose button.

3. Select Classifiers → Bayes → Naïve Bayes from the navigation hierarchy.

4. By default, under Test options, notice that WEKA specifies Cross-validation. We will use this option for our experiment because we have a single data file.

5. Click Start.

The results in the Classifier output window show that naïve Bayes achieves a very impressive 96.34% (658/683) classification accuracy. This obviously leaves little room for improvement. Do you suppose all nine attributes are equally important to the task of classification? Is there possibly a subset of the nine attributes, when selected as input to naïve Bayes, which leads to improved (or comparable level of) classification accuracy?

Before determining the answers to these questions, let us review WEKA's approach to attribute selection. It is not unusual for real-world data sets to contain irrelevant, redundant, or noisy attributes, which ultimately contribute to degradation in classification accuracy. In contrast, removing nonrelevant attributes often leads to improved classification accuracy. WEKA's supervised attribute selection filter enables a combination of evaluation and search methods to be specified, where the objective is to determine a useful *subset* of attributes as input to a learning scheme.

WEKA contains a Genetic Search class with default options that include a population size of $n = 20$ chromosomes, crossover probability $p_c = 0.6$, and mutation probability $p_m = 0.033$. Figure 27.9 shows the default options available in the Genetic Search dialog.

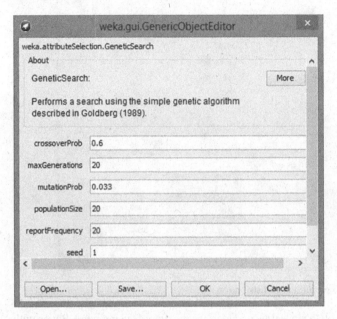

Figure 27.9   Genetic Search dialog.

As specified, the Genetic Search algorithm creates an initial set of 20 chromosomes. An individual chromosome in the initial population may consist of the attribute subset

1	4	6	7	9

where each of the five *genes* represents an attribute index. For example, the first gene in our example chromosome is the attribute *clump_thickness*, as represented by its index position = 1. In our configuration, the WrapperSubsetEval evaluation method serves as the fitness function $f(x)$ and calculates a fitness value for each chromosome. WrapperSubsetEval evaluates each of the attribute subsets (chromosomes) according to a specified learning scheme. In the example below we will specify naïve Bayes. This way, the usefulness of a chromosome is determined as a measure of the classification accuracy reported by naïve Bayes. In other words, the chromosomes leading to higher classification accuracy are more relevant and receive a higher fitness score.

Now, let us apply WEKA's Genetic Search class to our attribute set. To accomplish this task, we first have to specify the evaluator and search options for attribute selection.

1. Select the Classify tab.
2. Click the Choose button.

3. Select Classifiers → Meta → AttributeSelectedClassifier from the navigation hierarchy.

4. Now, next to the Choose button, click on the text "AttributeSelectedClassifier ..."

The AttributeSelectiedClassifier dialog appears as shown in Figure 27.10, where the default Classifier, Evaluator, and Search methods are displayed. Next, we will override these default options by specifying new classifier, evaluator, and search methods.

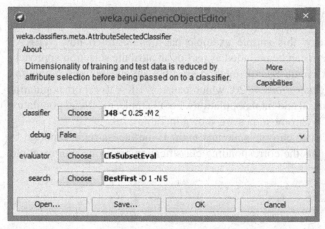

Figure 27.10   AttributeSelectedClassifier dialog.

1. Next to evaluator, press the Choose button.
2. Select AttributeSelection → WrapperSubsetEval from the navigation hierarchy.
3. Now, click on the text "WrapperSubsetEval" next to the evaluator Choose button. The WrapperSubsetEval dialog appears as shown in Figure 27.11. By default, WEKA specifies the ZeroR classifier.
4. Press the Choose button, next to classifier.
5. Here, select Classifiers → Bayes → Naïve Bayes from the navigation hierarchy.
6. Click OK to close the WrapperSubsetEval dialog. The evaluation method for AttributeSelection is now specified.
7. On the AttributeSelection dialog, press the Choose button next to search.
8. Select AttributeSelection → GeneticSearch from the navigation hierarchy.
9. Press OK to close the AttributeSelection dialog.

    The evaluator and search methods for attribute selection have been specified. Finally, we specify and execute the classifier.

10. Press the Choose button next to classifier.
11. Select Classifiers → Bayes → Naïve Bayes.
12. Press OK.

13. Now, under Test options, specify Use training set

14. Click Start

WEKA displays modeling results in the Explorer Panel. In particular, under Attributes, notice the list now shows seven predictor attributes, as shown in Table 27.7. That is, the two attributes *single_cell_size* and *mitoses* have been removed from the attribute list.

Naïve Bayes reports 96.93% (662/683) classification accuracy, which indicates the second model outperforms the first model by almost 0.05% (96.93% vs 96.34%). In this example, classification accuracy has increased where only seven of the nine attributes are specified as input. Although these results do not show a dramatic improvement in accuracy, this simple example has demonstrated how WEKA's Genetic Search algorithm can be included as part of an attribute selection approach.

By default, the Genetic Search method specifies default options *report frequency* = 20 and *maxgenerations* = 20, which cause WEKA to report population characteristics for the initial and final populations. For example, the initial population characteristics for the 20 chromosomes are shown in Table 27.8.

Here, each subset is a chromosome and *merit* is the fitness score reported by naïve Bayes, which equals the corresponding classification error rate. For example,

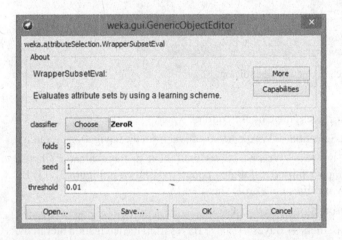

Figure 27.11   WrapperSubsetEval dialog.

TABLE 27.7   Attributes selected by the attribute selection method

```
Selected attributes:    1,2,3,4,6,7,8 : 7
                        clump_thickness
                        uniform_cell_size
                        uniform_cell_shape
                        marg_adhesion
                        bare_nuclei
                        bland_chromatin
                        normal_nucleoli
```

TABLE 27.8   Initial population characteristics reported by Genetic Search

```
Initial population
merit         scaled       subset
0.053         0.05777      4 6 7 9
0.04978       0.06014      1 2 3 4 7 9
0.03807       0.06873      1 2 3 4 6 9
0.05564       0.05584      6 7 8
0.13177       0            8
0.03953       0.06765      2 3 5 6 7 8
0.0448        0.06379      2 6 7
0.09048       0.03028      5 8
0.07028       0.0451       2
0.04275       0.06529      1 6 8 9
0.04187       0.06593      3 4 5 6 7 8
0.04275       0.06529      2 4 6 7 8
0.08492       0.03436      4 5
0.0612        0.05176      2 4 7
0.03865       0.0683       1 2 4 6 7 9
0.03807       0.06873      1 3 4 6 9
0.04275       0.06529      3 6 7 8 9
0.05329       0.05756      2 4 8
0.05271       0.05799      1 4 7 8
0.04275       0.06529      3 6 7 8 9
```

consider the chromosome {4, 6, 7, 9} reported in Table 27.8 with merit 0.053; this value corresponds[18] to the classification error rate reported by naïve Bayes using fivefold cross-validation when {4, 6, 7, 9} are specified as input.

Also, each chromosome's scaled fitness is reported in the *scaled* column, where WEKA uses the *linear scaling* technique to scale the values. By definition, the raw fitness and scaled fitness values have the linear relationship $f' = a \cdot f + b$, where f' and f are the scaled and raw fitness values, respectively. The constants a and b are chosen where $f'_{avg} = f_{avg}$ and $f'_{max} = C_{mult} \cdot f'_{avg}$. The constant C_{mult} represents the expected number of copies of the fittest individual in the population, and for small populations, it is typically set[19] to a value in the range of 1.2–2.0.

Therefore, by computing the average fitness values presented in Table 27.8, we obtain $f_{avg} = 0.055753$ and $f'_{avg} = 0.055755$, which agrees with the rule by which the constants a and b are chosen. Because the value for C_{mult} is not an option in WEKA, the fitness values from the last two rows from Table 27.8 are selected to solve the simultaneously equations for a and b, according to the relationship $f' = a \cdot f + b$:

$$0.05799 = 0.05271a + b$$
$$0.06529 = 0.04275a + b$$

---

[18]Actually, this value may differ slightly due to the value for the WrapperSubsetEval *threshold* option.
[19]WEKA sets this value internally.

Subtracting the second equation from the first, we obtain:

$$-0.0073 = 0.00996a$$

$$a = -\frac{0.0073}{0.00996} = -0.73293, \quad b = 0.096623$$

We use the definition $f'_{\max} = C_{\text{mult}} \cdot f_{\text{avg}}$ to determine $C_{\text{mult}} = \frac{f'_{\max}}{f_{\text{avg}}} = \frac{0.06873}{0.055753} = $ 1.23. Finally, observe that the fifth row in Table 27.8 has $f' = 0$. The raw fitness value of 0.13177 corresponds to the largest classification error in the population produced by chromosome {8}, and as a result, f' is mapped to zero to avoid the possibility of producing negatively scaled fitnesses.

In this exercise, we have analyzed a simple classification problem where Genetic Search was used to find an attribute subset that improved naïve Bayes classification accuracy, as compared to using the full set of attributes. Although this problem only has nine attributes, there are still $2^9 - 1 = 511$ possible attribute subsets that can be input to a classifier. Imagine building a classification model from a set of 100 inputs. Here, there are $2^{100} - 1 = 1.27 \times 10^{30}$ possible attribute subsets from which to choose. In situations such as these, Genetic Search techniques may prove helpful in determining useful attribute subsets.

Wisconsin Breast Cancer Database (January 8, 1991). Obtained from the University of Wisconsin Hospitals, Madison from Dr. William H. Wolberg.

THE R ZONE

Genetic algorithms

```
# Requires package "GA"
library("GA")
# Let fitness be the maximum of the
# function
n <- function(x) { dnorm(x,
    mean = 16, sd = 4) }
fit <- function(x) { n(x) }
ga1 <- ga(type="real-valued",
    fitness=fit, min = 0, max = 31)
summary(ga1)
plot(ga1)
ga1@solution
```

```
> summary(ga1)
+-----------------------------------+
|           Genetic Algorithm       |
+-----------------------------------+

GA settings:
Type                    = real-valued
Population size         = 50
Number of generations   = 100
Elitism                 =
Crossover probability   = 0.8
Mutation probability    = 0.1
Search domain
           x1
Min   0
Max  31

GA results:
Iterations              = 100
Fitness function value  = 0.09973557
Solution                =
           x1
[1,] 16

> ga1@solution
           x1
[1,] 16
```

R REFERENCES

R Core Team. *R: A language and environment for statistical computing*. Vienna, Austria: R Foundation for Statistical Computing; 2012. ISBN 3-900051-07-0, URL http://www.R-project.org/. Accessed 2014 Sep 30.

Scrucca, L (2013). GA: a package for genetic algorithms in R. *Journal of Statistical Software*, *53*(4), 1–37. URL http://www.jstatsoft.org/v53/i04/.

EXERCISES

CLARIFYING THE CONCEPTS

1. Match each of the following genetic algorithm terms with its definition or description.

Term	Definition
a. Selection	One of the candidate solutions to the problem.
b. Generation	Scales the chromosome fitness by the standard deviation of the fitnesses, thereby maintaining selection pressure at a constant rate.
c. Crowding	The operator that determines which chromosomes will reproduce.
d. Crossover	Genes in neighboring loci will often be crossed together, affecting the performance of the genetic algorithm.
e. Chromosome	The operator that introduces new information to the genetic pool to protect against premature convergence.
f. Positional bias	A feed-forward, completely connected, multilayer network.
g. Uniform crossover	A cycle through the genetic algorithm.
h. Mutation	One particularly fit chromosome generates too many clones and close copies of itself, thereby reducing population diversity.
i. Sigma scaling	The selection condition requiring that the genetic algorithm retains a certain number of the fittest chromosomes from one generation to the next.
j. Gene	The operator that performs recombination, creating two new offspring by combining the parents' genes in new ways.
k. Elitism	Each gene is randomly assigned to be that of either one parent or the other, with 50% probability.
l. Neural Network	A single bit of the candidate solution.

2. Discuss why the selection operator should be careful to balance fitness with diversity. Describe the dangers of an overemphasis on each.

3. Compare the strengths and weaknesses of using backpropagation and genetic algorithms for optimization in neural networks.

WORKING WITH THE DATA

4. Continue the example in the text, where the fitness is determined by the Normal (16, 4) distribution. Proceed to the end of the third iteration. Suppress mutation, and perform crossover only once, on the second iteration at locus four.

5. Calculate the child vectors for the whole arithmetic crossover example in the text. Use the parents indicated in the section on simple arithmetic crossover, with $\alpha = 0.5$. Comment on your results.

CHAPTER 6 HANDS-ON ANALYSIS

6. (Extra credit). Write a computer program for a simple genetic algorithm. Implement the example discussed in the text, using the Normal (16, 4) fitness function. Let the crossover rate be 0.6 and the mutation rate be 0.01. Start with the population of all integers 0–31. Generate 25 runs and measure the generation at which the optimal decision of $x = 16$ is encountered. If you have time, vary the crossover and mutation rates and compare the results.

7. Repeat the procedure using the *breast_cancer.arff* data set with WEKA by selecting an attribute subset using Genetic Search. This time, however, specify naïve Bayes with *use kernel estimator = true* for both attribute selection and 10-fold cross-validation. Now, contrast the classification results using the full set of attributes, as compared to the attribute subset selected using Genetic Search. Does classification accuracy improve?

## CHAPTER 28

IMPUTATION OF MISSING DATA

28.1 NEED FOR IMPUTATION OF MISSING DATA

In this world of big data, the problem of missing data is widespread. It is the rare database that contains no missing values at all. How the analyst deals with the missing data may change the outcome of the analysis, so it is important to learn methods for handling missing data that will not bias the results.

Missing data may arise from any of several different causes. Survey data may be missing because the responder refuses to answer a particular question, or simply skips a question by accident. Experimental observations may be missed due to inclement weather or equipment failure. Data may be lost through a noisy transmission, and so on.

In Chapter 2, we learned three common methods for handling missing data, which are as follows:

1. Replace the missing value with some constant, specified by the analyst.
2. Replace the missing value with the field mean (for numeric variables) or the mode (for categorical variables).
3. Replace the missing values with a value generated at random from the observed distribution of the variable.

We learned that there were problems with each of these methods, which could generate inappropriate data values that would bias our results. For example, in Chapter 2, a value of 400 cu. in. was generated for a vehicle whose cubic inches value was missing. However, this value did not take into account that the vehicle is Japanese, and there is no Japanese-made car in the database that has an engine size of 400 cu. in.

We therefore need *data imputation methods* that take advantage of the knowledge that the car is Japanese when calculating its missing cubic inches. In data imputation, we ask "What would be the most likely value for this missing value, given all the other attributes for a particular record?" For instance, an American car with 300 cu. in. and 150 hp would probably be expected to have more cylinders than a Japanese car with 100 cu. in. and 90 hp. This is called *imputation of missing data*. In

Data Mining and Predictive Analytics, First Edition. Daniel T. Larose and Chantal D. Larose.
© 2015 John Wiley & Sons, Inc. Published 2015 by John Wiley & Sons, Inc.

this chapter, we shall examine methods for imputing missing values for (i) continuous variables and (ii) categorical variables.

28.2 IMPUTATION OF MISSING DATA: CONTINUOUS VARIABLES

In Chapter 9, we introduced multiple regression using the *cereals* data set. It may be worthwhile to take a moment to review the characteristics of the data set by looking back at Chapter 9. We noted that there were four missing data values, which are as follows:

- Potassium content of Almond Delight
- Potassium content of Cream of Wheat
- Carbohydrates and sugars content of Quaker Oatmeal.

Before we use multiple regression to impute these missing values, we must first prepare the data for multiple regression. In particular, the categorical variables must be transformed into 0/1 dummy variables. We did so (not shown) for the variable *type*, turning it into a flag variable to indicate whether or not the cereal was cold cereal. We then derived a series of dummy variables for the variable *manufacturer*, with flags for Kellogg's, General Mills, Ralston, and so on.

We begin by using multiple regression to build a good regression model for estimating potassium content. Note that we will be using the variable *potassium* as the response, and not the original response variable, *rating*. The idea is to use the set of predictors (apart from potassium) to estimate the potassium content for our Almond Delight cereal. Thus, all the original predictors (minus potassium) represent the predictors, and *potassium* represents the response variable, for our regression model for imputing potassium content. Do not include the original response variable *rating* as a predictor for the imputation.

Because not all variables will be significant for predicting potassium, we apply the stepwise variable selection method of multiple regression. In stepwise regression,[1] the regression model begins with no predictors, then the most significant predictor is entered into the model, followed by the next most significant predictor. At each stage, each predictor is tested whether it is still significant. The procedure continues until all significant predictors have been entered into the model, and no further predictors have been dropped. The resulting model is usually a good regression model, although it is not guaranteed to be the global optimum.

Figure 28.1 shows the multiple regression results for the model chosen by the stepwise variable selection procedure. The regression equation is:

Estimated potassium

$$= -73.11 + 10.137(\text{Protein}) + 23.515(\text{Fiber}) + 1.6444(\text{Sugars})$$

$$+ 7.841(\text{Shelf}) + 70.61(\text{Weight}) - 22.1(\text{Kellogg's})$$

---

[1]See Chapter 9.

```
The regression equation is
Potass =  - 73.1 + 10.1 Protein + 23.5 Fiber + 1.64 Sugars + 7.84 Shelf
          + 70.6 Weight - 22.1 Kelloggs


74 cases used, 3 cases contain missing values


Predictor       Coef    SE Coef       T       P
Constant      -73.11      18.53   -3.94   0.000
Protein       10.137      2.946    3.44   0.001
Fiber         23.515      1.270   18.52   0.000
Sugars        1.6444     0.7334    2.24   0.028
Shelf          7.841      3.208    2.44   0.017
Weight         70.61      20.95    3.37   0.001
Kelloggs     -22.096      5.534   -3.99   0.000


S = 21.3976    R-Sq = 91.6%    R-Sq (adj) = 90.9%


Analysis of Variance

Source           DF        SS      MS       F       P
Regression        6    336060   56010  122.33   0.000
Residual Error   67     30676     458
Total            73    366736


Predicted Values for New Observations

New Obs    Fit   SE Fit       95% CI            95% PI
      1  77.97     4.41   (69.16, 86.77)   (34.36, 121.57)


Values of Predictors for New Observations

New Obs Protein    Fiber   Sugars   Shelf  Weight   Kelloggs
      1    2.00     1.00     8.00    3.00    1.00   0.000000
```

Figure 28.1   Multiple regression results for imputation of missing potassium values. (The predicted values section of this output is for Almond Delight only.)

To estimate the potassium content for Almond Delight, we plug in Almond Delight's values for the predictors in the regression equation:

Estimated potassium for Almond Delight

$$= -73.11 + 10.137(2) + 23.515(1) + 1.6444(8) + 7.841(3) + 70.61(1)$$

$$- 22.1(0) = 77.9672$$

That is, the estimated potassium in Almond Delight is 77.9672 mg. This, then, is our imputed value for Almond Delight's missing potassium value: 77.9672 mg.

We may use the same regression equation to estimate the potassium content for Cream of Wheat, plugging in Cream of Wheat's values for the predictors in the regression equation:

Estimated potassium for Cream of Wheat
$$= -73.11 + 10.137(3) + 23.515(1) + 1.6444(0) + 7.841(2) + 70.61(1)$$
$$- 22.1(0) = 67.108$$

The imputed value for Cream of Wheat's missing potassium value is 67.108 mg.

Next, we turn to imputing the missing values for the carbohydrates and sugars content of Quaker Oatmeal. A challenge here is that two predictors have missing values for Quaker Oatmeal. For example, if we build our regression model to impute carbohydrates, and the model requires information for sugars, what value do we use for Quaker Oats sugars, as it is missing? Using the mean or other such *ad hoc* substitute is unsavory, for the reasons mentioned earlier. Therefore, we will use the following approach:

Step 1. Build a regression model to impute carbohydrates; do not include sugars as a predictor.

Step 2. Construct a regression model to impute sugars, using the carbohydrates value found in step 1.

Thus, the values from steps 1 and 2 will represent our imputed values for sugars and carbohydrates. Note that we will include the earlier imputed values for potassium.

Step 1: The stepwise regression model for imputing carbohydrates, based on all the predictors except sugars, is as follows (to save space, the computer output is not shown):

Estimated carbohydrates
$$= 6.004 - 1.7741(\text{Fat}) + 0.06557(\text{Calories}) + 0.9297(\text{Protein})$$
$$+ 0.013364(\text{Sodium}) - 0.7331(\text{Fiber}) + 4.406(\text{Nabisco}) + 2.7(\text{Ralston})$$

(Note that sugars is not one of the predictors.) Then the imputed step 1 carbohydrates for Quaker Oats is as follows:

Estimated carbohydrates for Quaker Oats
$$= 6.004 - 1.7741(2) + 0.06557(100) + 0.9297(5) + 0.013364(0)$$
$$- 0.7331(2.7) + 4.406(0) + 2.7(0) = 11.682 \text{ g}$$

Step 2: We then replace the missing carbohydrates value for Quaker Oats with 11.682 in the data set. The stepwise regression model for imputing sugars is:

Estimated sugars
$$= 0.231 + 0.16307(\text{Calories}) - 1.5664(\text{Fat}) - 1.04574(\text{Carbohydrates})$$
$$- 0.8997(\text{Protein}) + 1.329(\text{Cups}) + 7.934(\text{Weight}) - 0.34937(\text{Fiber})$$
$$+ 1.342(\text{Ralston})$$

Estimated sugars for Quaker Oats

$$= 0.231 + 0.16307(100) - 1.5664(2) - 1.04574(11.682) - 0.8997(5)$$
$$+ 1.329(0.67) + 7.934(1) - 0.34937(2.7) + 1.342(0) = 4.572 \text{ g}$$

We insert 4.572 for the missing sugars value for Quaker Oats in the data set, so that there now remain no missing values in the data set.

Now, ambitious programmers may wish to (i) use the imputed 4.572 g sugars value to impute a more precise value for carbohydrates, (ii) use that more precise value for carbohydrates to go back and obtain a more precise value for sugars, and (iii) repeat steps (i) and (ii) until convergence. However, the estimates obtained using a single application of steps 1 and 2 above usually result in a useful approximation of the missing values.

When there are several variables with many missing values, the above step-by-step procedure may be onerous, without recourse to a recursive programming language. In this case, perform the following:

Step 1: Impute the values of the variable with the *fewest* missing values. Use only the variables with no missing values as predictors. If no such predictors are available, use the set of predictors with the fewest missing values (apart from the variable you are predicting, of course).

Step 2: Impute the values of the variable with the next fewest missing values, using similar predictors as used in step 1.

Step 3: Repeat step 2 until all missing values have been imputed.

28.3 STANDARD ERROR OF THE IMPUTATION

Clients may wish to have an idea of the *precision* of an imputed value. When estimating or imputing anything, analysts should try to provide a measure of the precision of their estimate or imputation. In this case, the *standard error of the imputation*[2] is used. The formula for the simple linear regression case is:

$$\text{Standard error of the imputation} = \text{SEI} = s \cdot \sqrt{1 + \frac{1}{n} + \frac{(x_p - \bar{x})^2}{(n-1)s_x^2}}$$

where s is the standard error of the estimate for the regression, x_p is the value of the known predictor for the particular record, $\bar{x}$ represents the mean value of the predictor across all records, and s_x^2 represents the variance of the predictor values.

For multiple regression (as used here), the formula for SEI is more complex and is best left to the software. Minitab reports SEI as "SE Fit." In Figure 28.1, where we were imputing Almond Delight's missing potassium value, the standard error of the imputation is SEI = SE Fit = 4.41 mg. This is interpreted as meaning that, in

---

[2]This is from the same formula used to find prediction intervals for the value of a randomly chosen y in simple linear regression.

repeated samples of Almond Delight cereal, the typical prediction error for imputing potassium, using the predictors in Figure 28.1, is 1.04 mg.

28.4 IMPUTATION OF MISSING DATA: CATEGORICAL VARIABLES

One may use any classification algorithm to impute the missing values of categorical variables. We will illustrate using CART (classification and regression trees, Chapter 8). The data file *classifyrisk* is a small data file containing 6 fields and 246 records. The categorical predictors are *maritalstatus* and *mortgage*; the continuous predictors are *income*, *age*, and number of *loans*. The target is *risk*, a dichotomous field with values *good risk* and *bad loss*. The data file *classifyrisk_missing* contains a missing value for the marital status of record number 19.

To impute this missing value, we apply CART, with *maritalstatus* as the target field, and the other predictors as the predictors for the CART model. Z-score standardization is carried out on the continuous variables. The resulting CART model is shown in Figure 28.2.

Record 19 represents a customer who has the following field values: *loans* = 1, *mortgage* = y, *age_Z* = 1.450, *income_Z* = 1.498, thus representing a customer who is older than average, with higher income than average, with a mortgage and one other loan. The root node split is on *loans*; we follow the branch down "loans in [0 1]." The next split checks whether *income_Z* is greater than 0.812. We follow the branch down "income_Z > 0.812," which ends at a leaf node containing 30 records,

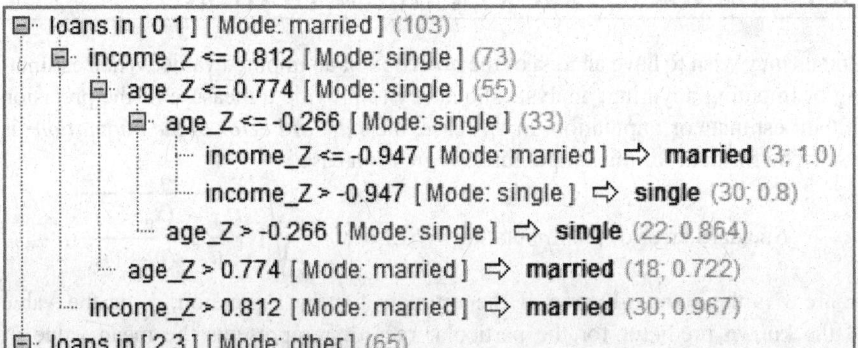

```
⊟·· loans in [ 0 1 ] [ Mode: married ] (103)
    ⊟·· income_Z <= 0.812 [ Mode: single ] (73)
        ⊟·· age_Z <= 0.774 [ Mode: single ] (55)
            ⊟·· age_Z <= -0.266 [ Mode: single ] (33)
                ┊··· income_Z <= -0.947 [ Mode: married ] ⇨ **married** (3; 1.0)
                └··· income_Z > -0.947 [ Mode: single ] ⇨ **single** (30; 0.8)
            └··· age_Z > -0.266 [ Mode: single ] ⇨ **single** (22; 0.864)
        └··· age_Z > 0.774 [ Mode: married ] ⇨ **married** (18; 0.722)
    └··· income_Z > 0.812 [ Mode: married ] ⇨ **married** (30; 0.967)
⊟·· loans in [ 2 3 ] [ Mode: other ] (65)
    ⊟·· loans in [ 0 1 2 ] [ Mode: married ] (49)
        ┊··· age_Z <= -0.682 [ Mode: married ] ⇨ **married** (13; 0.923)
        ⊟·· age_Z > -0.682 [ Mode: other ] (36)
            ┊··· income_Z <= 0.213 [ Mode: other ] ⇨ **other** (30; 0.667)
            └··· income_Z > 0.213 [ Mode: married ] ⇨ **married** (6; 1.0)
    └··· loans in [ 3 ] [ Mode: other ] ⇨ **other** (16; 1.0)
```

Figure 28.2   CART model for imputing the missing value of *maritalstatus*.

96.7% of which have a marital status of *married*. Thus, our imputed value for the marital status of record 19 is *married*, with a confidence level of 96.7%.

28.5 HANDLING PATTERNS IN MISSINGNESS

The analyst should remain aware that imputation of missing data represents replacement. The data value is now no longer missing; rather, its "missingness" has been replaced with an imputed data value. However, there may be information in the pattern of that missingness, information that will be wasted unless some indicator is provided to the algorithm indicating that this data value had been missing. For example, suppose a study is being made of the effect of a new fertility drug on premenopausal women, and the variable *age* has some missing values. It is possible that there is a correlation between the age of the subject and the likelihood that the subject declined to give their age. Thus, it may happen that the missing values for *age* are more likely to occur for greater values of *age*. Because greater age is associated with infertility, the analyst must account for this possible correlation, by flagging which cases have had their missing ages imputed.

One method to account for patterns in missingness is simply to construct a flag variable, as follows:

$$age\_missing = \begin{cases} 1 & \text{if age value imputed} \\ 0 & \text{otherwise} \end{cases}$$

Add *age_missing* to the model, and interpret its effect. For example, in a regression model, perhaps the *age_missing* dummy variable has a negative regression coefficient, with a very small p-value, indicating significance. This would indicate that indeed there is a pattern in the missingness, namely that the effect size of the fertility drug for those cases whose age value was missing tended to be smaller (or more negative). The flag variable could also be used for classification models, such as CART or C4.5.

Another method for dealing with missing data is to reduce the *weight* that the case wields in the analysis. This does not account for the patterns in missingness, but rather represents a compromise between no indication of missingness and completely omitting the record. For example, suppose a data set has 10 predictors, and Record 001 has one predictor value missing. Then this missing value could be imputed, and Record 001 assigned a weight, say, of 0.90. Then Record 002, with 2 of 10 field values missing, would be assigned a weight of 0.80. The specific weights assigned depend on the particular data domain and research question of interest. The algorithms would then reduce the amount of influence the records with missing data have on the analysis, proportional to how many fields are missing.

REFERENCE

The classic text on missing data is:

Little R, Rubin D. Statistical Analysis with Missing Data. second ed. Wiley; 2002.

THE R ZONE

Prepare Cereals data

```
# Read in Cereals dataset
cereal <- read.csv(file = "C:/.../cereals.txt",
    stringsAsFactors=FALSE,
    header=TRUE,
    sep="\t")
cereal$Cold <- c(rep(0, length(cereal$Type)))
cereal$Manuf_N <- cereal$Manuf_Q <- cereal$Manuf_K <- cereal$Manuf_R <-
    cereal$Manuf_G <- cereal$Manuf_P <- c(rep(0, length(cereal$Manuf)))
for (i in 1:length(cereal$Type)) {
    if(cereal$Type[i] == "C") cereal$Cold[i] <- 1
    if(cereal$Manuf[i] == "N") cereal$Manuf_N[i] <- 1
    if(cereal$Manuf[i] == "Q") cereal$Manuf_Q[i] <- 1
    if(cereal$Manuf[i] == "K") cereal$Manuf_K[i] <- 1
    if(cereal$Manuf[i] == "R") cereal$Manuf_R[i] <- 1
    if(cereal$Manuf[i] == "G") cereal$Manuf_G[i] <- 1
    if(cereal$Manuf[i] == "P") cereal$Manuf_P[i] <- 1
}
```

Build the regression model

```
reg1 <- lm(Potass ~ Calories +
    Protein + Fat + Sodium +
    Fiber + Carbo + Sugars +
    Vitamins + Shelf +
    Weight + Cups + Cold +
    Manuf_P + Manuf_R +
    Manuf_G + Manuf_K +
    Manuf_Q + Manuf_N,
    data = cereal)
step1 <- step(reg1,
    direction = "both")
summary(step1)
```

```
> summary(step1)

Call:
lm(formula = Potass ~ Calories + Protein + Fat + Fiber + Carbo +
    Sugars + Vitamins + Shelf + weight + Cold + Manuf_P + Manuf_K,
    data = cereal)

Residuals:
    Min      1Q  Median      3Q     Max
-44.006 -10.655  -0.201  12.593  55.608

Coefficients:
            Estimate Std. Error t value Pr(>|t|)
(Intercept) -41.3976    29.9285  -1.383  0.17164
Calories     -0.7050     0.5326  -1.324  0.19051
Protein      10.7344     3.6037   2.979  0.00415 **
Fat           8.5642     5.7527   1.489  0.14172
Fiber        24.5904     2.0583  11.947  < 2e-16 ***
Carbo         3.4000     2.4375   1.395  0.16811
Sugars        4.6504     2.2746   2.044  0.04523 *
vitamins     -0.1644     0.1263  -1.301  0.19815
Shelf         9.0983     3.4874   2.609  0.01141 *
weight       72.9586    36.2560   2.012  0.04861 *
Cold        -40.0808    22.3437  -1.794  0.07780 .
Manuf_P     -11.5908     8.3905  -1.381  0.17219
Manuf_K     -20.7905     6.3381  -3.280  0.00172 **
---
Signif. codes:  0 '***' 0.001 '**' 0.01 '*' 0.05 '.' 0.1 ' ' 1

Residual standard error: 20.61 on 61 degrees of freedom
  (3 observations deleted due to missingness)
Multiple R-squared: 0.9293,  Adjusted R-squared: 0.9154
F-statistic: 66.84 on 12 and 61 DF,  p-value: < 2.2e-16
```

Run the final regression model

```
# Include only predictors
# significant in the
# previous analysis
reg2<- lm(Potass ~ Protein +
    Fiber + Sugars + Shelf +
    Weight + Manuf_K,
    data = cereal)
summary(reg2)
```

```
> summary(reg2)

Call:
lm(formula = Potass ~ Protein + Fiber + Sugars + Shelf + Weight +
    Manuf_K, data = cereal)

Residuals:
    Min      1Q  Median      3Q     Max
-45.201 -15.013  -0.373  13.470  60.668

Coefficients:
            Estimate Std. Error t value Pr(>|t|)
(Intercept) -73.1079    18.5342  -3.944 0.000194 ***
Protein      10.1374     2.9456   3.442 0.001001 **
Fiber        23.5150     1.2698  18.518  < 2e-16 ***
Sugars        1.6444     0.7334   2.242 0.028263 *
Shelf         7.8412     3.2081   2.444 0.017155 *
Weight       70.6058    20.9513   3.370 0.001251 **
Manuf_K     -22.0963     5.5336  -3.993 0.000164 ***
---
Signif. codes:  0 '***' 0.001 '**' 0.01 '*' 0.05 '.' 0.1 ' ' 1

Residual standard error: 21.4 on 67 degrees of freedom
  (3 observations deleted due to missingness)
Multiple R-squared: 0.9164,  Adjusted R-squared: 0.9089
F-statistic: 122.3 on 6 and 67 DF,  p-value: < 2.2e-16
```

Use the model to estimate missing values

```
# Almond Delight is record 5
# Cream of Wheat is record 21
predict(reg2, newdata = cereal[5,])
predict(reg2, newdata = cereal[21,])
```

```
> predict(reg2, newdata = cereal[5,])
       5
77.96659
> predict(reg2, newdata = cereal[21,])
      21
67.10763
```

Prepare ClassifyRisk data, and open the required libraries

```
risk <- read.csv(file = "C:/ ... /classifyrisk.txt",
    stringsAsFactors=FALSE, header=TRUE, sep="\t")
risk$loans_n <- (risk$loans - min(risk$loans))/(max(risk$loans)-min(risk$loans))
# And so on for the continuous variables
library(rpart); library(rpart.plot)
# Make Record 19's marital status missing, use to create a new dataset
risk[19,4]<-NA; criskna <- risk
```

Apply CART to impute marital status

```
imp1 <- rpart(marital_status ~
    mortgage + loans_n + age_n +
    income_n,
    data = criskna, model = TRUE,
    method = "class")
rpart.plot(imp1)
# Predict marital status of Record 19
predict(imp1, criskna[19,])
```

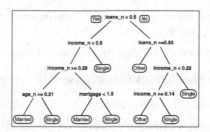

R REFERENCES

Milborrow S. (2012). rpart.plot: Plot rpart models. An enhanced version of plot.rpart. R package version 1.4-3. http://CRAN.R-project.org/package=rpart.plot.

R Core Team. *R: A language and environment for statistical computing*. Vienna, Austria: R Foundation for Statistical Computing; 2012. ISBN 3-900051-07-0, URL http://www.R-project.org/. Accessed 2014 Sep 30.

Therneau T, Atkinson B, and Ripley B (2013). rpart: Recursive Partitioning. R package version 4.1-3. http://CRAN.R-project.org/package=rpart.

EXERCISES

1. Why do we need to impute missing data?

2. When imputing a continuous variable, explain what we use for the set of predictors, and for the target variable.

3. When imputing a missing value, do we include the original target variable as one of the predictor variables for the data imputation model? Why or why not?

4. Describe what we should do if there are many variables with many missing values.

5. On your own, think of a data set where a potential pattern in missingness would represent good information.

6. State two methods for handling patterns in missingness.

HANDS-ON ANALYSIS

Use the *cereals* data set for Exercises 7–12. Report the standard error of each imputation.

7. Impute the potassium content of Almond Delight using multiple regression.

8. Impute the potassium content of Cream of Wheat.

9. Impute the carbohydrates value of Quaker Oatmeal.

10. Impute the sugars value of Quaker Oatmeal.

11. Insert the value obtained in Exercise 10 for the sugars value of Quaker Oatmeal, and impute the carbohydrates value of Quaker Oatmeal.

12. Compare the standard errors for the imputations obtained in Exercises 9 and 11. Explain what you find.

13. Open the *ClassifyRisk_Missing* data set. Impute the missing value for marital status.

Use the *ClassifyRisk_Missing2* data set for Exercises 14–15.

14. Impute all missing values in the data set. Explain the ordering that you are using.

15. Report the standard errors (for continuous values) or confidence levels (for categorical values) for your imputations in Exercise 14.

PART VIII

CASE STUDY: PREDICTING RESPONSE TO DIRECT-MAIL MARKETING

CHAPTER *29*

CASE STUDY, PART 1: BUSINESS UNDERSTANDING, DATA PREPARATION, AND EDA

In Chapters 29–31 we shall bring together much of what we have learned in this book in a detailed Case Study: *Predicting Response to Direct-Mail Marketing*. We follow the here in Chapter 29, we (i) enunciate our objectives in the Business Understanding Phase, (ii) get a feel for the data set in Part 1 of the Data Understanding Phase, prepare our data in the Data Preparation Phase, and extract some useful information in Part 2 of the Data Understanding Phase: exploratory data analysis (EDA). Then, in Chapter 30, we learn about possible segments in the customer database using clustering analysis and we investigate relationships among the predictors using principal components analysis. Finally, in Chapter 31, we apply the rich assortment of classification techniques at our disposal in the Modeling Phase, and make recommendations on which models to move forward with in the Evaluation Phase.

29.1 CROSS-INDUSTRY STANDARD PRACTICE FOR DATA MINING

The Case Study in Chapters 29–31 will be carried out using the cross-industry standard process for data mining (CRISP-DM). According to CRISP-DM, a given data mining project has a life cycle consisting of six phases, as illustrated in Figure 29.1. The details of CRISP-DM are discussed in Chapter 1; here, we but recapitulate the outline of the process.

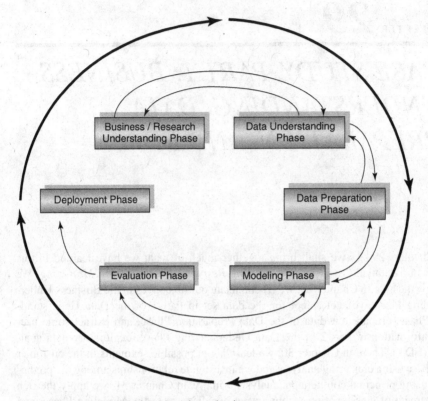

Figure 29.1   CRISP-DM is an iterative, adaptive process.

CRISP-DM: THE SIX PHASES

1. Business (or Research) Understanding Phase
2. Data Understanding Phase
3. Data Preparation Phase
4. Modeling Phase
5. Evaluation Phase
6. Deployment Phase

In practice, the data preparation phase often precedes or is interleaved with the data understanding (EDA) phase, as one may wish to clean up the data before trying to extract information from it. In this chapter, we approach these phases as follows:

29.2   BUSINESS UNDERSTANDING PHASE

In the business understanding phase, managers and analysts need to be crystal clear on communicating what the primary objectives of the project are. It often happens that lack of communication/understanding of the primary objectives leads analysts to fashion fine solutions to the wrong problems, like climbing to the top of the ladder, only to find that it is leaning against the wrong wall. To avoid this, a statement of the primary and secondary objectives of the analysis should be agreed upon, by both managers and analysts.

In this detailed Case Study, we are acting as analysts for a retail clothing store chain. The *clothing_store* data set[1] represents actual data provided by a clothing store chain in New England. Data were collected on 51 fields for 28,799 customers. More information about the data set is provided in the Data Understanding Phase below. Here follows the statement of the primary and secondary objectives of the analysis.

PRIMARY OBJECTIVE

Develop a classification model that will maximize profits for direct-mail marketing.

SECONDARY OBJECTIVE

Develop better understanding of our clientele through EDA, component profiles, and cluster profiles.

For this Case Study, our data mining task is a classification problem. We are to classify which customers will respond to a direct-mail marketing promotion, based on information collected about the customers. However, it will not be sufficient just to derive the classifier with the most accurate predictions. The analyst needs to consider how the classification problem fits into the client's business goals. As we said, for the clothing store, the primary objective is to *maximize profits*. Therefore, the goal of our classification model should also be to maximize profits, rather than simply to report impressive values for model accuracy, sensitivity, and specificity. To maximize profit, *data-driven misclassification costs* will be derived and applied.

---

[1] Available at the book web site: www.dataminingconsultant.com.

The specification of data-driven misclassification costs may be considered to belong to the business understanding phase. However, as we will not use the resulting cost matrix until the modeling phase, the derivation of these misclassification costs is postponed until the beginning of the modeling phase (see Chapter 30).

The secondary objective is to develop a better understanding of our customer database using market segment profiles. Specifically, we shall seek to uncover interesting clusters and principal components in our clientele, and, using profiles of these clusters and components, learn more about the different types of customers we have.

29.3   DATA UNDERSTANDING PHASE, PART 1: GETTING A FEEL FOR THE DATA SET

In the data understanding phase, we become more familiar with the data set using EDA, graphical and descriptive statistical methods for learning about data. The *Clothing_store_training_test* data set contains information about 28,799 customers, on the following 51 fields:

- Customer ID: unique, encrypted customer identification
- Zip code
- Number of purchase visits
- Total net sales
- Average amount spent per visit
- Amount spent at each of four different franchises (four variables)
- Amount spent in the past month, the past 3 months, and the past 6 months
- Amount spent the same period last year (SPLY)
- Gross margin percentage
- Number of marketing promotions on file
- Number of days the customer has been on file
- Number of days between purchases
- Markdown percentage on customer purchases
- Number of different product classes purchased
- Number of coupons used by the customer
- Total number of individual items purchased by the customer
- Number of stores the customer shopped at
- Number of promotions mailed in the past year
- Number of promotions responded to in the past year
- Promotion response rate for the past year
- Product uniformity (low score = diverse spending patterns)
- Lifetime average time between visits
- Microvision® Lifestyle Cluster Type

- Percent of returns
- Flag: credit card user
- Flag: valid phone number on file
- Flag: web shopper
- Fifteen variables providing the proportions spent by the customer on specific classes of clothing, including sweaters, knit tops, knit dresses, blouses, jackets, career pants, casual pants, shirts, dresses, suits, outerwear, jewelry, fashion, legwear, and the collectibles line. Also, a variable showing the brand of choice (encrypted).
- Target variable: response to promotion

Assume that these data are based on a direct-mail marketing campaign conducted last year. We shall use this information to develop classification models for this year's marketing campaign.

It is never a bad idea when beginning a new project to take a quick look at the actual data values. Here, Figure 29.2 shows some of the data values for the first 20 records for the first handful of fields.

	ID	Zip_code	Days_since_purchase	Purchase_visits	Total_net_sales	Credit_card	Ave_amount_spent	Brand	PSWEATERSraw
1	9955600066402	1001	208	2	368.46	0	184.23	11	0.18
2	9955600073501	1028	6	4	258.00	1	64.50	11	0.26
3	9955600076313	1056	327	2	77.00	0	38.50	11	1.00
4	9955600078045	1118	66	8	846.06	1	105.75	11	0.38
5	9955600078517	1107	49	1	87.44	0	87.44	11	0.20
6	9955600079035	1106	26	2	120.00	0	60.00	11	0.00
7	9955600081205	1108	98	3	450.98	0	150.32	11	0.16
8	9955600088237	1106	64	5	521.20	1	104.24	11	0.16
9	9955600088723	1118	145	1	782.08	1	782.08	11	0.12
10	9955600089274	1106	356	1	79.00	0	79.00	11	0.00
11	9955600093031	1104	264	1	318.50	0	318.50	11	0.24
12	9955600093053	1104	23	12	1663.46	1	138.62	11	0.25
13	9955600096452	1108	157	3	342.97	1	114.32	11	0.16
14	9955600099772	1201	144	7	632.08	1	90.29	11	0.38
15	9955600100984	1267	57	2	139.97	0	69.98	11	0.00
16	9955600102456	1267	118	1	172.99	0	172.99	16	0.00
17	9955600111322	1331	12	5	106.38	0	21.27	16	0.12
18	9955600113010	1373	276	1	87.48	0	87.48	16	0.85
19	9955600113573	1452	48	4	491.17	1	122.79	16	0.19
20	9955600114505	1462	29	4	107.21	0	26.80	16	1.00

Figure 29.2   A quick look at the data.

The ID field uniquely identifies each customer (not transaction) in the data set. Looking at the zip code field we immediately spot a problem. American zip codes have five digits; why do these have only four digits? Actually, this is a common problem with zip codes located in New England, which have zero as their initial digit. Somewhere along the line, the zip code field was set to a numeric variable, for which initial zeroes are omitted. We need to replace these initial zeros; one way to perform this is to derive a new zip code field with the following instruction:

if length(ZIP_CODE) = 4 then "0" >< ZIP_CODE else ZIP_CODE endif

where the "><" notation represents "concatenate." For example, the zip code for the first record in Figure 29.2, "1001," should really be "01001," the zip code for Agawam, Massachusetts.

The brand field is using digits to represent a categorical field. This is a potential minefield that may confuse downstream modeling algorithms. The field should be repopulated with letter values rather than numbers. Similarly, the credit card flag field uses 0/1 values, which certain algorithms may incorrectly try to apply operations to that should be reserved for continuous values (e.g., principal components analysis). Therefore, the analyst should be careful with fields like these, and may prefer to substitute F/T values for the 0/1 values. However, 0/1 values for a flag variable are useful as indicator variable predictors in regression and logistic regression. No other major problems leap out at us from Figure 29.2. Note that PSWEATERSraw represents a proportion, but may have been expressed as a percentage instead.

Figure 29.3 shows us an overview of some of the continuous predictors, including a histogram with an overlay of the response (dark = positive response), and some summary statistics. We note immediately that some of the predictors are quite skewed, and will benefit from transformations (discussed below). We may even get a hint of some EDA-flavored results: Responders seem to favor greater days on file and lower average days between purchases.

Field	Sample Graph	...	Min	Max	Mean	Std. Dev	Skewness
Gross_margin_%raw			-6.46	0.99	0.52	0.17	-5.90
Tot_#_promos_on_file			0	38	11.54	7.14	0.16
Days_on_file			1	717	436.92	192.97	-0.24
Ave_days_betw_purchases			1.00	717.00	171.27	146.97	1.61
Markdown_%			0.00	0.95	0.19	0.13	0.30
Tot_#_product_classes			1	37	7.13	5.34	1.30
Coupons_used			0	32	0.75	1.67	4.32
Num_indiv_items_purchased			1	743	17.16	24.80	6.56
Num_stores			1	33	2.34	1.61	2.43

Figure 29.3 Overview of some of the continuous predictors.

Analysts should never fail to account for missing data. As we discussed in earlier chapters, neglecting to account for missing data, or accounting for missing data in an inappropriate manner, can have deleterious effects on model efficacy. Thankfully, Figure 29.4 indicates that here are no missing values in our data.

Next, what is the overall proportion of responders to the direct-mail marketing promotion? Figure 29.5 shows that only 4762 of the 28,799 customers, or 16.54%, responded to last year's marketing campaign (1 indicates response, 0 indicates nonresponse.) As the proportion of responders is so small, we may decide to apply balancing to the data before modeling.

One of the variables, the Microvision Lifestyle Cluster Type, contains the market segmentation category for each customer, as defined by Nielsen Claritas. There are 50 segmentation categories, labeled 1–50; the distribution of the most prevalent 18 cluster types over the customer database is given in Figure 29.6.

Audit	Quality	Annotations			

Complete fields (%): 100%   Complete records (%): 100%

Field	Measurement		% Complete	Valid Records
Ⓐ Zip code	🔵 Nominal		100	28799
◇ Days since purchase	🔷 Continuous		100	28799
◇ Purchase visits	🔷 Continuous		100	28799
◈ Total net sales	🔷 Continuous		100	28799
◇ Credit card	🔵 Flag		100	28799
◈ Ave amount spent	🔷 Continuous		100	28799
◇ Brand	🔵 Nominal		100	28799
◈ PSWEATERSraw	🔷 Continuous		100	28799
◈ PKNIT TOPSraw	🔷 Continuous		100	28799

Figure 29.4   All fields and records are 100% complete: no missing data.

Value	Proportion	%	Count
0		83.46	24037
1		16.54	4762

Figure 29.5   Most customers are nonresponders.

Value	Proportion	%	Count
10		12.11	3488
1		9.43	2716
4		7.93	2284
16		6.57	1893
8		4.97	1430
15		4.61	1327
11		4.52	1301
18		4.25	1224
5		4.23	1219
23		4.02	1158
38		4.01	1155
3		3.15	906
12		3.1	893
6		2.86	823
25		2.24	646
20		1.85	532
24		1.69	487
35		1.68	483

Figure 29.6   The 20 most prevalent Microvision® Lifestyle Cluster Types.

The six most common lifestyle cluster types in our data set are:

1. Cluster 10. **Home Sweet Home**. Families, medium-high income and education, managers/professionals, technical/sales.

2. Cluster 1. **Upper Crust**. Metropolitan families, very high income and education, homeowners, manager/professionals.

3. Cluster 4. **Mid-Life Success**. Families, very high education, high income, managers/professionals, technical/sales.

4. Cluster 16. **Country Home Families**. Large families, rural areas, medium education, medium income, precision/crafts.

5. Cluster 8. **Movers and Shakers**. Singles, couples, students and recent graduates, high education and income, managers/professionals, technical/sales.

6. Cluster 15. **Great Beginnings**. Young, singles and couples, medium-high education, medium income, some renters, managers/professionals, technical/sales.

Overall, the clothing store seems to attract a prosperous clientele with fairly high income and education. Cluster 1, *Upper Crust*, represents the wealthiest of the 50 cluster types, and is the second most prevalent category among our customers. Unfortunately, however, the Microvision variable is more useful for customer description than for modeling, as its values do not help us discern between responders and nonresponders (not shown.) Now, normally, our policy is to retain variables for the modeling stage, even if they do not look significant at the EDA stage. However, because the Microvision variable contains so many different values, its inclusion in certain models (such as logistic regression) can degrade model performance. Thus, we will omit this variable from our modeling.

29.4 DATA PREPARATION PHASE

Now that we have a feel for the data set, we turn to the important task of preparing the data for analysis. There are several issues, starting with the unusual issue of negative amounts spent.

29.4.1 Negative Amounts Spent?

For many of the amounts-spent fields and the proportions-spent fields, some of the customers have negative values for the amount or proportion of money spent. See Figure 29.7, where the minimum values for a selection of these variables are negative. How can this be? Now, the data were collected within a particular time period, which is unspecified, perhaps a month or a quarter. It is possible for a customer to have bought some clothing in a prior period, and returned the purchased clothing in the time period from which the data are collected. If this customer also did not make any major purchases during the time period of interest, then the net sales for this customer would be negative.

These negative amounts and proportions represent a problem in two ways. First, if we are to apply a transformation, such as the natural log or square root transformation, then we would prefer to be dealing with nonnegative values. Second, if the customers with negative amount spent are more likely than those with zero amount spent to respond to the direct-mail solicitation, then our models may be confused by this, incorrectly expecting the negatives to not respond.

Field	Sample Graph		Min	Max	Mean	Std. Dev	Skewness
PSUITSraw			-0.59	1.00	0.03	0.13	5.01
POUTERWEARraw			-0.73	1.00	0.02	0.10	7.30
PJEWELRYraw			-0.11	1.00	0.01	0.04	9.76
PFASHIONraw			-0.67	1.00	0.03	0.08	5.82
PLEGWEARraw			-0.10	1.00	0.01	0.05	10.81
PCOLLSPNDraw			-0.44	1.00	0.07	0.18	3.03
Spent_at_AM_storeraw			-292.97	10642.72	14.06	142.88	27.02
Spent_at_PS_storeraw			-230.82	17946.90	147.52	411.12	11.04

Figure 29.7   The Min values indicate negative amounts spent. How can this be? What should we do about it?

Now, we have a range of options, for how to deal with these negative values.

- Option 1: Treat them as data-entry errors, and either delete the relevant records or apply imputation of missing data.
- Option 2: Leave them as they are.
- Option 3: Change the negative values to zero values.
- Option 4: Take the absolute value of the negative values.

To help us decide how to handle the negative amounts spent problem, let us compare the response rate of these negatives to two other types of customers, those with zero amount spent, and those with positive amount spent. Figure 29.8 shows that 21.57% of those with negative amount spent at the PS store responded positively, compared to 22.19% of those with positive amount spent, and 11.98% of those with zero amount spent. Thus, the customers with negative amount spent have a similar response rate to those with a positive amount spent, both of which are nearly double the response rate of those with zero amount spent. We therefore proceed to take the absolute value of all fields with negative amounts spent or negative proportions spent.

Response		Neg	Pos	Zero
0	Count	80	9914	14043
	Column %	78.43	77.81	88.02
1	Count	22	2828	1912
	Column %	21.57	22.19	11.98

Figure 29.8   Those with negative amount spent have a similar response rate to those with positive amount spent.

Moving to other variables, we turn to the customer ID. As this field is unique to every customer, and is encrypted, it can contain no information that is helpful for our task of predicting which customers are most likely to respond to the direct-mail marketing promotion. It should therefore be omitted from any analytic models. However, the customer ID field should be retained, for housekeeping tasks such as sorting. The zip code can potentially contain information useful in this task. Zip codes, although ostensibly numeric, actually represent a categorization of the client database by geographic locality. However, for the present problem, we set this field aside and concentrate on the remaining variables.

29.4.2   Transformations to Achieve Normality or Symmetry

Most of the numeric fields are right-skewed. For example, Figure 29.9 shows the distribution of *product uniformity*, a variable which takes large values for customers who purchase only a few different classes of clothes (e.g., blouses, legwear, pants), and small values for customers who purchase many different classes of clothes. Later we shall see that high product uniformity is associated with low probability of responding to the promotion. Figure 29.9 is right-skewed, with most customers having a relatively low product uniformity measure, while fewer customers have larger values. The customers with large values for product uniformity tend to buy only one or two classes of clothes. Note that there are spikes at 100 and at 50; these probably result from how product uniformity is calculated (details not available). It is possible that these spikes contain customers exhibiting specific behaviors, in which case the analyst could derive flag variables to investigate. However, as our time and space are limited, we must move on.

Many data mining methods and models, such as principal components analysis and logistic regression, function best when the variables are normally distributed, or, failing that, at least when they are symmetric. Therefore, we apply transformations

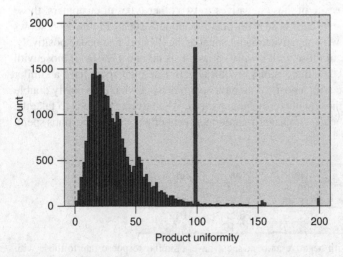

Figure 29.9   Most of the numeric fields are right-skewed, such as product uniformity.

to all of the numerical variables that require it, in order to induce approximate normality or symmetry. The analyst may choose from the transformations indicated in Chapter 8, such as the *natural log* (ln) transformation, the *square root* transformation, a *Box–Cox* transformation, or a *power* transformation from the ladder of reexpressions. For our variables that contained only positive values, we applied the natural log transformation. However, for the variables which contained zero values as well as positive values, we applied the square root transformation, as $\ln(x)$ is undefined for $x = 0$.

Figure 29.10 shows the distribution of product uniformity, after the natural log transformation. Although perfect normality is not obtained, the result is nevertheless much less skewed than the raw data distribution, allowing for smoother application of several data mining methods and models. Sadly, the spikes remain.

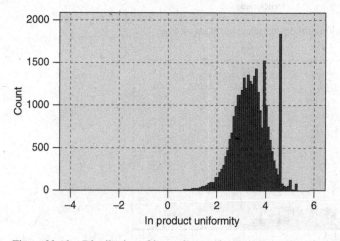

Figure 29.10   Distribution of *ln product uniformity* is less skewed, although the spikes remain.

Recall that the data set includes 15 variables providing the percentages spent by the customer on specific classes of clothing, including sweaters, knit tops, knit dresses, blouses, and so on. Figure 29.11 shows the distribution of the *percentage spent on blouses*. We see a spike at zero, along with the usual right-skewness, which calls for a transformation. The square root transformation is applied, with results shown in Figure 29.12. Note that the spike at zero remains, while the remainder of the data appear nicely symmetric.

The dichotomous character of Figure 29.12 motivates us to derive a flag variable for all blouse purchasers. Figure 29.13 shows the distribution of this flag variable, with about 58% of customers having purchased a blouse at one time or another. Flag variables were also constructed for the other 14 clothing percentage variables.

29.4.3   Standardization

When there are large differences in variability among the numerical variables, the data analyst needs to apply standardization. The transformations already applied do

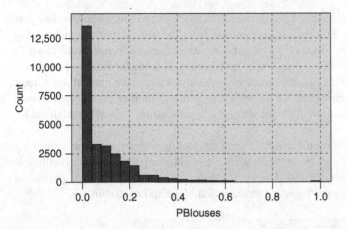

Figure 29.11   Distribution of the percentage spent on blouses.

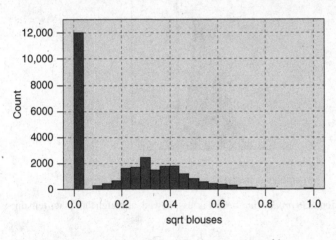

Figure 29.12   Distribution of *sqrt percentage spent on blouses*.

Value	Proportion	%	Count
F		41.66	11998
T		58.34	16801

Figure 29.13   Distribution of *blouse purchasers* flag variable.

help in part to reduce the difference in variability among the variables, but substantial differences still exist. For example, the standard deviation for the variable *sqrt spending in the last 6 months* is 10.03, while the standard deviation for the variable *sqrt # coupons used* is 0.73. To avoid the greater variability of the variable *sqrt spending in the last 6 months* overwhelming the variable *sqrt # coupons used*, the numeric fields should be normalized or standardized. Here, we choose to standardize the numeric fields, so that they all have a mean of zero and a standard deviation of one. For each variable, this is done by subtracting the mean of the variable, and dividing by the standard deviation, to arrive at the *z-score*. In this analysis, the resulting variable names are prefixed with a "Z" (e.g., *z sqrt # coupons used*). Other normalization techniques, such as min–max normalization, may be substituted for z-score standardization if desired.

29.4.4   Deriving New Variables

The creation of flag variables for blouse sales and the other item category sales represents deriving new variables, in order to provide greater insight into customer behavior, and hopefully to increase model performance. Further flag variables are constructed as follows. Figure 29.14 shows the histogram of the variable *z sqrt spending last 1 month*. Note the spike which represents the majority of customers who have not spent any money at the store in the past month. For this reason, flag (indicator) variables were constructed for *spending last 1 month*, as well as the following variables:

- Spending at the AM store (one of the four franchises), to indicate which customers spent money at this particular store.
- Spending at the PS store
- Spending at the AX store.
- Spending in the last 3 months.
- Spending in the last 6 months.
- Spending in the SPLY.
- Returns, to indicate which customers have ever returned merchandise.
- Response rate, to indicate which customers have ever responded to a marketing promotion before.
- Markdown, to indicate which customers have purchased merchandise which has been marked down.

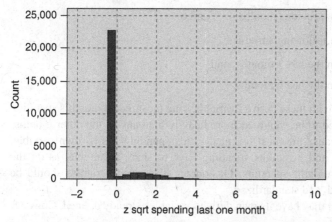

Figure 29.14   Histogram of *Z sqrt spending last 1 month* motivates us to create a flag variable to indicate which customers spent money in the past month.

- No flag is created for spending at the CC store, as *all* records in the database indicate non-zero amounts spent.

The data preparation phase offers the data miner the opportunity to clarify relationships between variables, and to derive new variables that may be useful for the analysis. For example, consider the following three variables:

- Amount spent (by customer) in the last month.
- Amount spent in the last 3 months.
- Amount spent in the last 6 months.

Clearly, the amount spent by the customer in the last month is also contained in the other two variables, the amount spent in the last 3 months and the last 6 months. Therefore, the amount spent in the last month is getting triple-counted. Now, the analyst may not wish for this most recent amount to be so heavily weighted. For example, in time-series models, the more recent measurements are the most heavily weighted. In this case, however, we prefer not to triple-count the most recent month, and must therefore derive two new variables, as shown in Table 29.1.

TABLE 29.1   New derived spending variables

Derived Variable	Formula
Amount spent in previous months 2 and 3	Amount spent in last 3 months −amount spent in last 1 month
Amount spent in previous months 4–6	Amount spent in last 6 months −amount spent in last 3 months

By "amount spent in previous months 2 and 3," we mean the amount spent in the period 90 to 30 days previous. We shall thus use the following three variables:

- Amount spent in the last month.
- Amount spent in previous months 2 and 3.
- Amount spent in previous months 4, 5, and 6.

And we shall omit the following variables:

- Amount spent in the last 3 months, and
- Amount spent in the last 6 months.

Note that, even with these derived variables, the most recent month's spending may still be considered to be weighted more heavily than any of the other months' spending. This is because the most recent month's spending has its own variable, while the previous 2 and 3 months spending have to share a variable, as do the previous 4, 5, and 6 months spending. Of course, all derived variables should be transformed as needed, and standardized.

The raw data set may have its own derived variables already defined. Consider the following variables:

- Number of purchase visits.

- Total net sales.
- Average amount spent per visit.

The *average amount spent per visit* represents the ratio:

$$\text{Average} = \frac{\text{total net sales}}{\text{number of purchase visits}}$$

As the relationship among these variables is functionally defined, it may turn out that the derived variable is strongly correlated with the other variables. The analyst should check this. For example, Figure 29.15 shows that there is strong correlation[2] among the variables *z ln total net sales*, *z ln ave spending per visit*, and *z ln total net sales*. This strong correlation shall bear watching; we shall return to this below. By the way, the correlation coefficients between the raw variables should be the same as the correlation coefficients obtained by the Z-scores of those variables.

z ln purchase visits		
Pearson Correlations		
z ln total net sales	0.76	Strong
z ln ave spending per visit	-0.30	Strong
z ln total net sales		
Pearson Correlations		
z ln purchase visits	0.76	Strong
z ln ave spending per visit	0.40	Strong
z ln ave spending per visit		
Pearson Correlations		
z ln purchase visits	-0.30	Strong
z ln total net sales	0.40	Strong

Figure 29.15   Check to make sure the derived variable is not correlated with the original variables.

29.5   DATA UNDERSTANDING PHASE, PART 2: EXPLORATORY DATA ANALYSIS

Having wrapped up our data preparation, we turn again to the Data Understanding Phase, this time to perform EDA. Recall that EDA allows the analyst to delve into the data set, examine the interrelationships among the variables, identify interesting subsets of observations, and develop an initial idea of possible associations among the predictors, as well as between the predictors and the target variable. And all of this is accomplished without worrying about fulfilling the assumptions required for modeling methods such as regression.

---

[2]For a sample size of 28,799, any correlation coefficient larger in absolute value than about 0.012 would be statistically significant at the $\alpha = 0.05$ level.

29.5.1   Exploring the Relationships between the Predictors and the Response

We shall return to the correlation issue later, but first we would like to investigate the variable-by-variable association between the predictors and the target variable, response to the marketing promotion. Ideally, the analyst should examine graphs and statistics for every predictor variable, especially with respect to the relationship with the response. However, the huge data sets prevalent in most data mining applications make this a daunting task. Therefore, we would like to have some way to examine the most useful predictors in an exploratory framework.

Of course, choosing the most useful variables is a modeling task, which lies downstream of our present phase, the EDA-flavored data understanding phase. However, a very rough tool for choosing some useful variables to examine at this early phase is correlation. That is, examine the correlation coefficients for each predictor with the response, and select for further examination those variables which have the largest absolute correlations. The analyst should of course be aware that this is simply a rough EDA tool, and linear correlation with a 0–1 response variable is not appropriate for inference or modeling at this stage. Nevertheless, this method can be useful for paring down the number of variables that would be helpful to examine at the EDA stage. Table 29.2 lists the top three predictors with the highest absolute correlation with the target variable, *response*.

We therefore examine the relationship between these selected predictors, and the response variable. First, Figure 29.16 shows a histogram of *Z ln Lifetime Average Time Between Visits*, with an overlay of *Response* (0 = no response to the promotion). It appears that records at the upper end of the distribution have lower response rates. In order to make the interpretation of overlay results more clearly, we turn to a normalized histogram, where each bin has the same height, shown in Figure 29.17.

Figure 29.17 makes it clear that the rate of response to the marketing promotion decreases as the lifetime average time between visits increases. This makes sense, as customers who visit the store more rarely will presumably be less likely to respond to the promotion. Note that presenting the normalized histogram alone is not sufficient, as it does not provide a feel for the original distribution of the variable. Thus, it is usually recommended to provide both the unnormalized and the normalized histograms.

Figure 29.18 shows the nonnormalized and normalized histograms for *z ln purchase visits*, illustrating that, as the number of purchase visits increases, the response rate increases as well. This is not surprising, as we might anticipate that the customers who shop at our stores often, purchase many different items, spend a lot of money, and buy a lot of different types of clothes, might be interested in responding to our

TABLE 29.2   Variables with largest absolute correlation with the target variable, *response*

Variable	Correlation Coefficient	Relationship
z ln Lifetime ave time between visits	−0.43	Negative
z ln Purchase visits	0.40	Positive
z ln # Individual items purchased	0.37	Positive

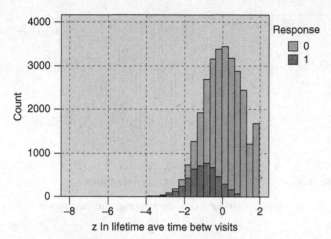

Figure 29.16   Histogram of *z ln lifetime average time between visits* with *response* overlay: may be difficult to interpret.

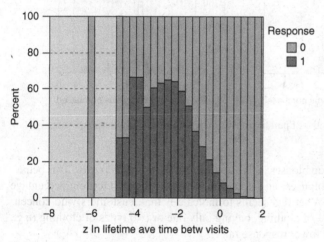

Figure 29.17   Normalized histogram of *z ln lifetime average time between visits* with *response* overlay: easier to discern pattern.

marketing promotion. Figure 29.19 shows the relationship between *z ln # individual items purchased* and the response variable. We see that, as the number of individual items purchased increases, the response rate increases as well.

We might expect that the three variables from Table 29.2 will turn out, in one form or another, to be among the best predictors of promotion response. This is further investigated in the modeling phase.

Next consider Figure 29.20, which shows the normalized histogram of *z sqrt percentage spent on blouses*, with an overlay of the *response* variable. Note from Figure 29.20 that, apart from those who spend nothing on blouses (the left-most bin),

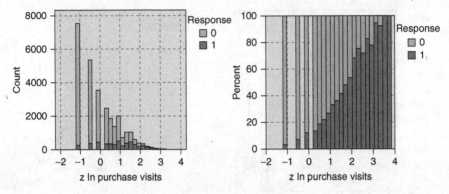

Figure 29.18   As the number of purchase visits increases, the response rate increases as well.

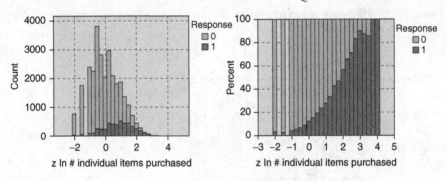

Figure 29.19   As the number of purchase visits increases, so does the response rate.

as the percentage spent on blouses increases, the response rate *decreases*. This behavior is not restricted to blouses, and is prevalent among all the clothing percentage variables (not shown). What this seems to indicate is that, customers who concentrate on a particular type of clothing, buying only one or two types of clothing (e.g., blouses), tend to have a lower response rate.

The raw data file contains a variable that measures product uniformity, and, based on the behavior observed in Figure 29.20, we would expect the relationship between product uniformity and response to be negative. This is indeed the case, as shown by the normalized histogram of *z ln product uniformity* in Figure 29.21. The highest response rate is shown by the customers with the lowest uniformity, that is, the highest diversity of purchasing habits, in other words, customers who purchase many different types of clothing.

Next, we turn to an examination of the relationship between the response and the many flag variables in the data set. Figure 29.22 provides a directed web graph of the relationship between the response (upper right) and the following indicator variables (counterclockwise from the response): credit card holder, spending months 4, 5, and 6, spending months 2 and 3, spending last 1 month, spending SPLY, returns, response rate, markdown, web buyer, and valid phone number on file. Web graphs

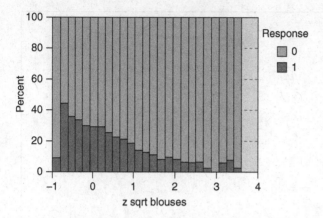

Figure 29.20   *z sqrt blouses*, with *response* overlay.

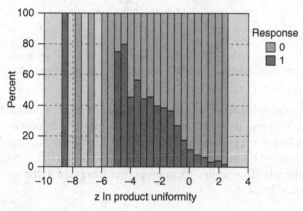

Figure 29.21   As customers concentrate on only one type of clothing, the response rate goes down.

are exploratory tools for determining which categorical variables may be of interest for further study.

In this graph, only the true values for the various flags are indicated. The darkness and solidity of the line connecting the flag variable with the response is a measure of the association of that variable with the response. In particular, these connections represent percentages of the "true" predictor flag values associated with the "true" value of the response. Therefore, more solid connections represent a greater association with responding to the promotion. Among the most solid connections in Figure 29.22 are the following:

- Web buyer
- Credit card holder
- Spending last 1 month
- Spending SPLY

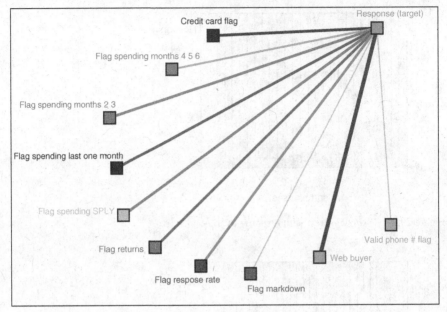

Figure 29.22 Directed web graph of relationship between the *response* and several flag variables.

We therefore examine the normalized distribution of each of these indicator variables, with the *response* overlay, as shown in Figure 29.23 (positive responses are darker). The counts (and percentages) shown in Figure 29.23 indicate the frequencies (and relative frequencies) of the predictor flag values, and do not represent the proportions shown graphically. To examine these proportions, we turn to the set of contingency tables in Figure 29.24.

Value /	Proportion	%	Count
F		95.65	27546
T		4.35	1253

Web buyer flag

Value /	Proportion	%	Count
F		61.7	17768
T		38.3	11031

Credit card flag

Value /	Proportion	%	Count
F		78.97	22744
T		21.03	6055

Spending last one month flag

Value /	Proportion	%	Count
F		76.05	21901
T		23.95	6898

Spending SPLY flag

Figure 29.23 Higher response rates are associated with (a) web buyers, (b) credit card holders, (c) customers who made a purchase within the past month, and (d) customers who made a purchase in the same period last year.

Consider the highlighted cells in Figure 29.24, which indicate the proportions of customers who have responded to the promotion, conditioned on their flag values. Web buyers (those who have made purchases via the company's web shopping option)

Response		F	T
0	Count	23346	691
	Column %	84.75	55.15
1	Count	4200	562
	Column %	15.25	44.85

Web buyer flag

Response		F	T
0	Count	16102	7935
	Column %	90.62	71.93
1	Count	1666	3096
	Column %	9.38	28.07

Credit card flag

Response		F	T
0	Count	20019	4018
	Column %	88.02	66.36
1	Count	2725	2037
	Column %	11.98	33.64

Spending last one month flag

Response		F	T
0	Count	19023	5014
	Column %	86.86	72.69
1	Count	2878	1884
	Column %	13.14	27.31

Spending SPLY flag

Figure 29.24   The statistics in these matrices describe the graphics from Figure 29.23.

are nearly three times as likely to respond compared to those who have not made a purchase via the Web (44.852% vs 15.247%). Credit card holders are also about three times as likely as noncredit card holders (28.066% vs 9.376%) to respond to the promotion. Customers who have made a purchase in the last month are nearly three times as likely to respond to the promotion (33.642% vs 11.981%). Finally, those who made a purchase in the SPLY are twice more likely to respond than those who did not make a purchase during the SPLY (27.312% vs 13.141%). We would therefore expect these flag variables to play some nontrivial role in the model building phase downstream.

29.5.2   Investigating the Correlation Structure among the Predictors

Recall that, depending on the objective of our analysis, we should be aware of the dangers of multicollinearity among the predictor variables. We therefore investigate the pairwise correlation coefficients among the predictors, and note those correlations that are the strongest. Table 29.3 contains a listing of the pairwise correlations that are the strongest in absolute value among the predictors.

Figure 29.25 shows a scatter plot of *z ln total net sales* versus *z ln # individual items purchased*, with a *response* overlay. The strong positive correlation is evident in

TABLE 29.3   Strongest absolute pairwise correlations among the predictors

Predictor	Predictor	Correlation
z ln Purchase visits	z ln # Different product classes	0.80
z ln Purchase visits	z ln # Individual items purchased	0.86
z ln # Promotions on file	z ln # Promotions mailed in last year	0.89
z ln Total net sales	z ln # Different product classes	0.86
z ln Total net sales	z ln # Individual items purchased	0.91
z ln Days between purchase	z ln Lifetime ave time between visits	0.85
z ln # Different product classes	z ln # Individual items purchased	0.93

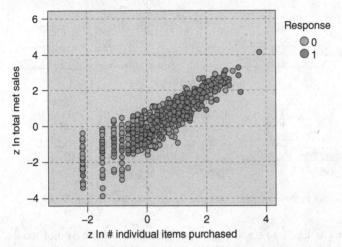

Figure 29.25 Scatter plot of a positive relationship: *z ln total net sales* versus *z ln # individual items purchased*, with response overlay.

that, as the number of items purchased increases, the total net sales tends to increase. Of course, such a relationship makes sense, as purchasing more items would presumably tend to result in spending more money. Also, at the high end of both variables (the upper right), responders tend to outnumber nonresponders, while at the lower end (the lower left), the opposite is true.

For an example of a negative relationship, we may turn to Figure 29.26, the scatter plot of *z gross margin percentage* versus *z markdown*, with *response* overlay. The correlation between these variables is −0.77, and so they did not make the list in Table 29.3. In the scatter plot, it is clear that, as markdown increases, the gross margin percentage tends to decrease.

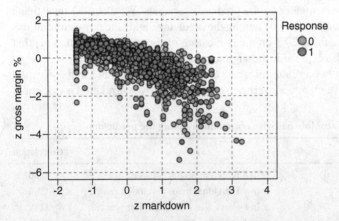

Figure 29.26 Scatter plot of a negative relationship: *z gross margin %* versus *z markdown*.

If the number of predictors is large, however, evaluating individual scatter plot may become tedious. This is because, for k predictors, there are $_kC_2$ possible two-dimensional scatter plots. For example, for 10 predictors, there are 45 possible scatter plots. It can be more convenient, therefore, to use matrix plots, which provide several scatter plots at one time. Figure 29.27 is an example of a matrix plot for the predictors *z ln days between purchases*, *z ln lifetime ave time betw visits*, and *z ln # individual items purchased*, with an overlay of response. The plots along the diagonal are histograms of the respective predictors. Note the positive relationship between *z ln days between purchases* and *z ln lifetime ave time betw visits* (plot in the middle of the left-hand column), which makes sense as customers who have shorter times between visits to the store are likely to have shorter times between purchases at the store. These customers tend toward the lower left of the plot, and indicate a greater response rate than the other customers. Also one may consider the negative relationship between *z ln days between purchases* and *z ln # individual items purchased* (plot in the lower left). It makes sense that, as customers wait longer between purchases, they will tend to make a lower overall number of individual items purchased. Also, there is a hint in the upper left of this last graph of a greater

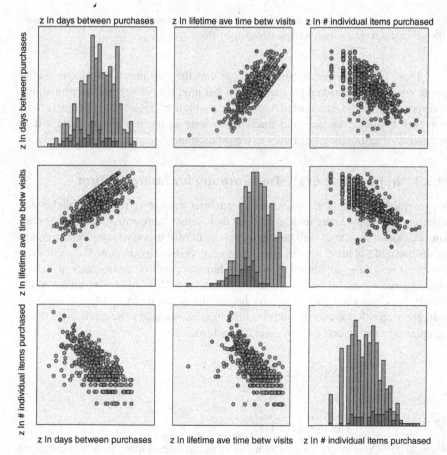

Figure 29.27   Matrix plot of three predictors, showing positive and negative relationships.

response rate, as these are the customers with smaller days between purchases, and higher number of individual items purchased.

A convenient method for examining the relationship between categorical variables and *response* is a contingency table, (or cross-tabulation), using a function of the response instead of raw cell counts. For example, suppose we are interested in the relationship between response to the promotion and two types of customers: those who have purchased sweaters and those who have made a purchase within the last month. Figure 29.28 contains such a cross-tabulation, with the cells representing the mean value of the target variable (response). As the target represents a dichotomous variable, the means therefore represent proportions.

flag sweaters	flag spending last one month	
	F	T
F	0.06	0.18
T	0.15	0.36

Figure 29.28   Cross-tabulation of spending within the last month versus sweater purchase, with cell values representing promotion response percentages.

Thus, in the cross-tabulation, we see that the customers who have neither bought sweaters nor made a purchase in the last month have only a 0.06 probability of responding to the direct-mail marketing promotion. However, customers who have both bought a sweater and made a purchase in the last month have a 0.36 probability of responding positively to the promotion.

29.5.3   Importance of De-Transforming for Interpretation

We provide an example to illustrate how analysts presenting results to clients and managers should take care to de-transform their statistical results. Figure 29.29 contains a cross-tabulation of web buyers versus credit card users, with the cells containing the mean of $z \ln purchase visits$ for the customers in each cell. Note that customers with positive values for both flag variables have the highest means, and customers with negative values for both have the lowest means. This is good information, but limited. We cannot tell from this information, the actual mean number of purchase visits for each cell. In order to find this information, we need to *de-transform*, which means to take the inverse of the original transformation.

Credit Card Flag	Web Buyer Flag	
	F	T
F	-0.35	0.47
T	0.48	1.17

Figure 29.29   Cross-tabulation of web buyers versus credit card users, with cells containing *z ln purchase visits*.

De-transforming a z value:

1. Find the mean $\bar{x}$ and standard deviation s used to perform the standardization.
2. Apply the following inverse Z transformation to obtain the original value: original value $= (z \text{ value}) \cdot s + \bar{x}$.

De-transforming a ln value:

1. Apply the following inverse ln transformation to obtain the original value: $e^{\ln \text{ value}} = \exp(\ln \text{ value})$.

Thus, to find the mean number of purchase visits for those customers who are both web buyers and credit card users, we need to (i) first apply the inverse Z transformation, and then (ii) apply the inverse ln transformation. The mean number of purchase visits for all customers is $\bar{x} = 1.14$ with standard deviation of $s = 0.93$ visits. Apply the inverse Z transformation gives us

$$\text{Original value} = (z \text{ value}) \cdot s + \bar{x} = (1.17) \cdot 0.93 + 1.14 = 2.2281$$

Then, applying the inverse ln transformation, we get:

$$e^{\ln \text{ value}} = e^{2.2281} = 9.28$$

Thus, the mean number of purchase visits for web buyers who are also credit card users is 9.28 visits. However, the mean number of purchase visits who are neither web buyers not credit card users is

$$\exp((z \text{ value}) \cdot s + \bar{x}) = \exp((-0.35) \cdot 0.93 + 1.14) = \exp(0.8145) = 2.26$$

Thus, customers who are both web buyers and credit card holders have more than three times as many purchase visits as customers who are neither web buyers nor credit card holders. These are results that are understandable and actionable by clients and managers.

Here in Chapter 29, we have illustrated how to use EDA to learn more about our customer clientele, which represents part of the secondary objective of our Case Study. Of course, much more could be done along these lines, but space limitations restrict us to the examples above. Next, in Chapter 30, we learn more about our customers through the use of principal components analysis and clustering analysis.

CASE STUDY, PART 2: CLUSTERING AND PRINCIPAL COMPONENTS ANALYSIS

Chapters 29–32 present a Case Study of *Predicting Response to Direct-Mail Marketing*. In Chapter 29, we opened our Case Study with a look at the primary and secondary objectives of the project, which are reprised here.

- **Primary objective:** Develop a classification model that will maximize profits for direct-mail marketing.

- **Secondary objective:** Develop better understanding of our clientele through exploratory data analysis (EDA), component profiles, and cluster profiles.

The EDA performed in Chapter 29 allowed us to learn some interesting customer behaviors. Here in this chapter, we learn more about our customers through the use of principal components analysis (PCA) and clustering analysis. In Chapter 31, we tackle our primary objective of developing a profitable classification model.

30.1 PARTITIONING THE DATA

The analyses we perform in Chapters 29–31 require cross-validation. We therefore partition the data set into a *Case Study Training Data Set* and a *Case Study Test Data Set*. The data miner decides the proportional size of the training and test sets, with typical sizes usually ranging from 50% training/50% test to 90% training/10% test. In this Case Study, we choose a partition of approximately 75% training and 25% test.

30.1.1 Validating the Partition

In Chapter 6, we discussed methods for validating that our partition of the data set is random, using some simple tests of hypothesis. However, such methods may become tedious when testing for dozens of predictors. Equivalent computational methods

Data Mining and Predictive Analytics, First Edition. Daniel T. Larose and Chantal D. Larose.
© 2015 John Wiley & Sons, Inc. Published 2015 by John Wiley & Sons, Inc.

exist for performing these tests on a large set of predictors. Figure 30.1 shows the results of F-tests (equivalent to t-tests in this case) performed on some of the continuous variables in our Case Study. (In *Modeler,* use the append node to put the training and test data sets together, then use the means node to examine for difference in means, based on the source input.) The null hypothesis is that there is no difference in means; the *Importance* field equals $1 - p\text{-value}$. None of the fields was found to be significant. Remember, that we might expect on average about 1 out of 20 tests to be significant, even if there is no difference in means.

Grouping field: Source					
*Cells contain: Mean, Standard Deviation, Standard Error, Count					
Field	1*	2*	F-Test	df	Importance
z ln purchase visits	0.00	-0.00	0.09	1, 28772	0.24
	1.00	0.98			▪ Unimportant
	0.01	0.01			
	21586	7188			
z days since purchase	-0.01	-0.01	0.02	1, 28772	0.11
	1.00	1.00			▪ Unimportant
	0.01	0.01			
	21586	7188			
z gross margin %	-0.00	0.01	0.74	1, 28772	0.61
	1.02	0.94			▪ Unimportant
	0.01	0.01			
	21586	7188			
z days on file	0.00	0.01	0.05	1, 28772	0.18
	1.00	1.00			▪ Unimportant
	0.01	0.01			
	21586	7188			

Figure 30.1   No significant difference in means for continuous variables.

Investigation of some noncontinuous variables (not shown) indicates no systematic deviations from randomness. We thus conclude that the partition is sound, and proceed with our analysis.

30.2   DEVELOPING THE PRINCIPAL COMPONENTS

PCA is useful when using models such as multiple regression or logistic regression, which become unstable when the predictors are highly correlated. However, PCA is also useful for uncovering natural affinities among groups of predictors, which may be of interest to the client. In other words, PCA is useful both for downstream modeling, and for its component profiles.

Figure 30.2 shows the variables input to our PCA. Note that all variables are continuous, and so do not include the flag or nominal variables, because PCA requires continuous predictors. Also, of course, the response variable is not included.

z ln purchase visits	z sqrt outerwear
z days since purchase	z sqrt jewelry
z gross margin %	z sqrt fashion
z days on file	z sqrt legwear
z markdown	z sqrt collectibles
z promotions mailed	z sqrt spending AM
z ln total net sales	z sqrt spending PS
z ln ave spending per visit	z sqrt spending CC
z sqrt tot promos on file	z sqrt spending AX
z sqrt percent returns	z sqrt spending last one month
z sqrt promo resp rate	z sqrt spending SPLY
z sqrt sweaters	z ln days between purchases
z sqrt knit tops	z ln # different product classes
z sqrt knit dresses	z sqrt # coupons used
z sqrt blouses	z ln # individual items purchased
z sqrt jackets	z ln stores
z sqrt career pants	z ln lifetime ave time betw visits
z sqrt casual pants	z ln product uniformity
z sqrt shirts	z sqrt # promos responded
z sqrt dresses	z sqrt spending months 2 3
z sqrt suits	z sqrt spending months 4 5 6

Figure 30.2   Predictors input to PCA.

PCA is applied to the training data set using these inputs, with minimum eigenvalue = 1.0, and using varimax rotation. The rotated results shown in Figure 30.3 show that 13 components were extracted, for a total variance explained of 68.591%.

Unfortunately, it turns out that the communalities for several of the predictors are rather low (<0.5, output not shown), given in Table 30.1. Low communalities mean that these variables share little variability in common with the set of other predictors. Thus, it makes sense to remove them as inputs from the PCA, and try again. PCA is again applied to the training data set, this time without the set of eight predictors from Table 30.1, using the same settings as previously. This time, Figure 30.4 shows that only 11 components are extracted, for a total variance explained of 75.115%.

TABLE 30.1   Set of predictors with low communality, that is, which do not share much variability with the remaining predictors

z sqrt knit tops	z sqrt dresses
z sqrt jewelry	z sqrt fashion
z sqrt legwear	z sqrt spending AX
z sqrt spending SPLY	z sqrt spending last one month

Component	Rotation Sums of Squared Loadings		
	Total	% of Variance	Cumulative %
1	8.847	21.064	21.064
2	4.135	9.846	30.910
3	2.010	4.785	35.695
4	2.000	4.763	40.457
5	1.881	4.479	44.936
6	1.308	3.115	48.052
7	1.304	3.104	51.156
8	1.300	3.094	54.250
9	1.239	2.951	57.201
10	1.210	2.880	60.081
11	1.206	2.870	62.952
12	1.191	2.836	65.787
13	1.178	2.804	68.591

Figure 30.3   Results from PCA to all continuous predictors.

Unfortunately, at this point, *z sqrt spending AM* exhibits relatively low communality (0.470) with the remaining predictors, a behavior reflected in both the training and test sets (not shown). This variable is therefore set aside, and PCA analysis is applied to the reduced set of predictors (omitting the eight in Table 30.1 and *z sqrt spending AM*). The results for the training set are shown in Figure 30.5. Eliminating another predictor from the PCA has again increased the cumulative variance explained, although this may be, in part, because omitting this variable has reduced the overall amount of variability to explain.

Before we move forward with this PCA solution, what is to become of the predictors that were omitted from the PCA model? As they have little correlation with the other predictors, they are to move on to the modeling stage without being subsumed into the principal components. PCA analysis of these nine predictors shows that, even among themselves, there is little correlation (Figure 30.6, for the training set). Further, only two components were extracted from this set of eight predictors, with less than 30% of the variance explained (not shown). Thus, these nine variables are free to move on to the modeling stage without the need for PCA. However, they will not contribute to the knowledge of our customer database that we will uncover using profiles of the principal components.

We therefore proceed with the PCA of all continuous predictors, except those in Figure 30.6.

Component	Rotation Sums of Squared Loadings		
	Total	% of Variance	Cumulative %
1	8.869	26.085	26.085
2	3.811	11.210	37.295
3	1.962	5.771	43.066
4	1.953	5.744	48.810
5	1.817	5.345	54.155
6	1.254	3.688	57.842
7	1.223	3.596	61.438
8	1.210	3.558	64.996
9	1.161	3.415	68.412
10	1.141	3.355	71.767
11	1.138	3.348	75.115

Figure 30.4   Eliminating low communality predictors reduced number of components and increased variance explained.

Component	Rotation Sums of Squared Loadings		
	Total	% of Variance	Cumulative %
1	8.805	26.682	26.682
2	3.842	11.643	38.325
3	1.967	5.961	44.286
4	1.951	5.911	50.197
5	1.813	5.492	55.689
6	1.225	3.712	59.401
7	1.224	3.708	63.109
8	1.208	3.661	66.769
9	1.156	3.504	70.274
10	1.151	3.488	73.762
11	1.126	3.413	77.175

Figure 30.5   Eliminating another predictor from the PCA has again increased the variance explained.

Communalities

	Initial	Extraction
z sqrt knit tops	1.000	.275
z sqrt knit dresses	1.000	.240
z sqrt jewelry	1.000	.368
z sqrt fashion	1.000	.444
z sqrt legwear	1.000	.226
z sqrt spending AM	1.000	.118
z sqrt spending AX	1.000	.352
z sqrt spending last one month	1.000	.370
z sqrt spending SPLY	1.000	.272

Figure 30.6   Little variance in common among the predictors not partaking in the PCA.

30.3   VALIDATING THE PRINCIPAL COMPONENTS

Just as with any modeling procedure, the analyst should validate the PCA, using cross-validation. Figure 30.7 contains the rotated component matrix for the training data set, showing which variables belong to which component. Values smaller than 0.5 are suppressed, to enhance interpretability. Compare with Figure 30.8, which shows the rotated component matrix for the test data set. The components are broadly similar between the training and test sets, with some minor differences. For example, the test set shows that *z sqrt spending PS* belongs to Component 1, while the training set disagrees. However, the test set component weight is only 0.502, barely above the 0.5 cutoff for suppression. So, we read this as good news for Component 1, because the training and test sets agree on all variables except this *z sqrt spending PS*, which may considered of dubious membership to Component 1.

Other minor differences between the training and test sets include the following. The component weights are not equal, but this is to be expected due to random noise. Components 3 and 4 are mischievously switched by the test data set, but retain their essence. However, broadly speaking, there is good agreement between the components extracted from the training and test data sets. We conclude therefore that our PCA is validated.

30.4   PROFILING THE PRINCIPAL COMPONENTS

Apart from their use to mitigate multicollinearity for downstream modeling, principal components are most useful for learning about how the variables interact. In fact, the analyst should always provide descriptive profiles of the principal components, both as a reality check for the analyst, as well as to enhance the client's understanding.

Rotated Component Matrix

	Component										
	1	2	3	4	5	6	7	8	9	10	11
z ln days between purchases	-.874										
z ln # individual items purchased	.871										
z ln lifetime ave time betw visits	-.849										
z ln purchase visits	.823										
z ln total net sales	.821										
z ln # different product classes	.812										
z days since purchase	-.732										
z sqrt spending months 4 5 6	.699										
z sqrt # coupons used	.694										
z ln product uniformity	-.679										
z ln stores	.635										
z sqrt promo resp rate	.633	.564									
z sqrt spending months 2 3	.633										
z promotions mailed		.880									
z sqrt tot promos on file		.850									
z days on file		.830									
z sqrt # promos responded	.626	.668									
z sqrt collectibles			.737								
z sqrt career pants			.666								
z sqrt jackets			.662								
z sqrt casual pants											
z gross margin %				.871							
z markdown				-.846							
z sqrt percent returns					-.828						
z ln ave spending per visit					.725						
z sqrt spending PS						.750					
z sqrt spending CC	.555					-.616					
z sqrt blouses							.787				
z sqrt sweaters							-.555				
z sqrt dresses								-.855			
z sqrt suits									.952		
z sqrt shirts										.859	
z sqrt outerwear											.906

Figure 30.7   Rotated component matrix (training data set), showing which variables belong to which component.

The analyst should ask, "Do these principal components (which are mathematical entities, after all) correspond to identifiable real-world commonsense behaviors?" If there is a problem with interpretability, then this may indicate some computational or procedural error upstream. If the principal components do correspond to real-world

Rotated Component Matrix

	Component										
	1	2	3	4	5	6	7	8	9	10	11
z ln days between purchases	-.873										
z ln # individual items purchased	.873										
z ln lifetime ave time betw visits	-.844										
z ln purchase visits	.822										
z ln total net sales	.816										
z ln # different product classes	.811										
z days since purchase	-.728										
z sqrt spending months 4 5 6	.696										
z sqrt # coupons used	.689										
z ln product uniformity	-.687										
z sqrt spending months 2 3	.638										
z ln stores	.637										
z sqrt promo resp rate	.614	.584									
z promotions mailed		.881									
z sqrt tot promos on file		.849									
z days on file		.828									
z sqrt # promos responded	.610	.684									
z gross margin %			.874								
z markdown			-.840								
z sqrt collectibles				.729							
z sqrt career pants				.684							
z sqrt jackets				.660							
z sqrt percent returns					-.828						
z ln ave spending per visit					.701						
z sqrt spending PS	.502					.747					
z sqrt spending CC	.542					-.618					
z sqrt blouses							.779				
z sqrt sweaters							-.567				
z sqrt dresses								-.844			
z sqrt suits									.952		
z sqrt shirts										.865	
z sqrt casual pants											
z sqrt outerwear											.883

Figure 30.8   Rotated component matrix for the test data set.

behaviors, then this acts as further validation of their "reality," as well as providing useful information for the client.

   To profile the components, we will work with the rotated component matrix generated by training set (Figure 30.7), which leveraged more records than the test set. Note that Component 1 is a large and complex component, consisting of many predictors, with both positive and negative component weights. This is often the case in PCA, with the first component often representing a general type of phenomenon such as "size," or "sales." In fact, without the varimax rotation, the first component would have been even larger. Table 30.2 indicates the positive and negative weighted predictors in Component 1.

TABLE 30.2 Predictors with positive and negative weights in Component 1 ("z ln" and "z sqrt" suppressed for clarity)

Positive Component Weight	Negative Component Weight
# Individual items purchased	Days between purchases
Purchase visits	Lifetime average time between visits
Total net sales	Days since purchase
# Different product classes	Product uniformity
Spending months 4 5 6	
# Coupons used	
Stores	
Promo response rate	
Spending months 2 3	
# Promos responded	
Spending at CC store	

We would describe Component 1 as measuring *"Sales Volume and Frequency."* This component measures sales volume and frequency in many ways, which are as follows:

- How many items are purchased?
- How often does the customer visit?
- How long does the customer go between purchases?
- What is the total amount spent?
- How many different types of item are bought?
- How consistent is the spending over time?
- How many different stores has the customer shopped at?
- How often does the customer respond to promotions?

All of these questions converge on what we have entitled *Component 1: Sales Volume and Frequency.* It is not surprising that these variables rise and fall together, and that they are thereby highly correlated.

WARNING: COMPONENTS ARE NOT CLUSTERS

It is important to note that principal components (unlike clusters) do not refer specifically to groups of similar customers (clusters), but rather to groups of similarly behaving predictors. For example, Component 1 does *not* consist of customers who have high sales volume. Rather, Component 1 represents a set of variables that "vary together," and are thereby correlated. Later, we will look at sets of customers, which are clusters, not components.

It would surprise no one if Component 1 was strongly predictive of response to the promotion. Figure 30.9a represents a histogram of the component values across all records in the training set, with an overlay of *response* (darker = positive). Figure 30.9b contains the normalized histogram. Thus, customers with high component values are associated with positive response. These customers have large values for the variables in the positive weight column in Table 30.2, and small values for the variables in the negative weight column. Conversely, customers with low values for Component 1 are associated with negative response.

Here follow brief profiles of the remaining 10 components.

- **Component 2: Promotion Proclivity.** This component consists of five predictors, all except one related to past promotion activity: Promotion response rate, Promotions mailed, Total number of promotions on file, and Number of promotions responded to. The fifth predictor measures how long the customer has been on file. All predictors have positive weights, meaning they are all positively correlated.

- **Component 3: Career Shopping.** This component consists of three related types of clothing: Career pants, Jackets, and Collectibles (defined as mostly suits and career wear). These positively correlated predictors measure career clothing purchases.

- **Component 4: Margin versus Markdown.** This component consists of two negatively correlated predictors: Gross margin percentage and Markdown

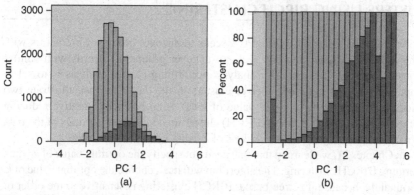

Figure 30.9   Component 1 values are highly predictive of *response*. (a) Histogram and (b) normalized histogram.

percentage. It makes sense that, as markdown increases, the margin will decrease. This component neatly captures this behavior.

- **Component 5: Spending versus Returns.** This component consists also consists of two negatively correlated variables: Average spending per visit and Percent returns. Evidently, those who have a high percentage of returns tend to have a low average spending amount per visit.

- **Component 6: PS Store versus CC Store.** Evidently these stores appeal to different groups of shoppers. If someone spends a lot at PS stores, they will tend not to spend much at CC stores, and vice versa.

- **Component 7: Blouses versus Sweaters.** It appears that shoppers tend not to buy blouses and sweaters together. The more spent on blouses, the less spent on sweaters, and vice versa.

- **Component 8: Dresses.** This is a singleton component containing only a single predictor: Dresses. In fact, each of the last four components is singleton. Note from Figure 30.3 that the eigenvalues for these components are each 1.2 or less, meaning that they explain about one predictor's worth of variability.

- **Component 9: Suits**. Singleton component: Suits. Perhaps surprising that it is not included in the Career Shopping component.

- **Component 10: Shirts**. Singleton component: Shirts.

- **Component 11: Outerwear**. Singleton component: Outerwear.

The question might arise: As the last four components are each singletons, why not just omit them, and extract only seven components? The answer is that the "singleton" label is a bit misleading. Each component contains loadings for each predictor; we have simply suppressed the small ones, in order to enhance interpretability. So, omitting these last four components would have effects beyond just these four predictors. Better to retain all 11 components.

30.5 CHOOSING THE OPTIMAL NUMBER OF CLUSTERS USING BIRCH CLUSTERING

Next, we turn to clustering. While PCA seeks to uncover groups of predictors with similar behavior, cluster analysis seeks to uncover groups of records with similar characteristics. One challenge for analysts performing cluster analysis is to select the optimal value of k, the number of clusters in the data. Here we illustrate two methods for selecting the optimal value of k, (i) using balanced iterative reducing and clustering using hierarchies (BIRCH) clustering on different sortings of the data and (ii) cycling through candidate values of k using k-means clustering.

In Chapter 21, we learned that one need not specify the optimal value of k when performing BIRCH clustering. The algorithm will itself choose the optimal value of k. Unfortunately, because it is tree-based, BIRCH clustering is sensitive to the order of the records scanned by the algorithm. In other words, it can report different clustering solutions for different sortings (orderings) of the data.

We shall then proceed as follows.

CHOOSING *K* USING BIRCH CLUSTERING

1. Sort the data several different ways.
2. Apply BIRCH clustering independently to each different sorting. Note the value of *k* chosen for each clustering model.
3. Approach a consensus as to the value of *k* most favored by the data.

We select five as the number of different sortings of the training data set. The *Modeler* stream flow is shown in Figure 30.10. First, four new sort variables are derived, Sort2 – Sort5 (Sort1 is considered to be the original data ordering). Each of these derived variables assigns a random real number between 0.0 and 1.0 to each record. The records are then separately sorted by each sort variable. Then, BIRCH clustering is performed on each of the five data orderings, the original plus the four random sortings. Table 30.3 shows the value of *k* favored by BIRCH for each sorting. The clear winner for the optimal number of clusters using BIRCH clustering is *k* = 2.

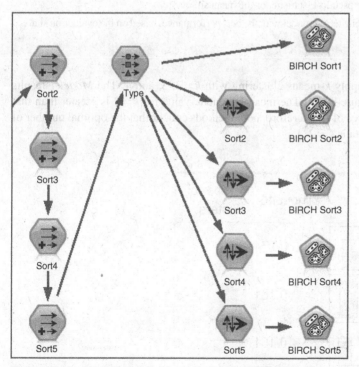

Figure 30.10   IBM/SPSS *Modeler* stream excerpt showing process for choosing *k* using BIRCH clustering.

TABLE 30.3 Value of _k_ favored by BIRCH clustering for each sorting

Sort1	Sort2	Sort3	Sort4	Sort5
2	2	2	2	2

30.6 CHOOSING THE OPTIMAL NUMBER OF CLUSTERS USING _k_-MEANS CLUSTERING

An alternate, and probably more widespread, method for selecting the optimal value for k is the following.

CYCLING METHOD FOR CHOOSING K

1. Select a clustering method, such as k-means. Select a range of plausible values for k, denoted as k_{low} through k_{high}.
2. Starting with k_{low}, cycle through the values of k, applying the clustering method at each value of k, until k_{high} is reached.
3. For each value of k, measure the goodness of the clustering model, using statistics such as the pseudo-F statistic, or the mean silhouette.
4. Select the clustering model with the best performance, based on the evaluation statistics of step 3.

Here, we apply k-means clustering with $k = 2$, 3, and 4. The _Modeler_ results are shown in Figure 30.11. The mean silhouette value for $k = 2$ is greater than that for the other values of k. Therefore, both methods concur that the optimal number of clusters in the data is $k = 2$.

Graph	Silhouette	Number of Clusters
	0.274	2
	0.181	3
	0.161	4

Figure 30.11 Mean silhouette is greatest for $k = 2$.

30.7 APPLICATION OF *k*-MEANS CLUSTERING

We thus proceed to apply *k*-means clustering to the set of predictors in the training data set, including all the continuous variables from Figure 30.2, along with all the flag variables and nominal variables. The principal components are not included as inputs to the clustering algorithm. Of course, the response should not be included as input to any modeling algorithm. Graphical summaries of the resulting two clusters are provided in Figure 30.12. Not all predictors were helpful in discriminating between the clusters; these are omitted from Figure 30.12.

30.8 VALIDATING THE CLUSTERS

We use cross-validation to validate our clusters. We apply *k*-means clustering to the test data set, using the same set of predictors used for the training data set. The graphical summary results are shown in Figure 30.13. The results are broadly similar to what we uncovered using the training data set. There are two clusters, the larger of which represents a large set of casual shoppers, while the smaller cluster represents the faithful customers (see the cluster profiles below). There are some differences, such as ordering of the variables, but, on the whole, the clusters are validated.

30.9 PROFILING THE CLUSTERS

We can use the information in Figure 30.12 to construct descriptive profiles of the clusters, which are as follows.

> **Cluster 1: Casual Shoppers** Cluster 1 is the larger cluster, containing 58.6% of the customers. Cluster 1 contains lower proportions of positive values for all flag variables listed in Figure 30.12. This indicates for example that Cluster 1 contains lower incidence of credit card purchases, lower response to previous promotions, lower spending in previous time periods, and lower proportions of purchases in most clothing classes. Cluster 1 contains newer customers (days on file), who nevertheless wait longer between purchases. The casual shoppers tend to focus on a small number of product classes, and to purchase only a few different items. They have fewer than average purchase visits, visit fewer different stores, and have lower total net sales. Their promotion response rate is lower than average, as well as the number of coupons used.

> **Cluster 2: Faithful Customers** Cluster 2 is the smaller cluster, containing 41.4% of the customers, and represents the polar opposite of Cluster 1 in most respects. Cluster 2 contains higher proportions of positive values for all the listed flag variables. This indicates, for example, that Cluster 1 contains greater use of credit cards, higher response to previous promotions, higher spending in previous time periods, and higher proportions of purchases in most clothing classes. The faithful Cluster 2 customers have been

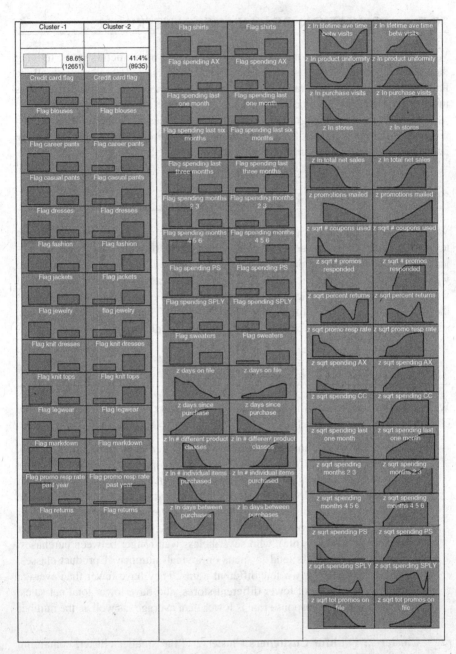

Figure 30.12   Graphical summaries of predictors, by cluster, for the training data.

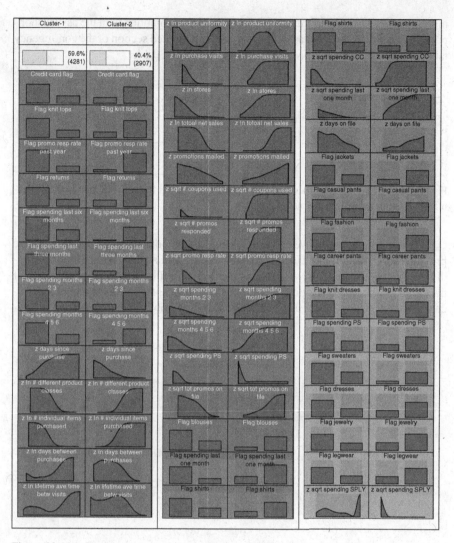

Figure 30.13   Graphical summaries of predictors, by cluster, for the test data set.

shopping with us for a long time, while having smaller durations between purchases. Cluster 2 customers shop for a wide variety of goods, and purchase a higher than average number of different items. They have higher than average purchase visits, visit more stores, and have higher total net sales. Their promotion response rate is higher than average, as well as the number of coupons used.

Without question, these clusters reflect different real-world categories of shoppers, thereby underscoring their validity. One can imagine the store clerks learning some of the faithful customers' names by sight, while not recognizing many of the casual shoppers. We might anticipate that the faithful customers cluster will have a much stronger response to the direct-mail marketing promotion than the casual shoppers. In fact, this is the case, as is shown by the highlighted section of the contingency table of cluster membership versus response in Figure 30.14.

Response		cluster-1	cluster-2
0	Count	11818	6187
	Column %	93.42	69.24
1	Count	833	2748
	Column %	6.58	30.76

Figure 30.14   Faithful customers are more than four times as likely to respond to the direct–mail marketing promotion as casual shoppers.

To summarize, we have extracted principal components and clusters that have provided some insight into customer behaviors, as well as uncovered groups of predictors that behave similarly. These have helped us fulfill our secondary objective of developing better understanding of our clientele. In Chapter 31, we construct classification models that will help us to address our primary objective: maximizing profits.

CASE STUDY, PART 3: MODELING AND EVALUATION FOR PERFORMANCE AND INTERPRETABILITY

31.1 DO YOU PREFER THE BEST MODEL PERFORMANCE, OR A COMBINATION OF PERFORMANCE AND INTERPRETABILITY?

This chapter and Chapter 32 address our primary objective with the Case Study of *Predicting Response to Direct-Mail Marketing*: that of developing a classification model that will maximize profits. However, recall that multicollinearity among the predictors can lead to instability in certain models, such as multiple regression or logistic regression. Unstable models lack interpretability, because we cannot know with confidence, for example, that a particular logistic regression coefficient is positive or negative. The use of correlated predictors for decision trees is problematic as well. For example, imagine a decision tree applied to a data set with correlated predictors x_2 and x_3. Suppose the root node split is made on the uncorrelated variable x_1. Then the left side of the tree may make splits based on x_2, while the right side of the tree makes splits based on x_3. Decision rules based on this tree will not capture the similarity of x_2 and x_3. Thus, we need to be wary of using correlated variables for classification.

As we have seen, the remedy for multicollinearity is to apply principal components analysis (PCA) to the set of correlated predictors. This solves the multicollinearity problem, but, as we shall see, somewhat degrades the performance of the classification model. The principal components capture less than 100% of the variability in the predictors, which represent a net loss of information. Therefore, the principal components usually do not perform as well at classification when compared to the original set of predictors. And, crucially, multicollinearity does not significantly affect point estimates of the target variable.

Data Mining and Predictive Analytics, First Edition. Daniel T. Larose and Chantal D. Larose.
© 2015 John Wiley & Sons, Inc. Published 2015 by John Wiley & Sons, Inc.

Thus, the analyst, together with the client, must consider the following question:

> "Are we looking for the best possible classification performance, such as the maximum profit for our classification model, with no interest at all in interpreting any aspects of the model, or, are we looking for a model with somewhat reduced performance but retaining complete interpretability?"

- If the primary objective of the business or research problem pertains *solely* to classification, with no interest in the interpretability of the model characteristics (e.g., coefficients), then substitution of the principal components for the collection of correlated predictors is not strictly required. In fact, these models usually outperform analogous PCA-based models. We investigate these types of classification models in Chapter 32.

- However, if the primary (or secondary) objective of the analysis is to assess or interpret the effect of the individual predictors on the response, or to develop a profile of likely responders based on their predictor characteristics, then substitution of the principal components for the collection of correlated predictors is strongly recommended. We examine these types of classification models here in this chapter.

31.2 MODELING AND EVALUATION OVERVIEW

An overview of our modeling and evaluation strategy for this chapter and Chapter 32 is given by the following:

MODELING AND EVALUATION OVERVIEW

1. Develop the cost-benefit table (cost matrix) using data-driven misclassification costs.
2. Provide a listing of the inputs to all models.
3. Establish the baseline model performance in terms of expected profit per customer contacted, in order to calibrate the performance of candidate models.
4. Use the built-in misclassification costs to apply the following classification algorithms to the training data set:
   a. Classification and regression trees (CART)
   b. C5.0 decision tree algorithm.
5. Apply rebalancing as a surrogate for misclassification costs for the following methods without built-in misclassification costs:
   a. Neural networks
   b. Logistic regression.

> **6.** Combine the predictions from the four classification models using model voting.
>
> **7.** Evaluate each of the above models using the test data set and the cost-benefit table to determine the most profitable model.
>
> **8.** (For this chapter only): Explain and interpret the most profitable model.

Because our strategy calls for applying many models that need to be evaluated and compared, we hence move fluidly back and forth between the modeling phase and the evaluation phase.

31.3 COST-BENEFIT ANALYSIS USING DATA-DRIVEN COSTS

We use the methods learned in Chapter 16 to derive our cost matrix. We are trying to predict whether or not our customers will respond to the direct-mail promotion. Now, supposing they do respond, how much can we expect them to spend? A reasonable estimate would be the average amount spent per visit for all 28,799 customers, which is $113.59 (Figure 31.1). (The median is another reasonable estimate, which we do not use in this Case Study. By the way, why is the mean larger than the median? Hint: Check out the maximum: Imagine spending an average of $1919.88 per visit to a clothing store.) Assume that 25% of this $113.59, or $28.40, represents the mean profit. Recall that this equals a "cost" of −$28.40. Also, assume that the cost of the mailing is $2.00.

Finally, we review the meaning of the cells of our contingency table, given in Table 31.1.

- **TN = True negative**. This represents a customer who we predicted would not respond, and would not in fact have responded.
- **TP = True positive**. This represents a customer who we predicted would respond, and would in fact have responded to the promotion.
- **FN = False negative**. This represents a customer who we predicted would not respond, but would in fact have responded to the promotion.
- **FP = False positive**. This represents a customer who we predicted would respond, but would not in fact have responded.

We are now ready to calculate our costs.

Count	28799
Mean	113.59
Min	0.49
Max	1919.88
Standard Deviation	86.98
Median	92.00

Figure 31.1 Summary statistics for *Average amount spent per visit*.

TABLE 31.1 **Generic contingency table for direct-mail response classification problem**

	Predicted Category	
Actual category	0 = Non-response	1 = Positive response
0 Non-response	TN = Count of true negatives	FP = Count of false positives
1 Positive response	FN = Count of false negatives	TP = Count of true positives

31.3.1 Calculating Direct Costs

- **True negative**. We did not contact this customer, and so did not incur the $2.00 mailing cost. Thus, the cost for this customer is $0.00.

- **True positive**. We did contact this customer, and so incurred the $2.00 mailing cost. Further, this customer would have responded positively to the promotion, providing us with an average profit of $28.40. Thus, the cost for this customer is $2.00−$28.40 = −$26.40.

- **False negative**. We did not contact this customer, and so did not incur the $2.00 mailing cost. Thus, the cost for this customer is $0.00.

- **False positive**. We did contact this customer, and so incurred the $2.00 mailing cost. But the customer lined his parakeet cage with our flyer and would not have responded to our promotion. Thus, the direct cost for this customer is $2.00.

These costs are summarized in the cost matrix in Table 31.2. Note that the costs are completely data-driven.

Software packages such as *IBM/SPSS Modeler* require the cost matrix to be in a form where there are zero costs for the correct decisions. Thus, we subtract $Cost_{TP} = -\$26.40$ from each cell in the bottom row, giving us the adjusted cost matrix in Table 31.3.

For interpretability, it is advisable now to divide each of the remaining nonzero adjusted costs by one of the remaining nonzero adjusted costs, so that one of the nonzero adjusted costs equals 1. This is so that the analyst may explain to managers

TABLE 31.2 **Data-driven cost matrix for the Case Study**

		Predicted Category	
		0	1
Actual category	0	$Cost_{TN} = \$0$	$Cost_{FP} = \$2$
	1	$Cost_{FN} = \$0$	$Cost_{TP} = -\$26.40$

TABLE 31.3 **Adjusted cost matrix**

		Predicted Category	
		0	1
Actual category	0	0	$Cost_{FP, Adj} = \$2$
	1	$Cost_{FN, Adj} = \$26.40$	0

or clients the relative cost of each classification error. For example, suppose we divide $Cost_{FP, Adj}$ and $Cost_{FN, Adj}$ each by $Cost_{FP, Adj} = 4$. This gives us $Cost^*_{FP, Adj} = \$1$ and $Cost^*_{FN, Adj} = \$13.20$. Thus, we may say that the cost of not contacting a customer who would actually have responded is 13.2 times greater than the cost of contacting a customer who would not actually have responded.

For decision purposes, Table 31.3 is equivalent to Table 31.2. That is, either cost matrix will yield the same decisions. However, Table 31.3 will not provide accurate estimates of the overall model cost when evaluating the classification models. Use Table 31.2 for this purpose.

31.4   VARIABLES TO BE INPUT TO THE MODELS

The analyst should always provide the client or end-user with a comprehensive listing of the inputs to the models. These inputs should include derived variables, transformed variables, or raw variables, as well as principal components and cluster membership, where appropriate. Figure 31.2 contains a listing of all the variables input to the classification models analyzed in this section (performance and interpretability) of the Case Study.

Note that all of the continuous variables have been both transformed and standardized, that many flag variables have been derived. In fact, only a handful of variables remain untouched by the data preparation phase, including the flag variables *Web Buyer* and *Credit Card Holder*.

	flag spending SPLY
Phone # on file	flag returns
Credit Card Flag	flag promo resp rate past year
Web Buyer Flag	flag markdown
Brand	flag spending months 4 5 6
flag sweaters	flag spending months 2 3
flag knit tops	z sqrt knit tops
flag knit dresses	z sqrt knit dresses
flag blouses	z sqrt jewelry
flag jackets	z sqrt fashion
flag career pants	z sqrt legwear
flag casual pants	z sqrt spending AM
flag shirts	z sqrt spending AX
flag dresses	z sqrt spending last one month
flag suits	z sqrt spending SPLY
flag outerwear	PC 1
flag jewelry	PC 2
flag fashion	PC 3
flag legwear	PC 4
flag collectibles	PC 5
flag spending AM	PC 6
flag spending PS	PC 7
flag spending CC	PC 8
flag spending AX	PC 9
flag spending last three months	PC 10
flag spending last one month	PC 11
flag spending last six months	Cluster

Figure 31.2   Input variables for classification models (performance and interpretability) section).

31.5 ESTABLISHING THE BASELINE MODEL PERFORMANCE

How will we know when our models are performing well? Is 80% classification accuracy good enough? 90%? 95%? In order to be able to calibrate the performance of our candidate models, we need to establish benchmarks against which these models can be compared. These benchmarks often come in the form of baseline model performance for some simple models. Two of these simple models are as follows:

- The "Don't send a marketing promotion to anyone" model.
- The "Send a marketing promotion to everyone" model.

Clearly, the company does not need to employ data miners to use either of these two models. Therefore, if the performance of the models reported by the data miner, after arduous analysis, is lower than the performance of either of the above baseline models, then the data miner better try again. In other words, the models reported by the data miner absolutely need to outperform these baseline models, hopefully, by a margin large enough to justify the project.

From Figure 31.3, we see that there are 6027 customers in the test data set who do not respond to the promotion, and 1161 who do respond. The contingency/costs table (adapted from Table 31.2) for the "Don't send to anyone" model is shown in Table 31.4.

- The final model cost for the "Don't send to anyone" model is of course $0.
- The per-customer cost is $0.

Value	Proportion	%	Count
0		83.85	6027
1		16.15	1161

Figure 31.3 Distribution of *Response* for the test data set.

So, we would not make any money by not sending a promotion to anyone, which is no surprise. Next, the contingency/costs table for the "Send to everyone" model is shown in Table 31.5.

- The final model cost for the "Send to everyone" model is $12,054 - $30,650.40 = -$18,596.40.
- The per-customer cost is -$2.59, where we recall that negative cost equals gain.

TABLE 31.4 Contingency/costs table for the "Don't send to anyone" model

		Predicted Category	
		0	**1**
Actual category	**0**	$6027 \cdot (\$0) = \$0$	$0 \cdot (\$2) = \$0$
	1	$1161 \cdot (\$0) = \$0$	$0 \cdot (-\$26.40) = \$0$

TABLE 31.5   Contingency/costs table for the "Send to everyone" model

		Predicted Category	
		0	**1**
Actual category	**0**	$0 \cdot (-\$2) = \$0$	$6027 \cdot (\$2) = \$12\,054$
	1	$0 \cdot (\$26.40) = \$0$	$1161 \cdot (-\$26.40) = -\$30,650.40$

So, we would gain an average of $2.59 per customer by sending a promotion to everyone. The revenue from the minority of customers responding would outweigh the mailing costs of sending to everyone.

Now, consider had we ignored misclassification costs, and chosen the model with the highest accuracy. The overall accuracy of the "Don't send to anyone" model is $6027/7188 = 0.8385$, which is much higher than the overall accuracy of the "Send to everyone" model, which is $1161/7188 = 0.1615$. Thus, had we erroneously ignored the misclassification costs, we would have chosen the "Don't send to anyone" model, based on higher accuracy. This egregious error would have cost our company tens of thousands of dollars. We know better. The "Don't send to anyone" model must be considered a complete failure, and shall no longer be discussed. However, the "Send to everyone" model is actually making money for the company. Therefore, it is this "Send to everyone" model that we shall define as our *baseline model*, and the profit of $2.59 per customer is defined as the *benchmark profit* that any candidate model should outperform.

31.6   MODELS THAT USE MISCLASSIFICATION COSTS

Misclassification costs may explicitly be specified using *Modeler*'s CART and C5.0 decision tree models, but may not using neural networks and logistic regression. So, at this point, we perform classification using the two algorithms where we can specify our misclassification costs: CART and C5.0. A CART model was trained on the training data set, and evaluated on the test data set. The contingency/costs table for the CART model is shown in Table 31.6, where the misclassification costs for the CART model were specified as $1 for false positive, and $13.20 for false negative.

- Total cost for the CART model is $-\$20,944$.
- Per-customer cost for the CART model is $-\$2.91$.

So, the CART model beats the "Send to everyone" model by $-\$2.91 + 2.59 = \$0.32$ per customer.

TABLE 31.6   Contingency/costs table for the CART model with misclassification costs

		Predicted Category	
		0	**1**
Actual category	**0**	$3299 \cdot (\$0) = \$0$	$2728 \cdot (\$2) = \$5456$
	1	$161 \cdot (\$0) = \$0$	$1000 \cdot (-\$26.40) = -\$26,400$

Next, a C5.0 decision tree model was run, with the misclassification costs given as $1 for false positive, and $13.20 for false negative. A C5.0 model was trained on the training set and evaluated on the test set. The contingency/costs table for the C5.0 model is shown in Table 31.7.

- Total cost for the C5.0 model is $-\$22,682.40$.
- Per-customer cost for the C5.0 model is $-\$3.16$.

TABLE 31.7 Contingency/costs table for the C5.0 model with misclassification costs

		Predicted Category	
		0	**1**
Actual category	**0**	$2637 \cdot (\$0) = \$0$	$3390 \cdot (\$2) = \$6780$
	1	$45 \cdot (\$0) = \$0$	$1188 \cdot (-\$26.40) = -\$29,462.40$

So, the C5.0 did even better than the CART model, beating the "Send to everyone" model by $-\$3.16 + 2.59 = \$0.57$ per customer.

31.7 MODELS THAT NEED REBALANCING AS A SURROGATE FOR MISCLASSIFICATION COSTS

In Chapter 16, we learned how to apply rebalancing as a surrogate for misclassification costs, where such costs cannot be expressly specified by the algorithm. In our Case Study, $Cost_{FN, Adj} > Cost_{FP, Adj}$, so that we multiply the number of records with positive responses in the training data by b, before applying the classification algorithm, where b is the *resampling ratio*, $b = Cost_{FN, Adj}/Cost_{FP, Adj} = 52.8/4 = 13.2/1 = 13.2$. We therefore multiply the number of records with positive responses (*Response* = 1) in the training data set by 13.2. This is accomplished by resampling the records with positive responses with replacement.

A neural network model was trained on the rebalanced training data set, and evaluated on the test data set, with the contingency/costs table shown in Table 31.8.

- Total cost for the neural network model is $-\$22,205.2$.
- Per-customer cost for the neural network model is $-\$3.09$.

TABLE 31.8 Contingency/costs table for the neural network model applied to the rebalanced data set

		Predicted Category	
		0	**1**
Actual category	**0**	$2768 \cdot (\$0) = \$0$	$3259 \cdot (\$2) = \$6518$
	1	$73 \cdot (\$0) = \$0$	$1088 \cdot (-\$26.40) = -\$28,723.20$

So, the neural network model did better than the CART model, but not as well as the C5.0 model, and beat the "Send to everyone" model by $-\$3.09 + 2.59 = \$0.50$ per customer.

Finally, a logistic regression model was trained on the rebalanced training data set, and evaluated on the test data set, with the contingency/costs table shown in Table 31.9.

- Total cost for the logistic regression model is −$21, 866.40.
- Per-customer cost for the logistic regression model is −$3.04.

TABLE 31.9   Contingency/costs table for the logistic regression model applied to the rebalanced data set

		Predicted Category	
		0	**1**
Actual category	**0**	$2757 \cdot (\$0) = \$0$	$3270 \cdot (\$2) = \$6540$
	1	$85 \cdot (\$0) = \$0$	$1076 \cdot (-\$26.40) = -\$28, 406.40$

So, the logistic regression model did better than the CART model, but not as well as the C5.0 model or the neural network model, and beat the "Send to everyone" model by −$3.04 + 2.59 = $0.45 per customer.

31.8   COMBINING MODELS USING VOTING AND PROPENSITY AVERAGING

Again, we combine models using model voting and propensity averaging. These methods were applied here, with mixed success. The single sufficient voting model predicts positive response if any of our four classification models (CART, C5.0, neural networks, logistic regression) predicts positive response. Similarly, twofold sufficient, threefold sufficient, and positive unanimity models were developed. The results are provided in Table 31.10. The threefold sufficient model performed best among the voting models, but still did not outperform the C5.0 singleton model.

Propensity averaging was also applied, with similar results. The propensities of positive response for the four classification models were averaged, and a histogram of the resulting mean propensity is shown in Figure 31.4. The analyst should try to determine a cutoff value where there are a high proportion of positive responses to the right, and a high proportion of negative responses to the left. It turns out that the optimal[1] cutoff was found to be *mean propensity* = 0.357, as shown in Table 31.10. This model predicts a positive response if the mean propensity to respond positively among the four models is 0.357 or greater. This model did well, but again did not outperform the original C5.0 model.

The reader is invited to try further model enhancements, if desired, such as the use of segmentation modeling, and boosting and bagging.

---

[1]Of course, to find the optimal cutoff, an exhaustive search is necessary of all possible cutoff points, which requires programming or scripting.

TABLE 31.10   Results from combining models using voting and propensity averaging (best performance in bold)

Model	Total Model Profit	Profit per Customer
"Send to All" model	$18,596.40	$2.59
CART model	$20,944.00	$2.91
C5.0 model	**$22,682.40**	**$3.16**
Neural network	$22,205.20	$3.09
Logistic regression	$21,866.40	$3.04
Single sufficient	$21,408.40	$2.98
Twofold sufficient	$22,411.60	$3.12
Threefold sufficient	$22,555.20	$3.14
Positive unanimity	$21,322.80	$2.97
Mean propensity 0.356	$22,553.60	$3.14
Mean propensity 0.357	$22,573.60	$3.14
Mean propensity 0.358	$22,508.40	$3.13

For clarity, profit rather than cost is listed, where profit = −cost. For completeness, the results from the singleton models are included as well.

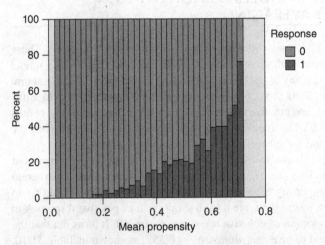

Figure 31.4   Mean propensity, with response overlay.

31.9   INTERPRETING THE MOST PROFITABLE MODEL

Recall that in this chapter, we are interested in both model performance and model interpretability. It is time to explain and interpret our most profitable model, the original C5.0 decision tree. Figure 31.5 contains the C5.0 decision tree, which is to read from left to right, with the root node split on the left.

```
⊟  Cluster = cluster-1 [ Mode: 0 ] (12,651)
   ⊟  PC 7 <= 2.76 [ Mode: 0 ] (12,550)
      ┈  Web Buyer Flag = T [ Mode: 1 ]  ⇨  1 (211; 0.237)
      ⊟  Web Buyer Flag = F [ Mode: 0 ] (12,339)
         ⊟  PC 1 <= -0.89 [ Mode: 0 ] (4,214)
            ⊟  flag spending last one month = T [ Mode: 1 ] (61)
               ┈  flag promo resp rate past year = T [ Mode: 0 ]  ⇨  0 (21; 1.0)
               ┈  flag promo resp rate past year = F [ Mode: 1 ]  ⇨  1 (40; 0.15)
            ⊟  flag spending last one month = F [ Mode: 0 ] (4,153)
               ⊞  PC 2 <= 0.44 [ Mode: 0 ] (2,722)
               ⊞  PC 2 > 0.44 [ Mode: 0 ] (1,431)
         ⊟  PC 1 > -0.89 [ Mode: 1 ] (8,125)
            ⊟  PC 1 <= 0.68 [ Mode: 1 ] (7,734)
               ⊞  PC 2 <= 0.73 [ Mode: 0 ] (6,932)
               ⊞  PC 2 > 0.73 [ Mode: 1 ] (802)
            ⊟  PC 1 > 0.68 [ Mode: 1 ] (391)
               ┈  PC 5 <= 1.14 [ Mode: 1 ]  ⇨  1 (334; 0.228)
               ⊞  PC 5 > 1.14 [ Mode: 0 ] (57)
   ┈  PC 7 > 2.76 [ Mode: 0 ]  ⇨  0 (101; 1.0)
⊟  Cluster = cluster-2 [ Mode: 1 ] (8,935)
   ⊟  PC 1 <= 1.11 [ Mode: 1 ] (5,960)
      ⊟  PC 1 <= 0.26 [ Mode: 1 ] (2,115)
         ┈  Web Buyer Flag = T [ Mode: 1 ]  ⇨  1 (69; 0.275)
         ⊟  Web Buyer Flag = F [ Mode: 1 ] (2,046)
            ⊟  flag markdown = T [ Mode: 1 ] (2,017)
               ⊞  PC 5 <= 0.45 [ Mode: 1 ] (1,406)
               ⊞  PC 5 > 0.45 [ Mode: 1 ] (611)
            ⊟  flag markdown = F [ Mode: 0 ] (29)
               ┈  flag promo resp rate past year = T [ Mode: 0 ]  ⇨  0 (28; 1.0)
               ┈  flag promo resp rate past year = F [ Mode: 1 ]  ⇨  1 (1; 1.0)
      ⊟  PC 1 > 0.26 [ Mode: 1 ] (3,845)
         ┈  Web Buyer Flag = T [ Mode: 1 ]  ⇨  1 (239; 0.381)
         ⊟  Web Buyer Flag = F [ Mode: 1 ] (3,606)
            ┈  PC 5 <= -0.39 [ Mode: 1 ]  ⇨  1 (1,117; 0.333)
            ⊟  PC 5 > -0.39 [ Mode: 1 ] (2,489)
               ⊞  PC 2 <= 0.10 [ Mode: 1 ] (739)
               ⊞  PC 2 > 0.10 [ Mode: 1 ] (1,750)
   ┈  PC 1 > 1.11 [ Mode: 1 ]  ⇨  1 (2,975; 0.482)
```

Figure 31.5   Our most profitable model, among the models chosen for performance and interpretability: the C5.0 decision tree.

Our root node split is on the clusters that we uncovered in Chapter 30. Recall that Cluster 1 contains *Casual Shoppers*, while Cluster 2 consists of *Faithful Customers*. We found that the *Faithful Customers* had a response proportion more than four times higher than the *Casual Shoppers*, so it is not surprising that our classification decision tree has found the clusters to have good discriminatory power between responders and non-responders. This is reflected in the decision tree: for Cluster 1, the mode is 0 (response = 0), while for Cluster 2, the mode is 1. As you look at Figure 31.5, keep in mind that all the nodes and information in the top half of the graph pertain to the *Casual Shoppers*, while all the nodes and information in the bottom half pertain to the *Faithful Customers*. The "+" symbols shown at certain splits indicate that there are further splits in the decision tree. But we did not have enough space to render the full decision tree on the page.

Let us begin by discussing the *Casual Shoppers*. The next split is on principal component 7, *Blouses versus Sweaters*, with the tiny minority of 101 casual shoppers who have bought lots of (PC 7 > 2.76) blouses (but not sweaters) being predicted not to respond. The next split is something to take note of: among the casual shoppers, *web buyers* are predicted to respond positively. Even though only 23.7% of these customers are actual responders, the 13.2 − 1 misclassification cost ratio makes it easier for the model to predict these customers as responders, rather than suffer the severe false negative cost. However, there are only a small number of these (211). Continuing with the vast majority of casual shoppers, we find the next split is on principal component 1, *Sales Volume and Frequency*. Note that this is the first split to partition off more than a couple of hundred records. This is because the first principal component is very large and quite predictive of response, as we saw in Chapter 30. In fact, PC 1 is the first split for our faithful customers. Unsurprisingly, the 4214 casual shoppers who have very low values for PC 1 (PC 1 ≤ −0.89) have a mode of non-response, while the remaining 8125 casual shoppers have a mode of positive response. For those with low values of PC 1, the next important split is on PC 2, *Promotion Proclivity*, where, unsurprisingly, the 802 casual shoppers who have very high values for PC 2 have a mode of positive response, while the remaining casual shoppers have a mode of non-response. For those with medium and high values of PC 1 (PC 1 > −0.89), the next split is again on PC 1, fine-tuning the remaining records. For the 7734 records that have PC values between −0.89 and 0.68, the next split is on PC 2, where high values have a mode of response and medium and low values have a mode of non-response.

Next, we turn to our *Faithful Customers*. The first split is on PC 1, *Sales Volume and Frequency*, with high values predicted to respond positively without further splits. Note the simplicity of this result: In this complicated data set, all we need to know to predict that a customer will respond positively is (i) that he or she belongs to the *Faithful Customers* cluster, and (ii) that he or she has high *Sales Volume and Frequency*. This is a rcsult that is simple, powerful, and crystal clear. Continuing, we find that the next split is also on PC 1, underscoring the importance of this large principal component. For faithful customers with PC 1 values of 0.26 or less, the next split is for *web buyer*, where only 69 positively responding records are split off. Next comes the *markdown* flag; that is, whether a customer bought an item that was marked down. But this split only partitions off 29 records. The next split is on principal component 5, *Spending versus Returns*. There are further splits here that would give us information on these 2017 records, but there was not enough room to show the splits here. For those with PC 1 values between 0.26 and 1.11, the next split is on *web buyer*, which, for the 239 web buyers, predicts positive response. Next comes principal component 5, *Spending versus Returns*: for low values, the prediction is positive response. For medium and high values of PC 5, there is a further split on PC 2, *Promotion Proclivity*.

In Chapter 32, we consider models that sacrifice interpretability for better performance.

CASE STUDY, PART 4: MODELING AND EVALUATION FOR HIGH PERFORMANCE ONLY

In this chapter, we are trading model interpretability for performance. We will take advantage of the fact that multicollinearity does not affect the model predictions, and not worry about substituting principal components for correlated predictors. In this way, as the set of original predictors contain more information than the set of principal components, we hope to develop models that will outperform those of Chapter 31, even while sacrificing interpretability.

32.1 VARIABLES TO BE INPUT TO THE MODELS

The models in this chapter will benefit from a greater number of input variables, including many of the continuous variables that were subsumed into the principal components in Chapter 31. The listing of the variables is provided in Figure 32.1. Note that cluster membership remains an input, even though the principal components do not.

32.2 MODELS THAT USE MISCLASSIFICATION COSTS

We begin using the two algorithms where we can specify our misclassification costs: classification and regression trees (CART) and C5.0. A CART model was trained on the training data set, and evaluated on the test data set. The contingency/costs table for the CART model is shown in Table 32.1, where the misclassification costs were specified as $1 for false positive, and $13.20 for false negative.

- Total cost for the CART model is −$23 366.
- Per customer cost for the CART model is −$3.25.

So, the "CART performance model" beats the "Send to everyone" model by −$3.25 + 2.59 = $0.64 per customer. Further, the CART performance model beat the

---

Data Mining and Predictive Analytics, First Edition. Daniel T. Larose and Chantal D. Larose.
© 2015 John Wiley & Sons, Inc. Published 2015 by John Wiley & Sons, Inc.

Predictors	flag spending last three months	z sqrt casual pants
	flag spending last one month	z sqrt shirts
Phone # on file	flag spending last six months	z sqrt dresses
Zip code	flag spending SPLY	z sqrt suits
Credit Card Flag	flag returns	z sqrt outerwear
Web Buyer Flag	flag promo resp rate past year	z sqrt jewelry
Brand	flag markdown	z sqrt fashion
flag sweaters	flag spending months 4 5 6	z sqrt legwear
flag knit tops	flag spending months 2 3	z sqrt collectibles
flag knit dresses	z ln purchase visits	z sqrt spending AM
flag blouses	z days since purchase	z sqrt spending PS
flag jackets	z gross margin %	z sqrt spending CC
flag career pants	z days on file	z sqrt spending AX
flag casual pants	z markdown	z sqrt spending last one month
flag shirts	z promotions mailed	z sqrt spending SPLY
flag dresses	z ln total net sales	z ln days between purchases
flag suits	z ln ave spending per visit	z ln # different product classes
flag outerwear	z sqrt tot promos on file	z sqrt # coupons used
flag jewelry	z sqrt percent returns	z ln # individual items purchased
flag fashion	z sqrt promo resp rate	z ln stores
flag legwear	z sqrt sweaters	z ln lifetime ave time betw visits
flag collectibles	z sqrt knit tops	z ln product uniformity
flag spending AM	z sqrt knit dresses	z sqrt # promos responded
flag spending PS	z sqrt blouses	z sqrt spending months 2 3
flag spending CC	z sqrt jackets	z sqrt spending months 4 5 6
flag spending AX	z sqrt career pants	Cluster

Figure 32.1   Listing of inputs to the models in this chapter.

TABLE 32.1   Contingency/costs table for the "performance CART model" with misclassification costs

		Predicted Category	
		0	**1**
Actual category	**0**	$3322 \cdot (\$0) = \$0$	$2705 \cdot (\$2) = \$5410$
	1	$71 \cdot (\$0) = \$0$	$1090 \cdot (-\$26.40) = -\$28\,776$

CART model from Chapter 31 by $-\$3.25$ to $-\$2.91 = \$0.34$. The performance model did indeed outperform the earlier CART model using the principal components, at least in terms of estimated model cost.

Next, a "performance C5.0 decision tree model" was run, with the misclassification costs given as $1 for false positive, and $13.20 for false negative. The contingency/costs table for the C5.0 model is shown in Table 32.2.

- Total cost for the C5.0 model is $-\$24\,294.40$.
- Per customer cost for the C5.0 model is $-\$3.38$.

So, the performance C5.0 model beat the "Send to everyone" model by $-\$3.38 + 2.59 = \$0.79$ per customer. This performance C5.0 model did better than the C5.0 model from Chapter 31 that used the principal components, by $-\$3.38$ to $-\$3.16 = \$0.22$.

TABLE 32.2 Contingency/costs table for the C5.0 model with misclassification costs

		Predicted Category	
		0	**1**
Actual category	**0**	$3509 \cdot (\$0) = \$0$	$2518 \cdot (\$2) = \$5036$
	1	$50 \cdot (\$0) = \$0$	$1111 \cdot (-\$26.40) = -\$29\,330.40$

32.3 MODELS THAT NEED REBALANCING AS A SURROGATE FOR MISCLASSIFICATION COSTS

Next, in order to use rebalancing as a surrogate for misclassification costs for our neural networks and logistic regression models, we multiplied the number of records with positive responses in the training data set by the resampling ratio $b = 13.2$.

A "performance neural network model" was trained on the rebalanced training data set, and evaluated on the test data set, with the contingency/costs table shown in Table 32.3.

- Total cost for the neural network model is $-\$24\,887.20$.
- Per customer cost for the neural network model is $-\$3.46$.

So, the neural network model beat the "Send to everyone" model by $-\$3.46 + 2.59 = \$0.87$ per customer. This performance neural network model scored better than the neural network model from Chapter 31 that used the principal components, by $-\$3.46$ to $-\$3.09 = \$0.37$ per customer.

Finally, a "performance logistic regression model" was trained on the rebalanced training data set, and evaluated on the test data set, with the contingency/costs table shown in Table 32.4.

- Total cost for the logistic regression model is $-\$23\,361.20$.
- Per customer cost for the logistic regression model is $-\$3.25$.

So, this logistic regression model beat the "Send to everyone" model by $-\$3.25 - 2.59 = \$0.66$ per customer. The performance logistic regression model also did better than the logistic regression model from Chapter 31 by $-\$3.25 + \$3.04 = \$0.21$.

TABLE 32.3 Contingency/costs table for the performance neural network model applied to the rebalanced data set

		Predicted Category	
		0	**1**
Actual category	**0**	$4109 \cdot (\$0) = \$0$	$1918 \cdot (\$2) = \$3836$
	1	$73 \cdot (\$0) = \$0$	$1088 \cdot (-\$26.40) = -\$28\,723.20$

TABLE 32.4   Contingency/costs table for the performance logistic regression model applied to the rebalanced data set

		Predicted Category	
		0	**1**
Actual category	**0**	$3346 \cdot (\$0) = \$0$	$2681 \cdot (\$2) = \$5362$
	1	$73 \cdot (\$0) = \$0$	$1088 \cdot (-\$26.40) = -\$28\,723.20$

32.4   COMBINING MODELS USING VOTING AND PROPENSITY AVERAGING

In Chapter 26, we learned how to combine models using model voting and propensity averaging. All of the "performance voting" combination models outperformed their counterparts from Chapter 31, but did not outperform the singleton performance neural network model above. Again, the threefold sufficient voting model had the best results among the voting models (Table 32.5). Propensity averaging was also applied, with similar results. The propensities of positive response for the four performance classification models were averaged, and a histogram of the resulting mean propensity is shown in Figure 32.2. A non-exhaustive search settled on the optimal cutoff to be *mean propensity* = 0.375, as shown in Table 32.5. This model predicts a positive response if the mean propensity to respond positively among the four models is 0.375 or greater. This model did well, but again did not outperform the singleton performance neural network model.

Again, the reader is invited to try further model enhancements, if desired, such as the use of segmentation modeling, and boosting and bagging.

TABLE 32.5   Results from combining performance models using voting and propensity averaging (best performance highlighted)

Model	Total Model Profit	Profit per Customer
"Send to All" model	$18 596.40	$2.59
CART model	$23 366.00	$3.25
C5.0 model	$24 294.40	$3.38
Neural network	**$24 887.20**	**$3.46**
Logistic regression	$23 361.20	$3.25
Single sufficient	$23 653.60	$3.29
Twofold sufficient	$24 136.40	$3.35
Threefold sufficient	$24 223.60	$3.37
Positive unanimity	23,895.2	$3.32
Mean propensity 0.374	$24 224.80	$3.37
Mean propensity 0.375	$24 236.80	$3.37
Mean propensity 0.376	$24 198.00	$3.37

For clarity, profit rather than cost is listed, where profit = −cost. For completeness, the results from the singleton models are included as well.

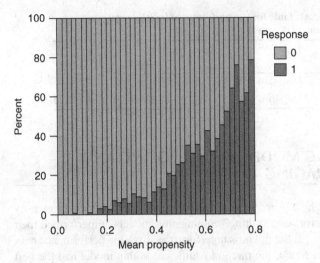

Figure 32.2 . Mean propensity, with response overlay.

32.5   LESSONS LEARNED

Clearly, the "performance" models in this chapter outperform the models in Chapter 31, which use the principal components. The average improvement in profit across the models in Table 32.5 over their counterparts in Chapter 31 is about $7 - 12\%$. Allowing the models to use the actual predictors rather than the principal components led to this increase in profitability. In other words, more information leads to better models.

· The downside of the performance models is lack of interpretability. It is symbolic here that the most profitable performance model is the neural network model, which is well-known for its lack of interpretability in any case. Where the neural network shines is when there are nonlinear associations in the data, which other types of models have difficulty in sifting through. This evidently is the situation in our clothing store data.

32.6   CONCLUSIONS

So, in the end, have we addressed our primary and secondary objectives?

- **Primary Objective**: Develop a classification model that will maximize profits for direct mail marketing.
- **Secondary Objective**: Develop better understanding of our clientele through EDA, component profiles, and cluster profiles.

In Chapters 29, 30, and 31, we developed a much better understanding of our clientele, using exploratory data analysis, component profiles, cluster profiles, and interpretation of the best performing model in Chapter 31. In Chapters 31 and 32, we have developed a set of models that will make a good bit of money for our clothing store company, to the tune of $3.46 per customer, an increase of $0.87 per customer over the "Send to everyone" model the company was probably using before the lessons learned from the Case Study a 25% increase in profits. In thus fulfilling the primary and secondary objectives for this Case Study, the predictive analyst has rendered valuable service, by leveraging existing data to enhance knowledge and profitability.

APPENDIX

DATA SUMMARIZATION AND VISUALIZATION

Here we present a very brief review of methods for summarizing and visualizing data. For deeper coverage, see *Discovering Statistics*, Second Edition, by Daniel Larose (W.H. Freeman, second edition, 2013).

PART 1: SUMMARIZATION 1: BUILDING BLOCKS OF DATA ANALYSIS

- *Descriptive statistics* refers to methods for summarizing and organizing the information in a data set.
  Consider Table A.1, which we will use to illustrate some statistical concepts.

- The entities for which information is collected are called *the elements*. In Table A.1, the elements are the 10 applicants. Elements are also called *cases* or *subjects*.

- A *variable* is a characteristic of an element, which takes on different values for different elements. The variables in Table A.1 are *marital status*, *mortgage*, *income*, *rank*, *year*, and *risk*. Variables are also called *attributes*.

- The set of variable values for a particular element is an *observation*. Observations are also called *records*. The observation for Applicant 2 is:

Applicant	Marital Status	Mortgage	Income ($)	Rank	Year	Risk
2	Married	Y	32,000	7	2010	Good

Data Mining and Predictive Analytics, First Edition. Daniel T. Larose and Chantal D. Larose.
© 2015 John Wiley & Sons, Inc. Published 2015 by John Wiley & Sons, Inc.

TABLE A.1   Characteristics of 10 loan applicants

Applicant	Marital Status	Mortgage	Income ($)	Rank	Year	Risk
1	Single	Y	38,000	2	2009	Good
2	Married	Y	32,000	7	2010	Good
3	Other	N	25,000	9	2011	Good
4	Other	N	36,000	3	2009	Good
5	Other	Y	33,000	4	2010	Good
6	Other	N	24,000	10	2008	Bad
7	Married	Y	25,100	8	2010	Good
8	Married	Y	48,000	1	2007	Good
9	Married	Y	32,100	6	2009	Bad
10	Married	Y	32,200	5	2010	Good

- Variables can be either *qualitative* or *quantitative*.
  - A *qualitative variable* enables the elements to be classified or categorized according to some characteristic. The qualitative variables in Table A.1 are *marital status*, *mortgage*, *rank*, and *risk*. Qualitative variables are also called *categorical variables*.
  - A *quantitative variable* takes numeric values and allows arithmetic to be meaningfully performed on it. The quantitative variables in Table A.1 are *income* and *year*. Quantitative variables are also called *numerical variables*.
- Data may be classified according to four *levels of measurement*: *nominal, ordinal, interval,* and *ratio*. Nominal and ordinal data are categorical; interval and ratio data are numerical.
  - *Nominal data* refer to names, labels, or categories. There is no natural ordering, nor may arithmetic be carried out on nominal data. The nominal variables in Table A.1 are *marital status*, *mortgage*, and *risk*.
  - *Ordinal data* can be rendered into a particular order. However, arithmetic cannot be meaningfully carried out on ordinal data. The ordinal variable in Table A.1 is *income rank*.
  - *Interval data* consist of quantitative data defined on an interval without a natural 0. Addition and subtraction may be performed on interval data. The interval variable in Table A.1 is *year*. (Note that there is no "year 0." The calendar goes from 1 BC to AD 1.)
  - *Ratio data* are quantitative data for which addition, subtraction, multiplication, and division may be performed. A natural 0 exists for ratio data. The interval variable in Table A.1 is *income*.
- A numerical variable that can take either a finite or a countable number of values is a *discrete* variable, for which each value can be graphed as a separate point, with space between each point. The discrete variable in Table A.1 is *year*.

- A numerical variable that can take infinitely many values is a *continuous variable*, whose possible values form an interval on the number line, with no space between the points. The continuous variable in Table A.1 is *income*.

- A *population* is the set of all elements of interest for a particular problem. A *parameter* is a characteristic of a population. For example, the population is the set of all American voters, and the parameter is the proportion of the population who supports a $1 per ton tax on carbon.
  - The value of a parameter is usually unknown, but it is a constant.

- A *sample* consists of a subset of the population. A characteristic of a sample is called *a statistic*. For example, the sample is the set of American voters in your classroom, and the statistic is the proportion of the sample who supports a $1 per ton tax on carbon.
  - The value of a statistic is usually known, but it changes from sample to sample.

- A *census* is the collection of information from every element in the population. For example, the census here would be to find from every American voter whether they support a $1 per ton tax on carbon. Such a census is impractical, so we turn to statistical inference.

- *Statistical inference* refers to methods for estimating or drawing conclusions about population characteristics based on the characteristics of a sample of that population. For example, suppose 50% of the voters in your classroom support the tax; using statistical inference we would *infer* that 50% of all American voters support the tax. Obviously, there are problems with this. The sample is neither random nor representative. The estimate does not have a confidence level, and so on.

- When we take a sample for which each element has an equal chance of being selected, we have a *random sample*.

- A *predictor variable* is a variable whose value is used to help predict the value of the *response variable*. The predictor variables in Table A.1 are all variables, except *risk*.

- A *response variable* is a variable of interest whose value is presumably determined at least in part by the set of predictor variables. The response variable in Table A.1 is *risk*.

PART 2: VISUALIZATION: GRAPHS AND TABLES FOR SUMMARIZING AND ORGANIZING DATA

2.1 Categorical Variables

- The *frequency* (or *count*) of a category is the number of data values in each category. The *relative frequency* of a particular category for a categorical variable equals its frequency divided by the number of cases.

- A (*relative*) *frequency distribution* for a categorical variable consists of all the categories that the variable assumes, together with the (relative) frequencies for each value. The frequencies sum to the number of cases; the relative frequencies sum to 1.
- For example, Table A.2 contains the frequency distribution and relative frequency distribution for the variable *marital status* for the data from Table A.1.

TABLE A.2   Frequency distribution and relative frequency distribution

Category of *Marital Status*	Frequency	Relative Frequency
Married	5	0.5
Other	4	0.4
Single	1	0.1
Total	10	1.0

- A *bar chart* is a graph used to represent the frequencies or relative frequencies for a categorical variable. Note that the bars do not touch.
  - A *Pareto chart* is a bar chart, where the bars are arranged in decreasing order. Figure A.1 is an example of a Pareto chart.
- A *pie chart* is a circle divided into slices, with the size of each slice proportional to the relative frequency of the category associated with that slice. Figure A.2 shows a pie chart of *marital status*.

2.2   Quantitative Variables

- Quantitative data are grouped into *classes*. The *lower (upper) class limit* of a class equals the smallest (largest) value within that class. The *class width* is the difference between successive lower class limits.

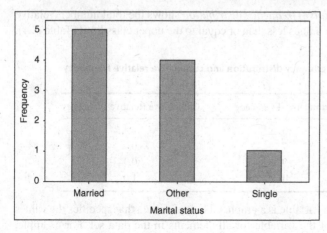

Figure A.1   Bar chart for *marital status*.

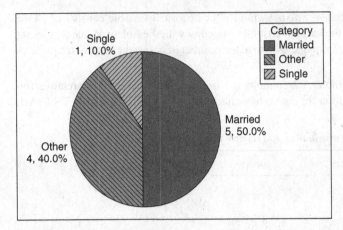

Figure A.2   Pie chart of *marital status*.

- For quantitative data, a *(relative) frequency distribution* divides the data into nonoverlapping classes of equal class width. Table A.3 shows the frequency distribution and relative frequency distribution of the continuous variable *income* from Table A.1.

TABLE A.3   Frequency distribution and relative frequency distribution of *income*

Class of *Income*	Frequency	Relative Frequency
$24,000–$29,999	3	0.3
$30,000–$35,999	4	0.4
$36,000–$41,999	2	0.2
$42,000–$48,999	1	0.1
Total	10	1.0

- A *cumulative (relative) frequency distribution* shows the total number (relative frequency) of data values less than or equal to the upper class limit (Table A.4).

TABLE A.4   Cumulative frequency distribution and cumulative relative frequency distribution of *income*

Class of *Income*	Cumulative Frequency	Cumulative Relative Frequency
$24,000–$29,999	3	0.3
$30,000–$35,999	7	0.7
$36,000–$41,999	9	0.9
$42,000–$48,999	10	1.0

- A *distribution* of a variable is a graph, table, or formula that specifies the values and frequencies of the variable for all elements in the data set. For example, Table A.3 represents the distribution of the variable *income*.

- A *histogram* is a graphical representation of a (relative) frequency distribution for a quantitative variable (Figure A.3). Note that histograms represent a simple version of *data smoothing* and can thus vary in shape depending on the number and width of the classes. Therefore, histograms should be interpreted with caution. See *Discovering Statistics*, Second Edition by Daniel Larose (W.H. Freeman), Section 2.4, for an example of a data set presented as *both* symmetric and right-skewed by altering the number and width of the histogram classes.

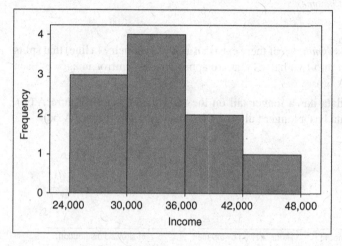

Figure A.3   Histogram of *income*.

- A *stem-and-leaf display* shows the shape of the data distribution while retaining the original data values in the display, either exactly or approximately. The leaf units are defined to equal a power of 10, and the stem units are 10 times the leaf units. Then each leaf represents a data value, through a stem-and-leaf combination. For example, in Figure A.4, the leaf units (right-hand column) are 1000's and the stem units (left-hand column) are 10,000's. So "2 4" represents $2 \times 10,000 + 4 \times 1000 = \$24,000$, while "2 55" represents two equal incomes of $25,000 (one of which is exact, while the other is approximate: $25,100). Note that Figure A.4, turned 90° to the left, presents the shape of the data distribution.

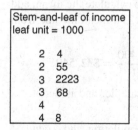

Figure A.4   Stem-and-leaf display of *income*.

- In a *dotplot*, each dot represents one or more data values, set above the number line (Figure A.5).

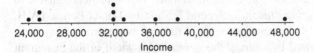

Figure A.5 Dotplot of *income*.

- A distribution is *symmetric* if there exists an axis of symmetry (a line) that splits the distribution into two halves that are approximately mirror images of each other (Figure A.6a).
- *Right-skewed* data has a longer tail on the right than the left (Figure A.6b). *Left-skewed* data has a longer tail on the left than the right (Figure A.6c).

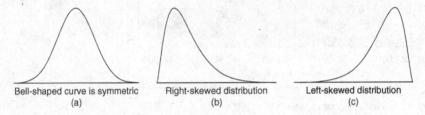

Figure A.6 Symmetric and skewed distributions.

PART 3: SUMMARIZATION 2: MEASURES OF CENTER, VARIABILITY, AND POSITION

- The *summation notation* $\sum x$ means to add up all the data values x. The sample size is n and the population size is N.
- *Measures of center* indicate where on the number line the central part of the data is located. The measures of center we will learn are the *mean*, the *median*, the *mode*, and the *midrange*.
  - The *mean* is the *arithmetic average* of a data set. To calculate the mean, add up the values and divide by the number of values. The mean income from Table A.1 is:

    $$\frac{38,000 + 32,000 + \cdots + 32,200}{10} = \frac{325,400}{10} = \$32,540$$

  - The *sample mean* is the arithmetic average of a sample, and is denoted $\bar{x}$ (*x*-bar).
  - The *population mean* is the arithmetic average of a population, and is denoted μ ("mew," the Greek letter for *m*).

- The *median* is the middle data value, when there are odd numbers of data values and the data have been sorted into ascending order. If there are even numbers, the median is the mean of the two middle data values. When the income data is sorted into ascending order, the two middle values are $32,100 and $32,200, the mean of which is the median income, $32,150.

- The *mode* is the data value that occurs with the greatest frequency. Both quantitative and categorical variables can have modes, but only quantitative variables can have means or medians. Each income value occurs only once, so there is no mode. The mode for *year* is 2010, with a frequency of 4.

- The *midrange* is the average of the maximum and minimum values in a data set. The midrange income is

$$\text{Midrange(income)} = \frac{(\max(\text{income}) + \min(\text{income}))}{2}$$
$$= \frac{48,000 + 24,000}{2}$$
$$= \$36,000$$

- *Skewness and measures of center.* The following are tendencies, and not strict rules:
  - For symmetric data, the mean and the median are approximately equal.
  - For right-skewed data, the mean is greater than the median.
  - For left-skewed data, the median is greater than the mean.

- *Measures of variability* quantify the amount of *variation*, *spread*, or *dispersion* present in the data. The measures of variability we will learn are the *range*, the *variance*, the *standard deviation*, and, later, the *interquartile range (IQR)*.

  - The *range* of a variable equals the difference between the maximum and minimum values. The range of *income* is: range = max(income) − min(income) = $48,000 − 24,000 = \$24,000$.

  - A *deviation* is the signed difference between a data value, and the mean value. For Applicant 1, the deviation in *income* equals $x - \bar{x} = 38,000 - 32,540 = 5460$. For any conceivable data set, the *mean deviation* always equals 0, because the sum of the deviations equals 0.

  - The *population variance* is the mean of the squared deviations, denoted as σ^2 (sigma-squared):

$$\sigma^2 = \frac{\sum (x - \mu)^2}{N}$$

  - The *population standard deviation* is the square root of the population variance: $\sigma = \sqrt{\sigma^2}$.

  - The *sample variance* is approximately the mean of the squared deviations, with n replaced by $n-1$ in the denominator in order to make it an *unbiased estimator* of σ^2. (An *unbiased estimator* is a statistic whose expected value equals its target parameter.)

$$s^2 = \frac{\sum (x - \bar{x})^2}{n - 1}$$

○ The *sample standard deviation* is the square root of the sample variance: $s = \sqrt{s^2}$.

○ The variance is expressed in *units squared*, an interpretation that may be opaque to nonspecialists. For this reason, the standard deviation, which is expressed in the original units, is preferred when reporting results. For example, the sample variance of *income* is $s^2 = 51,860,444$ *dollars squared*, the meaning of which may be unclear to clients. Better to report the sample standard deviation $s = \$7201$.

○ The sample standard deviation s is interpreted as the size of the *typical deviation*, that is, the size of the typical difference between data values and the mean data value. For example, incomes typically deviate from their mean by $7201.

• *Measures of position* indicate the relative position of a particular data value in the data distribution. The measures of position we cover here are the *percentile*, the *percentile rank*, the *Z-score*, and the *quartiles*.

○ The *pth percentile* of a data set is the data value such that p percent of the values in the data set are at or below this value. The 50th percentile is the median. For example, the median *income* is $32,150, and 50% of the data values lie at or below this value.

○ The *percentile rank* of a data value equals the percentage of values in the data set that are at or below that value. For example, the percentile rank of Applicant 1's income of $38,000 is 90%, as that is the percentage of incomes equal to or less than $38,000.

○ The *Z-score* for a particular data value represents how many standard deviations above or below the mean the data value lies. For a sample, the Z-score is:

$$Z\text{-score} = \frac{x - \bar{x}}{s}$$

For Applicant 6, the Z-score is

$$\frac{24,000 - 32,540}{7201} \approx -1.2$$

The income of Applicant 6 lies 1.2 standard deviations below the mean.

○ We may also find data values, given a Z-score. Suppose no loans will be given to those with incomes more than 2 standard deviations below the mean. Then, Z-score $= -2$, and the corresponding minimum income is:

$$\text{Income} = Z\text{-score} \cdot s + \bar{x} = (-2)(7201) + 32,540 = \$18,138$$

No loans will be provided to applicants with incomes below $18,138.

○ If the data distribution is normal, then the *Empirical Rule* states that:

• about 68% of the data lies within 1 standard deviation of the mean;

- about 95% of the data lies within 2 standard deviations of the mean;
- about 99.7% of the data lies within 3 standard deviations of the mean.

○ The *first quartile (Q1)* is the 25th percentile of a data set; the *second quartile (Q2)* is the 50th percentile (median); and the *third quartile (Q3)* is the 75th percentile.

○ The **IQR** is a measure of variability that is not sensitive to the presence of outliers. IQR = $Q3 - Q1$.

○ In the *IQR method for detecting outliers*, a data value x is an outlier if either
  - $x \leq Q1 - 1.5(\text{IQR})$, or
  - $x \geq Q3 + 1.5(\text{IQR})$.

- The *five-number summary* of a data set consists of the *minimum, Q1*, the *median, Q3*, and the *maximum*.

- The *boxplot* is a graph based on the five-number summary, useful for recognizing symmetry and skewness. Suppose for a particular data set (not from Table A.1) we have *min* = 15, *Q1* = 29, *median* = 36, *Q3* = 42, and *Max* = 47. Then the boxplot is shown in Figure A.7.

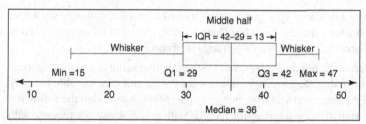

Figure A.7   Boxplot of left-skewed data.

○ The box covers the "middle half" of the data from Q1 to Q3.

○ The left whisker extends down to the minimum value which is not an outlier.

○ The right whisker extends up to the maximum value that is not an outlier.

○ When the left whisker is longer than the right whisker, then the distribution is left skewed and vice versa.

○ When the whiskers are about equal in length, the distribution is symmetric. The distribution in Figure A.7 shows evidence of being left-skewed.

PART 4: SUMMARIZATION AND VISUALIZATION OF BIVARIATE RELATIONSHIPS

- A *bivariate relationship* is the relationship between two variables.

- The relationship between two categorical variables is summarized using a *contingency table*, which is a cross-tabulation of the two variables, and contains a cell for every combination of variable values (i.e., for every contingency).

TABLE A.5 Contingency table for *mortgage* versus *risk*

| | | Mortgage | | |
		Yes	No	Total
Risk	Good	6	2	8
	Bad	1	1	2
	Total	7	3	10

Table A.5 is the contingency table for the variables *mortgage* and *risk*. The total column contains the *marginal distribution* for *risk*, that is, the frequency distribution for this variable alone. Similarly, the total row represents the marginal distribution for *mortgage*.

- Much can be learned from a contingency table. The *baseline proportion* of *bad risk* is 2/10 = 20%. However, the proportion of *bad risk* for applicants without a mortgage is 1/3 = 33%, which is higher than the baseline; and the proportion of *bad risk* for applicants with a mortgage is only 1/7 = 1%, which is lower than the baseline. Thus, whether or not the applicant has a mortgage is useful for predicting risk.

- A *clustered bar chart* is a graphical representation of a contingency table. Figure A.8 shows the clustered bar chart for *risk*, clustered by *mortgage*. Note that the disparity between the two groups is immediately obvious.

- To summarize the relationship between a quantitative variable and a categorical variable, we calculate summary statistics for the quantitative variable for each level of the categorical variable. For example, Minitab provided the following summary statistics for *income*, for records with *bad risk* and for records with *good risk*. All summary measures are larger for *good risk*. Is the difference significant? We need to perform a hypothesis test to find out (Chapter 4).

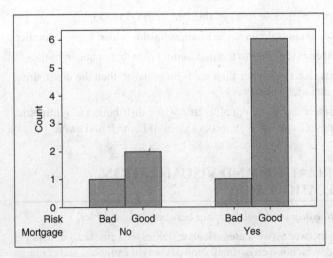

Figure A.8 Clustered bar chart for *risk*, clustered by *mortgage*.

Descriptive Statistics: Income						
Variable	Risk	Mean	StDev	Minimum	Median	Maximum
Income	Bad	28050	5728	24000	28050	32100
	Good	33663	7402	25000	32600	48000

- To visualize the relationship between a quantitative variable and a categorical variable, we may use an *individual value plot*, which is essentially a set of vertical dotplots, one for each category in the categorical variable. Figure A.9 shows the individual value plot for *income* versus *risk*, showing that incomes for *good risk* tend to be larger.

- A *scatter plot* is used to visualize the relationship between two quantitative variables, x and y. Each (x, y) point is graphed on a Cartesian plane, with the x axis on the horizontal and the y axis on the vertical. Figure A.10 shows eight scatter plots, showing some possible types of relationships between the variables, along with the value of the *correlation coefficient r*.

- The *correlation coefficient r* quantifies the strength and direction of the linear relationship between two quantitative variables. The correlation coefficient is defined as

$$r = \frac{\sum (x - \overline{x})(y - \overline{y})}{(n - 1)s_x s_y}$$

where s_x and s_y represent the standard deviation of the x-variable and the y-variable, respectively. $-1 \leq r \leq 1$.

  ○ In data mining, where there are a large number of records (over 1000), even small values of r, such as $-0.1 \leq r \leq 0.1$ may be statistically significant.

  ○ If r is positive and significant, we say that x and y are *positively correlated*. An increase in x is associated with an increase in y.

  ○ If r is negative and significant, we say that x and y are *negatively correlated*. An increase in x is associated with a decrease in y.

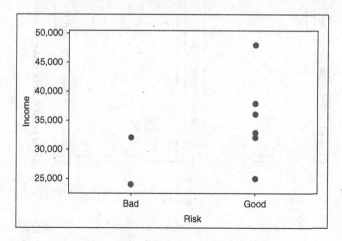

Figure A.9   Individual value plot of *income* versus *risk*.

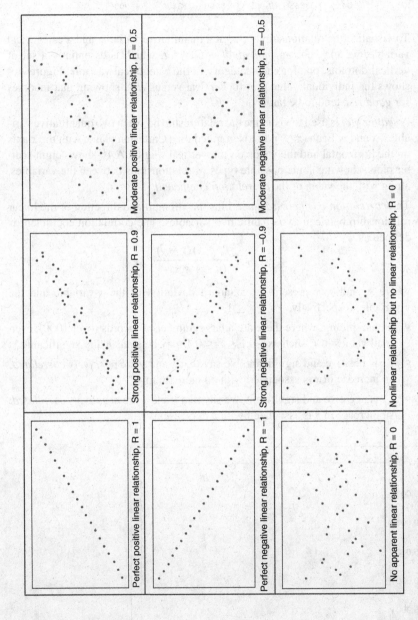

Figure A.10   Some possible relationships between *x* and *y*.

INDEX

Note: Page numbers in *italics* refer to Figures; those in **bold** to Tables

Data Mining and Predictive Analytics, First Edition. Daniel T. Larose and Chantal D. Larose.
© 2015 John Wiley & Sons, Inc. Published 2015 by John Wiley & Sons, Inc.

Printed in the United States
By Bookmasters